Laos

D0845128

Austin Bush,
Mark Elliot, Nick Ray

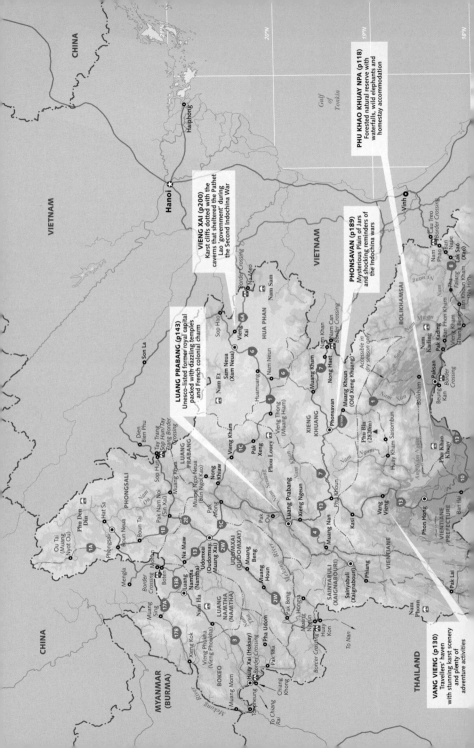

PHU KHAO KHUAY NPA (p118)
Forested natural reserve with waterfalls, wild elephants and homestay accommodation

VIENG XAI (p200)
Karst cliffs dotted with the caverns that sheltered the Pathet Lao 'government' during the Second Indochina War

PHONSAVAN (p189)
Mysterious Plain of Jars and shocking reminders of the Indochina wars

LUANG PRABANG (p143)
Unesco-listed former royal capital packed with dazzling temples and French colonial charm

VANG VIENG (p130)
Travellers' haven with stunning karst scenery and plenty of adventure activities

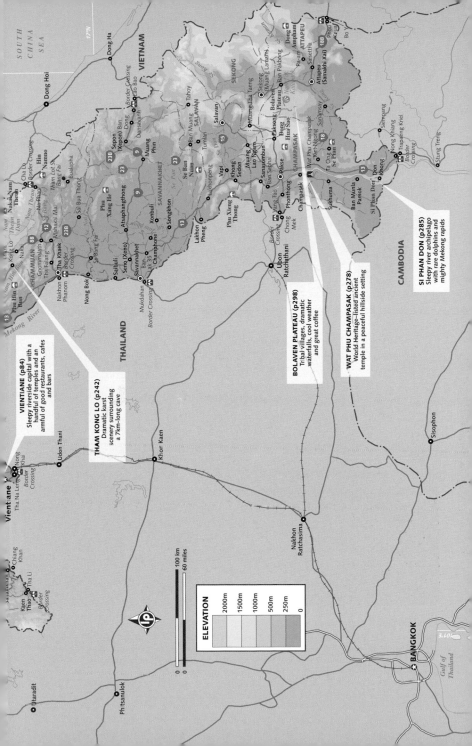

VIENTIANE (p84)
Sleepy riverside capital with a handful of temples and an armful of good restaurants, cafes and bars

THAM KONG LO (p242)
Dramatic karst scenery surrounding a 7km-long cave

BOLAVEN PLATEAU (p298)
Tribal villages, dramatic waterfalls, cool weather and great coffee

WAT PHU CHAMPASAK (p278)
World Heritage–listed ancient temple in a peaceful hillside setting

SI PHAN DON (p285)
Sleepy river archipelago with rare dolphins and mighty Mekong rapids

ELEVATION

2000m
1500m
1000m
500m
250m
0

100 km
60 miles

On the Road

AUSTIN BUSH Coordinating Author, **MARK ELLIOTT & NICK RAY**
It's a rare thing indeed when all the authors of a particular Lonely Planet guide are able to meet up *in situ*. But Team *Laos* was fortunate enough to arrange just such an encounter in Vientiane. Fuelled by numerous towers of Beerlao, we traded war stories, gossiped about our beloved employer and conducted some exceedingly in-depth 'research' at several watering holes. The result is a guide that we feel is collaborative, authoritative and fun, with, not surprisingly perhaps, the distinct hoppy aroma of a particular Lao brew… Pictured from left to right: Mark Elliott, Nick Ray and Austin Bush.

Laos Highlights

The former royal capital of Luang Prabang and the laid-back backpacker paradise of Si Phan Don are often cited as highlights of many travellers' visits to Laos. But in this low-key destination, something as simple as a spicy meal or making a new friend on a rural bus-ride can be equally memorable. Share your favourite Laos experience with the world at the Thorn Tree forum at www.lonelyplanet.com/thorntree. The following highlights are written by Austin Bush.

LAWRENCE WORCESTER

RIVERBOATS

Travelling on riverboats (p142) is a highlight in Laos, but when the water level is low you might have to get out and push!

THE GIBBON EXPERIENCE

We'd been on zip lines before. But the Gibbon Experience (p174) was a whole extra quantum of whizz.

2

MARK ELLIOT

AUSTIN BU

3

VIENG XAI CAVES

We realised that Laos had suffered in the Vietnam War but the scale of the suffering was only brought home to us with the brilliant audio-guide tour in beautiful Vieng Xai (p200), where local people and the Pathet Lao leadership lived in caves for nine years for protection from US bombers.

TREKKING NEAR PHONGSALI

Trekking around Phongsali (p231) we were fascinated by the Akha Nuqui people. At first the village women would run from our cameras shrieking. But once we'd been staying in their houses for a while they saw the digital photos we took of their kids and became keen to see their own portraits.

4

MARK ELLIOT

A NIGHT OUT IN VANG VIENG

As evening fell over the Nam Song (p130) and riverside bars closed, and the last few tubers drifted by, I met a group of friendly locals who were kind enough to take me out for local food and Beerlao, making it my best night in Vang Vieng.

JOHN ELK III

SWEET TREATS

You can put on a few pounds at Vientiane's excellent bakeries and cafes (p108), but it's definitely worth it.

AUSTIN BUSH

THE CLIFFS OF KHAMMUAN

The seemingly never-ending karst cliffs and mountains of Khammuan (p242) in central Laos are a definite highlight.

GRANT DIXON

PAMPERING IN VIENTIANE

Despite how hot it can be in Laos, I loved herbal saunas so much that at Vientiane's famous forest temple, Wat Sok Pa Luang (p97), I was sweating in its sauna almost every day I was in town.

8

JULIET COON

VIENTIANE BY BIKE

With its flat streets and lack of traffic, Vientiane is a great city to explore by bicycle (p98).

9

SARA-JANE CLELA

10

THE JOYS OF CENTRAL LAOS

I'd been to Laos several times previously but had always overlooked the centre of the country, so it was a genuine joy to discover this exceedingly beautiful area (p237).

AUSTIN BUSH

Contents

Regional Map Contents

Northern Laos p144

Vientiane &
Around p86

Central
Laos p238

Southern
Laos p266

Destination Laos

For centuries Laos was a buffer state, wedged between a pair of bigger neighbours, Thailand and Vietnam, and busy paying tribute to one, the other or both. In the 1960s and 1970s this balancing act came undone in spectacular fashion when, split down the middle in its role as a Cold War proxy for both American and communist forces, Laos became the most bombed country in history (see p35).

But nearly four decades after the end of the Second Indochina War, Laos is finally growing out of its role as buffer state and is becoming a crossroads in an increasingly globalised region. Pockets of pristine environment, diverse cultures and quite possibly the most chilled-out people on earth also mean that Laos is fast earning cult status among travellers.

Much of this change in Laos is relatively recent, having come in the years following the liberalisation policies of the late 1980s and early 1990s, and was largely funded by Western governments, financial institutions such as the World Bank and Asian Development Bank, and NGOs. But these contributors are increasingly being replaced by private enterprise and the world's newest superdonor – the People's Republic of China.

The physical signs are increasingly apparent. While most roads in Laos are still little more than country lanes, today many of the main routes are sealed, and Laos is now an important link in the so-called East–West Economic Corridor – a 1500km network of roads that connects four of the six Mekong countries. Laos will make some incidental money from the traffic on these roads, but the greater effect is in making its natural resources more accessible, and thus more open to development, most notably by the mining and energy sectors. If all goes to plan the money expected from a dizzying number of projects will allow Laos to help relieve poverty independently and break the reliance on foreign aid.

There are, however, a lot of real and potential downsides to this 'progress'. Having China as a major source of funding and as a political role model is unlikely to encourage the Lao government, which is already fearful of the effect opening up to the world will have on its culture and control, to adopt democratic reforms. In short, don't expect basic freedoms like speech, assembly or even uncensored song lyrics any time soon.

But it is this very cultural isolation that, ironically, has contributed to Laos's popularity as a tourist destination. The country still retains much of the tradition that has disappeared in a frenzy of bulldozers, concrete and reality TV elsewhere in the region. Village life is refreshingly simple and even in Vientiane it's hard to believe this sort of languid riverfront life exists in a national capital. Then, of course, there is the historic royal city of Luang Prabang, where watching as hundreds of saffron-robed monks move silently among centuries-old monasteries is as romantic a scene as you'll experience anywhere in Asia.

Away from the cities, the rivers that wind down to the Mekong, the forested mountains of the north, the gothic limestone karsts of central Laos and the 4000 riverine islands of the deep south are drawing travellers who are looking for nature, adventure or both. Kayaking, caving, rock-climbing and biking are all available, but it's the community-based trekking that is most popular because it combines spectacular natural attractions with the chance to experience the 'real Laos' with a village homestay (see the boxed text, p45) – while spending your money where it's needed most.

FAST FACTS

Area: 236,800 sq km

Border countries: Cambodia, China, Myanmar, Thailand, Vietnam

Population: 6.8 million (2009 estimate)

Official language: Lao

Literacy: 69%

GDP per capita (purchasing power parity): US$2110 (2008 estimate)

Inflation: 8.6% (2008 estimate)

Original name: Lan Xang Hom Khao (Million Elephants, White Parasol)

Approximate number of elephants in Laos today: around 2000

Laos's share of the Mekong River: 1865km

In recent years, the Lao government has recognised that ecotourism (see the boxed text, p73) has grown into a primary source of income and helps channel money to some of the poorest parts of society. And many small-scale projects, from community-based treks and tours in Khammuan Province to the Jhai Coffee Farmer Cooperative (see the boxed text, p300) on the Bolaven Plateau, are improving the deal for the rural poor.

But Laos's environment faces alarming threats. Unplanned or illegal logging has been a serious problem for years. But it's the dozens of hydroelectric dams (see the boxed text, p81) due to be built in the next decade, many by companies with poor reputations for looking after local communities or the environment, that have the potential to change ecosystems dramatically, rapidly and permanently.

The challenge for Laos is to balance all these competing interests, to make the most of its opportunities as a conduit of trade and tourist destination without being overwhelmed by the interests of others. For a country with much experience of being squeezed by outsiders, but little in the way of successful outcomes, it won't be an easy road. But for travellers with a desire to witness a country truly in flux, with one foot seemingly steadfast in a Communist-era time warp, and the other stepping towards a modern future, the Laos of today is a fascinating destination indeed.

Getting Started

With 30-day visas now available to most travellers when they arrive (p328), your most pressing pre-departure concerns are finding good books to read up on Laos, working out which route to take and getting enough cash to last you through the trip. Laos is a low-maintenance destination and an easy place to travel that's most rewarding to those ready to embrace the laid-back Lao way of life. Don't expect everything to be on time; do pack a smile and prepare to slide down a few gears.

WHEN TO GO

See Climate Charts p316 for more information.

The best time for visiting most of Laos is between November and February, when it rains the least and is not too hot. It's also Laos's main season for both national and regional *bun* (festivals; see p319).

If you plan to focus on the mountainous northern provinces, the early rainy season (around June) is not bad, as temperatures are moderate at higher elevations. The mountains are also (relatively) tolerable during the hot season (from March to May), although they're often obscured by smoke from swidden agriculture. Southern Laos, on the other hand, is best avoided during the hot season, when day-time temperatures break into the 40s and nights aren't much cooler.

The rainy season is not as bad as you might think. While it will rain – very heavily – the downpours are often fairly brief and can be bracketed by long periods of sunshine. The rains also clear dust from the skies and land, making everything clearer and brighter. Of course, there are downsides; unsealed roads can become quagmires and extensive travel in remote areas like Salavan, Phongsali and Sainyabuli might be impossible. River travel can be a good alternative during these months. If you intend to travel extensively by river, November is the best; flooding has usually subsided yet river levels are still high enough for maximum navigability. Between January and June, low water can make navigating some rivers difficult.

December to February and August are the peak tourist times. January, in particular, is very busy and booking ahead is advisable.

TRAVELLING RESPONSIBLY

Travelling responsibly in Laos involves little more than being considerate. Consider what impact your actions will have and you'll most likely do the right thing by yourself and the people and country of Laos. Environmental considerations include the obvious, such as avoiding littering and not having your towels washed every day, but are also impacted by the companies you choose to use for activities such as trekking; for green businesses in Laos see p375. Perhaps the most satisfying, sustainable and memorable responsible travel is using homestay accommodation. Not only do you bring money directly into the community, but you'll also get the chance to experience the 'real Laos' firsthand.

COSTS & MONEY

Laos is an inexpensive country to visit by almost any standards. Not including transport you could squeeze by on US$7 a day in the provinces, somewhat more in Luang Prabang and Vientiane. But that means slumming it in the very cheapest guesthouses and eating nothing but noodle soup. A budget of US$20 a day brings with it decent food and simple accommodation (p312) with basic attached bathroom. When you add air-con, hot water and *falang*

(Western) food, costs are around US$25 to US$30 per day if you economise. The sky's the limit if you plump for top-end dining and hotels (Luang Prabang's priciest suites cost more than US$1400) but such luxuries are limited to Vientiane, Luang Prabang and a very few tour-friendly locations.

Add to these estimates the cost of transport, which varies considerably depending on how fast you're moving. Flying domestically (p339) costs from US$80 to US$160 per sector. Long-distance boat rides typically cost around US$10 and are an attraction in themselves. Most bus trips cost between US$2 and US$20; see the boxed text, p114 for a better idea of costs. Also be sure to factor in enough for the various adventure activities that make Laos so special – eg from around US$18/35 a day in a group/alone for organised treks.

Most of your costs will be paid in Lao kip but, depending on where you are, you might be able to use US dollars, Thai baht and even Chinese yuan (RMB). Indeed in some border towns they're preferred. In this book we quote prices in the currency that any given establishment prefers. Credit cards are really only accepted in Vientiane and Luang Prabang. ATMs are still only available in a handful of provincial capitals so pack plenty of convertible cash (US dollars or Thai baht) especially if you're arriving at more remote borders or plan to go trekking before reaching a larger city.

READING UP

Relatively little has been written about Laos but there are enough books to keep you interested before you leave and while you're on the road.

Travel Literature

The classic travellers' account of Laos is Norman Lewis' *A Dragon Apparent: Travels In Cambodia, Laos and Vietnam*, written after the author's 1952 trip through French Indochina. It contains this passage on Laos: 'Europeans who come here to live, soon acquire a certain recognisable manner. They develop quiet voices, and gentle, rapt expressions'.

One Foot in Laos (1999) by Dervla Murphy is the veteran Irish writer's account of her lone bicycle trip through off-the-beaten-track Laos, written with passion for the local people. It includes some stinging assessments of travellers and modern ways.

Another Quiet American (2003), Brett Dakin's account of two years working at the National Tourism Authority of Laos, reveals a lot about what drives (or not) people working in Laos, both local and *falang*.

Foodies will appreciate *Ant Egg Soup* (2004), Natacha Du Pont De Bie's culinary-based travelogue that also includes recipes and illustrations.

More recent is *In the Naga's Wake* (2006) by Mick O'Shea, the Lao-based adventurer who details his epic kayaking trip down the Mekong River from source to sea.

Several classic travel narratives by 19th-century French visitors to Laos have been translated into English, including Henri Mouhot's *Travels in Siam, Cambodia, and Laos.* The book covers the 1858 to 1860 trip which resulted in the explorer's death – he's buried near Luang Prabang (p170).

Other Books

The vast majority of books on Laos are historical or political works and deal mainly with events of the last century or so.

For well-written, lucid histories it's hard to go past *A History of Laos* by Martin Stuart-Fox, who also wrote the history chapter in this book (p23), and *A Short History of Laos: The Land in Between* (2002) by Grant Evans. Both are wonderfully easy to read and don't require an in-depth foreknowledge of Laos. Evans's most recent title, *The Last Century of Lao Royalty: A*

DON'T LEAVE HOME WITHOUT ...

The range can be limited, but most of what you'll need while travelling can be found in Laos for less than you'd spend at home. There are, however, a few things you shouldn't forget, not least a deep well of patience, your sense of humour and a dose of perspective when a reality check is required. More tangible objects are:

- a sarong (for both women and men) to stay modest while bathing Lao style
- photos of family to show when language is a barrier
- a phrasebook to make that barrier more surmountable
- contraceptives and tampons if needed
- good sunscreen and mosquito repellent, and a small torch (flashlight) for caves and villages without electricity
- light wash-and-wear clothes
- slip-on shoes or sandals – cool to wear and easy to remove before entering a Lao home or temple
- a Leatherman (or similar) tool, sunglasses and a bandana if you're planning on motorbiking
- a sweater/pullover or light jacket for the cool season, mountainous provinces and overnight buses

---

Documentary History (2009), is a mixture of photos, letters, interviews and essays that detail one of the most obscure monarchies in modern history.

Those wishing to get their head around some of the more confusing aspects of Lao culture should pick up Robert Cooper's *Culture Shock! Laos* (2008). Cooper also started **Lao Insight Books** (www.acvientiane.com/bookshops/lao-insight), the Lao-based publishing company with a number of titles exclusively concerning Laos. Lao Insight books can be found at Cooper's Vientiane bookshop, Book Cafe (p85).

Several books have been written about Laos's role in the Second Indochina War. *The Ravens: Pilots of the Secret War of Laos* (1987), by Christopher Robbins, is a fast-paced account of the American pilots hired by the CIA to fly in Laos, where they weren't allowed to wear uniforms because the war didn't officially exist. *Shooting at the Moon: The Story of America's Clandestine War in Laos* (1998), by Roger Warner, and *The Blood Road: The Ho Chi Minh Trail and the Vietnam War* (2000), by John Prados, are well-respected accounts of the war, the CIA and Hmong role in it, and the Ho Chi Minh Trail.

For a first-person account of this period, *I Little Slave* (2006), by Bounsang Khamkeo, describes the French-educated author's account of surviving *samana,* the notorious re-education camps of post-revolutionary Laos, before emigrating to the United States.

Journalist Christopher Kremmer has written two entertaining books detailing his pursuit of the truth behind the final demise of the Lao monarchy in the late 1970s: *Stalking the Elephant Kings: In Search of Laos* (1998) and *Bamboo Palace: Discovering the Lost Dynasty of Laos* (2003).

Mekong (2000) by Milton Osborne is a more scholarly record of the role of the mighty Mekong River in regional history and modern politics. Anne Fadiman's award-winning *The Spirit Catches You and You Fall Down* (1997) looks at the tragic clash of cultures between a family of Hmong migrants and their American doctors.

There are very few novels set in Laos, the best of them probably being *The Honourable Schoolboy,* John Le Carré's Cold War thriller in which much of the action is set in surreal wartime Vientiane. More recently, Colin

TOP 10

Myanmar (Burma)

Vietnam

LAOS

FABULOUS FESTIVALS

Laos boasts a couple of festivals (p319) a month, year-round, not to mention public holidays. Here are the most impressive:

1 Makha Busa (Full Moon; national) February (p319)

2 Bun Wat Phu (Champasak) February (p281)

3 Elephant Festival (various locations in Sainyabuli Province) mid-February (p182)

4 Bun Pha Wet (national) March (p319)

5 Bun Pi Mai Lao (Lao New Year; Luang Prabang) April (p154)

6 Bun Bang Fai (Rocket Festival; national) May (p319)

7 Bun Khao Phansa (national) July (p319)

8 Bun Awk Phansa (national) October (p320)

9 Bun Nam (Boat Racing Festival; Vientiane, Savannakhet, Huay Xai) October (p100)

10 Bun Pha That Luang (Vientiane) October-November (p100)

OUTDOOR THRILLS – INTO THE WILD

There's no better country in Asia to get outside and adventurous.

1 Mounting a week-long expedition to Nong Fa in the Dong Amphan NPA (p311)

2 Boating through the 7km-long Tham Kong Lo cave (p242)

3 Being among the first to go on deep-forest 'tiger treks' from Vieng Thong (p203)

4 Kayaking down one of the Nam Ou's most spectacular sections between Muang Ngoi Neua and Nong Khiaw (p222)

5 Rock-climbing the caves and karsts of Vang Vieng (p133)

6 Playing Tarzan for three days zipping through forests and sleeping in wilderness treehouses on the brilliant Gibbon Experience (p174)

7 Trekking into timeless Akha villages in fascinating Phongsali province (see p231)

8 Blazing a trail to the virtually unvisited caves at Tham Lot Se Bang Fai and Hin Namno NPA (p253)

9 Riding a motorbike around southern Laos for a week (p297)

10 Climbing Phu Asa by elephant (p283)

LAO-STYLE MÚAN (FUN)

Just saying 'yes' to that weird-sounding dish, drink or experience is fun, Lao style.

1 Bumping along in the back of a *sǎwngthǎew* with loads of Lao people, chickens and rice (p340)

2 Challenging the locals to a game of *petang* (p48)

3 Drinking delicious Beerlao with ice (p64)

4 Ditching the tourist restaurants for an authentic Lao market meal (p62)

5 Sharing *lào-láo* (whisky) or a jar of *lào-hǎi* (jar liquor; home-brewed rice wine; p64)

6 Shopping for coffee and woven silk in the villages of southern Laos

7 Smiling at everyone you see

8 Taking a wash in the Mekong at Don Daeng (p281)

9 Tucking in to sticky rice and *làap* (meat salad) with your host family in a village homestay (p45)

10 Watching monks collect alms in early morning Luang Prabang (p155)

MOBILE PHONE NUMBERS IN LAOS

In 2010, another digit was introduced to Lao mobile phone numbers. Confusingly for travellers, the digit added corresponds to the number's provider, which can be identified by the first digit of the phone number (after the 020-). Thus, if a number begins with 4, 5 or 6, a 5 is added to beginning of the number (ie the former 020-560 6549 becomes 020-5560 6549); if a number begins with 7, a 7 is added; and if a number begins with 8 or 9, a 9 is added. For now there's no extra digit added if a number begins with 2 or 3, but this may change. We have aimed to provide numbers that were correct at the time of research, but be aware that you may see incorrect numbers on tourist information and that there may be further changes.

Cotterill's seven (and counting) well-received Dr. Siri books intertwine mystery and mysticism in post-revolutionary Vientiane.

INTERNET RESOURCES

Laos doesn't have a huge web presence, but it is improving. These are the best we've found this time around:

Lao Bumpkin (http://laobumpkin.blogspot.com) 'Travel, food and other things connected to Laos and the Lao people, or maybe not.'

how lao, brown cow (http://howlaobrowncow.com) Written by an Oregonian teaching English in northern Laos, this is a blog about travel, expat life and education, heavy on the Bob Dylan quotes.

BBC (http://news.bbc.co.uk/1/hi/world/asia-pacific/country_profiles/1154621.stm)

Library of Congress (http://rs6.loc.gov/frd/cs/latoc.html)

Ecotourism Laos (www.ecotourismlaos.com) Simple but stylish website full of information about the Lao environs, focussing on trekking and other ecotourism activities. Recommended.

lao*miao* (http://laomeow.blogspot.com) Up to date transportation details, mostly regarding northern Laos, culled from a variety of sources.

Lao National Tourism Administration (www.tourismlaos.org) Mostly up-to-date travel information from the government. Also has accurate exchange rates for the Lao kip and a good list of links.

Lao News Agency (www.kplnet.net) Best source of current news on Laos.

Library of Congress (www.loc.gov) Probably the most complete online resource about Laos, with thorough and regularly updated accounts of history, culture and politics.

Lonely Planet (www.lonelyplanet.com) The Thorn Tree forum is the place to get the latest feedback from the road.

Travelfish (www.travelfish.org) The most consistently updated website for independent travellers in Southeast Asia, including excellent coverage of Lao border crossings.

Vientiane Times (www.vientianetimes.org.la) Website of the country's only English-language newspaper, and operated by the government.

Itineraries
CLASSIC ROUTES

THE NORTH
One to Two Weeks/Huay Xai to Vientiane

The northern route has emerged as the standard Laos trip, but is still one of the best samplers for anyone who wants a good dose of the country in a relatively short time.

Enter Laos via ferry from Chiang Khong in Thailand to **Huay Xai** (p172) before boarding one of the slow boats that ply the Mekong to Luang Prabang. This two-day voyage requires an overnight stay in the small riverside village of **Pak Beng** (p179); the scenery along the Mekong River is a terrific mix of villages, limestone cliffs and intermittent forest.

Sightseeing in and around **Luang Prabang** (p143), Laos's atmospheric former royal capital, can easily occupy a week.

From here, continue southward along stunning Rte 13, stopping in **Vang Vieng** (p130), a modern-day travellers' centre surrounded by craggy, cave-studded limestone peaks. After a few days of river-tubing and cave hikes, head to **Vientiane** (p84), Laos's semibustling capital city.

Pass quiet village ports and rugged gorges boating along the Mekong to Luang Prabang, then follow Rte 13, which winds high into the mountains between Kasi and Vang Vieng toward Vientiane, to complete this 700km route.

THE SOUGH THE SOUTH   One to Three Weeks/Vientiane to Si Phan Don

This classic route takes you through the heartland of Lowland Lao culture, a world of broad river plains planted with rice, and homemade looms shaded by wooden houses on stilts.

Start in **Vientiane** (p84), the country's capital, and soak up the food, shopping, historical sights and nightlife (it gets quieter from here). Head south to **Tha Khaek** (p244), the archetypal sleepy Mekong riverside town, and go east on Rte 12 to explore the caves of **Khammuan Limestone** (p251) or take **The Loop** (p252) all the way around, stopping at the incredible **Tham Kong Lo** (p242).

Continue south to **Savannakhet** (p254), where you'll get a taste of how postcolonial Vientiane looked before it received a makeover from the Lao PDR government and international aid.

Roll on southward to **Pakse** (p267) and, if you don't have enough time to go east, through to tranquil **Champasak** (p276). This town is the base for seeing Laos's most important archaeological site, **Wat Phu Champasak** (p278), Angkor-style temple ruins stepping up the slopes of sacred Phu Pasak.

Make a final short hop to **Si Phan Don** (Four Thousand Islands; p285), an archipelago of idyllic river islands where the farming and fishing life hasn't changed much for a century or more. Swing in a hammock and relax, before moving on to Cambodia or heading to Thailand via Chong Mek.

This route covers about 700km of river plains and rolling hills, bridging clear streams and tracing traditional Lao villages as Rte 13 follows the Mekong south. Expect to move by bus, *săwngthăew*, motorbike and boat as you make your way south. Depending on time, take as many diversions east of Rte 13 as you can.

ROADS LESS TRAVELLED

NORTHERN WILDERNESS   Two to Three Weeks/Udomxai to Vietnam or Phonsavan

This route explores the little-visited mountain villages, rivers and caves of the north. Don't forget your phrasebook. Start in underrated **Udomxai** (p209) with a visit to the vast **Chom Ong Caves** (p213) plus pretty **Muang La** (p213), home to a 'magical' Buddha image.

Take the bumpy but scenic road to **Phongsali** (p231), a curious hill-town famous for its tea fields and top-quality green 'whisky'. Nowhere makes a better starting point for treks into timeless thatched-hut villages, many belonging to the Akha tribe, whose distinctive belief systems and photogenic costumes make any visit memorable. Return south on a one-day riverboat ride from **Hat Sa** (p233) to charming **Muang Khua** (p227). A new daily bus route links the town to Dien Bien Phu in Vietnam. Or you could continue another day down the beautiful Nam Ou (Ou River) to **Muang Ngoi Neua** (p207) and **Nong Khiaw** (p204). Both are traveller-friendly villages that share some of northern Laos' most stunning rural scenery. From Nong Khiaw, head east via 'tiger town' **Vieng Thong** (p203) to intriguing **Sam Neua** (p196). The main attraction there is an excursion to **Vieng Xai** (p200), where the communist Pathet Lao government spent nine years dodging US bombs by living in caves (from 1964 to 1973). The cave settings are gorgeous and the guided visits brilliant. From Sam Neua a daily bus to Vietnam takes a grand route past many more such caves. Or you could backtrack to **Phonsavan** (p189) and the mysterious **Plain of Jars** (p193).

Visit caverns, traditional villages and mysterious relics on this adventure that will take you along divergent paths leading to two of Laos's most remote and beautiful border crossings with Vietnam.

BOLAVEN & BEYOND   10 to 14 days/Pakse to Pakse

This trip into the remote provinces of southern Laos can be done by private vehicle, including small motorbikes, or more slowly – but more socially – by public transport. It's best in the dry season.

After a day or two getting organised in **Pakse** (p267), head up onto the **Bolaven Plateau** (p298) and to Laos's most impressive waterfall at **Tat Fan** (p298). At the coffee capital of **Paksong** (p299), you could stop to buy some java before continuing on to **Sekong** (p306), passing through Laven, Katang and other villages en route. Sleepy **Attapeu** (p308) is an easy place to hang out; interrupt your sunsets by the Se Kong with a bumpy day trip out to the village of **Pa-am** (p310) on the Ho Chi Minh Trail, and an overnight homestay in the **Se Pian NPA** (p311). Or undertake an overland adventure to the remote jungle-clad lake of **Nong Fa** (p311), formerly an R'n'R stop on the Ho Chi Minh Trail, now accessible by road.

Head back up Rte 16, through Sekong and turn north at Tha Taeng on a long, downhill laterite road to Beng. Check out **Salavan** (p303) for a day and, if the season is right, arrange transport along the rarely travelled road to **Tahoy** (p304), once an important marker on the Ho Chi Minh Trail and now a more peaceful but thoroughly remote home of the Ta-oy people.

Beautiful **Tat Lo** (p301) and its inevitable crowd of backpackers will be a shock after days with little, if any, contact with Westerners, and **Utayan Bajiang Champasak** (p276) makes an attractive lunch spot on the easy trip back to Pakse.

On this journey of roughly 650km you'll climb into the coffee-growing districts of the Bolaven Plateau, see spectacular waterfalls, and visit villages little changed since the end of the Second Indochina War.

TAILORED TRIPS

ACTION JACKSON TOUR

Laos has plenty on offer for those who like the outdoors. Start with a hike, kayak trip or bike ride in the **Nam Ha NPA** (p141) or zip through forests and sleep in treehouses at the **Gibbon Experience** (p174).

Head to **Vang Vieng** (p130), the activities capital of the country, where there are a myriad of rock-climbing, kayaking and biking options.

Go kayaking along the Nam Lik (Lik River), combining this with a spin on the **Nam Lik Jungle Fly** (p129) or a stay at the **Nam Lik Eco-Village** (p129). In **Vientiane** (p84), stop long enough for a massage at **Wat Sok Pa Luang** (p97) to work out some of the knots, before trekking into **Phu Khao Khuay NPA** (p118) in search of elephants.

Head south to Tha Khaek and get on a trek into the **Phu Hin Bun NPA** (p242), with its magical waterholes and incredible 7km-long boat ride through the **Tham Kong Lo** (p242) cave. If you fancy more tough trekking, head to **Pakse** (p267) and get yourself on a trek into the **Se Pian NPA** (p285), before rounding out your stay in Laos with an elephant ride to the mysterious temple ruins of **Phu Asa** (p283) or a boat trip around the pretty islands of **Si Phan Don**(p285).

LAO CULTURE TOUR

Start in **Vientiane**, probably the best place to dip your toe in the pool of Lao culture, and take a course in Lao cooking, weaving or language. With your newfound knowledge in hand, board a bus following the flow of the Mekong south to **Savannakhet** (p254), a bastion of Lao Loum (Lowland Lao) culture. Hire a motorcycle and explore the villages and temples of **Champhone** (p261) or do a homestay and gather forest products with locals in the sacred forest of **Dong Natad** (p260).

Head north to **Luang Prabang** (p143)to visit the city's numerous temples, where you can also join pious locals in making a ceremonial offering to the

saffron-robed monks during their *tak bat* dawn procession. From Luang Prabang, there are several fascinating options for exploring the ethnic diversity of northern Laos. Depending on the tribe you stay with, you might discover the power of names to the Hmong in **Ban Phakeo** (p195) observe Lenten papermaking in **Ban Nam Di** (p217), drink Boi K'Dang through long straws with the Khamu people near the **Chom Ong Caves** (p213), visit centuries-old tea slopes in **Ban Komaen** (p233) encounter Thai Lü elephant handlers around **Hongsa** (p181), or smoke giant bamboo bongs outside **Muang Sing** (p223) with the most visually distinctive of all Laotian peoples, the Akha.

History Professor Martin Stuart-Fox

PREHISTORY & TAI-LAO MIGRATION

The first modern humans (*Homo sapiens*) arrived in Southeast Asia around 50,000 years ago. Their stone-age technology remained little changed until a new Neolithic culture evolved about 10,000 years ago. This was the Hoabinhian, named after an archaeological site in northern Vietnam. Hoabinhian hunter-gatherers spread throughout much of Southeast Asia, including Laos. Their descendants produced the first pottery in the region, and later bronze metallurgy. In time they supplemented their hunting, fishing and gathering by horticulture and eventually rice cultivation, introduced down the Mekong River valley from southern China. These people were the ancestors of the present-day upland minorities, collectively known as the Lao Thoeng (Upland Lao), the largest group of which are the Khamu of northern Laos.

Other Lao Thoeng tribes live in southern Laos, including the Brao and the Katang. Like their northern cousins, they speak Austro-Asiatic languages, a group which includes Khmer. In fact southern Laos is believed to be the birthplace of the Cambodian people, from where they spread further south to establish the kingdom of Funan by the 2nd century CE. The earliest kingdom in southern Laos was identified in Chinese texts as Chenla, dating from the 5th century. Its capital was close to Champasak, near the later Khmer temple of Wat Phu. A little later Mon people (speaking another Austro-Asiatic language) established kingdoms on the middle Mekong – Sri Gotapura (Sikhottabong in Lao) with its capital near Tha Khaek, and Chanthaburi in the vicinity of Viang Chan (Vientiane).

Tai peoples probably began migrating out of southern China in about the 8th century. They included the Tai-Lao of Laos, the Tai-Syam and Tai-Yuan of central and northern Thailand, and the Tai-Shan of northeast Burma. They are called Tai to distinguish them from the citizens (Thai) of modern Thailand, though the word is the same. All spoke closely related Tai languages, practised wet-rice cultivation along river valleys, and organised themselves into small principalities, known as *meuang*, each presided over by an hereditary ruler, or *chao meuang* (lord of the *meuang*). The Tai-Lao, or Lao for short, moved slowly down the rivers of northern Laos, like the Nam Ou and the Nam Khan, running roughly from northeast to southwest, until they arrived at the Mekong, the Great River. They worshipped the ngeuk, powerful snake deities believed to inhabit these rivers, which if not propitiated could so easily tip frail canoes and drown their occupants. Most Lao peasants still believe that ngeuk exist.

Martin Stuart-Fox is Emeritus Professor at the University of Queensland, Australia. He has written seven books and over 70 articles and book chapters on the politics and history of Laos.

TIMELINE

1353	1479	1501
Fa Ngum establishes the Lao kingdom of Lan Xang and builds a fine capital at Xiang Dong Xiang Thong.	The Vietnamese emperor Le Thanh Tong invades Lan Xang, sending a large invasion force including many war elephants.	King Visoun comes to the throne and rebuilds the Lao kingdom, marking a cultural renaissance for Lan Xang. He installs the Pha Bang Buddha image in Luang Prabang.

THE KINGDOM OF LAN XANG

The first extended Lao kingdom dates from the mid-14th century. It was established in the context of a century of unprecedented political and social change in mainland Southeast Asia. At the beginning of the 13th century, the great Khmer king Jayavarman VII, who had re-established Cambodian power and built the city of Angkor Thom, sent his armies north to extend the Khmer empire to include all of the middle Mekong region and north-central Thailand. But the empire was overstretched, and by the mid-13th century the Khmer were in retreat. At the same time, the Mongol Yuan dynasty in China lost interest in further conquest in Southeast Asia.

This left a political vacuum in central Thailand, into which stepped Ramkhamhaeng, founder of the Tai-Syam kingdom of Sukhothai. To his north, his ally Mangray founded the Tai-Yuan kingdom of Lanna (meaning 'a million rice fields'), with his capital at Chiang Mai. Other smaller Tai kingdoms were established at Phayao and Xiang Dong Xiang Thong (Luang Prabang). In southern Laos and southern Thailand, however, the Khmer still held on to power.

We know that at this time Viang Chan was tributary to Sukhothai, and it may well be that Xiang Dong Xiang Thong was too. As the power of Sukhothai grew, it exerted more pressure on the Khmer. The Cambodian court looked around for an ally, and found one in the form of a young Lao prince, Fa Ngum, who was being educated at Angkor. Fa Ngum's princely father had been forced to flee Xiang Dong Xiang Thong after he seduced one of his own father's concubines. So Fa Ngum was in direct line for the throne.

The Khmer gave Fa Ngum a Khmer princess and an army, and sent him north to wrest the middle Mekong from the control of Sukhothai, and so divert

---

ALTERNATE ORIGINS

The early Lao text known as the Nithan (story of) Khun Borom recounts the myth of creation of the Lao peoples, their interaction, and the establishment of the first Lao kingdom in the vicinity of Luang Prabang. The creation myth tells how two great gourds grew at Meuang Thaeng (Dien Bien Phu, now in Vietnam) from inside which sounds could be heard. Divine rulers, known as khun, pierced one of the gourds with a hot poker, and out of the charred hole poured the dark-skinned Lao Thoeng. The khun used a knife to cut a hole in the other gourd, through which escaped the lighter-skinned Tai-Lao (or Lao Loum, Lowland Lao). The gods then sent Khun Borom to rule over both Lao Loum and Lao Thoeng. He had seven sons, whom he sent out to found seven new kingdoms in the regions where Tai peoples settled (in the Tai highlands of Vietnam, the Xishuangbanna of southern China, Shan state in Burma, and in Thailand and Laos). While the youngest son founded the kingdom of Xieng Khuang on the Plain of Jars, the oldest son, Khun Lo, descended the Nam Ou, seized the principality of Meuang Sua from its Lao Thoeng ruler, and named it Xiang Dong Xiang Thong (later renamed Luang Prabang).

1560	1638	1641–1642
King Setthathirat, grandson of King Visoun, moves the capital to Viang Chan because of the threat from Burma which was becoming a new power in the mainland.	The great Lao king, Suriya Vongsa, begins a 57-year reign known as the 'Golden Age' of the kingdom of Lan Xang.	The first Europeans to write accounts of Lan Xang arrive in Viang Chan providing information about trade and culture; descriptions of King Setthathirat's royal palace; and details of the king's power.

and weaken the Tai-Syam kingdom. In this he was successful. Sikhottabong acknowledged Fa Ngum's suzerainty. So did Xieng Khuang and a number of other Lao *meuang*. Only Viang Chan held out. Fa Ngum was acclaimed king in Xiang Dong Xiang Thong, before forcibly bringing Viang Chan into his growing empire. He named his new kingdom Lan Xang Hom Khao, meaning 'a million elephants and the white parasol'. Fa Ngum built a fine capital at Xiang Dong Xiang Thong and set about organising his court and kingdom. He appointed his Khmer generals to positions of power, even though this antagonised the local aristocracy. Tributary rulers had to journey to the capital every three years to renew their vows of fealty and present tribute.

Fa Ngum performed sacrifices to the *phii* (traditional spirits) of the kingdom, and to the ngeuk of the Mekong. But he also acquiesced to his wife's request to introduce Khmer Theravada Buddhism to Lan Xang. Here, according to the Lao chronicles, he began to run into problems. The Cambodian king despatched a large contingent of monks and craftsmen up the Mekong, but they only got as far as Viang Chan. There the image they were escorting, the famous Pha Bang, magically refused to move, and had to be left behind. Its reason for refusing to go on to the Lao capital was that it knew that Fa Ngum was not morally worthy. And it seems the Pha Bang was right. Fa Ngum began to seduce the wives and daughters of his court nobles, who decided to replace him. Fa Ngum was sent into exile in Nan (now in Thailand), where he died within five years. His legacy, however, stood the test of time. The Kingdom of Lan Xang remained a power in mainland Southeast Asia until early in the 18th century, able to match the power of Siam, Vietnam and Burma.

Fa Ngum was succeeded by his son Un Heuan, who took the throne name Samsenthai, meaning 300,000 Tai, the number of men, his census reported, who could be recruited to serve in the army. He married princesses from the principal Tai kingdoms (Lanna and Ayutthaya, which had replaced Sukhothai), consolidated the kingdom and developed trade. With his wealth he built temples and beautified his capital.

Following Samsenthai's long and stable reign of 42 years, Lan Xang was shaken by succession disputes, a problem faced by all Southeast Asian mandala (circles of power). A scheming queen, known only as Mahathevi (Great Queen), is said to have killed off a succession of youthful kings before seizing the throne herself. But she was overthrown by the nobility and sacrificed to the ngeuk (by being chained to a rock in the Mekong and drowned). The throne then passed to Samsenthai's youngest son, who took the throne name Xainya Chakkaphat (Universal Ruler). It was an arrogant claim, but he ruled wisely and well.

Tragedy struck at the end of his reign, when Lan Xang suffered its first major invasion. This was by Vietnam, whose emperor wanted revenge for a perceived insult. The story in the Lao chronicles is that a rare white elephant, a symbol of power and kingship throughout Southeast Asia, was captured and

By naming his kingdom Lan Xang Hom Khao, Fa Ngum was making a statement about power and kingship. Elephants were the battle tanks of Southeast Asian warfare, so to claim to be the kingdom of a million elephants was to issue a warning to surrounding kingdoms: 'Don't mess with the Lao!' A white parasol was the traditional symbol of kingship.

The Lao believe most *ngeuk* (snake deities) have been converted to become serpent protectors of Buddhism, called *naga* (in Lao *nak*). They still require propitiation, however, and annual boat races are held for their amusement. Many Buddhist temples (wat) have protective *naga* balustrades.

1707–1713	1826–1828	1867
Lan Xang is divided into three smaller and weaker kingdoms: Viang Chan, Luang Prabang and Champasak.	Chao Anou succeeds his two older brothers on the throne of Viang Chan and wages war against Siam for Lao independence. He is captured and Viang Chan is sacked by the Siamese armies.	Members of the French Mekong expedition reach Luang Prabang. Over the next 20 years the town is caught up in a struggle which sees the king being offered protection by France.

presented to Xainya Chakkaphat. Vietnamese emperor Le Thanh Tong asked for proof of its colour, so hairs were despatched in a fine box. Unfortunately, however, it was sent via Xieng Khuang, whose ruler wanted to thumb his nose at the Vietnamese. So he replaced the hairs with a small piece of dung.

Infuriated, the Vietnamese emperor sent a large invasion force against the Lao. After a bitter battle (recounted at length in the Lao chronicles, which even give the names of the principal war elephants), the Vietnamese captured and sacked Xiang Dong Xiang Thong. Xainya Chakkaphat fled and the Lao mounted a guerrilla campaign. Eventually the Vietnamese were forced to withdraw, their forces decimated by malaria and starvation. So great were their losses that the Vietnamese vowed never to invade Lan Xang again.

Consolidation of the Kingdom

The Lao kingdom recovered under one of its greatest rulers, who came to the throne in 1501. This was King Visoun, who had previously been governor of Viang Chan. There he had been an ardent worshipper of the Pha Bang Buddha image, which he brought with him to Xiang Dong Xiang Thong to become the palladium of the kingdom. For it he built the magnificent temple known as Wat Wisunarat (Wat Visoun), which though damaged and repaired over the years, still stands in Luang Prabang.

Visoun developed close relations with Chiang Mai, and enticed Lanna monks and craftsmen to his capital. He ordered a new version of the Lao chronicles composed, which he personally edited, and his reign marked a cultural renaissance for Lan Xang. Friendly relations with Lanna continued under Visoun's successor, his son Phothisarat. His grandson, Setthathirat, married a Lanna princess and briefly ruled over both kingdoms. But Lanna wanted its own king, and Setthathirat had trouble enough shoring up support in Lan Xang.

A new power had arisen in mainland Southeast Asia, the kingdom of Burma. It was the threat of Burma that in 1560 convinced Setthathirat to move his capital to Viang Chan. Before he did so, he built the most beautiful Buddhist temple surviving in Laos, Wat Xieng Thong. He also left behind the Pha Bang, and changed the name of Xiang Dong Xiang Thong to Luang Prabang in its honour. With him he took what he believed to be an even more powerful Buddha image, the Pha Kaew, or Emerald Buddha, now in Bangkok. Other reasons for the move included population movements (both the Khorat Plateau and southern Laos were by then Lao) and to seek improved trade links.

Setthathirat was the greatest builder in Lao history. Not only did he construct or refurbish several monasteries in Luang Prabang, besides Wat Xieng Thong, but he also did the same in Viang Chan. His most important building projects, apart from a new palace on the banks of the Mekong, were the great That Luang stupa, a temple for the Emerald Buddha (Wat Pha Kaeo), and endowment of a number of royal temples in the vicinity of the palace. The city was surrounded by a substantial wall and moat, 8km long.

Southeast Asian kingdoms were not states in the modern sense, with fixed frontiers, but varied in extent depending on the power of the centre. Outlying *meuang* (principalities) might transfer their allegiance elsewhere when the centre was weak. That is why scholars prefer the term *mandala*, a Sanskrit word meaning 'circle of power' (in Lao *monthon*).

1893	1907	1935
A French warship reaches Bangkok, guns trained on the palace. This forces the Siamese to give France sovereignty over all Lao territories east of the Mekong.	The present borders of Laos are established by international treaty. Vientiane (the French spelling of Viang Chan) becomes the administrative capital.	The first two Lao members join the Indochinese Communist Party (ICP), founded by Ho Chi Minh in 1930.

The Burmese threat persisted, however. When a Burmese army approached Viang Chan, Setthathirat abandoned the city to mount guerrilla attacks on Burmese supply lines. When the Burmese were forced to withdraw, he returned to celebrate his victory by building yet another temple (Wat Mixai). Burmese hostility disrupted Lao trade routes, so Setthathirat led an expedition down the Mekong to open a new route through Cambodia. But the Cambodians objected. In a great battle the Lao were defeated, and in their chaotic retreat Setthathirat disappeared.

It was over 60 years before another great Lao king came to the throne, a period of division, succession disputes and intermittent Burmese domination. In 1638 Suriya Vongsa was crowned king. He would rule for 57 years, the longest reign in Lao history and a 'golden age' for the kingdom of Lan Xang. During this time, Lan Xang was a powerful kingdom, and Viang Chan was a great centre of Buddhist learning, attracting monks from all over mainland Southeast Asia.

THE KINGDOM DIVIDED

Suriya Vongsa must have been stern and unbending in his old age, because he refused to intervene when his son and heir was found guilty of adultery and condemned to death. As a result, when he died in 1695 another succession dispute wracked the kingdom. This time the result was the division of Lan Xang. First the ruler of Luang Prabang declared independence from Viang Chan, followed a few years later by Champasak in the south.

The once great kingdom of Lan Xang was thus fatally weakened. In its place were three (four with Xieng Khuang) weak regional kingdoms, none of which was able to withstand the growing power of the Tai-Syam kingdom of Ayutthaya. The Siamese were distracted, however, over the next half century by renewed threats from Burma. In the end Ayutthaya was taken and sacked

---

FIRST CONTACT

The first European to have left an account of the Lao kingdom arrived in Viang Chan (Vientiane) in 1641. He was a merchant by the name of Gerrit van Wuysthoff, an employee of the Dutch East India Company, who wanted to open a trade route down the Mekong. He and his small party were royally accommodated and entertained during their eight-week stay in the Lao capital. Van Wuysthoff has more to say about the prices of trade goods than about Lao culture or religion, but he was followed a year later by a visitor who can offer us more insight into 17th-century Viang Chan. This was the Jesuit missionary, Giovanni-Maria Leria, who stayed in Viang Chan for five years. During that time he had singularly little success in converting anyone to Christianity, and eventually gave up in disgust. But he liked the Lao people (if not the monks) and has left a wonderful description of the royal palace and the houses of the nobility. He was also much impressed by the power of the king.

1945	1946	1949
The Japanese occupy Laos then force the king to declare independence; a nationalist resistance movement takes shape, the Lao Issara, and forms an interim government.	The French reoccupy Laos, sending the Lao–Issara government into exile.	France grants Laos partial independence within the Indochinese Federation and some of the Lao Issara leaders return to work for complete Lao independence from France.

Naga Cities of Mekong (2006) by Martin Stuart-Fox provides a narrative account of the founding legends and history of Luang Prabang, Vientiane and Champasak, and a guide to their temples.

by a Burmese army. Chiang Mai was already tributary to Burma, and Luang Prabang also paid tribute.

It did not take the Siamese long to recover, however. The inspiring leadership of a young military commander called Taksin, son of a Chinese father and a Siamese mother, rallied the Siamese and drove the Burmese out not just of central Siam, but from the north too. Chiang Mai became tributary to Siam. After organising his kingdom and building a new capital, Taksin sought new fields of conquest. The Lao kingdoms were obvious targets. By 1779 all three had surrendered to Siamese armies and accepted the suzerainty of Siam. The Emerald Buddha was carried off by the Siamese.

His success went to his head, however, and three years later Taksin, suffering delusions of spiritual grandeur, was deposed by his leading general. The new king, founder of the current Thai Chakri dynasty, titled himself Ramathibodi (later Rama I). He too built a new palace and capital at Bangkok, and quickly consolidated his power over tributary rulers. All Lao kings had to be endorsed by their Siamese overlord before they could assume their thrones, and all had to present regular tribute to Bangkok.

The Lao chafed under these conditions. When Chao Anou succeeded his two older brothers on the throne of Viang Chan, he determined to assert Lao independence. First he made merit by endowing Buddhist monasteries and building his own temple (Wat Si Saket). Then in 1826 he made his move, sending three armies down the Mekong and across the Khorat plateau. The Siamese were taken by surprise, but quickly rallied. Siamese armies drove the Lao back and seized Viang Chan. Chao Anou fled, but was captured when he tried to retake the city a year later. This time the Siamese were ruthless. Viang Chan was thoroughly sacked and its population resettled east of the Mekong. Only Wat Si Saket was spared. Chao Anou died a caged prisoner in Bangkok.

Paths to Conflagration: Fifty Years of Diplomacy and Warfare in Laos, Thailand and Vietnam, 1778-1828 (1998) by Mayoury Ngaosyvathn and Pheuiphanh Ngaosy-vathn provides the best account of the Lao revolt against Bangkok, from a Lao perspective.

For the next 60 years the Lao *meuang*, from Champasak to Luang Prabang, were tributary to Siam. At first these two remaining small kingdoms retained a degree of independence, but increasingly they were brought under closer Siamese supervision. One reason for this was that Siam itself was threatened by a new power in the region and felt it had to consolidate its empire. The new power was France, which had declared a protectorate over most of Cambodia in 1863.

Four years later a French expedition sent to explore and map the Mekong River arrived in Luang Prabang, then the largest settlement upstream from Phnom Penh. In the 1880s the town became caught up in a struggle that pitted Siamese, French and roving bands of Chinese brigands (known as Haw) against each other. In 1887 Luang Prabang was looted and burned by a mixed force of Upland Tai and Haw. Only Wat Xieng Thong was spared. The king escaped downstream. With him was a French explorer named Auguste Pavie, who offered him the protection of France.

1950	1953	1955
Lao communists (the Pathet Lao) form a 'Resistance Government'. Souphanouvong becomes the public face of the Resistance Government and president of the Free Laos Front.	Franco–Lao Treaty of Amity and Association grants full independence to Laos and a Lao delegation attends a conference in Geneva where a regroupment area is set aside for Pathet Lao Forces.	Pathet Lao leaders form the Lao People's Party (later Lao People's Revolutionary Party) with a broad political front called the Lao Patriotic Front (LPF).

FRENCH RULE

In the end French rule was imposed through gunboat diplomacy. In 1893 a French warship forced its way up the Chao Phraya River to Bangkok and trained its guns on the palace. Under duress, the Siamese agreed to transfer all territory east of the Mekong to France. So Laos became a French colony, with the kingdom of Luang Prabang as a protectorate and the rest of the country directly administered.

In 1900 Viang Chan (which the French spelled as Vientiane) was re-established as the administrative capital of Laos, though real power was exercised from Hanoi, the capital of French Indochina. In 1907 a further treaty was signed with Siam adding two territories west of the Mekong to Laos (Sainyabuli province, and part of Champasak). Siem Reap and Battambang provinces were regained by Cambodia at the same time.

French authorities in Saigon had hoped that their Lao territories would become the springboard for further expansion, to include all of what is today northeast Thailand. This whole area had been settled by Lao and ruled from Vientiane. By the early 20th century, however, French attention had shifted from Indochina to Europe, and from competition with Britain to friendship in the lead-up to WWI. This left up to 80% of all Lao still within the borders of Siam, while in French Laos, ethnic Lao comprised less than half the population. The rest were tribal minorities.

Over the next few years the French put into place the apparatus of colonial control. They built a mansion for the *résident-supérieur* (governor) on the site of the former royal palace, barracks for a small military detachment, a court house, a prison, and housing for interpreters and civil servants, most of whom were Vietnamese. Later came a hospital, covered market and schools. The sites of ancient monasteries were preserved, and in time new temples were constructed by the Lao population. Chinese shopkeepers and Vietnamese artisans arrived, along with a few French merchants. As they took up residence in the downtown area, near the Mekong, Lao villagers were pushed out. Even so, the town grew slowly, and by 1925 the population was still only around 8000.

In other parts of Laos the French presence was less obtrusive. In Luang Prabang, Savannakhet and Pakse town planning and services were slow to be introduced. In time spacious villas were constructed for senior French officials, and the Lao towns were graced by colonial French architecture. A heavily subsidised riverboat service linked the Lao Mekong towns to Phnom Penh and Saigon.

Nevertheless Laos remained a backwater. Despite French plans for economic exploitation, Laos was always a drain on the budget of Indochina. Corvée labour was introduced, particularly to build roads, and taxes were heavy, but the colony never paid its own way. Some timber was floated down the Mekong, and tin was discovered in central Laos, but returns were

The first Frenchman to arrive in Laos was Henri Mouhot, an explorer and naturalist who died of malaria in 1861 near Luang Prabang (where his tomb can still be seen).

1957	1960	1961
Formation of the First Coalition Government of National Union which collapses ater a financial and political crisis.	Guerrilla warfare covers large areas. A neutralist coup d'état is followed by the battle for Vientiane.	Orders given to the CIA to form a 'secret army' in northern Laos with links to the Vietnam War.

LACKLUSTRE COLONIALISTS

In 1940, the French population in Laos still only numbered around 600, more than half of whom lived in Vientiane. Most were colonial officials for whom a posting in Laos was no more than a step on the ladder of promotion. For most, their term of service was tedious, if undemanding. They kept up appearances, socialised and gossiped. A few, however, succumbed to the charm of the country, married Lao girls, and made Laos their home.

Not until the early 1940s did the French begin to make up for their previous neglect. By then Laos had only a handful of primary schools, one middle school, and no high school. Only 52 Lao graduated from middle school throughout the 1930s to progress to high school in Vietnam or France. Medical services were concentrated in a few towns, and the only decent hospital was in Vientiane. The few main roads were in poor repair, and the economy was undeveloped.

meagre. Coffee was grown in southern Laos, and opium in the north, most of it smuggled into China. The French tried hard to direct trade down the Mekong to Vietnam, but traditional trade routes across the Khorat Plateau to Bangkok were quicker and less costly.

The French introduced a three-tier system of administration into Laos. Ethnic minorities retained traditional links with local Lao leaders, who were supervised by Vietnamese civil servants, who were answerable to French officials. Taxes had traditionally been paid in the form of forest or agricultural products, but the French demanded cash. This introduced a market economy, but caused resentment. A series of anti-French rebellions broke out, first in the south and then in the north, led by traditional leaders who resented loss of authority. It took the French years of military campaigns to suppress them.

In the interwar years the French cast around for ways to make Laos economically productive. One plan was to connect the Lao Mekong towns to coastal Vietnam, by constructing a railway across the mountains separating the two colonies. The idea was to encourage the migration of industrious Vietnamese peasants into Laos to replace what the French saw as the indolent and easy-going Lao. Eventually Vietnamese would outnumber Lao and produce an economic surplus. The railway was surveyed and construction begun from the Vietnamese side, but the Great Depression intervened, money dried up, and the Vietnamisation of Laos never happened. Even so, in all the Mekong towns, with the exception of Luang Prabang, Vietnamese outnumbered Lao until most fled the country after WWII.

NATIONALISM & INDEPENDENCE

The independence movement was slow to develop in Laos. The French justified their colonial rule as protectors of the Lao from aggressive neighbours, particularly the Siamese. Most of the small Lao elite, aware of their own weakness, found this interpretation convincing, even though they resented the

1962	1964	1964–1973
Geneva Agreement on Laos establishes the Second Coalition Government that balances Pathet Lao and rightist representation with neutralist voting powers.	US begins air war against ground targets in Laos, mostly against communist positions on the Plain of Jars.	The Second Indochina War spills over into Laos. Both the North Vietnamese and US presence increases dramatically and bombing extends along the length of Laos.

presence of so many Vietnamese. The Indochinese Communist Party (ICP), founded by Ho Chi Minh in 1930, did not espouse separate independence for Vietnam, Laos and Cambodia. It only managed to recruit its first two Lao members in 1935. Until then all ICP members in Laos were Vietnamese civil servants or workers in the tin mines.

It took the outbreak of war in Europe to weaken the French position in Indochina. A new aggressively nationalist government in Bangkok took advantage of this French weakness to try to regain territory 'lost' 50 years before. It renamed Siam Thailand, and opened hostilities. A Japanese-brokered peace agreement deprived Laos of its territories west of the Mekong, much to Lao anger.

To counter pan-Tai propaganda from Bangkok, the French encouraged Lao nationalism. Under an agreement between Japan and the Vichy French administration in Indochina, French rule continued, though Japanese forces had freedom of movement. The Japanese were in place, therefore, when in early 1945 they began to suspect the French of shifting their allegiance to the allies. On 9 March the Japanese struck in a lightning coup de force throughout Indochina, interning all French military and civilian personnel. Only in Laos did a few French soldiers manage to slip into the jungle to maintain some resistance, along with their Lao allies.

The Japanese ruled Laos for just six months before the atomic bombing of Hiroshima and Nagasaki brought WWII to an end. During this time they forced King Sisavang Vong to declare Lao independence, and a nationalist resistance movement took shape, known as the Lao Issara (Free Lao). When the Japanese surrendered on 15 August, the Lao Issara formed an interim government, under the direction of Prince Phetsarat, a cousin of the king. For the first time since the early 18th century, the country was unified. The king, however, thereupon repudiated his declaration of independence in the belief that Laos still needed French protection. So tension quickly developed between Luang Prabang and Vientiane. The king dismissed Phetsarat as prime minister, so the provisional National Assembly of 45 prominent nationalists passed a motion deposing the king.

Behind these tensions were the French, who were determined to regain their Indochinese empire. After the war's end Chinese forces moved into Indochina north of the 16th parallel, and British Indian troops moved into the south to accept the surrender of the Japanese. The British soon handed command over to the French, enabling them to occupy southern Laos. In March 1946, while a truce held in Vietnam between the Viet Minh and the French, French forces struck north to seize control of the rest of Laos. The Lao Issara government was forced to flee to exile in Bangkok, leaving the French to sign a modus vivendi with the king reaffirming the unity of Laos and extending the king's rule from Luang Prabang to all of Laos. West Bank territories seized by Thailand in 1940 were returned to Laos.

'The Lao Issara formed an interim government, under the direction of Prince Phetsarat, a cousin of the king. For the first time since the early 18th century, the country was unified'

1974	1975	1979
Finally a ceasefire in Vietnam means an end to fighting in Laos and the formation of the Third Coalition Government.	Communist seizure of power and declaration of the Lao People's Democratic Republic (PDR). This ends 650 years of Lao monarchy.	Agricultural cooperatives abandoned and first economic reforms introduced.

The Kingdom of Laos became a member state of the new Indochinese Federation, with its own government and National Assembly. But the French were still very much in control. Those Lao who collaborated were denounced by the Lao Issara in Bangkok, which continued to support armed resistance.

By 1949 something of a stalemate had developed between the French and the Viet Minh in the main theatre of war in Vietnam. In order to shore up their position in Laos, the French granted the Lao a greater measure of independence. This partial independence was enough for Laos to gain recognition from Britain and the United States. A promise of amnesty for Issara leaders attracted most back to take part in the political process in Laos. Among the returnees was Souvanna Phouma, a younger brother of Phetsarat, who remained in Thailand. Meanwhile Souphanouvong, a half-brother of the two princes, led his followers to join the Viet Minh and keep up the anticolonial struggle.

RISE OF THE PATHET LAO

The decisions of the three princes to go their separate ways divided the Lao Issara. Those members who returned to Laos continued to work for complete Lao independence from France, but within the legal framework. Those who joined the Viet Minh did so in pursuit of an altogether different political goal – expulsion of the French and formation of a Marxist regime. Their movement became known as the Pathet Lao (Land of the Lao), after the title of the Resistance Government of Pathet Lao, set up with Viet Minh support in August 1950.

Cooperation between the Lao Issara and the Viet Minh went back to 1945, when, acting on Viet Minh instructions, Vietnamese in Laos backed the Lao Issara government. Joint Lao Issara–Viet Minh forces resisted the French reoccupation. Like the Lao Issara leaders, most Viet Minh in Laos fled the country, leaving the Mekong towns to be repeopled by Lao looking for jobs in the new Lao bureaucracy.

The architect of the Lao Issara–Viet Minh alliance was Prince Souphanouvong. He returned to Laos from Vietnam in time to take part in both the Lao Issara government (as foreign minister, though he would have preferred defence) and in the anti-French resistance. It was Souphanouvong who organised guerrilla resistance from bases in Thailand. He broke with his Issara-in-exile comrades when his close ties with the Viet Minh began to be questioned.

In August 1950 Souphanouvong became the public face of the Resistance Government and president of the Free Laos Front (Naeo Lao Issara), successor to the disbanded Lao Issara. Real power lay, however, with two other men, both of whom were members (as Souphanouvong then was not) of the Indochinese Communist Party. They were Kaysone Phomvihane, in

'Their movement became known as the Pathet Lao (Land of the Lao), after the title of the Resistance Government of Pathet Lao, set up with Viet Minh support in August 1950'

1986	1991	1995
The 'New Economic Mechanism' opens the way for a market economy and foreign investment.	Promulgation of the constitution of the Lao PDR. General Khamtay Siphandone becomes state president.	Luang Prabang is World Heritage–listed. Wat Phu, the ancient Khmer temple near Champasak, is listed shortly after.

charge of defence, and Nouhak Phoumsavan with the portfolio of economy and finance.

By that time the whole complexion of the First Indochina War had changed with the 1949 victory of communism in China. As Chinese weapons flowed to the Viet Minh, the war widened and the French were forced onto the defensive. In 1953 a Viet Minh force invaded northern Laos heading for Luang Prabang. The French flew in reinforcements, and the Viet Minh withdrew, turning over the whole region to the Pathet Lao. In order to protect Laos from another such invasion, the French established a substantial base in the remote mountain valley of Dien Bien Phu, close to the Lao border.

There was fought the deciding battle of the First Indochina War. The isolated French garrison was surrounded by Viet Minh forces, which pounded the base with artillery hidden in the hills. Supplied only from the air, the French held out for over two months before surrendering on 7 May. The following day a conference opened in Geneva that eventually brought the war to an end.

DIVISION & UNITY

As France had already granted full independence to Cambodia and Laos (in October 1953), it was as representatives of a free and independent country that the Lao delegation attended the conference in Geneva. After months of discussion it was agreed to divide Vietnam into north and south, each with a separate administration, but with the instruction to hold free and fair elections in both zones before the end of 1956. Cambodia was left undivided, but in Laos two northeastern provinces (Hua Phan and Phongsali) were set aside as regroupment areas for Pathet Lao forces. There the Pathet Lao consolidated their political and military organisation, while negotiating with the Royal Lao Government (RLG) to reintegrate the two provinces into a unified Lao state.

The first thing Pathet Lao leaders did was to establish a Lao Marxist political party. Previously Lao communists had been members of the Indochinese Communist Party, but in 1951 the ICP was disbanded and separate parties established for each state. Parties were founded immediately in Vietnam and Cambodia, but there were so few Lao members that it took time to recruit enough to constitute a party. Eventually the Lao People's Party was formed in 1955. (At its Second Congress in 1972 it was renamed the Lao People's Revolutionary Party, LPRP, which is today the ruling party of the Lao PDR.)

In good Marxist fashion, the LPP in 1956 established a broad political front, called the Lao Patriotic Front (LPF), behind which the Party could operate in secrecy. Souphanouvong was president of the Front, while Kaysone was secretary-general of the Party. Together with other members of the 'team' they led the Lao revolution throughout its '30-year struggle' (1945–1975) for

Kaysone Phomvihane was born in central Laos. As his father was Vietnamese and his mother Lao, he had a Vietnamese surname. He personally adopted the name Phomvihane, which is Lao for Brahmavihara, a series of four Buddhist heavens – an interesting choice for a committed Marxist.

power. Over this whole period no factionalism split the movement, which was one of its great strengths compared to the divisions among its opponents.

The first priority for the Royal Lao Government was to reunify the country. This required a political solution to which the Pathet Lao would agree. The tragedy for Laos was that when, after two centuries, an independent Lao state was reborn, it was conceived in the chaos of WWII, nourished during the agony of the First Indochina War, and born into the Cold War. From its inception, the Lao state was torn by ideological division, which the Lao tried mightily to overcome, but which was continuously exacerbated by outside interference.

In its remote base areas, the Pathet Lao was entirely dependent for weapons and most other kinds of assistance on the North Vietnamese, whose own agenda was the reunification of Vietnam under communist rule. Meanwhile the Royal Lao Government became increasingly dependent on the United States, which soon took over from France as its principal aid donor. Thus Laos became the cockpit for Cold War enmity.

From the Lao perspective, neutrality was the only realistic path for the country. And the only way to restore national unity was to bring the Pathet Lao into some kind of coalition government. To this the US was strongly opposed, seeing it as the thin end of a wedge that would lead to a communist seizure of power.

The Lao politician with the task of finding a way through both ideological differences and foreign interference was Souvanna Phouma. As prime minister of the RLG he negotiated a deal with his half-brother Souphanouvong which saw two Pathet Lao ministers and two deputy ministers included in a coalition government. The Pathet Lao provinces were returned to the royal administration. Elections were held, in which the LPF did surprisingly well. And the US was furious.

Between 1955 and 1958, the US gave Laos US$120 million, or four times what France had provided over the previous eight years. Laos was almost entirely dependent, therefore, on American largesse to survive. When that aid was withheld, as it was in August 1958 in response to the inclusion of Pathet Lao ministers in the government, Laos was plunged into a financial and political crisis. As a result, the first coalition government collapsed. It had lasted eight months.

With US support a right-wing government was installed in its place, without Pathet Lao representation, and Souvanna Phouma's neutralism was abandoned. Attempts to integrate Pathet Lao units into the Royal Lao Army collapsed, and the civil war resumed. A threatened military coup brought military strongman General Phoumi Nosavan to the Defence Ministry as deputy prime minister, again with American backing. Meanwhile under Kaysone's direction the Pathet Lao began building up their forces, recruit-

The Ravens: Pilots of the Secret War of Laos (1988) by Christopher Robbins tells the story of the American volunteer pilots based in Laos who supplied the 'secret army' and identified targets for US Air Force jets.

2001	2004	2005
A series of small bomb explosions worries the regime, which responds by increasing security.	Security is still tight when Laos hosts the 10th Asean summit in Vientiane, the largest gathering of world leaders ever assembled in Laos.	Ten-yearly census conducted putting population of Laos at 5,621,982.

ing especially from the tribal minorities in the mountainous areas where the Pathet Lao held power.

As guerrilla warfare resumed over large areas, moral objections began to be raised against Lao killing Lao. On 9 August 1960, the diminutive commanding officer of the elite Second Paratroop Batallion of the Royal Lao Army seized power in Vientiane while almost the entire Lao government was in Luang Prabang making arrangements for the funeral of King Sisavang Vong. Captain Kong Le announced to the world that Laos was returning to a policy of neutrality, and demanded that Souvanna Phouma be reinstated as prime minister. King Sisavang Vatthana acquiesced, but General Phoumi refused to take part, and flew to central Laos where he fomented opposition to the new government.

In this, he had the support of the Thai government and the US Central Intelligence Agency (CIA), which supplied him with cash and weapons. By December he was ready to march on Vientiane. The battle for the city was spirited, but lopsided. Kong Le withdrew to the Plain of Jars, until then garrisoned by the Royal Lao Army, where he joined forces with Pathet Lao units. The neutralist government still claimed to be the legitimate government of Laos, and as such received arms, via Vietnam, from the Soviet Union. Most of these found their way to the Pathet Lao, however. Throughout the country large areas fell under the control of communist forces. Offensives by the Royal Lao Army led to defeat and disaster. The US sent troops to Thailand, in case communist forces should attempt to cross the Mekong, and it looked for a while as if the major commitment of US troops in Southeast Asia would be to Laos rather than Vietnam.

THE SECOND COALITION & THE SECOND INDOCHINA WAR

At this point the new US administration of President John F Kennedy had second thoughts about fighting a war in Laos. In an about-face it decided instead to back Lao neutrality. In May 1961 a new conference on Laos was convened in Geneva. Progress was slow, however, because the three Lao factions could not agree on a political compromise that would allow a second coalition government to be formed. The right, under General Phoumi, was particularly recalcitrant. It took temporary suspension of US aid and a military defeat in northern Laos to convince the right to cooperate.

Eventually the 'three princes' (Souvanna Phouma for the neutralists, Souphanouvong for the Pathet Lao, and Boun Oum, hereditary prince of Champasak and then leader of the right) agreed to the composition of a second coalition government that balanced equal Pathet Lao and rightist representation (with four each), but left the neutralists with a voting majority (with 11 positions). Delegates of the 14 participating countries reassembled in Geneva in July 1962 to sign the international agreement guaranteeing Lao neutrality and forbidding the presence of all foreign military person-

During the Second Indochina War, Chinese military engineers built a network of roads into northern Laos. Though these roads assisted the Pathet Lao, they were never bombed by American aircraft, for fear that Chinese troops might join the war in northern Laos.

nel. In Laos the new coalition government took office buoyed by popular goodwill and hope.

Within months, however, cracks began to appear in the façade of the coalition. The problem was the war in Vietnam. Both the North Vietnamese and the Americans were jockeying for strategic advantage, and neither was going to let Lao neutrality get in the way. Despite the terms of the Geneva Agreements, both continued to provide their respective clients with arms and supplies. But no outside power did the same for the neutralists, who found themselves increasingly squeezed between left and right.

For the Vietnamese, Lao neutrality was designed to maintain existing de facto spheres of military control: the right in the Mekong lowlands; the Pathet Lao in the eastern highlands; a few neutralist units loyal to Souvanna Phouma in between. Moreover, Hanoi expected the Lao government to turn a blind eye to its use of Lao territory to infiltrate personnel and supplies into South Vietnam along what became known as the Ho Chi Minh Trail – as Cambodia did. For the Americans, Lao neutrality was designed precisely to prevent such infiltration.

For both sides the most strategically important area was the Plain of Jars, and this quickly became the principal battleground. As control of the plain would enable the US to threaten North Vietnam, Hanoi moved to prevent this – first by driving out Kong Le's neutralists; then by turning their attention to the CIA-trained Hmong 'secret army' (see the boxed text, p38) still supplied by the US in the mountains surrounding the plain.

By the end of 1963, as each side denounced the other for violating the Geneva Agreements, the Second Coalition Government had irrevocably broken down. Prime Minister Souvanna Phouma struggled to keep a façade intact, but Pathet Lao ministers had fled Vientiane, and neutralists had been cowered by the assassination of their foreign minister. It was in the interests of all powers, however, to preserve the façade of Lao neutrality, and international diplomatic support was brought to bear for Souvanna Phouma to prevent rightist generals from seizing power in coups mounted in 1964 and 1965.

In 1964 the US began its air war over Laos, with strafing and bombing of communist positions on the Plain of Jars. As North Vietnamese infiltration picked up along the Ho Chi Minh Trail, bombing was extended the length of Laos. According to official figures, the US dropped 2,093,100 tons of bombs on 580,944 sorties. The total cost was US$7.2 billion, or US$2 million a day for nine years. No one knows how many people died, but one-third of the population of 2.1 million became internal refugees.

During the 1960s both the North Vietnamese and the US presence increased exponentially. By 1968 an estimated 40,000 North Vietnamese regular army troops were based in Laos to keep the Ho Chi Minh Trail open and support some 35,000 Pathet Lao forces. The Royal Lao Army then numbered 60,000 (entirely paid for and equipped by the US), Vang Pao's forces were half that number (still under the direction of the CIA), and Kong Le's neutralists numbered 10,000. Lao forces on both sides were entirely funded by their foreign backers. For five more years this proxy war dragged on, until the ceasefire of 1973.

The turning point for the war in Vietnam was the 1968 Tet Offensive, which brought home to the American people the realisation that the war was unwinnable by military means, and convinced them of the need for a political solution. The effect in Laos, however, was to intensify both the air war and fighting on the Plain of Jars. When bombing was suspended over North Vietnam, the US Air Force concentrated all its efforts on Laos. The Pathet Lao leadership was forced underground, in the caves of Vieng Xai.

'In 1964 the US began its air war over Laos, with strafing and bombing of communist positions on the Plain of Jars. As North Vietnamese infiltration picked up along the Ho Chi Minh Trail, bombing was extended the length of Laos'

Though in much of Laos a 'tacit agreement' on spheres of control limited fighting between the two sides, on the Plain of Jars the ground war intensified. Instead of being used in guerrilla operations, units of the 'secret army' fought large-scale battles, in which they suffered heavy casualties.

But all the bombing was unable to staunch the flow of North Vietnamese forces down the Ho Chi Minh Trail (or trails). In January 1971 the one attempt by South Vietnamese forces to cut the Trail in southern Laos ended in defeat. The Pathet Lao claimed victory, but North Vietnamese forces did the fighting. Thereafter more of southern Laos fell to the Pathet Lao. By mid-1972, when serious peace moves got underway, some four-fifths of the country was under communist control.

In peace as in war, what happened in Laos depended on what happened in Vietnam. Not until a ceasefire came into effect in Vietnam in January 1973 could the fighting end in Laos. Then the political wrangling began. Not until September was an agreement reached on the composition of the Third Coalition Government and how it would operate; and it took another six months before security arrangements were in place for it to take office. The government reflected the changed balance of political power. Souvanna Phouma as prime minister was the sole neutralist, with other ministries equally divided between left and right.

It soon became clear that the Pathet Lao was unified, coordinated and following a well thought-out plan, formulated at the 1972 Second Congress of the Lao (LPRP). By contrast, the political right was fragmented and demoralised by the withdrawal of its US backer. This gave the communists the initiative, which they never lost.

REVOLUTION & REFORM

In April 1975, first Phnom Penh and then Saigon fell to superior communist forces. Immediately the Pathet Lao brought political pressure to bear on the right in Laos. Escalating street demonstrations forced leading rightist politicians and generals to flee the country. USAID was also targeted and hundreds of Americans began leaving Laos. Throughout the country, town after town was peacefully 'liberated' by Pathet Lao forces, culminating with Vientiane in August.

Souvanna Phouma, who could see the writing on the wall, cooperated with the Pathet Lao in order to prevent further bloodshed. Hundreds of senior military officers and civil servants voluntarily flew off to remote camps for 'political re-education', in the belief that they would be there only months at most. But Pathet Lao leaders had lied, just as they lied in promising to keep the monarchy. Hundreds of these inmates remained in re-education camps for several years.

With the rightist leadership either imprisoned or in Thailand, the Pathet Lao moved to consolidate power. At all levels of government, people's committees took administrative control, at the direction of the LPRP. In November an extraordinary meeting of what was left of the Third Coalition Government bowed to the inevitable and demanded formation of a 'popular democratic regime'. Under pressure, the king agreed to abdicate, and on 2 December a National Congress of People's Representatives assembled by the Party proclaimed the end of the 650-year-old Lao monarchy and the establishment of the Lao People's Democratic Republic (Lao PDR).

Unlike the military victories of communists in Cambodia and Vietnam, the Lao communists took power by 'quasi-legal' means. Their path to power had always used such means, by entering into coalition governments and demanding strict adherence to agreements, while continually strengthening their revolutionary forces. This strategy was the brainchild of Kaysone

Backfire: The CIA's Secret War in Laos and its Link to the War in Vietnam (1995) by Roger Warner provides an informed account of the range of CIA activity in Laos.

THE 'SECRET ARMY' & THE HMONG

After Laos gained independence in 1953, the United States trained and supplied the Royal Lao Army as part of its strategy to combat communism in Southeast Asia. In 1961, CIA agents made contact with the Hmong minority living on and around the Plain of Jars. They spread a simple message: 'Beware of the Vietnamese; they will take your land', handed out weapons and gave basic training. There were also some vague promises of Hmong autonomy. At the time, the plain was in the hands of neutralists and Pathet Lao, backed by North Vietnamese. To protect more vulnerable communities, several thousand Hmong decided to relocate to mountain bases to the south of the plain. Their leader was a young Hmong army officer named Vang Pao.

In October 1961 President John F Kennedy gave the order to recruit a force of 11,000 Hmong under the command of Vang Pao. They were trained by several hundred US and Thai Special Forces advisors and parachuted arms and food supplies by Air America, all under the supervision of the CIA.

The Hmong were a tough and independent people who had migrated into Laos in the early 19th century from China, where they had suffered persecution. They preferred to live at high altitudes, where they practised slash-and-burn agriculture and grew opium as a cash crop. In 1918 they rose in rebellion against the French administration, a rebellion that took the French four years to suppress. In the late 1930s a division occurred within the Hmong leadership over who had the right to represent the community under the French. In the First Indochina War, because of this division, though a majority of Hmong sided with the French (and later the Royal Lao Government), a substantial minority joined the Pathet Lao. The Hmong who formed the 'secret army' were those who had previously fought for the French.

With the neutralisation of Laos and formation of the Second Coalition Government in 1962, US military personnel were officially withdrawn. Even as it signed the 1962 Geneva Agreements, however, the US maintained its covert operations, in particular the supply and training of the 'secret army' for guerrilla warfare. The CIA's secret headquarters was at Long Cheng, but the largest Hmong settlement, with a population of several thousand, was at Sam Thong.

Over the next 12 years the Hmong 'secret army' fought a continuous guerrilla campaign against heavily armed North Vietnamese regular army troops occupying the Plain of Jars. They were supported throughout by the United States, an operation kept secret from the American public until 1970. So while American forces fought in Vietnam, a 'secret war' was also being fought in Laos. The Hmong fought because of their distrust of the communists, and in the hope that the US would support Hmong autonomy, but they paid a high price. In September 1969 a 'secret army' offensive, with heavy US air support, recaptured the Plain of Jars. Within six months a communist counteroffensive drove them back into the mountains, with terrible casualties.

As the war dragged on, so many Hmong were killed that it became difficult to find recruits. Boys as young as 12 were sent to war. The 'secret army' was bolstered by recruits from other minority groups, including Yao (Mien) and Khamu, and by whole battalions of Thai volunteers. By the early 1970s it had grown to more than 30,000 men, about a third of them Thai.

Not until 1970 did heavily censored transcripts of 1969 Congressional Hearings reveal the existence of the 'secret army' to the American people. Though the war in northern Laos was from then on no longer secret, no one then knew what the war had cost the Hmong. When a ceasefire was signed in 1973, prior to formation of the Third Coalition Government, the 'secret army' was officially disbanded. Thai volunteers returned home and Hmong units were absorbed into the Royal Lao Army. Hmong casualty figures have been put at 12,000 dead and 30,000 more wounded, but could well have been higher.

Years of warfare had bred deep distrust, however, and as many as 120,000 Hmong out of a population of some 300,000 fled Laos after 1975, rather than live under the Lao communist regime. Most were resettled in the United States. It should be noted that of those Hmong who sided with the Pathet Lao, several now hold senior positions in the Lao People's Revolutionary Party (LPRP) and in government.

Phomvihane, who in addition to leading the LPRP became prime minister in the new Marxist–Leninist government. Souphanouvong was named state president.

The new regime was organised in accordance with Soviet and North Vietnamese models. The government and bureaucracy were under the strict direction of the Party and its seven-member Politburo. Immediately the Party moved to restrict liberal freedoms of speech and assembly, and to nationalise the economy. People were forced to attend interminable 'seminars' to be indoctrinated into the Pathet Lao view of the world. As inflation soared, price controls were introduced. In response, most members of the Chinese and Vietnamese communities who still remained crossed the Mekong to Thailand. Thousands of Lao did the same. Eventually around 10% of the population, including virtually all the educated class, fled as refugees, setting Lao development back at least a generation.

The new communist government faced a daunting task. The economy of the rightist zone, particularly in the Mekong towns, had been entirely dependent on the injection of American aid. When this was terminated, the economy collapsed. The situation was aggravated by government policies and Thai closure of the border; and though Soviet, Eastern European and Vietnamese advisors poured in, levels of aid from the communist bloc were insufficient to replace American spending. A badly planned and executed attempt to cooperativise agriculture made things even worse.

The regime did not persecute Buddhism to anything like the extent the Khmer Rouge did in Cambodia, but it did curtail Buddhist religious life. Younger monks were encouraged to leave the Sangha (monastic order), while those who remained had to work for a living. The people were told not to waste their wealth on Buddhist festivals. Many monks fled to Thailand. The annual rocket festival, held to encourage a copious monsoon, was cancelled. That year there was a drought. People shrugged: the *naga* (mythical water serpent deities) had been offended. Next year the authorities allowed the festival to go ahead – and the rains were copious.

Though thousands of members of the 'secret army' and their families fled Laos, those who remained still resisted communist control. The Hmong insurgency dragged on for another 30 years. In 1977, fearing the king might escape his virtual house arrest to lead resistance, the authorities arrested him and his family and sent them to Vieng Xai, the old Pathet Lao wartime HQ. There they were forced to labour in the fields. The king, queen and crown prince all eventually died, probably of malaria and malnutrition, though no official statement of their deaths has ever been made.

By 1979 it was clear that policies had to change. Kaysone announced that people could leave cooperatives and farm their own land, and that private enterprise would be permitted. That year Vietnam invaded Cambodia to dispose of the Khmer Rouge, and China invaded northern Vietnam to teach Hanoi a lesson. Laos sided with Vietnam, and relations with the Chinese

The Politics of Ritual and Remembrance: Laos Since 1975 (1998) by Grant Evans provides a penetrating study of Lao political culture, including attitudes to Buddhism and the 'cult' of communist leader Kaysone.

RE-EDUCATION

Re-education camps were all in remote areas. Inmates laboured on road construction, helped local villagers, and grew their own vegetables. Food was nevertheless scarce, work hard, and medical attention inadequate or nonexistent. Except for a couple of high-security camps for top officials and army officers, inmates were allowed some freedom of contact with local villagers. Some even took local girls as partners. Escape was all but impossible, however, because of the remoteness of the camps. Only those showing a contrite attitude to past 'crimes' were released, some to work for the regime, but most to leave the country to join families overseas.

US AID-ING & ABETTING

The US had several hundred advisors in Laos, but no ground forces. Advisors were attached to the US embassy, the huge US Agency for International Development, or worked for Air America. Many more US military personnel supported the war from bases in Thailand. In Laos itself, civilians outnumbered the military, especially those working for USAID, which functioned as a parallel government. Their presence generated a demand for housing and other services, including entertainment. Bars and nightclubs sprang up, some renowned for their sexually explicit floor shows, and prostitution became rife.

The promise of employment or adventure attracted other foreigners to Vientiane, which had something of a frontier town feel to it. Drugs were freely available. Marijuana, used by the Lao for flavouring certain soups, could be bought in the markets, along with Lao tobacco. Opium, a traditional medicine, could also be purchased, or smoked in 'dens' across the city. One such was a disused theatre, with the best cubicles on the raised stage – until pressure from the US embassy brought about its closure.

In the Mekong towns, the war seemed far away and hardly intruded on everyday affairs. After all, fighting was not supposed to be happening in a country whose neutrality had been endorsed by international agreement. But war spending and the large American presence did bring some prosperity. New villas were built to rent to foreigners, motor traffic markedly increased and young Lao adopted the latest in American fashions, including flared jeans and long hair.

A substantial amount of American aid found its way into private Lao pockets, to be spent on parties, entertainment and travel abroad. Criticism of the lavish lifestyles of the wealthy was voiced especially by senior monks in the name of Buddhist morality, and was quickly seized upon by Pathet Lao propaganda, which warned that Lao culture and Lao youth were being corrupted by the decadent American culture.

deteriorated. They were no better with Thailand, which was supporting insurgency against the Vietnamese-installed regime in Cambodia.

Reforms were insufficient to improve the Lao economy. Over the next three years a struggle took place within the Party about what to do. The Soviet Union was getting tired of propping up the Lao regime, and was embarking on its own momentous reforms. Meanwhile Vietnam had Cambodia to worry about. Eventually Kaysone convinced the Party to do what the Chinese were doing: open the economy up to market forces, and the country to foreign aid and investment from the West, while retaining a tight monopoly on political power. The economic reforms were known as the 'new economic mechanism', and were enacted in November 1986.

Economic improvement was slow in coming, partly because relations with Thailand remained strained. In August 1987 the two countries fought a brief border war over disputed territory. The following year, relations were patched up, and with China too. The first elections for a National Assembly were held, and a constitution at last promulgated. Slowly a legal framework was put into place, and by the early 1990s foreign direct investment was picking up and the economy was on the mend.

MODERN LAOS

In 1992 Kaysone Phomvihane died. He had been the leading figure in Lao communism for more than a quarter of a century. The Party managed the transition to a new leadership with smooth efficiency, much to the disappointment of expatriate Lao communities abroad. General Khamtay Siphandone became both president of the Party and prime minister. Later he relinquished the latter to become state president. His rise signalled control of the Party by the revolutionary generation of military leaders. When

Khamtay stepped down in 2006, he was succeeded by his close comrade, General Chummaly Sayasone.

The economic prosperity of the mid-1990s rested on increased investment and foreign aid, on which Laos remained very dependent. The Lao PDR enjoyed friendly relations with all its neighbours. Relations with Vietnam remained particularly close, but were balanced by much improved relations with China. Relations with Bangkok were bumpy at times, but Thailand was a principal source of foreign direct investment. In 1997 Laos joined the Association of Southeast Asian Nations (Asean).

The good times came to an end with the Asian economic crisis of the late 1990s. The collapse of the Thai baht led to inflation of the Lao kip, to which it was largely tied through trading relations. The Lao regime took two lessons from this crisis: one was about the dangers of market capitalism; the other was that its real friends were China and Vietnam, both of which came to its aid with loans and advice.

The economic crisis sparked some political unrest. A small student demonstration calling for an end to the monopoly of political power by the LPRP was ruthlessly crushed and its leaders given long prison sentences. Lao dissidents in Thailand attacked a border customs post, provoking a swift Lao military response. A series of small bombings in Vientiane and southern Laos was also blamed on expatriate Lao dissidents, while Hmong 'brigands' were held responsible for attacks on transport in the north. In one attack, two Swiss cyclists were killed. Fearful of the effect on its burgeoning tourist industry, the government responded by increasing security.

Post-war Laos: The Politics of Culture, History and Identity (2006) by Vatthana Pholsena expertly examines how ethnicity, history and identity intersect in Laos.

The Lao authorities adopted a two-pronged approach. Pressure was placed on Thailand as an Asean member state to crack down on Lao dissidents in Thailand; while internally the Lao military went after the Hmong. In 2003 Western journalists for the first time made contact with Hmong insurgents. Their reports revealed an insurgency on the point of collapse. Renewed military pressure forced some Hmong to surrender, while others made their way to refuge in Thailand. Or so they thought. The Thai classified the Hmong as illegal immigrants; negotiations for resettlement in third countries stalled, and in December 2009, despite widespread international condemnation, some 4,000 Hmong were forcibly repatriated to an uncertain fate in Laos.

Security was still tight when Laos hosted the 10th Asean summit in Vientiane at the end of November 2004. This was the largest international gathering of world leaders ever assembled in Laos. A new multi-storey hotel was built and over 3000 delegates and 800 journalists attended. Despite prior bomb threats, the summit went off without incident, much to the relief of the Lao authorities. A similar success greeted the 25th Southeast Asian Games held in Vientiane in December 2009. Thousands of athletes attended from eleven Asean countries to compete in 28 sports. Laos did remarkably well to come seventh, winning 110 medals, including 33 gold. These two very different events boosted both Lao confidence and Lao nationalism.

Laos would never have been able to hold the 2009 Southeast Asian Games if China had not built a new national stadium, and Vietnam and Thailand provided other sporting facilities. But the secret agreement to hand over a large area of land in Vientiane for a housing development to the company that built the stadium met with widespread popular anger when it became known. This incident drew two things to public attention: the growing influence of China, and increasing high-level corruption.

In the decade to 2010, China greatly increased investment in Laos to almost equal that of Thailand. While official aid built such flashy projects as the National Cultural Center in downtown Vientiane, Japan remained the largest aid donor. However, Chinese companies invested in major projects in mining, hydropower and plantation agriculture and timber. Meanwhile, cross-border trade grew apace. Increased economic power brought political influence at the expense of Vietnam, though Lao–Vietnamese relations remained close and warm. Senior Lao Party cadres still take courses in Marxism–Leninism in Vietnam.

Increased investment brought increased exports and increased revenue for the government. Mining royalties are now a significant source of government revenue, as is the giant Nam Theun II hydroelectric dam, completed at the end of 2010. But much of this new wealth finds its way into the pockets of Party officials. Indeed, corruption has become widespread at all levels, much to the annoyance of many common folk. They argue that the government spends little on education and health – especially in the rural areas inhabited by ethnic minorities – so the gap between rural- and urban-living standards continues to widen.

Bamboo Palace: Discovering the Lost Dynasty of Laos (2003) by Christopher Kremmer builds on his personal travelogue told in *Stalking the Elephant Kings* (1997) to try to discover the fate of the Lao royal family.

PROSPECTS FOR THE 21ST CENTURY

However, prospects for Laos are relatively positive. Despite dissatisfaction over a lack of freedoms (of expression, association, and the press – essential to the development of a civil society) and rising levels of corruption, the LPRP faces minimal internal challenge to its authority. The Party seems set, therefore, to remain in power indefinitely – or at least for as long as it has the support of communist regimes in China and Vietnam.

New investments in hydropower and mining (gold, copper and bauxite) will bring a steady income into government coffers. Light industries, including textiles, face a more uncertain future as the Asean Free Trade Agreement (AFTA) comes into force and Laos eventually joins the World Trade Organisation (WTO). Forestry is another important resource.

Tourism, especially cultural, and ecotourism are growth industries. In 1995 Luang Prabang was placed on the Unesco World Heritage list, and Wat Phu, the ancient Khmer temple near Champasak, followed. Other parts of the country are opening up to ecotourism, including the Bolaven Plateau in the south, the Plain of Jars, and the far north. An added attraction is that many of the country's colourful minority tribes live in these regions. Laos attracted 1.7 million tourists in 2008 (well over half of them Thai), and the figure was expected to top 2 million in 2010.

Laos does not suffer severe population pressure, but there is a steady migration into the cities due to increasing disparities between urban and rural living standards. The government has shown little inclination to address this problem, or to improve the abysmally low education standards. Neither is there much focus on improving the poor health facilities available for the rural population faced with endemic diseases such as malaria, and HIV/AIDS. Some NGOs and foreign aid programs are trying to help, but human resources remain poorly developed.

Feature-film making resumed in Laos in 1997 – after a period of several years when only documentaries were produced – with the release of *Than Heng Phongphai* (The Charming Forest) directed by Vithoun Sundara. This was followed in 2001 by *Falang Phon* (Clear Skies After Rain), and in 2004 by *Leum Teua* (Wrongfulness), also directed by Sundara.

Reforms and new political movements will both be necessary for the country to prosper. Corruption remains a major problem, and laws are flouted because the legal system is under the control of the Party. The LPRP is now Marxist–Leninist in nothing but name. Rather, it exercises a single-party dictatorship, whose justification, many argue, is increasingly nationalistic. This may appeal to Lowland Lao, but less to the tribal minorities. Care will be needed to maintain social cohesion. It remains to be seen whether the Party has the resourcefulness to meet the challenges ahead.

The Culture

THE NATIONAL PSYCHE

It's hard to think of any other country with a population as laid back as Laos. *Baw pen nyăng* (no problem) could be the national motto. On the surface at least, nothing seems to faze the Lao and, especially if you're arriving from neighbouring China or Vietnam, the national psyche is both enchanting and beguiling. Of course, it's not as simple as 'people just smiling all the time because they're happy', as we heard one traveller describe it. The Lao national character is a complex combination of culture, environment and religion.

To a large degree 'Lao-ness' is defined by Buddhism, specifically Theravada Buddhism, which emphasises the cooling of the human passions. Thus strong emotions are a taboo in Lao society. *Kamma* (karma), more than devotion, prayer or hard work, is believed to determine one's lot in life, so the Lao tend not to get too worked up over the future. It's a trait often perceived by outsiders as a lack of ambition.

Lao commonly express the notion that 'too much work is bad for your brain' and they often say they feel sorry for people who 'think too much'. Education in general isn't highly valued, although this attitude is changing with modernisation and greater access to opportunities beyond Laos's borders. Avoiding any undue psychological stress, however, remains a cultural norm. From the typical Lao perspective, unless an activity – whether work or play – contains an element of *múan* (fun), it will probably lead to stress.

The contrast between the Lao and the Vietnamese is an example of how the Annamite Chain has served as a cultural fault line dividing Indic and Sinitic zones of influence. The French summed it up as: 'The Vietnamese plant rice, the Cambodians watch it grow and the Lao listen to it grow.' And while this saying wasn't meant as a compliment, a good number of French colonialists found the Lao way too seductive to resist, and stayed on.

The Lao have always been quite receptive to outside assistance and foreign investment, since it promotes a certain degree of economic development without demanding a corresponding increase in productivity. The Lao government wants all the trappings of modern technology – the skyscrapers seen on socialist propaganda billboards – without having to give up Lao traditions, including the *múan* philosophy. The challenge for Laos is to find a balance between cultural preservation and the development of new attitudes that will lead the country towards a measure of self-sufficiency.

Laos: Culture and Society (2000), by Grant Evans (ed), brings together a dozen essays on Lao culture, among them a profile of a self-exiled Lao family that eventually returned to Laos, and two well-researched studies of the modernisation and politicalisation of the Lao language.

Ethnic Groups of Laos, Vols 1-3 (2003) by Joachim Schliesinger is a well-respected modern ethnography of Laos. Schliesinger's scheme enumerates and describes 94 ethnicities in detail.

LIFESTYLE

Maybe it's because everything closes early, even in the capital, that just about everyone in Laos gets up before 6am. Their day might begin with a quick breakfast, at home or from a local noodle seller, before work. In Lao

---

RESPONSIBLE TRAVEL

- Always ask permission before taking photos.
- Don't prop your feet on chairs or tables while sitting.
- Never touch any part of someone else's body with your foot.
- Refrain from touching people on the head.
- Remove your shoes before entering homes or temple buildings.

Loum (Lowland Lao, see p48) and other Buddhist areas, the morning also sees monks collecting alms, usually from women who hand out rice and vegetables outside their homes in return for a blessing.

School-age children will walk to a packed classroom housed in a basic building with one or two teachers. Secondary students often board during the week because there are fewer secondary schools and it can be too far to commute. Almost any family who can afford it pays for their kids to learn English, which is seen as a near-guarantee of future employment.

Given that most Lao people live in rural communities, work is usually some form of manual labour. Depending on the season, and the person's location and gender (women and men have clearly defined tasks when it comes to farming), work might be planting or harvesting rice or other crops. Unlike neighbouring Vietnam, the Lao usually only harvest one crop of rice each year, meaning there are a couple of busy periods followed by plenty of time when life can seem very laid back.

During these quiet periods, men will fish, hunt and repair the house, while women might gather flora and fauna from the forest, weave fabrics and collect firewood. At these times there's something wonderfully social and uncorrupted about arriving in a village mid-afternoon, sitting in the front of the local 'store' and sharing a *lào-láo* (whisky) or two with the locals, without feeling like you're stealing their time.

Where vices are concerned, *lào-láo* is the drug of choice for most Lao, particularly in rural areas where average incomes are so low that Beerlao is beyond most budgets. Opium is the most high-profile of the other drugs traditionally used – and tolerated – in Laos, though recent crop-clearing has made it less available. In cities, *yaba* (methamphethamine), in particular, is becoming popular among young people.

Because incomes are rock-bottom in Laos – US$100 per month could be considered middle-class – the Lao typically socialise as families, pooling their resources to enjoy a *bun wat* (temple festival) or picnic at the local waterfall together. The Lao tend to live in extended families, with three or more generations sharing one house or compound, and dine together sitting on mats on the floor with rice and dishes shared by all.

Most Lao don some portion of the traditional garb during ceremonies and celebrations – the men a *phàa bjang* (shoulder sash), the women a similar sash, tight-fitting blouse and *phàa nung* (sarong). In everyday life men wear neat but unremarkable shirt-and-trousers combinations. However, it's still normal for women to wear the *phàa nung* or *sin* (sarong). Other ethnicities living in Laos – particularly Chinese and Vietnamese women – will wear the *phàa nung* when they visit a government office, or risk having any civic requests denied.

The Laos Cultural Profile (www.culturalprofiles.net/Laos) is established by Visiting Arts and the Ministry of Information and Culture of Laos covering a broad range of cultural aspects, from architecture to music. It's an easy entry point to Lao culture.

POLITICS & THE ECONOMY

At first glance the politics and economy of Laos seem simple enough: a one-party system is controlled by ageing revolutionaries that themselves have become a new elite, who have the power to control the exploitation of the country's natural resources, can squash any dissent and cooperate enough with foreign donors to keep the aid dollars coming in. But this generalisation is just that – the reality is more complex.

Laos is indeed a single-party socialist republic, with the only legal political entity being the ruling Lao People's Revolutionary Party (LPRP). President Chummaly Sayasone is both the head of state and the head of the LPRP; the head of government is Prime Minister Bouasone Bouphavanh. Both were appointed to their five-year terms by the 115-member National Assembly in June 2006. The National Assembly itself was elected in April 2006 and now

FEELING THE 'REAL LAOS'

A lot of travellers come looking for the 'real Laos', but few know exactly what that is. For about 80% of the population the 'real Laos' is village life, and the best way to really get a feel for how the Lao live is to spend a night or two in a homestay.

A homestay is, as the name suggests, staying with a family in their home, sleeping, eating and living just as they do. So what can you expect? The details vary from place to place, depending on ethnicity, geography and wealth, but the usual experience is described here.

Villages are small, dusty/muddy depending on the season, and full of kids. You'll be billeted with a family, usually with a maximum of two travellers per family. Toilets will be the squat variety, with scoop flush, in a dark hut at the corner of the block. You'll bathe before dinner, either in a nearby stream or river, or by using a scoop to pour water over yourself from a well, 44-gallon drum or concrete reservoir in your family's yard. Bathing is usually a public event – don't forget a sarong. Don't expect a mirror.

Food will be simple fare, usually two dishes and sticky rice. In our experience it's almost always been delicious, but prepare yourself for a sticky rice extravaganza – it's not uncommon to encounter the starch at every single meal. Even if the food doesn't appeal, you should eat something or your host will lose face. Dinner is usually served on mats on the floor, so prepare to sit lotus-style or with legs tucked under. Don't sit on pillows as that's bad form, and always take off your shoes before entering the house.

Your meal will most likely be followed by a communal drinking session. If you're lucky this will mean cold bottles of Beerlao, but more likely it will revolve around homemade rice alcohol served from a communal cup. The stuff can be pretty harsh, but if you can stomach it, it's a great icebreaker, and some of our best nights in Laos have been spent this way.

Sleeping will probably be under a mosquito net on a mattress on the floor, and might change to 'waking' once the cocks start crowing outside your window.

It might not be luxurious but homestay is very much the 'real Laos' and is a thoroughly worthwhile and enjoyable experience. Just remember that for most villagers, dealing with *falang* tourists is pretty new and they are sensitive to your reactions. Their enthusiasm will remain as long as their guests engage with them and accept them, and their lifestyle, without undue criticism. To get the most out of it take a phrasebook and photos of your family, and, most importantly, a torch, flip-flops, a sarong and toilet paper.

consists of 113 LPRP members and two non-partisan independents. There was, and remains, no legal opposition.

Change seems to come slowly in Laos, but when it does most policies and decisions come from an 11-member Politburo and a 55-member Central Committee – two powerful vestiges of the Soviet-style system adopted after the Pathet Lao takeover in 1975. Their decisions are rubber-stamped by the National Assembly.

Few outside the inner sanctum really understand the political scene, but it's accepted that the LPRP is loosely split between an older, more conservative guard and younger members pushing for limited reform. Cynics will tell you the infighting is mainly for the control of the lucrative kickbacks available to those who control the rights to Laos's rich natural resources. Others say the reformers' primary motivation is to alleviate poverty more quickly by speeding up development. The reality most likely lies somewhere between these two extremes.

Economically, Laos is in an interesting period. After the dark times of the Asian financial crisis in the late 1990s, the economy reported 6.4% growth in 2009, the second highest in Asia. However, other numbers don't look so hot. The World Bank rates Laos as one of the least-developed countries in East Asia, with more than 75% of people living on less than US$2 a day. More than three-quarters of the population still live as subsistence farmers

Foreign ethnographers who have carried out field research in Laos have identified anywhere from 94 to 134 different ethnic groups.

and gross domestic product was just an estimated US$5.2 billion in 2008. Major exports are timber products, garments, electricity and coffee, in that order. In recent years tourism has become one of the main earners of foreign income, much of which flows directly into the pockets of those who need it most.

Foreign aid remains a constant of the Laos economy, as it has been since the 1800s. First the French established a basic infrastructure, followed by massive wartime investment by the USA. Soviet and to a lesser extent Vietnamese assistance saw Laos into the 1990s, when the Japanese and Western governments and NGOs started picking up the development tab. Laos's reliance is unsurprising when you consider there is little effective taxation and the country is only now, for the first time, developing notable export capacity (in hydropower). Put simply, the money needed for building roads, bridges, schools, hospitals etc didn't exist at home, so someone else had to foot the bill, or allow Laos to continue languishing in poverty.

In recent years China has started spending some of its enormous surplus in Laos. Apart from the obvious investment in infrastructure such as roads, dams and plantations, this has two significant effects. First, Chinese aid comes with few strings attached, meaning for example that roads, plantations and dams are built by Chinese companies with little or no concern for local people or environments. This is in contrast to the usual carrot and stick approach of Western donors, who supply aid in various forms that is dependent on the Lao government improving their systems and getting involved in the development, rather than just sitting back and waiting for the dollars to roll in. Of course, not all Western aid programs are perfect – most are far from it – but most at least pay some attention to factors like governance and environmental impact.

Second, if one of your largest donors is the biggest regional political power and a one-party state just like you, it could be argued that it may not be the sort of role model that will encourage political or economic reform.

The development of hydroelectric and mining operations is expected to reduce Laos's reliance on foreign aid to a certain extent. Mines, such as the gold and copper operation at Sepon, are beginning to contribute to the government coffers. Dams like Nam Theun 2 will do likewise. Just who benefits from these projects, and how many will feel their negative impacts, is debatable. While foreign companies extract sizeable profits from their operations in Laos, the taxes and concession fees they pay may take a long time to trickle down to the average Lao family.

POPULATION

Laos has one of the lowest population densities in Asia, but the total population has more than doubled in the last 30 years, and continues to grow quickly. A third of Laos's 6.8 million inhabitants live in cities in the Mekong River valley, chiefly Vientiane, Luang Prabang, Savannakhet and Pakse. Another third live along other major rivers.

This rapid population growth comes despite the fact that almost one in 10 Lao fled the country after the 1975 communist takeover. Vientiane and Luang Prabang lost the most inhabitants, with approximately a quarter of the population of Luang Prabang going abroad. During the last 10 to 15 years this emigration trend has been reversed so that the influx of immigrants – mostly repatriated Lao, but also Chinese, Vietnamese and other nationalities – now exceeds the number of émigrés.

Most expatriate Westerners living in Laos are temporary employees of multilateral and bilateral aid organisations. A smaller number are employed by foreign companies involved in mining, petroleum and hydropower.

Article 9 of the current Lao constitution forbids all religious proselytising, and the distribution of religious materials outside churches, temples or mosques is illegal. Foreigners caught distributing religious materials may be arrested and expelled from the country.

SPORT

Like most poor countries, you won't read much about Laos when the Olympic circus sets up its tent. Laos has never won an Olympic medal, or much else in the international sporting arena, but that doesn't mean it's a complete sporting black hole.

Laos has a few traditional sports and these are as often an excuse for betting as they are a means of exercise. *Kátâw* (p47) and *múay láo* (Lao boxing, p47) certainly do involve exercise – and these are taken increasingly seriously as international competition raises their profiles. Cockfighting, however, does not involve exercise. Cockfights follow the usual rules, except that in Laos the cocks are not fitted with blades so they often survive the bout. If you want to watch (or not), keep your eyes and ears open, particularly on Sundays and public holidays.

In ethnic Tai areas you might find the more off-beat 'sport' of beetle fighting. These bouts involve notoriously fractious rhinoceros beetles squaring off while a crowd, usually more vociferous after liberal helpings of *lào-láo*, bets on the result. The beetles hiss and attack, lifting each other with their horns, until one decides it no longer wants to be part of this 'entertainment' and runs. If you bet on the runner, you lose. Beetle bouts are limited to the wet season.

Kids in Laos are likely to be seen chasing around a football (or at least something that resembles a football). Opportunities for pursuing football professionally are few, limited by an almost complete lack of quality coaching, pitches, and youth leagues where players can get experience of proper competition. Laos does, however, rank higher than its Southeast Asian neighbours in FIFA standings, and interprovincial matches at the National Stadium in Vientiane or in modest stadia in provincial capitals draw relatively large crowds.

Kátâw

Kátâw, a contest in which a woven rattan or plastic ball about 12cm in diameter is kicked around, is almost as popular in Laos as it is in Thailand and Malaysia.

Traditional *kátâw* involved players standing in a circle (the size of the circle depending on the number of players) and trying to keep the ball airborne by kicking it soccer-style. Points were scored for style, difficulty and variety of kicking manoeuvres.

A modern variation on *kátâw* – the one used in local or international competitions – is played with a volleyball net, using all the same rules as in volleyball except that only the feet and head are permitted to touch the ball. It's amazing to see the players perform aerial pirouettes, spiking the ball over the net with their feet. You're most likely to see *kátâw* in school yards, wats and public spaces, usually in the afternoon.

Múay Láo (Lao Boxing)

The Lao seem to have an almost insatiable appetite for televised kickboxing, whether the pictures are coming from Thailand (*múay thái*) or are of a local fight, known as *múay láo* (Lao kickboxing). *Múay láo* is not nearly as developed a sport in Laos as its counterpart in Thailand, and is mostly confined to amateur fights at upcountry festivals, but on most weekends you'll see the bigger fights broadcast on TV.

All surfaces of the body are considered fair targets and any part of the body except the head may be used to strike an opponent. Common blows include high kicks to the neck, elbow thrusts to the face and head, knee hooks to the ribs and low crescent kicks to the calf. A contestant may even

Due to Laos's ethnic diversity, 'Lao culture' only exists among the Lowland Lao or Lao Loum, who represent about half the population. Lao Loum culture predominates in the cities, towns and villages of the Mekong River valley.

Festivals of Laos (2010) by Martin Stuart-Fox and Somsanouk Mixay covers the full annual cycle of Lao festivals, from New Year to That Luang, with the added bonus of Steve Northup's stunning photographs.

PETANG

While you'll see plenty of *kátâw* and football, the sport you'll most likely be able to actually play is *petang*. Introduced by the French, *petang* is obviously a local corruption of pétanque. All over Laos you'll see small courts made of packed dirt or gravel. There's usually a certain level of improvisation with the 'playing arena'; the backboard might be a length of coconut trunk, and the throwing circle is usually a bike tyre.

While it's been around for decades, Lao involvement in international competition – presumably televised – has sparked a renewed interest in the game. In the 2005 Southeast Asian Games, Laos won gold in the men's singles and silver in the men's doubles, and in subsequent competitions the country has bagged another 16 medals including four gold, significant achievements for success-starved Laos.

As you travel around you'll see games are usually played in the afternoon and the players are usually men. If the game doesn't look like a life-and-death battle it's fine to ask to join in. The aim of the game is to get your *boule* (steel ball) as close to the *cochonnet* (piglet) as possible. Petang is supposed to be played between teams of two or three, though in practice it depends on how many boules and bodies are available. For technique, just watch and learn – and be careful not to injure any passing child or chicken.

---

grasp an opponent's head between his hands and pull it down to meet an upward knee thrust.

International boxing *(múay sǎakǫn)* is gaining popularity in Laos and is encouraged by the government in spite of the obvious Lao preference for the bang-up Southeast Asian version.

ETHNIC GROUPS

Laos is often described as less a nation state than a conglomeration of tribes and languages. And depending on who you talk with, that conglomeration consists of between 49 and 134 different ethnic groups. (The lower figure is that now used by the government.)

While the tribal groups are many and varied, the Lao traditionally divide themselves into four categories – Lao Loum, Lao Tai, Lao Thoeng and Lao Soung. These classifications loosely reflect the altitudes at which the groups live, and, by implication (it's not always accurate), their cultural proclivities. To address some of these inaccuracies, the Lao government recently reclassified ethnic groups into three major language families – Austro-Tai, Austro-Asiatic and Sino-Tibetan. However, many people you meet won't know which language family they come from, so we'll stick here with the more commonly understood breakdown.

Just over half the population are ethnic Lao or Lao Loum, and these are clearly the most dominant group. Of the rest, 10% to 20% are tribal Tai, 20% to 30% are Lao Thoeng ('Upland Lao' or lower-mountain dwellers, mostly of proto-Malay or Mon-Khmer descent) and 10% to 20% are Lao Soung ('Highland Lao', mainly Hmong or Mien tribes who live higher up).

The Lao government has an alternative three-way split, in which the Lao Tai are condensed into the Lao Loum group. This triumvirate is represented on the back of every 1000 kip bill, in national costume, from left to right: Lao Soung, Lao Loum and Lao Thoeng.

Small Tibeto-Burman hill-tribe groups in Laos include the Lisu, Lahu, Lolo, Akha and Phu Noi. They are sometimes classified as Lao Thoeng, but like the Lao Soung they live in the mountains of northern Laos.

Lao Loum

The dominant ethnic group is the Lao Loum (Lowland Lao), who through superior numbers and living conditions – in the fertile plains of the Mekong

River valley or lower tributaries of the Mekong – have for centuries domi-nated the smaller ethnic groups living in Laos. Their language is the national language; their religion, Buddhism, is the national religion; and many of their customs – including the eating of sticky rice and the *bąasĭi* ceremony (see p53) – are interpreted as those of the Lao nation, even though they play no part in the lives of many other ethnic groups.

Lao Loum culture has traditionally consisted of a sedentary, subsistence lifestyle based on wet-rice cultivation. The people live in raised homes and, like most Austro-Tais, are Theravada Buddhists who retain strong elements of animist spirit worship.

The distinction between 'Lao' and 'Thai' is a rather recent historical phenomenon, especially considering that 80% of all those who speak a lan-guage recognised as 'Lao' reside in northeastern Thailand. Even Lao living in Laos refer idiomatically to different Lao Loum groups as 'Tai' or 'Thai', for example, Thai Luang Phabang (Lao from Luang Prabang).

Lao Tai

Although they're closely related to the Lao, these Tai (or sometimes Thai) subgroups have resisted absorption into mainstream Lao culture and tend to subdivide themselves according to smaller tribal distinctions. Like the Lao Loum, they live along river valleys, but the Lao Tai have chosen to reside in upland valleys rather than in the lowlands of the Mekong floodplains.

Depending on their location, they cultivate dry (mountain) rice as well as wet (irrigated) rice. The Lao Tai also mix Theravada Buddhism and animism, but tend to place more importance on spirit worship than do the Lao Loum.

Generally speaking, the various Lao Tai groups are distinguished from one another by the predominant colour of their clothing, or by the general area of habitation; for example, Tai Dam (Black Tai), Tai Khao (White Tai), Tai Pa (Forest Tai), Tai Neua (Northern Tai) and so on.

Lao Thoeng

The Lao Thoeng (Upland Lao) are a loose affiliation of mostly Austro-Asiatic peoples who live on midaltitude mountain slopes in northern and southern Laos. The largest group is the Khamu, followed by the Htin, Lamet and smaller numbers of Laven, Katu, Katang, Alak and other Mon-Khmer groups in the south. The Lao Thoeng are also known by the pejorative term *khàa*, which means 'slave' or 'servant'. This is because they were used as indentured labour by migrating Austro-Thai peoples in earlier centuries and more recently by the Lao monarchy. They still often work as labourers for the Lao Soung.

The Lao Thoeng have a much lower standard of living than any of the three other groups described here. Most trade between the Lao Thoeng and other Lao is carried out by barter.

The Htin (also called Lawa) and Khamu languages are closely related, and both groups are thought to have been in Laos long before the arrival of the Lowland Lao, tribal Thai or Lao Soung. During the Lao New Year celebrations in Luang Prabang the Lowland Lao offer a symbolic tribute to the Khamu as their historical predecessors and as 'guardians of the land'.

Lao Soung

The Lao Soung (Highland Lao) include the hill tribes who live at the highest altitudes. Of all the peoples of Laos, they are the most recent immigrants, hav-ing come from Myanmar, Tibet and southern China within the last 150 years.

The largest group is the Hmong, also called Miao or Meo, who number more than 300,000 in four main subgroups, the White Hmong, Striped

'Lao Tai groups are distin-guished from one another by the pre-dominant colour of their clothing, or by the general area of habitation'

Hmong, Red Hmong and Black Hmong (the colours refer to certain clothing details). They are found in the nine provinces of the north, plus Bolikhamsai in central Laos.

The agricultural staples of the Hmong are dry rice and corn raised by the slash-and-burn method. The Hmong also breed cattle, pigs, water buffaloes and chickens, traditionally for barter rather than sale. For years their only cash crop was opium and they grew and manufactured more than any other group in Laos. However, an aggressive eradication program run by the government (with support from the USA) has eliminated most of the crop. The resulting loss of a tradeable commodity has hit many Hmong communities very hard. The Hmong are most numerous in Hua Phan, Xieng Khuang, Luang Prabang and northern Vientiane provinces.

The second-largest group are the Mien (also called Iu Mien, Yao and Man), who live mainly in Luang Nam Tha, Luang Prabang, Bokeo, Udomxai and Phongsali. The Mien, like the Hmong, have traditionally cultivated opium poppies. Replacement crops, including coffee, are taking time to bed in and generate income.

The Mien and Hmong have many ethnic and linguistic similarities, and both groups are predominantly animist. The Hmong are considered more aggressive and warlike than the Mien, however, and as such were perfect for the CIA-trained special Royal Lao Government forces in the 1960s and early 1970s (see the boxed text, p38). Large numbers of Hmong–Mien left Laos and fled abroad after 1975.

Other Asians

As elsewhere in Southeast Asia, the Chinese have been migrating to Laos for centuries to work as merchants and traders. Most come direct from Yunnan but more recently many have also arrived from Vietnam. Estimates of their numbers vary from 2% to 5% of the total population. At least half of all permanent Chinese residents in Laos are said to live in Vientiane and Savannakhet. There are also thousands of Chinese migrant workers in the far north.

Substantial numbers of Vietnamese live in all the provinces bordering Vietnam and in the cities of Vientiane, Savannakhet and Pakse. For the most part, Vietnamese residents in Laos work as traders and own small businesses, although there continues to be a small Vietnamese military presence in Xieng Khuang and Hua Phan Provinces. Small numbers of Cambodians live in southern Laos.

RELIGION
Buddhism

About 60% of the people of Laos – mostly Lowland Lao, with a sprinkling of tribal Tais – are Theravada Buddhists. Theravada Buddhism was apparently introduced to Luang Prabang (then known as Muang Sawa) in the late 13th or early 14th centuries, though there may have been contact with Mahayana Buddhism during the 8th to 10th centuries and with Tantric Buddhism even earlier.

King Visoun – a successor of the first monarch of Lan Xang, King Fa Ngum – declared Buddhism the state religion after accepting the Pha Bang Buddha image from his Khmer sponsors. Today the Pha Bang is kept at Wat Manorom (p156) in Luang Prabang. Buddhism was fairly slow to spread throughout Laos, even among the lowland peoples, who were reluctant to accept the faith instead of, or even alongside, *phii* (earth spirit) worship.

Theravada Buddhism is an earlier and, according to its followers, less corrupted school of Buddhism than the Mahayana schools found in east Asia

Two slim books of *Lao Folktales*, collected by Steve Epstein, retell some of Laos's better-known folklore. They're great for kids and offer an interesting insight into Lao humour and values.

POST-REVOLUTION BUDDHISM

During the 1964–73 war years, both sides sought to use Buddhism to legitimise their cause. By the early 1970s, the Lao Patriotic Front (LPF) was winning this propaganda war as more and more monks threw their support behind the communists.

Despite this, major changes were in store for the Sangha (monastic order) following the 1975 takeover. Initially, Buddhism was banned as a primary-school subject and people were forbidden to make merit by giving food to monks. Monks were also forced to till the land and raise animals in direct violation of their monastic vows.

Mass dissatisfaction among the faithful prompted the government to rescind the ban on the feeding of monks in 1976. By the end of that year, the government was not only allowing traditional alms-giving, it was offering a daily ration of rice directly to the Sangha.

In 1992, in what was perhaps its biggest endorsement of Buddhism since the Revolution, the government replaced the hammer-and-sickle emblem that crowned Laos's national seal with a drawing of Pha That Luang, the country's holiest Buddhist symbol.

Today the Department of Religious Affairs (DRA) controls the Sangha and ensures that Buddhism is taught in accordance with Marxist principles. All monks must undergo political indoctrination as part of their monastic training, and all canonical and extracanonical Buddhist texts have been subject to 'editing' by the DRA. Monks are also forbidden to promote *phǐi* (earth spirit) worship, which has been officially banned in Laos along with *sainyasqat* (magic). The cult of *khwǎn* (the 32 guardian spirits attached to mental/physical functions), however, has not been tampered with.

One major change in Lao Buddhism was the abolition of the Thammayut sect. Formerly, the Sangha in Laos was divided into two sects, the Mahanikai and the Thammayut (as in Thailand). The Thammayut is a minority sect that was begun by Thailand's King Mongkut. The Pathet Lao saw it as a tool of the Thai monarchy (and hence US imperialism) for infiltrating Lao political culture.

For several years all Buddhist literature written in Thai was also banned, severely curtailing the teaching of Buddhism in Laos. This ban has since been lifted and Lao monks are even allowed to study at Buddhist universities throughout Thailand. However, the Thammayut ban remains and has resulted in a much weaker emphasis on meditation, considered the spiritual heart of Buddhist practice in most Theravada countries. Overall, monastic discipline in Laos is far more relaxed than it was before 1975.

and the Himalayas. It's sometimes referred to as the 'Southern' school since it took the southern route from India through Sri Lanka and Southeast Asia.

Theravada doctrine stresses the three principal aspects of existence: *dukkha* (suffering, unsatisfactoriness, disease), *anicca* (impermanence, transience of all things) and *anatta* (nonsubstantiality or nonessentiality of reality – no permanent 'soul'). Comprehension of *anicca* reveals that no experience, no state of mind, no physical object lasts. Trying to hold onto experience, states of mind, and objects that are constantly changing creates *dukkha*. *Anatta* is the understanding that there is no part of the changing world we can point to and say 'This is me' or 'This is God' or 'This is the soul'.

The ultimate goal of Theravada Buddhism is *nibbana* (Sanskrit: *nirvana*), which literally means the 'blowing-out' or 'extinction' of all causes of *dukkha*. Effectively it means an end to all corporeal or even heavenly existence, which is forever subject to suffering and which is conditioned from moment to moment by *kamma* (action). In reality, most Lao Buddhists aim for rebirth in a 'better' existence rather than the supra-mundane goal of *nibbana*. By feeding monks, giving donations to temples and performing regular worship at the local wat, Lao Buddhists acquire enough 'merit' (Pali *puñña*; Lao *bun*) for their future lives. And it's in the pursuit of merit that you're most likely to see Lao Buddhism 'in action'. Watching monks walking through their neighbourhoods at dawn to collect offerings of food from people who are kneeling in front of their homes, is a memorable experience.

Lao Buddhists visit the wat on no set day. Most often they'll visit on *wán pha* (literally 'excellent days'), which occur with every full, new and quarter moon, ie roughly every seven days. On such a visit, typical activities include the offering of lotus buds, incense and candles at various altars and bone reliquaries, offering food to the monks, meditating, and attending a *thêt* (*Dhamma* talk) by the abbot.

MONKS & NUNS
Unlike other religions in which priests, nuns, rabbis, imams etc make a lifelong commitment to their religious vocation, being a Buddhist monk or nun can be a much more transient experience. Socially, every Lao Buddhist male is expected to become a *khúu-bạa* (monk) for at least a short period in his life, optimally between the time he finishes school and starts a career or marries. Men or boys under 20 years of age may enter the Sangha (monastic order) as *néhn* (novices) and this is not unusual since a family earns merit when one of its sons takes robe and bowl. Traditionally the length of time spent in the wat is three months, during the *phansǎa* (Buddhist lent), which coincides with the rainy season. However, nowadays men may spend as little as a week or 15 days to accrue merit as monks or novices. There are, of course, some monks who do devote all or most of their lives to the wat.

There is no similar hermetic order for nuns, but women may reside in temples as *náang sǐi* (lay nuns), with shaved heads and white robes.

Spirit Cults
No matter where you are in Laos the practice of *phǐi* (spirit) worship – sometimes called animism – won't be far away. *Phǐi* worship predates Buddhism and despite being officially banned it remains the dominant non-Buddhist belief system. But for most Lao it is not a matter of Buddhism *or* spirit worship. Instead established Buddhist beliefs coexist peacefully with respect for the *phǐi* that are believed to inhabit natural objects.

An obvious example of this coexistence is the 'spirit house', which you'll see in or outside almost every home. Spirit houses are often ornately decorated miniature temples, built as a home for the local spirit. Residents must share their space with the spirit and go to great lengths to keep it happy, offering enough incense and food that the spirit won't make trouble for them.

In Vientiane you can see Buddhism and spirit worship side-by-side at Wat Si Muang (p94). The central image at the temple is not a Buddha figure but the *lák méuang* (city pillar), in which the guardian spirit for the city is believed to reside. Many local residents make daily offerings before the pillar, while at the same time praying to a Buddha figure. A form of *phǐi* worship you might actually partake in is the *bạasǐi* ceremony; see the boxed text.

Outside the Mekong River valley, the *phǐi c*ult is particularly strong among the tribal Thai, especially the Tai Dam, who pay special attention to a class of *phǐi* called *then*. The *then* are earth spirits that preside not only over the plants and soil, but over entire districts as well. The Tai Dam also believe in the 32 *khwǎn* (guardian spirits). *Mǎw (*master/shaman), who are specially trained in the propitiation and exorcism of spirits, preside at important Tai Dam festivals and ceremonies. It is possible to see some of the spiritual beliefs and taboos in action by staying in a Katang village during a trek into the forests of Dong Phu Vieng NPA (p262).

The Hmong–Mien tribes also practise animism, plus ancestral worship. Some Hmong groups recognise a pre-eminent spirit that presides over all earth spirits; others do not. The Akha, Lisu and other Tibeto-Burman groups mix animism and ancestor cults.

Lao Buddha: The Image & Its History (2000), by Somkiart Lopetcharat, is a large coffee-table book containing a wealth of information on the Lao interpretation of the Buddha figure.

BĄASĬI (BACI)

The *bqasĭi* ceremony is a peculiarly Lao ritual in which guardian spirits are bound to the guest of honour by white or orange strings tied around the wrists. Among Lao it's more commonly called *su khwăn*, meaning 'calling of the soul'.

Lao believe everyone has 32 spirits, known as *khwăn*, each of which acts as a guardian over a specific organ or faculty – mental and physical. *Khwăn* occasionally wander away from their owner, which is really only a problem when that person is about to embark on a new project or journey away from home, or when they're very ill. Then it's best to perform the *bqasĭi* to ensure that all the *khwăn* are present, thus restoring the equilibrium. In practice, *bqasĭi* are also performed at festivals, weddings, and when special guests arrive – hence villagers often hold a *bqasĭi* when trekkers arrive during a community-based trek.

The *bqasĭi* ceremony is performed seated around a *pha khwăn*, a conical shaped arrangement of banana leaves, flowers and fruit from which hang cotton threads. A village elder, known as the *măw phon*, calls in the wandering *khwăn* during a long Buddhist mantra while he, and the honoured guests, lean in to touch the *pha khwăn*. When the chanting is finished, villagers take the thread from the *pha khwăn* and begin tying it around the wrists of the guests.

At this point the ceremony becomes a lot of fun. Villagers move around the room, stopping in front of guests to tie thread around their wrists. They'll often start by waving the thread across your hand, three times outwards accompanied by 'out with the bad, out with the bad, out with the bad', or something similar, and three times in with 'in with the good'. As they tie they'll also wish you a safe journey and good health, with the more comedic calling for beautiful wives, many children etc.

After the ceremony everyone shares a meal. You're supposed to keep the threads on your wrists for three days and then untie, not cut, them.

Other Religions

A small number of Lao – mostly those of the remaining French-educated elite – are Christians. An even smaller number of Muslims live in Vientiane, mostly Arab and Indian merchants whose ancestry as Laos residents dates as far back as the 17th century. Vientiane also harbours a small community of Chams, Cambodian Muslims who fled Pol Pot's Kampuchea in the 1970s. In northern Laos there are pockets of Muslim Yunnanese, known among the Lao as *jǐin háw*.

WOMEN IN LAOS

For the women of Laos roles and status vary significantly depending on their ethnicity, but it's fair to say that whatever group they come from they are seen as secondary to men. As you travel around Laos the evidence is overwhelming. While men's work is undoubtedly hard, women always seem to be working harder, for longer, with far less time for relaxing and socialising.

Lao Loum women gain limited benefits from bilateral inheritance patterns, whereby both women and men can inherit land and business ownership. This derives from a matrilocal tradition, where a husband joins the wife's family on marriage. Often the youngest daughter and her husband will live with and care for her parents until they die, when they inherit at least some of their land and business. However, even if a Lao Loum woman inherits her father's farmland, she will have only limited control over how it is used. Instead, her husband will have the final say on most major decisions, while she will be responsible for saving enough money to see the family through any crisis.

This fits with the cultural beliefs associated with Lao Buddhism, which commonly teaches that women must be reborn as men before they can attain nirvana, hence a woman's spiritual status is generally less than that of a man. Still, Lao Loum women enjoy a higher status than women from other ethnic groups, who become part of their husband's clan on marriage and rarely inherit anything.

Women in Laos face several other hurdles: fewer girls go to school than boys; women are relatively poorly represented in government and other senior positions; and although they make up more than half the workforce, pay is often lower than male equivalents. If a Lao woman divorces, no matter how fair her reasons, it's very difficult for her to find another husband unless he is older or foreign.

In the cities, however, things are changing as fast as wealth, education and exposure to foreign ideas allows, and in general women in cities are more confident and willing to engage with foreigners than their rural counterparts. Women are pushing into more responsible positions, particularly in foreign-controlled companies.

ARTS

The focus of most traditional art in Lao culture has been religious, specifically Buddhist. Yet, unlike the visual arts of Thailand, Myanmar and Cambodia, Lao art never encompassed a broad range of styles and periods, mainly because Laos has a much more modest history in terms of power and because it has only existed as a political entity for a short period. Furthermore, since Laos was intermittently dominated by its neighbours, much of the art that was produced was either destroyed or, as in the case of the Emerald Buddha (p92), carted off by conquering armies.

Laos's relatively small and poor population, combined with a turbulent recent history, also goes some way toward explaining the absence of any strong tradition of contemporary art. This is slowly changing, and in Vientiane and Luang Prabang modern art in a variety of media is finding its way into galleries and stores.

Weaving (see the boxed text, p59) is the one art form that is found almost everywhere and has distinct styles that vary by place and tribal group. It's also the single most accessible art the traveller can buy, often from the artist herself – weavers are almost always women.

Literature & Film

Of all classical Lao literature, *Pha Lak Pha Lam,* the Lao version of the Indian epic the Ramayana, is the most pervasive and influential in the culture. The Indian source first came to Laos with the Hindu Khmer as stone reliefs at Wat Phu Champasak and other Angkor-period temples. Oral and written versions may also have been available; eventually, though, the Lao developed their own version of the epic, which differs greatly both from the original and from Thailand's *Ramakian.*

Lao Textiles and Traditions (1997), by Mary F Connors, is useful to visitors interested in Lao weaving; it's the best overall introduction to the subject.

Of the 547 Jataka tales in the *Pali Tipitaka* (tripartite Buddhist canon) – each chronicling a different past life of the Buddha – most appear in Laos almost word-for-word as they were first written down in Sri Lanka. A group of 50 'extra' or apocryphal stories, based on Lao-Thai folk tales of the time, were added by Pali scholars in Luang Prabang between 300 and 400 years ago. Laos's most popular Jataka is an old Pali original known as the Mahajati or Mahavessandara (Lao: Pha Wet), the story of the Buddha's penultimate life. Interior murals in the *sim* (ordination hall) of many Lao wat typically depict this Jataka as well as others.

Contemporary literature has been hampered by decades of war and communist rule. The first Lao-language novel was printed in 1944, and only in 1999 was the first collection of contemporary Lao fiction, Ounthine Bounyavong's *Mother's Beloved: Stories from Laos,* published in a bilingual Lao and English edition. Since then, a growing number of Lao novels and short stories have been translated into Thai, but very few have seen English-language translations. The most recent of these was 2009's *When the Sky Turns Upside Down: Memories of Laos,* a translation of short stories, some of which date back 60 years, by prominent Lao authors Dara Viravongs Kanlaya and Douangdeuane Bounyavong.

Not surprisingly, Laos also has one of the quietest film industries in Southeast Asia, and 2008's *Good Morning, Luang Prabang* is only the sixth feature film produced in the country since 1975. Starring Lao-Australian heartthrob Ananda Everingham and led by Thai director Sakchai Deenan, the film features a predictably 'safe' love-based plot that nonetheless, allegedly required the constant monitoring by the Lao authorities during filming.

The Betrayal (Nerakhoon, 2008) is a documentary directed by American Ellen Kuras, with the help of the film's main subject, Thavisouk Phrasavath (who also received a co-director credit). Shot over a 23-year period, the film documents the Phrasavath family's experience emigrating from Laos to New York City after the communist revolution, and was showcased at the 2008 Sundance Film Festival.

Traditional Music of the Lao (1985), by Terry Miller, although mainly focused on northeast Thailand, is the only book-length work yet to appear on Lao music, and is very informative.

Music & Dance

Lao classical music was originally developed as court music for royal ceremonies and classical dance-drama during the 19th-century reign of Vientiane's Chao Anou, who had been educated in the Siamese court in Bangkok. The standard ensemble for this genre is the *sep nyai* and consists of *khâwng wóng* (a set of tuned gongs), the *ranyâat* (a xylophone-like instrument), the *khui* (bamboo flute) and the *pii* (a double-reed wind instrument similar to the oboe).

The practice of classical Lao music and drama has been in decline for some time – 40 years of intermittent war and revolution has simply made this kind of entertainment a low priority among most Lao. Generally, the only time you'll hear this type of music is during the occasional public performance of

---

JONNY OLSEN, 30

How did you originally hear about the *khâen* and Lao music? I used to work in a Thai restaurant with Lao and Thai people. I heard the *khâen* from a CD my coworker had.

How long did it take you to play the *khâen*? I have been playing *khâen* for six years. I first learned it in Northeast Thailand. Then I went to Laos to learn other styles of playing.

How do Lao people react to a foreigner playing their music? Lao people are always welcoming towards me. They are surprised that I, a foreigner, can play their national instrument. I'm happy and proud to be able to promote the Lao culture through playing the *khâen* and singing Lao folk songs.

Are you only interested in performing purely traditional Lao music, or have you ever been tempted to add any Western musical elements? My music is a mix of modern styles and traditional Lao folk melodies. My new album will be a mix of hip-hop, dance, and Lao folk. A lot of the songs are aimed at being purely humorous. In the future, I want to try to mix blues with Lao folk music.

Where's a good place in Vientiane to check out live Lao music? Any big festival like Bun Pha That Luang (p320) will have a lot of Lao music.

What's it like being a celebrity in Laos? Even though I am famous in Laos I still remain humble. The last thing I ever want to do is be arrogant and act like I'm a superstar. I'm still surprised and happy to see fans come up and talk to me. Some say hello to me, some are surprised and ask for an autograph, some are shy and don't say anything.

Jonny is an American who sings in Lao and plays the khâen *(mouth organ), a Lao instrument*

the *Pha Lak Pha Lam*, a dance-drama based on the Hindu Ramayana epic (see Literature, p54).

Not so with Lao folk and pop, which have always stayed close to the people. The principal instrument in folk, and to a lesser extent in pop, is the *kháen* (common French spelling: *khene*), a wind instrument that made of a double row of bamboo-like reeds fitted into a hardwood soundbox and made airtight with beeswax. The rows can be as few as four or as many as eight courses (for a total of 16 pipes), and the instrument can vary in length from around 80cm to about 2m. An adept player can produce a churning, calliope-like dance music.

When the *kháen* is playing you'll often see people dancing the *lám wóng* (circle performance), easily the most popular folk dance in Laos. Put simply, in the *lám wóng* couples dance circles around one another until there are three circles in all: a circle danced by the individual, a circle danced by the couple, and one danced by the whole crowd. Watch for a few minutes and you'll soon get the hang of it.

MĂW LÁM

The Lao folk idiom also has its own musical theatre, based on the *măw lám* tradition. *Măw lám* is difficult to translate but roughly means 'master of verse'. Led by one or more vocalists, performances always feature a witty, topical combination of talking and singing that ranges across themes as diverse as politics and sex. Very colloquial, even bawdy, language is employed. This is one art form that has always bypassed government censors and it continues to provide an important outlet for grass-roots expression.

Other diverse instruments, including electric guitar, electric bass and drums, may supplement the basic *kháen*/vocalist ensemble. Versions that appear on Lao national TV are usually much watered down to suit 'national development'.

There are several different types of *măw lám*, depending on the number of singers and the region the style hails from. *Măw lám khuu* (couple *măw lám*), for example, features a man and woman who engage in flirtation and verbal repartee. *Măw lám jót* (duelling *măw lám*) has two performers of the same gender who 'duel' by answering questions or finishing an incomplete story issued as a challenge – not unlike free-style rap.

Northern Lao *kháen*-based folk music is usually referred to as *kháp* rather than *lám*. Authentic live *măw lám* can be heard at temple fairs and on Lao radio. CDs can be purchased in larger towns and cities. Born-and-bred American artist Jonny Olsen (also known as Jonny Khaen; see p55) has become a celebrity in Laos for his *kháen*-based music.

North Illinois University has pages of information on Lao culture, language, history, folklore and music at www.seasite. niu.edu/lao- including recordings of the *kháen*.

LAO POP

Up until 2003 performing 'modern' music was virtually outlawed in Laos. The government had decided it just wasn't the Lao thing, and bands such as local heavy metal outfit Sapphire, who chose to play anyway, were effectively shut down. Instead the youth listened to pirated Thai and Western music, while Lao-language pop was limited to the *lûuk thûng*, syrupy arrangements combining cha-cha and bolero rhythms with Lao-Thai melodies.

Then the government decided that if Lao youth were going to listen to modern pop, it might as well be home-grown. The first 'star' was Thidavanh Bounxouay, a Lao-Bulgarian singer more popularly known as Alexandra. Her brand of pop wasn't exactly radical, but it was decidedly upbeat compared with what went before. In the last couple of years other groups have followed: the three guys and girl in Overdance wear matching outfits and produce expectedly poppy tunes. Girl-band Princess and pop-rock group

Awake are also popular, while Aluna is evolving from a Kylie Minogue copy to something less poppy.

In recent years, slightly edgier rock bands such as Crocodile and Leprozy have emerged, the latter of which have even played relatively high-profile gigs in Thailand. The hard-rock band Cells is another example of a Lao band for whom success has been much more rewarding in Thailand, where they've played big and relatively lucrative gigs in Bangkok. They perform mostly original songs and their singer also writes for other local artists.

There's also a tiny but burgeoning school of Lao-language hip hop that until recently was almost exclusively associated with Los Angeles and that city's Lao Diaspora. However, in recent years a domestic scene has developed around homegrown acts such as Hip Hop Ban Na and L.O.G., the latter of which scored a chart-topping hit in Thailand.

This is an exciting new era for Lao music, but it's not as revolutionary as it might seem. Original, non-pirated CDs sell for just 10,000K to 20,000K, so most musicians must work a day job. Indeed, Aluna might be a celebrity in Laos, but you'll still find her working behind reception in her family's Vang Vieng guesthouse. And the government's stance could best be described as pragmatic. Before recording, all songs must be vetted by government censors, who can and do change lyrics and video clips. Even after an album has been passed, some songs might not be approved for broadcast on radio. Needless to say, controversial social comment is at a premium.

In Vientiane, recordings by many if not all of the artists mentioned above are available at the open-air market near Pha That Luang and at Talat Sao Mall. Some can also be caught live at venues in Vientiane, though you're more likely to see them at outdoor gigs to celebrate major holidays.

Architecture

As with all other artistic endeavour, for centuries the best architects in the land have focussed their attention on Buddhist temples (see the boxed text, p58). The results are most impressive in Luang Prabang.

However, it's not only in temples that Laos has its own peculiar architectural traditions. The *that* (stupas) found in Laos are different to those found anywhere else in the Buddhist world. Stupas are essentially monuments built on top of a reliquary which itself was built to hold a relic of the Buddha – commonly a hair or fragment of bone. Across Asia they come in varying shapes and sizes, ranging from the multilevel tapered pagodas found in Vietnam to the buxom brick monoliths of Sri Lanka. Laos has its own unique style combining hard edges and comely curves. The most famous of all Lao stupas is the golden Pha That Luang (p95) in Vientiane. It is the national symbol.

Traditional housing in Laos, whether in the river valleys or in the mountains, consists of simple wooden or bamboo-thatch structures with leaf or grass roofing. Among Lowland Lao, houses are raised on stilts to avoid flooding during the monsoons and allow room to store rice underneath, while the highlanders typically build directly on the ground. The most attractive Lowland Lao houses often have a starburst pattern in the architraves, though these are increasingly difficult to find.

Colonial architecture in urban Laos combined the classic French provincial style – thick-walled buildings with shuttered windows and pitched tile roofs – with balconies and ventilation to promote air circulation in the stifling Southeast Asian climate. Although many of these structures were torn down or allowed to decay following independence from France, today they are much in demand, especially by foreigners. Luang Prabang and Vientiane both boast several lovingly restored buildings from this era. By contrast, in

'Traditional housing in Laos consists of simple wooden or bamboo-thatch structures with leaf or grass roofing'

TEMPLE ARCHITECTURE: A TALE OF THREE CITIES

The *uposatha* (Lao *sĭm;* ordination hall) is always the most important structure in any Theravada Buddhist wat. The high-peaked roofs are layered to represent several levels (usually three, five, seven or occasionally nine), which correspond to various Buddhist doctrines. The edges of the roofs almost always feature a repeated flame motif, with long, fingerlike hooks at the corners called *chaw fâa* (sky clusters). Umbrella-like spires along the central roof-ridge of a *sĭm,* called *nyâwt chaw fâa* (topmost *chaw fâa*) sometimes bear small pavilions (*naga*s – mythical water serpents) in a double-stepped arrangement representation of Mt Meru, the mythical centre of the Hindu-Buddhist cosmos.

There are basically three architectural styles for such buildings – the Vientiane, Luang Prabang and Xieng Khuang styles.

The front of a *sĭm* in the **Vientiane style** usually features a large verandah with heavy columns supporting an ornamented overhanging roof. Some will also have a less-ornamented rear verandah, while those that have a surrounding terrace are Bangkok-influenced.

In **Luang Prabang**, the temple style is akin to that of the northern Siamese (Lanna) style, hardly surprising as for several centuries Laos and northern Thailand were part of the same kingdoms. Luang Prabang temple roofs sweep very low, almost reaching the ground in some instances. The overall effect is quite dramatic, as if the *sĭm* were about to take flight. The Lao are fond of saying that the roof line resembles the wings of a mother hen guarding her chicks.

Little remains of the **Xieng Khuang** style of *sĭm* architecture because the province was so heavily bombed during the Second Indochina War. Pretty much the only surviving examples are in Luang Prabang and to look at them you see aspects of both Vientiane and Luang Prabang styles. The *sĭm* raised on a multilevel platform is reminiscent of Vientiane temples, while wide sweeping roofs that reach especially low are similar to the Luang Prabang style, though they're not usually tiered. Cantilevered roof supports play a much more prominent role in the building's overall aesthetic, giving the *sĭm*'s front profile a pentagonal shape. The pediment is curved, adding a grace beyond that of the typical Luang Prabang and Vientiane pediments.

A fourth, less common style of temple architecture in Laos has been supplied by the Tai Lü, whose temples are typified by thick, whitewashed stucco walls with small windows, two- or three-tiered roofs, curved pediments and *naga* (water serpent) lintels over the doors and steps. Although there are examples of Tai Lü influence in a few Luang Prabang and Muang Sing temples, their main location is in Sainyabuli Province.

the Mekong River towns of Tha Khaek, Savannakhet and Pakse, French-era buildings are decaying at a disturbing rate.

Buildings erected in post-Revolution Laos followed the socialist realism school that was enforced in the Soviet Union, Vietnam and China. Straight lines, sharp angles and an almost total lack of ornamentation were the norm. More recently, a trend towards integrating classic Lao architectural motifs with modern functions has taken hold. Prime examples of this include Vientiane's National Assembly and the Luang Prabang airport, both of which were designed by Havana- and Moscow-trained architect Hongkad Souvannavong. Other design characteristics, such as those represented by the Siam Commercial Bank on Th Lan Xang in Vientiane, seek to gracefully reincorporate French colonial features ignored for the last half-century.

Sculpture

Of all the traditional Lao arts, perhaps most impressive is the Buddhist sculpture of the period from the 16th to 18th centuries, the heyday of the kingdom of Lan Xang. Sculptural media usually included bronze, stone or wood and the subject was invariably the Lord Buddha or figures associated with the Jataka (*sáa-dók;* stories of the Buddha's past lives). Like other Buddhist sculptors, the Lao artisans emphasised the features thought to be peculiar to the historical Buddha, including a beaklike nose, extended earlobes and tightly curled hair.

Two types of standing Buddha image are distinctive to Laos. The first is the 'Calling for Rain' posture, which depicts the Buddha standing with hands held rigidly at his side, fingers pointing towards the ground. This posture is rarely seen in other Southeast Asian Buddhist art traditions. The slightly rounded, 'boneless' look of the image recalls Thailand's Sukhothai style, and the way the lower robe is sculpted over the hips looks vaguely Khmer. But the flat, slablike earlobes, arched eyebrows and aquiline nose are uniquely Lao. The bottom of the figure's robe curls upward on both sides in a perfectly symmetrical fashion that is also unique and innovative.

The other original Lao image type is the 'Contemplating the Bodhi Tree' Buddha. The Bodhi tree ('Tree of Enlightenment'), refers to the large banyan tree that the historical Buddha purportedly was sitting beneath when he attained enlightenment in Bodhgaya, India, in the 6th century BC. In this image the Buddha is standing in much the same way as in the 'Calling for Rain' pose, except that his hands are crossed at the wrists in front of his body.

The finest examples of Lao sculpture are found in Vientiane's Haw Pha Kaeo (p92) and Wat Si Saket (p92), and in Luang Prabang's Royal Palace Museum (p148).

Traditional Khamu houses often have the skulls of domestic animals hanging on a wall with an altar beneath. The skulls are from animals the family has sacrificed to their ancestors, and it is strictly taboo to touch them.

Handicrafts

Mats and baskets woven of various kinds of straw, rattan and reed are common and are becoming a small but important export. You'll still see minority groups actually wearing some of these baskets, affirming that until recently most Lao handicrafts were useful as well as ornamental. In villages it's possible to buy direct from the weaver, though you might need to commission your basket in advance and allow at least a day for the job to be finished. Or you could weave it yourself, under instruction from the experts for a small fee. Among the best baskets and mats are those woven by the Htin (Lao Thoeng).

Among the Hmong and Mien hill tribes, silversmithing plays an important role in 'portable wealth' and inheritances. In years past, the main source of

---

TEXTILES

Laos boasts over a dozen weaving styles across four regions. Southern weavers, who often use foot looms rather than frame looms, are known for the best silk weaving and for intricate *mat-mii* (ikat or tie-dye) designs that include Khmer-influenced temple and elephant motifs. In these provinces, beadwork is sometimes added to the embroidery. One-piece *phàa nung* (sarongs) are more common than those sewn from separate pieces.

In northeastern Laos, tribal Tai produce *yìap ko* (weft brocade) using raw silk, cotton yarn and natural dyes, sometimes with the addition of *mat-mii* techniques. Large diamond patterns are common.

In central Laos, typical weavings include indigo-dyed cotton *mat-mii* and minimal weft brocade (*jók* and *khit*), along with mixed techniques brought by migrants to Vientiane.

Gold and silver brocade is typical of traditional Luang Prabang patterns, along with intricate patterns and imported Thai Lü designs. Northerners generally use frame looms; the waist, body and narrow *sín* (bottom border) of a *phàa nung* are often sewn together from separately woven pieces.

Natural sources for Lao dyes include ebony (both seeds and wood), tamarind (seeds and wood), red lacquer extracted from the *Coccus iacca* (a tree-boring insect), turmeric (from a root) and indigo. A basic palette of five natural colours – black, orange, red, yellow and blue – can be combined to create an endless variety of other colours. Other unblended, but more subtle, hues include khaki (from the bark of the Indian trumpet tree), pink (sappanwood) and gold (jackfruit and breadfruit woods).

silver was French coins, which were either melted down or fitted straight into the jewellery of choice. In northern villages it's not unusual to see newer coins worn in elaborate head dress.

The Lowland Lao also have a long tradition of silversmithing and goldsmithing. While these arts have been in decline for quite a while now, you can still see plenty of jewellers working over flames in markets around the country.

Paper handcrafted from *săa* (the bark of a mulberry tree) is common in northwestern Laos, and is available in Vientiane and Luang Prabang. Environmentally friendly *săa* is a renewable paper resource that needs little processing compared with wood pulp.

See Shopping p324 for more on handicrafts in Laos.

Food & Drink

Lao food doesn't have the variety and depth of the more famous cuisines of neighbouring China, Thailand and Vietnam, but you can eat well in Laos if you take the time to learn a little about the cuisine while you're there. While few people travel to this country with food as their prime objective, a little experimentation can take you a long way towards appreciating the cuisine and can be very rewarding.

It's little surprise that Lao food is similar to Thai cuisine, given the long interwoven history the two countries share. But while dishes such as *làap* (meat salad) and *tąm màak-hung* (*som tam*; papaya salad) will be familiar to anyone with even a basic knowledge of Thai food, there are some aspects of Lao cuisine that are unmistakably Lao.

STAPLES & SPECIALITIES

Travellers already hip to Thai cuisine will experience déjà vu with the Lao emphasis on simple, fresh ingredients coarsely blended into rustic dishes. Herbs like basil, mint, coriander and lemongrass lend bright tones to the mix, balanced by the spicy bitterness of roots and rhizomes (the thick, underground stem of certain plants), the tang of lime juice and Kaffir lime leaves, the pungent salt of fish sauce or shrimp paste and the fire of fresh chillies.

The overwhelming staple, and for many poor Lao, virtually the only thing consumed on a daily basis, is rice. Specifically sticky rice. An entirely different variety of rice than long-grained rice, sticky or glutinous rice is prepared by steaming rather than boiling. First the grains are soaked for at least four hours and sometimes as long as overnight. The rice is then strained and steamed over boiling water in pointed bamboo baskets called *huat*. After about 10 to 15 minutes of steaming, the rice is flipped and steamed another 10 minutes. The finished rice is kept warm in lidded, permeable bamboo baskets called *típ khào*.

Other essential ingredients include locally raised *phák* (vegetables), *pạa* (fish), *kai* (chicken), *pét* (duck), *mŭu* (pork) and *sìin ngúa* (beef) or *sìin khwái* (water buffalo). Because of Laos's distance from the sea, freshwater fish is more common than saltwater fish or shellfish. When meats are used, Lao cooks prefer to emphasise savoury tones imparted by grilling, roasting or mixing with cooked ingredients that are inherently savoury, such as roasted rice.

To salt the food, various fermented fish concoctions are used, most commonly *pạa dàek*, a coarse, native Lao preparation that includes chunks of fermented freshwater fish, or *nâm pạa*, a thin sauce of fermented anchovies.

Ant Egg Soup (2004), by Natacha du Pont de Bie, is a well-written account of the author's encounters with food while travelling through Laos, garnished with recipes and line drawings.

TRAVEL YOUR TASTEBUDS

You haven't really been to Laos if you haven't dabbled in:

- Beerlao – the national beverage
- *jąew màak len* – a rich, generally salty dip of roasted tomatoes, chillies and shallots
- *khai phųn* – dried seasoned river moss, a Luang Prabang speciality
- *kôy pạa* – chunks of freshwater fish blended with herbs, lime juice and roasted ground sticky rice
- *lào hǎi* – fermented rice wine served in a large clay jar with long reed straws
- *nǎem khào* – balls of cooked rice mixed with sour pork sausage and fried whole, then broken into a saladlike dish eaten with fresh leaves and herbs; a Vientiane speciality
- *sìin sawǎn* – thin sheets of dried spiced beef, a dish associated with Savannakhet

See the Health chapter (p350) for warnings on eating *pạa dàek*. *Phŏng súu lot* – *ajinomoto* (MSG) – is also a common seasoning, and in Laos you may even see it served as a table condiment in noodle restaurants.

Fresh *nâm màak náo* (lime juice), *sĭi-khái* (lemongrass), *bại sálanae* (mint leaf) and *phák hăwm* (coriander leaf) are added to give the food its characteristic tang. Other common seasonings include *khaa* (galingale), *màak phét* (hot chillies), *nâm màak khăam* (tamarind juice), *khĭing* (ginger) and *nâm màak phâo* or *nâm káthí* (coconut milk). Chillies are sometimes served on the side in dips called *jǫew*. In Luang Prabang, *năng khwái hàeng* (dried skin of water buffalo) is quite a popular ingredient.

One Lao dish you're likely to encounter is *làap*, which is a Lao-style salad of minced meat, fowl or fish tossed with lime juice, *khào khûa* (roasted, powdered sticky rice), mint leaves and chillies. It can be very hot or rather mild, depending on the cook. Meats mixed into *làap* are sometimes raw *(díp)* rather than cooked *(súk)*. *Làap* is typically served with a large plate of lettuce, mint and various other fresh herbs depending on season and availability. Using your fingers you wrap a little *làap* in the lettuce and herbs and eat it with balls of sticky rice, which you roll by hand.

Many Lao dishes are quite spicy because of the Lao penchant for *màak phét*. But the Lao also eat a lot of Chinese and Vietnamese food, which is generally less spicy. *Fŏe* (rice noodle soup) is popular as a snack and for

Eat Like a Native: Laos is a handy fold-out guide to Lao cuisine and Lao-language food terms, available at some book stores in Laos.

WANTED: REAL LAO FOOD

Food-minded visitors to Laos expecting to find the variety of authentic local restaurants and dishes available in neighbouring Thailand and Vietnam will most likely be disappointed. Although in the larger towns you'll inevitably find a decent number of restaurants and some street-side carts, the majority of restaurants in Laos serve foreign cuisines (predominately Chinese or Vietnamese), or, more commonly in tourist areas, a significantly gentrified version of Lao food. And unlike elsewhere in much of Southeast Asia, most street food in Laos is take-away only, available at the markets that spring up every evening in most Lao towns. This is a frustrating state of affairs for foodies, particularly in the case of evening markets, as these are often the best places to sample authentic local food. But if you're as serious about sampling real Lao dishes as we are, a cheap set of plates, bowls and silverware is a worthwhile investment. We've also found that most guesthouses are willing to let you borrow their plates and cutlery if you sweeten the pot by agreeing to buy a few bottles of their Beerlao (in this deal, everybody wins).

Once you've got the logistics sorted out, the most ubiquitous evening-market dishes you're likely to come across are *kheuang pîng* (grilled foods). *Pîng kai* (grilled chicken) is a favourite, and involves taking a chicken (whole or in pieces) and rubbing it with a marinade of garlic, coriander root, black pepper and salt or fish sauce before cooking it slowly over hot coals. *Pîng pạa* is prepared by scaling a fish, rubbing it with a thick layer of salt and stuffing a handful of lemongrass stems down its throat before slowly grilling it. You'll also come across grilled duck, goat, pig snouts, cow teats, intestines and a variety of delicious grilled sausages.

Other characteristically Lao dishes you probably won't see on restaurant menus include *jǫew*, chilli-based dips taken with sticky rice and fresh or parboiled vegetables, and *kǫeng*, thick soups typically combining a bit of meat with fresh herbs and vegetables. Steaming is another popular method of cooking, and *mók pạa*, fish combined with herbs and steamed in a banana-leaf packet, is another Lao staple. Regardless of the cooking method, all Lao dishes are accompanied by *khào nĭaw (*sticky rice).

Thankfully, the one authentic Lao dish you can almost always figure on being able to sit down to eat is also arguably the most emblematic Lao dish of all: *tạm màak-hung* (generally known as *tạm sòm* in Vientiane), a spicy, tangy salad made by pounding shredded green papaya, lime juice, chillies, garlic, *pạa dàem* and various other ingredients together in a large mortar.

breakfast, and is almost always served with a plate of fresh lettuce, mint, basil, coriander, mung bean sprouts and lime wedges to add to the soup as desired. Especially in the south, people mix their own *fŏe* sauce of lime, crushed fresh chilli, *kápí* (shrimp paste) and sugar at the table using a little saucer provided for the purpose.

Another common noodle dish, especially in the morning, is *khào pjak sèn*, a soft, round rice noodle served in a broth with pieces of chicken or deep-fried crispy pork belly. Many *khào pjak sèn* vendors also sell *khànŏm khuu*, small deep-fried, doughnut-like Chinese pastries. Some vendors even leave a pair of scissors on each table so that you can cut the pastries up and mix them into your soup. It may sound strange, but it's very tasty.

Khào pûn, fresh rice noodles topped with a sweet and spicy *nâm káthí* (coconut sauce), is another popular noodle dish. These noodles are also eaten cold with various Vietnamese foods popular in urban Laos, particularly *nǎem néuang* (barbecued pork meatballs) and *yáw* (spring rolls).

Rice is the foundation for all Lao meals (as opposed to snacks), as is the case elsewhere in Southeast Asia. Although the Lao generally eat *khào nǐaw* (sticky or glutinous rice), *khào jâo* (ordinary white rice) is also common in the major towns.

In Vientiane, Savannakhet, Pakse and Luang Prabang, French bread *(khào jíi)* is popular for breakfast. Sometimes it's eaten plain with *kąa-féh nóm hâwn* (hot milk coffee), sometimes it's eaten with *khai* (eggs) or in a baguette sandwich that contains Lao-style pâté, and vegetables. Or you can order them *sai nâm nóm:* sliced in half lengthwise and drizzled with sweetened condensed milk. Fresh Lao baguettes can be superb. Croissants and other French-style pastries are also available in the bakeries of Vientiane and Luang Prabang.

Fish and Fish Dishes of Laos (2003), by Alan Davidson, is a thorough description of Laos's diverse freshwater fish cookery. The late Davidson was British ambassador to Laos in the 1970s and author of the esteemed *Oxford Companion to Food.*

DRINKS
Nonalcoholic Drinks
WATER

Water purified for drinking purposes is simply called *nâm deum* (drinking water), whether it is boiled or filtered. *All* water offered to customers in restaurants or hotels will be purified, so don't fret about the safety of taking a sip. In restaurants you can ask for *nâm pao* (plain water, which is always either boiled or taken from a purified source) served by the glass at no charge, or order plain or carbonated water by the bottle. In remote villages you'll often be served water with a distinct colour – usually yellow or red – and a smoky taste. This water is safe to drink and the colour comes from a root which is boiled with the water, the specific root differing depending on where you are.

COFFEE & TEA

Lao-grown coffee has a strong reputation (see the boxed text, p300). Traditionally, pure Lao coffee is roasted by wholesalers, ground by vendors and filtered through a sock-like cloth bag just before serving. The result is thick, black, strong and delicious. Increasingly, however, restaurants and hotels in particular are serving Nescafé or similar instant coffee to foreigners. To make sure you get real Lao coffee ask for *kąa-féh láo* (Lao coffee) or *kąa-féh bǫh-láan* (old-fashioned coffee).

Brewed coffee is usually served in small glasses and mixed with sugar and a startling amount of sweetened condensed milk. Once you've mixed it all up it's delicious, but if you don't want either be sure to specify *kąa-féh dạm* (black coffee) followed with *baw sai nâm-tąan* (without sugar). An almost addictive variation is *òh-lîang* (iced coffee with sugar). Only in better hotels and restaurants will you find real milk.

In central and southern Laos coffee is almost always served with a chaser of hot *nâm sáa* (weak and often lukewarm Chinese tea), while in the north it's typically served with a glass of plain hot water.

Both Indian-style (black) and Chinese-style (green or semicured) teas are served in Laos, some of the latter now being grown on the Bolaven Plateau and elsewhere. An order of *sáa hâwn* (hot tea) usually results in a cup (or glass) of black tea with sugar and condensed milk. As with coffee you must specify beforehand if you want black tea without milk and/or sugar. Ask for *sáa hâwn* followed by *baw sai nóm* (without milk) and/or *baw sai nâm-tạan* (without sugar). Chinese tea is traditionally served in restaurants for free. For stronger fresh Chinese tea, request *sáa jịin*.

> The blog Thai & Lao Food (http://thai-laos-food. blogspot.com) features a variety of Lao recipes with helpful videos.

Alcoholic Drinks
BEER

It's hard to overestimate how important Beerlao is to the people of Laos – and not just as a means of getting drunk. In a country with so few exports and virtually zero in the way of international recognition, the constant approval of their national brew is a source of great pride. The distinctive yellow crates can be seen in all but the most remote parts of the country and despite competition from Tiger, and to a lesser degree, Carlsberg and Heineken (all of which cost more), most people still opt for the local brew.

For more on Beerlao, see the boxed text.

BEERLAO

As the Head Brewmaster of the Lao Brewery Company, Sivilay Lasachack is singularly responsible for the quality of Beerlao, the country's unofficial national brew. But there's a catch: 'I don't like to drink,' acknowledged Lasachack in a 2009 NPR interview. Nonetheless, the middle-aged Lao woman must be doing something right, as Beerlao is almost certainly the country's most recognised brand, and is considered by many to be the best beer in Southeast Asia.

Beerlao dates back to 1973, when the then Lao Beer and Ice Factory was founded in Vientiane with the help of French businessmen. When the communists seized power in 1975, the brewery was renamed as the Lao Brewery Company, taken over by the state and run with the occasional support of brewers from Laos's communist allies in Eastern Europe. With the collapse of the Soviet Union in the 1990s, the brewery was on its own, and this is where Sivilay Lasachack comes in. Having studied brewing in the former Czechoslovakia, she returned to Laos, and in an effort to make the brewery more self-sufficient, decided to introduce rice as malt, rather relying entirely on the more expensive imported barley. She also started recycling yeast and chose to model the beer after a classic Czech-style pilsner. The result is today's Beerlao, a beer that is light and slightly sweet, boasting 5% alcohol.

Beerlao comes in the ubiquitous 630ml bottles but is also available in 330ml cans. A draught version (*bịa sót:* fresh beer) is tastier yet, but it has a limited distribution. Beerlao Dark (a unique dark lager with 6.5% alcohol) and more recently Beerlao Gold (a premium beer brewed with 'sapphire aroma hops') can be found in larger cities and towns. Lanexang is a slightly cheaper and stronger (5.5% alcohol) beer aimed towards working-class locals.

Since 2006, 50% of the Lao Brewery Co. Ltd. has been owned by Denmark's Carlsberg, with the other half still controlled by the communist state. In 2008 the brewery produced 210 million litres of beer at its two factories outside Vientiane and Pakse, and within Laos commands a staggering 99% market share. The overwhelming majority of Beerlao is consumed domestically, with only about one percent exported (mostly to Cambodia). The brewery hopes to increase this to 10% in the next decade, not by costly ad campaigns, but rather through word of mouth marketing, much like another once-obscure national brewery, Mexico's Corona, did during the 1970s.

If you'd like to learn more about Beerlao or see where it's made, the brewery, located 12km southeast of Vientiane at Tha Deua, offers free tours on weekdays from 10am onwards.

DISTILLED SPIRITS

Beerlao might be the source of much national pride but rice whisky, known as *lào-láo*, is responsible for many more sore heads. This is partly because it's so much cheaper than beer and partly because the Lowland Lao, in particular, just like it.

Chances are you'll be invited to partake in festivities with a neat shot of *lào-láo* at some point. In a Lao home the pouring and drinking of *lào-láo* at the evening meal takes on ritual characteristics. Usually towards the end of the meal, but occasionally beforehand, the hosts bring out a bottle of the stuff to treat their guests. The usual procedure is for the host to pour one jigger of *lào-láo* onto the floor or a used dinner plate first, to appease the house spirits. The host then pours another jigger and downs it in one gulp. Jiggers for each guest are poured in turn; guests must take at least one offered drink or risk offending the house spirits.

The best *lào-láo* is said to come from Phongsali and Don Khong, the northern and southern extremes of the country, but it's available virtually everywhere, usually for between 2000K and 5000K per 750ml bottle.

Tourist hotel bars in the larger cities carry the standard variety of liquors.

WINE

Decent French and Italian wines are abundantly available in Vientiane at restaurants, shops specialising in imported foods and in some shops that sell nothing but wine. Some restaurants and hotels in Luang Prabang, Savannakhet and Pakse also stock wine. Other wines are more scarce, though we saw quite a few Australian wines around. Whatever the origin, wine is much cheaper than it is in Thailand because the import tax is lower, so it's worth stocking up if you're heading across the border.

Luang Prabang is famous for a type of light rice wine called *khào kam*, a red-tinted, somewhat sweet beverage made from sticky rice. It can be quite tasty when properly prepared and stored, but rather mouldy-tasting if not.

In rural provinces, a rice wine known as *lào-hǎi* (jar liquor) is fermented by households or villages. *Lào-hǎi* is usually drunk from a communal jar using long reed straws.

CELEBRATIONS

Temple festivals *(bun wat)* make good opportunities to taste real home-cooked Lao food as temple regulars often bring dishes from home to share with other temple visitors. Chances are vendors will also set up foodstalls offering everything from *khûa fǒe* (fried rice noodles) to *pîng kai* (grilled chicken).

The annual boat races (p320), usually held in October in towns along the Mekong River, are another great chance to graze at long lines of vendor booths; *nǎem khào* is particularly popular at these events.

During *tut jiin* (Chinese New Year), also known by its Vietnamese name Tet, Laos's Chinese population celebrates with a week of house-cleaning, lion dances, fireworks and feasting. The most impressive festivities take place in Vientiane's Chinatown (at the north end of Th Chao Anou) and 'mooncakes' – thick, circular pastries filled with sweet bean paste or salted pork – are on sale all over town.

WHERE TO EAT & DRINK

Aside from evening markets and occasional street vendors (see the boxed text, p63), the cheapest and most dependable places to eat are *hâan fǒe* (noodle shops) and *talàat sâo* (morning markets). Most towns and villages have at least one morning market (which often lasts all day despite the name) and several *hâan fǒe*. The next step up is the Lao-style cafe (*hâan kheuang deum;*

'the cheapest and most dependable places to eat are *hâan fǒe* (noodle shops) and *talàat sâo* (morning markets)'

drink shop) or *hâan kĭn deum* (eat-drink shop), where a more varied selection of dishes is usually served. Most expensive is the *hâan qahăan* (food shop), where the menu is usually posted on the wall or on a blackboard (in Lao).

Many *hâan qahăan* serve mostly Chinese or Vietnamese food. The ones serving real Lao food usually have a large pan of water on a stool – or a modern lavatory – somewhere near the entrance for washing the hands before eating (Lao food is traditionally eaten with the hands).

Many restaurants or food stalls, especially outside Vientiane, don't have menus and fewer still have menus in English. In these parts it's worth memorising the names of a few standard dishes. Most provinces also have their own local specialities and if you have an adventurous palate it's well worth asking for *qahăan phêun méuang* (local food), allowing the proprietors to choose for you.

Especially in the larger cities along the Mekong River, the number of Western-style restaurants is growing fast. Vientiane and Luang Prabang in particular boast dozens of restaurants serving a wide variety of cuisine, from Japanese and North Korean to fine French fare, all at very reasonable prices.

> You'll see turkeys free-ranging their way around most villages in Laos, but you'll rarely see them on the table, as they are reserved for ceremonial occasions such as weddings. They were introduced in the early 1960s by the US-government aid organisation USAID, to bring much-needed protein to rural communities.

VEGETARIANS & VEGANS

Almost all Lao dishes contain animal products of one kind or another. Two principal seasonings, for example, are fish sauce and shrimp paste. Some dishes also contain lard or pork fat.

Vegetarian or vegan restaurants are virtually nonexistent, but menus at tourist-oriented restaurants in larger towns and cities will often have vegetarian dishes available.

Outside of tourist areas, vegetarians and vegans will have to make an effort to speak enough Lao to convey their culinary needs. The best all-around phrase to memorise is 'I eat only vegetables' *(khàwy kĭn tae phák)*. If you eat

---

A TASTE FOR THE WILD *Andrew Burke*

Driving through southern Laos with a Lao friend a few years ago we came across a snake slowly slithering its way across the road. We stopped for a look and a moment later a group of villagers walked over the hill about 150m in front of us, and a man on a bike pedalled over the crest about 200m behind us. Then they saw the snake…

Immediately several members of the group dropped what they were carrying and started bolting towards the snake. But this race was always going to be won by the guy pedalling frantically down the slope. A few seconds later he glided past and ran over the snake before calmly dismounting and strolling up to the stunned serpent. He grabbed it by the tail and swung it into the road, and a second later it was dead. The family ahead stopped running with a groan of disappointment and the guy stood holding up the snake, grinning with self-satisfaction. 'This is very special food,' he said, before heading home to grill it for lunch with his cousin.

Back in the car my friend, who was a little disappointed it wasn't him heading off to the grill, explained that most snakes were delicious (you guessed it, they taste a bit like chicken). 'Yes, and there are lots of wild animals in these forests that the villagers like to eat,' he added. While the number of rural people who can afford to buy domestically raised meat is rising, many still depend on wildlife they catch themselves for protein. And when you get off the main routes you'll see people selling and eating deer, wild pigs, squirrels, civets, monitor lizards, jungle fowl and pheasants, dhole (wild dogs), rats and just about any bird they can bring down with a slingshot or catch in a net.

In part this practice is due to the expense involved in animal husbandry, and partly due to the Lao preference for the taste of wild game. Either way, the eating of endangered species causes much consternation among wildlife conservationists (see p77) – and anyone who's walked through a virtually silent forest and wondered what happened to all the game.

Andrew authored the previous two editions of this guidebook.

eggs you can add *sai khai dâi* (it's OK to add egg) to your food vocabulary. Dairy products such as cheese won't be much of a concern since they're rarely served in Lao restaurants.

HABITS & CUSTOMS

Eating in Laos is nearly always a social event and the Lao avoid eating alone whenever possible. Except for the 'rice plates' and the noodle dishes, Lao meals are typically ordered 'family style', which is to say that two or more people order together, sharing different dishes. Traditionally, the party orders one of each kind of dish, for example, one chicken, one fish, one soup. One dish is generally large enough for two people.

Most Lao consider eating alone to be rather unusual; but then as a *falang* (Westerner) you are an exception anyway. In Chinese or Thai restaurants a cheaper alternative is to order dishes *làat khào* (over rice).

Most Lao dishes are eaten with *khào nǐaw* (glutinous or sticky rice). *Khào nǐaw* is served up in lidded baskets called *típ khào* and eaten with the hands. The general practice is to grab a small fistful of rice from the *típ khào,* then roll it into a rough ball that you then use to dip into the various dishes. As always, watching others is the best way to learn.

If *khào jâo* (normal steamed rice) is served with the meal, then it is eaten with a fork and spoon. The spoon, held in the right hand, is used to scoop up the rice and accompanying dishes and placing it in the mouth. The fork, held in the left hand, is merely used to prod food onto the spoon.

Chopsticks *(mâi thuu)* are reserved for dining in Chinese restaurants (where rice is served in small Chinese bowls rather than flat plates) or for eating Chinese noodle dishes. Noodle soups are eaten with a spoon in the left hand (for spooning up the broth) and chopsticks in the right (for grasping the noodles and other solid ingredients).

Dishes are typically served all at once rather than in courses. If the host or restaurant staff can't bring them all to the table because of a shortage of help or because the food is being cooked sequentially from the same set of pots and pans, then the diners typically wait until all the platters are on the table before digging in.

The Lao don't concern themselves with whether dishes are served piping hot, so no one minds if the dishes sit in the kitchen or on the table for 15 minutes or so before anyone digs in. Furthermore it's considered somewhat impolite to take a spoonful of food that's steaming hot as it implies you're so ravenous or uncivilised that you can't wait to gorge yourself.

COOKING COURSES

Cooking courses are available in Luang Prabang (p157), Udomxai (p211) and Vientiane (p99).

EAT YOUR WORDS

Want to know *làap* from *lào-láo*? *Khào kam* from *khào nǐaw*? Get behind the cuisine by getting to know the language of the food scene. For pronunciation guidelines see p357.

Traditional Recipes of Laos (1981) is the English translation of the handwritten recipes of Phia Sing, a former cook in the Lao royal palace of Luang Prabang.

Simple Laotian Cooking (2003), by Penn Hong-thong, is a collection of nearly 200 recipes along with straightforward expositions on the tools and techniques required to closely approximate Lao cuisine.

THE RIGHT TOOL FOR THE JOB

If you're not offered chopsticks, don't ask for them. When *falang* (Westerners) ask for chopsticks to eat Lao food, it only puzzles the restaurant proprietors. An even more embarrassing act is trying to eat sticky rice with chopsticks. Use your right hand instead. For ordinary white rice, use the fork and spoon provided (fork in the left hand, spoon in the right, or the reverse for left-handers).

Useful Words & Phrases

What do you have that's special?	*mii nyǎng phi-sèt baw*	ມີຫຍັງພິເສດບໍ່
Do you have...?	*mii ... baw*	ມີ ... ບໍ່
I didn't order this.	*khàwy baw dâi sang náew nìi*	ຂ້ອຍບໍ່ໄດ້ສັ່ງແບບນີ້
I eat only vegetables.	*khàwy kịn tae phák*	ຂ້ອຍກິນແຕ່ຜັກ
(I) don't like it hot and spicy.	*baw mak phét*	ບໍ່ມັກເຜັດ
(I) like it hot and spicy.	*mak phét*	ມັກເຜັດ
I'd like to try that.	*khàwy yàak láwng kịn boeng*	ຂ້ອຍຢາກລອງກິນເບິ່ງ
Please bring (a)...	*khǎw ... dae*	ຂໍ ... ແດ່
bill	*saek*	ແຊັກ
bowl	*thùay*	ຖ້ວຍ
chopsticks	*mâi thuu*	ໄມ້ທູ
fork	*sâwm*	ສ້ອມ
glass	*jàwk*	ຈອກ
knife	*mĩit*	ມີດ
menu	*láai-kạan qa-hǎan*	ລາຍການອາຫານ
plate	*jạan*	ຈານ
spoon	*buang*	ບ່ວງ

Food Glossary

STAPLES

qa-hǎan tha-léh	ອາຫານທະເລ	seafood
bọe	ເບີ	butter
kai	ໄກ່	chicken
khai	ໄຂ່	egg
khào	ເຂົ້າ	rice
kûng	ກຸ້ງ	shrimp/prawns
nóm sòm	ນົມສົ້ມ	yoghurt
pạa	ປາ	fish
phak	ຜັກ	vegetables
sìin mǔu	ຊີ້ນໝູ	pork
sìin ngúa	ຊີ້ນງົວ	beef

BREAD & PASTRIES

khào jịi	ເຂົ້າຈີ່	plain bread (usually French-style)
khào jịi páa-tê	ເຂົ້າຈີ່ປາເຕ	baguette sandwich
khúa-sawng	ຄົວຊຸ່ງ	croissants
pá-thawng-kó	ປະຖ່ອງໂກະ	'Chinese doughnuts' (*youtiao* in Mandarin)
(*khào-nǒm khuu*)	(ເຂົ້າໜົມຄູ່)	

CONDIMENTS, HERBS & SPICES

bại hǒh-la-pháa	ໃບໂຫລະພາ	sweet basil
hǔa sǐng khái	ຫົວສິງໄຄ	lemongrass
jaew	ແຈ່ວ	dipping sauces
kẹua	ເກືອ	salt

khĭing	ຂີງ	ginger
màak khăam	ໝາກຂາມ	tamarind
màak phét	ໝາກເຜັດ	chilli
nâm màak náo	ນ້ຳໝາກນາວ	lime juice
nâm pqa	ນ້ຳປາ	fish sauce
nâm sá-ìu	ນ້ຳສະອິ້ວ	soy sauce
nâm sòm	ນ້ຳສົ້ມ	vinegar
nâm-tqan	ນ້ຳຕານ	sugar

DRINKS

bja	ເບຍ	beer
bja sót	ເບຍສົດ	draught beer
jàwk	ຈອກ	glass
kâew	ແກ້ວ	bottle
kqa-féh dqm	ກາເຟດຳ	hot Lao coffee with sugar, no milk
kqa-féh nóm hâwn	ກາເຟນົມຮ້ອນ	hot Lao coffee with milk & sugar
kqa-féh nóm yén	ກາເຟນົມເຢັນ	iced Lao coffee with sugar, no milk
lào-láo	ເຫ້ຼາລາວ	rice whisky
nâm	ນ້ຳ	water
nâm deum	ນ້ຳດື່ມ	drinking water
nâm hâwn	ນ້ຳຮ້ອນ	hot water
nâm kâwn	ນ້ຳກ້ອນ	ice
nâm nóm	ນ້ຳນົມ	plain milk
nâm màak kîang	ນ້ຳໝາກກ້ຽງ	orange juice/soda
nâm sŏh-dqa	ນ້ຳໂສດາ	soda water
nâm tôm	ນ້ຳຕົ້ມ	boiled water
nâm yén	ນ້ຳເຢັນ	cold water
òh-lîang	ໂອລ້ຽງ	iced Lao coffee with milk & sugar
oh-wantin	ໂອວັນຕິນ	Ovaltine
sáa hâwn	ຊາຮ້ອນ	hot tea with sugar
sáa nóm hâwn	ຊານົມຮ້ອນ	hot tea with milk & sugar
sáa nóm yén	ຊານົມເຢັນ	iced tea with milk & sugar
sáa wăan yén	ຊາຫວານເຢັນ	iced tea with sugar

EGG DISHES

jeun khai	ຈືນໄຂ່	plain omelette
khai dqo	ໄຂ່ດາວ	fried egg
khai khùa	ໄຂ່ຂົ້ວ	scrambled egg
khai tôm	ໄຂ່ຕົ້ມ	hard-boiled egg

FISH & SEAFOOD

Pîing kûng	ປີ້ງກຸ້ງ	grilled prawns
jeun pqa	ຈືນປາ	crisp-fried fish
jeun kûng	ຈືນກຸ້ງ	fried prawns
nèung pqa	ໜຶ້ງປາ	steamed fish
pqa sòm-wăan	ປາສົ້ມຫວານ	sweet & sour fish

pqa dúk	ປາດຸກ	catfish
pǐing pqa	ປີ້ງປາ	grilled fish

FRUIT

âwy	ອ້ອຍ	sugarcane
màak kûay	ໝາກກ້ວຍ	banana
màak kîang	ໝາກກ້ຽງ	mandarin orange
màak hung	ໝາກຫຸ່ງ	papaya
màak lín-jii	ໝາກລິ້ນຈີ່	lychee
màak mïi	ໝາກມີ້	jackfruit
màak móh	ໝາກໂມ	watermelon
màak muang	ໝາກມ່ວງ	mango
màak náo	ໝາກນາວ	lime
màak nat	ໝາກນັດ	pineapple
màak ngaw	ໝາກເງາະ	rambutan
màak nyám nyái	ໝາກຍຳໃຍ	longan (dragon's eyes)
màak phâo	ໝາກພ້າວ	coconut
màak sïi-dqa	ໝາກສິດາ	guava

MEAT SALADS (LÀAP)

làap kai	ລາບໄກ່	chicken *làap*
làap mǔu	ລາບໝູ	pork *làap*
làap pqa	ລາບປາ	fish *làap*
làap sìin	ລາບຊີ້ນ	beef *làap*

NOODLE DISHES

fŏe	ເຝີ	rice noodle soup with vegetables & meat
fŏe hàeng	ເຝີແຫ້ງ	rice noodles with vegetables & meat, no broth
fŏe khùa	ເຝີຂົ້ວ	fried rice noodles with vegetables & meat
khào pûn	ເຂົ້າປຸ່ນ	white flour noodles served with sweet-spicy sauce
làat nàa	ລາດໜ້າ	thin fresh rice noodles with gravy
mii hàeng	ໝີ່ແຫ້ງ	yellow wheat noodles with vegetables & meat
mii nâm	ໝີ່ນ້ຳ	yellow wheat noodles in broth, with vegetables & meat
phát sá-yîu	ຜັດສະອິ້ວ	fried rice noodles with soy sauce

RICE DISHES

khào nèung	ເຂົ້າໜຶ້ງ	steamed white rice
khào nïaw	ເຂົ້າໜຽວ	sticky rice
khào làat kqeng	ເຂົ້າລາດແກງ	curry over rice
khào mǔu dqeng	ເຂົ້າໝູແດງ	'red' pork (char siu) with rice
khào nàa pét	ເຂົ້າໜ້າເປັດ	roast duck over rice
khào phát (khào khùa) …	ເຂົ້າຜັດ (ເຂົ້າຂົ້ວ)	fried rice with …
kai	ໄກ່	chicken
kûng	ກຸ້ງ	shrimp/prawns

| *mǔu* | ໝູ | pork |
| *pu̯u* | ປູ | crab |

SNACKS

khào khìap kûng	ເຂົ້າຂຽບກຸ້ງ	shrimp chips
mán fa-lang je̯un	ມັນຝລັ່ງຈືນ	fried potatoes
pîng kai	ປີ້ງໄກ່	grilled chicken
ta̯m màak-hung	ຕຳໝາກຫຸ່ງ	spicy green papaya salad
thua di̯n je̯un	ຖົ່ວດິນຈືນ	fried peanuts
yáw díp	ຍໍດິບ	fresh spring rolls
yáw je̯un	ຍໍຈືນ	fried spring rolls

SOUP

ka̯eng jèut	ແກງຈືດ	mild soup with vegetables & pork
ka̯eng jèut tâo-hûu	ແກງຈືດເຕົ້າຮູ້	mild soup with vegetables, pork & bean curd
khào pìak...	ເຂົ້າປຽກ...	rice soup with ...
kai	ໄກ	chicken
mǔu	ໝູ	pork
pa̯a	ປາ	fish
tôm yám pa̯a	ຕົ້ມຍຳປາ	fish & lemongrass soup with mushrooms

STIR-FRIED DISHES

kai phát khı̌ing	ໄກ່ຜັດຂີງ	chicken with ginger
mǔu sòm-wǎan	ໝູສົ້ມຫວານ	sweet & sour pork
ngúa phàt nâm-mán hǎ̱wy	ງົວຜັດນ້ຳມັນຫອຍ	beef in oyster sauce
phát phák	ຜັດຜັກ	stir-fried mixed vegetables

VEGETABLES

hǔa phák bua	ຫົວຜັກບົ່ວ	onion (bulb)
hǔa phák thíam	ຫົວຜັກທຽມ	garlic
ká-lam pi̯i	ກະລ່ຳປີ	cabbage
ká-lam pi̯i dàwk	ກະລ່ຳປີດອກ	cauliflower
màak khěua	ໝາກເຂືອ	eggplant
màak len	ໝາກເລັ່ນ	tomato
màak ta̯eng	ໝາກແຕງ	cucumber
màak thua di̯n	ໝາກຖົ່ວດິນ	peanuts (groundnuts)
mán fa-lang	ມັນຝລັ່ງ	potato
naw mâi	ໜໍ່ໄມ້	bamboo shoots
phák kàat hǔa	ຜັກກາດຫົວ	Chinese radish (daikon)
phák sá-lat	ຜັກສະລັດ	lettuce
thua	ຖົ່ວ	beans
thua ngâwk	ຖົ່ວງອກ	bean sprouts
thua nyáo	ຖົ່ວຍາວ	long green beans
tôn phák bua	ຕົ້ນຜັກບົ່ວ	onion (green 'scallions')

Environment

The environment in Laos has long benefited from the country's small population, which, until recently, has exerted relatively little pressure on the ecosystem. But with a growing poor population, for whom wildlife equals protein and forests mean potential fields, the environment is increasingly under strain. Add to that the ongoing problems of legal and illegal logging and increased mining and agriculture, plus a renewed desire to sell its rivers to foreign hydropower developers, and Laos is seeing its previously pristine environment disappear at an alarming rate.

Yet tourism is increasingly being recognised as a lucrative natural resource, and may be the key to preserving Laos's few remaining natural areas. In 2009, tourism was the Lao PDR's second-largest foreign income earner, and estimates suggest that about half of that money is from visitors who came to experience Laos's natural beauty (see the boxed text).

THE LAND

The Mekong River is known as Lancang Jiang (Turbulent River) in China; Mae Nam Khong in Thailand, Myanmar and Laos; Tonle Thom (Great Water) in Cambodia and Cuu Long (Nine Dragons) in Vietnam.

Covering an area slightly larger than Great Britain, landlocked Laos shares borders with China, Myanmar, Thailand, Cambodia and Vietnam. Rivers and mountains dominate, folding the country into a series of often-spectacular ridges and valleys, rivers and mountain passes, extending westward from the Lao–Vietnamese border.

Mountains and plateaus cover well over 70% of the country. Running about half the length of Laos, parallel to the course of the Mekong River, is the Annamite Chain, a rugged mountain range with peaks averaging between 1500m and 2500m in height. Roughly in the centre of the range is the Khammuan Plateau, a world of dramatic limestone grottoes and gorges where vertical walls rise hundreds of metres from jungle-clad valleys. At the southern end of the Annamite Chain, covering 10,000 sq km, the Bolaven Plateau is an important area for the cultivation of high-yield mountain rice, coffee, tea and other crops that flourish in the cooler climes found at these higher altitudes.

The larger, northern half of Laos is made up almost entirely of broken, steep-sloped mountain ranges. The highest mountains are found in Xieng Khuang Province, including Phu Bia, the country's highest peak at 2820m, though this remains off-limits to travellers for now. Just north of Phu Bia stands the Xieng Khuang plateau, the country's largest mountain plateau, which rises 1200m above sea level. The most famous part of the plateau is the Plain of Jars (p193), an area somewhat reminiscent of the rolling hills of Ireland – except for the thousands of bomb craters. It's named for the huge prehistoric stone jars that dot the area, as if the local giants have pub-crawled across this neighbourhood and left their empty beer mugs behind.

Much of the rest of Laos is covered by forest, most of which is mixed deciduous forest. This forest enjoys a complex relationship with the Mekong and its tributaries, acting as a sponge for the monsoon rains and then slowly releasing the water into both streams and the atmosphere during the long dry season.

THE MEKONG & OTHER RIVERS

Springing forth over 4000km from the sea, high up on the Tibetan Plateau, the Mekong River so dominates Lao topography that, to a large extent, the entire country parallels its course. Although half of the Mekong's length runs through China, more of the river courses through Laos than through

ECOTOURISM IN LAOS *Steven Schipani*

With forests covering about half of the country, 21 National Protected Areas, 49 ethnic groups, over 650 bird species and hundreds of mammals, it's no mystery why Laos is known as having some of Southeast Asia's healthiest ecosystems and is a haven for travellers looking to get off the beaten path. Nowadays there are many tour companies and local tour guides offering forest trekking, cave exploration, village homestays and special river journeys to where the roads don't go. These types of activities are very popular in Laos and their availability has exploded over the past decade. Following the success of the Nam Ha Ecotourism Project in Luang Namtha Province, which began in 1999, the ecotourism industry has grown from the bottom up and today the Lao Government is actively promoting ecotourism as one way to help reduce poverty and support the protection of the environment and local culture. It is estimated that culture- and nature-based tourism generates more than half of the country's US$300 million in annual tourism revenue.

The Lao National Tourism Administration defines ecotourism as: 'Tourism activity in rural and protected areas that minimizes negative impacts and is directed towards the conservation of natural and cultural resources, rural socio-economic development and visitor understanding of, and appreciation for, the places they are visiting.' A few Lao tour operators and guesthouses have taken this definition to heart and operate their businesses in a way that upholds the principles of Lao ecotourism.

Up north in Luang Namtha, the Boat Landing Guesthouse (see p219) is Laos's first ecolodge and winner of several international awards; for expertly led treks in Luang Namtha try the Jungle Eco Guide Service (p218) and try to book Mr Bouakhet as your guide. Visit one of the National Protected Areas (NPAs) with Green Discovery (p344), which has offices in Luang Namtha as well as Tha Khaek, Vientiane, Pakse and Vang Vieng. In Luang Prabang, Tiger Trail (p344) has partnered with local communities to offer treks, elephant rides and boat trips in the Nam Khan Valley. In the south, high quality eco-accommodation can be found in Champasak Province's Kingfisher Eco-Lodge (p284), nestled inside the Xe Pian NPA. For a chance to see wild elephants, don't miss the village-operated Elephant Tower at Ban Na (p120), about an hour from Vientiane. There are also locally-run ecoguide services attached to the Provincial Tourist Information Centres in Khammuan, Luang Namtha, Luang Prabang, Savannakhet and Champasak Provinces offering one to four day trips at fair prices. These can be booked on a walk-in basis – see Where to Trek (p79) and www.ecotourismlaos.com for details.

Unfortunately, some unscrupulous companies label everything as 'ecotourism', therefore it is important to determine who is actually upholding the principles of ecotourism, and who is simply greening their pockets. Some questions to ask to ensure you are on the right track are:

- Does my trip benefit local people financially, help to protect biodiversity and support the continuation of traditional culture? How?
- What will I learn on this trip, and what opportunities will local people have to learn from me?
- Are facilities designed in local style, do they use local, natural construction materials, and conserve energy and water? Is there local food on the menu?
- Will I be led by a local guide who is from the area?
- Is there a permit, entrance fee or other fee included in the price of the trip that is directed towards conservation activities?
- Are there sensible limits in place concerning group size and frequency of departures to minimize negative environmental impacts?

Supporting businesses that can give clear, positive and believable answers to these questions will most likely result in an enjoyable, educational experience, where you'll make more than a few local friends along the way. It also raises the profile of sustainable business operators, hopefully encouraging others to follow their example. See www.ecotourismlaos.com for further information on environmentally sustainable tourism in Laos.

any other Southeast Asian country. At its widest, near Si Phan Don in the south, the river can expand to 14km across during the rainy season; spreading around thousands of islands and islets on its inevitable course south.

The Mekong's middle reach is navigable year-round, from Heuan Hin (north of the Khemmarat Rapids in Savannakhet Province) to Kok Phong in Luang Prabang. However these rapids, and the brutal falls at Khon Phapheng (p295) in Si Phan Don, have prevented the Mekong from becoming the sort of regional highway other great rivers have.

The Mekong: Turbulent Past, Uncertain Future (2000), by Milton Osborne, is a fascinating cultural history of the Mekong that spans 2000 years of exploration, mapping and war.

The fertile Mekong River flood plain, running from Sainyabuli to Champasak, forms the flattest and most tropical part of Laos. Virtually all of the domestic rice consumed in Laos is grown here, and if our experience seeing rice packaged up as 'Produce of Thailand' is any indication, then a fair bit is exported via Thailand, too. Most other large-scale farming takes place here as well. The Mekong and, just as importantly, its tributaries are also an important source of fish, a vital part of the diet for most people living in Laos. The Mekong valley is at its largest around Vientiane and Savannakhet, which, not surprisingly, are two of the major population centres.

Major tributaries of the great river include the Nam Ou (Ou River) and the Nam Tha (Tha River), both of which flow through deep, narrow limestone valleys from the north, and the Nam Ngum (Ngum River), which flows into the Mekong across a broad plain in Vientiane Province. The Nam Ngum is the site of one of Laos's oldest hydroelectric plants, which provides power for Vientiane area towns and Thailand. The Se Kong (Kong River) flows through much of southern Laos before eventually reaching the Mekong in Cambodia, and the rivers Nam Kading (Kading River) and Nam Theun (Theun River) are equally important in central Laos.

All the rivers and tributaries west of the Annamite Chain drain into the Mekong, while waterways east of the Annamites (in Hua Phan and Xieng Khuang Provinces only) flow into the Gulf of Tonkin off the coast of Vietnam.

WILDLIFE

Laos boasts one of the least disturbed ecosystems in Asia due to its overall lack of development and low population density. Least disturbed, however, does not mean undisturbed, and for many species the future remains uncertain.

The World Conservation Union (www.iucn.org) believes wildlife in Laos has a much better chance of surviving than in neighbouring Vietnam. Lending weight to this is the Vietnam warty pig (Sus bucclentus), a species found in Laos but last recorded in Vietnam in 1892 and until recently considered extinct.

Animals

The mountains, forests and river networks of Laos are home to a range of animals both endemic to the country and shared with its Southeast Asian neighbours. Nearly half of the animal species native to Thailand are shared by Laos, with the higher forest cover and fewer hunters meaning that numbers are often greater in Laos. Almost all wild animals however are threatened to some extent by hunting and habitat loss; see Environmental Issues, p78.

In spite of this Laos has seen several new species discovered in recent years, while others thought to be extinct have turned up in remote forests. Given their rarity, these newly discovered species are on the endangered list (see p75).

As in Cambodia, Vietnam, Myanmar and much of Thailand, most of the fauna in Laos belong to the Indochinese zoogeographic realm (as opposed to the Sundaic domain found south of the Isthmus of Kra in southern Thailand or the Palaearctic to the north in China).

Notable mammals endemic to Laos include the lesser panda, raccoon dog, Lao marmoset rat, Owston's civet and the pygmy slow loris. Other important exotic species found elsewhere in the region include the Malayan and Chinese pangolins, 10 species of civet, marbled cat, Javan and crab-eating mongoose, the serow (sometimes called Asian mountain goat) and goral (another type of goat-antelope), and cat species including the leopard cat and Asian golden cat.

Among the most notable of Laos's wildlife are the primates. Several smaller species are known, including the Phayre's leaf monkey, François' langur, Douc langur and several macaques. Two other primates that are endemic to Laos are the concolour gibbon and snub-nosed langur. But it's the five species of gibbon that attract most attention. Sadly, the black-cheeked crested gibbon is endangered, being hunted both for its meat and to be sold as pets in Thailand. Several projects are underway to educate local communities to set aside safe areas for the gibbons.

ELEPHANTS

Laos might once have been known as the land of a million elephants, but these days only about 2000 remain. For an animal as threatened as the Asiatic elephant, this population is one of the largest in the region. Exact figures are hard to come by, but it's generally believed that there are about 800 wild elephants, roaming in open-canopy forest areas predominantly in Sainyabuli Province west of Vientiane, Bolikhamsai Province in the Phu Khao Khuay NPA (p118), and along the Nakai Plateau in central eastern Laos.

Hunting and habitat loss are their main threats. In areas such as the Nakai Plateau, Vietnamese poachers kill elephants for their meat and hides, while the Nam Theun 2 hydropower project in Khammuan Province has swallowed up a large chunk of habitat. The Wildlife Conservation Society (WCS) has an ongoing project in this area, with a long-term aim of establishing a 'demonstration site that will serve as a model for reducing human-elephant conflict nationwide.'

Working or domesticated elephants are also found in most provinces, totalling between 1100 and 1350 countrywide. They have traditionally been used for the heavy labour involved in logging and agriculture, but modern machinery is rapidly putting them out of work. As a result, the mahouts (elephant keepers and/or drivers) in some elephant villages are working with NGOs to find alternative income through tourism. Projects in Kiet Ngong (p283) in Champasak Province, and Hongsa (p181) in Sainyabuli Province offer elephant trekking, and the yearly elephant festival (p182) is growing in popularity as a tourist event. Working elephants are most visible in Sainyabuli, Udomxai, Champasak and Attapeu Provinces.

Despite these problems, Laos is in the rare position of having the raw materials – enough elephants and habitat – to ensure the jumbos have a long and healthy future. What is missing is money and, perhaps, sufficient political will.

ENDANGERED SPECIES

To a certain extent, all wild animals in Laos are endangered due to widespread hunting and gradual but persistent habitat loss. Laos ratified the UN Convention on International Trade in Endangered Species of Wild Flora and Fauna (CITES) in 2004, which, combined with other legal measures, has made it easier to prosecute people trading species endangered as a direct result of international trade. But in reality you won't need 20/20 vision to pick out the endangered species – both dead and alive – on sale in markets around the country. Border markets, in particular, tend to attract the most valuable species, with Thais buying species such as gibbons as pets, and Vietnamese shopping for exotic food and medicines.

Of the hundreds of species of mammals known in Laos, several dozen are endangered according to the IUCN's Redlist (www.iucnredlist.org).

Odd-shaped rocks are venerated across Laos. Even in what appears to be the middle of nowhere, you'll see saffron robes draped over rocks that look vaguely like turtles, fishing baskets, stupas etc. Local legends explain how the rocks came to be or what they were used for, and some are famous around the country.

Wildlife Trade in Laos: The End of the Game (2001), by Hanneke Nooren & Gordon Claridge, is a frightening description of animal poaching in Laos.

These range from bears, including the Asiatic black bear and Malayan sun bear, through the less glamorous wild cattle such as the gaur and banteng, to high-profile cats like the tiger, leopard and clouded leopard. Exactly how endangered they are is difficult to say. Camera-trapping projects (setting up cameras in the forest to take photos of anything that goes past) are being carried out by various NGOs and, in the case of the Nakai Nam Theun NPA, by the Nam Theun 2 dam operators themselves.

The Nakai Nam Theun research is part of a deal brokered by the World Bank that ensures US$1 million a year is set aside for environmental study and protection in the dam's catchment area. Results of camera trapping in the Nakai Nam Theun NPA have been both encouraging and depressing. The cameras returned photos of limited numbers of several species, but also a hunter posing proudly with his kill – not quite the shots they were hoping for.

The WCS is focussing its conservation activities on species including the Asian elephant, Siamese crocodile, tiger, western black crested gibbon and Eld's deer, one of several endangered deer species including barking deer and sambar. For more details, see www.wcs.org.

Some endangered species are so rare they were unknown until very recently. Among these is the spindlehorn (*Pseudoryx nghethingensis;* known as the *saola* in Vietnam, *nyang* in Laos), a horned mammal found in the Annamite Chain along the Laos–Vietnam border in 1992. The spindlehorn, which was described in 14th-century Chinese journals, was long thought not to exist, and when discovered it became one of only three land mammals to earn its own genus in the 20th century. Unfortunately, horns taken from spindlehorn are a favoured trophy among certain groups on both sides of the border.

In 2005 WCS scientists visiting a local market in Khammuan Province discovered a 'Laotian rock rat' laid out for sale. But, what was being sold as meat turned out to be a genetically distinct species named the *Laonastes aenigmamus.* Further research revealed it to be the sole survivor of a prehistoric group of rodents that died out about 11 million years ago. If you're very lucky you might see one on the cliffs near the caves off Rte 12 in Khammuan Province.

Among the most seriously endangered of all mammals is the Irrawaddy dolphin (see the boxed text, p292).

The giant Mekong catfish may grow up to 3m long and weigh as much as 300kg. Due to Chinese blasting of shoals in the Upper Mekong, it now faces extinction in the wild.

Birds

Those new to Laos often ask: 'Why can't I hear more birds?' The short answer is 'cheap protein' (see p80). If you can get far enough away from people, you'll find the forests and mountains of Laos do in fact harbour a rich selection of resident and migrating bird species. Surveys carried out by a British team of ornithologists in the 1990s recorded 437 species, including eight globally threatened and 21 globally near-threatened species. Some other counts rise as high as 650 species.

Notable among these are the Siamese fireback pheasant, green peafowl, red-collared woodpecker, brown hornbill, tawny fish-owl, Sarus crane, giant ibis and the Asian golden weaver. Hunting keeps urban bird populations noticeably thin. In 2008, scientists from the WCS and the University of Melbourne conducting research in central Laos discovered a new bird species, the bare-faced bulbul, the first bald songbird to be spotted in mainland Asia, and the first new bulbul to have been discovered in the last century.

Up until a few years ago, it wasn't uncommon to see men pointing long-barrelled muskets at upper tree branches in cities as large as Savannakhet and Vientiane. Those days are now gone, but around almost every village you'll hear hunters doing their business most afternoons.

RESPONSIBLE TRAVEL IN LAOS – WILDLIFE CONSERVATION

Throughout your travels in Laos the opportunity to buy or consume wildlife is likely to come about. In the interests of wildlife conservation, the Wildlife Conservation Society, Lao PDR strongly urges you not to partake in the wildlife trade. While it's true that subsistence hunting is permitted by the Government of Lao PDR for local rural villagers, the sale and purchase of *any* wildlife is illegal in Laos. The wildlife trade is damaging to biodiversity and to local livelihoods.

While strolling through rural and city markets you'll come across wild animals for sale as meat or live pets. In a misguided attempt to do the right thing travellers have been known to buy these live animals in order to release them. While it might feel like this is a positive step towards thwarting the wildlife trade it actually has the opposite effect with vendors, unaware of the buyer's motivation, interpreting the sale as increased demand.

Be prepared for some bizarre and disturbing items on restaurant menus and in food markets in Laos. While it may be tempting to experience the unusual, it's strongly recommended that the following animals be avoided: soft shelled turtles, rat snakes, mouse deer, sambar deer, squirrel, bamboo rat, muntjac deer and pangolins. Many of these species are endangered or are a source of prey for endangered species.

Thinking of purchasing a stuffed wild animal? A bag or wallet made from animal skin? Or perhaps an insect in a framed box? Think again. The money made in the sale of these peculiar trinkets goes directly towards supporting the illegal wildlife trade. Also to be avoided are the rings and necklaces made from animal teeth (sellers may tell you that this is buffalo bone, but it's just as likely that it's bear or wild pig bone) and the bottles of alcohol with snakes, birds, or insects inside. Though widely sold, this trade is illegal in Laos, and you'll most likely find your new libido-enhancing snake oil confiscated by customs in your home country anyway. Keep an eye out for products with a CITES-certified label. These are legal to buy in Laos and take home.

For many species of wildlife in Laos, populations are at critically low levels. The WCS Lao PDR program (www.wcs.org/international/Asia/laos) is collaborating with the Vientiane Capital City government to monitor and control wildlife trade. If you observe wildlife trading please contact the local authorities.

By the Wildlife Conservation Society, Lao PDR (www.wcs.org/international/Asia/laos)

Plants

According to the UN Food and Agriculture Organization, in 2005 forest covered more than 69% of Laos. Of these woodlands about 11% can be classified as primary forest. Laos ranks 17th worldwide in terms of forest cover as a percentage of total land cover.

Most indigenous vegetation in Laos is associated with monsoon forests, a common trait in areas of tropical mainland Southeast Asia that experience dry seasons lasting three months or longer. In such mixed deciduous forests many trees shed their leaves during the dry season to conserve water. Rainforests – which are typically evergreen – don't exist in Laos, although nonindigenous rainforest species such as the coconut palm are commonly seen in the lower Mekong River valley. There are undoubtedly some big trees in Laos, but don't expect the sort of towering forests found in some other parts of Southeast Asia – the conditions do not, and never have, allowed these sorts of giants to grow here.

Instead the monsoon forests of Laos typically grow in three canopies. Dipterocarps – tall, pale-barked, single-trunked trees that can grow beyond 30m high – dominate the top canopy of the forest, while a middle canopy consists of an ever-dwindling population of prized hardwoods, including teak, padauk (sometimes called 'Asian rosewood') and mahogany. Underneath there's a variety of smaller trees, shrubs, grasses and – along river habitats – bamboo. In certain plateau areas of the south, there are dry dipterocarp forests in which the forest canopies are more open, with less of a middle layer

Around 85% of Laos is mountainous terrain, and less than 4% is considered arable.

and more of a grass-and-bamboo undergrowth. Parts of the Annamite Chain that receive rain from both the southwestern monsoon as well as the South China Sea are covered by tropical montane evergreen forest, while tropical pine forests can be found on the Nakai Plateau and Sekong area to the south.

In addition to the glamour hardwoods, the country's flora includes a toothsome array of fruit trees, bamboo (more species than any country outside Thailand and China) and an abundance of flowering species such as the orchid. However, in some parts of the country orchids are being stripped out of forests (often in protected areas) for sale to Thai tourists; look for the markets near the waterfalls of the Bolaven Plateau (see p298) to see them. In the high plateaus of the Annamite Chain, extensive grasslands or savanna are common.

NATIONAL PROTECTED AREAS (NPAS)

Laos boasts one of the youngest and most comprehensive protected area systems in the world. In 1993 the government set up 18 National Biodiversity Conservation Areas, comprising a total of 24,600 sq km, or just over 10% of the country's land mass. Most significantly, it did this following sound scientific consultation rather than creating areas on an ad hoc basis (as most other countries have done). Two more were added in 1995, for a total of 20 protected areas covering 14% of Laos. A further 4% of Laos is reserved as Provincial Protected Areas, making Laos one of the most protected countries on earth.

The areas were renamed National Protected Areas (NPAs) a few years ago. And while the naming semantics might seem trivial, they do reflect some important differences. The main one is that an NPA has local communities living within its boundaries, unlike a national park, where only rangers and those working in the park are allowed to live and where traditional activities such as hunting and logging are banned. Indeed, forests in NPAs are divided into production forests for timber, protection forests for watershed and conservation forests for pure conservation.

The largest protected areas are in southern Laos, which, contrary to popular myth, bears a higher percentage of natural forest cover than the north. The largest of the NPAs, Nakai-Nam Theun, covers 3710 sq km and is home to the recently discovered spindlehorn, as well as several other species unknown to the scientific world a decade ago.

While several NPAs remain difficult to access without mounting a full-scale expedition, several others have become much easier to reach in recent years. The best way in is usually by foot; for a list of the trekking possibilities see the boxed text, Where to Trek.

The wildlife in these areas – from rare birds to wild elephants – is relatively abundant. The best time to view wildlife in most of the country is just after the monsoon in November. However, even at these times you'll be lucky to see very much. There are several reasons for this, the most important of which is that ongoing hunting mean numbers of wild animals are reduced and those living are instinctively scared of humans. It's also difficult to see animals in forest cover at the best of times, and many animals are nocturnal.

For fuller descriptions of all Laos's National Protected Areas, see the comprehensive website www.ecotourismlaos.com

ENVIRONMENTAL ISSUES

Flying over Laos it's easy to think that much of the country is blanketed with untouched wilderness. But first impressions can be deceiving. What that lumpy carpet of green conceals is an environment facing several inter-related threats.

For the most part they're issues of the bottom line. Hunting endangers all sorts of creatures of the forest but it persists because the hunters can't afford to buy meat from the market. Forests are logged at unsustainable

---

WHERE TO TREK

The best way to get into the wilderness is on a trek into one of Laos's National Protected Areas (NPAs). Most treks have both a cultural and environmental focus, with trekkers sleeping in village homestays (p45) and your money going directly into some of the poorest communities in the country.

These treks are mostly run by small local tour operators and have English-speaking guides. They can be organised once you arrive or in advance by phone, and are the cheapest trekking options available. Some larger companies, most notably Green Discovery (www.greendiscovery laos.com), Tiger Trail (www.laos-adventures.com) and Buffalo Tours (www.buffalotours.com) offer more elaborate trekking, often combining walking with mountain biking, kayaking and/or rafting. Guides will likely be more experienced but the trips are also more expensive.

To give you an idea of what's available, we've outlined the various trekking options in northern Laos (p188), central Laos (p239) and southern Laos (p267). For more general information on trekking in Laos, see p314 and p234.

---

rates because the timber found in Laos is valuable and loggers see more profit in cutting than not. And hydropower projects affect river systems and their dependent ecologies – including the forests – because Laos needs the money hydroelectricity can bring, and it's relatively cheap and easy for energy companies to develop in Laos.

Laws do exist to protect wildlife and, as mentioned, plenty of Laos is protected as NPAs. But most Laotians are completely unaware of world conservation issues and there is little will and less money to pay for conservation projects, such as organised park rangers, or to prosecute offenders. Lack of communication between national and local governments and poor definitions of authority in conservation areas just add to the issues.

One of the biggest obstacles facing environmental protection in Laos is corruption among those in charge of enforcing conservation regulations. Illegal timber felling, poaching and the smuggling of exotic wildlife species would decrease sharply if corruption among officials was properly tackled.

However, there is some good news. With the support of several dedicated individuals and NGOs, ecotourism (see the boxed text, p73) is growing to the point where some local communities are beginning to understand – and buying into – the idea that an intact environment can be worth money. Added to that, the government has mainly avoided giving contracts to companies wanting to develop large-scale resorts; though the same can't be said for many non-tourism projects. Air pollution and carbon emissions are about as low as you'll find anywhere in the region because most Lao still live at or just above a subsistence level and there is little heavy industry. Laos has one of the lowest per capita energy-consumption rates in the world.

One long-standing environmental problem has been the unexploded ordnance (UXO) contaminating parts of eastern Laos where the Ho Chi Minh Trail ran during the Second Indochina War. Bombs are being found and defused at a painstakingly slow rate, but progress is being made.

Thus the major challenges facing Laos's environment are the internal pressures of economic growth and external pressures from the country's more populated and affluent neighbours – particularly China, Vietnam and Thailand – who would like to exploit Laos's abundant resources as much as possible.

Hydropower Projects

At the time of writing the electricity industry lobby in Laos was proudly reporting on its website (www.poweringprogress.org) that since the 1990s seven hydroelectric dams had begun operation and construction is currently

proceeding on eight more. In addition to this, the Lao government is planning another 16 and investigating the feasibility of another 44 hydropower
projects, eight of which would potentially dam the Mekong itself.

Hydropower is a relatively clean source of energy and to a certain extent
dams in Laos are inevitable (see the boxed text, p81). But these are truly staggering numbers, with a potentially serious impact on the ecology of almost
every major river system in the country.

Aside from displacing tens of thousands of people, dam projects inundate
large swaths of forest (rarely agricultural land), permanently change the
water flows, block or change fish migrations, thus affecting the fisheries
local people have been relying on for centuries, and alter the ecosystems that
support forests and the species that live in them. These forests are also the
source of myriad nontimber products that contribute to local livelihoods,
and the effects on these are often severe.

Like solar and wind power, hydropower is a potential source of sustainable
and renewable energy when coupled with responsible land/resource planning
and development. The question is, does Laos – and the companies looking
to cash in on the resource – have the latter?

Habitat Loss

Deforestation is another major environmental issue in Laos. Although the
official export of timber is tightly controlled, no one really knows how much
teak and other hardwoods are being smuggled into Vietnam, Thailand and
especially China. The policy in northern Laos has been to allow the Chinese
to take as much timber as they want in return for building roads. The Lao
army is still removing huge chunks of forest in Khammuan Province and
from remote areas in the country's far south, near the Se Pian and Dong Hua
Sao NPAs, much of it going to Vietnam. The national electricity-generating
company also profits from the timber sales each time it links a Lao town or
village with the national power grid, clear-cutting a wider-than-necessary
swath along Lao highways. Increasingly large-scale plantations and mining –
also largely funded by Laos's neighbours – are also leading to significant
habitat loss.

Essentially, the Lao authorities express a seemingly sincere desire to conserve the nation's forests – but not at the cost of rural livelihoods. In most
rural areas 70% of non-rice foods come from the forest. Thus forest destruction, whether as a result of logging or dam-building, will lead to increased
poverty and reduced local livelihoods.

Other pressures on the forest cover come from swidden (slash-and-burn)
methods of cultivation, in which small plots of forest are cleared, burnt for
nitrogenation of the soil, and farmed intensively for two or three years, after
which they are infertile and unfarmable for between eight and 10 years.
Considering the sparse population, swidden cultivation is probably not as
great an environmental threat as logging. But neither is it an efficient use
of resources.

Forestry per se is not all bad, and effective management could maintain
Laos's forests as a source of income for a long time to come. Creating NPAs
has been a good start, but examples of forest regeneration and even planting
high-value trees for future harvest are rare. All too often the name of the
game is short-term gain.

Hunting & Overfishing

The majority of Lao citizens derive most of their protein from food culled
from nature, not from farms or ranches. How threatening traditional hunting habits are to species survival in Laos is debatable given the nation's

Margin notes

Marco Polo was probably the first European to cross the Mekong, in the 13th century, and was followed by a group of Portuguese emissaries in the 16th century. Dutch merchant Gerrit van Wuysthoff arrived by boat in the 17th century. In 1893 the French and Siamese signed the Treaty of Bangkok, desig-nating the Mekong as the border between Siam and French Indochina.

Several NGOs are working in Laos to help preserve, promote and protect the environment. See what they're doing at:

ElefantAsia (www.elefantasia.org)

Traffic East Asia (www.traffic.org)

Wildlife Conservation Society (www.wcs.org)

World Conservation Union (IUCN; www.iucn.org/lao/)

World Wildlife Fund (www.wwf.org or www.panda.org)

extremely sparse population. But, combined with habitat loss, hunting for food is placing increasing pressure on wildlife numbers.

The cross-border trade in wildlife is also potentially serious. Much of the poaching that takes place in Laos's NPAs is allegedly carried out by

DEVELOPING THE MEKONG: RELIEVING POVERTY OR DAM CRAZY?

For millennia the Mekong River has been the lifeblood of Laos and the wider Mekong region. As the region's primary artery, about 60 million people depend on the rich fisheries and other resources provided by the river and its tributaries. The Mekong is the world's 12th-longest river and 10th-largest in terms of volume. But unlike other major rivers, a series of rapids have prevented it from developing into a major transport and cargo thoroughfare, or as a base for large industrial cities.

Except in China, the Mekong's mainstream is not dammed. However, the greater river system has long been seen as a potentially lucrative source of hydroelectricity. And with the regional demand for power rising rapidly, plans to turn Laos into the 'battery of Southeast Asia' have been revived after almost two decades of stagnation and the Asian financial crisis.

For a country as poor as Laos there are definite benefits. Selling electricity to Thailand, Vietnam and China will bring much-needed foreign exchange to the economy. In theory, this windfall can be spent on developing the country while at the same time reducing its reliance on foreign aid and loans. It's an attractive proposition, and one that the Laos government and several international agencies seem happy to pursue.

The first, and biggest, was the Nam Theun 2 dam in Khammuan Province, finished in 2010. This controversial hydropower project was over a decade in the planning, and as such is probably one of the most studied dam projects in history. Dozens of research projects were carried out because the dam needed World Bank approval before investors would commit, and the World Bank was under sustained pressure to reduce the negative impacts as much as possible. Some organisations questioned whether the environmental impacts could be adequately reduced at all.

However, not all projects are as big or get as much publicity as Nam Theun 2. When the World Bank finally approved the project in 2005, it was the equivalent of opening hydropower's Pandora's Box. In the ensuing period a flurry of agreements have been signed between the Laos government and private developers, all looking for a slice of the hydropower pie. At the time of writing more than 30 hydropower projects were either being built or were in the advanced stages of planning in Laos, raising the question of whether the government has gone 'dam' crazy. Nine dams proposed for the Mekong River's mainstream have proved especially controversial.

For critics, including the rivers watchdog, International Rivers, the answer is a resounding yes. They claim that these lower profile dams have potentially far greater environmental and social impacts because there is no transparency and they are much harder to monitor. Although the government requires full environmental impact assessments for all hydropower schemes, if they have been carried out, few have been released to the public.

The negative impacts associated with dams include both the obvious and more difficult to see. Obvious effects include displacement of local communities, loss of livelihood, flooding upstream areas, reduced sediment flows and increased erosion downstream with resulting issues for fish stocks and the fisherman who work the rivers. Less immediately visible, but with a potentially much greater influence in the long term, are the changes these dams will have on the Mekong's flood pulse, which is critical to the fish spawning cycle, and thus the food source of millions of people.

All up, this is a hugely complex issue. For more information, visit these websites:

Asian Development Bank (www.adb.org)
International Rivers (www.internationalrivers.org)
Laos Energy lobby (www.poweringprogress.org)
Mekong River Commission (www.mrcmekong.org)
Save the Mekong Coalition (www.savethemekong.org)
WWF (www.panda.org)

Vietnamese hunters who have crossed into central Laos illegally to round up species such as pangolins, civets, barking deer, goral and raccoon dogs to sell back home. These animals are highly valued for both food and medicinal purposes in Vietnam, Thailand and China, and as the demand in those countries grows in line with increasing wealth, so too do the prices buyers are prepared to pay.

Foreign NGOs run grass-roots education campaigns across Laos in an effort to raise awareness of endangered species and the effects of hunting on local ecosystems. But as usual, money is the key to breaking the cycle. And while hunters remain dirt poor, the problem seems here to stay.

In more densely populated areas such as Savannakhet and Champasak provinces, the overfishing of lakes and rivers poses a danger to certain fish species. Projects to educate fishermen about exactly where their catch comes from, and how to protect that source, have been successful in changing some unsustainable practices. One area given particular attention is fishing using explosives. This practice, whereby fishermen throw explosives into the water and wait for the dead fish to float to the surface, is incredibly destructive. Most fishermen don't realise that for every dead fish they collect from the surface, another two or three lie dead on the riverbed. The practice is illegal in Laos, and anecdotal evidence suggests education and the law have reduced the problem.

While opium has been cultivated and used in Laos for centuries, the country didn't become a major producer until the passing of the 1971 Anti-Narcotics Law, a move that helped drive up regional prices steeply.

Vientiane & Around

Laos is booming. Driven by rising foreign investment, foreign-aid workers and a more urbane youth, change is coming quickly. However, even with all this dynamism you won't see words like 'hustle' and 'bustle' being used to describe Vientiane, which can still mount a strong argument for being the most relaxed capital city on earth.

Vientiane means 'Sandalwood City', and is actually pronounced Wiang Chan; the French are responsible for the modern transliteration. The combination of tree-lined boulevards and dozens of temples impart an atmosphere of timelessness, while the kaleidoscopic architectural styles reflect its historic influences, from classic Lao through Thai, Chinese, French, US and Soviet.

As Laos continues to open itself to the world, Vientiane is where the struggle between a communist past and inevitably more capitalist future is most dramatically played out. Lao bands sing lyrics censored by the government to dancing youths who'd look at home in any Western bar. The Lao National Museum still has displays glorifying victory over capitalist foreign imperialists, but across the road the first international fast-food franchise has opened.

Of course, Vientiane is not only about witnessing change. The 6400 Buddhas at Wat Si Saket, the religious art of Haw Pha Kaeo, and Laos' gilded national symbol, Pha That Luang, speak of the city's historical importance. Patuxai and the surreal Xieng Khuan (Buddha Park) may have less artistic merit, but like the city itself, they're not short of appeal.

HIGHLIGHTS

- Explore forgivingly flat and relatively car-free Vientiane on two wheels with our **cycling tour** (p98)
- Treat yourself to a traditional sauna and massage at **Wat Sok Pa Luang** (p97) or a **herbal sauna** (p97)
- Enjoy authentic French cuisine at a cafe such as **Le Banneton** (p108) or restaurant such as **chez philippe** (p107)
- Tube, climb, kayak, cycle or walk through the rivers and imposing limestone karst terrain around **Vang Vieng** (p130)
- Discover the emerging ecotourism area of Nam Lik basin by staying at the **Nam Lik Eco-Village** (p129) and zipping 40m above the jungle at **Nam Lik Jungle Fly** (p129)

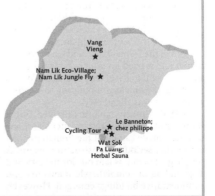

VIENTIANE

ວຽງຈັນ

☎ 021 / pop 262,000

HISTORY

Set on a bend in the Mekong River, Vientiane was first settled around the 9th century AD and formed part of one of the early Lao valley *meuang* (city-states) that were consolidated around the 10th century. The Lao who settled here did so because the surrounding alluvial plains were so fertile and initially the Vientiane *meuang* prospered and enjoyed a fragile sovereignty.

In the ensuing 10 or so centuries of its history, Vientiane's fortunes have been mixed. At various times it has been a major regional centre; at other times it has been controlled by the Vietnamese, Burmese and Siamese.

The height of Vientiane's success was probably in the years after it became the Lan Xang capital in the mid-16th century. (King Setthathirath moved the capital of the Lan Xang kingdom from the city now known as Luang Prabang.) Several of Vientiane's wats were built following this shift and the city became a major centre of Buddhist learning.

It didn't last. Periodic invasions by the Burmese, Siamese and Chinese, and the eventual division of the Lan Xang kingdom took their toll on the city.

It wasn't until the Siamese installed Chao Anou (a Lao prince who had been educated in Bangkok) on the throne in 1805 that the city received an overdue makeover. Chao Anou's public works included Wat Si Saket (p92), built in 1815.

Unfortunately, Chao Anou's attempts to assert Lao independence over the Siamese (see p27) resulted in the most violent and destructive episode in Vientiane's history.

In 1828 the Siamese defeated Chao Anou's armies and wasted no time in razing the city and carting off much of the population. Wat Si Saket was the only major building to survive, and the city was abandoned.

In 1867, French explorers arrived but it wasn't until late in the century, after Vientiane had been made capital of the French protectorate, that serious reconstruction began. A simple grid plan was laid out for the city and a sprinkling of colonial-style mansions and administrative buildings emerged. However,

Vientiane was always low in the French order of Indochinese priorities, as the modest building program testifies.

In 1928 the 'city' was home to just 9000 inhabitants – many of them Vietnamese administrators brought in by the French – and it wasn't until the end of WWII that Vientiane's population began to grow with any vigour. It was a growth fed primarily by Cold War dollars, with first French and later American advisors arriving in a variety of guises.

After a couple of coups d'état in the politically fluid 1960s, Vientiane had by the early '70s become a city where almost anything went. Its few bars were peopled by an almost surreal mix of spooks and correspondents, and the women who served them.

Not surprisingly, things changed with the arrival of the Pathet Lao (PL) in 1975. Nightclubs filled with spies were the first to go and Vientiane settled into a slumber punctuated by occasional unenthusiastic concessions to communism, including low level collectivisation and an initial crackdown on Buddhism. These days the most noticeable leftovers from the period are some less-than-inspired Soviet-style buildings. Things picked up in the 1990s and in recent years Vientiane has seen a relative explosion of construction, road redevelopment and vehicular traffic, much of it financed by China, the country that will most likely have the most signficant influence on Vientiane's future.

ORIENTATION

Vientiane curves along the Mekong River following a meandering northwest–southeast axis, with the central district of Muang Chanthabuli at the centre of the bend. Most of the government offices, hotels, restaurants and historic temples are located in Chanthabuli, near the river. Some old French colonial buildings and Vietnamese-Chinese shophouses remain, set alongside newer structures built according to the rather boxy social realist school of architecture.

Wattay International Airport (Map p86) is around 4km northwest of the centre. The Northern Bus Station (Map p86), where long-distance services to points north begin and end, is about 2km northwest of the centre. The Southern Bus Station (Map p119) deals with most services heading south and is 9km northeast of the centre on Rte 13. The border with Thailand at the Thai-Lao Friendship

Bridge (Map p119) is 19km southeast of the city.

Street signs are limited to major roads and the central, more touristy part of town. Where they do exist, the English and French designations vary (eg route, *rue*, road and avenue) but the Lao script always reads *thanǒn* (Th). Therefore, when asking directions it's always best to just use *thanǒn*.

The parallel Th Setthathirath (which is home to several famous temples) and Th Samsènethai are the main streets in central Vientiane. Heading northwest they both eventually lead to Th Luang Prabang and Rte 13 north. In the other direction they run perpendicular to and eventually cross Th Lan Xang, a major boulevard leading from the presidential palace past Talat Sao (Morning Market) to Patuxai (Victory Gate) and, after turning into Th Phon Kheng, to Rte 13 south and the Southern Bus Station.

The *meuang* of Vientiane are broken up into *bân* (Ban), which are neighbourhoods or villages associated with local wats. Wattay International Airport, for example, is in Ban Wat Tai – the area in which Wat Tai is located.

Maps

Hobo Maps *Vientiane* (www.hobomaps.com; US$2) is probably the best generally available map of the city; get it at bookshops and PhimPhone Markets (p109).

INFORMATION
Bookshops

Vientiane's handful of bookshops sell everything from years-old reports by development organisations to the more predictable travel guides and maps.

Book-Cafe (Map p90; ☎ 020-5689 3741; 53/2 Th Hengboun; ❧ 8am-8pm) Run by Robert Cooper, the author of several books on Laos and Thailand, this tiny shop stocks a wealth of books on Laos, as well as a general selection of used books.

Kosila Bookshop (Map p90; ☎ 020-224 0964; Th Chanthakoummane; ❧ 9am-5pm) Mostly used books.

Monument Books (Map p90; ☎ 243 708; www.monument-books.com; 124 Th Nokèokoummane; ❧ 9am-8pm Mon-Thu, 9am-9pm Fri & Sat, 9am-6pm Sun) The city's flashest bookshop stocks a range of new books on Asia, plus maps, magazines and postcards.

Oriental Bookshop (Map p90; ☎ 215 352; 121 Th Chao Anou; ❧ 8.30am-10pm) Mr Ngo stocks a huge selection of obscure and sometimes antiquated books on Laos. Coffee and Internet (per hr 5000K) are also available.

State Book Shop (Map p90; ☎ 212 475; cnr Th Setthathirath & Th Manthatourath; ❧ 8am-noon & 1-4pm Mon-Fri) Although English-language books here number in the low single digits, this longstanding government-run shop is a fascinating place to pick up communist-era mementos such as a Lao-language Karl Marx poster or a Lao–Latvian dictionary.

Vientiane Book Center (Map p90; ☎ 212 031; 32/05 Th Fa Ngoum; ❧ 8.30am-5pm) Friendly owner has a variety of mostly used books.

Cultural Centres
Centre Culturel et de Coopération Linguistique

(Map p90; ☎ 215 764; www.centredelangue.org; Th Lan Xang; ❧ 8.15am-6.15pm Mon-Fri, 9.30am-4.30pm Sat) The French Centre, as it's known, has a busy schedule of movies, musical and theatrical performances, a library and French and Lao language classes.

Emergency

Ambulance (☎ 195)
Fire (☎ 190)
Police (☎ 191)
Tourist Police (Map p90; ☎ 251 128; Th Lan Xang)

Immigration

Located in the Ministry of Public Security building across the road from Talat Sao, Vientiane's **Immigration Office** (Map p90; ☎ 212 250; Th Hatsady; ❧ 8am-noon & 1-4pm Mon-Fri) is the place to go for extensions or other visa-related issues. See p329 for details on extending your Lao visa.

Internet Access

Travellers will be pleased to find that internet cafes are now entirely ubiquitous and cheap in most of central Vientiane, as this wasn't always the case.

There's a row of internet cafes on the north side of Th Setthathirath between Nam Phu (the fountain) and Th Manthatourath, open from 9am to 11pm and charging 6000K an hour. Wi-fi, often for free, is also available at many of Vientiane's cafes.

Other places to get online:

Maison du Cafe (Map p90; ☎ 219 743; 119 Th Manthatourath; ❧ 8am-10pm; per hr 6000K) This shop offers ticketing services and coffee in addition to internet. International calls can be made for 4000K per min.

Oriental Bookshop (Map p90; ☎ 215 352; 121 Th Chao Anou; ❧ 8.30am-10pm; per hr 5000K) This bookshop also offers several computers with internet access.

True Coffee (Map p90; ☎ 260 417; 111 Th Setthathirath; ❧ 8am-10pm) Offers internet access via

VIENTIANE & AROUND

VIENTIANE

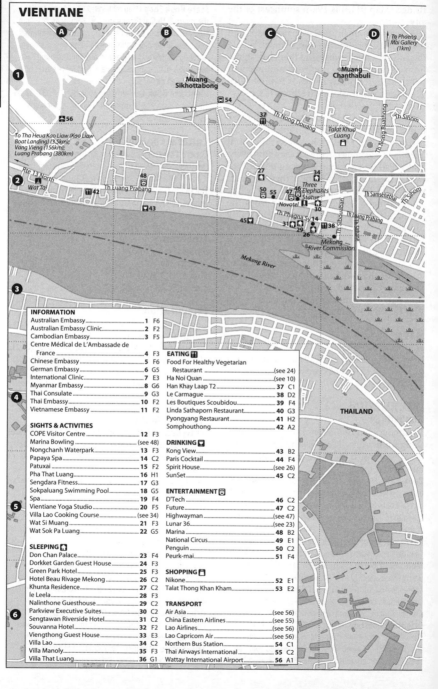

INFORMATION
Australian Embassy............................ **1** F6
Australian Embassy Clinic................... **2** F2
Cambodian Embassy........................... **3** F5
Centre Médical de L'Ambassade de
  France.. **4** F3
Chinese Embassy................................ **5** F6
German Embassy................................. **6** G5
International Clinic.............................. **7** E3
Myanmar Embassy.............................. **8** G6
Thai Consulate................................... **9** G3
Thai Embassy.................................... **10** F2
Vietnamese Embassy......................... **11** F2

SIGHTS & ACTIVITIES
COPE Visitor Centre.......................... **12** F3
Marina Bowling........................... (see 48)
Nongchanh Waterpark....................... **13** F3
Papaya Spa....................................... **14** C2
Patuxai... **15** F2
Pha That Luang................................. **16** H1
Sengdara Fitness............................... **17** G3
Sokpaluang Swimming Pool................ **18** G5
Spa.. **19** F4
Vientiane Yoga Studio....................... **20** F5
Villa Lao Cooking Course................ (see 34)
Wat Si Muang................................... **21** F3
Wat Sok Pa Luang............................. **22** G5

SLEEPING
Don Chan Palace............................... **23** F4
Dorkket Garden Guest House............. **24** F3
Green Park Hotel............................... **25** F3
Hotel Beau Rivage Mekong................ **26** C2
Khunta Residence............................. **27** C2
le Leela... **28** F3
Nalinthone Guesthouse..................... **29** C2
Parkview Executive Suites................. **30** C2
Sengtawan Riverside Hotel................ **31** C2
Souvanna Hotel................................ **32** F2
Viengthong Guest House.................... **33** E3
Villa Lao.. **34** C2
Villa Manoly.................................... **35** F3
Villa That Luang............................... **36** G1

EATING
Food For Healthy Vegetarian
  Restaurant................................ (see 24)
Ha Noi Quan............................... (see 10)
Han Khay Laap T2............................ **37** C1
Le Carmague.................................... **38** D2
Les Boutiques Scouibidou.................. **39** F4
Linda Sathaporn Restaurant............... **40** G3
Pyongyang Restaurant....................... **41** H2
Somphouthong.................................. **42** A2

DRINKING
Kong View... **43** B2
Paris Cocktail.................................... **44** F4
Spirit House................................. (see 26)
SunSet.. **45** C2

ENTERTAINMENT
D'Tech... **46** C2
Future.. **47** C2
Highwayman.............................. (see 47)
Lunar 36..................................... (see 23)
Marina.. **48** B2
National Circus................................. **49** E1
Penguin.. **50** C2
Peurk-mai... **51** F4

SHOPPING
Nikone.. **52** E1
Talat Thong Khan Kham..................... **53** E2

TRANSPORT
Air Asia....................................... (see 56)
China Eastern Airlines................... (see 55)
Lao Airlines................................. (see 56)
Lao Capricorn Air......................... (see 56)
Northern Bus Station........................ **54** C1
Thai Airways International.................. **55** C2
Wattay International Airport............... **56** A1

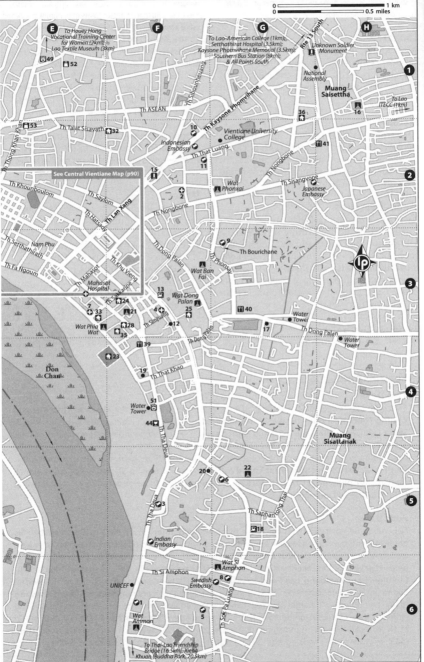

in-shop computers (per hr 8000K) or wi-fi (per hr 10,000K), accessible by pre-paid cards.

Laundry
Most hotels and guesthouses offer laundry services. Otherwise, several laundries and dry-cleaners are on Th Samsènethai just east of Th Chao Anou. Typical rates are about 10,000K per kg.

Media
Laos's only English-language newspaper is the government-run *Vientiane Times* (4500K), which carries the occasional critical piece in its six editions a week. French-speakers should look for *Le Rénovateur*.

Medical Services
Vientiane's medical facilities can leave a lot to be desired, so for anything serious make a break for the border and the much more sophisticated hospitals in Thailand. **Aek Udon International Hospital** (☎ in Thailand 04234 2555; www.aekudon.com) can dispatch an ambulance to take you to Udon Thani. Less serious ailments can be dealt with in Vientiane.

In Vientiane, try:
Australian Embassy Clinic (Map p86; ☎ 353 840; Th Tha Deua; ☽ 8.30am-12.30pm & 1.30-5pm Mon-Fri) For nationals of Australia, Britain, Canada, PNG and NZ only, this clinic's Australian doctor treats minor problems during office hours; it doesn't have emergency facilities.
Centre Médical de L'Ambassade de France (French Embassy Medical Center; Map p86; ☎ 214 150; cnr Th Khu Vieng & Th Simeuang; ☽ 8.30am-noon & 4.30-7pm Mon, Tue, Thu & Fri, 1.30-5pm Wed, 9am-noon Sat) Open to all, but visits outside regular hours by appointment only.
International Clinic (Map p86; ☎ 214 022; Th Fa Ngoum; ☽ 6-7am, noon-2pm & 5-9pm) Part of the Mahasot Hospital, probably the best place for not-too-complex emergencies. Some English-speaking doctors.
Setthathirath Hospital (off Map p86; ☎ 351 156) A Japanese-funded overhaul means this hospital, located northeast of the city, is relatively well equipped.

Money
For cash, licensed moneychanging booths can be found in much of central Vientiane, particularly along Th Setthathirath between Th François Ngin and Th Pangkham. You can also change cash at various shops, hotels or markets for no commission but at poor rates. See p323 for more information.

Banks listed here change cash and travellers cheques and issue cash advances (mostly in kip, but occasionally in US dollars and Thai baht) against Visa and/or MasterCard. Many now have ATMs that work with foreign cards,

---

VIENTIANE IN...

Two Days
Start with Lao coffee and the *Vientiane Times* before embarking on the **Monument to Mekong Cycling Tour** (p98). This will take you through most of Vientiane's main sights, including **Wat Si Saket** (p92), **Haw Pha Kaeo** (p92) and **Talat Sao** (p113). Top off your day with riverside cocktails at **Spirit House** (p109). On day two consider getting some motorised wheels and leaving the city centre to check out the myriad concrete Buddhas and Hindu deities at **Xieng Khuan** (p96). On the way back stop at **Pha That Luang** (p95) for great afternoon photos. Enjoy a fine French meal at **chez philippe** (p107) or **L'Adresse de Tinay** (p107), followed by a night on the town at **D'Tech** (p110) or **Lunar 36** (p110).

Four Days
Depending on what time you crawl out of bed on day three, make **PVO** (p105), arguably the home of Vientiane's best baguette sandwiches and fruit shakes, your lunch destination. From here it's just a short walk to the **COPE Visitor Centre** (p93), where you could easily spend a couple hours checking out excellent exhibits and watching the powerful documentaries. After a light Lao dinner at **Khambang Lao Food Restaurant** (p104), head around the corner to the **Herbal Sauna** (p97) for a good healthy Lao-style sweat. Rehydrate with draught Beerlao at **Bor Pennyang** (p109) before calling it a night. Day four can be spent educationally, by enrolling in a Lao cooking course at **Villa Lao** (p99), or indulgently, by shopping at the **handicraft and textile shops** (p112) of Th Nokèokoummane, rummaging for bizarre communist mementos at the **State Book Shop** (p85) or picking and choosing from the handmade soaps and oils at **T'Shop Lai Gallery** (p112).

but it's often cheaper to get a cash advance manually; see p322 for the low-down. All are open 8.30am to 3.30pm Monday to Friday.

ANZ (Map p90; ☎ 222 700; 33 Th Lan Xang) Main branch has two ATMs and can provide cash advances on Visa or MasterCard for a flat fee of 45,000K. Additional ATMs can be found on Th Setthathirath (Map p90) and Th Fa Ngoum (Map p90).

Bank of Ayudhya (Map p90; ☎ 214 575; 79/6 Th Lan Xang) Cash advances on Visa cards here carry a 1.5% commission.

Banque pour le Commerce Extérieur Lao (BCEL; Map p90; ☎ 213 200; cnr Th Pangkham & Th Fa Ngoum) Has an exchange booth and ATM on Th Fa Ngoum and three additional ATMs (!) attached to the main building. Can provide cash advances on Visa or MasterCard for a 3% fee. Another ATM can be found near Nam Phu on Th Setthathirath (Map p90).

Joint Development Bank (Map p90; ☎ 213 535; 75/1-5 Th Lan Xang) Has an ATM and charges a 3% transaction fee on cash advances. Also has an ATM on Th Fa Ngoum (Map p90).

Krung Thai Bank (Map p90; ☎ 213 480; Th Lan Xang) Also has an exchange booth on Th Fa Ngoum (Map p90).

Lao-Viet Bank (Map p90; ☎ 214 377; Th Lan Xang)

Siam Commercial Bank (Map p90; ☎ 227 306; 117 Th Lan Xang) Can provide cash advances for Visa or MasterCard for a transaction fee of 250B.

Thai Military Bank (Map p90; ☎ 216 486; cnr Th Samsènethai & Th Khounboulom) Cash advance on Visa only for 200B.

Post

Post, Telephone & Telegraph (Map p90; cnr Th Lan Xang & Th Khu Vieng; ☏ 8am-5pm Mon-Fri, 8am-noon Sat & Sun) Come here for poste restante.

Telephone

International calls can be made from most internet cafes for about 4000K per minute (see p85). Local calls can be made from any hotel lobby, often for free.

Lao Telecom Numphu Centre (Map p90; ☎ 214 470; Th Setthathirath; ☏ 8am-5pm Mon-Fri, 8.30am-2pm Sat) Has fax and international-call facilities for 2000K a minute (1000K a minute for domestic calls).

Tourist Information

Between Talat Sao and Patuxai, the ground-floor office of the government's **Tourist Information Centre** (Map p90; ☎ 212 251; www.tourismlaos.gov.la, www.ecotourismlaos.com; Th Lan Xang; ☏ 8.30am-noon & 1-4pm Mon-Fri) has finally become a place that is really worth a visit. The disorganised chaos of the past has been replaced by

an attractive, easy-to-use room with descriptions of each province and what you'll find there. When we visited staff spoke English and were able to answer most of our questions. You can pick up brochures and some regional maps, and staff can provide detailed information on visiting Phu Khao Khuay NPA (p118).

Travel Agencies

For a list of reputable agencies able to organise tours, see p344. Central Vientiane has plenty of agencies that can book air tickets and in some cases Thai train tickets, including the following:

Green Discovery (www.greendiscoverylaos.com) Nam Phu (Map p90; ☎ 223 022; Th Setthathirath; ☏ 8am-10pm); Th Hengboun (Map p90; ☎ 251 564; Th Hengboun; ☏ 8am-10pm) Two locations provide a large range of tours offered as well as normal travel agent services. Good reputation.

Lasi Ticketing (Map p90; ☎ 222 851; www.lasiglobal.com; 5 Th François Ngin; ☏ 8am-5pm Mon-Sat) The friendly women at this professional agency can book all manner of tickets.

DANGERS & ANNOYANCES

By international standards Vientiane has a very low crime rate, but readers' reports and local anecdotes suggest there's an increasing risk of getting mugged. Be especially careful around the BCEL Bank on the riverfront where bag-snatchers, usually a two-man team with a motorbike, have been known to strike; common sense should be an adequate defence. Violent crime against visitors is extremely rare.

The repaving of most streets in the centre of town has improved the situation, but manhole covers seem to be given less importance here than you might be used to and at the time of writing there were still more than enough stormwater drains and open sewers big enough to swallow you – a thoroughly shitty end to any day.

SIGHTS

With urban sprawl a fairly recent phenomenon in Vientiane it's no surprise that the bulk of sights are concentrated in a small area in the centre of the city. Except for Xieng Khuan (Buddha Park), all sights are easily reached by bicycle and, in most cases, on foot. Only the more prestigious temples are listed here; if you're interested in visiting the city's minor temple sights, consider doing our bicycle tour

VIENTIANE & AROUND

CENTRAL VIENTIANE

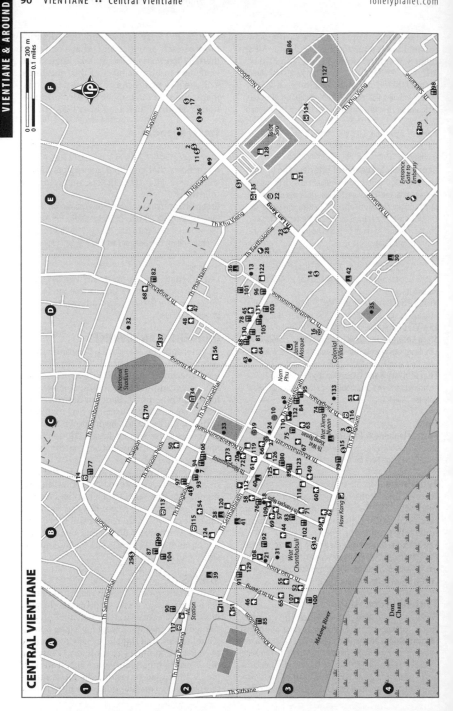

of the city (p98). Most wats welcome visitors after the monks have collected alms in the morning until about 6pm.

Wat Si Saket
ວັດສີສະເກດ

Built between 1819 and 1824 by Chao Anou, **Wat Si Saket** (Wat Sisaketsata Sahatsaham; Map p90; cnr Th Lan Xang & Th Setthathirath; admission 5000K; 🕑 8am-noon & 1-4pm) is believed to be Vientiane's oldest surviving temple. And it shows; this beautiful temple-cum-national museum is in dire need of a facelift.

Chao Anou, who was educated in the Bangkok court and was more or less a vassal of the Siamese state, had Wat Si Saket constructed in the early Bangkok style but surrounded it with a thick-walled cloister similar to – but much smaller than – the one that surrounds Pha That Luang (p95). The stylistic similarity to their own wats might have motivated the Siamese to spare this monastery when they crushed Chao Anou's rebellion (p27), even as they razed many others. The French restored the temple in 1924 and again in 1930.

In spite of the Siamese influence, Wat Si Saket has several unique features. The interior walls of the cloister are riddled with small niches that contain more than 2000 silver and ceramic Buddha images. More than 300 seated and standing Buddhas of varying sizes and materials (wood, stone, silver and bronze) rest on long shelves below the niches, most of them sculpted or cast in the characteristic Lao style. Most of the images are from 16th- to 19th-century Vientiane but a few hail from 15th- to 16th-century Luang Prabang.

Along the western side of the cloister is a pile of Buddhas that were damaged during the 1828 Siamese-Lao war. And in the *sim* (ordination hall) a slightly damaged Khmer-style Naga Buddha – which depicts the Buddha seated on a coiled cobra deity (*naga*), sheltered by the *naga*'s multiheaded hood – is also on display just in front of the main seated Buddha; it is believed to date from the 13th century and was brought from a nearby Khmer site.

The *sim* is surrounded by a colonnaded terrace in the Bangkok style and topped by a five-tiered roof. The interior walls bear hundreds of Buddha niches similar to those in the cloister, as well as beautiful – but decaying – Jataka murals depicting stories of the

Buddha's past lives. Portions of the Bangkok-style murals are unrestored 1820s originals, while others are from various markedly less proficient contemporary restorations.

The flowered ceiling was inspired by Siamese temples in Ayuthaya and is similar in style to floral designs from Versailles. At the rear interior of the *sim* is an altar with several more Buddha images, bringing the total number of Buddhas at Wat Si Saket to about 6400 – though we didn't count them ourselves. The standing Buddha to the left on the upper altar is said to have been cast to the same physical proportions as Chao Anou. The large, gilt wood candle stand in front of the altar is thought to be an original, carved in 1819.

On the verandah at the rear of the *sim* is a 5m-long wooden trough carved to resemble a *naga*. This is the *háang song nâm pha* (image-watering rail), which is used during Lao New Year to pour water over Buddha images for ceremonial cleansing.

To the far left of the entrance to the cloister, facing Th Lan Xang, is a raised *hǎw tại* (Tripitaka library) with a Burmese-style roof, being renovated at the time of research. The scriptures once contained here are now in Bangkok.

Haw Pha Kaeo
ຫໍພະແກ້ວ

Once a royal temple built specifically to house the famed Emerald Buddha, **Haw Pha Kaeo** (Map p90; Th Setthathirath; admission 5000K; 🕑 8am-noon & 1-4pm) is today a national museum of religious art. It is about 100m southeast of Wat Si Saket.

According to the Lao, the temple was originally built in 1565 by command of King Setthathirath, who on inheriting the Lan Xang throne moved the capital from Luang Prabang to Vientiane and brought with him the so-called Emerald Buddha (Pha Kaeo in Lao, which means 'Jewel Buddha Image' – the image is actually made of a type of jade). Wat Pha Kaeo also served as Setthathirath's personal place of worship. Following a skirmish with the Lao in 1779, the Siamese stole the Emerald Buddha and installed it in Bangkok's Wat Phra Kaew. Later, during the Siamese-Lao war of 1828, Vientiane's Wat Pha Kaeo was razed.

The temple was finally rebuilt with French help between 1936 and 1942, supposedly following the original plan exactly. However, the 'original' 16th-century plan looks nothing like its contemporaries, instead bearing an uncanny resemblance to 19th-century Bangkok-style *sim*. The floor and the main wooden door at the southern end – with its angels carved in high relief that are reminiscent of Angkorean apsaras – are notable survivors of the original remains.

These aside, today's Haw Pha Kaeo is impressive mainly for its size. Some of the best examples of Buddhist sculpture found in Laos are kept here, with a dozen or so prominent sculptures displayed along the surrounding terrace. These include Dvaravati-style stone Buddhas from between the 6th and 9th centuries; several bronze standing and sitting Lao-style Buddhas – including the 'Calling for Rain' (standing with hands at his sides), 'Offering Protection' (palms stretched out in front) and 'Contemplating the Tree of Enlightenment' (hands crossed at the wrist in front) poses; and a collection of inscribed Lao and Mon stelae. Most of the Lao bronzes are missing their *usnisa* (flame finial).

Inside the *sim* are more Buddhist sculptures (including a wooden copy of the Pha Bang), some Khmer stelae, various wooden carvings, palm-leaf manuscripts and a bronze frog drum. A 17th-century bronze 'Calling for Rain' Buddha, tall and lithe, is particularly beautiful; also unique is a 17th-century Vientiane-style bronze Buddha in the 'European pose' – with the legs hanging down as if seated on a chair. Attendants will point you to the most interesting pieces.

The *sim* is surrounded by a landscaped garden, which is also home to a single stone jar from the Plain of Jars.

COPE Visitor Centre
ສູນຂັ້ນຜູ້ຄົນພິການແຫ່ງຊາດ

COPE (Cooperative Orthotic & Prosthetic Enterprise) is the main source of artificial limbs, walking aids and wheelchairs in Laos. Its excellent **Visitor Centre** (Map p86; ☎ 218 427; www.copelaos.org; Th Khu Vieng; admission free; ☉ 9am-6pm), part of the organisation's National Rehabilitation Centre, offers a myriad of interesting and informative multimedia exhibits about prosthetics and the UXO (unexploded ordnance) that make them necessary. Several powerful documentaries are shown on a rolling basis in a comfortable theatre, and there's a gift shop and cafe, 100% of the proceeds of which go to supporting COPE's projects in Laos.

Patuxai
ປະຕູໄຊ

Reminiscent of the Arc de Triomphe in Paris, the **Patuxai** (Map p86; Th Lan Xang; admission 3000K; ☉ 8am-4.30pm Mon-Fri, 8am-5pm Sat & Sun) is Vientiane's most prominent monument. The name is approximately equivalent to Arch (*pátuu*, also translated as 'door' or 'gate') of Triumph (*xái*, from the Sanskrit *jaya* or 'victory'), but unlike its Parisian namesake the Patuxai boasts four, rather than two, archways. It was built in the 1960s with US-purchased cement that was supposed to have been used for the construction of a new airport. Hence it's sometimes called 'the vertical runway'.

From a distance, Patuxai looks much like its French source of inspiration. Up close, however, the Lao design is revealed. The bas-relief on the sides and the temple-like ornamentation along the top and cornices are typically Lao, though the execution is at times shoddy. Don't miss the sign on the southwest corner, which in a few lines reflects both Laos's endearing honesty and naivety to 'First World' preoccupations like marketing. One sentence reads: 'From a closer distance, it appears even less impressive, like a monster of concrete'; talk about brutal honesty.

A stairway leads through two levels stuffed with souvenir T-shirts (seriously, there are thousands) to the top levels, from where the views are grand. Photography is supposed to be banned from the top.

Patuxai is within walking distance of the town centre and work in recent years has transformed the surrounding field into the most popular park in Vientiane. It's a good place to soak up the atmosphere of modern Laos, with the Chinese-donated musical fountain a big hit in the late afternoon.

Lao National Museum
ພິພິດທະພັນປະຫວັດສາດແຫ່ງຊາດລາວ

With a limited collection of historical and revolutionary exhibits, the **Lao National Museum** (Map p90; ☎ 212 461; Th Samsènethai; admission 10,000K; ☉ 8am-noon & 1-4pm) will never be confused with the Louvre. But it does serve to sum up the country's ongoing struggle to come to grips with its own identity, so it's worth a look.

The museum is housed in a large administrative building originally built as the colonial police commissioner's office in the 1920s. It became a museum in the 1990s and until recently it was known as the 'Lao Revolutionary

Museum'. While the displays start with predictable themes such as prehistory and Laos's ethnic groups, upstairs the emphasis quickly moves to the Pathet Lao's lengthy struggle for power. Among the typical exhibits are items like rice baskets, spoons and even dried herbs used by prominent revolutionaries 'during the fighting against the US imperialists', enough historic weaponry to arm all the extras in a Rambo film, and a modest collection of industrial items produced by Laos during the '90s, such as a few generic pharmaceuticals.

While these things might not have you panting with expectation – and let's face it, individually they are as unexciting as they sound – the real value in visiting the museum is to compare the older rooms to those upgraded more recently. The latter emphasise cultural influences, traditional musical instruments, Khmer sandstone sculptures that illustrate the Khmer influence on Laos, and rooms that deal with other historical periods that have nothing to do with the communist victory. Whether consciously or not, it appears to reflect a slow move away from the hardline socialist ideals that the Pathet Lao fought for, and which dominated domestic policy in the 15 to 20 years after 1975, towards a more broad-based, nationalist view of history and national identity. Most exhibits are labelled with at least some English.

Wat Si Muang
ວັດສີເມືອງ

The most frequently used grounds in Vientiane are those of **Wat Si Muang** (Map p86; cnr Th Setthathirath, Th Samsènethai & Th Tha Deua; 6am-7pm daily, until 10pm on special days), the site of the *lák*

meuang (city pillar/phallus), which is considered the home of the guardian spirit of Vientiane (see the boxed text).

The large *sĭm* (destroyed in 1828 and rebuilt in 1915) was constructed around the *lák meuang,* and consists of two halls. The large entry hall features a copy of the Pha Kaeo, the Emerald Buddha, and a much smaller, rather melted-looking seated stone Buddha that allegedly survived the 1828 inferno. Locals believe it has the power to grant wishes or answer troubling questions, and the practice is to lift it off the pillow three times while mentally phrasing a question or request. If your request is granted, then you are supposed to return later with an offering of bananas, green coconuts, flowers, incense and candles (usually two of each).

The pillar itself is located in the rear hall, and is believed to date from the Khmer period, indicating the site has been used for religious purposes for more than 1000 years. Today it is wrapped in sacred cloth, and in front of it is a carved wooden stele with a seated Buddha in relief.

Behind the *sĭm* is a crumbling laterite *jĕhdii* (stupa), almost certainly of Khmer origin. Devotees deposit broken deity images and pottery around the stupa's base so the spirits of the stupa will 'heal' the bad luck created by the breaking of these items. In front of the *sĭm* is a little public park with a statue of King Sisavang Vong (1904–59).

Kaysone Phomvihane Memorial
ຫໍພິພິດທະພັນແລະອະນຸສາວະລີໄກສອນ ພົມວິຫານ

Opened in 1995 to celebrate the late president's 75th birthday, the **Kaysone Phomvihane**

NO SACRIFICE TOO GREAT

Legend has it that a group of sages selected the site for Wat Si Muang in 1563, when King Setthathirath moved his capital to Vientiane. Once the spot was chosen, a large hole was dug to receive the heavy stone pillar (probably taken from an ancient Khmer site nearby) that would become the *lák meuang* (city pillar). When the pillar arrived it was suspended over the hole with ropes. Drums and gongs were sounded to summon the townspeople to the area and everyone waited for a volunteer to jump in the hole as a sacrifice to the spirit.

Depending on who's relating it, the legend has several conclusions. What is common to all of them is that a pregnant woman named Sao Si leaps in and the ropes are released, killing her and in the process establishing the town guardianship. Variations include her leaping in upon a horse, and/or with a diminutive monk.

However, Lao scholars think that if there is any truth to this story it is likely to have occurred much earlier than Setthathirath's time, in the pre-Buddhist Mon or Khmer periods when human sacrifice was ritually practised…and that Sao Si's legendary leap might not have been her choice at all.

Memorial (off Map p86), near Km 6 on Rte 13 south, serves as a tribute to Indochina's most pragmatic communist leader. The memorial is actually two jarringly different sites. Kaysone's former house is a model of modesty suggesting he might have lived in less luxury than any other world leader. In contrast the museum is a vast Vietnamese-style celebration of the cult of Kaysone, a cult he never encouraged.

The **museum** (admission 5000K; 8am-noon & 1-4pm Tue-Sun) is impossible to miss, with its mega-sized bronze statue of Kaysone out front flanked by large sculptures in the Heroes of Socialism style, complete with members of various ethnic groups and a sportsman looking like a super-serious Superman. The building is a stark contrast, too, and is filled with a remarkably complete collection of memorabilia of both Kaysone and the Party. These include a mock-up of Kaysone's childhood home in Savannakhet, his desk from the French school he attended at Ban Tai and a model of a portion of 'Kaysone Cave' in Hua Phan Province, complete with revolver, binoculars, radio and other personal effects.

In contrast, Kaysone's **house** (admission 3000K; 8am-4pm Tue-Sun) is a remarkably modest affair, yet fascinating both because of its history and that it remains virtually untouched since the great man died in 1992. The house is inside the former USAID/CIA compound, a self-contained headquarters known as 'Six Klicks City' because of its location 6km from central Vientiane. It once featured bars, restaurants, tennis courts, swimming pools, a commissary and assorted offices from where the Secret War (p38) was orchestrated. During the 1975 takeover of Vientiane, Pathet Lao forces ejected the Americans and occupied the compound. Kaysone lived here until his death.

A Lao People's Revolutionary Party (LPRP) guide will show you through the house, with Kaysone's half-empty bottles of Scotch, tacky souvenirs from the Eastern Bloc, white running shoes, notepads and original Kelvinator air-conditioners. Even the winter coats he wore on visits to Moscow remain neatly hanging in the wardrobe.

It's possible to cycle here or take any transport on Rte 13 south. Kaysone's house is a bit trickier to find, so it's easiest to backtrack; after visiting the museum, return south, the way you came. Upon reaching the first stop light, turn right and continue 1km until you see the sign on your right that says 'Mémorial du Président Kaysone Phomvihane'.

Pha That Luang
ພະທາດຫລວງ

The most important national monument in Laos, **Pha That Luang** (Map p86; Th That Luang; admission 5000K; 8am-noon & 1-4pm) is a symbol of both the Buddhist religion and Lao sovereignty. Its full official name, Pha Chedi Lokajulamani, means World-Precious Sacred Stupa, and an image of the main stupa appears on the national seal and in countless other places. Legend has it that Ashokan missionaries from India erected a *thâat* or reliquary stupa here to enclose a piece of the Buddha's breastbone as early as the 3rd century BC. Excavations have found no trace of this, but did find suggestion of a Khmer monastery that might have been built near here between the 11th and 13th centuries AD.

When King Setthathirath moved the Lan Xang capital from Luang Prabang to Vientiane in the mid-16th century, he ordered the construction of Pha That Luang in its current form on the site of the Khmer temple. Construction began in 1566 and in succeeding years four wats were built around the stupa, one on each side. Only two remain today, **Wat That Luang Neua** to the north and **Wat That Luang Tai** to the south. Wat That Luang Neua is the residence of the Supreme Patriarch (Pha Sangkhalat) of Lao Buddhism. The main building is a reconstruction from the early 20th century.

The monument itself looks almost like a gilded missile cluster from a distance. Surrounding it is a high-walled cloister with tiny windows, added by King Anouvong in the early 19th century as a defence against invaders. Even more aggressive-looking than the thick walls are the pointed stupas themselves, which are built in three levels (see the boxed text, p96).

In 1641 Gerrit van Wuysthoff, an envoy of the Dutch East India Company, visited Vientiane and was received by King Suriya Vongsa in a reportedly magnificent ceremony at Pha That Luang. The Lan Xang kingdom was at its peak at this time and van Wuysthoff was deeply impressed by the 'enormous pyramid, the top of which was covered with gold leaf weighing about a thousand pounds'.

Unfortunately, the glory of Lan Xang and Pha That Luang was only to last another 60

VIEWING PHA THAT LUANG

Each level of Pha That Luang has different architectural features in which Buddhist doctrine is encoded; visitors are supposed to contemplate the meaning of these features as they walk around. The first level is an approximately square base measuring 68m by 69m that supports 323 *siimáa* (ordination stones). It represents the material world, and also features four arched *hǎw wái* (prayer halls), one on each side, with short stairways leading to them and beyond to the second level.

The second level is 48m by 48m and is surrounded by 120 lotus petals. There are 288 *siimáa* on this level, as well as 30 small stupas symbolising the 30 Buddhist perfections *(páalamíi sǎam-síp thâat)*, beginning with alms-giving and ending with equanimity.

Arched gates again lead to the next level, a 30m by 30m square. The tall central stupa, which has a brick core that has been stuccoed over, is supported here by a bowl-shaped base reminiscent of India's first Buddhist stupa at Sanchi. At the top of this mound the superstructure, surrounded by lotus petals, begins.

The curvilinear, four-sided spire resembles an elongated lotus bud and is said to symbolise the growth of a lotus from a seed in a muddy lake bottom to a bloom over the lake's surface, a metaphor for human advancement from ignorance to enlightenment in Buddhism. The entire *thâat* was regilded in 1995 to celebrate the Lao PDR's 20th anniversary, and is crowned by a stylised banana flower and parasol. From ground to pinnacle, Pha That Luang is 45m tall.

---

years or so. Repeated damaging assualts were carried out during the 18th century by invading Burmese and Siamese armies. Then, in 1828, a Siamese invasion ransacked and depopulated Vientiane to such an extent that Pha That Luang remained abandoned, and eventually dismantled by treasure seekers, until it was (badly) restored by the French in 1900.

That restoration left the stupa looking a bit too chunky and none too attractive, at least that's what the locals thought. In a victory of town planning over history, the orientation was changed so that the main entrance faced south, rather than east. This meant the wide new Th That Luang ran straight up to the stupa, but didn't fit with traditional Buddhist doctrine, which has most temples and religious monuments facing east.

In fairness to the French, they did try to fix it. Changing the orientation back was clearly too hard, but between 1931 and 1935 a French university department dismantled the stupa and rebuilt it in the original Lao-style lotus-bud shape. For guidance they used the drawings of French explorer and architect Louis Delaporte, who had stumbled on the abandoned and overgrown Pha That Luang in 1867 and made a number of detailed sketches of the monument.

Pha That Luang is about 4km northeast of the centre of Vientiane at the end of Th That Luang. Facing the compound is a statue of King Setthathirath. The temple is the site of a major festival, Bun Pha That Luang, held in early November (see p100).

Lao Textile Museum
ພິພິດທະພັນຜ້າໄໝບູຮານລາວ

What began as a private **museum** (off Map p84; ☎ 030-525 8293; www.ibiss.co.jp/laomuseum/access.html; admission 30,000K; ☯ 9am-4pm), established by the family that runs Kanchana Boutique (p113), has subsequently become, with the help of several foreign NGOs, something of a Lao cultural centre. The emphasis at this leafy traditional Lao compound is predominately on textiles, and in addition to a wooden house filled with looms and antique Lao textiles representing several ethnic groups, the museum also offers courses in weaving and dyeing (see p100), and a shop.

The museum also offers Lao cooking classes, although these didn't yet appear to be up and running during our visit, and on Saturdays, lessons on traditional Lao music, although the latter are only for those with experience playing Lao instruments and who are fluent in the Lao language. For both of these we'd advise calling the museum or Kanchana Boutique in advance.

The museum is located about 3km northeast of the National Circus (Hong Kanyasin); Kanchana Boutique can provide a map.

Xieng Khuan (Buddha Park)
ຊຽງຂວັນ

In a field by the Mekong River about 24km south of central Vientiane, **Xieng Khuan** (Buddha Park or Suan Phut; Map p118; admission 5000K, camera 3000K; ☯ 8am-4.30pm, sometimes longer) is a park full of

Buddhist and Hindu sculpture that is a monument to one eccentric man's quite bizarre ambition.

Xieng Khuan was designed and built in 1958 by Luang Pu (Venerable Grandfather) Bunleua Sulilat, a yogi-priest-shaman who merged Hindu and Buddhist philosophy, mythology and iconography into a cryptic whole. Originally, Bunleua is supposed to have studied under a Hindu *rishi* (sage) who lived in Vietnam. Legend has it that their meeting was fortunate, to say the least, as while Bunleua was walking in the mountains he fell through a sinkhole and landed in the *rishi*'s lap. As you do. Bunleua developed a large following in Laos and northeastern Thailand, and moved to Thailand around the time of the 1975 Revolution. In 1978 he established the similarly inspired Wat Khaek in Nong Khai, Thailand. He died in 1996.

The concrete sculptures at Xieng Khuan (which means 'Spirit City') are bizarre but compelling in their naive confidence. They include statues of Shiva, Vishnu, Arjuna, Avalokiteshvara, Buddha and numerous other deities, all supposedly cast by untrained artists under Luang Pu's direction.

The large pumpkin-shaped concrete monument in the grounds has three levels joined by interior stairways. The levels are said to represent hell, earth and heaven, and lead to the roof and panoramic views of the park.

A few drink vendors offer fresh coconuts, soft drinks and beer.

Xieng Khuan is a definite favourite among kids.

GETTING THERE & AWAY

Bus 14 (5000K, 24km, one hour) leaves the Talat Sao terminal every 15 or 20 minutes throughout the day and goes all the way to Xieng Khuan. Alternatively, charter a tuk-tuk (about US$10 return, depending on your bargaining skills) or hop on a shared jumbo (5000K) as far as the old ferry pier at Tha Deua and walk or take a *săam-lâaw* (three-wheeled taxi) the final 4km to the park. Going by motorbike is popular.

ACTIVITIES
Bowling

Lao Bowling Centre (Map p90; ☎ 218 661; Th Khoun-boulom; per frame before/after 7pm 10,000/12,000K; ☺ 9am–midnight) A short stroll from town, and includes several snooker tables (24,000K per hr).

Marina Bowling (Map p86; ☎ 216 978; Th Luang Prabang; per frame 8000–12,000K; ☺ 1–11.30pm) This nightclub also offers bowling.

Gyms & Yoga

Sengdara Fitness (Map p86; ☎ 414 061; 5/77 Th Dong Palan; ☺ 6am–10pm Mon-Sat, 8am–10pm Sun) Vientiane's first Western-style mega-gym, with stacks of machines, sauna, pool, massage, aerobics and yoga classes, and a juice bar and restaurant. A one-day pass costs 32,000K.

Tai-Pan Hotel (Map p90; ☎ 216 906; 22/3 Th François Ngin; per visit US$7.50) Small fitness room and sauna; central location.

Vientiane Yoga Studio (Map p86; ☎ 020-7760 8365; www.vientianeyoga.com; Th Sok Pa Luang; 90-min class 50,000K) This home-bound studio, the city's only dedicated yoga space, offers both regular (see website for class schedule) and private tuition by a certified Australian instructor.

White Lotus Yoga & Massage (Map p90; ☎ 217 492; Th Pangkham; ☺ 10am–10pm) Offers yoga instruction on a regular basis; inquire for dates and times.

Massage/Sauna

Herbal Sauna (Map p90; ☎ 020-5504 4655; off Th Chao Anou; ☺ 1–9pm) Located near the river, this place offers Lao-style herbal saunas (15,000K) provided in separate rooms for men and women. The fee includes a cloth (for men) and towel; women must pay an additional 2000K for the rental of a sarong. In addition to the sauna it also offers a variety of massage, including Lao (per hour 40,000K), oil (per hour 65,000K) and foot (per hour 40,000K).

Papaya Spa (Map p86; ☎ 216 550; www.papayaspa.com; Th Phagna Sy; ☺ 9am–7pm) In an old French villa west of town (follow the many signs), this is one of the classiest massage operations in town. Services include Lao massage (per hour 110,000K), Swedish oil massage (per hour 210,000K), facials, waxing, body scrubs, reflexology and saunas.

The Spa (Map p86; ☎ 285 113; www.the-spa-laos.com; Th That Khao; ☺ 10am–10pm) This attractive house-bound spa offers a menu of services from massage (per hour 86,000K) to herbal sauna (50,000K).

Wat Sok Pa Luang (Map p86; Th Sok Pa Luang; ☺ 2–8pm) In a shaded, almost semirural setting that is entirely in keeping with its name (*wat paa* means 'forest temple'), this temple is famous for its herbal saunas (15,000K) and expert massage (per hr 35,000K). Taxi, jumbo (motorcycle taxi) and tuk-tuk drivers all know how to get to Wat Sok Pa Luang, with tuk-tuk drivers charging 40,000K.

White Lotus Yoga & Massage (Map p90; ☎ 217 492; Th Pangkham; ☺ 10am–10pm) Just north of Nam Phu; foot massage (50,000K), traditional Laos massage (per hour 50,000K). It also offers regular yoga instruction; stop in for dates and times.

Running

The **Vientiane Hash House Harriers** (www.laohash .com) welcomes runners to its two weekly hashes. The Saturday hash is the more challenging run and starts at 3.45pm from Nam Phu. It's followed by food and no shortage of Beerlao. Monday's easier run starts at 5pm from varying locations – look for maps at the Scandinavian Bakery (p108) or Europcar (p342), where owner **Joe Rumble** (☎ 020-5551 1293) is more than happy to help out.

Swimming

There are several places in Vientiane where you can work on your strokes or simply take a cooling dip. If you have kids, make a bee-line for **Nongchanh Waterpark** (Map p86; ☎ 219 386; www.nongchanhwaterpark.com; Th Khu Vieng; adult/ child 30,000/20,000K; ☽ 10am-6.30pm), a collection of slides and pools. The **Vientiane Swimming Pool** (Map p90; ☎ 020-5552 1002; Th Lé Ky Huong; adult/ child 10,000/7000K; ☽ 8am-7pm) is central and usually fine for swimming laps. Further afield, the 25m-long **Sokpaluang Swimming Pool** (Map p86; ☎ 350 491; Th Sok Pa Luang; adult/child 7000/5000K; ☽ 8am-8pm) in southeastern Vientiane also has a children's pool and changing rooms. Several hotels welcome nonguests, including the **Settha Palace Hotel** (Map p90; ☎ 217 581; Th Pangkham; admission US$7.50) with its decadent pool and surrounding bar, as well as the **Lane Xane Hotel** (Map p90; ☎ 214 100; www.lanexanghotel.com.la; Th Fa Ngoum; admission 30,000K) and **Tai-Pan Hotel** (Map p90; ☎ 216 906; 22/3 Th François Ngin; admission US$7.50).

MONUMENT TO MEKONG CYCLING TOUR

With its wide flat streets and still relatively few cars, Vientiane is a great city to explore via bicycle. Our bike tour of the city covers about 7km and will take between four and six hours, depending on how often you stop, eat, drink and shop. We suggest starting in the cool hours of the morning and thus have included breakfast and lunch stops; if you're doing the tour later you could simply regard these as lunch and dinner stops, but be aware that some attractions, such as Talat Khua Din, are best visited early in the day.

Begin your day by getting yourself to Th Nokèokoummane and charging up with coffee and a crispy croissant at one of the street's

excellent French bakeries such as **Le Banneton** (**1**; p108). There's a bike rental place virtually next door, or if this doesn't work, there's a few more on adjacent Th François Ngin; most open at 7am and charge about 10,000K per day.

Hop on your bike, turn on to one-way Th Setthathirath and passing **Nam Phu (2)**, Vientiane's underwhelming fountain, continue about 1km until you reach the stoplight, where on your right is the **Presidential Palace (3)**, a vast beaux-arts-style chateau originally built to house the French colonial governor. After independence King Sisavang Vong (and later his son Sisavang Vatthana) of Luang Prabang used it as a residence when visiting Vientiane; these days it is used mainly on ceremonial occasions.

Directly opposite the palace is **Wat Si Saket** (**4**; p92), with its thousands of Buddha figures, and just up the road, **Haw Pha Kaeo (5**; p92), the national museum for religious objects. By arriving in the morning you'll beat most of the crowds, but don't get there too early, as both places don't open until 8am. Conversely, if you do the tour later in the day, keep in mind that Wat Si Saket and Haw Pha Kaeo close between noon and 1pm.

Continuing in the same direction along Th Setthathirath, cross Th Mahasot and turn left down Th Gallieni. You'll know you're in the right place by the white walls of the **French Embassy (6**; p318) on your left and the towering **Catholic Church (7)** on your right. Continue northwest along this street until you reach the T-intersection with Th Khu Vieng; on the opposite side is the barely noticeable entrance to **Talat Khua Din (8**; p113), one of Vientiane's largest fresh food markets.

Continuing northwest along Th Khu Vieng, turn right onto Th Lan Xang, a street sometimes (very) generously described as the 'Champs Elysées of the East'. At this point you're directly in front of Vientiane's biggest market, **Talat Sao (9**; p113), a great place to fill your bicycle basket up with Lao textiles.

Continuing northeast along Th Lan Xang, you'll pass by the **Tourist Information Centre (10**; p89), a chance to pick up maps or brochures. At this point you're also only 500m from **Patuxai (11**; p93), which is worth climbing for unbeatable views of the city.

Circle around Patuxai and continue southwest along Th Lan Xang. Turn right into quiet Th Bartholomie. Buzz past the walls of the **US**

MONUMENT TO MEKONG CYCLING TOUR

embassy (**12**; p318) and continue to **That Dam (13)**, where legend has it that the gold that covered this stupa was carted off by the Siamese during their pillaging of 1828. If you can pass here without being swallowed by the giant *naga* that allegedly lurks beneath, continue southwest and turn right onto Th Samsènethai.

Continue two blocks until, on your left hand side you see the gaudy Chinese-funded **Lao National Culture Hall (14**; p111). Directly opposite this is the **Lao National Museum (15**; p93), worth a stop to gain some insight into ancient and modern Laos.

Continue another 500m along one-way Th Samsènethai until you reach the stoplight. Turn left and head southwest along Th Sihom, continuing straight through the next stoplight, after which the road turns into Th Khounboulom. Continue about 250m southwest along this street until you reach **Khambang Lao Food Restaurant (16**; p104). This family-run place is central Vientiane's best Lao restaurant and your lunch break destination.

Do a U-turn and backtrack a block northeast along Th Khounboulom until you reach **Wat In Paeng (17)**, famed for the artistry displayed in the *sìm*'s stucco relief. Weaving to Th Setthathirath via Th Chao Anou, park your bike at **Wat Ong Teu Mahawihan (18)** and visit the temple's namesake, a 16th-century bronze Buddha measuring 5.8m tall and weighing several tonnes. The *sìm* that houses the Buddha is also famous for the wooden facade over its front terrace, a masterpiece of Lao carving. Take a break at shady and little-visited **Wat Hai Sok (19)** before your final temple stop, **Wat Mixai (20)**, with its Bangkok-style *sìm* and heavy gates, flanked by two *nyak* (guardian giants). From here it's a short ride to either Th Nokèokoummane or Th François Ngin to return your bike.

Finish the day by walking southeast towards the Mekong, find a seat at one of the **riverfront food and drink vendors (21**; p104) and soothe your aching legs with the healing properties of Beerlao.

COURSES
Cooking
As well as being a great place to stay (p101), **Villa Lao** (Map p86; ☎ /fax 242 292; lessons 300,000K) offers cooking courses at 9am and 2pm by appointment, involving a trip to the market, preparation of three dishes of your choice and sampling your creations. The price is per lesson, so the more people involved, the cheaper it will be. The **Lao Textile Museum** (p96) also offers cookery courses, in theory at least, but details were hard to come by when we stopped by. Hopefully things will be clearer by the time you read this.

Language Courses
For details on Vientiane language schools that teach Lao see p317.

Weaving & Dyeing
You can learn how to dye textiles using natural pigments and then weave them on a traditional loom at the **Houey Hong Vocational**

Training Center for Women (off Map p86; ☎ 560 006; www.houeyhongcentre.com; Ban Houey Hong; ⏱ 8.30am-4.30pm Mon-Sat). The NGO group, run by a Lao-Japanese woman, established this centre north of Vientiane to train disadvantaged rural women in the dying art of natural dyeing and traditional silk-weaving practices. Visitors can look for free or partake in the dyeing process (120,000K, two hours, two scarves) or weaving (200,000K, whole day). You keep the fruits of your labour. Transportation to and from the centre is provided for an additional 33,000K. The centre's contact point and commercial venture in Vientiane is **True Colour** (Map p90; ☎ 214 410; Th Setthathirath).

Classes in weaving and dyeing are also available at the **Lao Textile Museum** (off Map p86; ☎ 030-525 8293; www.ibiss.co.jp/laomuseum/access .html; lessons US$50), run by the folks who own Kanchana Boutique (p113). Lessons must be arranged in advance, and some English is spoken, although those truly interested should probably bring a translator.

Vipassana Meditation

Every Saturday from 4pm to 5.30pm monks lead a session of sitting and walking meditation at **Wat Sok Pa Luang** (Map p86; ☎ 231 1938; Th Sok Pa Luang); see p97. Both Lao and foreigners are welcome and there's no charge. There's usually a translator for the question period held after the meditation.

FESTIVALS & EVENTS

You can rest assured that whatever the festival, celebrations in Vientiane will be as vigorous as anywhere in the country.

Bun Pha That Luang (That Luang Festival), usually in early November, is the largest temple fair in Laos. Apart from the religious fervour, the festival features a trade show and a number of carnival games. The festivities begin with a *wíen thíen* (circumambulation) around Wat Si Muang, followed by a procession to Pha That Luang, which is illuminated all night for a week. The festival climaxes on the morning of the full moon with the *ták bàat* ceremony, in which several thousand monks from across the country receive alms food. That evening there's a final *wíen thíen* around Pha That Luang, with devotees carrying *pɑɑsàat* (miniature temples made from banana stems and decorated with flowers and other offerings). Fireworks cap off the evening and everyone makes merit or merry until dawn.

Another huge annual event is **Bun Nam** (River Festival) at the end of *phansǎa* (the Buddhist rains retreat) in October, during which boat races are held on the Mekong River. Rowing teams from all over the country, as well as from Thailand, China and Myanmar, compete; the riverbank is lined with food stalls, temporary discos, carnival games and beer gardens for three days and nights. Vientiane is jam-packed during Bun Nam, and given how far away the boat racing is and how difficult it is to find a vantage point, we think smaller towns like Vang Vieng and Muang Khong are better bets, though Muang Khong doesn't usually hold its festival until early December, around National Day.

SLEEPING

Vientiane's dozens of guesthouses and hotels range from US$5-a-night cells to opulent colonial-era affairs where no luxury is spared. Most rooms, particularly those at the cheaper end, suffer from capital-city syndrome – meaning they cost more than they would elsewhere.

Most accommodation is within walking distance to the centre of town and comparing options is easy enough on foot. Some mid-range and top-end places are a little further away, but it's usually only a couple of kilometres. Accommodation is listed by price, from cheapest up, and divided into budget (up to the equivalent of US$19), midrange (US$20 to US$80) and top end (US$81 and up).

Budget

The cheapest places in town at the time of research were **Sabaidy Guest House** (Map p90; ☎ 213 929; p_vily@hotmail.com; 110 Th Setthathirath; dm/d/tr 20,000/50,000/75,000K), and **Mixok Guest House** (Map p90; ☎ 251 606; Th Setthathirath; s/d/tr 35,000/45,000/60,000K), though the price is really the only reason you'd stay.

Other budget options:

ourpick Mixay Guesthouse (Map p90; ☎ 213 679; 56 Th Nokèokoummane; d 45,000K, r 55,000-135,000K) This is one of Vientiane's cheapest guesthouses, but still manages to provide good service and accommodation. The rooms are very basic but clean, and the atmosphere is equally laid-back. Some rooms have hot-water bathrooms, many others have no windows – check a few. It's very popular, so unless you're booking ahead, don't be surprised if it's full.

Syri 1 Guest House (Map p90; ☎ 212 682; Th Saigon; r 50,000-150,000K; ⚫) Rooms at this rambling old house range from an enormous studio to compact doubles, some without windows or bathroom. The uniting factor is the antiquated furniture, heaps of charm, lots of inviting communal areas and a true guesthouse feel. Don't confuse it with the Syri 2.

RD Guesthouse (Map p90; ☎ 262 112; www.rdlao .com; 37-01 Th Nokèokoummane; dm US$6, r US$12-17; ⚫) The rooms at RD (Relax & Dream away) are utterly characterless, but clean and conveniently located, and a library and communal kitchen are perks.

Saysouly Guest House (Map p90; ☎ 218 383/4; www. saysouly.com; 23 Th Manthatourath; r US$7-15; ⚫) Two minutes' walk from Nam Phu and popular with backpackers, this three-storey place offers basic but clean rooms, some with shared bathrooms. Service can't exactly be described as enthusiastic, but the atmosphere is busy and social, and the balconies can be a good place to meet other travellers.

Soukchaleun Guest House (Map p90; ☎ 218 723; 121 Th Setthathirath; r with fan/air-con 100,000/130,000K; ⚫) The Soukchaleun has a homey atmosphere that, unfortunately, doesn't extend into the rather characterless rooms. Nonetheless it's tidy, the atmosphere is pretty friendly, and the location great – front rooms have views over Wat Mixai.

Lao Youth Inn (cnr Th François Ngin & Th Fa Ngoum **Map p90**; ☎ 217 130; 29 Th Fa Ngoum; r US$10-18; ⚫ ; Th François Ngin **Map p90**; Th François Ngin; r US$12; ⚫) Service at the Lao Youth Inn's original location at the corner of Th Fa Ngoum and Th François Ngin is patchy at best, and the setting somewhat hectic, but the location is convenient, and the light green paint job gives the otherwise bare rooms a bit of character. A better bet is the hotel's newest branch, just up Th François Ngin, across from the entrace to Wat Mixay, where newer rooms in a markedly more sedate setting go for a reasonable US$12.

Orchid Guesthouse (Map p90; ☎ 252 825; Th Fa Ngoum; r US$11-20; ⚫) In the heart of the action along the riverfront, the Orchid's rooms are simple and clean but those without bathroom or air-conditioning (US$11) are a bit pricey. It's welcoming and has a communal rooftop balcony overlooking the Mekong.

Dragon Lodge (Map p90; ☎ 250 112; dragon lodge2002@yahoo.com; 311-312 Th Samsènethai; r 100,000-180,000K; ⚫) Although the rooms here are large and well kitted out, they can also be musty and a bit dark. However the chilled-out bar downstairs (which also has handy travel information) makes this an easy decision for those who emphasise socialising over comfort.

Phonepaseuth Guest House (Map p90; ☎ 212 263; www.laoguesthouse.com; 97 Th Pangkham; r with fan/air-con US$12/18; ⚫) Centrally located near Nam Phu, this guesthouse has a range of rooms, some windowless, so look at several. The staff can't be described as welcoming but its location keeps it popular.

Viengthong Guest House (Map p86; ☎ 212 095; viengthongguesthouse@hotmail.com; 8 Th Fa Ngoum; s/tw US$15/20; ⚫) In a quiet *soi* (street) along the northwest side of Wat Phia Wat, the Viengthong mixes laid-back service (ie slow but smiling) with good-value rooms, a quiet location and some trippy wat-style murals. The rooms in the newer building are actually minisuites and are excellent value at US$20.

our pick **Villa Lao** (Map p86; ☎ /fax 242 292; www. villa-lao-guesthouse.com; off Th Nong Douang; r 480-720B; ⚫ ⚫) If the location was a bit more convenient, this would be the most atmospheric budget place in Vientiane. Located about 1.5km west of town, Villa Lao (the former Thongbay Guesthouse) is a leafy, manicured compound containing two large traditional houses. The cheapest rooms are bare, are fan-cooled and have shared bathrooms, and all rooms are large and cool with low-lying beds. The English-speaking owners are passionate about Lao food, can recommend good restaurants and can organise cooking classes (p99). Bikes can be hired.

Asian Pavilion Hotel (Map p90; ☎ 213 430-2; 379 Th Samsènethai; s/d/ste 500/600/800B; ⚫ ⚫) In its pre-Revolutionary incarnation, this was the Hotel Constellation (immortalised in John Le Carré's *The Honourable Schoolboy*) and was frequented by all sorts of secret-agent types during the '60s and '70s. Unfortunately little has changed since those days, and the huge girth of the 'Asian suite' rooms and the hefty discount are the only real draws.

Douang Deuane Hotel (Map p90; ☎ 222 301-3; DD_hotel@hotmail.com; Th Nokèokoummane; s/tw/tr incl breakfast 120,000/170,000/220,000K; ⚫ ⚫ ⚫) A recent facelift and the combination of location, price, and simple but clean, medium-sized rooms with fridge, phone and satellite TV make the Douang Deuane a good value. With this in mind, don't waste your breath by trying to bargain – it ain't gonna happen.

Vayakorn House (Map p90; ☎ 241 911; www.vayakorn. jimdo.com; 91 Th Nokèokoummane; s/d US$17/26; ☒ ☎) Two blocks west of Nam Phu, Vayakorn's stylish and spacious rooms are a bargain. All have polished floors, satellite TV and spotless bathrooms, though the singles are pretty small. Nearby, the same people run the midrange Vayakorn Inn.

Also recommended:

Phonethip Guesthouse (Map p90; ☎ 217 239; 72 Th In Paeng; r 80,000-120,000K; ☒) Quiet family-run place with range of rooms – look at a few.

Souphaphone Guesthouse (Map p90; ☎ 261 468; www.souphaphone.net; just off Th François Ngin; r US$20; ☒ ☐) Attractive wood furnishings and large rooms provide this otherwise unremarkable hotel with a bit of class.

Souvanna Hotel (Map p86; ☎ 223 576; Th Talat Sisavath; r 400B; ☒) Clean, comfy and cheap – the only downside being that it's a trek to get 'downtown' and tuk-tuks can be hard to find at night. There are a couple of similar places in the vicinity.

Villa That Luang (Map p86; ☎ 413 370; www.villa -thatluang-guesthouse.com; 307 Th That Luang; s/d incl breakfast 130,000/150,000K; ☒ ☐) The rooms here are a bit past their prime, but boast a real homey feel and ample amenities make it a comfortable place to stay.

Midrange

Many midrange hotels accept Visa and MasterCard, but guesthouses probably won't.

GUESTHOUSES

Nalinthone Guesthouse (Map p86; ☎ 243 659; namrin nvte@yahoo.com; Th Fa Ngoum; r US$20-25; ☒ ☐ ☎) This family-run, modern place on the river lacks a little in atmosphere but the clean and comfortable rooms are great value considering the position – the doubles with river views (US$20) are the pick.

ourpick Mali Namphu Guest House (Map p90; ☎ 215 093; www.malinamphu.com; 109 Th Pangkham; r incl breakfast US$22-45; ☒ ☐ ☎) Rates have doubled here since the last edition, making this former budget place now a midranger, but the attractive 40 rooms built around a pleasant courtyard still remain one of the city's better value places to stay. The rooms vary in size and are not huge, but they are spotless, and the staff are both efficient and eager to please.

Lani Guest House (Map p90; ☎ 214 919; www.lani guesthouse.com; 281 Th Setthathirath; s US$28-33, d/tr US$39/44; ☒) Just off busy Th Setthathirath, north of Wat Hai Sok in the centre of town, this colonial-era mansion has a tranquil, historic feel. High ceilings, antiques, Lao handi-crafts and no TVs in the 12 rooms contribute to the atmosphere. And it's that – the ambience – you're paying for here, not luxury; you can get much better equipped rooms for less elsewhere.

Dorkket Garden Guest House (Map p86; ☎ 020-5571 2288; www.dorkketgarden.com; Th Sakkarine; r US$35-45; ☒ ☎) Like staying at your grandparents' house, but in a good way. The rooms here are in a stately low-rise villa or in a tidy brick annex, and are united by a familiar homey atmosphere and garden that encourages relaxing. Recommended.

Villa Manoly (Map p86; ☎ /fax 218 907; manoly20@ hotmail.com; r US$35-45; ☒ ☒) In a quiet street off Th Fa Ngoum between Wat Si Muang and the Mekong, the Manoly is a large French-era villa (plus a newer building) fronted by a large garden with a pool. The rooms are not quite as classy as the exterior and lobby suggest, but all have hardwood and terrazzo floors, high ceilings and vintage furnishings.

HOTELS

Lao Silk Hotel (Map p90; ☎ 213 976; www.laosilkhotel .com; Th François Ngin; r US$25-35; ☒ ☎) Brand-spanking new at the time of research, this tall hotel offers 20 virtually identical and rather tight rooms all featuring double beds. Price depends on view and the size of room.

Auberge Sala Inpeng (Map p90; ☎ 242 021; www .salalao.com; Th In Paeng; r incl breakfast US$25-40; ☒) Located on a quiet leafy street reminiscent of Luang Prabang, the accommodation here also suggests upcountry Laos with its handful of semi-detached wooden bungalows in an attractive garden. Although the cheapest rooms are small and lack TVs, this is a place to stay for the atmosphere not the amenities.

ourpick Hôtel Khamvongsa (Map p90; ☎ 218 415; www.hotelkhamvongsa.com; Th Khounboulom; r incl breakfast US$25-50; ☒ ☎) This French-era building has recently been renovated and expanded into an intimate, attractive, and very good value midrange hotel. Although the majority of rooms are located in the newer building out the back, all are reminiscent of the colonial era with attractive furnishings in dark woods and tall ceilings. The more expensive rooms include kitchenettes. Staff are confident and helpful.

Vayakorn Inn (Map p90; ☎ 215 348; www.vayakorn .jimdo.com; 19 Th Hèngbounnoy; r US$35; ☒ ☎) On a quiet street just off increasingly hectic Th Setthathirath, this new hotel has comfortable and attractive single or double rooms, all of which feature balconies. A good value.

our pick **Day Inn Hotel** (Map p90; ☎ 222 985; dayinn@laopdr.com; 59/3 Th Pangkham; s/d/tw/tr incl breakfast US$35/40/45/65; ⊠ �🛜) Charming service, a well-maintained, tidy atmosphere and large, airy rooms make the Day Inn a great choice. The price isn't exactly a steal, but wi-fi is free, and if you're arriving by air, the price includes airport pick-up.

Intercity Hotel (Map p90; ☎ 242 842-4; www.rama yana-laos.com; 24-25 Th Fa Ngoum; r incl breakfast US$35-75; ⊠ 🛜) The somewhat gaudy exterior and lobby of this hotel conceals markedly more subtle rooms complete with high ceilings, polished wood floors and big windows. All front rooms have Mekong views. Professional service.

Lane Xang Hotel (Map p90; ☎ 214 100; www.lane xanghotel.com.la; Th Fa Ngoum; r incl breakfast US$38-95, ste incl breakfast $64-178; ⊠ 🖥 🛜 🖺) Built in the 1960s on the site of a prominent Lan Xang-era wat, this hotel facing the Mekong was once the classiest place in town. The rooms on the 4th floor were renovated for the 2009 SEA Games and are considered 'deluxe', but their counterparts could use a face-lift, and even with buffet breakfast, airport pickup and free wif-fi, are probably a touch overpriced.

our pick **Hotel Beau Rivage Mekong** (Map p86; ☎ 243 375; Th Fa Ngoum; www.hbrm.com; s incl breakfast US$39, d incl breakfast US$47-57; ⊠ 🛜) Don't be put off by the preponderance of pink; this Australian-owned boutiqueish hotel on the banks of the Mekong has heaps of character, and is a particularly great place for couples. All of the 16 rooms are stylishly laid out and furnished with a pink, blue or green theme, and those with Mekong views (US$57), terrazzo baths and small balconies are best.

Lao Orchid Hotel (Map p90; ☎ 264 134; www.lao-or chid-hotel.com; Th Chao Anou; d/ste incl breakfast US$45/65; ⊠ 🛜) The Lao Orchid is one of a new breed of tastefully designed hotels that have opened in Vientiane over the last few years. The 33 well-equipped rooms are fitted out with an emphasis on wood and silk, and the service is a step up from the standard. All rooms have a balcony, but ask for one at the front to take in the Mekong views. Good value.

Sengtawan Riverside Hotel (Map p86; ☎ 219 362; www.sengtawan.com; r incl breakfast US$45-100; ⊠ 🛜) One of a couple of similarly priced new places near the river, the rooms here are largely characterless, but large and comfortable.

le Leela (Map p86; ☎ 214 048; www.leleela.com; r incl breakfast US$55-75; ⊠ 🛜) This refurbished mansion, located on a quiet street off Th Fa Ngoum between Wat Si Muang and the Mekong, is probably the most stylish of Vientiane's new hotels. Minimalism rules here, mixed tastefully with elements of the house's colonial-era origins, although the quality of some of the furnishings suggests IKEA rather than Chippendale, possibly explaining the hotel's relatively low rates. Some of the rooms here are quite large and feature inviting balconies; ask to see a few.

Tai-Pan Hotel (Map p90; ☎ 216 906, 216 909; www. taipanhotel-vientiane.com; 2-12 Th François Ngin; r incl breakfast US$70-154; ⊠ 🖥 🛜 🖺) Near the riverfront, the Tai-Pan is very reliable with good service and has become popular with people on business. The best rooms have balconies, so it's worth requesting one. Prices drop during low season.

Top End

All Vientiane's top-end establishments are hotels, and most of them have business centres, pool and at least one restaurant. Major credit cards are accepted.

Ansara (Map p90; ☎ 213 514; www.ansara.com; off Th Fa Ngoum; r/ste incl breakfast US$80/120; ⊠ 🖥 🛜) Opened only a few days before we left Laos, this hotel stands to be a formidable midrange/ top end contender in central Vientiane. The attractive rooms, hidden down a quiet lane near Wat Chanthabuli, look over a garden behind the faux colonial-era main structure, and boast thoughtful perks such as laptop, stereo and Jaccuzzi.

Lao Plaza Hotel (Map p90; ☎ 218 800; www.laoplaza hotel.com; 63 Th Samsènethai; r incl breakfast US$140-200, ste incl breakfast US$270-560; ⊠ 🛜 🖺) This busy 142-room complex, occupying an entire block east of the Lao National Museum, boasts four-star rooms with views across the city. Discounts are available if you book online.

Green Park Hotel (Map p86; ☎ 264 097; www. greenparkvientiane.com; 248 Th Khu Vieng; r incl breakfast US$145-450; ⊠ 🛜 🖺) We tend to agree with the guestbook author who wrote that the Green Park is 'an oasis in a dusty city'. Resembling something of a Lao village set around a courtyard pool, the 34 rooms here have details like bathroom gardens that put it a cut above the rest. Good choice if you can afford it, though do book ahead.

Don Chan Palace (Map p86; ☎ 244 288; www. donchanpalacelaopdr.com; off Th Fa Ngoum; r incl breakfast

US$150-300; ❌ 💻 🛜 🖲) On an island in the
Mekong believed to be home to a powerful
naga, this gargantuan monstrosity was built
for the Asean conference in 2004, somehow
managing to bypass Vientiane's seven-storey
height limit. It's certainly luxurious and the
views are great, but lacks the atmosphere
you'll find in Vientiane's other offerings at
this price range.

Settha Palace Hotel (Map p90; ☎ 217 581;
www.setthapalace.com; 6 Th Pangkham; standard/deluxe incl
breakfast US$170/182, ste US$252-363; ❌ 💻 🛜 🖲)
The Settha Palace is Vientiane's classic colonial hotel, and is probably the best hotel in
town. It has been beautifully restored, with
custom-made rosewood furniture, plank
floors and landscaped gardens. The 29 tastefully appointed rooms have wi-fi (per hour
US$5) and black-and-white Venetian marble
bathrooms (the deluxe rooms with bathtubs),
but don't expect acres of space.

APARTMENTS
If you're going to be here for a while check out
these luxury apartment complexes: **Parkview
Executive Suites** (Map p86; ☎ 250 888; Th Luang Prabang;
❌ 💻 🛜 🖲) and the French-run **Khunta
Residence** (Map p86; ☎ 251 199; www.khuntaresidence.
com; off Th Luang Prabang; ❌ 🛜 🖲).

Many of Vientiane's newish small hotels
such as **City Inn** (Map p90; ☎ 281 333; www.cityinnvien
tiane.com; Th Pangkham; r incl breakfast 550,000K; ste incl
breakfast 810,000-900,000K; ❌ 🛜) and **Phasouk
Residence** (Map p90; ☎ 243 415; www.phasoukresidence.
com; 57/4 Th Wat Xieng Nyean; r/ste US$55/75; ❌ 💻 🛜)
also operate equally well as serviced apart-
ments for those with generous housing
allowances.

EATING
It'd be a stretch to label Vientiane as a culinary destination, but the city boasts an
abundance of solid restaurants spanning a
remarkably wide swathe of cuisines, ranging from North Korean to southern French.
Although quality can vary, value is a near
universal, and in particular, the city is a great
place to indulge in French food, even if you
are on a budget.

Lao
Paradoxically and frustratingly, an authentic
and tasty Lao restaurant can be somewhat
hard to find in Vientiane, particularly in the
city centre. Self-catering is an option (see the

boxed text p62), or you can try one of the
following.

Riverfront food and drink vendors (Map p90; ⏱ 4-
10pm) For years the east bank of the Mekong
River has been one of Vientiane's culinary
highlights, and we've enjoyed many a sunset
while eating *pîng kai* (grilled chicken), *tąm
màak-hung* (papaya salad) and drinking cheap
Beerlao. Unfortunately, at the time of writing,
the entire riverfront was in the process of
being gentrified and the state of the vendors
post-renovation had yet to be determined.

Ban Anou night market (Map p90; ⏱ 5-9pm)
This night market sets up every afternoon in
a small street off the north end of Th Chao
Anou. From grilled meats to a huge array of
jąew, chili-based dips taken with par-boiled
veggies and sticky rice, it has the largest variety of authentic Lao dishes in town – the only
caveat being that there's no seating, so be sure
to ask your guesthouse in advance if you can
borrow some of their plates and bowls.

Han Sam Euay Nong (Map p90; Th Chao Anou;
mains 8000-20,000K; ⏱ 8am-7pm) Cheap, tidy and
tasty, this busy family-run restaurant embod-
ies everything we like in an eatery. It's also one
of the few places in the touristy downtown
area to serve authentic Lao flavours. Must-
have dishes include *năem khào*, crispy balls of
deep-fried rice and sour pork sausage shredded into a saladlike dish and eaten with fresh
leaves and herbs, several types of *tąm màak-
hung*, and the delicious *khào pûn nâm jąew*,
thin rice noodles served in a clear pork broth
with slices of pork, bamboo and herbs. There's
no sign here, but the restaurant is located
directly adjacent to the Lao Orchid Hotel.

Han Ton Phai (Map p90; ☎ 252 542; Th Hengboun;
mains 10,000-20,000K; ⏱ 9am-10pm) This very local
Lao place surprisingly has an English menu,
but there's really no reason to look any further than the restaurant's speciality, *kôy pąa*
(10,000K to 20,000K), a chunky salad of
freshwater fish and fresh herbs. There's no
English-language sign, so keep an eye open
for the billboard that says 'traditional food'.

Khambang Lao Food Restaurant (Map
p90; ☎ 217 198; 97/2 Th Khounboulom; mains 10,000-
70,000K; ⏱ 11.30am-2.30pm & 5.30-9pm) This third-
generation restaurant, basically an extension
of the family's living room, serves what is
almost certainly the best Lao food in central
Vientiane. We're confident you could blindly
choose from the menu and put together an
outstanding meal, but it'd be a pity if you

OODLES OF NOODLES

Noodles of all kinds are popular in Laos, and Vientiane has the country's greatest variety. The most popular noodle of all is undoubtedly fŏe, the local version of Vietnamese pho, served with beef or pork and accompanied, Lao-style, by a huge plate of fresh herbs and vegetables and a ridiculous amount of condiments. Central Vientiane's most popular fŏe joint is Pho Dung (p106). Also popular are khào pûn, the thin rice noodles known as khànŏm jeen in Thailand, taken in Laos with a spicy curry-like broth as is done at Amphone (p105), or sometimes in a clear pork broth (khào pûn nâm jqew), available at Han Sam Euay Nong (p104). There's also khào pìak sèn, thick rice- and tapioca-flour noodles served in a slightly viscuous broth with crispy deep-fried pork belly or chicken. A good place to sample this dish is **Rice Noodle – Lao Porridge** (Map p90; ☎ 020-5541 4455; Th Hengboun; mains 8000K; ⏰ 4pm-1am).

Other popular noodles include mìi (traditional Chinese egg noodle), particularly prevalent in the unofficial Chinatown area bounded by Th Hengboun, Th Chao Anou, Th Khounboulom and the western end of Th Samsènethai, and băn kuan, Lao for bánh cuôn, a freshly-steamed rice noodle filled with minced pork, mushrooms and carrots, a Vietnamese specialty that is popular in Laos. Look for it in the mornings near the intersection of Th Chao Anou and Th Hengboun.

missed the house special roasted fish; the áw lám, described on the menu as 'spicy beef stew', a thick stew of meat and herbs; or the sài ua, Luang Prabang style sausage. Insiders also know to order jqew màak len, a dip of roasted tomatoes, chillies and shallots not mentioned on the menu.

Soukvemarn Lao Food (Map p90; ☎ 214 441; www .laofoods.com; 89/12 Ban Sisaket; mains 12,000-45,000K; ⏰ 11am-2pm & 6-10pm) Although the prices put Soukvemarn in the tourist bracket, the dishes at this family-run restaurant are authentically Lao. Examples include kqeng pqa khai mot, fish soup with ant larvae – in season, and mok pqa, fish steamed with herbs in a banana leaf packet.

Han Khay Laap T2 (Map p86; ☎ 020-5551 3491; Th T2; mains 15,000-30,000K; ⏰ 8am-3pm; 🚑) If you're heading north, then make plans to have lunch at this local foodie fave, not far from the Northern Bus Station on Th T2. The friendly English-speaking owners specialise in everything beef, from the eponymous (and delicious) làap to kheuang nái ngúa, a thick soup with beef offal, as well as a couple of fish dishes such as kôy pqa (a làap-like dish of fish) and kqeng sôm pqa (a sour fish soup). There's no English-language sign, so keep your eyes peeled for the T2 amid Lao script, roughly across from the imposing Khounxay Hotel.

Amphone (Map p90; ☎ 020-7771 1138; Th Wat Xieng Nyean; mains 15,000-60,000K; ⏰ 11am-2pm & 5-10pm) On the surface, Amphone looks like Lao for tourists, but locals eat here and the menu has a good selection of traditional and not-so-traditional Lao dishes. Trying one of the

four set meals (80,000K) is a good way to sample what's available, otherwise stop by on a weekday during lunch when the restaurant serves hearty (and tasty) bowls of mìi kathi (15,000K; rice noodles served with a pork- or beef-based coconut milk broth) and khào pûn (fresh rice noodles with a soupy fish broth). Recommended.

Somphouthong (Sin Daad Savan; Map p86; ☎ 020-5504 4444; Th Luang Prabang; sets 33,000-120,000K; ⏰ 4pm-midnight) Sìin daad, DIY Korean-style barbecue, is obviously not Lao, but it's so popular in the country that we felt inclined to include it in this category. This place, known locally as Sin Daad Savan, is one of Vientiane's most longstanding and favourite destinations for the dish. There's no English menu, but it's really just a matter of choosing your protein (they've got everything from pork to crocodile; see p67 if you're having language issues) and indicating whether you want sut nyai (big set) or sut nôy (small).

Makphet (Map p90; ☎ 260 587; Th Setthathirath; mains 40,000-55,000K; ⏰ 11am-9pm Mon, Wed, Fri & Sat, 11am-2pm & 6-9pm Tue & Thu) Run by Friends International (www.friends-international. org), this small restaurant trains homeless youths to cook and wait tables. It's a good choice for those intimidated by Vientiane's more authentic Lao restaurants. An attached shop sells handicrafts made by underprivileged families.

Other Asian

PVO (Map p90; ☎ 214 444; 344 Th Samsènethai; mains 8000-18,000K; ⏰ 6am-7pm Mon-Sat, 6am-2pm Sun) This is the third and hopefully final incarnation of this Vietnamese restaurant-slash-motorcycle rental. The combo sounds odd, but this is one of the better places in town to grab lunch, and in addition to several tasty spring roll–based Vietnamese dishes (14,000K to 18,000K), PVO does some of the best *khào jįi pá-tê* (half/whole baguette 8000/16,000K) in town, and by our reckoning, possibly Vientiane's best fruit shakes. For motorcycle rental, go to p116.

Ali (Map p90; ☎ 217 958; 52 Th Pangkham; mains 10,000-70,000K; ☺ 9.30am-10.30pm) Ali has a more diverse menu than Vientiane's other Indian places, and the execution is also above par. Lots of vegetarian choices, and a few Malaysian dishes are also available.

Pho Dung (Map p90; ☎ 213 775; 158 Th Hengboun; noodle soup 12,000-15,000K; ☺ 6am-2pm) Arguably the best and undoubtedly the most popular *fǒe* (rice noodle soup) in central Vientiane. Run by a friendly Vietnamese family used to dealing with foreigners, the gargantuan bowls here are served Lao-style, ie with heaps of optional seasonings and immense plates of fresh veggies and herbs.

Linda Sathaporn Restaurant (Map p86; ☎ 415 355; cnr Th Dong Palang & Th Phonsay; mains 13,000-45,000K; ☺ 8am-10pm) Linda Sathaporn's fat menu filled with pictures of its varied tasty Thai dishes make it worth the trip. It's very popular with Thais, and with smart service, large portions and ample veggie options, it's easy to see why. Seating is inside or in the more pleasant shaded courtyard out the back.

Korean Restaurant (Map p90; ☎ 020-208 7080; Th Hengboun; mains 30,000-180,00K; ☺ 9am-11pm) Lacklustre name aside, this Korean-run place is great for sampling what is currently the most popular foreign cuisine in Southeast Asia. Most locals go directly for the Korean barbecue (80,000K), but we liked the kimchi stew (30,000K), served Korean-style with heaps of side dishes.

Han Khay Khao Jii Pate (Map p90; ☎ 223 726; Th Samsènethai; ☺ 6am-8pm) Along the strip of road boasting several vendors selling the Vietnamese baguette sandwiches, we reckon that this shop does the best *khào jįi pá-tê* (half/whole baguette 11,000/22,000K). There's no English-language sign here, but the shop is directly adjacent to Europcar.

Ha Noi Quan (Map p86; Th Kaysone Phomvihane; mains 15,000-25,000K; ☺ 11am-10pm) This quasi-outdoor restaurant, located next door to the Thai embassy, has a short menu of tasty and authen-

tic northern Vietnamese dishes. There's *pho* (noodle soup with beef or chicken), *bánh mì* (baguette sandwiches), *bánh cuôn* (a freshly-steamed rice noodle filled with minced pork), and *bún* (fresh rice noodles served with grilled pork). Choices run low by evening, so best make this a lunch destination.

our pick **Vieng Sawan** (Map p90; ☎ 213 990; Th Hengboun; mains 16,000-46,000K; ☺ 11am-10pm) In the middle of Chinatown, Vieng Sawan is a bustling open-sided restaurant that offers a fun eating experience. It specialises in *năem néuang* (Vietnamese barbecued pork meatballs) and many varieties of *yáw* (spring rolls), usually sold in 'sets' *(sut)* with *khào pûn*, fresh lettuce leaves, mint, basil, various sauces for dipping, sliced starfruit and green banana. You can also order *sìin joom* here, thin slices of raw beef which customers boil in small cauldrons of broth and eat with dipping sauces.

Pyongyang Restaurant (Map p86; ☎ 263 118; Th Nongbone; mains 17,000-120,000K; ☺ 11am-10pm) Owned by the same people as the Phnom Penh restaurant of the same name, this Pyongyang is even more surreal. Waitresses direct from North Korea, trained to sing and dance since childhood, will take your order one minute and step up to the microphone the next to perform perfectly choreographed dance routines and/or play electric guitar and drums (it starts about 7.30pm, and only if there are enough customers). It's a complete trip. Don't, however, let them order for you, as you'll be served only the most expensive dishes on what is a relatively pricey menu.

our pick **YuLaLa Cafe** (Map p90; ☎ 020-5510 4050; Th Hengboun; mains 35,000-45,000K; ☺ 11.30am-2pm & 6-9.30pm Tue-Sun) This cozy place serves food that can only be described as Japanese/French/Lao fusion. Amazingly, Saya and Aya pull it off, and the huge chalkboard menu includes dishes such as fried tofu with tomato-based sauce and Japanese-style croquettes. There are appetising-sounding daily specials and lunch sets that include rice, vegetable soup and homemade pickled veggies. Really the only problem here is scoring one of the few tables during peak hours.

No's (Map p90; ☎ 265 000; Th Hengboun; sushi sets 60,000-100,000K, buffet 85,000K; ☺ 11.30am-2pm & 5.30-10.30pm) Considering Laos's landlocked position, sushi is about as exotic as it gets, and this restaurant's modern design also suggests an expensive meal, but sushi sets are affordable, and come Tuesday there's an all you can eat sushi buffet.

> **BIG DEAL**
>
> Don't fret if the wine list starts where your lodging budget ends; many of Vientiane's best French restaurants offer set lunch specials, typically involving two courses and a dessert for around 60,000K to 85,000K. Particularly worth investigating are the offerings at chez philippe, Le Carmague, Le Silapa and Le Vendôme, the latter of which at 22,000K, must be the cheapest French food just about anywhere in the world.

French

It is no surprise that this former French colony should boast so many French restaurants, but their overall high quality is surprising. When you consider that this fine dining experience will cost a fraction of what you'd pay at home, it gets even better.

Paradice (Map p90; ☎ 312 836; Th Lan Xang; mains 25,000-45,000K; ✕ 11am-7pm Mon-Sat; ☎) In the grounds of the Centre Culturel et de Coopération Linguistique, this airy, comfortable cafe serves basic but tasty French and Asian dishes; think croque-monsieur and a crisp salad. Don't miss the delicious ice creams and chocolates.

Le Vendôme (Map p90; ☎ 216 402; Th In Paeng; mains 20,000-75,000K; ✕ 10am-2pm Mon-Fri, 5-10pm daily) Tucked away in an old house in a quiet street behind Wat In Paeng, Le Vendôme's menu features entire sections for terrines and soufflés, in addition to pasta and wood-fired pizzas. But most diners let the chef do the choosing, particularly at lunch, when the restaurant serves a revolving weekday special for only 22,000K.

Le Silapa (Map p90; ☎ 219 689; 17/1 Th Sihom; mains US$10-24; ✕ 11.30am-2pm & 6-10pm) We somewhat reluctantly put Le Silapa in this category, as although the restaurant calls itself French, the chefs are Canadian, and the menu, with its frequent emphasis on sweet and sour flavours, can only be described as international. Nonetheless it's has been serving some of the most proclaimed upscale cuisine in Vientiane for years, complemented by refined surrounds and discreet service.

Le Carmague (Map p86; ☎ 264 189; 164 Th Sibouaban; mains 60,000-120,000K; ✕ 11am-2pm & 6.30-10pm Mon-Sat) Housed in an atmospheric colonial-era brick and wood building, this restaurant focusses on the specialties of the eponymous southern French province. Dishes such as Carmague style buffalo stew or tatin arlésienne, a traditional pie of Arles, form a menu quite unlike that of the restaurant's resident countrymen.

chez philippe (Map p90; ☎ 213 334; Th Setthathirath; mains 45,000-250,000K; ✕ 11.30am-2pm & 6-10pm) You probably didn't even notice this restaurant, located directly above PhimPhone Market, but it's serving some of the city's best upscale cuisine. Creative dishes such as Split pea soup with snails and croutons, and the restaurant's modern interior set chez philippe apart from Vientiane's more traditional French restaurants.

L'Adresse de Tinay (Map p90; ☎ 020-5691 3434; New Lao Paris Hotel, 118 Th Samsènethai; mains 120,000-145,000K; ✕ 6-11pm) Chef Tinay was born in Laos but raised in France, and after 16 years of cooking there, thankfully for us, has decided to come back home. Virtually the entire menu changes on a monthly basis but fortunately for the diners, Tinay's starter made with goat cheese from an organic farm in Vang Viang, and his excellent confit duck served as cassoulet with Toulouse sausage and sweet garlic cream, are constants.

Other International

More expats and travellers means a demand for a greater variety of cuisines, a demand that Vientiane seems to be meeting fairly well. There are also plenty of eateries offering a combination of cuisines. And while you should justifiably be wary of any kitchen purporting to know *làap* as well as lasagne, there are a few here that manage to do their multicultural menus justice.

Sticky Fingers Café & Bar (Map p90; ☎ 215 972; 10/3 Th François Ngin; mains 14,000-68,000K; ✕ 10am-11pm Tue-Sun; ☎) Sticky Fingers has the atmosphere of a Sydney cafe and serves tasty cuisine that could be described as 'modern international'. Generous happy-hour drink specials and free wi-fi are even more reasons to stop by.

Khop Chai Deu (Map p90; ☎ 251 564; 54 Th Setthathirath; mains 18,000-60,000K; ✕ 8am-midnight; ☎) In a remodelled colonial-era villa near Nam Phu, Khop Chai Deu has been a traveller's favourite for years because of its range of well-prepared

Lao, Thai, Indian and assorted Western fare, and lively ambience.

Istanbul (Map p90; ☎ 020-7797 8190; Th François Ngin; mains 20,000-90,000K; ☒ 10am-10pm; ☒ ☎) Istanbul claims to be the only Turkish restaurant in Laos. The menu opens up to several pages of meat dishes, but delve a bit further and you'll find lots of veggie dishes, meat-free *mezze*, homemade yogurt and yeasty homemade pitas. A warning: those who fear garlic best stay far, far away.

Chokdee Café (Map p90; ☎ 020-5610 3434; Th Fa Ngoum; mains 20,000-95,000K; ☒ 11am-11pm) Belgium isn't exactly celebrated for its food, but this cozy Tintin-themed place may just change your mind. Come Friday or Saturday, the restaurant serves vast pots of moules-frites, Belgian-style mussels served with a variety of sauces and fried potatoes (59,000K to 69,000K) that are taken, naturally, with one of more than 10 Belgian beers. Every other day there's a good selection of Belgian and Lao dishes.

Aria (Map p90; ☎ 222 589; www.arialao.org; 8 Th François Ngin; mains 35,000-208,000K; ☒ 11am-2.30pm & 5.30-11pm) If there's a better pie in town, then we haven't found it. But the best pizzas at this white-tablecloth, Italian-run place don't run cheap, so it makes sense to stop by during the weekday pizza and pasta buffet (58,000K, 11.30am to 2.30pm Monday to Friday). Otherwise, if budget isn't an obstacle, the homemade pasta and gelati, unusual imported ingredients and an expansive menu make this an intriguing dinner destination.

Vegetarian

At the time of research Vientiane only had two dedicated veggie restaurants, in addition to a **vegetarian stall** (mains 8000-12,000K; ☒ 9am-6pm) on the 3rd floor of Talat Sao Mall (p113), although meat-free options are easy to come by at other restaurants such as YuLaLa Cafe (p106), Linda Sathaporn Restaurant (p106), Ali (p106), Istanbul (p108), and chez philippe (p107).

Khouadin Vegetarian (Map p90; ☎ 215 615; buffet 17,000K; ☒ 7am-2pm) A tidy oasis in the mess behind Talat Sao, this simple restaurant serves precooked but thoroughly recommended vegetarian dishes. Great for a fast, tasty lunch.

Food For Healthy Vegetarian Restaurant (Map p86; ☎ 020-7771 0985; 178 Th Sakkarine; buffet 20,000K; ☒ 10am-2pm Mon-Fri) The friendly people here offer a generous buffet of meat-free dishes.

Located a few doors down from Dorkket Garden Guest House.

Bakeries & Cafes

Sleepy Vientiane is, somewhat paradoxically, probably the best place in Southeast Asia to get caffeinated. The coffee is generally quite good, and the baked goods, whether they're Swedish or French, are amazingly authentic, ubiquitous and inexpensive to boot.

Scandinavian Bakery (Map p90; ☎ 215 199; www.scandinavianbakerylaos.com; Nam Phu; pastries 7000-9000K; ☒ 7am-9pm; ☎) This long-running favourite on Nam Phu sells fresh bread, pies, ice cream, sandwiches (17,000K to 25,000K), real Scandinavian-style pastries and cakes.

Croissant d'Or (Map p90; ☎ 223 741; 96/1 Th Nokèokoummane; ☒ 7am-8pm; ☎) The coffee, breakfast sets (15,000K to 27,000K) and fine pastries (3000K to 12,000K) particularly the eclairs, make this petit French-run cafe a long-time favourite.

our pick **Le Banneton** (Map p90; ☎ 217 321; Th Nokèokoummane; pastries 10,000-20,000K; ☒ 7am-7pm Mon-Sat, 7am-1.30pm Sun) In addition to being the best bakery in town, Le Banneton serves equally kick-ass coffee drinks (10,000K to 15,000K) and a diverse and interesting menu of lunchtime sandwiches (33,000K to 40,000K), ranging from baguettes to paninis. If it had wi-fi and beds we'd probably never have left.

Joma Bakery Café (Map p90; ☎ 215 265; www.joma.biz; Th Setthathirath; coffee 10,000-21,000K, sandwiches 16,000-26,000K; ☒ 7am-9pm; ☎) Free wi-fi, ample air-conditioning, great coffee and a Starbucks-like ambiance draw the crowds here, but for baked goods and pastries Vientiane has much stronger choices.

Café Sinouk (Map p90; Th Samsènethai; coffee 10,000-25,000K; ☒ 8am-8pm) Operated by one of the biggest producers of Lao coffee, this modern cafe is also a great place to pick up a bag of domestic beans. It's directly adjacent to the Asian Pavillion Hotel.

Self-Catering

For the largest selection of fresh groceries and the best prices, you should stick to the markets. But if there's something 'Western' you're yearning for, or a bottle of wine, check out the following minimarkets and wine cellars.

Les Boutiques Scoubidou (Map p86; ☎ 214 073; Th Tha Deua; ☒ 8am-9pm) Brie de Meaux, sel de

10,000 FRUIT SHAKES

OK, not quite that many, but we did sample more than our fair share of Vientiane's fruit smooth-ies during the research for these pages, and reveal our favourites here. At the top of the heap is **PVO** (Map p90; ☎ 214 444; 344 Th Samsènethai; ☺ 6am-7pm Mon-Sat, 6am-2pm Sun) whose shakes (7000K to 9000K), supplemented with a splash of milk, are successfully able to balance that razor edge of sweet and sour (although if we're splitting hairs, on occasion it could use a bit more fruit). The runner up is **Noy's Fruit Heaven** (Map p90; ☎ 030-526 2369; 60/2 Th Hengboun; ☺ 7am-9pm), an exceedingly cheery place with an exclamation mark-laden menu of expertly-manipulated fruit shakes (5000K to 7000K) and fresh juices (6000K to 15,000K), although don't come if you're in a hurry. The southern side of Th Samsènethai near Nam Phu boasts several fruit shake vendors aimed at foreigners such as **House of Fruit Shake** (Map p90; ☎ 212 200; Th Samsènethai; ☺ 7am-8pm), although our research indicates that the prices are highest and the quality the most inconsistent. For something a bit more Lao, head to the area colloquially known as Centre Point, near the corner of Th Samsènethai and Th Chao Anou, where every evening from about 5pm to 9pm locals down fruit shakes and other drinks by the side of the road.

Guérande, cassoulet de porc: this tiny deli stocks just about every imagineable French necessity and/or luxury (depending on how you look at it).

PhimPhone Market (Map p90; 94/6 Th Setthathirath; ☺ 8am-9pm Mon-Sat) The mother of all PhimPhones, this store near Nam Phu has a wide selection of imported goods, including canned and frozen foods, magazines, personal hygiene and women's products such as tampons.

PhimPhone Market 2 (Map p90; ☎ 214 609; cnr Th Samsènethai & Th Chanthakoummane; ☺ 8.30am-8.30pm) This is a smaller branch of the Phimphone market and includes a small wine cellar.

Vins de France (Map p90; ☎ 217 700; 354 Th Samsènethai; ☺ 8am-8pm) Vins de France (the sign says 'baràvin') is one of the best French wine cellars in Southeast Asia. Even if you don't like wine, it's worth popping in for a look at a place so completely out of character with its surrounds. If you do like wine, the US$7 degustation might be a wise investment.

VanSom (Map p90; ☎ 212 196; 110/01 Th Samsènethai; ☺ 8am-8pm Mon-Sat) Another well stocked and equally slick wine cellar.

DRINKING

Vientiane is no longer the illicit pleasure palace it was when Paul Theroux described it, in his 1975 book *The Great Railway Bazaar*, as a place in which 'the brothels are cleaner than the hotels, marijuana is cheaper than pipe tobacco and opium easier to find than a cold glass of beer'. Nowadays, brothels are strictly prohibited, Talat Sao's marijuana stands have been removed from prominent display and cold Beerlao has definitely replaced opium as the nightly drug of choice. Most of the bars, restaurants and discos close by 11.30pm or midnight.

Bars open and close at a remarkable rate in Vientiane, though the recent trend has been leaning more heavily on the opening side. If you're looking for something cheaper and more local than the expat bars, try the strip of open-air vendors along the Mekong, although at research time virtually the entire area was under construction.

Spirit House (Map p86; ☎ 262 530; 105 Th Fa Ngoum; ☺ 7am-midnight) The friendly bartenders here will do everything within their power to get you to order a mojito, but the bar is well-stocked and the comprehensive drinks menu actually features many, many cocktails without rum or mint in them. Food is available, and it's almost certainly the classiest place in Vientiane to gaze at the Mekong.

Bor Pennyang (Map p90; ☎ 020-7787 3965; Th Fa Ngoum; ☺ 10am-midnight; ☺) The rooftop bar of this four-storey building is a classic Southeast Asian melting pot of backpackers, crusty local expats and Lao bargirls. And why not? The combination of great views over the Mekong, draught Beerlao and a reliable range of music appeal to just about everybody.

SunSet (Map p86; ☎ 251 079; ☺ 11am-11pm) At the west end of the dirt road along the riverfront, the 'Sunset Bar' is a Vientiane institution. The rustic wooden platform made of old boat timbers has been serving Beerlao at sunset for years, and was the only such bar to survive the government's first riverfront gentrification (the second phase of this was ongoing at the time of research). The friendly and enterprising proprietors also offer local food and interesting snacks.

Samlo Pub (Map p90; ☎ 222 308; Th Setthathirath; ☉ 4pm-2am) The Samlo stays open later than most, making it a favourite haunt of working girls and their fans, but it's also a good place to watch live sports. Either way, it's the perfect launching pad to a fun late night.

Kong View (Map p86; ☎ 520 522; off Th Luang Prabang; dishes 25,000-70,000K; ☉ 11am-midnight) This stylish balcony, suspended over a quiet section of the Mekong, functions equally well as a beer garden or dinner destination. The menu definitely verges to the Thai side of the river, but you could always go for the 'Assorted Lao' snacks, a platter of all the Lao dishes we love most including *khai phụn* (dried, seasoned river moss), *jạew màak len* (a dip of roasted tomatoes) and *sâi ua* (Luang Prabang style sausage).

Hare & Hound (Map p90; Th François Ngin; ☉ 11am-2pm & 5pm-midnight Mon-Fri, 5pm-midnight Sat-Sun) Even if it is the only one, the Hare & Hound is still Vientiane's most authentic British pub, down to the English owner, Union Jack paint job and a menu that features dishes (mains 25,000K to 125,000K) ranging from bangers and mash to steak and kidney pie. Import beers, draught Beerlao and a jukebox round things out.

Paris Cocktail (Map p86; ☎ 353 919; Th Tha Deua; ☉ 5pm-midnight; ☎) This cozy cocktail bar sports a short but sweet menu of classic drinks and 'Tony's Creations' (try the pineapple ginger Collins). Friendly 'tenders, a generous happy hour (5pm to 8pm) a good soundtrack and free wi-fi round out the package.

Jazzy Brick (Map p90; ☎ 020-244 9307; 47/1 Th Setthathirath; ☉ 6pm-late) Run by a Laotian who studied in Australia, the Jazzy Brick is a cut above most of its competitors on the style front. It's ostensibly a cocktail bar and the cocktails are well mixed, but the prices (drinks 40,000K to 50,000K) are difficult to justify in a town as cheap as Vientiane.

Loft (Map p90; ☎ 242 991; Th Khounboulom; ☉ 7pm-midnight) Imagine your high-school gymnasium stuffed with lounge chairs, reflecting pools and beautiful waitresses, and you begin get an idea of Loft. We're not entirely convinced that Vientiane needed an upscale cocktail lounge,

but it should come as a surprise to no one that it would be as quirky as this.

GQ Bar & Massage (Map p90; ☎ 020-247 3389; Th Chao Anou; ☉ 8pm-1am) Central Vientiane's only gay bar also offers massage (Lao/oil per hr 40,000/50,000K), giving you an idea of what goes on here…

ENTERTAINMENT

Like everything else, Vientiane's entertainment scene is picking up as money and politics allows, though the range remains fairly limited. You could make your way through all of Vientiane's live music venues and nightclubs in a couple of big nights out, though this is better than the couple of hours it would have taken a few years ago. By law, entertainment venues must close by 11.30pm, though most push it to about midnight.

Live Music & Nightclubs

DJs have only recently caught on in Vientiane, and even places that look like discos tend to be more dance hall, with live bands interdispersed by the occasional recorded track. Music ranges from electrified Lao folk (for *lám wóng,* circular dancing) to quasi-Western pop, but is usually dominated by the latest Thai hits. There is generally no charge to enter most nightclubs, but the Beerlao is more expensive than elsewhere.

Conveniently, three of the better clubs are within walking distance of each other on the way to the airport. **D'Tech** (Map p86; ☎ 213 570; Th Samsènethai; ☉ 8pm-1am), at the Novotel, is popular with Vientiane's beautiful people, and is a fun place to dance to Thai pop and top 40 hits. A block away, and sharing virtually the same building are **Future** (Map p86; Th Luang Prabang; ☉ 8pm-midnight) and **Highwayman** (Map p86; Th Luang Prabang; ☉ 8pm-midnight; cover 3000K), both of whom blast a mix of recorded music to a young Lao crowd. Just up the road, **Penguin** (Map p86; ☎ 020-5655 5552; Th Luang Prabang; ☉ 8pm-midnight) offers more traditional Lao-style entertainment, with live music, sofa seating, and if you're as lucky as we were, slow dancing.

Other locales are:

Lunar 36 (Map p86; ☎ 244 288; www.donchanpalace laopdr.com; 3rd fl, Don Chan Palace, off Th Fa Ngoum; ☉ 8pm-3am; cover 30,000K) At the time of research this was Vientiane's heaviest disco – most likely because it's the only one open late. Nonetheless the mix of Lao and foreign music is as eclectic as the clientele, and it's really the only place buzzing on weeknights. The cover charge gets you a large Beerlao.

Anou Cabaret (Map p90; ☎ 213 630; cnr Th Hengboun & Th Chao Anou; ☯ 8pm-midnight) On the ground floor of the Anou Paradise Hotel, the cabaret has been swinging along for years. It's a funny place, with old crooners and a palpable 1960s feel.

Wind West (Map p90; ☎ 020-200 0777; Th Luang Prabang; ☯ 5pm-1am) A Western-US-style bar and restaurant, Wind West (yes, Wind, that's not a typo) has live Lao and Western rock music most nights – the music usually starts about 10pm. Depending on the night it can be heaving, or completely dead.

Peurk-may (Map p86; ☎ 315 536; Th Tha Deua; ☯ 6pm-midnight) The name means 'tree bark', a design theme that dominates this self-designated 'Acoustic Guitar Bar'. Thai folk and pop dominates, and even if you're not a fan of the genre, the conversation-level volume and the enticing Thai/Lao menu (mains 16,000K to 65,000K) make Peurk-may a good low-key destination.

Tawan Daeng (Map p90; Th Pangkham; ☯ 5pm-midnight) This Bangkok-style live-music hall, essentialy the lounge of the Lane Xang Hotel, plays host to a thick crowd of urban Lao (if such a term can be used) clientele who come to rock out to Thai, Western and Lao music. Accompany your tunes with a bottle of 100 Pipers and some Lao-style drinking snacks (10,000K to 20,000K).

Marina (Map p86; ☎ 216 978; Th Luang Prabang; ☯ 8pm-1am) This popular club, being renovated at the time of research, also offers bowling until 11.30pm.

Traditional Music & Dancing

In addition to the below, six types of traditional Lao dance can be seen nightly from 7.30pm to 11pm in the Lane Xang Hotel (p102). The **Lao National Culture Hall** (Map p90; Th Samsènethai) also hosts similar performances on occasions, but with no publicly available schedule of events you'll need to keep a close eye on the *Vientiane Times* for an announcement.

Lao National Opera Theatre (Map p90; ☎ 260 300; Th Khounboulom; admission 70,000K; show ☯ 7-8.30pm Tue, Thu & Sat) This state-sponsored performance venue features a smorgasbord of Lao entertainment ranging from self-proclaimed 'Lao oldies' to Lao boxing and traditional performances of *Pha Lak Pha Lam*, the Lao version of the Indian epic the Ramayana.

AN IDIOT'S GUIDE TO TUK-TUKS & JUMBOS

Three different types of tuk-tuk/jumbo operate in Vientiane and if you know the difference it can save you money and a lot of argument.

Tourist tuk-tuks

You'll find these loitering in queues outside popular tourist spots, such as at Nam Phu. In theory, chartering a tuk-tuk should be no more than 10,000K for distances of 1km or less, but these guys will usually show you a laminated card with a list of fares at least double what a Lao person would pay. Bargaining is essential but probably won't get you far because there is an agreement within the queue that tuk-tuks won't leave without a minimum fare, which while lower than the outrageous printed fare is still significantly more than locals would pay.

Wandering tuk-tuks

These tuk-tuks will pick you up anywhere and negotiate a fare to anywhere – prices are lower than tourist tuk-tuks and rise as you head further away from main roads. If you're going somewhere within the centre of town, you can probably get away with handing the driver 5000K and telling him where you want to go. It's best not to hail a wandering tuk-tuk near a queue of tourist tuk-tuks as he'll likely be harassed by drivers in the queue.

Fixed route share jumbos

The cheapest tuk-tuks are more like buses, starting at tuk-tuk stations and operating along set routes for fixed fares. The biggest station is near Talat Sao and one very useful route runs to the Friendship Bridge (5000K, compared with about 200B for a charter). Just turn up and tell them where you want to go.

Phatoke Laoderm (Map p90; ☎ 263 981; www .phatokelaoderm.com; Senglao Hotel, 47/1 Th Chao Anou; admission US$12; show ⊗ 7-9.30pm Mon-Sat) This hotel-bound dinner theatre is popular with tour groups and combines traditional Lao performance and dishes from Luang Prabang.

Cinema

Lao cinemas died out in the video shop tidal wave of the 1990s.

Centre Culturel et de Coopération Linguistique (Map p90; ☎ 215 764; www.centredelangue.org; Th Lan Xang; admission 10,000K; screenings 6.30pm Tue & Thu, 5.30pm Sat) The French Centre screens French films (usually subtitled in English) on a regular basis.

Circus

National Circus (Hong Kanyasin; Map p86; Th Thong Khan Kham) The old 'Russian Circus' established in the 1980s is now known as Hong Kanyasin. It performs from time to time in the National Circus venue, in the north of town. Check for dates in the *Vientiane Times*.

SHOPPING

Just about anything made in Laos is available for purchase in Vientiane, including hill-tribe crafts, jewellery, traditional textiles and carvings. The main shopping areas in town are Talat Sao (Morning Market), the eastern end of Th Samsènethai (near the Asian Pavilion Hotel), Th Pangkham and along Th Nokèokoummane.

Handicrafts, Antiques & Art

Several shops along Th Samsènethai, Th Pangkham and Th Setthathirath sell Lao and Thai tribal and hill-tribe crafts. The Lao goods are increasingly complemented by products from Vietnam and Thailand, such as lacquer work and Buddha images. Many of the places listed in the Textiles and Clothing section also carry handicrafts and antiques.

Carterie du Laos (Map p90; ☎ 241 401; 118/2 Th Setthathirath; ⊗ 9am-5pm) This shop has a wide range of postcards, cards, posters and books, and a few small souvenirs.

Handicraft Products of Ethnic Groups (Map p90; Th Khu Vieng; ⊗ 8am-4pm) Opposite Talat Sao, this market-style place sells handicrafts from around Laos. The quality is variable, but at the least this is a good place to get an idea what is out there and how much it costs.

Satri Lao (Map p90; ☎ 244 384; Th Setthathirath; ⊗ 9am-8pm Mon-Sat, 10am-7pm Sun) With a name like Satri Lao (Lao Woman), it shouldn't come as a surprise that this three-storey shop has a predominately female-oriented selection of local and imported clothes and handicrafts, from miniskirts and bikinis made from Hmong weavings to herbal soaps.

treasures of asia (Map p90; ☎ 222 236; 86/7 Th Setthathirath; ⊗ noon-7pm Mon-Fri) This tiny gallery holds the original works of established Lao artists, many of whom are featured in the book *Lao Contemporary Art*, also available here.

T'Shop Lai Gallery (Map p90; ☎ 223 178; www.art isanslao.com; off Th In Paeng; ⊗ 8am-8pm Mon-Sat, 10am-6pm Sun) This beautiful shop is well worth a look if you're interested in modern and traditional art in a range of media, furniture and interesting handicrafts, as well as fragrant handmade soaps and oils. The owner is committed to promoting fair-trade products.

Textiles & Clothing

Downtown Vientiane is littered with stores selling textiles. Th Nokèokoummane is the epicentre; Talat Sao is also a good place to buy fabrics. You'll find antiques as well as modern fabrics, plus utilitarian items such as shoulder bags (some artfully constructed around squares of antique fabric), cushions and pillows.

To see Lao weaving in action, seek out the weaving district of Ban Nong Buathong, northeast of the town centre in Muang Chanthabuli. About 20 families (many originally from Sam Neua in Hua Phan Province) live and work here, including a couple of households that sell textiles directly to the public; the **Phaeng Mai Gallery** (off Map p86; ☎ 243 121; www.phaengmaigallery.com; 110 Th Nong Buathong; ⊗ 8am-5pm Mon-Sat), in a white, two-storey house, is among the best, and features an army of weavers out the back plus a free museum of antique textiles. It's out past the National Circus – most tuk-tuk drivers know it and will charge about 30,000K one way.

Carol Cassidy Lao Textiles (Map p90; ☎ 212 123; www.laotextiles.com; 84-86 Th Nokèokoummane; ⊗ 8am-noon & 2-5pm Mon-Fri, 8am-noon Sat, or by appointment) Lao Textiles sells high-end contemporary, original-design fabrics inspired by older Lao weaving patterns, motifs and techniques. The American designer, Carol Cassidy, employs Lao weavers who work out the back of the attractive old French-Lao house. It is internationally known, with prices to match.

Couleur d'Asie (Map p90; ☎ 223 008; www.couleur dasie.net; 201 Th François Ngin; ✆ 9am-5pm Mon-Sat) The owner, a French-Vietnamese dress designer with Paris fashion-school experience, manages to fuse Lao and Western styles into some attractive designs at reasonable prices.

Kanchana Boutique (Map p90; ☎ 213 467; 102 Th Chanthakoummane; ✆ 8am-9pm Mon-Sat) This shop carries what is possibly the most upscale selection of Lao silk in town (the most expensive designs, some of which sell for several thousand US dollars, are kept in an adjacent room), and the friendly owners can arrange a visit to, or even lessons in weaving and dyeing, at their Lao Textile Museum (p96).

KPP Handicraft Promotion Enterprise of Sekong Province (Map p90; ☎ 241 421; cnr Th Setthathirath & Th Chao Anou; ✆ 9am-8pm) This modest-looking place sells fair-trade textiles from the Bolaven Plateau province of Sekong.

Nikone (Map p86; ☎ 212 191; nikone@laotel.com; ✆ 8am-5pm Mon-Sat) Located out near the National Circus, this is another good place to see weaving and dyeing in action.

True Colour (Map p90; ☎ 214 410; Th Setthathirath; ✆ 9am-8pm Mon-Sat) This store sells textiles and clothes made in the Houey Hong Vocational Training Center for Women (p99).

Other stores on Th Nokèokoummane that are worth a look include **Khampan Lao Handicraft** (Map p90; ☎ 222 000; ✆ 8am-9pm), with textiles from the Sam Neua area at very reasonable prices; upmarket **Mixay Boutique** (Map p90; ☎ 216 592; ✆ 9am-8pm), which deals in locally-made silks; and **Camacrafts** (Mulberries; Map p90; ☎ 241 217; www.mulberries.org; ✆ 10am-6pm Mon-Sat), which stocks silk clothes and weavings from Xieng Khuang Province, plus some bed and cushion covers in striking Hmong-inspired designs.

Markets

Talat Sao (Map p90; Th Lan Xang; ✆ 7am-4pm) Vientiane's most famous market is a sprawling collection of stalls offering fabrics, ready-made clothes, jewellery, cutlery, toiletries, bedding, hardware and watches, as well as electronic goods and just about anything else imaginable. Unfortunately, at the time of research the exterior of the market was being renovated and the original 1960s-era facade was encased in rebar and concrete. We can only assume that the results will resemble the adjacent Talat Sao Mall, something of a Lao version of Bangkok's MBK, with stalls selling mobile phones and clothes, and on the 3rd floor, several shops selling Lao music CDs (see p55 for some recommended artists).

Talat Khua Din (Map p90; Th Khu Vieng; ✆ 5am-1pm) East of Talat Sao and beyond the bus terminal, this rather muddy market offers fresh produce and meats, as well as flowers, tobacco and other assorted goods.

Talat Thong Khan Kham (Map p86; cnr Th Khan Kham & Th Dong Miang; ✆ 5am-3pm) This market north of the centre in Ban Khan Kham is open all day, but is best in the morning. It's one of the biggest in Vientiane and has virtually everything, from food to tools. Nearby are basket and pottery vendors.

GETTING THERE & AWAY
Air
Departures from Vientiane's Wattay International Airport are perfectly straightforward. The Domestic Terminal is in the older, white building east of the more impressive International Terminal. There is an (often unmanned) information counter in the arrivals hall, and food can be found upstairs in the International Terminal.

See p332 for details on air transport to Laos, p338 for information on flights within Laos.

AIRLINE OFFICES
See also Travel Agencies, p89.
Air Asia (Map p86; ☎ 513 029; www.airasia.com; Wattay Airport International Terminal; ✆ 8am-5pm) Operates thrice-weekly flights between Vientiane and Kuala Lumpur (US$152).
China Eastern Airlines (Map p86; ☎ 212 300; www .flychinaeastern.com; Th Luang Prabang; ✆ 8.30-11.30am & 1.30-4.30pm Mon-Sat, to 11.30 Sun) Same building as Thai Airways, China Eastern conducts flights between Vientiane and Kunming (US$190).
Lao Airlines (www.laoairlines.com) Airport Office (Map p86; ☎ 512 028; ✆ 4am-8pm); Head Office (Map p90; ☎ 212 051-4; 2 Th Pangkham; ✆ 8am-noon & 1-4pm Mon-Sat, to noon Sun) Conducts domestic flights between Vientiane and Huay Xai (US$106), Luang Prabang (US$80, 40 minutes, two or three daily), Luang Namtha (US$106, three times weekly), Pakse (US$111) and Phonsavan (US$80, five times weekly), Savannakhet (US$106, three times weekly), Udomxai (US$106, three times weekly), and international flights between Vientiane and Bangkok (US$115, twice daily), Chiang Mai (US$155), Hanoi (US$125, twice daily), Kunming (US$155, once daily), Phnom Penh (US$165, once daily) and Siem Reap (US$165, four times weekly).
Lao Capricorn Air (Map p86; ☎ 513 009; www .laocapricornair.net; ✆ 7am-7pm; Wattay Airport Domestic Terminal) Operates domestic flights between

Vientiane and Sainyabuli (US$82, twice weekly), Phongsali (US$119, twice weekly) and Sam Neua (US$93, three times weekly).

Thai Airways International (Map p86; ☎ 222 527; www.thaiairways.com; Th Luang Prabang; ⊗ 8.30am-

5pm Mon-Fri, to noon Sat) Operates twice-daily flights between Vientiane and Bangkok (7070B).

Vietnam Airlines (Map p90; ☎ 217 562; www.vietnam airlines.com; 1st fl, Lao Plaza Hotel, Th Samsènethai; ⊗ 8am-noon & 1.30-4.30pm Mon-Fri, to noon Sat) From

---

LEAVING VIENTIANE BY BUS

All services depart daily except where noted, though times do change so use this as a guide only. Note that in Laos roads are poor and buses break down, so it might take longer than advertised. In addition to domestic departures, there are now several buses to various Thai cities from the Talat Sao bus station. For buses to China (terminating in Kunming), contact the **Tong Li Bus Company** (☎ 242 657) at the Northern Bus Station. For Vietnam, buses leave the Southern Bus Station daily at 7pm for Hanoi (230,000K, 24 hours) via Vinh (160,000K, 16 hours), Danang (230,000K) via Hue (180,000K, 19 hours), and on Mondays, Thursdays and Sundays at 7pm, for Ho Chi Minh City (500,000K, up to 48 hours); contact **S.P.T.** (☎ 720 175) for details.

Destination	Fare (kip)	Distance (km)	Duration (hr)	Departures
Northern Bus Station				
Huay Xai	180,000	869	24	5.30pm (fan)
	200,000		22-30	5.30pm (air-con)
Luang Namtha	140,000	676	21-24	8.30am (fan)
	150,000		18-20	5pm (air-con)
Luang Prabang	95,000	384	10-11	6.30am, 7.30am, 9am, 11am, 1.30pm, 4pm, 6pm, 7.30pm (air-con)
	115,000		9-12	8am, 9am, 8pm (VIP)
Phongsali	160,000	811	25-28	6.45am (fan)
Phonsavan	95,000	374	10-11	6.30am, 8am, 9.30am, 11am, 4pm, 6.40pm (air-con)
	115,000		9-10	8pm (VIP)
Sainyabuli	90,000	485	14-16	4pm (fan)
	110,000		12	6pm (air-con)
Sam Neua	150,000	612	22-24	7am, 9.30am, noon (fan)
	160,000		20-22	2pm (air-con)
Udomxai	110,000	578	16-19	6.45am, 1.45pm (fan)
	130,000		15-17	6.30pm (air-con)
	155,000		5-17	4pm (VIP)
Southern Bus Station				
Attapeu	130,000	812	22-24	9.30am, 5pm (fan)
	190,000		14-16	8.30pm (VIP)
Don Khong	130,000	788	16-19	10.30am (fan)
Lak Sao	50,000	334	6-8	5am, 6am, 7am (fan)

Vientiane conducts flights to and from Hanoi (US$145), Ho Chi Minh City (US$190) and Phnom Penh (US$180).

Boat

Passenger boat services between Vientiane and Luang Prabang have become almost extinct as most people now take the bus, which is both faster and cheaper.

A regular slow boat makes the trip from Vientiane to Pak Lai, 115km away. Boats leave Monday, Wednesday and Saturday at 8am (100,000K, about eight hours). Six-passenger

Destination	Fare (kip)	Distance (km)	Duration (hr)	Departures
Paksan	25,000 30,000-40,000	143	3-4 3-4	7am-3pm (tuk-tuk) Take any bus going south
Pakse	100,000	677	16-18	Every 30 mins from 12.30pm to 4pm (fan)
	130,000		11-12	5.15am, 7.15am, 6pm, 6.30pm, 7pm, 7.30pm, 8pm (air-con)
	150,000		8-10	7.15am, 8.30pm, 9pm (VIP)
Salavan	120,000	774	15-20	4.30pm, 7.30pm (fan)
	150,000		16	7.30pm (air-con)
	180,000		13	8pm (VIP)
Savannakhet	65,000	457	8-11	Every 30 mins from 5.30am (fan), or any bus to Pakse
	95,000		8-10	8.30pm (VIP)
Tha Khaek	50,000	332	6	4am, 5am, 6am (fan), or any bus to Savannakhet or Pakse
	75,000		5	1pm (VIP)
Nong Khiang	130,000	818	16-20	11am (fan)
Talat Sao Bus Station				
Khon Kaen	52,000		4	8.15am, 2.45pm (air-con)
Nakhon Ratchasima	82,000		7	7.30am (air-con)
Nong Khai	17,000		1.5	7.30am, 9.30am, 12.40pm, 2.30pm, 3.30pm, 6pm (air-con)
Udon Thani	24,000		2.5	8am, 10.30am, 11.30am, 2pm, 4pm, 6pm (air-con)
Vang Vieng	30,000		3-4	7am, 9.30am, 1pm, 3pm (fan)

héua wái (speedboats) also do the same route when there's enough passengers, and if you have the cash will go all the way to Luang Prabang – a full day's trip for at least US$300 for the boat. The boats depart from Tha Heua Kao Liaw (Kao Liaw Boat Landing), 7.7km west of the Novotel (3.5km west of the fork in the road where Rte 13 heads north) in Ban Kao Liaw; a sign says 'Kaolieu Harbour'. It's best to go the day before you plan to travel.

Bus

Our table (p114) gives timetable information. Buses use three different stations in Vientiane, all with some English-speaking staff, and food and drink stands. The **Northern Bus Station** (Map p86; ☎ 261 905; Th T2), about 2km northwest of the centre, serves all points north of Vang Vieng, including China. Destinations and the latest ticket prices are listed in English.

The **Southern Bus Station** (Map p119; ☎ 740 521; Rte 13 South), commonly known as Dong Dok Bus Station or just *khíw lot lák káo* (Km 9 Bus Station), is 9km out of town and serves everywhere south. Buses to Vietnam depart from here.

The final departure point is the **Talat Sao bus station** (Map p90; ☎ 216 507), from where desperately slow local buses run to destinations within Vientiane Province, including Vang Vieng, and some more distant destinations, though for the latter you're better going to the Northern or Southern stations. The Thai-Lao International Bus also uses this station for its trips to Khon Kaen, Nakhon Ratchasima, Nong Khai and Udon Thani; see p114 for details.

Train

In March 2009 tracks were extended from Nong Khai's train station across the Thai-Lao Friendship Bridge to Dongphasy in Laos, effectively forming Laos's first railway line. At research time the government announced plans to extend the tracks an additional 9km, part of a greater plan that will see the commencement of a national railway grid sometime in the next five years, but for now Laos boasts a grand total of 3.5km of rolling track. For the details on train travel between Thailand and Laos see p117.

GETTING AROUND

Central Vientiane is entirely accessible on foot. For exploring neighbouring districts, however, you'll need transport.

To/From the Airport

Wattay International Airport is about 4km northwest of the city centre, which makes the US$6 flat fare for a taxi (US$8 for a minivan) more than a little steep. The fare is set by the government and the US$6 takes you anywhere in Vientiane (to the Thai-Lao Friendship Bridge is US$10). Only official taxis can pick up at the airport, and even the drivers think the fare is too high because it costs them business.

If you're on a budget and don't have a lot of luggage, simply walk 500m to the airport gate and cross Th Luang Prabang and hail a shared jumbo (5000K per person), or even a bus (4000K). Prices on shared transport will rise if you're going further than the centre.

From Talat Sao bus station, tuk-tuk drivers charge 200B and jumbo drivers 80B to 120B. The number 30 Tha Pa and the number 49 Nong Taeng buses from Talat Sao bus station make the journey for 4000K.

Bicycle

Cycling is a cheap, easy and recommended way of getting around mostly flat Vientiane. Loads of guesthouses and several shops hire out bikes for about 10,000K per day; you won't need a map to find them.

Bus

There is a city bus system, but it's oriented more towards the distant suburbs than the central Chanthabuli district. Most buses leave from Talat Sao bus station; the number 14 Tha Deua bus to the Thai-Lao Friendship Bridge runs from 6am to 5.30pm and costs 5000K.

Car & Motorcycle

Small motorcycles are a popular means of getting around Vientiane and can be hired throughout the centre of town. In particular, there are a couple places on the west side of Th Nokèokoummane near the **Douang Deuane Hotel** (Map p90; Th Nokèokoummane). The place directly in front of the hotel is the cheapest and rents 110cc bikes for 70,000K per day, but 80,000K to 85,000K per day was closer to the average going rate in Vientiane at research time.

Other vehicle rental places:

Boualian (Map p90; ☎ 219 649; Th Samsènethai; per day 70,000-90,000K) Next to to the New Lao Paris Hotel, this motorcycle rental place also provides other tourist services.

Europcar (Asia Vehicle Rental; Map p90; ☎ /fax 223 867; www.avr.laopdr.com; 354-356 Th Samsènethai; 🕐 8am-5.30pm Mon-Fri, 8.30am-1pm Sat & Sun) Undoubtedly the most reliable place to hire cars, with or without drivers. Offers 4WDs, vans, sedans, as well as motorcycles. Recommended.

jules classic rental (Map p90; ☎ 020-7760 0813; www.bike-rental-laos.com; Th Setthathirath; per day US$25-50; 🕐 7am-9pm) Jules specialises in 'bikes with personality', ranging from dirt bikes such as a 250cc Yamaha WR-F to road warriors such as the Kawasaki W650. He can also provide comprehensive insurance, trip consultation, one-way service and a full range of equipment and clothing.

LaoWheels (☎ 021-223 663, 020-5550 4604; lao wheels@yahoo.co.uk) You could always let Vientiane-based Christophe Kittirath do the driving for you; he speaks fluent French, good English, is a good driver and knows Laos like the back of his van. Send him an email or call about rates.

PVO (Map p90; ☎ 020-5555 9922; Th Fa Ngoum; per day 80,000-100,000K) In addition to the standard Japanese scooters, this Vietnamese restaurant also hires 250cc bikes, usually Honda Bajas, for 250,000K a day, less for longer hire. Recommended.

Jumbo & Tuk-Tuk

Drivers of jumbos and tuk-tuks will take passengers on journeys as short as 500m or as far as 20km. Understanding the various types of tuk-tuk is important (see the boxed text, p111) if you don't want to be overcharged. Tourist tuk-tuks are the most expensive; share jumbos that run regular routes around town (eg Th Luang Prabang to Th Setthathirath or Th Lan Xang to That Luang) are much cheaper – usually about 5000K per person.

Taxi

Car taxis of varying shapes, sizes and vintages can often be found stationed in front of the larger hotels or at the airport. Bargaining is the rule for all, the exception being **Meter Taxi Service** (☎ 454 168). Drivers from this company often wait for fares on Th Pangkham, roughly across from the Day Inn Hotel (p103).

CROSSING THE THAI BORDER AT NONG KHAI & VIENTIANE

The Thai-Lao Friendship Bridge (Saphan Mittaphap Thai-Lao) spans the Mekong River between Nong Khai in Thailand and Tha Na Leng in Laos, approximately 20km from Vientiane. Tuk-tuks are available from Nong Khai's train station (20B) and bus station (50B) to the Thai border post at the bridge. You can also hop on the Thai-Lao International Bus from Nong Khai bus station (55B, 1½ hours) or Udon Thani bus station (80B, two hours), both of which terminate at Vientiane's Talat Sao bus station. If flying into Udon Thani, a tuk-tuk from the airport to the city's bus station should cost about 100B.

Regardless of where you're coming from, once in Nong Khai don't be tempted to use a tuk-tuk driver to get your Lao visa, no matter what they tell you – it will take far longer than doing it yourself, and you'll have to pay for the 'service'. Insist they take you straight to the bridge.

After passing the **Thai border post** (☎ in Thailand 0 4240 2244; 🕐 6am-10pm), you'll board a bus (15B, five minutes) that takes you over the bridge to the **Lao border post** (🕐 6am-10pm). There, a 30-day visa on arrival is available for US$20 to US$42, depending on your nationality (for more details on Lao visas see p328). If you don't have a photo you'll be charged an extra US$2, and be aware that an additional US$1 'overtime fee' is charged from 6am to 8am and 6pm to 10pm on weekdays, as well as on weekends and holidays. The last obstacle is a US$1/40B 'entry fee', and all that remains is to choose between minivan (100B), tuk-tuk (250B) or taxi (300B) for the remaining 19km to Vientiane.

It's also possible to cross the brige by train, as tracks have been extended from Nong Khai's train station 3.5km into Laos, terminating at Dongphasy Station, about 23km from central Vientiane. From Nong Khai there are two daily departures (9.30am and 4pm, fan/air-con 20/50B, 15 minutes) and border formalities are taken care of at the respective train stations.

From Vientiane, the easiest and cheapest way to the bridge is to cross on the Thai-Lao International Bus, which conducts daily departures for the Thai cities of Khon Kaen, Nakhon Ratchasima, Nong Khai and Udon Thani (see the boxed text, p114, for details). Alternative means of transport between Vientiane and the bridge include taxi (300B), tuk-tuk (shared/charter 5000K/200B), jumbo (200B to 300B) or the number 14 Tha Duea bus from Talat Sao bus station (5000K) between 6am and 5.30pm.

The **Talat Sao taxi stand** (Map p90; 7am-6pm) at the corner of Th Lan Xang and Th Khu Vieng, across from Talat Sao, is where you'll find taxis to the Friendship Bridge (300B).

A car and driver costs about US$30 to US$40 per day as long as the vehicle doesn't leave town. If you want to go further afield, eg to Ang Nam Ngum or Vang Vieng, expect to pay more.

AROUND VIENTIANE

There are several places worth seeing within an easy trip of Vientiane. Some make good day trips while others could detain you much longer.

PHU KHAO KHUAY NPA

ສວນອຸດທິຍານແຫ່ງຊາດພູເຂົາຄວາຍ

Covering more than 2000 sq km of mountains and rivers to the east of Vientiane, the underrated **Phu Khao Khuay NPA** (www.trekkingcentrallaos.com) is the most easily accessed protected area in Laos. Treks ranging in duration from a couple of hours to three days have been developed in close consultation with two villages on the edge of the NPA, Ban Na and Ban Hat Khai.

Phu Khao Khuay (pronounced poo cow kwai) means 'Buffalo Horn Mountain', a name derived from local legend, and is home to three major rivers that flow off a sandstone mountain range and into the Ang Nam Leuk Reservoir. It boasts an extraordinary array of endangered wildlife, including wild elephant, gibbon, Asiatic black bear, clouded leopard, Siamese fireback pheasant and green peafowl. About 88% of the NPA is forested, though only 32% has been classified as dense, mature forest. Depending on elevation, visitors may encounter dry evergreen dipterocarp (a Southeast Asian tree with two-winged fruit), mixed deciduous forest, conifer forest or grassy uplands. Several impressive waterfalls are accessible as day trips from Vientiane.

But while all of this is undoubtedly impressive – even more so if you actually get to see the endangered wildlife – by far the greatest attraction at Phu Khao Khuay is its herd of wild elephants (see the boxed text, p120).

Detailed information on trekking, accommodation and getting to and from Phu Khao Khuay can be found at the Tourist Information Centre (p89) in Vientiane. Trekking in Phu Khao Khuay costs 140,000K

per person per day, and you must also purchase a permit to enter the NPA (40,000K) and contribute to the village fund (50,000K). If trekking from Ban Hat Khai you'll also have to pay for boat transportation (70,000K per boat, up to five passengers).

Ban Na
ບ້ານນາ

The lowland farming village of Ban Na, 82km northeast of Vientiane, is home to about 600 people. The village is typical Lao, with women weaving baskets from bamboo (skills they will happily impart for a small fee) and men tending the fields. But it's the local herd of elephants that is most interesting to visitors (see the boxed text, p120).

Village guides lead one-, two- and three-day treks from Ban Na, including through elephant territory to Keng Khani (three to four hours one way), through deep forest to the waterfall of **Tat Fa** (four to five hours) and to the elephant observation tower at **Pung Xay** (4km). The trek to this tower is not the most spectacular in Laos, but if you're lucky your overnight stay will be. The tower overlooks the elephants' favourite salt lick, which they visit at dusk or later. Trekkers sleep in the tower (100,000K per person) on the floor, with guides who cook a local dinner. We've met people who have had a fantastic time, seen 10 elephants and raved about this larger-than-life taste of the Laos wilderness. Others, however, have seen nothing and come away disappointed. So it's important to remember these pachyderms are wild and there's only about a 50/50 chance (perhaps less) they'll turn up. If you go, take a torch and a flash if you want photos, and/or go when the moon is full. It's also worth mentioning that the tower can only sleep 12 people, and gets quite busy during November to March, the months you're most likely to see elephants.

En route to Ban Na it's worth stopping briefly at **Wat Pha Baht Phonsan**, which sits on a rocky outcrop at Tha Pha Baht, beside Rte 13 about 2km south of Ban Na. The wat is revered for its large *pha bàat* (Buddha footprint) shrine, monastery and substantial reclining Buddha figure. You'll know it by the large and well-ornamented 1933-vintage stupa.

Ban Hat Khai
ບ້ານຫາດໄຂ່

Along with Ban Na, the village of Ban Hat Khai is a launch point for treks into Phu Khao

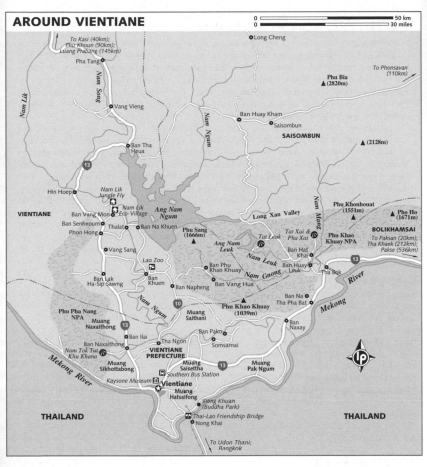

AROUND VIENTIANE

Khuay NPA. Destinations include the huge cliff, views and beautiful landscape of **Pha Luang** (three to four hours one way), and the forested areas around **Huay Khi Ling** (two to three hours one way). A trek taking in both these areas takes two or three days, depending on the season; you sleep in the forest. Boats can be arranged here to take you upriver to **Pha Xai**.

Waterfalls

Phu Khao Khuay's three most impressive waterfalls are accessed from the road running north from Rte 13, just before Ban Tha Bok. **Tat Xai** cascades down seven steps, and 800m downstream **Pha Xai** plunges over a 40m-high cataract. There's a pool that's good for swim-ming, though it can get dangerous during the wet season.

Tat Leuk is much smaller but makes a beautiful place to camp for the night. You can swim above the falls if the water isn't flowing too fast, and the Visitor Centre has some information about the area, including a detailed guide to the 1.5km-long **Huay Bon Nature Trail**. The guy who looks after the Visitor Centre can arrange local treks for about 80,000K to 150,000K, and rents quality four-person tents for 40,000K, plus hammocks, mat-tresses, mosquito nets and sleeping bags for 10,000K each. There's a very basic restaurant, best supplemented with food you bring from outside, and small library of wildlife books and a pair of binoculars.

THE SWEET-TOOTHED ELEPHANTS OF BAN NA

The farmers of Ban Na grow rice and vegetables, but a few years ago they began planting sugar cane after being encouraged by a local sugar company. What they didn't count on was the collective sweet tooth of the elephants in the nearby mountains. It wasn't long before these jumbos had sniffed out the delights in the field below and were happily eating the sugarcane, pineapples and bananas planted around Ban Na. Not surprisingly, the farmers weren't happy. They decided the only way to get rid of the elephants was to rip up the sugarcane and go back to planting boring (and less lucrative) vegetables.

It was hoped the 30-odd elephants would take the hint and return to the mountains, but they didn't. Instead, they have made the lowland forests, bamboo belt and fields around Ban Na their home. The destruction they cause is significant, affecting both the environment and finances of Ban Na. The only way the villagers can continue to live with the elephants (ie not shoot them) is by making them pay their way. The result is elephant ecotourism. This was working well, and the number of elephants had actually grown to about 40, until in 2009 when the bodies of six murdered elephants were found. The elephants were stripped of their tusks and hind legs, suggesting that they were killed by poachers rather than vengeful villagers. The locals we talked to seemed genuinely upset about the killings, although plans to build a sugar refinery nearby – with the resulting demand for locally produced sugarcane – could yet again change the village's opinion of the creatures.

Sleeping & Eating

Homestay-style accommodation is also available in both Ban Na and Ban Hat Khai for 30,000K per person, per night, with an additional 25,000K per person for food. The prices do not include transport from Vientiane and are not negotiable. All monies go to the village and NPA. To contact Ban Na directly, call Lao-speaking **Mr Bounthanom** (☎ 020-220 8286); at Ban Hatkhai contact **Mr Khammuan** (☎ 020-224 0343). Or, get anyone else who speaks Lao to call for you.

If you need a bed en route there are two decent guesthouses in Tha Bok.

Getting There & Away

Buses from Vientiane's Southern Bus Station leave regularly for Ban Tha Bok and Paksan. For Wat Pha Baht Phonsan and Ban Na get off at Tha Pha Bat near the Km 81 stone; the shrine is right on Rte 13 and Ban Na is about 2km north – follow the signs.

For Ban Hat Khai, keep on the bus until a turn-off left (north) at Km 92, just before Ban Tha Bok. If you have your own transport, continue 8km along the smooth laterite road until you cross the new bridge. Turn right at the Y-intersection and it's 1km to Ban Hat Khai and another 9km to Tat Xai; turn left, continue another 6km and Tat Leuk is accessible via a rough 4km road. Alternatively, villagers in Ban Hat Khai can arrange motorcyle pick up from Ban Tha Bok for 15,000K one way if you call ahead.

Note that as you come from Vientiane there are three signed entrances to Phu Khao Khuay, the second leads to Ban Na and the third to Ban Hat Khai and the waterfalls.

VIENTIANE TO VANG VIENG

On the way to Vang Vieng are a few interesting stopover possibilities. The **Nam Tok Tat Khu Khana** waterfall (also called Hin Khana) is easy to reach via a 10km dirt road, leading west from Rte 13 near the village of Ban Naxaithong, near Km 17.

At **Vang Sang**, 65km north of Vientiane via Rte 13, a cluster of 10 high-relief Buddha sculptures on cliffs is thought to date from the 16th century. Two of the Buddhas are more than 3m tall. The name means 'Elephant Palace', a reference to an elephant graveyard once found nearby. To reach Vang Sang, follow the sign to the Vang Xang Resort, near the Km 62 marker, then take the laterite road around a small lake, up the hill and right until you reach the shaded forest at the end.

A bit further north is the prosperous town of Phon Hong, the turn-off for Thalat and **Ang Nam Ngum**, a vast artificial lake created when the Nam Ngum was dammed in 1971. The highest peaks of the former river valley became forested islands after the valley was inundated, and following the 1975 PL conquest of Vientiane, an estimated 3000 prostitutes, petty

(Continued on page 129)

LAND OF A MILLION ELEPHANTS

Elephants were once so important to Laos that they formed the country's name. Lan Xang means Land of a Million Elephants, and is a vivid illustration of the animal's ubiquity and importance in this former kingdom. Although the number of elephants has since waned, in today's Laos it's still possible to cross paths with these immense creatures, and your encounter might be via a Lao Loum elephant handler in the north, in one of Laos's protected areas, or in the form of a depiction on one of the country's stunning religious monuments.

JANE SWEENEY

THE PEOPLE OF LAOS

For a country with relatively little in the way of bona fide sights, the people are often cited as a highlight of any trip to Laos. The friendliness and kindness of Laos's citizens are just as impressive as their ethnic diversity, which conservative estimates reckon spans at least 49 separate ethnic groups. The following is a breakdown of the four generally accepted ethnic groups in Laos and the people within those groups that you're most likely to encounter.

CLINT LUCAS

① Lao Loum

The country's dominant ethnic group, the Lao Loum (Lowland Lao; p48) have defined what it means to be Lao. Adherents of Theravada Buddhism, the Lao Loum live near the flood plains of the Mekong River where they have traditionally subsisted upon wet-rice cultivation.

② Lao Thoeng

Despite the name, the Lao Thoeng (Upland Lao; p49) are not ethnically Lao at all, but rather an ad hoc conglomeration of Austro-Asiatic and Mon-Khmer peoples. They tend to live in elevated areas throughout the country.

③ Lao Tai

They belong to the same ethno-linguistic group as the Lao Loum, however the Lao Tai (p49) reside in higher upland valleys in the north and centre of the country and still cling to animistic beliefs that precede Buddhism.

④ Lao Soung

The Lao Soung (Highland Lao; p49) tend to live at the highest elevations, predominately in northern Laos. The group consists of relatively recent immigrants from Myanmar and China who are often associated with slash-and-burn agriculture.

ANTHONY PLUMMER

RELIGIOUS PILGRIMAGES

Even the most devout atheist can find something of interest in Laos's numerous and diverse religious monuments. From Khmer-era temples like Wat Phu Champasak where you can pretend to be a modern-day Indiana Jones, to quiet observation of the whirlwind of donation and devotion at Vientiane's Wat Si Muang, your experience can range from the spiritual to the adventurous.

CAROL WILEY

GRANT DIXON

❶ Pha That Luang

The unofficial symbol of Laos, this immense golden spire (p95) in Vientiane, allegedly encasing a piece of the Buddha's breastbone, has been inspiring awe in foreign visitors for centuries.

❷ Wat Phu Champasak

One of the most stunningly located of the Khmer vestiges, Wat Phu (p278) is nestled on the slopes of the very phallic Sri Lingaparvata, more commonly known as Phu Pasak.

❸ Wat Si Saket

An ancient Buddha statue sits amongst thousands of silver and porcelain images in the gloriously unrestored temple compound (p92) that offers you a glance into the Vientiane of yesterday.

❹ Wat Xieng Thong

Luang Prabang's most visited temple (p153) dates back to the 16th century and is virtually the sole survivor of the city's unique indigenous architectural style. Locals wear traditional costumes to Bun Pi Mai Lao (Lao New Year) celebrations.

❺ Tham Pa Fa

Apparently forgotten for several centuries, hidden in the limestone peaks around blue lagoons, this Buddha-filled cave (p249) in central Laos was rediscovered in 2004. It will most likely inspire you to think, What else is out there?

❻ Wat Si Muang

There's hardly a dull moment at Vientiane's busiest temple (p94), which sees a nearly constant stream of worshippers, wishers, monks and donors.

❼ Morning Alms Round

Daily at dawn, many Lao Buddhists make humble offerings to processions of saffron-robed monks. The scene is magical in Luang Prabang (p155) but tourist insensitivity there threatens to trivialise the age-old ceremony. See p155 for tips.

OUTDOOR ADVENTURES

For those pining for that extra dose of fresh air, there's hardly a better destination in Southeast Asia. The locals have begun to realise this as well, and the outdoor options in today's Laos range from world-class rock climbing in Vang Vieng to so-called 'tiger treks' in the north. And best of all, because the industry is still in its infancy, your visit often contributes directly to the people living in these areas.

AUSTIN BUSH

❶ Phakeo Trek in Phonsavan

Doing the Phakeo Trek (p195) combines a visit to the Plain of Jars with beautiful ridge-top scenery, a stay in a classic Hmong village and a climb up a layered waterfall.

❷ DIY Trekking Around Muang Ngoi Neua

If you like the idea of hiking for a few hours between villages (p188) with neither guide nor group, the straightforward but very picturesque pathways behind glorious Muang Ngoi Neua offer the perfect getaway.

❸ Exploring the Nam Kading & the Nam Kading NPA

The Nam Kading (p240) is quite possibly the clearest and most beautiful river in Laos. Boat rides along it and multiday hikes in the area surrounding it are great ways to experience this delightfully untouristed area.

❹ Culture-Based Hill-Tribe Trekking

In northernmost Laos, it's possible to make guided treks (p231) into timeless Akha villages where many local women still dress in distinctive indigo costumes with ornate silver headgear. Staying overnight is a great way to learn about their sometimes astonishing beliefs.

❺ Nature-Based Trekking

An alternative to the popular hill-tribe route is to shun people altogether and spend a few days wandering through one of Laos's protected natural areas. Options range from 'tiger treks' (p203) outside Vieng Thong to hikes among surreal limestone cliffs in the centre of the country (p242).

❻ The Gibbon Experience

You might not actually see any of Laos's rare gibbons during your three-day Gibbon Experience (p174), but there's a good chance of feeling like you're a gibbon yourself as you 'fly' on an incredible network of zip wires.

FOOD

Yes, Laos lacks the culinary reputation and diversity of its neighbours, but those who fancy full-flavoured rustic cuisine are bound to find something tastily memorable. With this in mind, there's no better introduction to the country's cuisine than the unofficial Lao holy trinity of *pîng kai* (grilled chicken), *khào nǐaw* (sticky rice), and *tqm màak-hung*, a spicy, tangy salad of pounded green papaya.

CAROL W

❶ Làap

We dare you to grow tired of *làap* (p62), the ubiquitous meat 'salad' supplemented with fresh herbs, chilli, roasted rice powder and lime juice. A lesser-known alternative is *kôy pqa*, a *làap*-like dish made with chunks of freshwater fish.

❷ Night Markets

If you're having trouble finding authentic Lao food in restaurants, head to the local night market, where rustic grilled foods and sticky rice rule. Go native and try *jqew*, chilli-based dips eaten with fresh or par-boiled vegetables.

❸ Noodles

From *fŏe* (Vietnamese-style rice noodle soup), to *khào pìak sèn* (soft, round noodles in a viscous broth with pieces of chicken or deep-fried crispy pork belly), noodles (p62) are a delicious staple of Lao food.

❹ Beerlao

Beerlao, the unofficial national brew (p64), is virtually the only beer available in Laos. Fortunately, one taste is enough to convince most travellers that this is not an entirely negative state of affairs.

(Continued from page 120)

criminals and drug addicts were rounded up from the capital and banished to two of these islands; one each for men and women. Today the Nam Ngum hydroelectric plant generates most of the electricity used in the Vientiane area and sells power to Thailand. Ang Nam Ngum is dotted with picturesque little islands and it is well worth arranging a cruise. Boats can be hired from Ban Na Khuen, which is also home to the area's best accommodation and restaurants, for 150,000K for a half-day or 300,000K for a full day.

At the village of Ban Senhxoum, just past Km 80, turn right and continue about 7km along the smooth laterite road and you'll reach a quiet but emerging ecodestination revolving around the banks of Nam Lik. In addition to being a great place to stay, the **Nam Lik Eco-Village**, a riverside resort located on the west bank of the Nam Lik, is a good base for outdoor activities such as orchid walks, kayaking in the river or mountain biking. It's also a good jumping off point for the area's flashest attraction, the **Nam Lik Jungle Fly** (☎ 020-5662 2001; www.laosjunglefly.com; admission US$62). Opened in early 2010, the jungle fly consists of a series of 14 ziplines and rope bridges spanning a total of 2km. The ziplines tower as high as 37m over attractive secondary-growth jungle offering great views of the Nam Lik, and visits can be approached as a day trip or combined with camping. Getting there involves a 10-minute boat ride up the Nam Lik, which means bookings must be made in advance and can be done at the various branches of **Green Discovery** (www.greendiscoverylaos.com) such as its offices in Vientiane (p89) and Vang Vieng (p135).

North of Hin Hoep, at the market village of Ban Tha Heua, you'll reach the turnoff to the **(Former) Saisombun Special Zone**. After 30 years as a no-go zone, off-limits due to an armed insurgency by Hmong rebels that has persisted since 1975, the Lao government has decided the Saisombun Special Zone is no longer required. The zone was actually a 4506-sq-km area of rugged mountains and plateaus at the northeast corner of Vientiane Province, stretching into Xieng Khuang Province. It was established because the area is home to a large population of Hmong, and was the home of **Long Cheng**, the 'secret city' from where the Hmong and CIA operated during the Second Indochina War.

Saisombun was formerly a launching point for rafting trips along the Nam Ngum, now an impossibility since the construction of the Nam Ngum II dam. War buffs may be interested in visiting Long Cheng, but what remains of the former base (now a Lao military base) is still very much off limits, and individual travel is still likely to raise suspicion, and the only likely way is to go through an established tour agency (p344).

Sleeping & Eating

Basic accommodation is available intermittently along the entire stretch of Rte 13 from Vientiane to Vang Vieng. If you're cycling from Vientiane, a good initial stop is **Vang Xang Resort** (☎ 021-211 526; r 60,000K), located about 65km north of Vientiane.

Around Ang Nam Ngum, **Ban Na Khuen**, a short distance from the dam, is the best place in the area to sleep and eat. **Salapa Fisherman's Haven** (☎ 030-526 6026; www.salapafishermans.com; bungalows incl breakfast US$30; 🖼) offers attractive bungalows looking over the reservoir. The owner, a Lao who lived in France for 30 years, is a fishing enthusiast and can provide equipment and advice. If you prefer to eat rather than catch, **Nam Ngeum** (☎ 020-5551 3521; mains 15,000-50,000K), one of a handful of restaurants at Ban Na Khuen, gets good reviews for its tasty *kâwy pǫa* (tart and spicy fish salad), *kǫeng pǫa* (fish soup) and *neung pǫa* (steamed fish with fresh herbs).

Located on the west bank of the Nam Lik just outside Ban Vang Mon, the highly recommended **Nam Lik Eco-Village** (☎ 020-5550 8719, 020-202 6817; www.namlik.com; bungalows US$10-50) plays hosts to a variety of visiting scientists, entomologists and orchid nerds, in addition to those simply looking for a rural escape. The resort consists of 12 spacious bungalows and a good restaurant, and the emphasis on activities in the surrounding forest and involvment of locals thoroughly justify the 'Eco' label. Just up the river, the **Nam Lik Jungle Fly** (☎ 020-5662 2001; www.laosjunglefly.com) offers tent accommodation on a hilltop overlooking the Nam Lik, and at research time claimed it would also soon begin work on a lodge and five treetop bungalows. Bookings and price inquiries can be made at **Green Discovery** (www.greendiscoverylaos.com) offices in Vientiane (p89) and Vang Vieng (p135), the most likely jumping-off points for the attraction.

Getting There & Away

From Vientiane's Talat Sao Bus Station buses leave every hour from 6.30am to 5.30pm bound for Thalat (12,000K, 2½ hours, 87km), the largest city near Ang Nam Ngum; from Thalat you can take a *săwngthăew* to Ban Na Khuen (15,000K), or Salapa Fisherman's Haven can pick you up if you're staying at the resort. Taxis in Vientiane usually charge from US$35 to US$50 return to the lake. Ask the driver to take the more scenic Rte 10 through Ban Khuen for the return trip.

Both Nam Lik Eco-Village and Nam Lik Jungle Fly provide transportation if booked in advance. Otherwise, from Vientiane, you can hop on any bus bound for Vang Vieng and get off at Ban Senhxoum (25,000K, about three hours), calling Nam Lik Eco-Village or hitching a ride the remaining 7km to Ban Vang Mon.

VANG VIENG
ວັງວຽງ
☎ 023 / pop 33,612

Vang Vieng's main attraction has long been its dramatic setting. The limestone cliffs that provide the town with its stunning backdrop are honeycombed with unexplored tunnels and caverns – a true spelunker's heaven. Meanwhile, the Nam Song (Nam Xong), the river that gracefully borders the town at the foot of these cliffs, plays host to kayakers and travellers floating along on tractor inner tubes – a pastime so thoroughly enjoyable and popular that it has become one of the rites of passage of the Indochina backpacking circuit.

Yet over the last decade, the area's natural beauty and potential as a base for outdoor activities have increasingly been eclipsed by Vang Vieng's role as a party destination. Sections of the Nam Song now resemble open-air raves-slash-amusement parks, while in town, loud DJ-led and bucket-fuelled parties on Don Khang (aka 'the island') blast on until 3am. And active pursuits such as rock climbing and mountain biking seem to come a distant second to the notorious Vang Vieng pastime of sitting on an axe pillow, sucking down a shake laced with marijuana/mushrooms/opium/*yaba (methamphetamine)* and tripping through endless reruns of *Friends/ The Simpsons/Family Guy*. Although these have had relatively little impact on the natural environment, the profile of the town has changed, and the reason travellers first came here – to experience small-town Laos in a stunning setting – has seemingly been forgotten.

The good news is that it's easy enough to escape this scene by staying a bit away from the centre. It's also reassuring that the locals seem to have accepted this influx of *falang* without losing their sense of humour. And as Vang Vieng continues to evolve, its accommodation options have too. There are still plenty of cheap guesthouses where you can sleep off a hangover between long nights in the island bars, but there are now also more luxurious offerings.

Information
Internet cafes are just about everywhere in central Vang Vieng, most charging around 300K per minute.

Agricultural Promotion Bank (Th Luang Prabang) Exchanges cash only.

BCEL Th Luang Prabang (☎ 511 434); Old Market (🕙 8.30am-3.30pm) Has two branches in town, both with ATMs; the smaller branch near the Old Market exchanges cash, travellers cheques and handles cash advances on Visa, MasterCard and JCB.

BKC Bookshop (🕙 7am-7pm) Second-hand novels plus guidebooks and maps.

Post office (☎ 511 009) Beside the old market.

Provincial Hospital (☎ 511 604) The flash new hospital is a reflection of the money coming into Vang Vieng. It now has X-ray facilities and is fine for broken bones, cuts, malaria and most noninternal injuries.

Dangers & Annoyances
Most visitors leave Vang Vieng with nothing more serious than a hangover, but this tranquil setting is also the most dangerous place in Laos for travellers. Visitors die every year from river accidents, drug misadventures and while caving. Theft can also be a problem, with fellow travellers often the culprits. Take the usual precautions and don't leave valuables outside caves.

ON THE RIVER
Whether tubing or kayaking down the Nam Song, rivers can be dangerous. Wearing a life jacket is advisable, especially during the wet season when waters flow up to four times faster than normal.

When tubing, it's worth asking how long the trip should take (durations vary depending on the time of year) so you can allow plenty of time to get back to Vang Vieng before dark – it's black by about 6pm in winter.

The multistorey high riverside rope swings, ziplines and in particular the massive slide

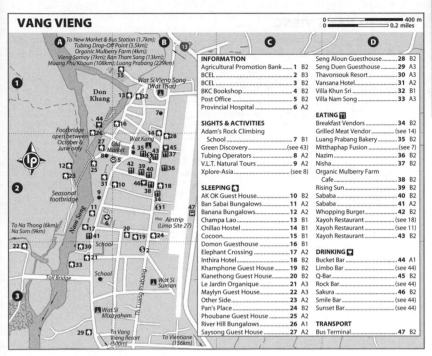

VANG VIENG

Labels within map: To New Market & Bus Station (1.7km); Tubing Drop-Off Point (3.5km); Organic Mulberry Farm (4km); Vieng Samay (7km); Ban Tham Sang (13km); Muang Phu Khoun (108km); Luang Prabang (229km)

Wat Si Vieng Song (Wat That)
Don Khang
Footbridge open between October & June only
Wat Kang
Old Market
Seasonal footbridge
Nam Song
To Na Thong (6km); Na Som (9km)
Airstrip (Lima Site 27)
School
Toll Bridge
School
Wat Si Suman
Luang Prabang
Wat Si Mixayaham
To Vang Vieng Resort (500m)
To Vientiane (156km)

0 ——— 400 m
0 ——— 0.2 miles

(known colloquially as the 'slide of death') have been the source of many injuries and the deaths of several travellers.

Finally, don't forget that while tubing the Nam Song might be more fun when you're off your head, it's also more dangerous.

DRUGS

With so many drugs washing around Vang Vieng it's no surprise that the local police are particularly adept at sniffing out spliffs, especially late at night, and if you're caught with a stash of marijuana (or anything else) it can be expensive. The normal practice is for police to take your passport and fine you US$500. If you don't have much cash on you, you might be able to negotiate the fine downwards. But ultimately you have broken the law and will have to pay something. Don't expect a receipt, and don't bother calling your embassy.

If you must use opium, don't mix it with too much else and certainly not with lime juice. We haven't tested this theory (our dedication to research doesn't go quite that far), but several Vang Vieng residents told us that at least one traveller has died after using

opium and having an innocuous-sounding glass of lime juice! According to local folklore, this mix has long been used by hill-tribe women who suicide as an ultimate act of protest against a bad husband.

CAVING

The caves around Vang Vieng are often spectacular, but being caves they come with certain hazards – they're dark, slippery and disorienting. It's easy to get lost, especially if your torch batteries die. It's well worth hiring a guide at the cave (see p132).

Sights & Activities

Vang Vieng has evolved into Laos's number-one adventure destination, with kayaking, rafting, caving, trail- and mountain-biking and world-class rock climbing all available. These activities tend to be more popular than the sights, which are mainly monasteries dating from the 16th and 17th centuries. Among these, **Wat Si Vieng Song** (Wat That), **Wat Kang** and **Wat Si Suman** are the most notable. Over the river are a couple of villages to which Hmong have been relocated, which

AROUND VANG VIENG

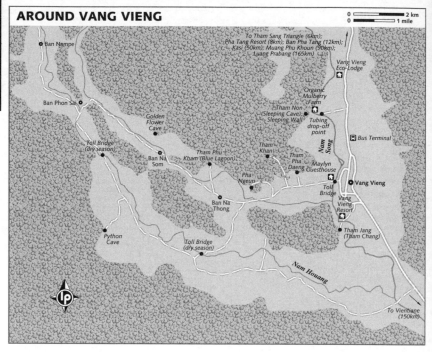

are accessible by bicycle or motorbike (see the boxed text, p134).

CAVES

Following, we've described several of the most accessible *thàm* (caves). Most are signed in English as well as Lao, and an admission fee is collected at the entrance to each cave. A guide (often a young village boy) will lead you through the cave for a small fee; bring water and a torch (flashlight), and be sure your batteries aren't about to die.

For more extensive multicave tours, most guesthouses can arrange a guide. Trips including river tubing and cave tours cost around US$10/17 for a half-/full day.

Tham Jang (Tham Chang)
ຖ້ຳຈັງ

The most famous of the caves, **Tham Jang** (Tham Chang; Map p132; admission 15,000K; ⏰ 8am-11.30am & 1-4.30pm), was used as a bunker in defence against marauding *jíin háw* (Yunnanese Chinese) in the early 19th century (*jàng* means 'steadfast'). Stairs lead up to the main cavern entrance.

The main cave chamber isn't the most impressive, and nowadays is quite gentrified, but it does afford magnificent views over the river valley through an opening in the limestone wall. A cool spring at the foot of the cave feeds into the river and you can swim up here about 80m into the cave. You can swim outside the cave for free; not a bad option.

To get there, walk or cycle south to the Vang Vieng Resort where you must pay a 2000K fee to cross the grounds, plus another 2000/3000K to park your bike/motorcycle. To reach the cave, turn left at the far side of the bridge.

Tham Phu Kham
ຖ້ຳພູຄຳ

Vast **Tham Phu Kham** (Blue Lagoon; Map p132; admission 10,000K) is considered sacred by Lao and is popular largely due to the lagoon at the foot of the cave. The beautiful green-blue waters are perfect for a dip after the stiff climb. The main cave chamber contains a Thai bronze reclining Buddha, and from here deeper galleries branch off into the mountain. To get there, cross the bridge and pedal or motorcycle 6km along a scenic but unpaved road to the village of Ban Na Thong. From Ban Na Thong follow the signs towards the cliff and a stiff 200m climb through scrub forest.

Be forewarned that locals have taken to referring to other caves, including the similarly named and nearby Tham Phu Thong, as Blue Lagoon, but Tham Phu Kham is the original.

Tham Sang Triangle

A popular half-day trip that's easy to do on your own takes in Tham Sang plus three other caves within a short walk. Begin this caving odyssey by riding a motorcycle or taking a jumbo 13km north along Rte 13, turning left a few hundred metres beyond the barely readable Km 169 stone. A rough road leads to the river, where you cross a toll bridge (5000K), or during the wet season, a boatman will ferry you across to Ban Tham Sang (20,000K return). Tham Sang itself is right here, as is a small restaurant.

Tham Sang (Tham Xang; admission 5000K), meaning 'Elephant Cave', is a small cavern containing a few Buddha images and a Buddha 'footprint', plus the (vaguely) elephant-shaped stalactite that gives the cave its name. It's best visited in the morning when light enters the cave.

From Tham Sang a path takes you about 1km northwest through rice fields to the entrances of **Tham Loup** and **Tham Hoi** (combined admission 10,000K). The path isn't entirely clear, but the local kids are happy to show you the way for a small fee. The entrance to Tham Hoi is guarded by a large Buddha figure; reportedly the cave continues about 3km into the limestone and an underground lake. Tham Loup is a large and delightfully untouched cavern with some impressive stalactites.

About 400m south of Tham Hoi, along a well-used path, is the highlight of this trip, **Tham Nam** (admission 10,000K). The cave is about 500m long and a tributary of the Nam Song flows out of its low entrance. In the dry season you can wade into the cave, but when the water is higher you need to take a tube from the friendly woman near the entrance; the tube and headlamp are included in the entrance fee. Dragging yourself through the tunnel on the fixed rope is fun.

If you've still got the energy, from Tham Nam a path leads about 2km south along a stream to **Tham Pha Thao**, a cave said to be a couple of kilometres long with a pool in the middle. Otherwise, it's an easy 1km walk

back to Ban Tham Sang. This loop is usually included in the kayaking/trekking/tubing combo trip run by most Vang Vieng tour operators.

KAYAKING

Kayaking is almost (but not quite) as popular as tubing and trips typically include visits to caves and villages and traverse a few rapids, the danger of which depends on the speed of the water. There are loads of operators and prices are about US$10/17 per person for a half-/whole day. Kayaking trips to Vientiane along the Nam Lik involve a lot of paddling and part of the trip is by road, and are only possible when the water is high enough.

Not all guides are as well trained as they could be. Before using a cheap operator, check the equipment and the guides' credentials, and ask other travellers.

ROCK CLIMBING

In just a few years the limestone walls around Vang Vieng have gained a reputation as some of the best climbing in Southeast Asia. More than 200 routes have been identified and most have been bolted. The routes are rated between 4a and 8b, with the majority being in or near a cave. The most popular climbing spots are at **Tham Non (Sleeping Cave)**, with more than 20 routes, and the tougher **Sleeping Wall** nearby, where some routes have difficult overhangs.

The climbing season usually runs between October and May, with routes too wet at other times. **Adam's Rock Climbing School** (☎ 020-5501 0832; www.laos-climbing.com; lessons per day 1000B) is the only dedicated climbing outfit in the area and offers fully outfitted courses ranging in skill from beginner to advanced. Adam himself is one of the most experienced climbers in the area (see p137), his guides get good reports and equipment rental is also available. **Green Discovery** (☎ 511 440; www.greendiscoverylaos.com) conducts three-day beginners' courses and when available, can provide a handy climbing guide to the area.

TUBING

Virtually everyone who comes to Vang Vieng goes tubing down the Nam Song in an inflated tractor-tyre tube. The activity has become such a popular rite of passage on the Southeast Asia backpacker circuit that full-fledged bars, mud pits, towering rope swings and a huge slide have been set up on islands and beaches along the route. In fact, the **tubing drop-off point** (Map p132), 3.5km north of town, just before the turn off to the Mulberry Farm, has become something akin to an open-air disco, albeit one with an astonishingly beautiful natural setting. The sound of trance music blasting against the limestone cliffs and hundreds of ravers dancing on bamboo platforms results in an unreal scene, and is worth checking out even if tubing doesn't appeal.

The **tubing operators** (8.30am-7pm) have formed a cartel so all tubing is organised from

WEST VANG VIENG LOOP

To get right into the heart of the limestone karsts rising out of the rice paddies opposite Vang Vieng, consider this loop by motorbike or mountain bike (see Map p132). Joe of Maylyn Guest House claims to have done the entire 33km loop in an hour, but we reckon it's best approached as a day trip, with stops at the various caves, viewpoints and swimming holes. It's best done on a trail bike, though possible on smaller motos or mountain bikes. The latter half of the loop involves a few dry season toll-bridge crossings, the lack of which would make doing the entire loop difficult, if not impossible during the wet season. Other than Joe at Maylyn Guest House, the best guide to the area is the Hobo Maps *Vang Vieng* (www.hobomaps.com; US$2) map, which includes heaps of helpful details including handy references to the numbered power poles that run along part of the road.

Heading west from Maylyn Guest House you'll see hand-painted signs to various caves along the first couple of kilometres of the path, only some of which are visit-worthy, and all of which charge 10,000K for admission and/or guiding. Worth considering are **Tham Pha Daeng** (admission 10,000K), the turn off to which is located after pole 16. There's a cave pool and the area is allegedly the best place to watch the bats stream from their caves every evening. The 2km walk to **Tham Khan** (admission 10,000K), approached via a 1.5km side road after pole 24, is probably more worthwhile than the long, but claustrophobic cave.

At the Hmong village of Ban Phone Ngeun about 3km from Maylyn Guest House, turn right just after pole 42, opposite two basic shops. A flagged road leads past the local school to a desk where the local kids will collect a fee of 10,000K to take you on the steep 45 minute hike to the top of **Pha Ngeun**, a rocky cliff where the locals have built a few basic observation decks offering arguably the most dramatic views of the area.

Returning to the main road, keep right at the next intersection where you'll pass through the Lao Loum village of **Ban Na Thong**. After 2km you'll come to another fork and a sign pointing right to **Tham Phu Kham** (Blue Lagoon; p132), about 700m along a track. Don't confuse this with nearby Tham Phu Thong, also referred to by locals as the Blue Lagoon, but more like a muddy pond. The natural pool at Tham Phu Kham is a great place to stop for a refreshing swim, particularly if you scaled Pha Ngeun, and equally refreshing organic fruit shakes are sold before the entrance to the cave.

Back on the main track, continue west and you'll soon be in **Ban Na Som**, a village of Hmong who have been resettled here. Around here the vegetation on the karsts is scarred by slash-and-burn farming. Just beyond Na Som are signs to **Golden Flower Cave.** Reaching it involves walking through rice fields, climbing a fence and following two white arrows for a few minutes. The cave is about 50m up the hill – look into the undergrowth for the vague stairs. It's barely worth the effort.

Continuing west a beautiful stretch of track hugs the edge of the karsts and crosses a couple of streams that could be difficult in the wet, and eventually comes to **Ban Phon Sai**. Here the track joins with a better dirt road, but first you need to cross the Nam Houang (Houang River), which is tricky in the wet season.

You have a choice now: continue 5km west through more dramatic scenery to **Ban Nampe**, a pretty village but nothing more, or start heading back east along the southern route. About 6km southeast of Ban Phon Sai, over another couple of creeks, signs point across a small bridge to a track to **Python Cave**, about 800m away. Once you've seen this, it's plain sailing back to Vang Vieng. Keep along the road, then go left at the junction (follow the power poles), immediately cross a stream and soon you'll be back on the main track, loop complete.

a small building across from where the old market once was. It costs 55,000K to rent a tube plus a 60,000K refundable deposit. Life jackets are available and you can rent a dry bag for 20,000K. The fee includes transport to the tubing drop-off point, but keep in mind that you must return the tube before 6pm, otherwise you'll have to pay a 20,000K late fee. If you lose your tube, you have to pay US$7.

This is fair enough, but it gets dodgy when you've finished the trip, have planted yourself at one of the island bars and a kid offers to take your tube back for you. What a good idea, you might think. If you do think that, you'll have someone knocking on your door the next morning asking for US$7. The other thing you should remember is to take something – a sarong, perhaps – to put on when you finish the trip and have to walk through town. The locals don't appreciate people walking around in bikinis or Speedos as much as you might think.

In times of high water, rapids along the Nam Song can be quite daunting; see Dangers & Annoyances p130.

Tours

Several companies operate so-called adventure tours out of Vang Vieng. Prices and standards vary, though the following have good reputations:

Green Discovery (☎ 511 230; www.greendiscovery laos.com; Th Luang Prabang; ◷ 8am-9.30pm) Green Discovery is the biggest and most reliable operator, offering trekking, kayaking, rock climbing and caving.

V.L.T Natural Tours (☎ 020-5520 8283; www.vang viengtour.com) Good-value kayaking and trekking. Vone (a guide) gets good feedback.

Xplore-Asia (☎ 020-252 5180; www.xplore-asia.com) Good for kayaking.

Sleeping

Vang Vieng has some of the best-value rooms in Laos, and prices often fall even further in low season. The downside is that although a centrally-located river front hotel for a few US dollars a night may seem like a steal, the noise across the water from Don Khang (p138) has become a serious annoyance as of late, with the riverside hotels and guesthouses catching the full brunt of competing bars that now stay open as late as 4am. Also, particularly if you're staying in the centre of town, early-morning construction-related noise can also be an issue, with new hotels going up all the time.

BUDGET

Khamphone Guest House (☎ 511 062; r 200-400B; ⊠) Khamphone's three buildings on the southern edge of town offer good-value rooms; the 400B options with TV, air-con and fridge are best.

Le Jardin Organique (☎ 511 420; r 200-400B, bungalows 600B; ⊠) This place lost its riverfront position a few years ago, and currently feels hemmed in by larger structures on virtually every side, but the atmosphere remains upbeat and service friendly. The large bungalows, at 600B, are a good deal.

Chillao Hostel (☎ 511 035; dm 20,000K, r 40,000-90,000K; ⊠ ▯ ☞) The former Bountang Guest House, this classic backpacker hostel features an eclectic variety of exceedingly cheap, but acceptable rooms. Those on the top floor boast great views, while all boast air-con and tall ceilings. A communal area has a pool table and computers, and bikes can be rented. Friendly and enthusiastic service.

Pan's Place (☎ 511 484; www.pansplacelaos.com; r 40,000-75,000K; ▯) You'll find places with better facilities elsewhere, but the cheery and helpful staff and commune-like atmosphere at Pan's are something lacking at most of the city's guesthouses. There are several types of rooms, so ask to look at a few.

Villa Khun Sri (☎ 511 697; r 50,000-80,000K; ⊠ ☞) We love the simple rooms in this atmospheric 80 year-old wooden house, and expect that the expansion, being done with antique wood, will maintain the same atmosphere. The only downside is that noise from Don Khang (see p138) can be an issue here. The same Lao-Thai family also runs **Champa Lao** (☎ 511 698; r 20,000-80,000K; ☞), located just across the street, another old-style Lao guesthouse with a similarly good feel.

Seng Duen Guesthouse (☎ 511 138; r 50,000-80,000K; ⊠ ▣) The rooms themselves are unexceptional, but their setting in this tidy pool-equipped villa just outside of town, and the friendly English-speaking staff that run them, make this a solid choice.

Kianethong Guest House (☎ 511 069; www.kanaeng .com/kianethong.html; r 60,000-100,000K; ⊠) The 40-plus rooms here are reminiscent of a US–style motel, and likewise are cheap, tidy and reliable. It's also far enough from the party strip that you can sleep at night.

Domon Guesthouse (☎ 511 210; r 80,000-150,000K; ⊠ ☞) Of several large new hotels to have gone up on the banks of the Nam Song north of the old market, this is the most ostentatious of the lot. Rooms are large, and those on the river side have great views, though noise from revellers on Don Khang can make it hard to sleep.

Seng Aloun Guesthouse (☎ 511 203; r 100,000-150,000K; ✹) The east side of Th Luang Prabang is home to several big and cheap guesthouses, although at many, atmosphere can be hectic and service an afterthought. Slightly more expensive than most, Seng Aloun makes up for this with a quiet setting just outside the main strip and friendly service.

Also recommended:

AK OK Guest House (☎ 511 396; r 60,000K) This simple family-run place on a quiet back street is probably about as close as you can get to what staying in Vang Vieng used to be like back in the day.

Phoubane Guest House (☎ 511 306; r 35,000-300,000K; ✹) The cheapest bungalows here share a common bathroom, while newer bungalows, right on the river, boast en suites and air-con.

Saysong Guest House (☎ 511 130; www.saysong -guesthouse-riverhill-bungalows.com; r US$8-12; ✹ 🔲) Although not as flashy as its newer neighbours, this family-run place has a good atmosphere, popular communal balconies and a mix of rooms.

River Hill Bungalows (☎ 511 130; www.saysong -guesthouse-riverhill-bungalows.com; r 150,000K; ✹) Run by the same people that operate Saysong Guest House, River Hill Bungalows is attractive, but you'd have to be a seriously dedicated party animal to stay directly on noisy Don Khang.

MIDRANGE & TOP END

Inthira Hotel (☎ 511 070; www.inthirahotel.com; r incl breakfast US$20-34; ✹ 🔲 ☎) This style-conscious hotel is indicative of a boutique trend that appears to be emerging in Vang Vieng. The 28 rooms are comfortable and attractive, although without the benefit of a mountain view or waterfront setting, feel somewhat overpriced. The hotel's (relatively) posh restaurant is served by Xayoh Restaurant (p138).

Cocoon (☎ 511 035; www.thecocoonlaos.com; r incl breakfast US$20-49; ✹ 🔲 🖳) This resort has an expansive riverside location reminiscent of a park complete with volleyball court, pool, a riverside lounging deck and pétanque piste. However unless you plan on taking advantage of all of these facilities, the rather basic bungalows are generally overpriced.

Thavonsouk Resort (☎ 511 096; www.thavonsouk .com; r incl breakfast 250,000-450,000K; ✹ 🔲) We've been assured that Thai celebs have stayed here, and there was a pretty flash Benz parked out the front during our visit, but the main vibe at Thavonsouk is that of comfort, not bling. It's one of Vang Vieng's earliest hotels, and its recently remodeled 52 rooms now range from mock-Tudor bungalows to mock colonial-era villas, all of which are comfortable and casual. Recommended.

Ban Sabai Bungalows (☎ 511 088; r incl breakfast US$32-40; ✹ 🔲) These modern bungalows in a serene riverside setting are a good choice. Some rooms have a bathtub and there are two romantic 'singles' with a double bed and balcony over a pond. There is a riverside bar-restaurant.

our pick **Elephant Crossing** (☎ 511 232; www .theelephantcrossinghotel.com; r incl breakfast US$42-48; ✹ 🔲 ☎) With almost every room boasting a balcony overlooking the Nam Song and out to the dramatic karsts, it's hard to beat this place. That the rooms are comfortable, relatively stylish and fair value doesn't hurt, either. Prices fall by US$10 in the low season.

Vansana Hotel (☎ 511 598; www.vansanahotel-group .com; r incl breakfast 400,000-500,000K; ✹ 🔲 🖳) The 38 rooms here are comfortable if not desperately stylish, though quite a few don't have a view. It does, however, have a very nice pool, which nonguests can use for 20,000K.

Villa Nam Song (☎ 511 637; www.villanamsong.com; r incl breakfast US$70-120; ✹ 🔲 🖳) The 16 rooms here don't take full advantage of their waterfront setting and the great views, but the entire compound is something of an oasis of calm in increasingly hectic Vang Vieng. The service here gets good reports, and the hotel's restaurant is probably one of the better places on the river for a sundowner.

OUT OF TOWN

If Vang Vieng town isn't your bag, head out of town for a quieter location. In addition to what's listed here, a couple of places located just across the Nam Song boast a rustic almost farm-like atmosphere, although with noisy Don Khang just across the way, this is almost certainly not the case at night. **Other Side** (☎ 020-5512 6288; bungalows 30,000-75,000K) has simple bungalows, the cheapest of which share bathrooms. Next door, **Banana Bungalows** (☎ 020-5501 4937; bungalows 30,000-75,000K) offers a nearly identical setup. Both are quite popular.

our pick **Maylyn Guest House** (☎ 020-5560 4095; jophus_foley@hotmail.com; r 50,000-80,000K) The Maylyn's 19 rooms are set in a lush, butterfly-filled garden beside a stream. The mix of bungalows and rooms with and without bathrooms aren't luxurious, but they're clean and the atmosphere is good. Owner Joe can advise on various hikes in the surrounding peaks and the West Vang Vieng Loop (p134), and rents bicycles.

Organic Mulberry Farm (Map p132; ☎ 511 220; www .laofarm.org; r 50,000-250,000K) Known locally as *săran máwn phúu dĭn dąeng* (Phoudindaeng Mulberry Farm), this organic farm 4km north of Vang Vieng raises mulberry trees for silk and tea production, as well as other organic produce for its restaurants on site and in town (see p138). The farm accepts volunteers and provides accommodation, ranging from basic dorms to newer bungalows perched over the mulberry bushes. It must be noted that noise from the adjacent tubing drop-off point (see p133) has made this a markedly less peaceful place to stay in recent years.

Vang Vieng Resort (Map p132; ☎ 511 050; bungalows 350-500B; 🏊) Slightly south of town but near the river and opposite Tham Jang, Vang Vieng Resort is quiet and the cottages are comfortable, if ageing a bit.

Vang Vieng Eco-Lodge (Map p132; ☎ 020-224 7323; r US$15-25) About 7km north of town (look for the sign after the Km 162 stone), calling this an 'ecolodge' might be overstating it but the scenic location and attractive bungalows are still a good option away from the crowds.

Eating

You know by the time you sit down for your third meal that something is amiss in the Vang Vieng restaurant scene. 'This looks a lot like the menu at that other place,' is commonly heard. Usually followed by something like: 'Hang on, it *is* the same!' The sad truth is that several restaurants, particularly those TV bars on the main street, do serve virtually identical fare aimed squarely at perceived Western tastes. And as with most places offering such a varied selection of cuisines (usually including Lao, Thai, Chinese, Italian, American, French and with a veggie option), none of it is done particularly well.

There are, however, a few decent eateries which even have their own menus. Most restaurants are open from about 7am or 8am until about 11pm, though in the low season hours can be shorter. Note that this is just a small selection of restaurants we know to be reliable. You don't need a guidebook to find the others, just look around.

For Lao food, a string of **breakfast vendors** (Th Luang Prabang; mains 5000-7000K; 🕙 6-9am) set up shop every morning, across from the Organic Mulberry Farm Cafe, serving basic but tasty

---

SANGTHONG (ADAM) NIESELT, 27

Who were the first people to climb at Vang Vieng? The first rock climbing was in 2002 by a half-French half-Lao guy called David. The first place he bolted was at Pha Daeng, 2km west of Vang Vieng by the Nam Song.

And you? When and where did you learn how to climb? I would say that I am the first Lao rock climber ever! I started rock climbing in 1997 in the south of Thailand. After six years in Krabi as a rock climbing instructor, and after three and a half years of climbing in Germany and France, I came to Vang Vieng and started my rock climbing business in 2005.

How would you describe the climbing at Vang Vieng compared to other places in the world? I think Vang Vieng is the number one rock climbing place in Asia. There is so much limestone from Vang Vieng all the way up to China, and most of it forms high cliffs, over 200 metres.

Is Vang Vieng only for expert climbers, or it is a good place for beginners to learn how to climb too? This is the right place to learn how to rock climb for beginners. Mostly we put beginners on 4a and 5a only, not any harder than that. The bungalows and guesthouses in Vang Vieng are very cheap and near the river, and the food is tasty.

What is the future of rock climbing in Vang Vieng? In Vang Vieng now we have about 200 routes, from 4a to 8b, and still more routes, from 6b+ to 7a+, are being developed. We'd love to have a pro climber who can drill new routes, they just have to bring their own drill, bolts and hangers. In the future I think Vang Vieng will also have caving, canyoning, and maybe even bungee jumping, base jumping, ballooning and sky diving!

Adam is a native of Laos who started, and runs, Adam's Rock Climbing School in Vang Vieng (www.laos-climbing.com)

HAPPINESS IS A STATE OF MIND

'Don't worry, be happy' could be the national motto for Laos, but in some backpacker centres the term 'happy' has taken on a wholly different connotation. In the TV bars of Vang Vieng and the riverside bungalows of Si Phan Don (p285) seeing the word 'happy' in front of 'shake', 'pizza' or anything else does not, as one traveller was told, mean it comes with extra pineapple. The extra is usually marijuana, added in whatever quantity the shake-maker deems fit. However, it could also be mushrooms, yaba (methamphetamine) or opium, and these usually cost more, so orders must be specific.

For many travellers 'happy' is a well-understood alias, but there are others who innocently quaff down their shake or pizza only to spend the next 24 hours somewhere near the outer reaches of the galaxy paranoia, with no idea why. So if you'd prefer not to be nine miles high for your tubing trip, then avoid the 'happy' meals and steer well clear of anything described as 'ecstatic'. If you do fancy floating down both literally and figuratively, then at least consider wearing a life jacket.

---

dishes such as *bạng kụan* (freshly-steamed rice noodles filled with minced pork) and rice porridge. In the evenings, hit the strip of Th Luang Prabang directly north of Chillao where popular **Mitthaphap Fusion** (☎ 020-225 4515; Th Luang Prabang; ☻ 5-10pm; BBQ set 25,000-40,000K) serves *siin dàat*, do-it-yourself Korean-style BBQ, and a **grilled meat vendor** (Th Luang Prabang; mains 15,000K; ☻ 1-9pm) does *ping mùu*, grilled pork and delicious *nǎem khào*, balls of cooked rice mixed with sour pork sausage, both of which are served with platters of fresh leaves and herbs; there's no English language sign, so look for the wooden shack adjacent to Chilllao.

The Indian restaurants are predictably popular, especially with vegetarians. Tiny **Nisha** (☎ 511 579; Th Luang Prabang; mains 12,000-35,000K) lacks atmosphere but the food is reliable. A few metres south is another branch of the domestic Indian food empire **Nazim** (☎ 511 214; Th Luang Prabang; mains 12,000-60,000K).

Organic Mulberry Farm Cafe (☎ 511 174; Th Luang Prabang; mains 13,000-35,000K) Great about the fresh organic produce, pity about the dull quasi-Asian menu... Nonetheless, this is about as good as it gets in Vang Vieng, and this popular restaurant is a particularly good destination for vegetarians. You can also eat at the organic farm itself (p137).

Sababa (mains 15,000-40,000K) With two branches in town, Sababa ('Cool' in Hebrew) is allegedly run by a Lao Jew, boasts a Hebrew-language menu, and not surprisingly, is the best place in town to find your inner falafel. The chicken shnitzel also gets good reviews.

Luang Prabang Bakery (☎ 511 145; mains 18,000-60,000K) This long-running bakery serves oversized but only decent pastries, good

Western-style coffee and a menu that ranges from breakfast to pizza.

Xayoh Restaurant (☎ 511 088; Th Luang Prabang; mains 30,000-48,000K) We suspect that Xayoh may be the origin of the genre-spanning menu that's now available at virtually every restaurant in town. They probably do the dishes better than most, and also have outlets at Ban Sabai Bungalows (p136) and Inthira Hotel (p136).

Whopping Burger (mains 30,000-70,00K; ☻ 5-11pm) As the name suggests, the burgers here are ridiculously large, but are also very tasty, and arrive served with a garlic mayonnaise on slightly sweet home made buns. The friendly Japanese chef/owners also do equally whopping dishes of pasta. The sign isn't entirely clear, so look for the tray of cooling buns out the front.

Rising Sun (☎ 020-5539 7535; pies 35,000K) This Irish pub claims to do the best pies in Vang Vieng. We reckon they're the *only* one in town doing Cornish pasties and steak and ale, and served with fries or 'real mash', they're one of the more authentic Western-style meals in town.

Drinking

You can drink in every guesthouse and restaurant in town and you won't need a guidebook to track down the most happening places. In general, they're split into the open-air, anything-goes bars on Don Khang (aka 'the island'), and more familiar-looking places on or just off Th Luang Prabang. Most places in town close by midnight or 1am, while the Don Khang bars were open as late as 4am during our visit, but this could very well change.

On Don Khang, **Bucket Bar, Rock Bar, Limbo Bar, Smile Bar** and **Sunset Bar** are all competing for your business. We trust you to sniff out the best party.

In town, **Q-Bar** (Th Luang Prabang; 8am-1am) was the heavingest bar and the only non-island destination where people were dancing during our visit. **Sakura** (5-11.30pm;), branch of a popular Lijiang, China bar, is a friendly and fun place to drink – ask Punky to make you a Lao mojito – and surfing on the wi-fi is free.

Getting There & Away

Buses, minibuses and *såwngthåew* depart from the **bus terminal** (511 657; Rte 13) about 2km north of town, although if you're coming in from Vientiane you'll most likely be dropped off at or near the **bus stop** (Rte 13) near the former runway, a short walk from the centre of town. When leaving Vang Vieng, be aware that, even if you purchased your tickets at the bus station, the more expensive minibuses and air-con buses often cater predominately to *falang* and will circle town, picking up people at their guesthouses, adding as much as an additional hour to the departure time.

Heading north, buses for Luang Prabang stop at the bus terminal for about five minutes en route from Vientiane about every hour between 11am and 8pm. All the services below also stop at Kasi and Phu Khoun (for Phonsavan). For transport from Luang Prabang, see p168.

Heading south, there are several bus options to Vientiane, all of which are shown below. Alternatively, *såwngthåew* (30,000K,

3½ to 4½ hours) leave about every 20 minutes from 5.30am until 4.30pm and as they're often not full can be quite enjoyable. For transport from Vientiane, see p113.

Getting Around

Vang Vieng is easily negotiated on foot. Renting a bicycle (per day 10,000K) or mountain bike (per day 20,000K to 30,000K) is also popular; they're available almost everywhere. Most of the same places also rent motorcycles for about 40,000K per day. For cave sites out of town you can charter *såwngthåew* near the old market site – expect to pay around US$10 per trip up to 20km north or south of town.

VANG VIENG TOWARDS LUANG PRABANG

The road between Vang Vieng and Luang Prabang winds its way up over some stunningly beautiful mountains and back down to the Mekong at Luang Prabang. If you suffer from motion sickness, take precautions before you begin.

Roughly 20km north of Vang Vieng, **Ban Pha Tang** is a pretty riverside village named after Pha Tang, a towering limestone cliff. The town's bridge offers a very photogenic view of its namesake. The only accommodation in the area is the ageing but comfortable **Pha Tang Resort** (020-5531 9573; Rte 13; r 70,000-110,000K), about 3km south of the town, literally at the base of Pha Tang.

In the middle of a fertile valley filled with rice fields, **Kasi**, 56km north of Vang Vieng, is a lunch stop for bus passengers and truck drivers travelling on this route. The surrounding

BUSES FROM VANG VIENG

Destination	Fare (kip)	Distance (km)	Duration (hr)	Departures
Luang Prabang	90,000	168	6-8	9am, 2pm (minibus)
	80,000			10am (air-con)
	100,000			12pm, 5pm (VIP)
				Phonsavan
	90,000	219	6-7	9.30am (minibus)
Vientiane	30,000	156	3-4	5.30am, 6.30am, 7am, 12.30pm, 2pm (fan)
	70,000			9am (minibus)
	60,000			10am, 1pm, 2pm (air-con)

area is full of interesting minority villages, and there are allegedly even a few big caves in the area, but few people bother to stop as there isn't much in the way of tourist infrastructure. If you've got trailblazing on your mind, you can base yourself at **Somchit Guesthouse** (☎ 020-220 8212; Rte 13; r 60,000-150,000K), an expansive and tidy hotel about 1km north of the city. Another option is to book a basic room at **Vanphisith Guest House** (☎ 023-700 084; Rte 13; r 60,000K), conveniently located near the bus stop restaurants and within walking distance of the town's exchange booth.

While Kasi town isn't memorable, the road on towards Luang Prabang certainly is, despite the ravages of slash and burn agriculture. For around 50km to Phu Khoun (p171) you'll ascend through some of the most spectacular limestone mountains that you'll find anywhere in Laos.

Northern Laos

If a careless god grabbed a giant sheet of green paper and crumpled it into a ball, the contours would resemble northern Laos. At every turn, convoluted rivers curl through layers of mountain ridges. Hidden amid these lush folds, the former royal capital of Luang Prabang is by far Laos' most magical city and the region's tourist magnet. By contrast, other northern towns are functional places, rebuilt after wholesale bombing during the 20th-century Indochina wars. During that terrible period, much of the population hid for years in caves around lovely Vieng Xai and majestic Nong Khiaw. Add to this the Lao predilection for rebuilding rather than restoring the few old temples that did survive, and you'll understand why there are so few historic buildings to be found. But that's not why you come to northern Laos. What appeals here is the rural life. Thatch, bamboo and timber houses abound, giving virtually any village a timeless, photogenic quality. The relatively sparse population forms an intriguing melting pot of cultures, best explored while trekking. River trips also offer a wonderful way to discover the bucolic scenery as well as a practical alternative to tortuous bus rides.

This chapter starts with Luang Prabang, loops anticlockwise from Huay Xai around to Muang Sing, then finishes with relatively isolated Phongsali Province.

HIGHLIGHTS

- Go wat-hopping and market-shopping in regal **Luang Prabang** (p143)
- Zip-line high above forested valleys and into rustic tree-houses on the **Gibbon Experience** (p174) near Huay Xai
- Take a boat ride or kayak down the Nam Ou between **Muang Ngoi Neua** (p207) and **Nong Khiaw** (p204)
- Play amateur anthropologist in homestays with some of Laos' last traditionally costumed tribal families on treks out of **Phongsali** (p231)
- See for yourself what it meant to spend nine years hiding from aerial bombardment at the haunting **Vieng Xai caves** (p200)
- Amble through Xieng Khuang's **Plain of Jars** (p193)
- Drive to Vang Vieng along scenic **Rte 13** (p171)
- Trek into the forests of **Nam Ha NPA** (p218)

Climate

The ideal season to visit northern Laos is roughly November to mid-February when there's little rain and skies are reasonably clear. Days typically range from warm to hot once the sun burns through the chilly morning mists, but you'll often need a decent jacket to deal with colder night-time temperatures in higher mountainous areas (particularly Luang Namtha, Phongsali, Xieng Khuang and Hua Phan provinces).

Wrap yourself up warmly if motorcycling before 10am. As the dry season continues, river levels drop and by February some sections of the Mekong and Nam Tha might be too low for navigation. March is a bad time to visit the whole region as the air becomes choked with smoke and visibility is severely reduced thanks to the widespread fires of slash-and-burn agriculture. In April the searing heat of the Mekong Valley is tempered by a week of good-humoured water throwing

---

WHICH RIVER TRIP?

Until the 1990s, riverboats were an essential form of inter-city passenger transport in Laos. Today villagers in roadless hamlets still travel by river, while several longer distance routes remain possible thanks in significant part to tourist interest. In each case the journey is an attraction in itself.

Mekong Longboats

- **Luang Prabang–Pak Ou** (four hours return; p169) The typical tourist taster for those with no time for anything longer.

Mekong Slowboats

- **Huay Xai–Pak Beng** or **Pak Beng–Luang Prabang** (one day; p176) Both sectors are very pleasant one-day rides. Boats are designed for 70 passengers but are sometimes seriously overcrowded. The seats are usually very hard, but you can get up and walk around. There's a toilet on board and usually a stall selling biscuits and overpriced beer.

- **Huay Xai–Luang Prabang** (two days; p177) Take the *Luang Say*, and travel in relative luxury on a boat that is a similar size to the Mekong slowboats but carries only 40 passengers. Packages are pricey but include meals, sightseeing stops and excellent overnight accommodation in Pak Beng.

- **Pak Lai–Vientiane** (one day; p187) Completely untouristy, but only runs once or twice a week.

Mekong Speedboats

- **Huay Xai–Luang Prabang** (one day; p177) Scarily fast, potentially dangerous and excruciatingly uncomfortable if you're not both small and supple.

- **Xieng Kok–Muang Mom** (three hours; p178) There's similar speedboat dangers and problems but it's virtually the only way to see this attractive stretch of the Mekong.

Nam Tha Boats

- **Luang Namtha–Huay Xai longboat** or **Na Lae–Huay Xai longboat** (two days; p222) Escape the tourist trail on an open boat with a maximum capacity of around six. One night is spent in the boatman's village. Scenery is attractive but only gets at all dramatic for a one-hour section around Ban Phaeng. When the river levels are low there's lots of rapids-shooting. Trying to organise this one can get pricey or time-consuming.

- **Hat Sat–Muang Khua, Muang Khua–Nong Khiaw, Nong Khiaw–Luang Prabang riverboats** (one day each; Muang Khua p229, Nong Khiaw p206) A traveller favourite; covered boats usually depart daily on each sector. Boats typically hold up to 20 people in sometimes cramped conditions. Bring your own snacks. Arguably the most scenically dramatic sections of any navigable river in Laos are an hour or two's ride in either direction from Nong Khiaw. Much of that you can see from the twice-daily boat between Nong Khiaw and Muang Ngoi Neua (90 minutes upstream, 70 minutes downstream).

during the Pi Mai festival (p154) – a time when accommodation can be booked out and transport gets particularly crowded. Rain is likely after Pi Mai in the far north, though the rainy season typically peaks between June and September. Rains are not constant, and in between showers the sky clears and the rice paddies glow emerald green. But unpaved roads can become impassably muddy, trekking paths can get slippery, leeches may appear in the grass and river fords become awkward to cross.

Getting There & Around

Road journeys in northern Laos are slow and exhausting. Only the most major routes are asphalted and even these are generally so narrow and winding that it's rare to average more than 30km per hour. On unpaved roads progress is further hampered by mud in wet conditions, while in the dry season, traffic creates vast dust clouds making travel extremely unpleasant by bike or *săwngthăew* (pick-up trucks fitted with benches in the back for passengers). Follow the local example and wear a face-mask. Or consider engaging a private chauffeured minivan if you can afford the cost (roughly US$100 per day, only available from major towns). Fortunately for adventure motorcyclists with decent trail bikes, many secondary roads have virtually no traffic.

A delightful, if often even slower, alternative to road travel is to use the river boats (see the boxed text); also see the boxed text on p340 for details of boat types. Think twice before opting for a 'speedboat' – a surfboard with a strap-on car engine might be safer. And more comfortable.

ROUTE CHOICES

There are essentially only two practicable roads linking the north to the rest of Laos. By far the easiest, most popular and most spectacular is Rte 13 from Luang Prabang to Vang Vieng. The alternative, via Sainyabuli and Pak Lai, is painfully dusty and less scenic, although it does allow you to make the utterly untouristed link to Vientiane by riverboat (see p187). A third possibility, Rte 10 from Muang Khoun to Paksan, is under very slow reconstruction, but for now it's a nightmarish slog that can be impassable for days.

For an overview of routes between Luang Prabang and the neighbouring countries, see p334.

LUANG PRABANG & AROUND

Laos's former royal capital is an enchanting place to idly watch the day glide by from a riverside bar-terrace or a fine French restaurant. More active visitors might prefer the surrounding countryside, which has plenty of waterfalls and caves to explore, kayaking and cycling options and a couple of elephant camps for budding mahouts. Few visitors fail to take at least one trip down the Mekong, and many who'd planned a two-day visit end up staying for weeks.

LUANG PRABANG

ຫລວງພະບາງ
☎ 071 / pop 70,000

Magical Luang Prabang (Louang Phabang) is one of Southeast Asia's most alluring destinations. While lacking any world-beating 'sights', it's thoroughly pervaded by a heady, intangible charm – a unique place where time runs slowly amid fragrances of frangipani and fresh coffee. Silent palms drool over gold-and-claret wats, while saffron-clad monks seem to float along the tree-shaded streets. Colonial and pseudo-colonial buildings emphasise the tropical torpor, with many characterful structures now tastefully reworked into handicraft stores, patisseries and boutique hotels. The whole scene is encircled by hazy green mountains at the confluence of the Nam Khan and Mekong River, whose cafe-lined banks offer a procession of enchanting viewpoints.

Unesco World Heritage status means a blessed ban on buses and trucks in the old centre where most road users are on foot or bicycle. Although the city teems with foreign visitors, this is not a party destination. Most restaurants stop serving before 10pm, bars shut at 11.30pm, and by midnight silence reigns.

History

Legend has it that Luang Prabang's founder was Phunheu Nhanheu, a sexually ambiguous character with a bright red face and a stringy body like Dougal from *Magic Roundabout*. His/her ceremonial effigies are kept hidden within Wat Wisunarat, only appearing during Bun Pi Mai (p154), but models are widely sold as souvenirs.

NORTHERN LAOS

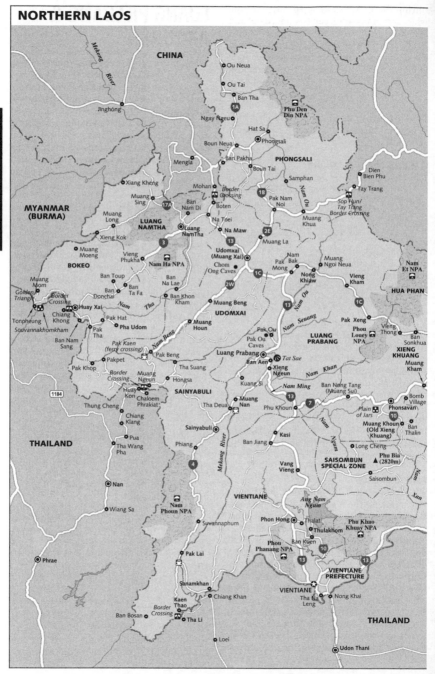

Known as Muang Sawa (Muang Sua) from 698, then Xiang Dong Xiang Thong (City of Gold) from the 11th century, a city state here passed between the Nanzhao (Yunnanese), Khmer and greater Mongol empires over several centuries. It flourished at the heart of Lan Xang, following that kingdom's creation in 1353 by Khmer-supported conqueror Fa Ngum. In 1512, Lan Xang's King Visoun accepted the Pha Bang (p149), a celebrated Buddha image, as a gift from the Khmer monarchy. The city was renamed in its honour as Luang (Great/Royal) Prabang (Pha Bang).

Although Viang Chan (Vientiane) became the capital of Lan Xang in 1560, Luang Prabang remained the main source of monarchical power. When Lan Xang broke up following the death of King Suriya Vongsa in 1695, one of Suriya's grandsons set up an independent kingdom in Luang Prabang, which competed with kingdoms in Vientiane and Champasak.

From then on, the Luang Prabang monarchy was so weak that it was forced to pay tribute at various times to the Siamese, Burmese and Vietnamese. The reversal of China's Taiping Rebellion caused several groups of 'Haw' militias to flee southern China and reform as mercenary armies or bandit gangs. The best known of these was the Black Flag Army who devastated Luang Prabang in 1887, destroying and looting virtually every monastery in the city. In the wake of the attack, the Luang Prabang kingdom chose to accept French protection, and a French commissariat was established in the royal capital.

The French allowed Laos to retain the Luang Prabang monarchy, and imported Vietnamese workers to erect the brick-and-stucco offices and villas that give the city its distinctive colonial atmosphere. Luang Prabang quickly became a favourite post for French colonials seeking a refuge as far away from Paris as possible – even during French Indochina's last years, prior to WWII, a river trip from Saigon to Luang Prabang took longer than a steamship voyage from Saigon to France.

The city survived Japanese invasion and remained a royalist stronghold through the Indochina wars, as such avoiding the US bombing that destroyed virtually every other northern Lao city. Through the 1980s, collectivisation of the economy resulted in a major exodus of business-people, aristocracy and intelligentsia. With little money for or interest

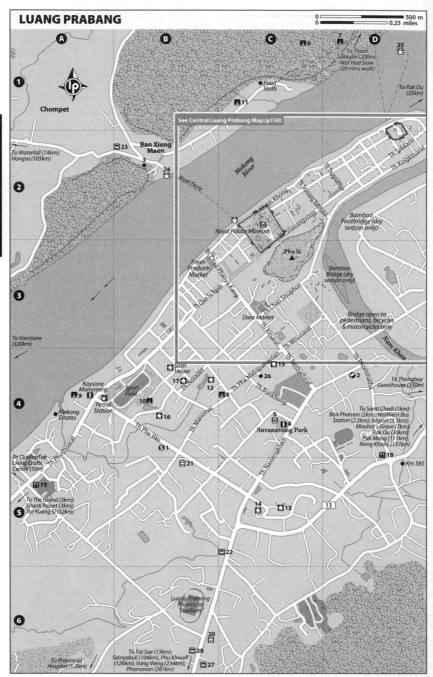

in conserving the city's former regal-colonial flavour, Luang Prabang became a ghost of its former self. But after 1989, newly relegalised private enterprise meant that long-closed shops reopened and once-dilapidated villas were converted into hotels and guesthouses. The city received Unesco World Heritage status in 1995, accelerating the process, raising the city's international profile and, in principle, ensuring that any new development in the old city remains true to the architectural spirit of the original – guidelines that have been rather loosely interpreted in some cases. Such has been the city's international popularity in the 21st century that in some quarters, guesthouses, restaurants, boutiques and galleries now outnumber real homes. Some fear that this is leading to a 'museumising' of the old city, while architectural purists lament the over-flamboyant renovations to certain wats. But the overall result remains an unparalleled delight while the many newer constructions

are at least in pseudo-traditional style – a vast improvement over mouldering 1970s Soviet concrete.

Orientation

The historic centre occupies the peninsula formed between the Mekong River and Nam Khan and surveyed by the stupa-topped hill whose name, Phu Si (Pu-si, Phousy), raises many a cheap guffaw from native English speakers.

Traditionally the town is divided into minuscule 'villages' (ban), often named for the local wat. Many official addresses use that system rather than street names, which have changed at least three times over the last 20 years. So don't be surprised to find widely varying addresses on maps and visit-cards. The main street heading northeast up the peninsula is currently called Th Phothisarat (Phothisalat) southwest of the palace, Th Sisavangvong in its middle reach and Th Sakkarin (Sakkaline Rd) at the northeastern end. The road that runs along the Mekong waterfront is variously known as Souvannakhamphong, Oun Kham and Suvannabanlang, although most locals call it Th Khem Khong (Mekong Riverside Rd). Understandably for directions, most locals use landmarks rather than street names.

Various commercial city maps are available, but by far the most accurate and comprehensive is the regularly updated *Hobo Maps Luang Prabang* (www.hobomaps.com; 25,000K) which marks virtually every business and around 200 guesthouses with a very useful series of indexes.

Information
BOOKSHOPS

Both **L'Etranger Books & Tea** (Map p150; ☎ 020-5537 7826; Th Kingkitsarat; ☯ 7am-10pm Mon-Sat, 10am-10pm Sun) and **YensaBai Books & Art** (Map p150; ☎ 260 195; www.yensabaiart.com; Th Chao Sisuphon; ☯ 8am-10pm) buy, sell and exchange used books and sell new ones. Both have small libraries offering paid loans from collections that include some otherwise hard-to-find, locally relevant titles. **Monument Books** (Map p150; ☎ 254 954; www.monument-books.com; Th Thugnaithao; ☯ 8am-9pm) stocks new guidebooks, maps, coffee-table books and works on Lao history. If you can't find a Hobo Map in the bookshops, try at **Oui's Guesthouse** (Map p150; Th Kingkitsarat) or the **Scandinavian Bakery** (Map p150; Th Sisavangvong).

NORTHERN LAOS

IMMIGRATION

If you apply before it has expired, it's usually possible to extend your Lao visa for up to 30 extra days (US$2 per day) at the **Immigration Office** (Map p150; ☎ 212 435; Th Wisunarat; ☒ 8.30am-4.30pm Mon-Fri).

INTERNET ACCESS

It's increasingly common to find wi-fi in midrange hotels and better cafes but obviously you'll need your own laptop. There are numerous internet cafes, many within travel agencies. Most charge around 100K per minute, with a 20-minute minimum. Beware that many such computers are riddled with viruses. If your laptop is playing up or your camera's flash memory has been zapped by viruses, **DSCom** (Map p150; ☎ 253 905; ☒ 9.30am-noon & 1-6pm Mon-Sat) might be able to save the day. Fuang speaks good English.

Good internet access can be found at:

Broadband Internet (Map p150; Th Phommatha; per min 150K; ☒ 7.30am-10.30pm) Consistently fast connection speeds.

Internet Shop (Map p150; Th Sisavangvong; per min 100K, 300K per min after 10pm; ☒ 8am-11pm) Central spot with bearable connection. Numerous other options in tour agencies nearby.

Manivong Hi-Speed Internet (Map p150; Th Chao Sisuphon; per min 150K, minimum 2000K; ☒ 8am-midnight) Decent connection, opens late, drinks for sale and more attractively appointed than most.

Viva Travel (Map p150; ☎ 245 590; Th Chao Fa Ngum; per min 100K, 2000K minimum; ☒ 7am-9pm) Handy for Th Hoxieng guesthouses.

MEDICAL SERVICES

Provincial Hospital (Off Map p146; ☎ 254 025; Ban Naxang) A doctor's consultation (100,000K) costs double at weekends or after 4pm when few staff are available anyway. For anything serious consider flying to Thailand.

MONEY

There are half a dozen ATMs in town. Several tour companies on Th Sisavangvong offer cash advances on Visa or MasterCard for around 3% commission. They'll change money too but rates tend to be poor. Better options:

BCEL (Map p146; Th Phu Vao; ☒ 8.30am-3.30pm Mon-Sat) Exchange money, cash travellers cheques, make cash advances on Visa and MasterCard or use the 24-hr ATM. Several more helpfully central branches offer the same services but should your cash card get 'swallowed', retrieve it at this main branch.

Minipost Booth (Map p150; Th Sisavangvong; ☒ 7.45am-8.30pm, cash advances 9am-3pm) Changes most major currencies at fair rates and is open daily. After 6pm it's easy to miss, hidden behind market stalls.

POST

Post Office (Map p150; Th Chao Fa Ngum; ☒ 8.30am-3.30pm & 5-10pm Mon-Sat)

TELEPHONE

Most internet cafes in town have Skype and MSN Messenger and can offer international calls at 2000K per minute.

The Minipost Booth sells Unitel mobile phone SIM cards for 10,000K which includes 10,000K credit.

TOURIST INFORMATION

Provincial Tourism Department (Map p150; ☎ 212 487; www.tourismlaos.com; Th Sisavangvong; ☒ 8am-4pm Mon-Fri) In an attractively appointed old colonial building, the office sells passable city maps (20,000K) and gives away various brochures. Staff we encountered were friendly but spoke poor English and seemed incapable of much problem solving.

Sights

ROYAL PALACE MUSEUM (HO KHAM)
ຫໍພິພິດຕະພັນພະລາຊວັງ(ຫໍຄຳ)

Perfectly framed by an avenue of tall Palmyra palms, the former **Royal Palace** (Map p150; ☎ 212 470; Th Sisavangvong; admission 30,000K; ☒ 8am-11am & 1.30-3.30pm Wed-Mon) was built in 1904, blending traditional Lao and French beaux-arts styles. It was the main residence of King Sisavang Vong (r 1905–59) whose chubby-featured **statue** stands outside. Exhibits are well labelled in English and by the time you read this there should be a new audio-guide to add context to the most interesting items (entry charges might rise as a result). Note that you must be 'appropriately dressed' to enter, which means no sleeveless shirts or short shorts. For 2000K you can hire a wrap to attain a suitably decorous modesty.

The main palace building is approached from the south. Italian marble steps lead into an entry hall where the centrepiece is the gilded dais of the former Supreme Patriarch of Lao Buddhism. To the right, the **king's reception room** has walls covered in light-suffused Gauginesque canvases of Lao life, painted in 1930 by French artist Alix de Fautereau. A line of centuries-old Khamu metal drums leads back to the main **throne room** whose golden trimmed walls are painted deep red and encrusted with a feast of naive mosaic-work in coloured mirror-glass. Side galleries here display a collection of small Buddhas, some 16th-century, that were recovered from destroyed or looted stupas, including That Makmo (p154).

Behind the throne room are the former royal family's decidedly sober **residential quarters**, with some rooms preserved much as they were when the king departed in 1975. The **children's room**, however, displays gamelan-style musical instruments and a series of masks for Ramayana dance-dramas. These were once a classic entertainment for the Lao court and have now been partly revived at the Phrolak-Phralam Theatre (p167), albeit largely for tourist consumption.

Beneath, but entered from the western side, is a series of **exhibition halls** used for temporary exhibits. Separate outbuildings display the **'Floating Buddha'** collection of meditation photographs and the five-piece **Royal Palace Car Collection**, including two 1960s Lincoln Continentals and a rare, wing-edged 1958 Edsel Citation.

Pha Bang

No single treasure in Laos is more historically resonant than the **Pha Bang**, an 83cm-tall gold-alloy Buddha for which the whole city is named. Its arrival here in 1512 spiritually legitimised the Lan Xang royal dynasty as Buddhist rulers. Legend has it that the image was cast around the 1st century AD in Sri Lanka, though it is stylistically Khmer and more likely dates from the 14th century. The Siamese twice carried the Pha Bang off to Thailand (in 1779 and 1827) but it was finally restored to Lao hands by King Mongkut (Rama IV) in 1867.

Nearing completion in the southeast corner of the palace gardens, **Wat Ho Pha Bang** is a soaring, multi-roofed temple designed to eventually house the Pha Bang Buddha. The building's glitzy red-and-gold interior already sports a multilevel 'throne' space for the image and also houses a 16-man gilt palanquin on which the Pha Bang is paraded through town during the classic Pi Mai celebrations (p154).

For now, however, the Pha Bang lives in an easy-to-miss little room surrounded by engraved elephant tusks and three silk screens embroidered by the former queen. To find it, walk east along the palace's exterior south

terrace and peep in between the bars at the eastern end. Note that persistent rumours claim that the image on display here is actually a copy and that the original is stored in a vault in either Vientiane or Moscow. The 'real' one supposedly has gold leaf over the eyes and a hole drilled through one ankle.

WAT MAI SUWANNAPHUMAHAM
ວັດໃໝ່ສຸວັນນະພູມອາຮາມ

Beside the palace, **Wat Mai** (Map p150; Th Sisavangvong; admission 10,000K; ☺ 8am-5pm) is one of the city's most sumptuous monasteries. Its wooden *sim* (ordination hall) has a five-tiered roof in archetypal Luang Prabang style, while the unusually roofed front verandah features detailed golden reliefs depicting scenes from village life, the Ramayana and Buddha's penultimate birth.

When built in 1821 to replace a 1796 original, this was the *mai* (new) monastery. The name has stuck. It was spared destruction in 1887 by the Haw gangs who reportedly found it too beautiful to harm. Since 1894 it has been home to the Sangharat, the head of Lao Buddhism.

PHU SI
ພູສີ

Dominating the old city centre, the abrupt 100m-tall hill of Phu Si is crowned by a 24m gilded stupa called **That Chomsi** (Map p150; admission 20,000K; ☺ 6.30am-7pm). Viewed from a distance, especially when floodlit at night, the structure seems to float in the hazy air. Visiting it, however, the main attraction is the series of city views. Beside a flagpole on the same summit there's a small remnant anti-aircraft cannon left from the war years.

Ascending Phu Si from the north side (329 steps), take a quick look at little **Wat Pa Huak** (Map p150; admission by donation), one of the few city temples not to have been colourfully (over) renovated. The carved wood facade shows Buddha riding Airavata, the multi-trunked elephant from Hindu mythology that featured on Laos's national flag before 1975. The temple's interior retains extensive fragments of some unique 1860 murals showing historic scenes along the Mekong River. Notice the visiting Chinese diplomats and warriors arriving by river and horse caravans.

Reaching That Chomsi is also possible from the south and east sides. Two such paths climb through large **Wat Siphoutthabat Thippharam**

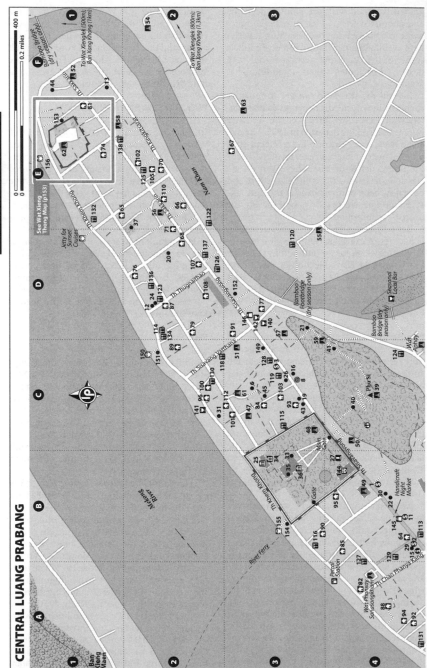

CENTRAL LUANG PRABANG

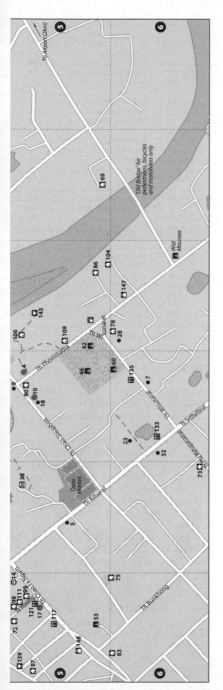

(Map p150) to a curious miniature shrine that protects a **Buddha Footprint** (Map p150; admission free). If this really is his rocky imprint, then the Buddha must have been the size of a brontosaurus. Directly southwest of here a series of new gilded Buddhas are nestled into rocky clefts and niches around **Wat Thammothayalan**. The monastery is free to visit if you don't climb beyond to That Chomsi.

TAEC
Especially if you're planning a trek, visiting this professionally presented three-room **museum** (Traditional Arts & Ethnology Centre; Map p150; ☎ 253 364; www.taeclaos.org; admission 20,000K; ☻ 9am-6pm Tue-Sun) is a must to learn about northern Laos's various hill-tribe cultures. There's just enough to inform without overloading a beginner. If you want more information, watch the video or ask to leaf through the books of a small library cabinet in the museum's delightful cafe. TAEC is within a former French judge's mansion that was among the city's most opulent buildings of the 1920s.

XIENG MOUANE AREA
ວັດຊຽງມ່ວນ

Over the gilded and carved wooden facade, **Wat Pa Phai** (Map p150) has a classic Tai–Lao fresco depicting everyday scenes of late 19th-century Lao life. The grand colonial mansion across the road, now the **French Cultural Centre**, is used mainly for language courses. Footpaths lead back from the commercial main drag into a little oasis of palm-shaded calm around the **Villa Xieng Mouane** (Map p150), an authentic traditional longhouse on tree-trunk stilts that is now partly used as an occasional exhibition centre. Beside it, the **Heritage House Information Centre** (Map p150; ☻ 8.30am-4pm Mon-Fri) has computers on which you can peruse a series of photos and descriptions of the city's numerous Unesco-listed historic buildings.

Behind is **Wat Xieng Mouane** (Map p150), a large monastery whose *sim* dates back to 1879. A training centre here teaches young monks woodcarving, painting, Buddha-casting and other skills necessary to maintain Luang Prabang's temples. Such activities came to a virtual halt after the 1975 revolution and have a fair amount of ground to recover, judging from the unrefined examples sold in their little **showroom** (☻ 8.30-10.30am & 1.30-4pm).

Next door, the garden around the little **Wat Choumkhong** (Map p150) is particularly

NORTHERN LAOS

attractive when its poinsettia trees blush red. Built in 1843, the monastery takes its name from a Buddha statue that was originally cast from a melted-down gong.

A series of lanes and narrow linking passages run down to the enchanting **Mekong riverfront** with its shuttered colonial-era house-fronts, river-facing terrace cafes and curio shops. Interesting **Fibre2Fabric** (Map p150; ☎ 254761; www.fibre2fabric.org; admission free; ✆ 8am-9pm) combines a small museum-style display of original minority costumes with explanations of traditional production techniques. Sign up in advance to attend their intimate free weekly **talks** (✆ 6pm Mondays).

THE UPPER PENINSULA

The northern tip of the peninsula formed by the Mekong River and the Nam Khan is jam-packed with glittering palm-fronded monasteries. Well before dawn they resonate mysteriously with drum beats and as the morning mists swirl they disgorge a silent procession of saffron-clad monks. The most celebrated monastery is Wat Xieng Thong (p153), but several others are quieter, less touristy, and intriguing in their own right.

Dated 1737 but rebuilt a century ago, **Wat Pakkhan** (Map p150) has a simple, appealingly archaic look with angled support struts holding up the lower of its two superposed roofs. Across the road, the ochre colonial-era villa that now forms **Unesco offices** was once the city's customs office.

A fine viewpoint overlooks the river junction from outside Hotel Mekong Riverside. At the peninsula's far tip, a **bamboo bridge** (toll 5000K return) that's rebuilt each dry season crosses the Nam Khan, allowing access to a 'beach' and basic sunset-watching bar and offering a shortcut to Ban Xang Khong (p157), 1km northeast.

The most prominent building of **Wat Souvannakhili** (Wat Khili; Map p150) looks more like a colonial mansion than a monastery but the small *sim* is a classic of now-rare Xieng Khuang style.

Rich ruby red walls with intricate gold overlay gives **Wat Sensoukaram** (Map p150; Th Sakkarin) one of the most dazzling facades of all of Luang Prabang's temples. The name reportedly refers to the initial donation of 100,000K made to build it, a handsome sum back in 1718.

NORTHERN LAOS

Wat Xieng Thong

ວັດຊຽງທອງ

Luang Prabang's best-known and most visited **monastery** (Map p150; admission 20,000K; 🕙 6am-5.30pm) is centred on a 1560 *sim* that's considered a classic of local design. Its roofs sweep low to the ground and there's an idiosyncratic 'tree of

WAT XIENG THONG

0 _____ 50 m

life' mosaic set on its west exterior wall. Inside, gold stencil-work includes dharma wheels on the ceiling and exploits from the life of legendary King Chanthaphanit on the walls. During 1887 when the Black Flag army sacked the rest of the city, Xieng Thong was one of just two temples to be (partially) spared. The Black Flag's leader, Deo Van Tri, had studied here as a monk earlier in his life and used the desecrated temple as his headquarters during the invasion.

Dotted around the *sim* are several stupas and three compact little chapel-halls called *hăw*. **Hăw Tai**, shaped like a tall tomb, was origi-nally a 'library' but now houses a standing Buddha. The other two sport very striking external mirror-shard mosaics depicting local village life and the exploits of Siaw Sawat, a hero from a famous Lao novel. The **Hăw Pa Maan** ('success' Buddha sanctuary) remains locked except during the week following Pi Mai. The **Hăw Tại Pha Sai-nyàat** (reclining Buddha sanctuary) was dubbed La Chapelle Rouge – Red Chapel – by the French. It con-tains an especially rare reclining Buddha that dates from the construction of the temple. This one-of-a-kind figure has an exquisitely sinuous upper-body with a right hand seeming to gesture 'Oh, whatever!'. The contrastingly rectilinear feet emerge on die-straight legs from beneath monastic robes that curl upward like rocket fumes.

Fronted in especially lavish gilt-work, the **Hóhng Kép Mien** is a garage for a ceremonial carriage designed to carry the huge golden funeral urns of the Lao royalty. This glittering vehicle is festooned with seven red-tongued *naga* snakes that contrast amusingly with the prosaic Bridgestone tyres of its undercarriage.

WAT WISUNARAT (WAT VISOUN) AREA
ວັດວິຊຸນນະລາດ

Two of Luang Prabang's most historically important temples lie amid Palmyra palms in pleasant if traffic-buzzed grounds (admission free) offering glimpsed views up towards Phu Si. A lumpy hemispherical stupa here is commonly nicknamed **That Makmo** (Map p150), which translates as 'Watermelon Stupa'. Originally constructed in 1503, it was pillaged for hidden treasures during the 1887 destructions and the latest renovation (1932) coated the stupa in drearily grey concrete.

BUN PI MAI (LAO NEW YEAR)

In the middle of April when the dry season reaches its hottest peak, Lao New Year (Pi Mai) marks the sun's passage from the zodiac sign of Pisces into Aries. The old year's spirit departs and the new one arrives amid a series of celebrations and a frenzy of good-hearted water throwing. Festivities are especially colourful in Luang Prabang where many people dress in traditional clothes for certain major events which stretch over seven days.

Pi Mai in Luang Prabang

- **Day 1** – The old spirit departs, people give their homes a thorough cleaning and at Hat Muang Khoun, a Mekong River island beach near Ban Xieng Maen, locals gather to build and decorate miniature sand stupas for good luck.
- **Day 2** – Civic groups mount a colourful, costumed parade down Luang Prabang's main avenue from Wat Pha Mahathat to Wat Xieng Thong.
- **Day 3** – A 'rest day' without parades when the devout take time to wash Buddha images at their local wat.
- **Day 4** – In the early morning people climb Phu Si to make offerings of sticky rice at the summit stupa. Then in the afternoon they participate in *baci* (bąasǐi; sacred string-tying ceremonies, see p53) with family and friends.
- **Day 5** – In a solemn procession, the Pha Bang (p149) leaves the Royal Palace Museum and is taken to a temporary pavilion erected in front of Wat Mai Suwannaphumaham (p149).
- **Day 6** – The new spirit arrives. This day is considered especially crucial, and cleansing rituals extend to the bathing of Buddhist holy images – particularly the Pha Bang, temporarily at Wat Mai – by pouring water onto them through wooden sluice pipes shaped like *naga* (mythical water serpents). Senior monks receive a similar treatment, and younger Lao will also pour water over the hands (palms held together) of their elderly relatives in a gesture of respect.
- **Day 7** – A colourful final procession carries the Pha Bang from Wat Mai back to the museum.

Practicalities

Overlaying all the traditional ceremonies, Pi Mai is nowadays mainly a festival of fun and water throwing. This being the height of the hot season, being anointed with a cup or two of cold water can indeed be refreshing. However, bucket-loads hurled into passing tuk-tuks are less amusing especially if you haven't thought to bag up your valuables. Remember that foreigners are not exempt from the soaking and indeed some are guilty of egging on locals to use high-powered water canons that are far removed from the original spirit of the event.

Transport can be hard to find at this time and hotel occupancy (and prices) will be at a peak, especially in Luang Prabang.

TAK BAT – THE MONKS' ALMS PROCESSION

Daily at dawn, saffron clad monks pad barefoot through the streets while pious townsfolk place tiny balls of sticky rice in their begging bowls. It's a quiet, meditative ceremony through which monks demonstrate their vows of poverty and humility while lay Buddhists gain spiritual merit by the act of respectful giving.

Although such processions occur all over Laos, Old Luang Prabang's peaceful atmosphere and extraordinary concentration of mist-shrouded temples means that the morning's perambulations along Th Sakkarin and Th Kamal create an especially romantic scene. Sadly, as a result, tourists are progressively coming to outnumber participants. Despite constant campaigns begging visitors not to poke cameras in the monks' faces, the amateur paparazzi seem incapable of keeping a decent distance. Sensitive, non-participating observers should ideally:

- stand across the road from the procession or better still watch inconspicuously from the window of their hotel (where possible)
- refrain from taking photos or at best do so from a considerable distance with a long zoom. Never use flash
- maintain the silence (arrive by bicycle or on foot, don't chatter)

If it's genuinely meaningful to you, you may take part in the ceremony – meaningful in this case implies not wanting to be photographed in the process. Joining in takes some preparation and knowledge to avoid causing unspoken offence. Don't be pushed into half-hearted participation by sales-folk along the route. Such vendors contribute to the procession's commercialisation and many sell over-priced, low-grade rice that is worse than giving nothing at all. Instead, organise some *Kao Kai Noi* (the best grade sticky rice) to be cooked to order by your guesthouse. Or buy it fresh-cooked from the morning market before the procession. Carry it in a decent rice-basket, not a plastic bag. Before arriving, dress respectfully as you would for a temple (covered upper arms and chest, skirts for women, long trousers for men). Wash your hands and don't use perfumes or lotions that might flavour the rice as you're handing it out.

Once in situ:

- remove shoes
- put a sash or scarf across your left shoulder
- women should kneel with feet folded behind (don't sit), men may stand
- avoid making eye-contact with the monks

Facing That Makmo, **Wat Wisunarat** (Map p150; Th Wisunarat; admission 20,000K; 8am-5pm) takes its name from Chao Wisunarat (King Visoun), who founded it in 1513. Though touted as one of Luang Prabang's oldest operating temples it's actually an 1898 reconstruction built following the Black Flag raids. As a rather meagre return for paying the entrance fee you can peruse a sizeable collection of old gilded 'Calling for Rain' Buddhas with long sinuous arms held to each side. Along with some medieval ordination stones, these were placed for their protection here having been rescued from various abandoned or ravaged temples.

Smaller **Wat Aham** (admission 20,000K; 8am-5pm) was the residence of the Sangharat (Supreme Patriarch of Lao Buddhism) until superseded by Wat Mai (p149) two hundred years ago. Colourful, if unsophisticated, murals of Buddhist history and (sometimes gruesome) morality tales cover the interior walls but there are no translations nor interpretations to justify the entrance fee.

SOUTH OF THE CENTRE

Hop on a bicycle to discover the following sites.

Behind a manicured new park featuring a large clapping **statue of the 'Red Prince'** (Map p146; see also p32) lies the sobering **UXO Laos Information Centre** (Map p146; ☎ 252 073; www.uxolao.gov.la; admission by donation; 8-11.45am & 2-4pm Mon-Fri). Visiting the latter helps to get a grip on the devastation Laos suffered in the Second Indochina War, and how nearly 40 years later, death or injury from unexploded ordnance remains an everyday reality in several provinces.

NORTHERN LAOS

If you miss it here, there's a similar centre in Phonsavan.

Winding lanes to the west lead to **Wat Manorom** (Wat Mano, Wat Manolom; Map p146; Th Pha Mahapatsaman), set amid frangipani trees just outside what were once the city walls (now invisible). Possibly the oldest temple-site in Luang Prabang, the *sim* contains a sitting 6m-tall bronze Buddha originally cast in 1372. During the 1887 disasters the statue was hacked apart but surviving elements were reconstituted in 1919 and in 1971 the missing limbs were replaced with concrete falsies covered in gold leaf.

Wat Pha Mahathat (Wat That; Map p150) is named for a venerable Lanna-style stupa erected in 1548. The 1910 *sim* in front has carved wooden windows and portico, rosette-gilded pillars and exterior reliefs retelling tales of the Buddha's past lives.

Traditionally the cremation site for Lao royalty, legend has it that **Wat That Luang** (Map p146; admission 10,000K; 8am-6pm) was originally established by Ashokan missionaries in the 3rd century BC. However, the current large *sim* is a 1818 rebuild whose leafy column-capitals look more Corinthian than Indian. The *sim* is bracketed by two stupas, the larger of which is plated with an armour of corroded old brass plates. It reputedly contains the ashes of King Sisavang Vong, even though it was built in 1910, fifty years before his death.

Further south the modern Vietnamese–Lao temple of **Wat Phabaht** (Map p146; admission 10,000K) is fronted by a distinctive if kitschy array of spires. Behind is a shady Mekong-front terrace from which steps lead down to another gigantic holy footprint hidden beneath a turquoise shelter.

Just beyond the extensive **Talat Market**, a tiny lane leads 200m towards the Mekong emerging at the excellent **OckPopTok Living Crafts Centre** (off Map p146; 212 597; www.ockpoptok.com; admission free; 9am-5pm), a beautifully laid-out traditionally styled workshop where weavers, spinners and batik-makers produce top-quality fabrics. Free tours of the centre start roughly half-hourly and give a superb insight into silk production and dye-making. Watching master craftsmen and women at work one becomes vividly aware of the extraordinary patience and skill required.

If you're waiting for a tour, there's plenty of information to peruse along with a great river-view cafe serving drinks and excellent Lao food. A multi-dish lunch costs 85,000K for two people including a beer. Or try a cup of the surprisingly pleasant worm-poo tea – yes, a unique infusion made from silk-worm droppings. Weaving and dyeing courses are possible here, see p158.

ACROSS THE MEKONG RIVER

For a very different 'village' atmosphere, cross the Mekong to Muang Chomphet. Above the ferry landing a branch of **Laos Jewel Land Travel** (Map p146; www.laosjewelland.com; 8am-4pm) sells district sketch maps (3000K) and rents mountain bikes (per day 50,000K). However, you'll need neither bike nor map to visit the series of attractive monasteries that are scattered east along the riverbank from the traffic-free village of Ban Xieng Maen.

First founded in 1592, **Wat Xieng Maen** (Map p146; admission 5000K) gained a hallowed air in 1867 by housing the Pha Bang (p149) – on its way back to Luang Prabang after 40 years in Thai hands – for seven nights. The monastery's current, colourful *sim* contains an attractive 'family' of Buddhas and has stencilled columns conspicuously inscribed with the names of US donors who paid for their renovation.

Ban Xieng Maen's long, narrow, brick-edged 'street' slowly degrades into a rough track. It eventually becomes little more than a rocky footpath. At about this point climb an obvious 123-step stairway to find the 1888 **Wat Chomphet** (Map p146; admission 5000K) fronted by greying twin pagodas. The hilltop temple is little more than a shell but the site offers undisturbed views of the town and river.

Continuing east you'll find the enchanting **Wat Longkhun** (Map p146; admission 5000K) set amid bougainvillea and starburst Palmyra palms. When the coronation of a Luang Prabang king was pending, it was customary for him to spend three days in retreat at Wat Longkhun before ascending the throne. Today various monastic outbuildings retain a cohesive rustic style, while the central *sim* features old murals with a curious sense of perspective. One scene depicts giant fish attacking shipwrecked sailors.

If you ask at the ticket desk they should give you the key and torches (flashlights) required to visit **Tham Sakkalin** (off Map p146; admission included in the Wat Longkhun ticket price). It's three minutes' walk further east then up a few stairs beneath some overhanging bougainvillea. Flicking the switch to the right of the door only partially il-luminates this slippery, 100m-long limestone cave. A few Buddha fragments are kept in a niche to the right as you descend but the only really remarkable feature here is the inexplicable heat that the cave seems to produce.

Around 20 minutes' walk further east is the operational if rather decrepit little **Wat Had Siaw** (off Map p146; admission free) – take the unpromising right fork about halfway along just after the main path turns inland. You'll pass a lonely hut and cross a one-plank stream-bridge before arriving.

Beyond Wat Had Siaw a path climbs a wooded hill that's all a-chirrup with birdsong and is topped with a new **gilt Buddha** sat on a seven-headed snake (fifteen minutes' walk).

Getting There & Away
Once they have a handful of passengers, cross-river boats (local/foreigner 2000/5000K) depart from near the Navigation Office. Alternatively boatmen at various other points on the Luang Prabang waterfront will run you across to virtually any point on the north bank for around 20,000K per boat. If water levels allow, a good excursion idea is to hire such a boat to the Wat Longkhun jetty then walk back via Ban Xieng Maen to the main crossing point. However, reaching Wat Longkhun by boat isn't always practicable due to seasonally changing sandbanks.

ACROSS THE NAM KHAN RIVER
In the dry season, once water levels have dropped significantly, a pair of **bamboo footbridges** (toll 2000K) are constructed, making for easy access to the Nam Khan's east bank and its semi-rural neighbourhoods. When the river is high (June to November), the bridges disappear and access becomes circuitous – via the 'Old Bridge' by bicycle or motorbike, via the northern bus station by car.

Crossing the southern bamboo bridge you'll climb steps past the highly recommended garden cafe, Dyen Sabai (p164), emerging beside **Wat Punluang** (Map p150). The dusty unpaved road to the left leads 2km to the interesting craft village of Ban Xang Khong, passing **Watpakha Xaingaram** (Map p150) with its ruined shell of a temple, peaceful riverside **Wat Phonsaat** (Map p150), and **Wat Xiengleck** (off Map p150), which sports a wobbly old brick stupa in an Angkor Wat–style state of atmospheric dilapidation. Half a kilometre

beyond, **Ban Xang Khong** (off Map p150) has a 400m-strip of old houses and **craft boutiques** where you can watch weavers and paper-makers at work, buy examples of their work and sometimes organise practical courses to learn for yourself. The most visually striking gallery-workshop is **Artisans du Mekong** (off Map p150; ☎ 254 981; ☻ 8.30am-4pm), an ensemble of buildings in temple-archaic style behind a giant 'tusk' gateway. The raised floor-seat cafe serves tea and coffee and a selection of snacks.

Activities
MASSAGE & SAUNA
Options are abundant for herbal saunas and Lao, Khamu or Swedish massage. The cheapest places (including a trio on Th Khem Khong and several on central Th Sisavangvong) charge from 40,000K per hour for body or foot massage; 60,000K with oils. The following take a little more searching out:

Dhammada (Map p150; ☎ 212 642; www.dhammada.com; Namneua Lane; per hr foot/oriental/aromatherapy massage 100,000/100,000/160,000K; ☻ 11am-11pm) Reckoned to be the best in town. A stylish-rustic place beside a meditative lotus pond.

Lao Red Cross (Map p150; ☎ 252 856; Th Wisunarat; ☻ massage 9am-9pm, sauna 5-8pm) Housed in a nicely preserved Lao–French building with half-timbered walls, the decor is simple and prices are low. Take your own towel or sarong.

Spa Garden (Map p150; ☎ 212 325; massage 60,000-350,000K, sauna/manicure 30,000/60,000K) Garden setting with various relaxation and detox packages.

FITNESS
Pack Luck Gym (Map p150; before/after 4pm 30,000/50,000K; ☻ 6am-9pm Mon-Fri, 7am-9pm Sat & Sun) New, high-quality work-out equipment in a somewhat ragged historic building. Steam room open 5pm to 8pm.

Courses
COOKING
Tamarind (Map p150; ☎ 020-7777 0484; www.tamarindlaos.com; Ban Wat Nong; one-day US$28; ☻ Mon-Sat) Sign up one day before at Tamarind restaurant and arrive there the next morning before 9am. You'll be whisked off to Phosy Market to learn about choosing local herbs and vegetables, then on to the class in an attractive rural pavilion overlooking a fish pond. Transport and ingredients are included. The experience is thoroughly recommended, but be prepared to be on your feet all day.

Tamnak Lao (Map p150; ☎ 212 239; www.tamnaklao.net; Th Sakkarin; day/evening 250,000/200,000K; ☻ 10am & 6pm) Full-day cooking classes including market shopping or shorter three-hour evening classes set behind the well-known Tamnak Lao restaurant.

MASSAGE

Dhammada (Map p150; ☎ 212 642; www.dhammada. com; Namneua Lane) Offers one- to five-day massage courses costing US$60 to $350.

WEAVING

OckPopTok Living Crafts Centre (off Map p146; ☎ 212 597; www.ockpoptok.com; half-/one-/two-/three-day courses US$45/55/100/150) Try your hand at a range of textile arts by taking a small group class in dyeing, weaving or ikat. Teachers are master craftsmen, all materials and excellent Lao lunches are included and you get to keep your handiwork. Half-day bamboo basket-making courses cost US$35. If you want to stay on site, a new four-room guesthouse is nearing completion. You can book via OckPopTock's central gallery-shops (p167).

Some weavers in Ban Xang Khong (p157) offer informal courses on request.

Walking Tour

After an early stroll through the **Morning Market** (1; p166), arrive as **TAEC** (2; p151, not open Monday) which opens at 9am. Peruse the excellent little exhibition on northern Laos's ethnic mosaic or simply enjoy great coffee and croissants at attached Le Patio (p166). Suitably fuelled, try to weave your way through the untouristed little maze of residential homes to reach the southern flank of Phu Si. Climb to **That Chomsi** (3; p149) before the day gets too hot. Or, if the air looks too hazy for views, continue instead around the hill via Buddha's oversized **footprint** (4; p149) and descend to the main commercial street through **Wat Siphoutthabat Thippharam** (5; p149). If you can arrive by 11am, visit the **Royal Palace Museum** (6; p148) to see how Lao royalty lived until 1975. Then meander through the palm-shaded footpaths of **Ban Xieng Mouane** (7) to reach the **Mekong Waterfront** (8) with its inviting cafe terraces and Lao-French colonial houses. If you didn't already explore them at dawn after the Monks' Alms Procession (p155), dip into a selection of atmospheric wats as you wander up the spine of the peninsula. Don't miss the most famous monastery of all, **Wat Xieng Thong** (9; p153). Stroll back, taking in a stretch of the lovely **Nam Khan waterfront** (10) and, in the dry season, cross the bamboo bridge for a

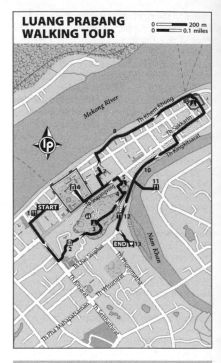

LUANG PRABANG WALKING TOUR

0 ———— 200 m
0 ———— 0.1 miles

WALK FACTS

This walk meanders through the heart of the historic city in a leisurely four to six hours, assuming plenty of stops. We suggest starting bright and early to miss the afternoon heat on Phu Si; and avoiding Mondays and Tuesdays to fit in with museum opening times. But if you accept that it's the overall atmosphere and cafe scene that makes Luang Prabang special rather than any particular sights, the walk can work any time.

---

well-deserved lunch at delightful **Dyen Sabai** (11; p164). If the bridge isn't there (June to November), unwind in **Lao Lao Garden** (12; p164), or seek the secret path to **Utopia** (13; p166).

Tours

Luang Prabang has an abundance of travel agents vying for your patronage for half- to multiday tours. Tours to waterfalls and the Pak Ou Caves (p169) are particularly popular and prices are generally competitive, but it still pays to shop around. Many agencies, notably those lining Th Sisavangvong, also book flights, rent bicycles, change money and arrange visas (but note that Vietnamese visas and Lao visa extensions are easy and cheaper to arrange yourself). The following agencies aren't necessarily the cheapest but have a wider range of offerings including regional trekking, kayaking and biking trips, are well organised and/or stand out for their ecotourism projects and community involvement.

Green Discovery (Map p150; ☎ 212 093; www.green discoverylaos.com; Th Sisavangvong)

Lao Youth Travel (Map p150; ☎ 253 340; www .laoyouthtravel.com)

Tiger Trail (Map p150; ☎ 252 655; www.laos-advent ures.com, www.biking-laos.com, www.trekking-in-laos .com; Th Sisavangvong)

Festivals & Events
Large numbers of visitors converge on Luang Prabang for both the 'water throwing' festival **Bun Pi Mai** (Lao New Year, p154) in April, so advance bookings are wise at such times. Daily after dawn, monks' alms-processions pass conveniently in front of central Wat Ho Siang, with another looping more atmospherically around the upper peninsula. Please read the boxed text, p155 before attending such processions.

Sleeping
Accommodation costs are considerably higher in Luang Prabang than elsewhere in Laos. Rates given here are for the high season (October to March). Prices briefly climb higher for Pi Mai (mid April) and Christmas, but will typically fall at least 25% from May. The choice is bewildering, with hundreds of existing options and a new guesthouse opening on average every 18 days. You'll generally pay a hefty premium for any address northeast of the palace. Compact, pretty and generally good value Ban Hoxieng is a delightful little network of formerly residential lanes tucked behind the main post office, with a great concentration of good value yet relatively central choices. A selection of budget- and lower-midrange places south of Phu Si are generally less atmospheric but there's a knot of good bars nearby. Bigger hotels, some aimed at package tours and Thai/Chinese groups, are mostly further south, notably along Th Phu Vao. Few are special enough to warrant the out-of-centre location.

BUDGET
In Luang Prabang anything under US$20 can be considered 'budget'. Many rooms costing under 100,000K are cramped and rather unpleasant but there are exceptions.

Central Luang Prabang
X3 Hostel/Xayana Guesthouse (Map p150; ☎ 260 680; www.mylaohome.com; Ban Hua Xieng; dm/d 30,000/150,000K; ☒) The 8-bed dorms offer unparalleled value for solo budget travellers and comfort that's far ahead of the more famous but depressingly ropey SpicyLaos Backpackers. New, clean bunks have super-thick mattresses and the shared bathrooms are decent. Private rooms are a much poorer deal.

Paphai Guesthouse (Map p150; ☎ 212 752; s/d with shared bathroom 50,000/80,000K) The family atmosphere, rock-bottom prices and superb location nearly compensate for very basic rooms with bamboo-weave walls that share just-bearable bathrooms and hot showers.

Mala Guesthouse (Map p150; ☎ 212 800; r 50,000K) The four rooms are basic, cramped and dingy but they're cheap and central on the loveliest lane in town.

Saylom Khemkhong Guesthouse (Map p150; ☎ 212 304; Th Khem Khong; s/d without bathroom 50,000/60,000K) If you accept the taped-up floorboards, bars on the windows and discolouring of the sheets, this cheapie has relatively big and well-lit rooms, the shared bathroom water runs hot and helpful manager Mr Wong speaks decent English. A large, Spartan sitting area upstairs faces the Mekong.

Padichith Guesthouse (Map p150; ☎ 212 134; without/with bathroom 70,000/80,000K) It's nothing fancy, and natural light is limited, but the beds are comfy and even the shared bathroom has hot water. Bananas, coffee and drinking water are free. There are several similarly priced alternatives in the same crooked alley.

Sengphet Guesthouse (Map p150; ☎ 253 534; Th Hoxieng; without/with bathroom 70,000/100,000K; ☒) A friendly budget place that's a notch above most at this price with simple Lao paintings to spice up the walls. Unwind in the tree-shaded front yard.

Soutikone Guesthouse 1 & 2 (Map p150; ☎ 253 990; r 80,000-180,000K; ☒) The interiors aren't luxurious but those at Soutikone 1 are almost totally panelled in varnished wood giving the vague impression of 1920s ocean liner cabins. Rooms vary considerably and some have oddities like doorways to nowhere, missing windows or unfinished bathrooms. A small, shared balcony gives oblique Mekong glimpses. The cheapest rooms are around the corner in noticeably older, far less polished Soutikone 2.

Pak Houay Guesthouse (Map p150; ☎ 020-5650 4726; pakhouaygh@hotmail.com; Ban Wat Nong; r 90,000K; ✗) Apart from a little cracked paintwork, these unrefined rooms are remarkably good value for such a central location. Each has simple stencil artwork and air-con, plus there's a little swing seat out front among the pot-plants.

Vilayvanh Guesthouse (Map p150; ☎ 252 757; r 100,000K; ✗ 💻) This sparkling clean new guesthouse is excellent value and quietly tucked down a pretty residential alley. Plug-in internet, coffee, drinking water and bananas are all free for guests.

Symoungkhoun Guesthouse (Map p150; ☎ 254 901; Th Sakkarin; r 120,000-150,000K; ✗) Simple but clean box rooms that are about the cheapest you'll find with a direct view of the monks' dawn alms procession.

Phonemaly Guesthouse (Map p150; ☎ 253 504; Th Hoxieng; r 130,000K; ✗) This pair of new but traditionally styled wooden houses has very much the feel of a real home yet all the conveniences of a better guesthouse. The best timber-clad rooms are upstairs. Obliging family owners ensure a free supply of bananas and coffee.

Souksavath Guesthouse (Map p150; ☎ 212 043; Th Hoxieng; r 130,000K; ✗ 🛜) A tasteful new guesthouse with partly wood-panelled rooms and a front shared balcony. Wi-fi is free but temperamental.

Manichan Guesthouse (Map p150; ☎ 020-5692 0137; www.manichanguesthouse.com; with/without bathroom US$20/15) Upper rooms with bright, two-coloured walls share a bathroom that's worthy of a boutique hotel and a wide terrace with Phu Si views. The ground-floor rear units come with paintings and ensuite bathrooms with screened showers.

Pakam Guesthouse (Map p150; ☎ 253 436; Ban Pakam; r 150,000K) This neat little guesthouse has unfussy but very clean rooms featuring comfortable beds and writing desks. Upstairs a small balcony offers residential views.

South of the Centre

Phuvao Guesthouse (Map p146; ☎ 212 004; r/bungalow 40,000/70,000K) Three of the seven simple bamboo & wood bungalows have extensive views from modest balconies and all have a fan, hot water and kitschy patterned sheets. Cheaper

rooms occupy a barracks-style concrete block with slightly stained and tired bedding but they are large, well ventilated and unusually cheap for Luang Prabang. No English is spoken and fellow guests will more likely be amorous locals than tourists.

Suan Phao Guesthouse (Map p146; ☎ 252 229; without/with bathroom 50,000/80,000K) In a shady coconut grove facing a lotus pond, the cheapest rooms are neater than you'd fear while the ensuites are clean, fresh and come with mosquito nets and hot water showers. Minimal English is spoken.

Khounsavanh Guesthouse (Map p150; ☎ 212 297; Ban Thongchaleum; r without bathroom 60,000K, with bathroom 100,000-130,000K; ✗) Ranged around a scrubby lawn, Khounsavanh is the most appealing of several budget guesthouses strung along a quiet if mosquito-prone lane near Dara Market. The cheapest rooms are very simple but the best air-con ensuite versions share a wide open terrace with views of Phu Si's summit temple spire.

Jaliya Guesthouse (Map p150; ☎ 252 154; Th Pha Mahapatsaman; r 70,000K; ✗) A long-term favourite with backpackers, the best rooms here are scrupulously clean, set behind an attractive garden and come with hot showers. The same street offers several other inexpensive options, food stalls and an internet place.

Mao Pha Shak Guesthouse (Map p150; ☎ 212 513; Ban Visoun; r 70,000-100,000K; ✗) A neat, tidy, fair-value new guesthouse down a quiet side alley. Two rooms have oblique river views.

Thony 1 Guesthouse (Map p150; ☎ 212 805; Ban Visoun; r 80,000-160,000K; ✗) A mixed bag of rooms with banana-shaded views of the old bridge and free internet. There are several other bland budget options nearby.

Sakura Guesthouse (Map p146; ☎ 213 026; Th Pha Mahapatsaman; r 150,000K; ✗) A step up from most surrounding box-room options, the Sakura has good beds, minibars, satellite TV and curious pebble-tile showers along with distinctive bedposts in some rooms.

MID-RANGE

Most prices drop around 30% in the low season.

Central Luang Prabang

LJB Smooth Hotel (Map p150; www.ljbsmooth-hotel.com; Ban Aham ☎ 254 706; Th Phommatha; r US$20-30; Peninsula ☎ 253 927; r US$55-60, tr $70; ✗) The Ban Aham address suffers a little from road noise and lower rooms have awkward door systems but room standards are high for the price and there are several lively bars nearby. The peninsula branch doesn't look much from the road but inside it's crammed with curious design ideas, tapered doors, silk-weavers' poles as curtain rails and a large ecstatic Buddha lounging above the wooden stairway. An archway leads through to each room's rainforest shower.

Phounsab Guesthouse (Map p150; ☎ 212 975; phounsabguesthouse@yahoo.com; Th Sisavangvong; r US$25-40; 🗶) Slap-bang in the heart of the old-city's commercial centre, the Phounsab's newer rooms are set back off a narrow courtyard and the great-value front ones are big and breezy with wooded trim and polished board floors.

Villa Senesouk (Map p150; ☎ 212 074; senesouk@ laohotel.com; Th Sakkarin; r US$30-50; 🗶) The morning monks' procession passes right outside the cheaper rooms – the lower ones slightly dark, the upper ones brighter and sharing a wat-view balcony. Tucked away across a garden-courtyard, the 'new' block is designed to look like a traditional family home. Wood-panelled rooms here have full mod-cons, the US$50 options offering more space than slightly cramped $40 ones.

Hoxieng 2 Guesthouse (Map p150; ☎ 212 703; Th Hoxieng; r with/without balcony US$35/30; 🗶) Hoxieng 2 feels like a real boutique hotel with art and traditional pottery adorning the corridors and little lobby area. Some of the nine suave rooms have flat-screen TVs and roomy bathrooms with a tub and rainforest shower. Don't con-

fuse this with Hoxieng 1 across the street, which is altogether more ordinary.

Thatsaphone Guesthouse (Map p150; ☎ 020-5567 1888; Ban Xieng Mouane; r US$30; 🗶 🛜) Bird song and wafting traditional music fill the air around the leafy central lane where you'll find this attractive ten-room guesthouse. Rooms are small but stylishly appointed with pebbles and basket-basins in the bathrooms, flat-screen TVs and free wi-fi. Some rooms need better ventilation.

Xieng Mouane Guesthouse (Map p150; ☎ 252 152; 86/6 Ban Xieng Mouane; d/f 300,000/383,000K; 🗶) This white two-storey colonial house has snug rooms with local fabric wall-hangings, sparkling-clean floors and slightly dated bathrooms. The palm-shaded courtyard garden creates an oasis of calm.

Pumalin Guesthouse (Map p150; ☎ 212 221; pumalin guesthouse@gmail.com; Th Hoxieng; r US$35-45; 🗶 🛜) Rosewood steps lead across a tiny carp pool on the way up to brand new rooms that combine stylish bathroom fittings with semi-traditional woodwork interiors, top quality linens and free wi-fi. The best room (201) has a private balcony with oblique glimpses of the Mekong. Rates include a daily breakfast; the menu changes daily.

Luang Prabang River Lodge (Map p150; ☎ 253 314; www.luang-prabang-river-lodge.com; Th Khem Khong; US$40-60; 🗶 🛜) This shuttered colonial corner house has an alluring patio draped in floral vines and framed by a lychgate and old bomb-casings. Interiors have clean lines

---

GOODWILL ACTIVITIES

Give back to the local community by making the most of some commendable enterprises in Luang Prabang. Pop into **Big Brother Mouse** (Map p150; ☎ 254 937; www.bigbrothermouse.com; ☀ 8am-8pm) and buy some books to distribute to local children. As well as promoting literacy, the idea is that it's more beneficial for visitors to hand out books than candy. Founded by a retired American publisher, the staff are local college and high-school students who contribute to the books' content and illustrations as well as office admin. Volunteers are welcome at 9am Monday to Saturday to help run two-hour English classes for local kids.

In a similar project, **Luang Prabang Library** (Map p150; ☎ 254 813; www.communitylearninginter national.org; Th Sisavangvong; ☀ 8am-5pm Tue-Sun) collects US$2 donations to provide local books for a 'book-boat' library that sails to remote villages. US$200 provides a whole mini-library with the possibility that donors join the river trip that delivers 'their' stock. Next door to the library the **Children's Cultural Centre** (Map p150; ☎ 253 732; cccLuangPrabang@gmail.com; Th Sisavangvong; ☀ 9am-3pm Tue-Sat) seeks donations of virtually anything recyclable or resalable to provide after-school activities for kids. And you can donate used, washed clothing to the **Lao Red Cross** (Map p150; ☎ 252 856; Th Wisunarat; ☀ 9am-8pm) or even give blood (9am to 4pm, days vary), a precious commodity in Laos as anywhere.

and restrained decor and a few rooms offer Mekong views.

Pack Luck Villa Guesthouse (Map p150; ☎ 253 373; r US$45-55; 🏋) This imaginatively upgraded colonial-era building looks enchanting at night when soft light picks out the flecks of gold leaf on its colourful walls. Rooms are a little tight but the three with upper balconies overlook the monks' morning passeggiata. All have striking fabrics and paper lanterns as demonstrated by the head-turning bed display that dominates the foyer.

La Maison de Xanamkieng (Map p150; ☎ 255 123; www.xanamkieng.com; r from US$50; 🏋 🛜) Rosewood floors, designer grey walls, hip bathrooms and warm decor all make for a pleasant midrange boutique hotel. A couple of rooms are lacking in natural light.

Khoum Xiengthong Guesthouse (Map p150; ☎ 212 906; www.khoumxiengthong-gh.com; Th Sisalernsak; r US$50-70; 🏋 🛜) Pamper yourself with virginal white linens, fresh orchids and a real walk-in shower. Some rooms have latter-day four-poster beds. The neo-traditional house is tucked into a peaceful corner of the monastery quarter with access across a tiny pond.

Ancient Luang Prabang Hotel (Map p150; ☎ 212 264; www.ancientLuangPrabang.com; Th Sisavangvong; s/d incl breakfast 595,000/637,500K; 🏋 🛜) The term 'ancient' is entirely misleading for this 12-room modernist construction which uses half its space on a fashion-conscious cafe and acres of suspended wooden stairway. Drapes over the beds and view baths create a strong visual image in the double rooms. Front-facing rooms overlook the night market so they're great for people-watching but not for early sleepers.

Sala Luang Prabang (Map p150; ☎ 252 460; http://salaprabang.salalao.com; Th Khem Khong; r US$65-80; 🏋) This professionally managed hotel is in fact a collection of six nearby houses along the Mekong waterfront, some retaining original elements of colonial-era tiling, others entirely revamped. If you can, look at a few before deciding which one to take. Stylishly re-clad with raw stonework, the reception is in a 19th-century house that was once home to Laos's 1954 transition prime minister. Upper balconies cascade with vivid bougainvillea.

Apsara (Map p150; ☎ 254 670; www.theapsara.com; Th Kingkitsarat r incl breakfast US$70-120; Rive Droite r US$140-195; 🏋 🖼) Refurbished in 2010, the main two-storey hotel has enticing elements of 1930s Shanghai-retro style and even the cheapest rooms are airily spacious with TVs consciously absent. Upper rooms come with riverview balconies. Across the Nam Ou by private drag-ferry, the indulgent new Apsara Rive Droite offers full-on modernist studios, a garden and a river-front swimming pool.

Chang Inn (Map p150; ☎ 253 553; www.the-chang.com; Th Sakkarin; r 680,000-765,000K; 🏋) The lounge foyer of this enticing place sports a melange of dark woods, Chinese vases, mother-of-pearl inlay furniture and old clocks. Wooden mock-deer trophies lead down a short corridor to petite rooms with sepia photos and polished rosewood floors. A leafy brick-floored garden lies behind.

Other possibilities include the following:
Kongsavath Guesthouse (Map p150; ☎ 212 994; khongsavath@hotmail.com; Th Khem Khong; r US$25/35; 🏋) Good value if you get one of the big Mekong terrace rooms, less so for the darker options behind.

Ancient Phoneheung (Map p150; ☎ 255 123; www.ancientLuangPrabang.com; s/d US$50/55; 🏋 🛜) Six new yet classical rooms featuring curious sunken bathtubs as performance spaces within the bedroom.

Lao Wooden House (Map p150; ☎ 260 283; www.laowoodenhouse.com; Th Khounswa; r US$55; 🏋) Well-appointed half timbered guesthouse-hotel typical of the neat, pleasant pseudo-traditional new buildings that are appearing constantly in the old quarter.

View Pavilion Hotel (Map p150; ☎ 255 918; www.the-view-pavilion-hotel.com; downstairs/upstairs r US$80/100; 🏋 🛜) Take one of four upstairs rooms for unexpectedly fabulous views of Luang Prabang's craggy green mountain backdrop.

SOUTH OF THE CENTRE

Villa Suan Maak (Noix d'Arec Guesthouse; Map p146; ☎ 252 775; www.villa-suan-maak-laos.com; Th Noradet; r incl breakfast downstairs/upstairs US$20/35; 🏋) The centrepiece here is a homely little colonial villa where two shuttered upper rooms feature local fabrics, columns and views across the quiet patch of garden. Newer downstairs rooms are tacked around the old house and are well appointed, if sometimes underlit. Common areas feature curious chairs fashioned from cartwheels and Khamu bronze drums.

Villa Sayada (Villa Shayada; Map p150; ☎ 254 872; www.villa-shayada-laos.com; Th Phommatha; r US$20-25; 🏋) Opposite Wat Visoun, this nine-room mini-hotel is stuffed with heavy furniture, tartan cushions and some uninspired 'art' but amply makes amends with generously sized rooms, hung fabrics, handmade lamps and decent hot showers.

Lane Xang Guesthouse (Map p150; ☎ 212 794; villa lanexang@yahoo.com; Th Wisunarat; s/tw/f US$30/45/55; ✷) Lane Xang appeals for its old-world architectural blend of half-timbered colonial and traditional Lao styles, but rooms feel a little tired.

ourpick **Ban Lao Hotel** (Map p146; ☎ 252 078; www.banlaohotel.com; Th Thammamikalath; s/d US$42/54, s/d deluxe US$54/66; ✷ 🖳 🤝) Tastefully comfortable rooms are set behind a late-colonial era mansion that's 'hollowed out' so that you can see the garden's palms and jackfruit trees as you check in. Deluxe rooms come on sturdy stilts over fountain walls and swing seats. Breakfast (included) is served in a large pavilion perched over a pond. It's peaceful, and excellent value.

Across the Nam Khan

Thongbay Guesthouse (off Map p146; ☎ 253 234; www.thongbay-guesthouses.com; without/with river view US$28/34) Subtle lighting and immaculately managed foliage intersperse the Thongbay's close-packed wood-and-thatch bungalows, most of which overlook the Nam Khan. Facilities include balconies, minibar and good tiled bathrooms with step-in shower. The downside is an isolated location on an unpaved backstreet.

BelAir Boutique Resort (Map p150; ☎ 254 699; www.lebelairhotels.com; r/bungalow US$75/90; ✷ 🤝) BelAir's thatched cottages might look rustic from the outside, but within all is modern and well chosen including curtained display-baths and sunset-facing private balconies. Standard rooms are large and similarly stylish in a complex that's widely spaced amid palm trees and beautifully manicured lawns. Service is obliging, and breakfast is served in an idyllic riverview restaurant. Complimentary shuttles run to town five times daily, last return 9.20pm.

TOP END

Many walk-in rates (as quoted below) are intimidatingly fierce, but booking well ahead through websites like www.agoda.com might save you 50% or more.

Ramayana Boutique Hotel & Spa (Map p150; ☎ 255 055; www.ramayana-laos.com; d/ste US$90/150; ✷ 🤝) This picture-perfect heritage building is a half-timbered palace-mansion built by French 19th-century colonists then used as a meeting hall by a Lao prince. Revamped as an atmospheric 15-room hotel, not all rooms are equal but the best suites offer a striking mix of neo-antique furniture and traditionally

influenced modern art. Light sleepers might be annoyed by the pre-dawn bustle of the morning market nearby.

Villa Santi (Map p150; ☎ 252 157; www.villasantihotel.com; Th Sakkarin; s/d/ste US$105/110/240; ✷) This well-run operation combines three very different sections. The original 19th-century villa, once home to King Sisavang Vong's wife, has just six vast 'royal' suites, plus an upstairs breakfast room with an enviable road-view terrace. Many 'deluxe' (ie standard) rooms are in a quiet, evocative central annex while many more are in fact in a well-appointed 'resort'. The latter has a swimming pool and tennis court but it's 5km south of town.

The Grand (off Map p146; ☎ 253 851; www.grandluangprabang.com; r US$120-135; 🖳 🤝) On a peaceful bend of the Mekong 5km southwest of town, The Grand is a large, colonial-style complex set amid lawns and ornamental pools. Rooms have balconies and views, dark wood furnishings, curious carved bed-boards and parquet floors, but bathrooms could be livelier and there are a few signs of wear. In the extensive grounds the slightly run-down Xieng Keo Palace is the former home of Laos's WWII-era prime minister Prince Phetsarath. It's now maintained as an unpublicised free museum with photos and oddments of furniture upstairs. The river-front terrace is ideal for a sundowner cocktail (US$4.80).

Chang Heritage (Map p150; ☎ 255 031; www.the-chang.com; r US$170-250) This 'village' of close-packed oriental cottages based on traditional building designs occupies a prime Nam Khan riverside spot. The reception is overloaded with enthralling knickknacks but some rooms are dark, small and overpriced at rack rates.

Maison Souvannaphoum (Map p150; ☎ 212 200; www.coloursofangsana.com; Th Phothisarat; r from US$264; ✷ 🖳 🤝) This two-storey former royal residence has been very stylishly reworked, service is flawless and the spa is tempting but the hotel feels slightly cramped behind a busy major road.

Auberge les 3 Nagas (Map p150; ☎ 253 888; www.alilahotels.com/3nagas; Th Sakkarin; r US$234-312, ste US$318-568; ✷) Straddling both sides of Th Sakkarin in two impeccably restored historic villas, boutique rooms display a discrete old-meets-new panache. Some half-timbered interiors feature four-poster beds, suites come with a private courtyard or balcony and a stylish common sitting area features mounted fabrics with a modernist sweep of spiral stairs.

NORTHERN LAOS

La Résidence de Phou Vao (Map p146; ☎ 212 530; www.residencephouvao.com; r US$427-510, ste US$569; ☒ ☒) There's no better high-end choice in Luang Prabang with seamless, proactive service and impeccable, timelessly stylish rooms. The infinity pool reflects distant Phu Si hill, is flanked by elements of mock Angkor-esque ruins and backed by a top-notch neo-colonial style restaurant where only the prices (mains US$22-44) are intimidating.

Eating

Several enchanting restaurants are dotted along the main strip with many more along the riverbanks, though by no means do all offer great food.

LAO

Luang Prabang has a unique cuisine all of its own. Archetypal dishes include ubiquitous local sausages and a soup-stew called orlam (*áw lám*) made with meat, mushrooms and eggplant with special bitter-spicy wood-chips added for flavouring (don't swallow them!). A great local snack is *khái pâen* (Mekong riverweed). Reminiscent of *nori* seaweed, it is formed into squares, briefly fried in seasoned oil, topped with sesame seeds and ideally served with *jąew bąwng*, a sweet-spicy jam-like condiment made with chillies and dried buffalo skin.

Lao Lao Garden (Map p150; Th Kingkitsarat; mains 18,000-35,000K; ☽ 8am-11pm) Fun, al fresco restaurant, where tables are scattered between prettily lit foliage that rises up a steep hill. It's great for a wide range of foods including orlam and buffalo stew, but the cook-it-yourself Lao hotpot-barbecue (*sìn daat,* 45,000K to 78,000K for a group) is a particular favourite. Complimentary 'welcome' shots of fruit laolao are commonly dispensed.

our pick **Dyen Sabai** (Map p150; ☎ 020-5510 4817; Ban Phan Luang; mains 20,000-35,000K; ☽ 8am-11pm) One of Luang Prabang's best-kept secrets for fabulous Lao food, the eggplant dip and the fried Mekong riverweed are as good as you'll find. Most seating is on recliner cushions in rustic open-sided pavilions that climb the lush wooded slope across the Nam Kham river. It's a short easy stroll across the lower bamboo bridge in the dry season but a circuitous cycle ride at other times. Happy hour two-for-one cocktails from noon to 7pm also makes this an ideal drinking spot.

Tamarind (Map p150; ☎ 020-7777 0484; www.tamarindlaos.com; Ban Wat Nong; mains 25,000-40,000K; ☽ 8am-9pm) Cosy Tamarind offers both superb traditional and creative 'Mod-Lao' cuisine, including a variety of brilliant sampling platters. The experience is considerably enhanced by helpfully detailed explanations of the ingredients and how dishes are eaten. Wash it all down with one of their divine fruit coolers.

Kon Kai (Map p150; ☎ 020-213 1112; Th Kingkitsarat; mains 25,000-45,000K; ☽ 8am-10pm) Tasty local, Thai and Chinese food arrives at your table at one of the loveliest Nam Khan river terraces plus prices here are cheaper than those of many nearby competitors. The luscious pork in garlic terrifies local vampires.

Café Toui (Map p150; ☎ 253 397; Th Sisavang Vatthana; dishes/set meals from 20,000/70,000K; ☽ 10am-10pm) Gilt motifs on magenta walls give this compact little Lao eatery a pleasant vibe.

Roots & Leaves (Map p150; ☎ 254 870; www.rootsinlaos.com; mains 28,000-40,000K, set lunch/dinner 90,000/225,000K, beer 16,000K; ☽ 7.30am-10pm) The outdoor setting sees tables ranged beneath palms around a lotus pond, where an artificial 'island' forms a stage for performances by local musicians. Differing dinner shows are performed here, generally 7pm to 9pm Monday to Saturday, but there are seasonal variations so check before you book (100,000K reservation deposit). It's advisable to bring some mosquito repellent.

Tamnak Lao (Map p150; ☎ 252 525; Th Sakkarin; mains 35,000-150,000; ☽ 9am-4pm & 6-10pm) Plenty of Lao and Luang Prabang options served in an archetypal half-timbered house with sturdy arched balconies overlooking the street. Service is obliging but prices somewhat inflated.

Coconut Garden (Map p150; ☎ 260 436; www.elephant-restau.com; Th Sisavangvong; meals 35,000-150,000K; ☽ 8am-9pm; ⓢ) An excellent 100,000K vegetarian set meal provides five top-quality Lao dishes allowing a single diner to create the subtle palate of flavours that you'd normally only get from a multiperson feast. Should you want something Western, their spaghetti carbonara (40,000K) is about the best in town. With front and rear yards it's a great spot for lunch, but at night the alluring upper dining room loses appeal by morphing into a sports bar.

OTHER ASIAN

Nisha Restaurant (Map p150; Ban Xieng Mouane; mains 12,000-32,000K; ☽ 9am-10.30pm) Fluorescent strips light a haphazardly whitewashed house-restaurant whose minimal aesthetics are amply compensated by good value Indian curries. Our malai kofta (tofu-raisin-cashew balls in semi-sweet curry) was superb.

Nazim Indian Food (Map p150; ☎ 253 493; Th Sisavangvong; mains 12,000-35,000K; ☾ 11am-11pm) The biriyanis and faux-tandoori chicken are as half-hearted as the decor but the crispy dosai are creditable and the kitchen keeps cooking till 11pm, unusually late for Luang Prabang.

Big Tree Café (Map p150; ☎ 020-7777 6748; www. bigtreecafe.com; Th Khem Khong; snacks 13,000-15,000K, mains 18,000-45,000K; ☾ 9am-9pm) Genuine Korean food along with Japanese, Western and local-fusion options (try tofu orlam) are served in a gallery of Adri Berger's framed Lao photos (for sale).

Sushi (Map p150; ☎ 020-7751 8300; snacks 20,000-35,000K, meal sets 45,000-60,000K, sushi 30,000-150,000K; ☾ 10am-10.30pm) The interior feels like a converted Ikea showroom and when fresh fish isn't delivered there might not be much sushi after all. However, a delicious range of other Japanese favourites include *gyoza*, *katsudon* and *katsukare*. Sets come with miso soup, daikon pickles and rice.

Café de Malee (Map p150; ☎ 020-5467 6176; Th Khem Khong; mains 25,000-75,000K; ☾ 7.30am-9.30pm Wed-Mon) Authentic Thai and excellent Thai-fusion food served at outdoor tables in front of a Mekong-facing house whose rectilinear lines look like the study for a 1960s book of 'modern' architecture.

WESTERN

Blue Lagoon (Map p150; ☎ 253 698; www.blue-lagoon -cafe.com; ☾ 11am-10pm) Well-cooked meals, some with a Germanic twist, are served in the multileveled timber-framed restaurant or amid the banana fronds and fairy lights of the open courtyard.

Café Namphu (Café 56; Map p150; Th Chao Fa Ngun; espresso 10,000K; ☾ 7am-10pm; ☎) Good coffee and tapas, both Spanish and Lao, served in a two-level cafe whose attractive art-filled upper section looks over the rusty roofs of Ban Hoxieng. Formerly Café 56. Free wi-fi.

L'Elephant Restaurant (Map p150; ☎ 252 482; www. elephant-restau.com; Ban Wat Nong; European mains 90,000-210,000K, Lao mains 30,000-70,000K; ☾ 11.30am-10.30pm) A classic open-sided corner building uses lazily turning ceiling fans and part-lowered bamboo blinds to create a brilliantly under-stated colonial-era vibe. The menu offers some of Luang Prabang's most reliably cooked

European food like duck in Grand Marnier or dill-sauce scallops.

Pizza Sasa (Map p150; ☎ 020-5433 2494; Ban Wat That; pizzas 40,000-70,000K; ☾ 4.30-10pm) Small, expat favourite for thin-crust pizza made in a real wood-fired oven. Last orders for pizza is 9pm.

Restaurant Le Calao (Map p150; ☎ 212 100; www.calaoinn.laopdr.com; Th Khem Khong; French mains 90,000-150,000K, Lao mains 55,000K; ☾ 5-10.30pm) Romantic in the night-time candlelight, the Calao's terrace tables front an archetypal 1904 colonial-era house. French food is cooked with considerable aplomb, many rich sauces using Roquefort or foie gras with refined subtlety. Portions are small but beautifully presented, house wine costs 65,000K per half-litre carafe. Order ahead for fondues, raclette or *pissaladière* (southern-French pizza).

BAKERIES & CAFES

Many unexotic shop-stalls serve strong Lao coffee at around 5000K a cup. However if you're seeking out European pastries and espresso-style coffee there's a growing selection to tempt you. Most serve light meals too.

Le Café Ban Vat Sene (Map p150; ☎ 252 482; Th Sakkarin; snacks 7000-35,000K, coffee/beer 10,000/15,000K; ☾ 6.30am-7.30pm; ☎) Sit in wicker chairs at old-style desk-tables, read the newspaper to Bossanova jazz and enjoy friendly unobtrusive service in this relaxed colonial-era shophouse-cafe. The croissants are the best in town whether served hot (7000K) or filled with smoked ham, salad and béchamel sauce (32,000K). Wi-fi is free if you spend 50,000K.

Le Banneton (Map p150; ☎ 030-513 1170; Th Sakkarin; snacks from 9000K, coffee 11,000K; ☾ 6.30am-5.45pm) Bakes what's probably the best bread in town, offers buttery *pains au chocolat*, and the well-pitched cafe area invites you to linger.

Saffron (Map p150; www.saffroncoffee.com; espresso 10,000K; ☾ 6am-9pm Mon-Sat) Top-quality coffee is sourced from Lao growers and served on a Mekong-front terrace. Good wraps and breakfasts are also available.

JoMa Bakery Café (Map p150; ☎ 252 292; www.joma. biz; Th Chao Fa Ngum; snacks 12,000-35,000K; ☾ 7am-9pm; ☒ ☎) Behind a shuttered colonial-era facade you'll find thick grey walls affecting a curious designer-damp look beneath large modern-art canvases. The croissants are anaemic but the coffee is reliable, the quiches tasty, the sandwiches, soups and salads all popular and the delicious hot egg-cheese-ham bagel (23,000K) makes for a legendary hangover-cure. Free wi-fi.

Le Patio (Map p150; ☎ 253 364; TAEC; coffee/sandwiches from 15,000/29,000K; ☼ 9am-5.45pm Tue-Sun; ☞) Sip Phongsali smoked teas or Lao Arabica espressos and nibble delicious feta-olive baguette sandwiches on a shaded terrace with attractive mountain views, attached to the TEAC. Complementing the free wi-fi are handily placed power points for those with battery trouble.

QUICK EATS

A variety of well-filled French-bread sandwiches sell for 10,000K at makeshift **baguette stalls** (Map p150; ☼ 7am-10pm) facing the tourist office. Various fruit stalls too.

Night food stalls (Map p150; ☼ 6-10pm) Food stalls emerge at dusk on a narrow street behind the tourist office with illuminated communal tables so you don't have to eat on the hoof. There's no better place to taste a wide variety of cheap yet well-cooked local food. You can also sample mini-buffets of mildly spiced, tourist-oriented dishes (small/large serve-yourself platefuls 70,000/100,000K). There's even a 'vegan' stall. Whole roast fish stuffed with lemongrass is a bargain at around 15,000-20,000K.

Xieng Thong Noodle-Shop (Map p150; noodle soup 8000K; ☼ from 6.30am) The best *khào pìak sèn* (round rice noodles served in a broth with pieces of chicken or deep-fried crispy pork belly) in town is served from an entirely unexotic shop-front well up the peninsula. Stocks are usually finished by 2pm.

SELF-CATERING

Food markets are great for fresh fruit, vegetables and 'meat' in more versions than you can imagine.

Morning market (Map p150; ☼ 5.30am-4pm Sat, Sun, Mon) A colourful street market in Ban Pakam that's at its liveliest in the early morning when locals stock up on leafy greens, eggs, dried shrimp and live frogs.

Talat Phosy (Map p146) An extensive tile-roofed complex.

Mittabhab Market (Map p146) A lively, local affair.

Drinking

The main stretch of Th Sisavangvong northeast of the Palace has plenty of drinking places including two appealing wine bars and a mojito stand. Legal closing time is 11.30pm though occasionally some places stretch this a little. The local bowling alley, for some time the one exception where drinking regularly continued till 3am, closed in May 2010.

Ancient House (Map p150; ☎ 254 883; ☞) The half-timbered 1945 house in question is tastefully furnished with disconcertingly low ceilings and serves the city's cheapest beer (7500K), while the pleasant garden restaurant has a very wide range of food styles and many veggie options (mains 20,000K, hotpots from 35,000K). Wi-fi costs 10,000K for as long as you want.

Lao Lao Garden (Map p150; Th Kingkitsarat) This joyfully exotic place is the best of half a dozen close-packed drinking spots at the southern foot of Phu Si. Next door, Hive has contemporary music while House stocks Belgian beers at Belgian bar prices.

LPB (Map p150; Th Khem Khong) Of numerous open-air Mekong terraces, LPB has some of the best river views.

Satri Lounge (Map p150; ☞) Calm, suavely stylish bar with oriental touches, ample sofa space, chess to play and free wi-fi.

Ikon Club (Map p150; ☼ 6pm-late as possible) Cosy, Bohemian cocktail bar with 1930s chairs, a framed Doc Martens boot and a hidden upstairs room for occasional impromptu dancing.

Utopia (Map p150; Nam Khan Riverbank; ☼ 8am-11.30pm, kitchen till 11pm) This unique garden bar–restaurant complex consists of lush, moodily lit gardens, palm trees, statuettes and cushion-seat pavilions. 'Come for a drink, stay for a day' is their motto, and the service is slow enough to make that come true. But you might also linger for the languid Nam Khan views, bar games and occasional volleyball matches. Later in the evening, trancy music wafts through an ever more chilled-out crowd. Follow the signs down a winding maze of attractive residential alleys.

Entertainment
NIGHTCLUBS

Luang Prabang has only two dance places. Neither stay open much beyond 11.30pm.

Dao Fah (Map p146; ☎ 260 789; admission free; ☼ 9-11.30pm) This big-hall nightclub has oil-drum tables, laser lighting and a DJ who loves to do talk-over spots in Lao to the delight of young local groovers. Live bands play early evening then Thai/Lao pop takes over, sprinkled with mainstream Western sounds. It's close to the southern bus station.

Muangsua By Night (Map p146; ☎ 212 263; Th Vao; ☼ 9-11.30pm) In a 1960s-style low-ceilinged room behind the Muangsua Hotel, a Lao band plays an archetypal selection of lilting tunes to inspire local line-dancers. It's a curious time-warp experience that eschews any fashion sense.

THEATRE

Phrolak-Phralam Theatre (Map p150; Royal Palace Grounds; tickets 70,000-170,000K; ☺ shows 6pm or 6.30pm, Mon, Wed, Fri, Sat) The misleadingly named 'Royal Lao Ballet' puts on slow-moving traditional dances accompanied by a 10-piece Lao 'orchestra'. Performances last about 1¼ hours and include a Ramayana-based scene – it's well worth reading the typewritten notes provided at the entrance to have an idea of what's going on. Be aware that despite the nominal 'royal' connections, the theatre has all the glamour of a 1970s school hall. And that if all the seats are full (rare), guests who bought the very cheapest tickets could end up standing.

CINEMA

Pay for a drink and you can watch a movie of the day at L'Etranger Books & Tea (p147; screening at 7pm) and, weather permitting, at the open-air **Boulevard Café-Bar** (Map p150; Th Ho Xieng; ☺ 7.45pm Fri-Wed).

The Luang Prabang Film Festival (p320) runs every year in early December at several venues around town.

Shopping

The best areas for shopping are Th Sisavangvong and the Mekong waterfront, where characterful boutiques selling local art, gilded Buddhas, handmade paper products and all manner of tempting souvenirs abound. Many specialise in fabrics but **OckPopTok** (Map p150; www.ockpoptok.com; Centre ☎ 254 406; Th Sisavangvong; Ban Nong ☎ 254 761; ☺ 8am-9pm) is particularly notable for producing and selling its own naturally dyed Lao silk and cotton along with custom-tailored clothing. **Pathana Boupha Antique House** (Map p150; ☎ 212 262; 29/4 Ban Visoun; ☺ 8.30am-6pm) also carries high-quality textiles. The owner creates costumes for the annual Miss Luang Prabang contest, while her late father once made costumes and ornaments for use in the Royal Palace. The shop's main specialities are antique statuary, jewellery, silverwork and old coins. Its entrance is upstairs via the easily missed side entrance of an impressive old French mansion.

Silver shops (Map p150) are attached to several houses in Ban Ho Xieng, the traditional royal silversmiths' district.

For artistic photos of local scenes, **Kinnaly Gallery** (Map p150; ☎ 020-5555 7737; Th Sakkarin; www.kinnaly-lao.com; ☺ 9.30am-10pm) specialises in black and white, while the gallery at Big Tree Café (p165) has full-colour images available for sale.

HANDICRAFT NIGHT MARKET

Every evening this tourist-oriented but highly appealing **market** (Map p150; Th Sisavangvong; ☺ 5.30-10.30pm) fills the main road from the Royal Palace Museum to Th Kitsarat. Low-lit and quiet, it's devoid of hard selling and is possibly the most tranquil market in Asia. Tens of dozens of traders sell silk scarves, wall hangings, Hmong appliqué blankets, T-shirts, clothing, shoes, paper, silver, bags, ceramics, bamboo lamps and more. Prices are remarkably fair but cheaper 'local' creations often come from China.

Getting There & Away

AIR

Around 4km from the city centre, **Luang Prabang International Airport** (off Map p146; ☎ 212 173) is decidedly modest, though big expansion plans are afoot. For Bangkok (US$160, 100 minutes), **Bangkok Airways** (Map p150; ☎ 253 253, 253 334; Th Sisavangvong) and **Lao Airlines** (Map p146; ☎ 212 172; Th Pha Mahapatsaman; ☺ 8am-5pm Mon-Fri, 8am-3pm Sat) both fly twice daily. Lao Airlines also serves Vientiane (695,000K, 40 minutes, two or three daily), Chiang Mai (US$125, one hour, daily), Hanoi (US$130, one hour, five weekly) and Siem Reap, Cambodia (US$180) via Pakse (1,345,000K) on Monday, Thursday and Saturday. **Vietnam Airlines** (☎ 213 049; Airport) also flies to both Siem Reap (four times weekly) and Hanoi (twice daily).

BOAT

Read p340 for important notes on river travel. For slowboats to Pak Beng (110,000K, nine hours, 8am), buy tickets from the **Navigation Office** (Map p150; ☎ 253 756) behind the Royal Palace. Through-tickets to Huay Xai (220,000K, two days) are also available but you'll have to sleep in Pak Beng; curiously it's slightly cheaper to pay the fare to Pak Beng then buy the onward section there. This also allows you to stay a little longer in attractive Pak Beng should you like the place. The main

slowboat landing (Map p150) is directly behind the navigation office but departure points can vary according to river levels.

The comfortable, if pricey, **Luang Say Riverboat** (Map p150; ☎ 252 553, 212 092; www.luang say.com; 50/4 Th Sakkarin) departs on two-day rides to Huay Xai from a pier opposite Le Calao restaurant. Finding availability is easier in this direction than returning from Huay Xai. See p177 for more details.

Fast but uncomfortable and seriously hazardous six-person **speedboats** can shoot you up the Mekong to Tha Suang (120,000K, 2½ hours), Pak Beng (170,000K, three hours) and Huay Xai (280,000K, seven hours). However there are no fixed departure times and prices assume a full boat so unless you organise things through an agency, it's worth heading up to the **speedboat station** the day before to make enquiries. That's around 5km north of town: turn west off Rte 13 beside the Km 390 post then head 300m down an unpaved road that becomes an unlikely dirt track once you cross the only crossroads en route.

River levels permitting, **Mekong River Cruises** (Map p150; ☎ 071-254 768; www.cruisemekong.com; Ban Xieng Thong) makes lazy seven-day trips from Luang Prabang to Thailand's Golden Triangle on innovative new two-storey German-Lao riverboats with sun-deck and sixteen cabins in which you sleep as well as travel (departs Thursdays).

Numerous boats for the Pak Ou caves depart between 8.30am and lunchtime. A single boat to Nong Khiaw (120,000K, seven hours) departs around 9am assuming enough people signed up. Buy tickets at the easily missed little **longboat office** (Map p150; Th Khem Khong).

BUS & MINIBUS

Predictably enough, the **northern bus station** (off Map p146; ☎ 252 729; Rte 13, 700m beyond Km 387) and **southern bus station** (Bannaluang Bus Station; Map p146; ☎ 252 066; Rte 13, Km 383) are at opposite ends of town. Several popular bus routes are duplicated by minibuses/minivans from the **Naluang minibus station** (Map p146; ☎ 212 979; souknasing@ hotmail.com; Rte 13, 800m past Km 382), diagonally opposite the latter. Booking through agencies or guesthouses you'll generally pay around 25,000K extra. That includes a transfer to the relevant station but getting your own tuk-tuk is often quicker and slightly cheaper.

For less than double the bus fare, a great option is to gather your own group and rent a comfortable six-seater minivan. Prices in-

clude photo stops and you'll avoid the farcical petrol-stop and driver-buys-lunch shenanigans that typify many a public departure. Directly booked through the minibus station, prices are 850,000K to Phonsavan, 850,000K to Vang Vieng and 500,000K to Nong Khiaw including pick-up from your guesthouse.

Vientiane & Vang Vieng

From the southern bus station there are up to ten daily Vientiane services (express/VIP 125,000/145,000K, nine to 12 hours) via Vang Vieng (110,000K, six to eight hours) between 6.30am and 7.30pm. VIP buses leave at 9am. A plethora of morning minibuses to Vang Vieng (90,000K) depart from the Naluang minibus station. The scenery en route is consistently splendid.

Sainyabuli & Hongsa

Buses to Sainyabuli (50,000K, four hours) depart the southern bus station at 9am and 2pm. Dusty pickups to Hongsa (100,000K, five hours) start from the **Chomphet săwngthăew stand** (Map p146) across the river from Luang Prabang, departing at 8am, but only if customer numbers are sufficient.

Phonsavan & Vietnam

For Phonsavan (10 hours) there's an 8.30am minibus (95,000K) from Naluang minibus station and an 8am bus (ordinary/'express' 85,000/105,000K, 10 hours) from the southern bus station. Also from the southern bus station, a through bus to Vinh (Vietnam, 175,000K, around 21 hours) departs at 6.30pm on Thursday and Sunday.

Nong Khiaw & Sam Neua

For Nong Khiaw (50,000K, four hours), 9am minibuses start from Naluang minibus station. Alternatively, from the northern bus station use *săwngthăew* (35,000K) at 9am, 11am and 1pm or the 8.30am bus that continues to Sam Neua (120,000K, 17 hours) via Vieng Thong (100,000K, 10 hours). Another Sam Neua–bound bus (from Vientiane) should pull in sometime around 5.30pm.

Northwestern Laos & China

Until recently the sleeper bus to Kunming, China (420,000K, 24 hours) started from the **Beijing Hotel** courtyard (map p146), but at the time of research it was departing from the southern bus station at 7am, sometimes earlier. Pre-booking, and checking the departure location, is wise. From the northern bus station buses run to Udomxai (50,000K, five hours) at 9am, noon and 4pm, Luang Namtha (80,000K, nine hours) at 9am and Huay Xai (Borkeo, 110,000K, 15 hours) at 5.30pm and a VIP at 7pm (VIP, 135,000K).

Getting Around

Luang Prabang has no motorbike taxis, only tuk-tuks, plus the odd taxi-van from the airport charging a standardised 50,000K into town. These will cost more if over three people share the ride. From town back to the airport you might pay marginally less. From the old bridge you could walk to the terminal in around half an hour.

Around town locals often pay just 5000K for short tuk-tuk rides but foreigners are charged a flat 20,000K per hop. To the speedboat landing reckon on 50,000K for the vehicle.

A much more satisfying way to get around is by bicycle. They're rented by numerous shops and some guesthouses for 15,000-30,000K per day. Motorcycle rental typically costs US$15 a day or US$20 for 24 hours. However almost all agencies actually subcontract for **Naluang Rental** (☎ 212 979, 020-5577 2720; Naluang Minibus Station) who charge US$15 for 24 hours if you book directly with them.

Be careful to lock bicycles and motorbikes securely and don't leave them on the roadside overnight. Note that the peninsula's outer road is one-way anticlockwise; signs are easy to miss but although you'll see locals flouting the rule (and riding without helmets), police will occasionally fine foreigners for either infraction.

AROUND LUANG PRABANG

For those with limited time in Luang Prabang, agents vie to sell one day 'tours' combining the Pak Ou caves and Tat Kuang Si (prices from 105,000K). It's an odd combination, given that the sites are in opposite directions, but the advantage is that the vehicle to the Kuang Si waterfalls should be waiting when you return to the agency office from your boat trip. Note that tour prices don't include entry fees.

Pak Ou Caves

ຖ້ຳປາກອູ

The Nam Ou joins the Mekong beneath a dramatic karst formation that, from some

distance south, looks like a vast green eagle taking off. Facing it is the village of Ban Pak Ou, where a couple of river-front restaurants gaze out across the Mekong. On the other side (there's no bridge) are two famous **caves** (Tham Thing; admission 20,000K) cut into the limestone cliff. Both are crammed with Buddha images of various styles and sizes. A few steps from the river, the lower 'cave' is actually more of an overhang. A group of Buddhas pose perfectly as silhouettes against the grand riverine backdrop. To reach the upper cave, follow stairs to the left and climb for five sweaty minutes. This one is 50m-deep behind an old carved-wooden portal. If you didn't bring a torch (flashlight), you can borrow one for a suitable donation from a desk at the front.

Appealing as the scene may be, the caves themselves are less of an attraction for many visitors than the Mekong boat trip from Luang Prabang to get there. So be aware that you'll see the exact same section of river should you do a Luang Prabang–Pak Beng or Luang Prabang–Nong Khiaw boat trip (see the boxed text p142). Between January and April, villagers along the Mekong sandbanks en route pan for gold using large wooden platters.

BAN XANG HAY

Whether by road or by boat, most visitors en route to Pak Ou stop at this 'Lao Lao Village' where the narrow footpath-streets behind the very attractive (if mostly new) wat are full of weavers' looms, colourful fabric stalls and a few stills producing the wide range of liquors sold.

GETTING THERE & AWAY

Luang Prabang's longboat office sells return boat tickets to Pak Ou (per person/boat 50,000/300,000K return) taking two hours upstream, 1¼ hours back and giving you around an hour at the caves plus 20 minutes at Ban Xang Hay. Departures are most numerous around 8.30am but generally continue all morning. Travel agencies and guesthouses sell the same tickets for a little more, often including a tuk-tuk transfer.

An alternative is to go by road to Ban Pak Ou (30km, around 150,000K return for a tuk-tuk) then take a motor-canoe across the river (20,000K return). Ban Pak Ou is 10km down a decent unpaved road that turns off Rte 13 near Km 405.

Tat Kuang Si

ຕາດກວາງຊີ

Bikinis, bears and beautiful mature trees make curious bedfellows in this appealing if busy **jungle park** (admission 20,000K; ⏰ 7.30am-5.30pm) 30km southwest of town. The park is centred on a many-tiered **waterfall** that is one of Laos's most impressive, especially in the dry season. A five-minute forest walk from the restaurant-ringed carpark brings you to the first of several cascades. These tumble into limpid opal-blue pools that are popular for swimming or rope-jump dives and there are even a few changing booths (bring togs and towels). Five minutes further you'll reach the main waterfall, a powerful beauty whose longest leap is around 25m. The best views are from the footbridge at its base but you can climb to the top via exhaustingly steep footpaths on either side (around 15 minutes up). The one to the right is a slippery scramble while the one on the left is better maintained with sections of steps. Unless water is very high you can easily wade through the top pools to link the two routes.

When you entered the park you'll have noticed a well-designed **bear enclosure** (www.bearlao.com; no extra charge). The inmates here have been confiscated from poachers and are kept here in preference to releasing them to the same certain fate. Souvenirs are sold to fund their feeding.

Many cheap eateries line the entrance carpark at the top end of the Khamu village of Ban Thapene. Ten minutes' walk downhill towards Luang Prabang, **Viradesa Guesthouse** (☎ 020-7755 9808; Rte 2501, 900m past Km 23; r 70,000K) has four overpriced bare-board bungalows with mattresses on the plank floors, private cold-tap bathrooms and no mosquito nets.

GETTING THERE & AWAY

Tuk-tuks from Luang Prabang typically charge 120,000K for one person, 200,000K for several. Some folks manage to cobble together an impromptu group by meeting fellow travellers beside the baguette sellers' area near the tourist office. Or pay 45,000K per person and let an agency do the organising for you.

Visiting Kuang Si by hired motorcycle is very pleasant now that the road is decently paved and allows stops in villages along the way. By bicycle, be prepared for two long, steady hills to climb.

An appealing alternative is to charter a boat down the Mekong to Ban Ou (one hour downstream) from which the remaining 5km to the falls should be easy to hitch: Rte 2501 to the falls turns 90 degrees away from the river directly behind Ban Ou's wat. Some boatmen, however, have been known to drop passengers at different villages from which there's no choice but to charter a 'friend's' tuk-tuk.

Tat Sae

ນ້ຳຕົກຕາດແຊ້

The wide, multi-level cascade pools of this **waterfall** (admission 15,000K; ⏰ 8am-5pm) are a particularly memorable sight from August to November. They dry up almost completely by February and, unlike Tat Kuang Si, there's no single long-drop centrepiece. But several year-round gimmicks keep visitors coming, notably **elephant rides** (per person 120,000K; ⏰ 8am-3.30pm) and a loop of 14 **Zip Lines** (☎ 020-5429 0848; www.flightofthenature.com; per person 300,000K) allowing you to 'fly' around and across the falls. Only two of those lines are over 100m long so don't imagine a serious competitor to the Gibbon Experience (p174).

Part of the attraction of a visit is getting there on a very pleasant seven-minute boat ride (10,000K per person return, 20,000K minimum) that starts from **Ban Aen**, a peaceful Lao village that's just 1km east of Rte 13 – turn east at Km 371.5. By tuk-tuk, the 30-minute ride south of Luang Prabang costs from around 100,000K return including a couple of hours' wait. Ban Aen's **car park** (bike parking 3000K) is five minutes' walk short of the river and home to a second set of elephant rides (100,000K per person).

Ban Phanom & Beyond

ບ້ານພະນົມ/ສຸສານຫນູຫິດ

If you climbed Phu Si you'll surely have spied a large octagonal stupa near the 'New Bridge' painted a dazzling golden hue. This is the 1988 **Santi Chedi** (Peacefulness Pagoda; donation expected; ⏰ 8-10am & 1.30-4.30pm Mon-Fri), whose five interior levels are painted with all manner of Buddhist stories and moral admonitions. It's on a gentle rise, 1km off Rte 13 beside the road to **Ban Phanom**, a prosperous weaving- and handicrafts-village less than 1km further east. A mostly unpaved road initially follows the Nam Khan east and south, looping round eventually after 14km to **Ban Kok Gniew**, the 'pineapple village' at Km372 on Rte 13, just 500m short of the turning to Tat Sae waterfall.

The road is dusty and gently hilly but quiet and scenic with some attractive karst scenery and several points of interest. Around 4.5km from Ban Phanom, a steep signed track descends in around 300m to the whitewashed **tomb of Henri Mouhot**. Mouhot was a French Explorer best known for 'discovering' Angkor Wat. He perished of malaria in Luang Prabang during 1861, scrawling in his diary 'Have pity on me, O my God' before expiring. His heavily bearded statue at the site looks altogether more cheerful and in the drier months the riverside 'beach' beneath becomes a popular picnic and swimming spot.

Less than 2km further along the road are the mural-daubed old wat and gilded stupa of **Ban Noun Savath**. The scene is especially photogenic in afternoon light with a large karst-hump mountain forming a perfect backdrop. Just before reaching the village you'll pass the **All Lao Elephant Camp** (☎ 253 522; www.alllaoservice.com; ✆ 8am-3pm). Elephant rides lasting around 90 minutes start at 8am, 9.30am, 11.30am and 1.30pm with elephant bathing at 2.30pm. For longer mahout courses and riding-kayaking combination trips (there are dozens of possibilities), contact its Luang Prabang office (map p150; Th Sisavangvong).

Around 5km beyond, the German-organised **Elephant Village** (☎ 252 417; www.elephantvillage-laos.com, www.elephant-park-project.org) is another such place with similar offerings and is worth biking to if only to enjoy the riverside setting facing a splendid karst ridge. Elephant Village is down the spur road that dead-ends after 2km in Ban Xieng Lom village.

Both elephant camps offer comfortable accommodation, and two more luxurious bungalow resorts near Elephant Village both have gorgeous views. German-run **Lao Spirit** (☎ 030-514 0111; www.lao-spirit.com; r US$90-120, from US$75 May-Sep) is closer to the river and has a convivial collection of thatched cottages on sturdy brick stilts. Road access is 1.7km off the Phanom road but on foot it's just ten minutes' walk from the Elephant Village.

Higher up the same hill, Canadian-owned **Zen Namkhan** (☎ 030-514 2411; www.zennamkhan resort.com; r US$130-150; ✆ ✆) takes the exclusive boutique hotel approach. Expansive, stylishly minimalist bungalows enjoy wide-view balconies and inside-outside showers. Service is highly attentive. The spring-fed swimming pool is ecofriendly in refraining from chlorination but as a result is a little slimy underfoot.

Towards Vang Vieng

Rte 13 to Vang Vieng is spectacular. Stop at Km 354, near an unnamed thatched **shack-cafe**, for cinemascopic views across meandering valleys towards green dragon-toothed mountains. **Phongsaat** (Km 347) is a mixed Khamu-Hmong strip village at the base of a forest-draped crag. **Ban Phoudam** (Km 309) has a handful of restaurants with sweeping views at its southern end. Just beyond, **Kiewkacham** (Km 308) has a market and three basic **guesthouses** (r 40,000-60,000K) offering a possible rest spot for cyclists after around five hours' pedalling from Luang Prabang. Marked 'Clean Toilet, Awesome View', **Kiokalam II Guesthouse** (☎ 252 571) has cramped box rooms but Western toilets and new mattresses, along with a hidden viewpoint that really is awesome.

There are more views from **Kyomailo hamlet** (Km 296) and around **Phu Khoun** (Km 257), a transit village at the Rte 7 junction (for Phonsavan). At least four basic guesthouses at Phu Khoun have tatty rooms from 40,000K. The **Onth Bun Mixay Guesthouse** (☎ 020-5534 2375; without/with bathroom 60,000/70,000K) is a better central option with big, new beds, shiny tiled floors (walls less clean) and bucket bathrooms. The top option is **Phoukhoun Bankalao** (☎ 020-5550 4784; 500m past Km 253; r 110,000K), 3.5km further towards Vang Vieng on a chilly ridgetop, where a large restaurant aimed at coach groups has a splendid panorama not shared by the six sizeable guest rooms with sweetheart sheets, hot showers and fireplaces.

Beyond the pricey glass-walled **Phieng Fah Restaurant** (☎ 020-5522 5577; mains 25,000-40,000K; ✆ 8am-8pm), karst walls and limestone spires make the next 25km the most spectacular section of all. The twin prongs of Pha Phra viciously stab the air when viewed southbound descending towards **Nam Khene** (Km 233) a roadside hamlet whose restaurant and basic bungalows (50,000K) sadly fail to overlook the scene. **Kasi** (p139), 30km further south, has more accommodation choices.

THE MIDDLE MEKONG

The mighty Mekong threads together the provinces of Bokeo and Sainyabuli, along with Pak Beng in southern Udomxai. For many tourists the region is seen merely in passing between Thailand and Luang Prabang – typically on the two-day slowboat route from Huay Xai via Pak Beng – but there's plenty to interest the more adventurous traveller. Bokeo, meaning 'Gem Mine', takes its name from the sapphire deposits in Huay Xai district, and the province harbours 34 ethnicities despite a particularly sparse population. Sainyabuli Province, especially Hongsa, is synonymous with working elephants. Other than in Huay Xai and Pak Beng you'll need a decent phrasebook wherever you go. Western Sainyabuli remains particularly far off the traveller radar but if you want to be way ahead of the crowds, places like dramatic Khop district are 'last frontiers' with a complex ethnic mix and reputedly high proportion of still-pristine forests.

HUAY XAI (HOKSAY)

ຫ້ວຍຊາຍ

☎ 084 / pop 20,000

All that many travellers see of this Mekong river-town is the central strip of guesthouses and tour operators, plus the queue of tuk-tuks waiting to rush them to the bus station, river port or cross-river jetty to Thailand. The place feels less organised than Thailand and not as immediately beguiling as elsewhere in Laos, but step back just a little and you'll quickly find a backdrop of rich green hills and friendly outer villages. If you're doing the Gibbon Experience you'll need to stop the night here.

Information

Lao Development Bank Exchange Booth (☽ 8am-5pm daily) Handy booth right beside the pedestrian immigration window. Most major currencies exchanged into kip. US$ bills must be dated 2006 or later.

BCEL (☽ 8.30am-3.30pm Mon-Fri) Exchange and international 24-hour ATM.

Phongsavanh Bank (☽ 8.30am-4.30pm) Exchanges 11 currencies including Vietnamese dong seven days a week. Fronted by big bronze elephants.

Yon Computer (per 20 mins 5000K; ☽ 8am-10pm) High speed wi-fi and internet, plus computer repairs.

Laundry (10,000K per kg) Clothes machine-washed to order, with fabric softener.

Tourist Information Office (☎ 211 162; ☽ 8am-4.30pm Mon-Fri) Has free, OK tourist maps of the town and some suggestions for excursions around the province.

Sights

Huay Xai's modest tourist attractions include the Mekong views from several colourful wats. *Naga* stairs, ascending opposite the ferry access lane, emerge at the hilltop **Wat Jom Khao Manilat**, originally constructed in 1880. Commanding the rise directly above the speedboat landing, 3km south of the central area, **Wat Thadsuvanna Phakham** is a colourful new temple featuring a row of eight gilded Buddhas demonstrating the main meditation postures and disdaining Mekong views beneath floral foliage. **Wat Khonekeo Xaiyaram**, in Ban Khonekeo, has a lavish frontage with dazzling red, gold and green pillars and doors. **Wat Keophone Savanthanaram** features murals of gruesome torture scenes on the *sǐm*'s north wall while on the slope above, a long Buddha reclines behind chicken wire.

The very dilapidated shell of French-built **Fort Carnot** sits on the hilltop behind the Bokeo

---

CROSSING THE THAI BORDER AT CHIANG KHONG & HUAY XAI (HOKSAY)

Crossing the Lao–Thai **border** (☽ 8am-6pm) here is by Mekong riverboat (a bridge is planned eventually). Even if you're planning to head straight for Luang Prabang, don't let sneaky Thai-side signs like 'last chips', 'last drinks' etc mislead you into thinking that you won't find snacks for sale on the Lao side.

Pedestrians cross by longboat (three minutes), costing per person/big bag 30/10B from the Thai side, 10,000/3000K from the Lao side. Boats leave within a few minutes, even with only two or three passengers. As usual the Lao immigration post gives thirty-day tourist visas on arrival (most nationalities US$30 to US$40 plus a US$1 surcharge at weekends or after 4pm). If you don't have a passport-style mugshot they'll charge 40B extra. An exchange booth right beside Lao immigration (open till 5pm) converts currencies at a fair rate, eg selling US dollars to pay the visa fee or Thai baht for those heading into Thailand – arriving on the Thai side you'll need 30B to pay the port charge (or 60B after 4.30pm) and another 30B for the tuk-tuk to the bus station. The nearest Thai-side ATM is nearly 2km south.

A vehicle ferry crosses a few times daily (except Sunday) between the main Thai immigration point and the slowboat landing in Huay Xai, costing 500B for motorcycles, 1000B for cars (or 1500B on the 5pm sailing).

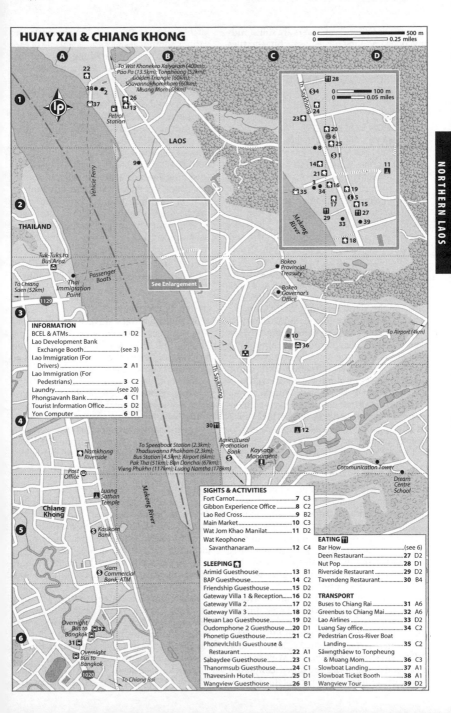

HUAY XAI & CHIANG KHONG

To Wat Khonekeo Xaiyaram (400m);
Pao Pa (13.5km); Tonpheung (52km);
Golden Triangle (60km);
Souvannakhomkham (60km);
Muang Mom (68km)

LAOS

THAILAND

Vehicle Ferry

Petrol Station

Tuk-Tuks to
Bus Area

Passenger Boats

To Chiang Saen (52km)

Thai Immigration Point

1129

Bokeo Provincial Treasury

Bokeo Governor's Office

To Airport (4km)

See Enlargement

Th Saykhong

Mekong River

Namkhong Riverside

Post Office

Luang Sathan Temple

Chiang Khong

Kasikorn Bank

Siam Commercial Bank; ATM

Overnight Bus to Bangkok

Overnight Bus to Bangkok

1020

To Chiang Rai

To Speedboat Station (2.3km);
Thadsuvanna Phakham (2.3km);
Bus Station (4.5km); Airport (6km);
Pak Tha (51km); Ban Donchai (67km);
Vieng Phukha (117km); Luang Namtha (178km)

Agricultural Promotion Bank

Kaysone Monument

Communication Tower

Dream Centre School

INFORMATION
BCEL & ATMs	**1**	D2
Lao Development Bank Exchange Booth	(see 3)	
Lao Immigration (For Drivers)	**2**	A1
Lao Immigration (For Pedestrians)	**3**	C2
Laundry	(see 20)	
Phongsavanh Bank	**4**	C1
Tourist Information Office	**5**	D2
Yon Computer	**6**	D1

SIGHTS & ACTIVITIES
Fort Carnot	**7**	C3
Gibbon Experience Office	**8**	C2
Lao Red Cross	**9**	B2
Main Market	**10**	C3
Wat Jom Khao Manilat	**11**	D2
Wat Keophone Savanthanaram	**12**	C4

SLEEPING
Arimid Guesthouse	**13**	B1
BAP Guesthouse	**14**	C2
Friendship Guesthouse	**15**	D2
Gateway Villa 1 & Reception	**16**	D2
Gateway Villa 2	**17**	D2
Gateway Villa 3	**18**	D2
Heuan Lao Guesthouse	**19**	D2
Oudomphone 2 Guesthouse	**20**	D1
Phonetip Guesthouse	**21**	C2
Phonevichith Guesthouse & Restaurant	**22**	A1
Sabaydee Guesthouse	**23**	C1
Thanormsub Guesthouse	**24**	C2
Thaveesinh Hotel	**25**	D1
Wangview Guesthouse	**26**	B1

EATING
Bar How	(see 6)	
Deen Restaurant	**27**	D2
Nut Pop	**28**	D1
Riverside Restaurant	**29**	D2
Tavendeng Restaurant	**30**	B4

TRANSPORT
Buses to Chiang Rai	**31**	A6
Greenbus to Chiang Mai	**32**	A6
Lao Airlines	**33**	D2
Luang Say office	**34**	C2
Pedestrian Cross-River Boat Landing	**35**	C2
Săwngthăew to Tonpheung & Muang Mom	**36**	C3
Slowboat Landing	**37**	A1
Slowboat Ticket Booth	**38**	A1
Wangview Tour	**39**	D2

Governor's Office. Two towers are still standing, one straddling the gateway, but the tiles are falling off the old barrack room roofs and the whole sparse site is very overgrown. Tucked in the valley behind is Huay Xai's vibrant **main market**.

Activities
THE GIBBON EXPERIENCE
The three-day **Gibbon Experience** (www.gibbonx. org, experience@gibbonx.org; all-inclusive €180, 9000B or 2,250,000K) is one of Laos's most unforgettable adventures but you must book way ahead and it's quite inappropriate for young children or those with physical disabilities, vertigo, arachnophobia etc. Essentially this is an extended chance to play Tarzan; living two nights in soaring tree houses within thickly forested hills and swinging high across intervening valleys on incredible zip lines, some over 500m long. Part of the price supports the conservation of the forest that's home to a species of gibbon once thought extinct in Laos. For those on the **'classic experience'** there's a good chance of hearing the gibbons' bizarre singing – a noise that starts like a rising penny whistle then oscillates like an alien spaceship taking off (and is almost as loud). Actually seeing gibbons is much rarer but some lucky groups do catch a fleeting glimpse. Unless making a pre-dawn trek to Tree-house 3, participants on the **'waterfall trek'** are far less likely to hear gibbons but that variant's longer hikes give an added sense of purpose and you get to sleep in two different tree-houses instead of just one. The waterfall for which it's named is a forgettable sideshow but in both variants the real highlight is the zip-lining which is the only way to reach your accommodation. That's in unique thatched tree-houses that are spaced sufficiently far from each other so that each feels entirely alone in the jungle. Often around 40m above the ground and set in natural amphitheatres with spectacular views, most of the tree-houses sleep eight people with bedding laid out beneath large cloth nets. Note that in general two people must sleep side-by-side, potentially a socially awkward predicament for solo travellers. Large spiders on the walls and rats rustling in the ceilings will be your companions too, but this is the jungle after all. Tree-houses 2 (Classic) and 4 (Waterfall) sleep just two people. Well-cooked meals consisting of rice and four accompaniments are zip-lined in from one of three rustic

kitchens while coffee, tea, hot chocolate and various additional snacks are available in each tree-house. Keeping anything edible in the provided strong box is essential to avoid the forest rats being attracted.

Booking around six weeks ahead is virtually essential, especially in the dry season. Pre-payment online through Paypal works well but do be patient as communication isn't always immediate. One day before your booked departure, check in at its **Huay Xai office** (☎ 212 021; ☽ office 8-11am & 2-7pm). Gloves (essential for using the zip-lines) are sold next door for 8000K. It's also advisable to bring a torch (flashlight), water bottle and maybe some playing cards, but otherwise leave most of your baggage in the office storeroom – everything you bring you must carry on your back over some steep hikes and on the zip lines. As there'll be no electricity for three days, don't forget to pre-charge camera batteries.

OTHER ACTIVITIES
Most **hill-tribe treks** advertised by Huay Xai agencies actually start from Vieng Phukha (p222) so you'll generally do better to book them there. One-day **tours** to Souvannakhomkham (p178), including a boat ride around the Golden Triangle (p178), are also offered but there are rarely enough travellers signing up to make the prices viable.

Lao Red Cross (☎ 211 935; ☽ 9am-9pm) offers Swedish-Lao massage for 30,000K per hour and a traditional herbal sauna (10,000K) from 4pm in a stately old mansion beside the Mekong.

Sleeping
The central drag is packed with guesthouses and many more are dotted at sporadic intervals for several kilometres towards the bus station. Oddly the inconvenient outer places including the once-plush Mekong Lao Hotel seem in general poorer value than the more central options. Condoms do the talking in several others.

Heuan Lao Guesthouse (☎ 211 163; s/d/tr 40,000/50,000/60,000K) Tatty yet perversely endearing in its dogged refusal to modernise the 1960s furniture, faded pheasant-print wall panels and cheap vinyl that covers the old wooden floorboards.

Phonetip Guesthouse (☎ 211 084; tw/tr without bathroom 40,000/60,000K, with solar/electric hot water r 50,000/60,000K) Simple, central and clean by budget standards, the cheapest options are just beds in boxes but there's a pleasant road-facing communal area to sit upstairs if you can grab a seat.

Friendship Guesthouse (☎ 211 219; s/d/tr/q from 45,000/60,000/90,000/125,000K) Rooms have the usual aged patches and beds can be creaky but the selling point here is the open roof with great views and three simple tables at which to enjoy them.

Thanormsub Guesthouse (☎ 211 095; r with fan/TV/air-con 70,000/90,000/120,000K; ✸) Airy but functional beneath a conspicuous blue roof.

Oudomphone 2 Hotel (☎ 211 308; r with fan/air-con 75,000/120,000K; ✸) Clean and neat with polished floors, tree-slice tables and a few oddments of local fabric to soften the concrete interiors. Bathrooms have hot water, though some are a little musty.

BAP Guesthouse (☎ 211 083; r with fan/TV/view/air-con 80,000/100,000/130,000/150,000K; ✸) BAP looks lovably old-fashioned from the outside, while the appealing wood-panelled rooms at the back have been recently refreshed. The English-speaking owner aggressively refuses to show rooms until they're paid for.

Phonevichith Guesthouse & Restaurant (☎ 211 765; Ban Khonekeo; r 300B; ✸) Colourful fabrics, fans and kitschy lamps add a little character to the decent rooms, which come with piping-hot showers and optional air-con (extra charge). The main attraction is the Mekong perch and handy proximity to the slowboat landing.

Thaveesinh Hotel (☎ 211 502; s/d/tw 65,000/78,000/90,000, with air-con 105,000/140,000/168,000; ✸) Rooms in this very central hotel are fair sized and clean if chintzy with pink curtains and windows that don't always shut securely. Heavy wooden furniture and ornaments decorate common areas and there's a rooftop breakfast room.

Gateway Villa Hotel (☎ 020-5521 3355; s/d 78,000/96,000K, s/d/tr with air-con 96,000/122,000/143,000K; ✸ 🖳) Combining three very different, disconnected buildings, high points here are the proactively helpful service and free breakfast at the stylish central cafe. Rooms come with good new linens but otherwise have little appeal, even in boutiquey new Gateway Villa 2. Above reception, Gateway Villa 1 is a dowdy if well located study in faded 1960s concrete with low ceilings and hardboard walls. Unmarked opposite the school, building 3's

air-con rooms feel like converted container boxes but the upstairs fan rooms share a great little Mekong view terrace – fine if you don't mind the odd cobweb and large associated spiders.

Arimid Guesthouse (Alimit; ☎ 211 040; s/d/tw/tr 80,000/80,000/90,000/100,000K, with air-con d/tr 150,000/180,000K; ✸) At first glance this collection of thatched bamboo bungalows has more atmosphere than the town's typical concrete box-hotels. However, while comfortable enough, the rooms are far from stylish and can be a little dingy. It's handy for the slowboat landing and the owner speaks French.

Sabaydee Guesthouse (☎ 211 252; fan/air-con 100,000/140,000K; ✸) Clean and bright, the Sabaydee offers smartly maintained – if largely unadorned – rooms with reliable hot water. Reclining wooden seats on the rear third floor create a gem of a communal chill-out area with a foliage-framed view of the Mekong. The owner speaks French.

Wangview Guesthouse (☎ 211 055; www.wangviewtour.net; r 500B; ✸) Handy for the slowboat landing, this smart new air-conditioned guesthouse makes good use of pale polished wood and provides bathrooms that are ample if sometimes a tad musty due to poor ventilation. Don't confuse this place with a second highly inconvenient Wangview Guesthouse way out west beyond the Pak Tha turning, or the Mekong-facing Wangview Resort, whose cabins suffer a karaoke onslaught at night.

Eating

Of three *falang*-style restaurants near the slowboat pier, that at Phonevichith Guesthouse has the best river views. Old ladies sell banana leaves full of sticky rice (3000K) and *mok* (5000K) as takeaway snacks from ad hoc tables around the corner on Rte 3.

Deen Restaurant (☎ 020-5590 1871; veg/non-veg curries 13,000/23,000K, fruit shake/lassi 7000/10,000K; ☯ 7am-10.30pm) This simple timber-walled shop-house is a fashion parade for calendar girls. It serves halal Indian food such as creamy tofu korma and fruit shakes with a hint of coconut. Breakfast offerings include pancakes and parathas.

our pick **Nut Pop** (☎ 211 037; mains 15,000-35,000K; pizza 42,000-50,000K; ☯ 4.30-10.30pm) Long coloured cylinders of twinkling lights entice you into this atmospheric timber deck surrounded by foliage. The cuisine is just as delightful, ranging from perfectly executed Lao and

Vietnamese dishes to inventive twists on pizza (try the Lao Discovery).

Riverside Restaurant (☎ 211 064; mains 20,000-60,000K; ☒ 7am-11pm) The Mekong terrace here offers a great vantage point from which to watch the ferry canoes shuttling to and fro to Thailand. The menu has a wide range of Thai and Lao food, plus Western breakfasts. It would also be ideal for a sunset beer if the music weren't so cheesy.

Bar How (veg/non-veg meals 22,000/24,000K; ☒ 6.30am-11pm; ☎) The funkiest little bar-restaurant on Huay Xai's main strip, Bar How is decorated with muskets and wine bottles. Mushrooms with ginger and sesame is one of many lip-smacking vegetarian choices and the rice is included in most quoted menu prices. You can use wi-fi on the terrace by arrangement with the next-door Yon Computer. Attached on the other side, a tiny shop sells a few second-hand books and 330ml bottles of locally made 'wines' (20,000K), some produced from ginger, others from Malacca fruits.

Tavendeng Restaurant (☎ 020-5568 4999; mains 25,000-80,000K; ☒ 7am-11pm) Predominantly aimed at Thai visitors, this large wooden dining complex features live music and exotic foods such as frog and fried crocodile.

Getting There & Away

For years, streams of Luang Prabang–bound travellers have piled into Huay Xai and jumped straight aboard a boat for the memorable descent of the Mekong. Today, improving roads mean that an ever-increasing proportion opt instead for the overnight bus. But although slightly cheaper than the slowboat, the bus is far less social, less attractive

---

RURAL RETREATS

Most rural accommodation in northern Laos is squarely aimed at the backpacker market. But if you want something a little more special book ahead at one of these:

- **Muang La Resort**, p214
- **Zen Namkhan**, p171
- **Nong Kiau Riverside**, p206
- **Auberge de la Plaine des Jarres**, p191
- **Pak Beng Lodge**, p180
- **Boat Landing Guesthouse**, p219

---

and leaves most travellers exhausted on arrival so isn't necessarily a great time-saver either.

AIR

Huay Xai's airport is oddly perched on a hillside off the city bypass, 1.5km northwest of the bus station. **Lao Airlines** (☎ 211 026, 211 494; ☒ 8am-noon & 1-5pm Mon-Sat) flies to/from Vientiane (895,000K) on Tuesday, Thursday and Saturday.

BOAT
Slowboats to Pak Beng & Luang Prabang

Slowboats currently depart from Huay Xai at 11am daily. Purchase tickets at the **slowboat ticket booth** (☎ 211 659) to Pak Beng (100,000K, one day) or Luang Prabang (two days, 200,000K, accommodation not included). Sales start at 8am on the day of travel. Buying a ticket from a travel agent (150,000K to Pak Beng) simply means you get an overpriced tuk-tuk transfer to the pier and then have to sit around awaiting departure.

'Seats' are typically uncomfortable wooden benches for which you'll value the expenditure of 10,000K for a cushion (sold at many an agency in town). Some boats also have a number of more comfy airliner-style seats. Certain folks choose to arrive at dawn to reserve these, ie to sit on them before anyone else as tickets aren't numbered. Every day is different and at the time of research the slowboats weren't as horrendously overcrowded as they had been in the past, but if they try to cram on too many passengers (over 70 or so), a tactic that really works is for later arrivals to simply refuse to get aboard until a second boat is provided. In one case that we observed, a second boat left half-empty when the earlier one had been crammed full. Some travellers prefer to arrive just before 11am, gambling on such a scenario. But it is indeed a gamble.

'Luxury' Slow Boats

To do the two-day river journey in more comfort, a popular if pricey alternative is the 40-seat **Luang Say** (☎ 020-5509 0718; www.luangsay.com; ☒ 8am-3pm). Packages include meals, guides, visits en route and a night's accommodation at the appealing Luang Say Lodge in Pak Beng (see p180). Departures are three or four times weekly in peak season (s/d €331/576, last-minute r US$458) and twice-weekly in the low season from May to September (s/d

€224/366). There's no service at all in June or when the Mekong is too low.

With some patience a small group could charter their own slowboat from around US$700 (highly negotiable).

Speedboats & Longboats

The **speedboat landing** (☎ 211 457; Rte 3, 200m beyond Km 202) is directly beneath Wat Thadsuvanna Phakham, 3km south of town. Six-passenger speedboats (*héua wái*) zip thrillingly but dangerously and with great physical discomfort to Pak Beng (per person/boat 160,000/960,000K, three hours) and Luang Prabang (360,000/2,040,000K, seven hours including lunch stop) typically departing around 8am. For speedboats to Xieng Kok (p227) it's cheaper to start from Muang Mom (p178).

For the two-day **longboat trip** to Luang Namtha (or to Na Lae in the dry season), charters cost around 6000B/US$200 if organised by agencies, about 1,300,000K when discussed directly with a boatman (something that's tough without spoken Lao). It's sometimes possible to find a longboat bound for Ban Khon Kham (p223) leaving after dawn from the speedboat landing in which case boatmen charge just 150,000K per person – from Ban Khon Kham you'll need to organise onward boats to Na Lae.

BUS & SĂWNGTHĂEW

Note that Huay Xai bound buses are usually marked 'Borkeo'. The bus station is 5km east of town. Buses to Luang Prabang (14 to 17 hours) via Luang Namtha and Udomxai depart at 9am, 11.30am, 1pm and 5pm. The 11.30am continues to Vientiane (230,000K, 22 to 30 hours). The 5pm Luang Prabang bus is a VIP service (135,000K) that includes blankets and seats that recline a little but certainly aren't ideal for sleeping. For Udomxai (80,000K, nine hours) there's also an 8.30am service. For Luang Namtha (55,000K, 4½ hours) additional buses leave at 9am and 12.30pm, or you could use China-bound services: the 8.30am to Mengla (110,000K, seven hours) runs daily; the 7.30am to Jinghong (also spelt Xienghuong or Xianghouang; 150,000K, 10 hours) currently operates Tuesday, Thursday and Saturday only.

Travel agency minibuses to Luang Namtha leave from central Huay Xai at around 9am (400B) but still arrive at Namtha's inconveniently out-of-town bus station.

Săwngthăew to Pak Tha depart from a small station directly above the speedboat landing. *Săwngthăew* to Tonpheung (30,000K) leave when full from beside the main market, very occasionally continuing to Muang Mom.

On the Thai side, buses leave from assorted offices around 2.5km south of Chiang Khong's Thai immigration post. To Chiang Rai (65B, 2¼ hours) local services leave hourly on the hour from 6am to 5pm in either direction. **Greenbus** (☎ Thailand 0066 5365 5732; www.greenbusthailand.com) has services to Chiang Mai at 6am, 9am (272B) and 11.40am (211B). Several overnight buses leave for Bangkok (493B to 739B, 10 hours) from nearby at 3pm and 3.30pm.

GETTING AROUND

Wangview Tour (☎ 211 055; www.wangviewtour.net; ☻ 8am-noon & 1.30-5pm) rents small, relatively new motorcycles (per half/full day 150/250B). Bicycles (per day 30,000K) and older motorbikes are available from the Thaveesinh Hotel.

Tuk-tuks line up on the main road just 50m beyond Lao immigration charging 15,000K per person to the speedboat or slow boat landings and 20,000K to the airport or bus station. The road here is one way so don't panic if they seem to head off in the 'wrong' direction.

On the Thai side, tuk-tuks wait just above the immigration post and beside a market close to Chiang Khong's various bus offices. Pay 30B between the two points.

AROUND HUAY XAI
North of Huay Xai

In 2008, Rte 3 was totally rebuilt from Huay Xai (Km 199 to 206) to Luang Namtha via Vieng Phukha (Km 87, p222). Nonetheless it has already become heavily degraded for a 60km section south of **Ban Sod** (Km 123), where good asphalt returns and after which are a series of layered ridge-top views. Access to the **Gibbon Experience** (p174) is from the tiny Hmong village of **Ban Toup**. That's 14km on the mud road from **Ban Donchai** (Rte 3, Km 137.7) but don't just show up – you're usually expected to start from Huay Xai. If you've prepaid and have made very explicit advance arrangements, it is possible to be met or dropped-off at Ban Donchai, saving two hours' journey when connecting to/from Luang Namtha. However, that will likely mean needing to sleep at Donchai, where the only accommodation is an extremely rustic three-room guesthouse (r 30,000K) attached to the village shop with rough plank floors and a shared terrace overlooking the stream.

West of Huay Xai

While not dramatically beautiful, Rte 3 west of Huay Xai is initially well paved and offers some curiosities as it approximately follows the Mekong to **Nam Keung** (Km 22). Then it leaves the riverside and becomes a flat, wide but painfully dusty unpaved affair – at least until roadworks are complete.

PAO PA

Pretty **Pao Pa** is a haphazardly re-gilded ancient Buddha rock, set beneath fronds of bougainvillea on a ledge overlooking the Mekong's rocky passage. To find it, descend for 20 seconds on foot from a point 500m west of the very conspicuous Vocational School (Km 13). There's a white on green sign in Lao.

TONPHEUNG

At Km 49, an (as yet unfinished) bypass forks right, while pot-holed old Rte 3 continues 1km to a T-junction. Turn left and make a west-southwest dogleg through **Tonpheung** (2.5km south) to head for Souvannakhomkham. Or turn right for Muang Mom (21km), passing **Chalernsup Guesthouse** (☎ 020-5579 0555; r with fan/air-con 200/500B; ✿) set in a dusty Mekong-front garden.

SOUVANNAKHOMKHAM

In a wide bend of the Mekong are the scattered ruins of **Souvannakhomkham**, an ancient city site refounded in the 1560s by Lan Xang king Sai Setthathirat. Today all you'll see are a few brick-piles that were once stupas plus a couple of crumbling Buddha statues all dotted widely about an expanse of almost-flat maize fields. The greatest concentration of sites lies 900m off the lane between Ban Don That and Ban Hanjin. Get there by heading 8km southwest from Tonpheung, turn right when you spot the '900' on an otherwise all-Lao script sign. Fork left just before arriving at the 7.2m-high seated **brick Buddha**, a very eroded figure that's the site's best known icon. The setting amid towering flame trees is quietly magical. And distantly visible across the Mekong on the Thai side shimmers a larger golden Buddha. Sadly Souvannakhomkham's access roads are infuriatingly rutted, dusty when dry and appalling muddy when wet, especially the short

cut back to Rte 3 via Ban Don That (emerging at an unmarked junction around 15km west of Nam Keung).

GOLDEN TRIANGLE

Around 5km north of Tonpheung, dusty Rte 3 abruptly undergoes an astonishing transformation. Suddenly you're gliding along a two-coloured paved avenue, lined with palm trees and immaculately swept by teams of cleaners. Golden domes and pseudo-classical charioteers rear beside you. No, you haven't ingested a happy pizza. This is Laos's' surreal Las Vegas, a casino and entertainment project still under construction but planned one day to cover almost 100 sq km. After 2.5km this surreal strip turns left and dead-ends after 600m at the Mekong beside another Disneyesque fantasy dome and a mini Big Ben. You've arrived at the famous Golden Triangle, where Thailand and Laos face off, with Myanmar sticking a long nosed sand bank between the two. Boat cruises potter past from the Thai side, while on the Lao bank speedboats await but foreigners can't cross the border without prearranged authorisation.

MUANG MOM

Rte 3's fairytale avenue turns back into a bumpy pumpkin before **Ban Siboun** (Km 58), a conspicuously wealthy village with a colourful new wat. The road ends at **Muang Mom** (Km 68), which is of interest mainly for those wishing to take a speedboat (per person/boat 900/3500K) up the Mekong to Xieng Kok (p227). There's no certain schedule and the route is impossible when river levels are low, typically January to May. Muang Mom's inconspicuous speedboat jetty is tucked behind the main wat. Around 300m further south along the riverfront is an unlabelled **guesthouse** (tw 200B) whose rooms are far more basic than you'd imagine from the grand cream-and-beige mansion containing them.

East of Huay Xai

PAK THA
ປາກທາ

The very rare travellers who venture down the Mekong to this pleasant if unremarkable port are usually hoping to score a cheap longboat ride up the Nam Tha towards Na Lae (p222) or Luang Namtha (p216). Finding a ride is by no means assured, but an advantage here is that any passing boat must stop and have relevant papers stamped at the Phone Tong boatmen's office. Officer Tong Dam working there speaks great French but minimal English.

Pak Tha's main town area is across the deep-cut Nam Tha from the boatmen's office, very close as the crow flies but 2km by road. After crossing the high concrete bridge, take the first major unpaved road right to find the market. Where that road peters out, take the last lane to the left to find Pak Tha's only formal accommodation, the **Souphany Guesthouse** (☎ 020-5598 3469; r 50,000K). It has cramped rooms and hard mattresses but the shared bucket-flush squat is clean enough and there are sunset views across the Mekong from the *petang* rectangle behind. A simple restaurant is attached and Boan Mee speaks some English.

Săwngthăew run occasionally to Huay Xai. The daily Pak Beng–Huay Xai slowboats stop briefly at the landing beneath the boatmen's office.

PAK BENG
ປາກແບ່ງ
☎ 084 / pop 20,000
This winding, one-street strip-town straggles above a steep-sided stretch of the Mekong. The numerous pretty river views are particularly striking when dry-season water levels drop to reveal jagged waterside rocks. However, the town makes little of its tourist potential and most travellers simply stop one night here when en route to Huay Xai or Luang Prabang by slowboat, or take a break here for lunch on Huay Xai–Luang Prabang speedboats. The modest **tourist office** (www.oudomxay.info; ⊙ 7am-noon & 2-9pm) can arrange guides and has maps of the town.

Hydroelectric power now lights the town 24 hours a day. Well, at least when there's water in the dam. Some days in the dry season (February to June) power cuts occur and at such times it's worth paying a little extra for a guesthouse with a generator.

Guesthouses can change money at dismal rates but there's no bank nor ATM. Thai baht are widely used. There are no internet cafes (yet) but if you buy a drink at the Luang Say or Pak Beng lodges the wi-fi is free.

Sights & Activities
Overlooking the Mekong are two monasteries: relatively modern **Wat Khok Kho**; and archaic little **Wat Sin Jong Jaeng**. The latter dates back to the early colonial period and although its eaves have been entirely repainted, an old, very faded mural remains on the *sĭm*'s eastern exterior. Look carefully and you'll spot a moustachioed figure with hat, umbrella and big nose, presumably representing an early European visitor.

Across the Mekong the **Elephant Camp** (☎ 071-254 130; from US$47) offers rides and bathtime observations of former working elephants by arrangement with Pak Beng Lodge for whose guests the project seems mostly aimed. Even if you don't plan to play with pachyderms, a pleasant excursion is to cross

NORTHERN LAOS

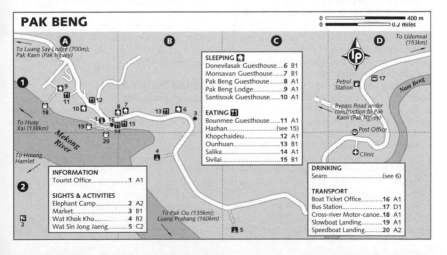

PAK BENG

0 — 400 m
0 — 0.2 miles

To Udomxai (153km)

To Luang Say Lodge (700m); Pak Kaen (Pak Nguey)

To Huay Xai (138km)

To Hmong Hamlet

Mekong River

To Pak Ou (135km); Luang Prabang (160km)

Petrol Station

Bypass Road under construction to Pak Kaen (Pak Nguey)

Post Office

Clinic

Nam Beng

SLEEPING
Donevilasak Guesthouse......6 B1
Monsavan Guesthouse......7 B1
Pak Beng Guesthouse........8 A1
Pak Beng Lodge................9 A1
Santisouk Guesthouse......10 A1

EATING
Bounmee Guesthouse......11 A1
Hashan..........................(see 15)
Khopchaideu....................12 A1
Ounhuan..........................13 B1
Salika..............................14 A1
Sivilai..............................15 B1

INFORMATION
Tourist Office....................1 A1

SIGHTS & ACTIVITIES
Elephant Camp..................2 A2
Market.............................3 B1
Wat Khok Kho..................4 B2
Wat Sin Jong Jaeng..........5 C2

DRINKING
Searo..............................(see 6)

TRANSPORT
Boat Ticket Office............16 A1
Bus Station......................17 D1
Cross-river Motor-canoe...18 A1
Slowboat Landing............19 A1
Speedboat Landing.........20 A2

the river (motor-canoe 5000K) then walk for about ten minutes diagonally right away from the river to a tiny, authentic **Hmong hamlet**.

The tourist office suggests a typical selection of local caves and waterfalls in the district and there are villages to explore if you can find a motorbike for rent – try asking at your guesthouse (individuals around the **market** ask an outrageous 40,000K per hour).

Most of the hillsides along the Udomxai road have been brutally deforested but one attractive stretch survives around 10km north of Pak Beng.

Sleeping

Prices are high by rural Lao standards. Touts meet boats, offering cheap digs from around 150B, generally tiny rooms with hard mattresses and shared facilities. For 300B you can get a decent room with hot shower (if electricity is working), though prices can rise further when demand is high. With sixteen relatively similar options within five minutes' walk it's worth comparing several options.

Santisouk Guesthouse (☎ 020-5578 1797; r old/new 200/400B) In the new building, expect stylishly rolled towels on comfy new beds, sash curtains and double-door arrangements to allow a good through-current of air. These rooms are better than the shamelessly overpriced Phetokxai Hotel opposite yet cost a third of the price. Rooms in the old building are contrastingly basic with hard beds and hardboard ceilings. A simple shared-view platform allows guests to contemplate the Mekong.

Donevilasak Guesthouse (☎ 212 315; r without/with bathroom 200/400B) The last guesthouse on the strip has three buildings. One is a dowdy old timber house with very basic box rooms sharing a bathroom (hot water). The others are decent sized and modern albeit with a little staining in the otherwise-good private bathrooms.

Pak Beng Guesthouse (☎ 020-5606 1428; r 300B) Neat, clean and central with fair-sized, high-ceilinged rooms and box-spring beds. Decor is minimal and toilets burp but showers are hot and the generator is reliable during blackouts.

Monsavan Guesthouse (☎ 212 619; r 400-500B) The polished wood floors and exterior are attractive and the relatively smart new rooms come with hot water, though walls are thin. Money exchange is possible at poor rates.

Pak Beng Lodge (☎ 212 304; www.pakbenglodge. com; s/d/ste from US$72/87/118; ☞) This enticing upmarket complex occupies a garden slope above the Mekong where all rooms have river views. The cheaper 'superior' rooms feature bamboo deckchairs on private balconies but it's the magnificent deluxe suites that really impress, a symphony of rosewood shutters, whitewashed pillars and terracotta tiles that crown a small hillock directly behind. Chill out in the indulgent upper lounge or take an in-room massage from US$10.

Luang Say Lodge (☎ 212 296; www.mekongcruises. com; per person half board low/high season US$72/119; ☞) In season this delightful traditionally styled wooden ecolodge is almost entirely reserved for guests on the Luang Say riverboat (p177), for whom a stay is included. But when low waters stop the boat, room prices fall substantially.

Eating & Drinking

There's a string of stomach-filling possibilities; most places have long menus and all charge approximately the same prices (mains 10,000-25,000K) for standard Lao, Thai and Western fare. By day, pick one with a good Mekong view like the **Bounmee Guesthouse**, **Salika** or **Sivilai**. The latter offers a 6pm happy hour (Beerlao 8000K). By night, colourful lanterns make **Ounhuan** a favourite. Indian restaurant **Hashan** also has appealing lighting and decor but the curries at **Khopchaideu** are more accomplished. Most eateries open around 7am and make 15,000K sandwiches to sell as take-away boat lunches. Most kitchens stop cooking around 9pm and by 10pm you might need to search a little even to find a beer. **Searo**, a one-room laser-lit nightspot, has occasional dancing.

The Luang Say Lodge's splendid bar-restaurant is ideal for enjoying Mekong views with a sundowner, and glasses of boxed wine cost only US$3.

Getting There & Away

The tiny **bus station** is at the northernmost edge of town with departures to Udomxai (35,000K, four hours) at 9am and noon plus a 3pm sǎwngthǎew to Muang Houn (20,000K, two hours).

The **downriver slowboat** to Luang Prabang departs between 9am and 10am (100,000K, around eight hours) with request stops possible at Pak Tha and Tha Suang (for Hongsa). The slowboat for Huay Xai (100,000K, around nine hours) departs 8am. For Muang Ngeun, request a stop at Pak Kaen (Pak Nguey) then hope that the connecting *săwngthăew* shows up. You could alternatively take a speedboat (50,000K per person) or tuk-tuk (120,000K charter) plus river ferry (5000K) to Pak Kaen then attempt to hitch, but traffic is very sparse and the port manager tries to charge hitchhikers a hefty commission (so walk away from the dock area).

Speedboats take around three hours to either Luang Prabang or Huay Xai, costing 170,000K per person assuming a crushed-full quota of six passengers (dangerous and highly uncomfortable). Arriving by speedboat, local boys will generally offer to carry your bags for about 5000K (after some bargaining). If your bags are unwieldy this can prove money well spent, as when river levels are low you'll need to cross two planks and climb a steep sandbank to reach the road into town. Accessing the slowboat landing is less awkward.

THA SUANG
pop 40

This scattering of homes is simply the Mekong jetty for Hongsa. Slowboats are met by Hongsa-bound *săwngthăew* (20,000K, 70 minutes). However, if less than 10 people get off the morning boat from Pak Beng you might have to charter (200,000K) or wait till around 4pm for the boat from Luang Prabang to come in. There's no through traffic whatsoever, so don't count on hitching. Should you get stranded, the first unmarked building on the right as you arrive off the boat is an extremely basic two-room guesthouse without light bulbs.

HONGSA
ຫົງສາ

☎ 074 / pop 6000

Especially for elephant-lovers, Hongsa makes a good journey break between Luang Prabang and Nan (Thailand, via Muang Ngeun). The centre is a grid of newer constructions but the town's stream-ribboned edges are backed by beautiful layered rice fields. The **Lao Development Bank** here is the nearest bank to the Thai border and exchanges baht, US$ and euros.

The most characterful of Hongsa's several monasteries is **Wat Simungkhun** (Wat Nyai). Its initiation pavilion (*hang song pa*) is fashioned in attractive naive style while the archaic, muralled *sim* sits on an oddly raised stone platform that allegedly covers a large

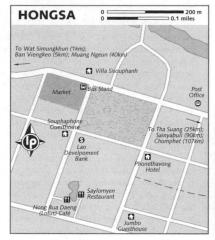

hole 'leading to the end of the world'. It's 1km west of the centre towards Muang Ngeun then 100m north after the first river bridge.

Given a day's notice some Hongsa guesthouses can organise 5km elephant rides across a wide valley of rice paddies and watermelon fields to **Ban Viengkeo** (returning by tuk-tuk). Many of Viengkeo's log-and-timber Tai Lü homes have weavers' looms beneath the high stilted floors and the village is the area's major centre for working elephants.

SLEEPING & EATING
During the elephant festival (see p182) Ban Viengkeo sprouts a rash of makeshift cafes and ample homestays for all comers. At other times, central Hongsa has all the accommodation and restaurants.

Villa Sisouphanh (☎ 211 791; r without bathroom 40,000K, d/tr with bathroom 60,000/80,000K, r with air-con 100,000K; 🐱) Rooms are lacklustre but the location is conveniently opposite the bus stand, a couple of bicycles are available to rent (per day 20,000K) and English-speaking Tuny can help arrange elephant activities given a day or two's warning.

Souphaphone Guesthouse (☎ 020-5587 7316; r old/new/air-con 50,000/70,000/100,000K; 🐱) The old block is slightly musty but the new one is marginally Hongsa's best deal with new beds, a shared balcony and a handy location opposite the bank, one block south of the bus stand.

Jumbo Guesthouse (☎ 020-5685 6488; www.lotuselephant.com; r 80,000K; 🖥) Brazil-born German anthropologist Monica invites travellers into

NORTHERN LAOS

ELEPHANTS A-GOGO

Laos was originally known as Lan Xang, the land of a million elephants, yet curiously no recent statistics accurately record how many remain. Especially in Sainyabuli province, working elephants have long been a mainstay of the logging industry, allowing tree trunks to be dragged out selectively without the clear-felling required for tractor access. Elephants are trained and worked by a mahout (handler) whose relationship with the animal is akin to a marriage and can last a lifetime. Elephants are generally owned by a consortium of villagers who share profits, costs and risks. To ensure a profit, owners need their animals to keep working but as a result, few working elephants have the energy for romance nor the time for a two-year maternity leave. With Lao elephants dying 15 times more often than they're born, the domestic elephant is likely to extinct within 50 years at 2010 rates, according to **ElefantAsia** (www.elefantasia.org), which is behind plans for an elephant nursery and hospital in Sainyabuli. It also organises the popular **Elephant Festival** (http://festival.elefantasia.org; admission free; ◔ mid-Feb), a vast two-day jamboree featuring music, theatre and many a beer tent as well as elephant parades and skills demonstrations. In past years the venue has rotated annually between Pak Lai, Sainyabuli and Ban Viengkeo (near Hongsa), but it might eventually find a permanent home in the latter. Meanwhile, numerous retired or 'unemployed' elephants have found alternative employment in tourism, notably around Luang Prabang and Pak Beng. Elefantasia's website offers various 'Read before you ride' tips to help tourists choose well-managed elephant camps, as not all are equal.

---

a family-style home where bathrooms are shared but the four rooms are tidy and inviting. A community feeling is fostered by group dinners but do check costs (sometimes substantial) for meals, breakfast and even tea. It's the best place in town for comprehensive local information and elephant rides are available with a day's notice. Next door, separately managed Jumbo Guesthouse 2 has new en-suite rooms but less character.

Phonethavong Hotel (☎ 211 785; r 150,000-250,000K; ⊠) This motel-style place has an L-shaped rank of haphazardly maintained rooms around a dusty car park. Wall cracks, peeling paint and splattered vinyl floors undermine its reputation as the best option in central Hongsa but outside, the communal area of rattan-chair seating is pleasant.

A block west of Jumbo Guesthouse, **Nong Bua Daeng (Lotus) Café** (mains 12,000-25,000K; ◔ 8am-9pm) and **Saylomyen Restaurant** are attractive thatched pavilions perched between fishponds but neither have written menus and there's minimal spoken English.

GETTING THERE & AWAY

The transport **ticket office** (☎ 020-5558 711) beside the market opens around 7.30am with vehicles departing for Sainyabuli (80,000K, four hours) and Muang Ngeun (40,000K, 1¼ hours) as soon as a decent quota of guests has piled aboard (usually before 9am). If custom proves sufficient an 8am pickup runs to

Chomphet, across the Mekong from Luang Prabang (120,000K, five hours) and an 8am *săwngthăew* runs to Tha Suang (20,000K, 70 minutes) arriving in time to connect with the Luang Prabang–bound slowboat.

MUANG NGEUN

ເມືອງເງິນ

This very quiet border 'town' is in fact a diffuse collection of predominantly Tai Lü villages interspersed by patches of rice-paddy. It's not worth a special visit but makes a very pleasant if spread-out place to explore if you're en route to/from Thailand. Around 2.5km east of the border post, head 1km north of the Hongsa–Nan road to find the sparse centre around a small, new **market** where traders can organise baht–kip exchange. There's no bank.

Continue 1.5km further north past a few governmental buildings to find **Wat Si Boun Yeun** (Ban Luang), the most appealing of Muang Ngeun's numerous temples. Perched above the modest Nam Yang river beside a new concrete bridge, its *sim* has old wooden shingles for roof tiles and uses rough-hewn old rosewood pillars inside. Notice the tiny, weather-worn wooded Buddhas left as votive offerings in niches of the little stupa behind. For bucolic scenery, follow the river west, 700m off the main road, through **Ban Keodonkhun** to an undistinguished sub-wat from which there are lovely sunset views. Or head 300m east from beside the school to find prettier **Wat Donsai**, ringed by shaggy ancient trees.

Around 1.3km further north up the main road, **Ban Khon** is a weaving centre sporting a neat line of close-packed, timber-top homes in contemporary Tai Lü style. **Wat Ban Khon** here is considered Muang Ngeun's most important monastery but a total rebuild in 2009 has left it without any great appeal.

Almost all of the eight guesthouses offer similar prices and room standards (bucket-flush squat toilet, water heater). **Wong Chaeng Kaew Guesthouse** (☎ 020-5523 2337; r 50,000K) shows signs of wear but is handily just 150m south of the market. Around 400m further south, **Deuanpen Guesthouse** (r without/with TV 50,000/60,000K) is mostly built on stilts above a gloopy green fishpond and has a quaint little open-sided drinking pavilion.

Phouxay Guesthouse (☎ 020-214 2826; Nan-Hongsa Rd; r 50,000K) is a line of ten reasonable bungalows sat on a slight rise with pleasant views, 800m west of the main junction towards Thailand (ie 1.8km from the market). Another trio of options lie a kilometre further west towards the border post.

From a tiny **'Passenger Car Station'** (☎ 020-245 0145, 020-244 4130) beside the market, *săwngthăew* run to Hongsa (40,000K, 1½ hours) departing between 2pm and 4pm, and to **Pak Kaen** (35,000K, one hour) at around 7.30am and 2pm, arriving in time for the Mekong slowboats to Huay Xai and Pak Beng.

LUANG PRABANG TO SAINYABULI

Attractive but painfully dusty, Rte 4 branches off Rte 13 at Km 362, ie 43km south of Luang Prabang. Landscapes of emerald rice fields are backed by towering horizons of eccentric-shaped mountains reaching a particular scenic crescendo during the long descent into **Muang Nan**, a one-horse, two-guesthouse town. Thereafter the road crosses a fertile former lake-bed ringed with bamboo-fuzzed mountain spikes. Then it descends abruptly to the Mekong at a minuscule settlement of snack shacks called **Pak Khon**. Until the Mekong Bridge is built (scheduled completion May 2013), crossing to the bigger Sainyabuli-side village of **Tha Deua** is by motorised canoe for pedestrians (5000K) and motorcycles (20,000K); by tug-ferry for vehicles and passengers (included in your bus ticket).

From the southwest corner of Tha Deua village, a pleasant, 15-minute walk passes Number 2 Sawmill, S-bends into attractive forest and brings you to a little wooden footbridge. This crosses a stream that emerges 100m upstream from beneath a Buddha image and tiny cave featuring the statue of a bearded ascetic. Across a shady picnic area the stream flows on over a cliff forming the pretty, 20m-high waterfall called **Tat Jao**. That's best seen by walking three minutes further then descending towards the Mekong, albeit on dangerously rotten wooden stairs.

A speedboat (800,000K for six people) could whisk you between Tha Deua and Luang Prabang in barely an hour versus nearly three hours by bus. But public boats rarely venture southeast where the Mekong is at its wildest. In 1909 a French steamer sank there while carrying much of the Lao royal crown jewels en route for a Paris exhibition. They were never recovered.

SAINYABULI (XAIGNABOURI)

ໄຊຍະບູລີ

☎ 074 / pop 17,000

One of Laos's 'elephant capitals', Sainyabuli (variously spelt Xaignabouri, Xayaboury, Sayabouli and Sayabouri) is a prosperous town backed to the east by an attractive range of high forested ridges. Making a self-conscious attempt to look urban, central Sainyabuli consists of overspaced avenues and showy new administrative buildings that are surprising for their scale but hardly an attraction. Starting around the tourist office and continuing south you'll find an increasing proportion of attractive wooden or part-timber structures, some with languid settings among arching palm trees. Overall it's a pleasant, friendly and entirely untouristed place whose popularity is likely to grow considerably once connecting roads are paved and the planned Elephant Sanctuary is developed. For the elephant festival see the boxed text.

Information

Tourist Office (☎ 030-518 0095; Sayaboury_ptd@tour ismlaos.org; ☷ 8.30-11am & 2-4pm Mon-Fri) Good free city maps, English-speaking staff and plans to organise trekking tours and rental of bikes and motorcycles.

BCEL (☷ 8.30am-3.30pm Mon-Fri) Changes money, ATM.

Post Office (☷ 8-11am & 1-5pm Mon-Fri)

Ticky Computer (Internet per hr 6000K; ☷ 8am-9pm)

Sights

Many spots along the riverside are rendered especially idyllic thanks to the dramatic ridge

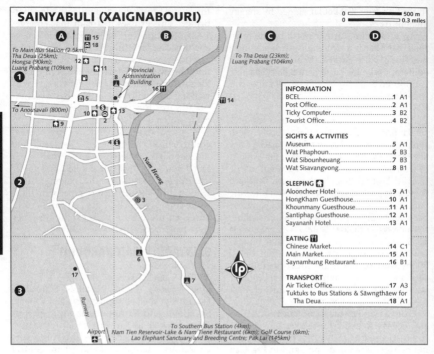

SAINYABULI (XAIGNABOURI)

0 — 500 m
0 — 0.3 miles

INFORMATION
BCEL..1 A1
Post Office.....................................2 A1
Ticky Computer.............................3 B2
Tourist Office................................4 B2

SIGHTS & ACTIVITIES
Museum...5 A1
Wat Phaphoun...............................6 B3
Wat Sibounheuang........................7 B3
Wat Sisavangvong.........................8 B1

SLEEPING
Alooncheer Hotel 9 A1
HongKham Guesthouse................10 A1
Khounmany Guesthouse...............11 A1
Santiphap Guesthouse.................12 A1
Sayananh Hotel............................13 A1

EATING
Chinese Market............................14 C1
Main Market.................................15 A1
Saynamhung Restaurant..............16 B1

TRANSPORT
Air Ticket Office...........................17 A3
Tuktuks to Bus Stations & Săwngthǎew for
Tha Deua.................................18 A1

of **Pak Kimin** reflected in the waters of the Nam Heung. One such viewpoint is tucked behind **Wat Sibounheuang**, the town's most evocative monastery. It sports a lopsided **gilded stupa** and reclining Buddha in a delightful garden setting where the bare-brick ruins of the tiny original *sim* are reckoned to be early 14th-century. The 'new' *sim* is covered in murals including anti-adultery scenes in a style reminiscent of Matisse. This building covers a mysterious 'hole' traditionally associated with *sinkhone* spirit-ghosts who are placated in the **Phaveth Festival** (13th-15th day of the third Lao month) leading up to the February full moon.

Other attractive Buddhist complexes include palm-framed **Wat Phaphoun** with an unusual diamond-shaped stupa, and more central **Wat Sisavangvong**, reportedly built by King Sisavang Vong on an older temple site.

The sweetly banal, one-room **museum** (admission free; 8.30-11am & 2-4pm Mon-Fri) has no English explanations. Around 1.5km due west, local martyrs are commemorated by the **Anousavali Stupa** atop a gentle rise with wide views across town.

A medicinal herbal **Spa Centre** and botanical conservation area is being developed around 13km south of town near Ban Heukeng surrounded by relatively well-preserved forest. A botanical pathway will allow for guided walks. Ask the tourist office for more information.

NAM TIEN
To fully appreciate the charm of Sainyabuli's setting, drive 9km southwest to the **Nam Tien reservoir-lake** where canoeing and other outdoor activities are slated to start in 2011. A restaurant here is perched above the dam, offering views across emerald rice paddies and wooded slopes towards a western horizon where **Pak Kimin** and **Pak Xang** ridges overlap. Directly below the dam, a modest but attractive nine-hole **golf course** (020-244 6666; per round 50,000K, club rental 100,000K) opens by arrangement. By 2011, a 10-minute boat ride should be whisking visitors across the reservoir to a new **Elephant Sanctuary** (www. elefantasia.org) incorporating an elephant hospital and breeding program (see the boxed text). Bungalows and a dormitory are under construction for overnight visitors who may

have the chance to ride, feed and bathe the elephants.

The 3km asphalt spur road to Nam Tien branches west off the Pak Lai road around 500m before the south bus station, just before a bridge (6.5km from central Sainyabuli).

Sleeping

Khounmany Guesthouse (☎ 211 342; without/ with TV 50,000/40,000K; ⊠) Plonked in one of Sainyabuli's incongruous central rice fields, this new, family-style guesthouse offers five clean, fair-sized rooms with squat toilets and hot showers.

Alooncheer Hotel (☎ 213 136; r 40,000-60,000K; r with air-con 60,000-100,000K; ⊠) This sizeable Hmong-owned complex is quiet yet central, its polished wood-panelled lobby is decorated with traditional instruments and most rooms have high ceilings, twee lamps, minibars and only a few stains. Very good value, but beware that the very cheapest rooms are a significant step down in quality.

HongKham Guesthouse (☎ 211 381; r 60,000K) There are many plusher rooms in town but the HongKham is central, tucked behind a traditional style timber-top house and run by a charming family who speak some English. Beds are comfy and new.

Santiphap Guesthouse (☎ 211 184; r 80,000K; ⊠) Clean, well appointed rooms with desks, aircon, TV and good linens make this one of Sainyabuli's best options. Front rooms can suffer from road noise and the bathrooms are slightly cramped, but the showers are piping hot. Tea and instant coffee are free.

Sayananh Hotel (☎ 211 116; r without/with TV 80,000/100,000K; ste 150,000K; ⊠) Conspicuous and central, this three-storey hotel has a grand-looking entrance that belies soulless, merely adequate rooms off corridors that could have featured in *The Shining*.

Eating

Saynamhung Restaurant (☎ 211 171; mains 25,000-70,000K; fried noodles 10,000K; beer 10,000K; ⊠ 7am-10pm) Contemplate the bamboo-banked river and the looming Pak Kimin massif as you dine on tasty Lao food whose culinary merits are undersold by the menu's clumsy English translations. The 'Stream Fish with Mushrooms' is actually a complex, delightfully well-balanced flavour-fest.

Nam Tiene Restaurant (☎ 020-5569 7696; fried rice 15,000K; fish by weight, other mains 25,000-50,000K; ⊠ 6.30am-11pm) Well-made, professionally presented food along with lovely reservoir views amply reward the excursion out to the Nam Tien dam.

Several cheaper eateries and barbecue vendors line the street between the tourist office and Sayananh Hotel. The **main market** (⊠ 8am-6.30pm) and sizeable **Chinese Market** are both functional, modern affairs. A **night market** (⊠ 6-10pm) near the central roundabout has food stalls for noodle soup, Lao grills, fresh fruits and *khànŏm* (traditional sweets). A simple local eatery beside the southern bus stand does great little pork chops (5000K) and less appetising bee-larvae roasted in banana leaf (3000K).

Getting There & Away

The **airport** is beside the main Pak Lai road, around 3km south of the centre. **Lao Capricorn Air** (Airport ☎ 213 152; www.laocapricornair.net; ticket office ☎ 213 153; ⊠ 8am-noon & 2-4pm Mon-Fri) flies to Vientiane on Monday and Friday at 10.50am.

CROSSING THE THAI BORDER AT HUAY KON & MUANG NGEUN

The **border post** (⊠ 8am-5pm) is around 2.5km west of Muang Ngeun junction. On the Lao side there's no restaurant nor any waiting transport but if you can persuade the immigration officer to call for you, the afternoon *săwngthăew* to Hongsa should be prepared to collect you. Or you might plod 900m east to the **Dougmala Guesthouse** (☎ 020-236 6793; r 60,000K) who can run you into town. Either should charge 5000K per person, minimum 20,000K.

From the Thai side, if you don't want to walk your bags across the 1km of no-man's-land you can pay 100B for a motorbike with luggage-carrying sidecar. The Thai border post, **Huay Kon**, is not quite a village but does have simple noodle shops serving 30B meals and a large market comes alive on Saturday morning just up the hill from immigration. The only public transport is a luxurious minibus (☎ 083-024 3675; ⊠) to Phrae (160B, five hours) via Nan (100B, three hours) departing from the border post at 11.45am. Northbound it leaves the bus stations in Phrae at 6am, and Nan at 8am.

Air tickets (695,000K) are sold from the tiny ticket office 800m further north, misleadingly marked Lao Air.

From the **main bus station** (☎ 213 173) 2.5km north of the centre, an 11am *săwngthăew* runs to Hongsa (80,000K, three hours) continuing some days to Muang Ngeun (100,000K), Xienghone (150,000K) and even Khop (200,000K) if there's enough passengers. For Luang Prabang (50,000K, four hours) direct buses depart at 9am and 2pm or you could use the Vientiane-bound services at 1pm or 4pm (the later 'VIP' bus costs 10% more). Journey times should drop to around 2½ hours once the Tha Deua bridge is built and the Luang Prabang road is asphalted (scheduled for completion May 2013).

A third Sainyabuli–Vientiane bus (departing 9.30am, dry-season only) runs via Pak Lai. Given the appallingly dusty road, that bus is a much better way to reach Pak Lai (50,000K, 4½ hours) than taking *săwngthăew*, which depart around 9am and noon from the **southern bus station**, a tiny stand 4km southwest of the airport.

Săwngthăew for Tha Deua plus tuk-tuks to the bus stations (main/south 10,000/15,000K per person) depart from the main market.

Tourist minivans direct from Luang Prabang to the Nam Tien reservoir should operate once the Elephant Sanctuary has been established.

SOUTH OF SAINYABULI
Sainyabuli to Pak Lai
Although major roadworks are underway, for now the mostly-unpaved Pak Lai–Sainyabuli route is a hellish ride. The road is almost impassably muddy after rain and appallingly dusty when dry. The endless clouds of dust are further stirred up by numerous logging trucks whose booty has seen the nearby hillsides virtually stripped of their once-majestic forests in recent years. Wear dustsheets and a mask.

The initially flat road leads through a succession of relatively prosperous rural towns set in attractive rice terraces. Then it climbs a narrow, brutally deforested valley beyond **Ban Nam Pouy** (Ban Nam Phui), where there's a guesthouse. A small roadside market in the rustic Hmong settlement of **Nam Gnap** (Nam Nyab) sells recently killed civets and other sorry exotica. The scenery sports a few small karst formations around **Na Mo**, beyond which a long, abrupt ridge to the west retains a rare

remnant of the area's once splendid tropical forest. Much of this region is officially within the 1150 sq km **Nam Phui NPA** whose western limit is just 1km from the school in **Phonsack**. Deeper in, where logging has been spared, these rugged, forested hills are thought to sustain extensive wildlife populations but exploring without permission will cause trouble.

Pak Lai
ปากลาย
☎ 074 / pop 12,000
Bustling and pleasant, this Mekong riverport is an almost unavoidable stop on the off-beat route between Sainyabuli and Loei in Thailand. The town follows a 5km curl of Rte 4 paralleled a block further east by a shorter riverside road that's sparsely dotted with historic structures in both Lao and French-colonial style. Exploring north to south, start at **Wat Sisavang** (Wat Sisavangvong), which sports some older monks' quarters as well as a gaudily ornate new bell tower and gateway. Next door, within the **District Administration Complex**, notice an old wooden building whose facade blends Tai Lü and art-nouveau design

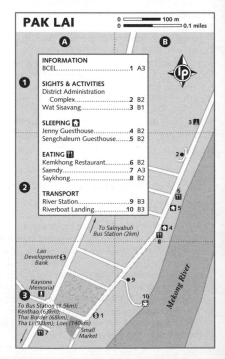

PAK LAI   0 — 100 m
0 — 0.1 miles

INFORMATION
BCEL...1 A3

SIGHTS & ACTIVITIES
District Administration
   Complex................................2 B2
Wat Sisavang.............................3 B1

SLEEPING 🏠
Jenny Guesthouse.....................4 B2
Sengchaleurn Guesthouse.......5 B2

EATING 🍴
Kemkhong Restaurant.............6 B2
Saendy.......................................7 A3
Saykhong..................................8 B2

TRANSPORT
River Station..............................9 B3
Riverboat Landing................10 B3

To Sainyabuli
Bus Station (2km)

Lao
Development
Bank

Kaysone
Memorial

To Bus Station (1.5km);
Kenthao (63km);
Tha Border (68km);
Tha Li (92km); Loei (140km)

Small
Market

Mekong River

NORTHERN LAOS

CROSSING THE THAI BORDER AT THAI LI & KAEN THAO

This quiet rural **border** (8am-6pm) is the home of yet another (but smaller) Friendship Bridge, this time over the Nam Heuang.

From Pak Lai, there are *sǎwngthǎew* to the border post at Kaen Thao at around 10am and noon (35,000K, 1¾ hours). After walking across the bridge you'll have to take a short *sǎwngthǎew* ride (20B) 8km to Tha Li before transferring to another *sǎwngthǎew* (35B) the remaing 46km to Loei, from where there are regular connections to Bangkok and elsewhere.

---

ideas. Within the next 500m you'll pass the main guesthouses, the river port and **BCEL Bank** (ATM, exchange available) before crossing a little old wooden bridge into an attractive village-like area of local homes beyond a small market.

The Elephant Festival is held every third year in Pak Lai, see the boxed text, p182 for more information.

SLEEPING & EATING

Brilliantly central, **Jenny Guesthouse** (020-236 5971; r fan/air-con 50,000/90,000K;) has hot showers and Mekong views from some rooms. The odd cobweb is forgivable, and helpful Chan speaks some English. Newer and just marginally fresher is the all air-con **Sengchaleurn Guesthouse** (020-206 8888; r 100,000K;) a block north. Next door within an older wooden building, the **Kemkhong Restaurant** (mains 20,000-40,000K; 6am-10.30pm) is good for a quiet 9000K beer with river views, **Saykhong** (mains 30,000-40,000K) beside Jenny Guesthouse is livelier and also overlooks the river. **Saendy** (Sandee; 020-236 5950; mains 15,000K-25,000K; 7am-9pm) does better yet cheaper food, and its tastefully low-key atmosphere would make it a *falang* favourite were there any foreigners in town.

GETTING THERE & AWAY

Bring a facemask and disposable clothes if you attempt the Pak Lai–Sainyabuli journey by *sǎwngthǎew* (50,000K, 4½ hours). These depart in both directions between 7.30am and 9.30am and once again around noon. Mud-crusted victims arrive at Pak Lai's little Sainyabuli bus station, 3km north of the centre. From there, tuk-tuks charge 7000K per person to the guesthouses or 10,000K to the southern bus terminal. That terminal has *sǎwngthǎew* to Kaen Thao, plus a 9am bus to Vientiane (80,000K, around six hours). A more appealing option to Vientiane is the riverboat, departing from the central **river station** on Monday (and some Thursdays)

at 9am (90,000K), taking roughly 7½ hours downstream, nine hours back up.

XIENG KHUANG & HUA PHAN PROVINCES

Lonely, narrow roads wind in seemingly endless ribbons across these green, sparsely populated northeastern provinces towards the mysterious 'Plain of Jars' (p193) and the fascinating Vieng Xai Caves (p200). Both are truly intriguing places to visit if you're en route to or from Vietnam, but might feel a little anticlimactic if you've made a special out-and-back trip. You could alternatively combine them as a loop trip from Luang Prabang with added stops in Nong Khiaw (p204) and Vieng Thong (p203) where talk of 'tiger treks' is causing a minor travel buzz. All of the above feature on Stray Asia's pricey *Long Thaang* bus loop (www.straytravel.asia). Almost anywhere else in either province is completely off the tourist radar.

The altitude (averaging over 1000m) ensures a climate that's not too hot in the hot season, not too cold in the cool season. In December and January, sweaters and a jacket will often be appropriate at night and in the early mornings, when seas of cloud fill the populated valleys and form other-worldly scenes for those looking down from passes or peaks.

History

Xieng Khuang's world-famous giant 'jars' (p193) along with Hintang's mysterious megaliths (p202) indicate a well-developed iron-age culture of which historical knowledge is astonishingly hazy. Whoever carved those enigmatic monuments had long since disappeared by the 13th-century when Xieng Khuang emerged as a Buddhist, Tai Phuan principality with a capital at today's Muang Khoun (p194). Both provinces spent subsequent centuries as either independent kingdoms or part of Annamese–Vietnamese vassal states known as Ai Lao and Tran Ninh. In 1832 the Vietnamese captured the Phuan king of Xieng Khuang, publicly executed him in Hué and made the kingdom a prefecture of Annam, forcing people to adopt Vietnamese dress and customs. Chinese Haw gangs ravaged the region in the late 19th century, pushing both provinces to accept Siamese and French protection.

Major skirmishes between the Free Lao and the Viet Minh took place from 1945 to 1946, and as soon as the French left Indochina the North Vietnamese started a build-up of troops to protect Hanoi's rear flank. By the end of the 1960s the area had become a major battlefield.

With saturation bombing by American planes obliterating virtually every town and village, much of the population had to live for their protection in caves, only emerging in 1973. At Vieng Xai, the most important of these caves also sheltered the Pathet Lao's anti-Royalist government.

North Vietnamese troops did their share of damage on the ground as well, destroying once-magnificent Muang Sui and much of royalist-held western Xieng Khuang province. After the conflict, infamous *samana* re-education camps appeared, notably in eastern Hua Phan, to 'rehabilitate' and punish former royalists with a mixture of hard labour and political indoctrination. Many continued into the 1980s and the possibility that a samana still

TREKKING IN NORTHERN LAOS

Northern Laos has won prizes for its 'ecotrekking' system, pioneered in Luang Namtha and the Nam Ha NPA. Registered agencies pledge to return a significant (and stated) percentage of profits to the villages visited and to abide by sensible ecologically friendly guidelines. Visiting remote off-road villages without a guide is of dubious legality. Fortunately, guides and any necessary trekking permits can usually be arranged very quickly by local agencies – the evening before departure in many cases. Costs excluding transport are typically around US$35 per person per day if alone, falling to under US$20 per person for a larger group. Agencies don't generally compete directly so comparing product is more relevant than comparing prices. Employing freelance guides might be cheaper but is discouraged as they'll rarely make contributions to village development funds. See the boxed text, p234 for cultural tips and visit the excellent website www.ecotour ismlaos.com for plenty more information. The following list is a generalised overview of what differentiates the various trekking centres.

Phongsali (p231) Nowhere is better for striking out into truly timeless villages where traditional costumes and arcane animist beliefs are still commonplace, particularly in the remote Akha communities. Many homes retain picture-book thatched roofs, at least for now. Virgin-forest treks are also possible near Boun Neua.

Luang Namtha (p216) Treks are very well organised and have numerous options, some combining trekking with other activities such as biking and kayaking. Forest hikes to Nam Ha NPA 'jungle camps' are especially popular. To reduce pressure on any single host village, most agents have unique routes. However, this inadvertently adds to the complexity of deciding just what you actually want to see and where you'll find it. Not all routes are equally inspiring.

Vieng Phukha (p222) A much less commercial starting point for Nam Ha forest treks.

Muang Long (p226) & **Muang Sing** (p223) Guided or DIY visits to colourful and relatively accessible Akha villages (where many local women still wear traditional costumes).

Udomxai (p209) A specialist agency makes Udomxai a popular centre for mountain biking, some itineraries combined with treks.

Muang Khua (p227) Limited options include a one-day trek visiting an Akha Pala village (where some local ladies wear curiously gaudy semi-traditional costumes), with plenty of views en route but minimal forest.

Phonsavan (p189) One unique trek combines a mossy archaeological site, accommodation in a roadless Hmong village and culminates with the ascent of a multi-stage waterfall to the 'Bomb Village'. It's a fascinating walk, but don't expect costumed tribesfolk in this area.

Muang Ngoi Neua (p207) Easy DIY day-walks to pretty villages or very inexpensive group treks with freelance guides, some including scenic boat trips.

remains near Sop Hao has never been officially confirmed nor denied. Meanwhile, decades after the conflict, UXO (see the boxed text, p199) remains very widespread especially in central and eastern Xieng Khuang, threatening local lives for generations to come.

PHU KHOUN TO PHONSAVAN

At Phu Khoun (p171), Phonsavan–bound Rte 7 branches east of Rte 13, the Luang Prabang–Vang Vieng road. Starting dramatically, it snakes for 15km along a high ridge, offering dazzling panoramas of distant mountains viewed between Hmong and Khamu villages. Beyond, the constant bends continue but landscapes become more staid, with mostly secondary forest and few views. Across the bridge in **Ban Namchat** are a pair of simple roadside cafes, the only eateries for miles around.

Worth a brief stop if you're driving by (but not a special excursion), **Ban Nong Tang** (Km 89) is set around a pond flanked by abrupt limestone outcrops. This was once **Muang Sui**, an historic city of antique Buddhist temples and quaint provincial architecture. However, during the Second Indochina War, Muang Sui became the headquarters of the Neutralist faction and 'Lima Site 108' (a landing site used by US planes). Late in the war, after the Royal Lao Army had been pushed out of Xieng Khuang Province, it was utterly razed by the North Vietnamese Army.

Close to Nong Tang lie several cliff-caves. UXO worries mean that visitors without a guide should stick to the best known, **Tham Pha** (admission 10,000K; ⏰ 8am-4.30pm), safely accessible by a 3.3km asphalted spur road (signed 'Buddha Cave' from Rte 7 directly west of the pond). The illuminated main-cave system sports an unrefined 5m-tall Buddha statue that is reputedly 1200 years old. Behind are sizeable water-eroded caverns but there's little to see apart from a handful of small Buddhas, a resonant 'gong' stalactite and an almost empty glass display case comically marked 'Valuable Antiques'. Exit the cave the way you came in, turn left and follow crumbling old concrete steps for five minutes around the rocky crag to find the much less-visited **Tham Sangja**. Looking eerily like a junkie's den, this rocky overhang-cave is still littered with ampoules and little glass medicine vials from the wartime era when it was used as a makeshift hospital. Further unlit

caves descend hazardously into the mountain from here.

Overlooking the pond in Ban Nong Tang, **Nong Tang Guesthouse** (☎ 312 070, 020-5556 1023; Km 89, Rte 7; r 50,000K) has a semi-dormant restaurant with a stilt platform, and a trio of tiny timber cabins, each with balcony, miniature desk and uncertain hopes of electricity.

East of Nong Tang the landscape consists mostly of low grassy hillocks, rice-valleys and sparse sprinklings of conifers. It's a look that's altogether different from almost anywhere else in northern Laos. Viewed from the air, the scene is polka-dotted with uncountable bomb-crater depressions.

PHONSAVAN

ໄຟນສະຫວັນ

☎ 061 / pop 60,000

Droves of visitors use Phonsavan as a base from which to visit the Plain of Jars (p193). The town itself has an unfinished feel and is very spread out with its two parallel main boulevards stretching for about 3km east–west. Fortunately a very handy concentration of hotels, restaurants and tour agents is crammed into a short if architecturally un-inspired 'strip' around the Nice Guesthouse. More shops, markets and facilities straggle along Rte 7. But the town is best appreciated from the surrounding hills, several of which are pine-clad and topped with small resorts.

The region has long been a centre of Phuan language and culture (part of the Tai-Kadai family). There's also a strong Vietnamese presence.

Information

The oddly located **Provincial Tourist Office** (☎ 312 217) has a series of information scrolls to peruse and is developing regional treks. Some town maps are free here, others cost 5000K.

Currency exchange is available at **Lao Development Bank**, at **BCEL** and from several travel agents. There are two ATMs along Rte 7. An **internet shop** (per min 200K; ⏰ 7am-10pm) beside Simmaly Restaurant has excellent connection speeds. The **Lao-Mongolian Friendship Hospital** (☎ 312 166) is OK for minor health needs.

Dangers & Annoyances

Don't underestimate the dangers of UXO (unexploded ordnance) to you; see p199.

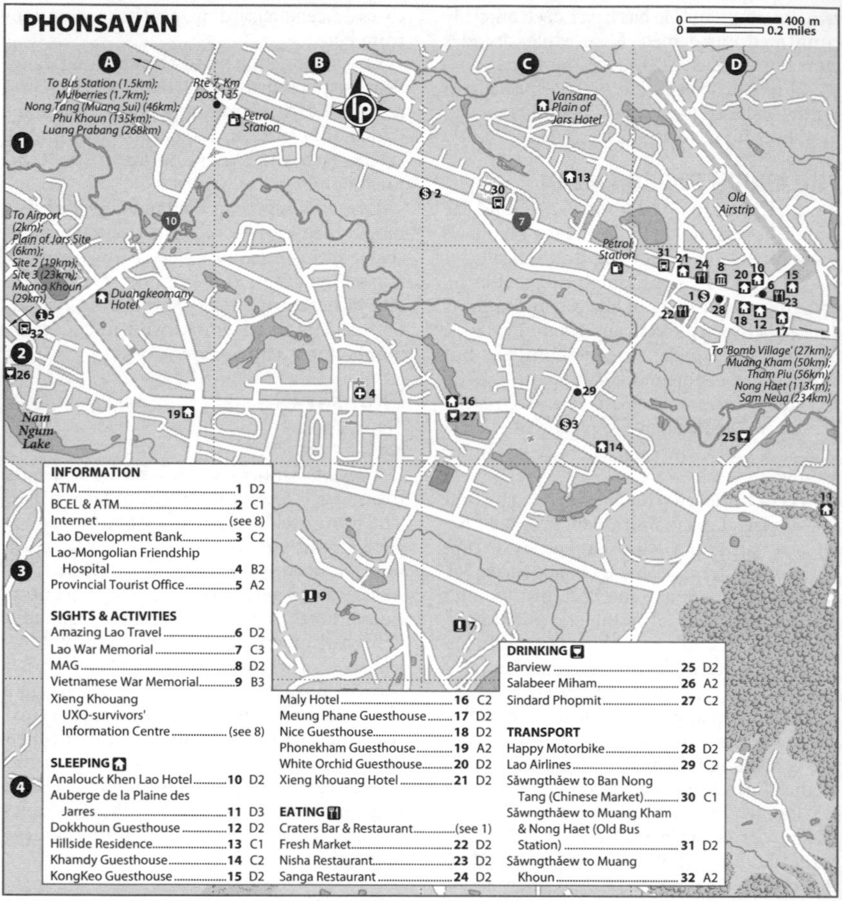
PHONSAVAN
0 400 m
0 0.2 miles
To Bus Station (1.5km); Mulberries (1.7km); Nong Tang (Muang Sui) (46km); Phu Khoun (135km); Luang Prabang (268km)
Rte 7, Km post 135
Petrol Station
Vansana Plain of Jars Hotel
Old Airstrip
To Airport (2km); Plain of Jars Site (6km); Site 2 (19km); Site 3 (23km); Muang Khoun (29km)
Duangkeomany Hotel
Petrol Station
To 'Bomb Village' (27km); Muang Kham (50km); Tham Piu (56km); Nong Haet (113km); Sam Neua (234km)
Nam Ngum Lake
INFORMATION
ATM 1 D2
BCEL & ATM 2 C1
Internet (see 8)
Lao Development Bank 3 C2
Lao-Mongolian Friendship Hospital 4 B2
Provincial Tourist Office 5 A2
SIGHTS & ACTIVITIES
Amazing Lao Travel 6 D2
Lao War Memorial 7 C3
MAG 8 D2
Vietnamese War Memorial 9 B3
Xieng Khouang UXO-survivors' Information Centre (see 8)
SLEEPING
Analouck Khen Lao Hotel 10 D2
Auberge de la Plaine des Jarres 11 D3
Dokkhoun Guesthouse 12 D2
Hillside Residence 13 C1
Khamdy Guesthouse 14 C2
KongKeo Guesthouse 15 D2
Maly Hotel 16 C2
Meung Phane Guesthouse 17 D2
Nice Guesthouse 18 D2
Phonekham Guesthouse 19 A2
White Orchid Guesthouse 20 D2
Xieng Khouang Hotel 21 D2
EATING
Craters Bar & Restaurant (see 1)
Fresh Market 22 D2
Nisha Restaurant 23 D2
Sanga Restaurant 24 D2
DRINKING
Barview 25 D2
Salabeer Miham 26 A2
Sindard Phopmit 27 C2
TRANSPORT
Happy Motorbike 28 D2
Lao Airlines 29 C2
Săwngthăew to Ban Nong Tang (Chinese Market) 30 C1
Săwngthăew to Muang Kham & Nong Haet (Old Bus Station) 31 D2
Săwngthăew to Muang Khoun 32 A2

Sights

Decades after America's 'secret' war on Laos, unexploded bombs and mines remain a devastating problem throughout this region. To understand just how bad things are, visit the thought-provoking UXO Information Centre run by **MAG** (Mines Advisory Group; ☎ 021-252 004; www.maginternational.org/laopdr; admission free; 🕑 8am-8pm) a British organisation that has been helping to clear Laos's unexploded ordnance since 1994. The centre's photos, slide shows and computer map-program underline the enormity of the bomb-drops and there are examples of (defused) UXO to ponder. Evening screenings show the powerful documentaries *Bomb Harvest* (2007, www.bombharvest.com) and *Bombies* (2001, www.itvs.org/bombies/film.html). Donations are highly encouraged: US$12 pays for the clearing of around 10 sq m and qualifies the giver for a commemorative T-shirt. Two doors away, the similarly insightful **Xieng Khouang UXO-survivors' Information Centre** (☎ 213 349; www.laos.worlded.org; 🕑 8am-8pm) displays prosthetic limbs, wheelchairs and bomb parts and gives further harrowing insight into the UXO problem.

About 1km apart at the south edge of town are two hilltop **memorials** (🕑 sunrise-sunset) to Pathet Lao and Vietnamese soldiers lost in the war.

Mulberries (☎ 021-561 271; www.mulberries.org; 🕑 8am-4pm Mon-Sat) is a fair-trade silk farm that offers interesting free visits. It's off Rte 7 just west of the main bus station.

Tours

Several agents on the main drag and virtually every guesthouse is ready to slot you into a one-day Plain of Jars tour visiting the three main sites. The going price is 120,000K including noodle-soup lunch and entry fees or 90,000K without. Getting that price takes a little shopping around and relies on there being at least seven fellow passengers. Don't expect too much insight from your guide.

Other advertised tours include trips to the 'Bomb Village' (p195) and Muang Khoun (p194), but these rarely garner enough custom for prices to be competitive. Try gathering your own group.

Amazing Lao Travel (☎ 260 026; ouanvat@yahoo.com) arranges the Phakeo Trek (p195), charging 340,000/700,000K per person in groups of eight/two.

Sleeping

CENTRAL STRIP

KongKeo Guesthouse (☎ 211 354, 020-5658 2683; www.kongkeojar.com; s/d 60,000/80,000K) Hidden at the southern end of the former airstrip, the KongKeo's rooms are Spartan, with shared bathroom and rucked carpets, though there are also half a dozen en-suite bungalows with solar-heated showers. The great selling point is the bamboo bar-restaurant hangout in front where fires are lit in sliced-open bomb casings and guests watch videos on the war era.

Dokkhoun Guesthouse (☎ 312 189; r from 60,000K) Rooms of varying standards occupy two multi-storey blocks. They compete on price and location but those we saw were battered, dark and dank with little sense of style.

Nice Guesthouse (☎ 312 454; d/tw 80,000/100,000K) This welcoming choice at the heart of Phonsavan's 'strip' has English-speaking staff and well maintained rooms that aren't overly big. Upstairs rooms share a narrow balcony.

White Orchid Guesthouse (☎ 312 403; r 80,000-200,000K) Wicker lamps and oddments of local fabric add character while map design bed-covers teach you Lao geography in the cramped 100,000K rooms with undersized beds. Much bigger but poorer value, the 200,000K rooms have heavy lacquered furniture but the same unsophisticated bathrooms.

Meung Phane Guesthouse (☎ 312 046; r US$10) Five ample-sized rooms with decent bathrooms set motel style round a parking yard.

Analouck Khen Lao Hotel (☎ 213 599; r 150,000-300,000K; 🗙) This modern five-storey tower offers a striking jump in quality over all nearby competitors for a modest extra price. Bright, clean and ample-sized 200,000K rooms are the best value with virginal white linens, kettle, fridge, shower booth and breakfast included. Independent electricity usually keeps the lift working when the rest of the town has power cuts.

Xieng Khouang Hotel (☎ 213 567; r US$24-30; 🛜) Very conspicuous, this brand-new but utterly soulless four-storey construction has only one selling point – the free wi-fi.

ELSEWHERE

Newer guesthouses are dotted sparsely all over Phonsavan. Many of these are better value than those on the strip but few are within walking distance of restaurants, so the money you might save on sleeping will be spent on transport.

Khamdy Guesthouse (☎ 020-7766 1555; r 50,000K) Despite cobwebs and a few patches of peeling paint, the large rooms are good value with OK beds and shiny new floor tiles. Without a car the location can feel pretty isolated.

Phonekham Guesthouse (☎ 020-5626 2675; d/tw 60,000/70,000K; 🖵) This odd new guesthouse lavishes inordinate space on a two-storey columned entrance hall that's spookily unadorned except for a single computer (free internet). Rooms are smart and spacious for the price, though the mattresses show springy teeth and the suburban location is awkwardly isolated.

Maly Hotel (☎ 312 031; www.malyht.laotel.com; s 150,000-400,000K; r 200,000-500,000K; 🗙 🛜) Way more atmospheric than most of Phonsavan's generic box-hotels, the Maly's rooms lead off a rambling warren of corridors and stairways decorated in local fabrics and giant masks. The cheapest basement rooms have slightly scuffed carpets but the best rooms are characterful suites, decorated with love and sporting corner-unit bathtubs for two. A cosy restaurant offers reliably good food, and locally relevant videos (in English) are available to watch in the lobby-lounge.

Hillside Residence (☎ 213 300; Ban Tai; r US$25) Set in a neat handkerchief of garden, this newly built half-timbered mansion looks like it belongs in a colonial hill-town. Rooms are petite and furniture could be more refined, but there's a pleasant family atmosphere. A shared upper sitting terrace and some upstairs rooms have their own balconies.

our pick **Auberge de la Plaine des Jarres** (☎ 020-5599 9192; auberge_plainjars@yahoo.fr; r US$60)

Crowning a different pine-forested hill overlooking the town, Phonsavan's most appealing option is a characterful series of wood-and-stone bungalows with fireplaces, board floors and paper-umbrellas for lamps. The bar-restaurant is delightful too, with sweeping views. It's professionally run, and English and French are spoken.

Eating

Wild matsutake mushrooms (*hét wâi*) and fermented swallows (*nok ąen dąwng*) are local specialities. Try the **fresh market**, or ask in Maly Hotel's restaurant. Several Vietnamese restaurants serve dog (*thit chó*).

Sanga Restaurant (Sa-Nga; ☎ 312 318; mains 10,000-20,000K; ◷ 11am-10pm) The venue is a large, banal concrete box-room but the meals are unexpectedly accomplished for such sensible prices. The chicken *làap* was especially decent while at 15,000K, the steak and chips is a popular bargain.

Nisha Restaurant (mains 14,000-35,000K; ◷ 6.30am-10pm) Tuck into delicious aloo ghobi, dosas, tikka masalas and rogan josh at this popular Indian diner with roughly painted timber walls.

Craters Bar & Restaurant (☎ 020-7780 5775; snacks 12,000-25,000K, meals 25,000-65,000K; ◷ 6.30am-10pm) This cosy, *falang*-pleasing cafe is full of bamboo and rattan furniture and decorated with faded framed photos of wartime bombardments. The menu includes club sandwiches, pizzas and even an Australian T-bone (65,000K), though a beaten-flat local steak costs half the price. Thai and Lao dishes are suitably tamed for Western palates.

Drinking

Of a handful of playfully lit bars around the old airstrip, only the bar at the KongKeo Guesthouse is really traveller oriented – it often screens UXO-related DVDs at night. Local-style open-sided beer pavilions further afield include **Barview** (☎ 020-234 5881), with sunset views over the rice fields, and **Sindard Phopmit** (☎ 020-234 4054; ◷ 8am-11pm), on stilts above one of Phonsavan's numerous ponds. Snacks include 'fried frogs' and 'scalded gut'. **Salabeer Miham** (☎ 020-5587 5207; ◷ 7.30am-late) is similar and has a 'swan' boat for punts on the pond. No spoken English.

Getting There & Away

Note that airline and bus timetables usually call Phonsavan 'Xieng Khuang', even though that was originally the name for Muang Khoun (p194).

AIR

Lao Airlines (☎ 212 027) flies to/from Vientiane (675,000K) on Monday, Wednesday, Friday, Saturday and Sunday. Some years a weekly flight to/from Luang Prabang operates in peak season.

BUS

International & Long Distance

Longer-distance bus tickets presold by travel agencies typically cost around 40,000K more than standard fares but include a transfer to the bus station, around 4km west of MAG. From here Vietnam-bound buses depart to Vinh (138,000K, 11 hours) at 6.30am on Tuesday, Thursday, Friday and Sunday, continuing seasonally on Mondays to Hanoi (185,000K). For Vientiane (95,000K, 11 hours) there are air-con buses at 7am, 8am, 10.30am, 4.30pm, 6.40pm and a VIP bus (115,000K) at 8pm. These all pass through Vang Vieng, to where there's an additional 7.30am departure (80,000K). For Luang Prabang (10 hours) both minivan (75,000K) and VIP bus (85,000K) depart at 8.30am. There's an 8am bus to Sam Neua (60,000K, eight to 10 hours) plus two Vientiane–Sam Neua buses that should pick up here once they finally dribble into town. A 7.30am bus is timetabled to Paksan (100,000K) but the road remains deplorable and road reconstruction isn't due to be completed until 2015.

Local services

Local buses and *sǎwngthǎew* use three different stands: for Muang Khoun (10,000K, four daily, last return 5pm) they start at Nam Ngam market; for Ban Nong Tang (10,000K, one hour, three daily) they start at the Chinese Market; for Muang Kham (20,000K, two hours, four daily) and Nong Haet (35,000K, four hours, four daily) they start at the old bus station.

Getting Around

Tuk-tuks cost from 5000K for a short hop, 10,000K to the bus station (or 5000K per person for groups), and 20,000K to the airport. **Happy Motorbike** (☎ 213 233; ◷ 7am-8pm) rents bicycles (per day 40,000K) and 100cc motorbikes (100,000K), ideal for reaching a selection of jar sites.

Chauffeured six-seater vans or 4WDs can be chartered through most guesthouses and hotels, but you're looking at US$150 to Sam Neua, US$120 to Luang Prabang.

AROUND PHONSAVAN
Plain Of Jars
ທົ່ງໄຫຫິນ

Giant, very ancient stone jars of unknown origin are scattered over hundreds of square kilometres around Phonsavan, giving the area the misleading name of Plain of Jars. In fact it's no more of a plain than the rice-bowl valleys at Muang Sing or Luang Namtha, and indeed most of the curious jar sites are on hills. But what is more fascinating about the jars themselves is the mystery of what civilisation made them. Remarkably, nobody knows. But that doesn't stop guides guessing, often amusingly randomly. Meanwhile, a fanciful legend claims that they were made to brew vast quantities of rice wine to celebrate the local people's 6th-century liberation from cruel overlords by the Tai-Lao hero Khun Jeuam. In some versions of this story, the jars were 'cast' from a type of cement made from buffalo skin, sand, water and sugar cane, then fired in 'kilns'. Some even claim that the cave beside Jar Site 1 housed one such kiln. In fact, however, the jars were fashioned from solid stone and archaeologists estimate they date from the Southeast Asian iron age, between 500 BC and 200AD.

Smaller jars have long since been carted off by collectors but around 2500 larger jars, jar fragments and 'lids' remain. As the region was carpet-bombed throughout the Indochina wars, it's miraculous that so many jars survived. Only seven of the 90 recorded jar-sites have so far been cleared of UXO, and then only within relatively limited areas. These sites, and their access paths, are delineated by easily missed red-and-white marker stones: stay on the white side to avoid very unpleasant surprises.

Sites 1, 2 and 3 form the bases of most tour loops. Phakeo (a trio of closely linked, overgrown sub-sights) is only accessible by two-day trek (p195). Although the Plain of Jars is northeastern Laos's most popular tourist attraction, even the main sites are remarkably low-key and can be virtually deserted if you arrive in the afternoon.

MAIN JAR SITES
Jar Site 1

The biggest and most easily accessible, **Site 1** (Hai Hin; admission 10,000K; ⏰ 8am-4pm Mar-Sep, 7am-

5pm Oct-Feb) features 334 jars or jar fragments relatively close-packed on a pair of hilly slopes pocked with bomb craters. The biggest, Hai Jeuam, weighs around 6 tonnes, stands over 2.5m high and is said to have been the mythical victory cup of Khun Jeuam. The site is just 8km southwest of central Phonsavan, 2.3km west of the Muang Khoun road – turn at the signed junction in Ban Hay Hin. The bare, hilly landscape is appealing, though in one direction the views of Phonsavan airport seem discordant. An information booth is planned near the entrance, where there's already a gift shop, rest pavilion and toilets.

Jar Sites 2 & 3

While the jars aren't as large nor as plentiful as at Site 1, Sites 2 and 3 both have charming yet very different locations and the journey to reach them offers glimpses of some typical local villages. For both sites, turn west of the Muang Khoun road at just past Km 8. Follow the unpaved road for 10km/14km to find the turnings for Sites 2/3, then follow muddy tracks for 1.5/1.8km respectively.

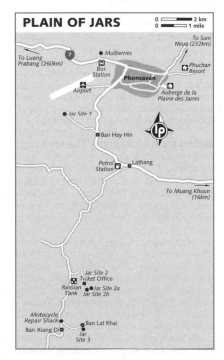

PLAIN OF JARS

Site 2 (Hai Hin Phu Salato; admission 10,000K) is a pair of hill-crests divided by a shallow gully that forms the access lane. That rises 700m from the ticket desk in what becomes a muddy slither in wet conditions. To the left in thin woodlands, look for a cracked stone urn through which a tree has managed to grow. To the right another set of jars sits on a grassy knoll with panoramas of layered hills, paddies and cow-fields. No refreshments are available here.

The 150-jar **Site 3** (Hai Hin Lat Khai; admission 10,000K) sits on a scenic hillside in thin, pretty woodland above Ban Lat Khai village. The access road to Lat Khai leads east beside a tiny motorbike repair hut just before Ban Xiang Di (Ban Siang Dii). The only 'sign' is a red 'III' and jar symbol spray-painted on an electricity pole – if you reach Xiang Di's petrol station you've come 400m too far. Within Lat Khai the Site 3 carpark is unsigned to the right after 1.8km. The ticket booth is beside a simple but pleasant restaurant. The jars are accessed by a little wooden footbridge then a 10-minute walk across rice fields and up.

Getting There & Away

All three main sites could be visited by rented motorbike from Phonsavan in around five hours, while Site 1 is within bicycle range. Alternatively, sign up the night before to join one of several regular guided minibus tours (p191). Most throw in a noodle-soup lunch at Site 3 and a quick stop to see the lumpy rusting remnant of an armoured vehicle in a roadside copse at Ban Nakho: its nickname, the 'Russian Tank', exaggerates the appeal.

Muang Khoun (Old Xieng Khuang)

ຊ຺ຽງຂວາງເກ່ົາ(ເມືອງຄູນ)

pop 4000

The region's ancient capital, Muang Khoun was ravaged in the 19th century by Chinese and Vietnamese invaders, then so heavily bombarded during the Second Indochina War that by 1975 it was almost completely abandoned. However, a handful of aged monuments survived and the good asphalt road from Phonsavan (30km) takes you through some attractive rice-terrace villages, several sporting Phuan-style houses built of sturdy timbers. Buying the Muang Khoun Visitor's Ticket (10,000K) at a booth at the western end of town supports site maintenance.

The main historic sights are a trio of grass-greened historic stupas, all walking distance

from the Khoun Guesthouse. One is directly behind in the grounds of the colourfully rebuilt active monastery, **Wat Si Phoum**. The other two are on a facing ridge, accessed via the brick-and-mud lane that climbs opposite the guesthouse, petering out into a narrow footpath. The 1576 **That Foun** (also called That Chomsi) is around 25m tall and built in the Lan Xang/Lanna style. It now has a distinct lean to its spire and you can climb right through a hole that was made by 19th-century Chinese Haw marauders, who tunnelled in to loot the priceless Buddha relics enshrined within. Five minutes' walk around the easy ridge track brings you to the stubbier remnants of the Cham-built 16th-century stupa **That Chom Phet**. Near the tall communications tower, look back to admire That Foun which, from this angle, appears to be lost amid pristine peaks and forests.

The main road continuing east from the guesthouse passes the shattered ruins of a former Phuan prince's palace (500m) and swerves south just before Km 30 after **Wat Phia Wat**. Of Wat Phia Wat's original 1582 building, just the base platform and a few brick columns survived a devastating 1966 bombing raid. But these columns photogenically frame an age-greyed, shell-shocked Buddha with a whiplash smile.

The unpaved road continuing east passes the small, very degraded **Jar Site 16** after around 5km. This road becomes increasingly difficult and finally dead-ends some 12km beyond at **Ban Thalin**, an interesting village without any commercial facilities that's used as the starting point for the Phakeo trek (p195).

SLEEPING & EATING

In a pleasant little garden area roamed by loveable dogs, the town's one accommodation option is **Khoun Guesthouse & Restaurant** (☎ 212 464, 030-517 1872; Km 29, Rte 10; r 40,000-80,000K). The 40,000K rooms are shabby hardboard coffin-boxes but the 60,000K rooms are new and acceptable with bucket mandi and ensuite toilet. The 80,000K version adds TV and hot water. The pleasant family restaurant has a limited menu, but Bii speaks some English.

GETTING THERE & AWAY

Buses to Phonsavan (10,000K, 45 minutes) depart at 8am, 11am, 2pm and 5pm. By motorbike it's possible to visit Muang Khoun plus the three main jar sites in one long day.

LOCAL VOICES – RESIDENT OF NA KAM PENG, 'BOMB VILLAGE'

Isn't it dangerous living in 'Bomb Village'? Of course. People are careful. But it's not always enough. Two of my young cousins were killed just last year. They knew not to play with bombies – we've all had MAG [Mines Advisory Group, p190] training – but there was a child from out of the area. For him the dangers were unknown. I guess he was fascinated by the toy-like ball. But it blew him up and took my cousins with him.

Why don't you move elsewhere? It sounds easy, but in fact the villagers moved here after the war from somewhere that was even more dangerous. Everything is relative. Of course, back then when everything was devastated, at least there was money to be made collecting war scrap and selling it to dealers. And now, well, we are close to the road, there's electricity too, and they might even pipe in clean water some day, though that will still take a few years.

The anonymous interviewee lives in Ban Tha Jok/Na Kam Peng, a village in rural Xieng Khuang known for its abundance of everyday items made from war scrap.

On maps, Rte 10/3908 appears to link Muang Khoun to Paksan via That Thom and a daily bus is timetabled that way from Phonsavan. However, during research that road was effectively impassable, buses had been stuck for three days in axle-deep mud and even trail bikes were struggling to get through.

Phakeo Trek

Organised through Phonsavan agencies (p191), this excellent two-day trek combines many essential elements of the Xieng Khuang experience. On the long first day, hike across secondary forested mountain ridges to a three-part jar site with a total of over 400 ancient jars and jar fragments, many moss-encrusted and shaded by foliage. The trek then descends into the roadless Hmong village of Ban Phakeo, whose shingle-roofed mud-floor homes huddle around a central rocky knoll. A purpose-built Hmong-style guest-shack provides a basic sleeping platform with space for eight hikers. There's no electricity. The next day, the hike descends into attractive semi-agricultural valleys then climbs up the cascades of a multi-terraced waterfall to arrive in the famous 'Bomb Village'.

Towards Vietnam & Sam Neua

Rte 7 east of Phonsavan runs to the Vietnamese border via the 'Bomb Village' and Nong Haet. At Muang Kham, narrow but asphalted Rte 6 strikes north via Nam Neun (two guesthouses) to the tiny junction village of Phoulao (aka Ban Ko Hing), where the attractive road to Sam Neua continues east, passing within 6km of the Hintang archaeological 'park' (p202) and right by Tat Saloei (p202). However, if you're not driving, none

of the minor attractions along these routes easily warrant the long waits and/or lengthy walks that are necessary to access them using extremely infrequent public transport.

BOMB VILLAGE & WATERFALL

In many Lao settlements you'll find the odd element of 'recycled' war debris but the Hmong double-village of Ban Tha Jok/Na Kam Peng has more than most, hence the nickname 'Bomb Village'. Although much has been sold for scrap you can still see cluster-bomb casings used to make the legs of rice barns, planting pots for herbs, barbecue braziers and, in one case, a whole over-engineered fence. The main concentration lies in minor lanes about 700m south of Rte 7, turning at Km 165 (27km east of Phonsavan). An impressive multistep waterfall drops into a nearby valley around 2km south (ask for directions).

MUANG KHAM & AROUND

Lurking at the toll gate 500m past Km 178 (43km east of Phonsavan), kids compete to sell *kao lam*, bamboo tubes filled with sticky rice sweetened with coconut and red bean. Located 700m past Km 185 (2.5km west of central Muang Kham), **Kham District Handicrafts Group** (☎ 030-517 0185) weave some high quality, fair-priced fabrics and have a small display on natural dyestuffs.

Central **Muang Kham** (Ban Chomthong, Km 188) is little more than a highway trading post with a market and a couple of guesthouses. The better of these is the once attractive **Sengdeuan Guesthouse** (☎ 061-212 415; r with cold/hot water 60,000/70,000K), which feels slightly neglected.

If you're driving the bumpy road towards Vietnam it's more pleasant to stay at the **Nam**

Hone Resort (☎ 020-246 1615; r from 50,000K), 20km east of Muang Kham – turn south at Km 204 then continue 5.5km down a spur road. The best rooms here have bamboo thatch walls, air-con and a bath. Into this, warm water is piped from unexotic hot springs that lie five minutes' walk away in pleasant woodlands.

For more accessible hot springs, visit **Ban Nam Hong Noi** (Nam Ounnoi; admission 5000K) 4km east of Muang Kham then 700m south of the Vietnam road. Scalding hot water trickles out into a waffle-shaped grid of low concrete separators then flows into a river that gurgles merrily across attractive rapids. Find the perfect bathing temperature by adjusting your place in the meeting waters. Use of a bathing ladle is included in the ticket price.

THAM PIU
ຖ້ຳພິວ

North of Muang Kham rises an imposing wall of abrupt wooded ridges and exposed limestone rock-faces. Carved into one such cliffside is **Tham Piu** (admission 5000K; ⏰ 7am-4pm), a cave where villagers sought protection from American bombers during the Indochina war. Hundreds died here in November 1968 when a US fighter plane fired a rocket into the cave and the site still holds major emotional resonance. Today the setting is pretty but the small museum in the car park adds little information to give meaning to a visit and its collection of photos and bomb fragments aren't directly related to the Tham Piu incident. The cave, ten minutes' climb via an obvious stairway, still shows signs of smoke damage while the floor is littered by small, unsophisticated memorial cairns. The cave mouth is wide enough to allow natural light into the main cavern but a torch (flashlight) would be useful to venture a little deeper.

The site is 2.6km up a degraded asphalt lane that heads west from the main road at a turning signed 'Tham Piew', around 4km north of Muang Kham.

SAM NEUA (XAM NEUA)
ຊຳເໜືອ
☎ 064 / pop 14,000

Behind a central disguise of well-spaced concrete modernity, Sam Neua offers eye-widening produce markets and a colourful ethnic diversity. The town is a logical transit point for visiting nearby Vieng Xai (p200) or catching the daily bus to Vinh in Vietnam and remains one of Laos's least-visited provincial capitals. At an altitude of roughly 1200m, you'll value a decent sweater in the dry winter period, at least by night and until the thick morning fog burns off. From April to October the lush landscapes are contrastingly warm and wet.

Information

The **Provincial Tourist Office** (☎ 312 567; ⏰ 8am-noon & 1.30-4pm Mon-Fri) has English-speaking staff who are eager to help. When that's closed it's worth asking for tips at the Khongmany Indian restaurant whose owner is helpful and well informed. **Agricultural Promotion Bank** (☎ 314 284) and **Lao Development Bank** (☎ 312 171) both exchange Thai baht and US dollars at fair rates. However, changing money is generally quicker through one of the **fabric-stalls** in the main market – they exchange Vietnamese dong and are open at weekends (till around 5pm). As yet there's no ATM in Sam Neua. **Tam.com Internet Service** (per min 170K; ⏰ 8am-10pm) is a relatively reliable internet cafe while Samneua Hotel offers decent wi-fi.

Sights

At the town's central junction stands the bizarre **Suan Keo Lak Meung Monument**. Four hooked concrete pincers hold aloft a glittery disco-ball that is intended to celebrate Sam

---

CROSSING THE VIETNAMESE BORDER AT NAM CAN & NAM KHAN

Direct buses to Vinh from Phonsavan (four weekly) and Luang Prabang (twice weekly) cross the lonely **Nam Can/Nam Khan border** (⏰ 8am-noon & 1.30-5pm) around 240km northwest of Vinh. The nearest town on the Lao side is Nong Haet, 13km west, with up to four daily bus services to Phonsavan (40,000K, four hours) and a *săwngthăew* to the border leaving around noon (20,000K). From the Vietnam side, 21km of hairpins wind down to the first small town, Mu'òng Xén. There's no public transport from the border but paid hitching or motorbike taxis are a possibility. Mu'òng Xén has a basic hotel and a bus to Vinh departing around 4pm, which should reach Con Cuông with ample time to connect with the 8pm Hanoi night-bus.

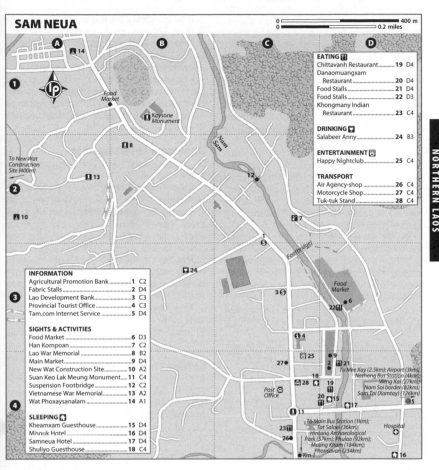

SAM NEUA

EATING 🍴
Chittavanh Restaurant................**19** D4
Danaomuangxam
   Restaurant.........................**20** D4
Food Stalls...............................**21** D4
Food Stalls...............................**22** D3
Khongmany Indian
   Restaurant.........................**23** C4

DRINKING 🍸
Salabeer Anny.........................**24** B3

ENTERTAINMENT 🎭
Happy Nightclub.......................**25** C4

TRANSPORT
Air Agency-shop.......................**26** C4
Motorcycle Shop.......................**27** C4
Tuk-tuk Stand..........................**28** C4

INFORMATION
Agricultural Promotion Bank **1** C2
Fabric Stalls...........................**2** D4
Lao Development Bank....................**3** C3
Provincial Tourist Office **4** C3
Tam.com Internet Service **5** D4

SIGHTS & ACTIVITIES
Food Market **6** D3
Han Kompoan **7** C2
Lao War Memorial......................**8** B2
Main Market..........................**9** D4
New Wat Construction Site..............**10** A2
Suan Keo Lak Meung Monument.....**11** C4
Suspension Footbridge..................**12** C2
Vietnamese War Memorial..............**13** A2
Wat Phoxaysanalam **14** A1

SLEEPING 🛏
Kheamxam Guesthouse..................**15** D4
Misouk Hotel **16** D4
Samneua Hotel **17** D4
Shuliyo Guesthouse....................**18** C4

To Mee Xay (2.5km); Airport (3km);
Nathong Bus Station (4km);
Vieng Xai (27km);
Nam Soi border (82km);
Sam Tai (Xamtay) (126km)

To Main Bus Station (1km);
Tat Saloei (36km);
Hintang Archaeological
Park (57km); Phulao (92km);
Muang Kham (184km);
Phonsavan (234km)

Neua's folk-song image as an 'indestructible jewel'. However, the effect is unintentionally comic with its backing of half-hearted fountains and a frieze full of communist triumphalist soldiers.

The **main market** is predominantly stocked with Chinese and Vietnamese consumer goods. However, some fabric stalls here stock regional textiles, and jewellers sell antique coins and silverware used for tribal headgear. Tucked away near the back, some stalls hawk gaudy collections of replica ethnic-style clothing.

Across the river, the fascinating **food market** is well stocked with fresh vegetables and meats, some rather startling. Field rats are displayed cut open to show the freshness of their entrails. Banana leaves might be stuffed with squirming insects. And there's plenty of dead furry wildlife that you'd probably prefer to see alive in the forests.

Apart from two modest old stupas that somehow survived the wartime bombs, the main road seems brash and modern. However, just metres away, enchanting river scenes are visible from the bike-and-pedestrian **suspension bridge**. For wide views over town you could sink a *lào-láo* at the ragged **Han Kompoan** cafe-shack, climb to the Lao or Vietnamese **war memorials**, or wind up to a big **new wat construction site**. Till it's finished, **Wat Phoxaysanalam** remains the town's main monastery. The tourist office can organise visits to local **weaving** houses.

Sleeping

There are around twenty guesthouses in town, with many budget options lying close to the market.

Kheamxam Guesthouse (☎ 312 111; r without bathroom 30,000K, r with bath/TV 50,000/70,000K) This pastel-hued, corner hotel offers good value no-nonsense rooms whose sole adornment is the demurely smiling face of a calendar pin-up girl. Airport and bus station transfers are available.

Shuliyo Guesthouse (☎ 312 462; r 70,000K) A curious mixture of heavy carved chairs, bouquets of plastic flowers and a Ho Chi Minh portrait welcome guests into this pleasant new family guesthouse. Varnished pale wood stairs lead up to neat rooms with OK bathrooms. Mattresses could be thicker.

Misouk Hotel (☎ 314 555; r small/large 100,000/150,000K) A large, new peach-coloured guesthouse just south of the hospital where attractively patterned patchwork quilts grace good, new beds and most rooms come with fridge and kettle. The large communal balcony space on the second floor has no seating but offers views across rice terraces that feel far from urban.

Samneua Hotel (☎ 314 777; snhotel_08@yahoo. com; s/d/tw 120,000/150,000/200,000K; 🖳 🛜) The small foyer looks unfinished but compact new rooms are well furnished in sturdy, pale woods adorned with carved motifs. There's plenty of communal sitting space and if you don't have a laptop to enjoy in-room wi-fi, use the guest computer in the curious all-window sun-room on the fourth floor.

Eating

Cheap *fŏe*, samosas and many harder-to-identify local morsels are sold from **food stalls** (🕙 dawn-dusk) opposite the main market and especially along the riverside lane leading to the food market.

Danaomuangxam Restaurant (☎ 314 126; mains US$1-1.50; 🕙 7am-9.30pm) This simple, box restaurant has no special charm and can get chilly at night but its relatively traveller-friendly menu includes cornflakes (5000K), breakfast omelettes (8000K) and beef with chips (20,000K).

Khongmany Indian Restaurant (☎ 020-5429 2445; mains 15,000-27,000K, sandwiches 8000-12,000K; 🕙 7am-9pm) Decor is simple but the great Indian food is supplemented by sandwiches, pancakes and a long list of breakfast options. The super-

helpful owner is a great source of local information. Location might change.

Chittavanh Restaurant (☎ 312 265; mains 30,000K; 🕙 7am-9.30pm) Savouring a delicious 15,000K Chinese fried tofu dish makes it worth braving the reverberant clatter of this cavernous concrete-box restaurant where vinyl tablecloths have been nailed into place and haphazard decor revolves around display cases of Pepsi cans.

Drinking & Entertainment

Don't assume you'll find any English speakers at the following.

Salabeer Anny (☎ 020-5566 4044) Twinkling with fairy lights, this thatched pavilion restaurant-bar overlooks Sam Neua's curious green heart where a large patch of central rice paddies have yet to be swallowed by urban development.

Mee Xay (☎ 020-9986 6139) Featuring twin *petang* strips, this pleasantly rustic bar is out of the centre, 500m before the airport. Grilled meat meals are available.

Happy Nightclub The most central dancespot, this one-room club pumps out mostly Thai hip-hop for crammed-together teenage revellers.

Getting There & Away

AIR

Sam Neua's little **Nathong Airfield** is 3km east of the centre towards Vieng Xai. A tiny central **agency-shop** (☎ 020-234 6106) sells tickets for **Lao Capricorn Air** (http://laocapricornair.net) flights to Vientiane (790,000K) on Tuesday, Thursday and Saturday. All too frequently the flights get cancelled just half an hour before departure. Phonsavan/Xieng Khuang airport is more reliable.

BUS

Sam Neua has two bus stations. Schedules change frequently so double check and certainly don't rely on timetables printed on tourist maps and notice boards.

Main bus station

The main station is on a hilltop 1.2km south of the central monument, just off the Vieng Thong road. From here buses leave to Vientiane (135,000K, 22 hours) via Phonsavan (10 hours) at 9am, noon and 2pm. An additional 8am Vientiane bus goes via Vieng Thong (40,000K, six hours), Nong

UXO & WAR JUNK

During the Indochina wars, Laos became the most heavily bombed nation in world history. Xieng Khuang province was especially hard-hit and even today, uncountable scraps of combat debris remain. Much of it is potentially deadly 'UXO' (unexploded ordnance), including mortar shells, white phosphorous canisters (used to mark bomb targets) and assorted bombs. Some of the most problematic UXO comes from cluster bombs, 1.5m-long torpedo-shaped packages of evil whose outer metal casing was designed to split open lengthwise in mid-air, scattering 670 tennis-ball-size bomblets ('bombies') over a 5000-sq-metre area. Once disturbed, a bombie would explode, projecting around 30 steel pellets like bullets killing anyone within a 20m radius. Almost 40 years after bombing ceased, roughly one person a day is still killed by UXO in Xieng Khuang. Tens of millions of bombies remain embedded in the land, causing an ever-present danger to builders, farmers and especially to young children, who fatally mistake them for playthings. And for impoverished villagers, the economic temptation to collect UXO to sell as scrap metal has caused numerous fatalities. Despite valiant ongoing clearance efforts, at current rates it would take an estimated 150 years to deal with the problem.

Cluster-bomb casings, which were not themselves explosive, have meanwhile found a wide range of more positive new uses. In some places you can see them reused as architectural features (see the boxed text, p195), feeding troughs, pots for growing spring onions or simply as ornaments around houses or hotels.

If you find any war debris don't be tempted to touch it. Even if it appears to be an exhibit in a collection, beware that some hotels display war junk that's never been properly defused and might remain explosive. Even if it isn't live and dangerous, Laos's legal code makes it illegal to trade in war leftovers of any kind. Purchase, sale or theft of any old weaponry can result in a prison term of between six months and five years.

Khiaw (80,000K, 13 hours), Luang Prabang (110,000K, 17 hours) and Vang Vieng. Minibuses to Vieng Thong (7.20am) and Luang Prabang (7.30am) duplicate parts of the same route.

Nathong Bus Station

The Nathong bus station is 1km beyond the airport on the Vieng Xai road at the easternmost edge of town. *Săwngthăew* to Vieng Xai leave five times daily, currently at 8am, 10am, 11am, 2.30pm and 4pm. If it leaves bang on time, the 8am service might just get you there just in time for the first caves tour, but it's very tight. Other services include 'Nameo' (actually the Nam Soi border post) at 8am (20,000K, three hours), Sam Tai (Xamtay) at 9.30am (34,000K, five to six hours) and Sop Hao at 8am and 1pm (19,000K, 2½ hours).

To Vietnam

A bus (sometimes minibus) departs daily to Thanh Hoa in Vietnam (180,000K, 11 hours). It currently starts from outside the Indian restaurant at 7am, swings up to the main bus station around 7.05am, trawls around the market then collects more passengers at the Nathong bus station around 8am. Wherever you board it's advisable to prepurchase your ticket at the main bus station or risk paying very considerably more than the true fare. 'Through tickets' to Hanoi (290,000K) still go via Thanh Hoa where you change bus. Returning from Thanh Hoa (8am), tickets should cost 200,000 dong but foreigners are often asked for significantly more.

MOTORCYCLE

A central **motorcycle shop** (☎ 312 255; ◷ 7am-6pm) rents low-quality motorbikes at 60,000K per day.

AROUND SAM NEUA

It doesn't take much effort to get into some timeless rural villages around Sam Neua. For random motorcycle trips you might try heading south from the hospital for a few kilometres or heading north up the unpaved lane directly to the right-hand side of Wat Phoxaysanalam. The latter winds its way after 11km to **Ban Tham**, just before which there's an inconsequential **Buddha cave** (to the left around 100m before the school and shop). But more appealing are rice terrace valleys around 4km out of Sam Neua where two picturesque villages across the river each sport spindly old greying stupas. With a decent motorbike you could day-trip to Vieng Xai. Or to Hintang (p202) via Tat Saloei (p202).

Vieng Xai

ວຽງໄຊ

☎ 064 / pop 9000

Vieng Xai's thought-provoking 'bomb-shelter caves' are set amid dramatic karst outcrops and offer a truly gripping opportunity to learn about northern Laos's unlucky 20th-century history. Imagine Vang Vieng, but with compelling history instead of happy tubing.

HISTORY

For centuries the minuscule hamlet of Long Ko sat peacefully here, lost amid deep ancient forests and towering karst outcrops. But in 1963, political repression and a spate of assassinations in Vientiane led the Pathet Lao leadership to retreat deep into the Hua Phan hinterland, eventually taking up residence in the area's caves. As the US Secret War gathered momentum, surrounding villages were mercilessly bombarded. Horrified and bemused, locals initially had no idea of who was attacking them, nor why. Still, for safety, they too retreated into the vastly expanded cave systems, over 450 of which eventually came to shelter up to 23,000 people. As the war dragged on, cave sites came to host printing works, hospitals, markets and even a metalwork factory. After almost a decade in the caves, the 1973 ceasefire allowed the refugees to tentatively emerge and construct a small town here. Indeed, until December 1975, it was the de facto capital of the Pathet Lao's Liberated Territories. The town was named Vieng Xai as that had been the secret codename of future president Kaysone Phomvihane while in hiding here. Decades later, many of Vieng Xai's cave sites still retain visible signs of their wartime roles, making the complex one of the world's most complete revolutionary bases to have survived from the cold war period.

ORIENTATION & INFORMATION

Twin roads run 1km south off Rte 3 to the busy market area. Beyond, the town retains the quiet, wide avenues and well-spaced houses of Kaysone's 1973 'capital' interspersed with man-made lakes, trees, flowers and several karst outcrops. Around 1km south of the market, a key feature for visitors is the **caves office** (Vieng Xai Caves Visiting Centre; ☎ 314 321, 020-266

9022; www.visit-viengxay.com; ☑ 8-11.30am & 1-4.30pm), which organises all cave visits, rents bicycles, has maps, a small book-exchange and a useful information board. There's even a display case full of old Lenin busts and assorted socialist iconography.

SIGHTS & ACTIVITIES
The Cave Tour

Joining a truly fascinating 18-point **tour** (admission 60,000K) is the only way to see Vieng Xai's seven most important war-shelter cave complexes, along with several 1970s postwar buildings associated with major liberation heroes. All are set in beautiful yet very natural gardens and backed by fabulous karst scenery. A local guide unlocks each site and can answer your questions. Meanwhile, an audioguide gives masses of first-hand background information and historical context, offering a moving, balanced and uniquely fascinating glimpse of how people struggled on through the war years. Compared to anything else you're likely to encounter in Laos, the sheer professionalism is mind-boggling. The production incorporates original interviews from local survivors and is enlivened with sound effects and accompanying music – the Hendrixesque soundtrack to the Air America piece is particularly memorable.

Most caves have minor elements of original furnishings. Some have 'emergency rooms', air-locked concrete caves-within-caves designed to protect top politburo members from possible chemical or gas attacks. No such attacks occurred but the emergency room of the **Kaysone Phomvihane Cave** still has its air-circulation pump in working order. Enjoy bamboo-framed views of town from the ledge of the **Nouhak Phoumsavan Cave** and look for two rocket-impact holes in the karst outcrop above the **Souphanouvong Cave**, once the hideout of Laos's famous 'Red Prince'. Almost all the main cave sites are well illuminated but bring a torch (flashlight) if you want to traverse the unadorned **hospital cave** (occasionally flooded).

Steps lead down from the hand-dug **Khamtay Siphandone Cave** to the **Barracks Caves**, extensive natural caverns that would have housed hundreds of conscripted liberation soldiers. Above is the **Artillery Cave** from whose open ledge spotters would watch for incoming American planes. The tour culminates in the **Xanglot Cave**, a wide double-ended cavern that was used as a wedding hall, cinema and even as a theatre. Incredibly, performers from Russia, China and Vietnam all managed to mount productions here during the war.

Tours start at 9am and 1pm from the caves office. By arrangement private visits are also possible at other times (costing an extra 50,000K per group) depending on guide availability. Seeing all 18 sites in the three hours available is possible without feeling unduly rushed, assuming you rent a bicycle (available for 10,000/20,000K per tour/day from the caves office) and that you'll listen to the longer audio tracks while travelling between the sites rather than waiting to arrive before pressing play.

Other sites

A newly restored **'market cave'** was due to open in 2010. **Tat Nam Neua** is an 80m waterfall, around 6km west near the Sam Neua road.

SLEEPING

There are half a dozen options. If built as planned, a new 18-room 'boutique ecolodge' should eventually provide profits to help fund the development of other cave sites.

Xah Cha Lern Guesthouse (☎ 020-5571 4106; r with bathroom 60,000K, s/tw/tr without bathroom 20,000/40,000/60,000K) Awkwardly located on the main Sam Neua–Vietnam road 1km north of Vieng Xai market, the ensuite rooms are small but relatively fresh in a peach-coloured new house. The cheapest rooms offer just mats on the floor.

Thavisay Hotel (r 40,000K) Despite a peaceful, crag-backed location near the town's most attractive lake, this two-storey 1974 eyesore has all the charm of a Soviet psychiatric hospital. Cold, characterless rooms have floors of loose tiles or ripped vinyl but ceilings are high and the water just might run warm…eventually.

Naxay 2 Guesthouse (☎ 314 330, 020-5521 0788; r 60,000K) Opposite the caves office, Vieng Xai's most comfortable option offers new, bamboo-lined bungalows around a patch of greenery backed by an impressive split-toothed crag. Beds are comfy, water heaters work and the attached beach-style cafe pavilion has a menu in English, though few of the items are actually available.

EATING

While several places claim to stay open till 10.30pm or 'all night', in reality many have run out of food by 8pm. By 9pm the town has virtually hibernated. The most attractive place

to dine is the **Thavisay Restaurant** (☎ 020-5571 8474; mains 15,000-40,000K), a thatched open-sided pavilion with associated bamboo stilt-booths perched on the lakeside near the Thavisay Hotel. Fish dishes are over-full of bones but the *làap* is good and the lemongrass soup is especially refreshing.

Several *fŏe* shops in the market serve rice and cheap noodle dishes till around 5pm.

GETTING THERE & AWAY

Săwngthăew to Sam Neua (10,000K, 50 minutes) leave at approximately 7am, 10am, 1pm, 2.30pm and 4pm from the market. Buses between Sam Neua and Sam Tai, Nam Soi or Thanh Hoa (one bus daily to each) bypass Vieng Xai 1km to the north but will usually stop on request. Visiting Vieng Xai by rented tuk-tuk from Sam Neua costs around 250,000K return per vehicle.

SAM NEUA TO VIETNAM

Two roads lead from Sam Neua to Vietnam. On a map the route via Sop Hao looks most promising but in reality it's unpaved and the border crossing is for locals only. However, the scenic route via fascinating Vieng Xai is open to all nationalities, Vietnamese visas permitting. It's narrow but paved and offers a feast of varied views. The best incorporate giant teeth of tree-dappled karst outcrop backing bucolic valleys layered with rice terraces. Several villages en route including **Ban Piang Ban** (Km 144.5) specialise in basket-making and bamboo crafts. Across the river at Km 169 is a **'steel cave'** where knives and agricultural tools were made on an almost industrial scale during the Second Indochina War (and, incredibly, for over a decade afterwards too). Today there's neither sign nor access bridge across the river but eventually the site is to be developed as an historical attraction.

Turn south at Km 164 for the recently asphalted spur road to **Sam Tai** (Xamtay), famous for producing magnificent textiles. It has a couple of guesthouses should you feel like getting well off the beaten track to investigate. Public access to the remote **Nam Sam NPA** beyond is not currently permitted.

SAM NEUA TO NONG KHIAW

From Sam Neua, Rte 6 runs along winding mountain ridges passing Hintang Archaeological Park (p202) and meeting Phonsavan-bound Rte 1 at minuscule Phoulao

---

CROSSING THE VIETNAMESE BORDER AT NA MEO & NAM SOI

If you're crossing the **Nam Soi/Na Meo border** (Km 175; ☯ 7.30-11.30am & 1.30-4.30pm), the easiest transport option is to take the direct bus between Sam Neua and Thanh Hoa (now daily, see p199) which passes close to Vieng Xai but doesn't enter town. Once you're in Thanh Hoa, there's a night train to Hanoi departing at 11.30pm and arriving antisocially early around 4am.

It's quite possible to reach the border by the 8am Na Meo *săwngthăew* from Sam Neua (three hours). However, organising onward transport from the Vietnamese side is complicated by unscrupulous operators who seem intent on keeping you in town.

Westbound, note that the Lao border post (Nam Soi) isn't a town. There's a trio of simple restaurant shacks but no accommodation and no waiting transport apart from the 11.30am *săwngthăew* to Sam Neua. If you're later than that, it might be wise to sleep in bigger Na Meo on the Vietnamese side where a selection of accommodation includes the relatively swish new **Yên Trang Hotel** (☎ Vietnam-37-359 2511).

Be sure to carry sufficient convertible currency if arriving in Laos this way: there's no ATM in Sam Neua, Vieng Thong or Nong Khiaw.

(Ban Kho Hing), 92km west of Sam Neua, where kilometre markings reset. Some travellers have managed to find a bed here but there's no formal guesthouse and only the simplest of shop-shacks. West of Phoulao the green mountains become much more heavily deforested until reaching the boundary of the Nam Et/Phou Louey NPA. That's best visited from Vieng Thong, which also makes a decent place to break the long journey. The only other place with accommodation en route is Vieng Kham, a river-spanning settlement about 50km east of Nong Khiaw. The long descent towards Nong Khiaw lasts many kilometres and offers some glimpses of superb scenery.

Tat Saloei

Also known as Phonesai Waterfall, this impressive series of cascades forms a combined drop of almost 100m. It's briefly visible from eastbound Rte 6 roughly 1km after Km 55 (ie 36km from Sam Neua), but easy to miss westbound. There are plans to develop a visitor centre and walking trails here.

Hintang Archaeological Park (Suan Hin)

ສວນຫິນ

Almost as mysterious as Xieng Khuang's more famous jars, this unique, unfenced collection of **standing stones** is thought to be at least 1500 years old. Spindly, rough-hewn uprights up to 3m tall are interspersed with **stone disks** that formerly covered funerary sites. Some are over a metre in diameter. Misleading comparisons to Britain's Stonehenge overplay the visual appeal but the 'families' of stones do have a certain magic and the group has been nominated for Unesco World Heritage status. Local mythology claims that the stones were originally cut using a magic axe wielded by a giant called Ba Hat whose plans to build a great city here were thwarted by the cunning of the Luang Prabang king.

Access is up a rough, rutted track that cuts south from Rte 6 at **Ban Phao** (Km 35.3), 57km from Sam Neua. This track can be impracticably muddy for vehicles after any rain. The main site is right beside the track after 6km, around 800m beyond the obvious radio mast summit. Some 2km back towards the main road, an orange sign points to the **Keohintang Trail**, which allows more intrepid visitors to seek out lesser-known megalith groups hidden along a partially marked two-hour hiking trail. Take the narrow rising path, not the bigger track that descends towards Ban Nakham. If you don't get lost, the trail should emerge back onto Rte 6 at **Ban Tao Hin** (Km 31.5), a tiny village without any facilities.

Chartered tuk-tuks from Sam Neua want around 450,000K return. If you're driving between Sam Neua and either Phonsavan or Udomxai, allow two hours extra for the very slow detour to the main site. By public transport you'll have to walk to and from Rte 6. Practicalities work out best if you're visiting between Sam Neua and Phonsavan – starting with the Vieng Thong–bound minibus you'll have around six hours for the walk before the last Phonsavan/Vientiane–bound bus rumbles past. If you don't want an overnighter, hop off 8km south of Phoulao in pleasant **Nam Neun** where there are restaurants and two cheap if semi-dormant guesthouses.

Vieng Thong (Muang Hiam)

ວຽງທອງ

☎ 064 / pop 4000

If you're travelling between Nong Khiaw and Sam Neua, stopping here for at least one night makes the long journey altogether more enjoyable – especially eastbound. US bombing destroyed the town's once-grand monastery but its surviving stupa, **That Hiam**, is on the rise beside the district administration buildings. The dazzling green rice fields around town are photogenic and short walks or bicycle rides can take you to pretty Tai Daeng, Hmong and Khamu villages. Many locals still refer to Vieng Thong by its original name Muang Hiam. Coming from a Tai Daeng word meaning 'watch out', that was highly suitable back when dangerous tigers roamed the surrounding forests. These days barely a dozen still survive, deep in the enormous Nam Et/Phou Louey NPA, but Vieng Thong is the main starting point to look for them on newly initiated **'tiger treks'** (see the boxed text, below). These are organised through the **Nam Et/Phou Louey NPA office** (☎ 810 008; dsenghalath@wcs.org, www.namet .org; ☼ 8am-noon & 1-4.30pm Mon-Fri). which is building a new Vieng Thong visitors' centre. This will allow you to learn more about the park's imaginative wildlife protection programs and to peruse remarkable animal photos snapped

by ingenious camera-traps dotted around the park (also online at http://programs.wcs.org/ laoswildlifephotoexhibition). The office is at the northwestern edge of town, 700m beyond the market area – cross the river (Nam Khao) on Rte 1, turn immediately right at Km 197 taking the unsurfaced Muang Pur (Meuagper) road, then swing immediately left up the 200m access lane.

Ten minutes walk further towards Muang Pur is a little **hot spring area**. At first glance there seems to be nothing here but a half-demolished brick building and a series of bathing pipes leading out of a scum-rimmed pond. However, if you wander back into the protected 'school forest' behind, the scene has an altogether lovelier aspect with a steaming stream meandering through an emerald green clearing dotted with little granite boulders. In places the bubbling, sulphurous water is scalding hot (so don't touch!) and clouds of midges can prove annoying but the setting is attractive amid some grand older trees. Big plans are afoot to totally redevelop the site over coming years.

SLEEPING & EATING

Dokchampa Guesthouse (☎ 810 005; r without/with bathroom 30,000/50,000K) New but very functional rooms with mosquito nets and limited or no natural light.

Dok Khoun Thong Guesthouse (☎ 810 017; r 50,000K) The most appealing of Vieng Thong's

---

NAM ET/PHOU LOUEY NPA

In this vast **National Protected Area**, rare civets, Asian Golden Cats, river otters, white-cheeked crested gibbons and the utterly unique Laotian warty newt (*Paramesotriton laoensis*) share 4200 sq km of relatively pristine forests with around a dozen **tigers**. Approximately half is an inaccessible core zone. The remainder includes 98 ethnic minority hamlets, to some of which treks may eventually be organised. Since 2010, two-day wildlife-watching excursions are being pioneered to the park's remote Nam Nern field station, a roadless former village site where a campsite and surrounding walking trails have been professionally cleared of UXO. Highlights of the trip include a night-time boat ride 'spotlighting' for animals and day-time guided hikes learning about wildlife tracking. Actually seeing a live tiger is unlikely but there's more hope of spotting Sambar and Barking Deer and for each significant sighting, nearby villages receive a small payment – a cleverly thought-out scheme that encourages the local population to work actively against poachers.

Trips are organised through the NPA office in Vieng Thong but contacting them well in advance is advisable since there's a limit of two departures per week. Tour costs (US$80/100 per person in groups of five/two people) include guides, cooks, food and camping equipment, with a significant proportion of the fee going into village development funds. The price also includes the 90-minute boat ride from Ban Sonkhua, around 50km east of Vieng Thong on Rte 1. Getting to Ban Sonkhua (not included) is possible on the morning public minibus from Vieng Thong or Phonsavan but be sure to discuss travel arrangements with the organisers.

NORTHERN LAOS

four options, this brand new guesthouse is tucked away behind the market, accessed by a lane starting beside the Souksakhone Guesthouse. Very clean, decent-sized rooms have hot showers, netted windows and comfortable new beds with love-message sheets and teddy-bear towels. There's a pleasant first-floor sitting area and attractive views across riverside fields from the rear terrace.

Tontavanh Restaurant (☎ 810 013; mains 10,000-20,000K) This typical-looking local eatery serves unexpectedly appetising food and even has a menu in English. Across Rte 1C the small market only really comes to life before dawn. A handful of restaurant-stands at the bus station offer varied delicacies such as frog-on-a-stick to passing travellers.

For rice-paddy views, try the rough-and-ready **salabeer bar** (beer 10,000K) just beyond the NPA Office en route to the hot springs. Karaoke alert.

GETTING THERE & AWAY

Westbound buses arriving from Sam Neua around noon, continue after lunch to Nong Khiaw (60,000K, 6½ hours), Pak Mong and Luang Prabang (130,000K, 10 hours). Eastbound, the best choice for Sam Neua is the 7am minibus (40,000K, six hours) as the two Sam Neua through-services (from Luang Prabang/Vientiane) both travel the road largely by night, leaving Vieng Thong somewhere around 6pm/2am respectively.

The bus and petrol stations are 300m along Rte 6 from the market at the eastern edge of town. Dok Khoun Thong Guesthouse has two bicycles for guest use and motorcycle rental might become possible in coming years.

MUANG NGOI DISTRICT

Tracts of green mountains are attractive wherever you go in northern Laos. But at Nong Khiaw and tiny, roadless Muang Ngoi Neua, the contours do something altogether more dramatic. At both places, vast karst peaks and towering cliffs rear dramatically out of the Nam Ou, creating jaw-droppingly beautiful scenes. Both villages make convenient rural getaways from Luang Prabang and are accessible by riverboat from Muang Khua. Nong Khiaw also makes an excellent rural rest stop between Luang Prabang and Vieng Thong or Sam Neua.

NONG KHIAW
ຫນອງຂຽວ
☎ 071 / pop 3500

Sleepy little Nong Khiaw is a pair of dusty streets on the west bank of the languid Nam Ou. On the river's scenic east bank (officially called Ban Sop Houn) is a selection of guesthouses and restaurants catering to travelllers. Linking the two, a high concrete bridge built in 1973 offers particularly mesmerising views of soaring limestone crags and haphazard chunks of mountain.

Beware that Nong Khiaw is alternatively known as Muang Ngoi (the name of the surrounding district) creating an obvious confusion with Muang Ngoi Neua (p207), a 90-minute boat ride further north.

Information

The tiny **post office** (⏰ 8.30am-5pm) exchanges baht and US dollars at very unfavourable rates, but the nearest bank is 16km west in Nam Bak. In emergencies, the reception at **Nong Kiau Riverside** (see p206) just might be able to do credit card cash advances. That resort is also the only place to offer internet (per min 500K) and wi-fi (per min/hr/day 300/25,000/40,000K), both temperamental. The **tourist information office** above the boat landing is rarely open.

Sights

It's hard to beat just standing on the bridge and gazing at the river. And do return to the bridge at dusk when fabulous star-shows turn the deep indigo sky into a pointillist canvas that subtly outlines the riverside massifs.

Around 2km east along remarkably quiet Rte 1C, the horizon's array of towering karst formations reaches a brief but particularly impressive climax. Just beyond, **Tham Pha Thok** (admission 5000K; ⏰ 7.30am-6.30pm) is a series of caves in an abrupt limestone cliff. This is where villagers and much of the Pathet Lao's Luang Prabang provincial government lived during the Second Indochina War to avoid American bombing. The first and most obvious cave is around 30m above ground level, accessed by a lichen-crusted wooden stairway. Much smaller but more exciting to visit (unless you're claustrophobic) is a second cave 300m around the cliff. Home to the region's main bank between 1968 and 1974, it's accessed through a narrow, twisting former siphon passage. It's pitch black inside the caves

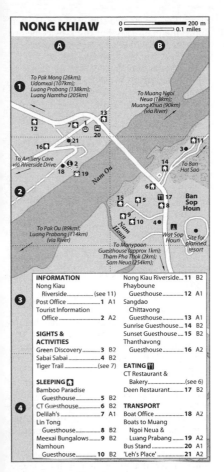

NONG KHIAW

0 _____ 200 m
0 _____ 0.1 miles

To Pak Mong (26km);
Udomxai (107km);
Luang Prabang (138km);
Luang Namtha (205km);

To Muang Ngoi
Neua (18km);
Muang Khua (90km)
(via River)

To Artillery Cave
via Riverside Drive

Nam Ou

To Ban
Hat Sao

Ban
Sop
Houn

To Pak Ou (89km);
Luang Prabang (114km)
(via River)

Nam Houn

To Manypoon
Guesthouse (approx 1km);
Tham Pha Thok (2km);
Sam Neua (254km);

Wat Sop
Houn

Site for
planned
resort

INFORMATION		
Nong Kiau		
Riverside	(see 11)	
Post Office	1	A1
Tourist Information		
Office	2	A2
SIGHTS &		
ACTIVITIES		
Green Discovery	3	B2
Sabai Sabai	4	B2
Tiger Trail	(see 7)	
SLEEPING		
Bamboo Paradise		
Guesthouse	5	B2
CT Guesthouse	6	B2
Delilah's	7	A1
Lin Tong		
Guesthouse	8	B2
Meexai Bungalows	9	B2
Namhoun		
Guesthouse	10	B2
Nong Kiau Riverside	11	B2
Phayboune		
Guesthouse	12	A1
Sangdao		
Chittavong		
Guesthouse	13	A1
Sunrise Guesthouse	14	B2
Sunset Guesthouse	15	B2
Thanthavong		
Guesthouse	16	A2
EATING		
CT Restaurant &		
Bakery	(see 6)	
Deen Restaurant	17	B2
TRANSPORT		
Boat Office	18	A2
Boats to Muang		
Ngoi Neua &		
Luang Prabang	19	A2
Bus Stand	20	A1
'Leh's Place'	21	A2

so bring a head-torch or rent one for 5000K at the ticket booth.

Activities

Well equipped **Green Discovery** (☎ 020-397 5637, 020-265 4792; www.nongkiauclimbing.com; Nong Kiau Riverside; ☺ 8am-9pm) organises various **kayaking** options including a three-day paddle-camping expedition to Luang Prabang (from 1,330,000K per person). A one-day trip starting with a longboat ride to Muang Ngoi then paddling back costs 350,000/410,000/600,000K per person assuming four/two/one participants in two-person kayaks. Experienced staff can accompany you up the grand riverside cliffs for a half-day's **rock climbing** (maximum difficulty grade 4)

costing 125,000K to 200,000K per person, or 300,000K if you take the three-pitch **abseiling** option to return.

Tiger Trail (☎ 020-5537 9661; www.laos-adventures. com, www.trekking-in-laos.com; Delilah's; ☺ 8-11.30am, 1-5pm & 6.30-9pm) organises full-day '100 Waterfalls' trips (170,000/250,000K per person for three/two people) taking you down the Nam Ou by boat for around 45 minutes, then climbing for around 90 minutes on foot through a succession of cascades. After bathing in the upper pools, hike on to a different riverside village for the boat back. Sign up one day before and depart at 9am.

Sabai Sabai offers massage (per hr 40,000K) and herbal steam baths (15,000K including sarong, towel and tea) to ease those post-trekking aches.

Sleeping

In the low season, prices become highly negotiable.

Sangdao Chittavong Guesthouse (☎ 020-5537 9677; without/with bathroom 30,000/70,000K) Well-spaced in a leafy west-bank garden are simple matted-wall huts with shared squat and bucket bath but also pleasant bamboo bungalows with clean en suite bathrooms. All have mosquito nets and views through the foliage towards the river.

Delilah's (r 40,000K) Near the bus stand, simple but popular rooms with shared bathrooms sit above a cafe-restaurant whose front terrace table has seats made of bomb casings.

Meexai Bungalows (☎ 030-923 0763; without/with bathroom 40,000/70,000K) Relatively new bamboo huts with tin roofs and well-functioning water heaters have diagonal glimpses of the river from little balconies; the best view is from Room 4.

Namhoun Guesthouse (☎ 020-5577 4462; without/with bathroom 40,000/70,000K) Six typical bungalows with private terraces face each other in a peaceful garden setting, but only Room 6 has any real river view.

CT Guesthouse (☎ 020-5577 4778; bungalow 60,000K) If you get one at the front, you'll probably forgive the tired, rickety state of the bamboo bungalows, thanks to the beguiling river views. However those at the rear get blasted with karaoke and have no view at all. There are ensuite squat toilets and water heaters but the bedcovers are old.

Bamboo Paradise Guesthouse (☎ 810 066; bungalow 60,000-80,000K; r 100,000K) Bungalows face the bridge with decent enough views; the sprung mattresses are firm and water heaters work. Six new rooms are under construction. The friendly owners can take you on a traditional net fishing trip (50,000K).

Sunrise Guesthouse (☎ 020-247 8799, 020-207 9587; bungalow 70,000-80,000K) Tightly packed little bungalows are slightly rough and come with squat toilets but all have river views – those from the upper level being less obscured by trees.

Sunset Guesthouse (☎ 810 033; without/with view from 110,000/200,000K) This array of bungalow-rooms have super river views. Patchwork bedspreads and paper lanterns add a little atmosphere and towels are folded like origami. However, compared to neighbouring options the prices are a startling step up for a relatively modest improvement in quality.

Nong Kiau Riverside (☎ 810 004, 020-5570 5000; www.nongkiau.com; r incl breakfast 320,000K; ☐ ☎) Nong Khiaw's top option by far, this delightful, quiet 'resort' consists of huge bungalows with high polished A-frame eaves, bamboo walls, tasteful lighting, writing desks and great hot showers. Views from the river-view balconies are unbeatable. Large, comfy, four-poster beds have high-slung mosquito nets but the rooms have minor niggles including a lack of bedside tables, glasses, storage space or balcony lamps.

If you arrive late in the high season most of the above are likely to be full. If so, you might have to resort to one of the following:

Phayboune Guesthouse (☎ 810 028; r/bungalow 50,000/70,000K) Cramped bungalows without views, and bigger, damp rooms in an uninspired concrete house behind the bungalows. No views, little charm.

Manypoon Guesthouse (☎ 020-5678 2525; Rte 1C; without/with bathroom 30,000/50,000K) Appealing mostly to amorous local couples, these pleasant new bungalows have OK beds and cold showers but are in an utterly isolated spot 1.3km east of town.

Lin Tong Guesthouse (☎ 020-5590 1169; without/with bathroom 30,000/70,000K) Jammed-together little huts without views, some very basic French is spoken.

Thanthavong Guesthouse (☎ 020-5503 3788; r 40,000K) Ultra-thin hardboard 'walls' divide unlovely rooms with dodgy mattresses and basic squats but at least the en-suite showers run hot.

Eating

A few traveller-oriented eateries line Rte 1C on the east bank while across the bridge the Sangdao Chittavong Guesthouse has a convivial fairy-lit restaurant with river-garden views. Two un-named stilt-cafes are perched above the main jetty but think twice before ordering food within an hour before your boat departure – cooking can take aeons.

Deen Restaurant (☎ 020-5578 4352; veg & non-veg mains 10,000-20,000K; ☽ 7am-10pm) Probably the best Indian food you'll find anywhere in rural Laos served in a setting that's pleasantly inviting at night but viewless and slightly gloomy by day.

CT Restaurant & Bakery (☎ 020-5577 4778; mains 15,000-45,000K; ☽ 7am-10pm) Right beside the bridge, this open-sided restaurant has the best views of any eatery in town. There's a little deck-chair chill-out corner and a bookshelf of well-thumbed paperbacks. On top of countless tasty Lao and Chinese options, the menu ranges from spaghetti to steak to French-bread pizzas. The mint-lemon shakes (8000K) are especially refreshing.

Getting There & Away
BOAT

River-boat rides are a highlight of visiting Nong Khiaw. For Luang Prabang (100,000K, five to eight hours), sign up one day before departure at the **boat office**. If at least ten people have signed up, a boat leaves around 11am (100,000K, six to nine hours). If fewer people travel, the minimum shared cost will be 1,000,000K per boat. Sometimes when water levels are very low, there are sections of the trip where you'll need to push the boat through shallows and/or take a 10km tuk-tuk ride around them. Plan ahead with suitable footwear.

Boats to Muang Ngoi Neua (20,000K, 1¼ hours) leave at 11am and 2pm. It's a lovely ride and in high season extra departures are possible as custom dictates. A few times weekly boats run all the way to Muang Khua (120,000K, seven hours) – if none are scheduled from Nong Khiaw you might still find a departure from Muang Ngoi Neua.

BUS & SĂWNGTHĂEW

The journey to Luang Prabang is possible in 2½ hours but in reality usually takes at least four. Minibuses or *săwngthăew* (35,000K) start at around 9am and 11am, plus there's a minivan (50,000K) at 1pm. Tickets are sold at the bus stand but the 11am service actually starts at the boat office, filling up with folks arriving off the boat(s) from Muang Ngoi. Having a pre-purchased ticket won't assure you a seat by the time it reaches the bus stand. On days when a boat arrives from Muang Khua there'll usually be additional Luang Prabang minivans departing at around 3pm from the boat office. Between 6pm and 7pm the minibus from Sam Neua passes through en route to Luang Prabang: it stops for just a few seconds outside the Sangdao Chittavong restaurant.

For Udomxai a direct minibus (40,000K, three hours) leaves at 11am. Alternatively take any westbound transport and change at Pak Mong (20,000K, 50 minutes). Above a Pak Mong pharmacy, the **Arronh Guesthouse** (☎ 020-213 6655; r 50,000K) is marginally the best of Pak Mong's three very lacklustre overnight options should you get stuck there.

Originating in Luang Prabang, the minibus to Sam Neua (130,000K, 12 hours) via Vieng Thong (110,000K, 5½ hours) makes a quick lunch stop in Nong Khiaw around 11.30am. Another Sam Neua bus (arriving from Vientiane) passes through at night.

Getting Around
Bicycle rental makes sense to explore local villages or reach the caves. Town-bicycles cost 20,000K per day from Tiger Trail. Mountain bikes cost 30,000K from unsigned **'Leh's Place'** shop nearby, or 50,000K from Green Discovery at Nong Kiau Riverside.

MUANG NGOI NEUA (BAN NGOI KAO)
ເມືອງງອຍເໜືອ
pop 800

Flanked in all directions by sculpted layers of majestic karst mountain and cliff, this totally roadless village enjoys one of northern Laos's prettiest riverside settings. The one 500m-long 'street' fires itself dead straight from the main monastery towards a dramatic pyramidal tooth of forest-dappled limestone. Uniquely for such a tiny place, budget accommodation abounds and English is widely spoken so you get the experience of a remote village without the inconvenience. Short unaided hikes take you into timeless neighbouring villages while kayaking trips are a great way to savour the memorable Nam Ou, which has its most scenically spectacular stretches either side of the village.

History
Muang Ngoi was once a regional centre but it was pulverised during the Second Indochina War, bombs destroying all three of its once-celebrated historic monasteries. Such was the devastation that a 'new' postwar Muang Ngoi (ie Nong Khiaw, p204) took over as the district headquarters, a potential confusion that still sometimes causes mix ups. The rebuilt village was 'discovered' by travellers in the late 1990s when its beauty and laissez-faire atmosphere gained it a major pre-Twitter-era buzz despite not featuring in any guidebooks. By 2002 virtually every guesthouse hosted dollar-a-night *falang*, some of whom stayed for months in a chilled-out opiate haze, but Laos's clamp down on drugs changed the atmosphere radically. Most of the very cheapest guesthouses closed or improved their facilities to cater for a (slightly) more demanding new generation of travellers who still enjoy the enchanting boat journeys from Nong Khiaw but are now more interested in hiking, kayaking and simply enjoying the riverscape. If you want to sleep for under a dollar, that's still possible in nearby Huay Bo (p209).

Information
Generators provide electricity but only from dusk till 9.30pm. There's ETL mobile phone coverage but no internet. In emergencies you could exchange US dollars at a few of the guesthouses but rates are unsurprisingly poor.

Dangers & Annoyances
Thefts from Muang Ngoi's cheaper guesthouses tend to occur when over-relaxed guests leave flimsy doors and shutters unsecured or place valuables within easy reach of long armed pincers – most windows here have no glass.

Sights & Activities
Such is the grandeur of the riverside views that you could happily linger all day just lazing on your balcony or sitting at one of the better-placed restaurant shacks. A little after dawn it's interesting to watch locals delivering alms to monks at the rebuilt monastery, **Wat Okadsayaram**.

Numerous freelance guides offer a wide range of walks to Lao, Hmong and Khamu villages and to regional waterfalls. Prices are remarkably reasonable and some visits, such as to the **That Mok** falls, involve boat rides. Others are easy hikes that you could do perfectly well unguided, possibly staying the night in one of three pretty outlying villages (see Around Muang Ngoi).

NORTHERN LAOS

Kayaking is a great way to appreciate the fabulous riverine scenery that stretches both ways along the Nam Ou. **Lao Youth Travel** (www. laoyouthtravel.com; ☯ 7.30-10.30am & 1.30-7pm) has its own kayaks and is handily located where the boat-landing path passes the two-storey Rainbow House.

Sleeping

None of the guesthouses are luxurious but many have inspiring views over the Nam Ou and its multilayered karst massifs. Savouring such views from your bungalow is one of Muang Ngoi's great attractions, so think twice before choosing an inland guesthouse just to save 10,000K.

Phetdavanh Guesthouse (dm/r from 20,000/40,000K) No views, no hammocks but its 24-hour power and a range of cheap rooms including various dormitory-style affairs keeps the travellers coming. More buildings are under construction.

Kaikeo Guesthouse (r 30,000K) These disconcertingly rough old riverfront bungalows are the cheapest in town. The access path is disturbingly dark at night but co-manager Sai (☎ 020-389 1827) is one of the friendliest and most helpful English speakers in town.

Saylom Guesthouse (r 40,000-50,000K) The main plus is that you're right above the boat landing, where the river is at its widest and most beautiful, in the one corner of town that's well lit and 'lively' at night (lively meaning that there are three nearby restaurants open till 9.30pm). Clean, concrete-walled rooms with solid, tiled floors and shutters (but no windowpanes) are set behind the restaurant. The bamboo-walled ones have unobstructed views. All have private flush toilet, hammocks and new mosquito nets.

Ning Ning Guesthouse (r from 50,000K) Sizeable wooden or bamboo thatch units set back a little from the boat landing.

River View Guesthouse (r 50,000K) Simple wooden en-suite rooms with vinyl floors stand on long concrete stilts. The beds are small but you get your own hammock and a shared terrace overlooks the river.

Aloune Mai Guesthouse (r 50,000K) Off the path and away from the river, the garden atmosphere is appealing but the very rustic rooms have rough wooden floors, low ceilings and slightly saggy beds.

Lattanavongsa 1 Guesthouse (r 80,000K) Pleasant cottage rooms that are a slight cut above

most Muang Ngoi alternatives with polished floors and gas-fired hot showers. They are set around a scrappy lawn where the boat-landing path meets the 'main street' behind steps that use bomb-casings for banisters.

Veranda (☎ 020-386 2021; r 80,000K) The five bamboo-weave bungalows form an arc around a sweep of river view. All have hammocks, embroidered bedspreads, good beds and solar heated showers. Were the floorboards slightly less rough one could imagine this marketed as a miniature boutique ecoresort.

Eating

Several guesthouses cook a range of local food and traveller fare. Our favourites for views are **Saylom**, nearby **Riverside Guesthouse** and more hidden **Suan Phao Guesthouse** towards the southern end of town. **Bamboo Garden Restaurant** has the most attractive atmosphere with its thatched roofed pavilion while the **Sky Bar** offers its own take on pizza beside the Aloune Mai Guesthouse.

Nang Phone Keo Restaurant (mains 8000-20,000K; ☯ 7.30am-9pm) is a Main St house-restaurant on whose deck you can get Muang Ngoi's most exotic dessert, a flaming plate of fried bananas flambéed in *lào-láo*. Also imaginative is the *falang* roll with peanut butter, banana, sticky rice and honey.

Getting There & Away

Boats to Nong Khiaw (20,000K, one hour) leave around 9am, with tickets on sale from 8am at the boat office beside Ning Ning Guesthouse. If the boat from Muang Khua is operating that day then it will pick up in Muang Ngoi for Nong Khiaw around 1.30pm. However, be prepared to stay another night if it doesn't arrive. Going to Muang Khua, a boat leaves at 9.30am if enough people sign up the day before on the list at the boat office. The price is 120,000K provided there are ten or more passengers. The first hour of the ride cuts through particularly spectacular scenery.

AROUND MUANG NGOI

Muang Ngoi Neua is a great place for making short hikes through clouds of white and orange butterflies into beautiful karst-edged countryside. Reaching the three closest villages is easy without guide or map. Start by heading east away from the river either along the continuation of the boat landing access track or on the path that starts opposite the

Nang Phone Keo Restaurant. These converge after five minutes. Around 25 minutes' walk further is a small tollbooth that charges foreigners 10,000K to continue. Your toll also allows access to the adjacent **Tham Kang**, a modest limestone cave set between poinsettia bushes and trumpet lilies. Inside you might spot a few bats and there's the eerie sight of a stream emerging through what at first glance look like giant stone jaws. For refreshments, cross a little bamboo bridge over the crystal clear Nam Ngoi river to the simple little **Cave View Restaurant** (mains 10,000-30,000K; beer 13,000K; ☺ 8am-6pm).

Five minutes' walk beyond, morning light emphasises ferric orange stripes in the pathside cliffs. In the easternmost of three small caves here you'll find a grey concrete Buddha with vaguely simian features sitting on a rock pile.

Continuing for 15 minutes you'll cross a stream (wading it is safer than risking the slippery stepping stones) and reach a large area of rice fields. Keep left just as you first enter the rice fields. Then at the next junction (three minutes later) bear left for Huay Sen (45 minutes) or right for Ban Na (15 minutes) and Huay Bo (40 minutes). Sticking to the convoluted but well-worn main path is wise as there are little hand-painted signposts at each of the few possible confusion points. All three villages offer very basic, ultra-cheap accommodation with shared outdoor squat toilets and associated restaurant shacks that are open if and when anyone happens to be around to cook.

For stilt-house architecture, **Huay Sen** has the most authentic vibe of the three villages. Its one **guesthouse** (r 10,000K) is a dismal set of four minuscule bamboo-boxes, but the enthusiastic owner speaks some English, can rustle up a decent fried rice and stocks an unusually flavoursome bamboo-macerated *lào-láo*. He also offers guided two-hour walks to neighbouring Hmong villages.

Ban Na's houses look less rustic but you can observe local weavers at work and both village guesthouses overlook a sea of rice fields with a jutting karst horizon. **OB Bungalows** (☎ 020-386 3225; r 10,000K) at the farthest end of the village has the better view and its new, relatively sizeable bamboo huts are particularly good value. **Chantanohm Guesthouse** (r 10,000K) has a pretty setting and features a *petang* rectangle and bomb casings.

The walk to **Huay Bo** is very attractive but requires fording one intermediate river (calf-deep in the dry season). You'll pass a particularly sharp limestone spike and follow beneath a high ridge. The village comprises mostly stilt and bamboo-weave houses albeit with a less serene atmosphere than in Huay Sen. Three simple side-by-side guesthouses all charge 5000K, possibly the cheapest anywhere in Laos. The friendly owner of **Konsavanh Guesthouse** (☎ 020-386 2043) speaks some English and has been known to take guests on hunting forays into the forests (50,000K).

NORTHWESTERN LAOS

Northern Udomxai and Luang Namtha Province form a mountainous tapestry of rivers, forests and traditional villages that are home to almost 40 classified ethnicities. Luang Namtha is the most developed of several traveller-friendly towns ranged around the 2224-sq-km Nam Ha National Protected Area (p218) with hiking, biking, kayaking and boating adventures all easily arranged at short notice. Udomxai is the regional transport hub, while Boten is the one China–Laos border open to international visitors.

UDOMXAI (OUDOMSAY, MUANG XAI)
ຊຸດົມໄຊ (ເມືອງໄຊ)
☎ 081 / pop 25,000

Booming Udomxai is a Laos–China trade centre and handy crossroads city that's about as metropolitan a place as you'll find in northern Laos. The brash main street and lack of a traveller vibe puts off many short-term visitors, but it takes minimal effort to find charm and interest nearby – the well-organised tourist office has many ideas to tempt you to stay longer.

Around 25% of Udomxai's population is Chinese, with the Yunnanese dialect as often heard as Lao in some businesses and hotels. There's also a small but active community of international expats, notably German.

Information
The **tourist office** (Provincial Tourism Department of Oudomxay; ☎ 211 797, 212 483; www.oudomxay.info; ☺ 7.30-11.30am & 1.30-6pm Mon-Fri Apr-Sep, 8am-noon & 1.30-4pm Mon-Fri Oct-Mar) has masses of information about onward travel, accommodation and local sights. Its professional flyers and

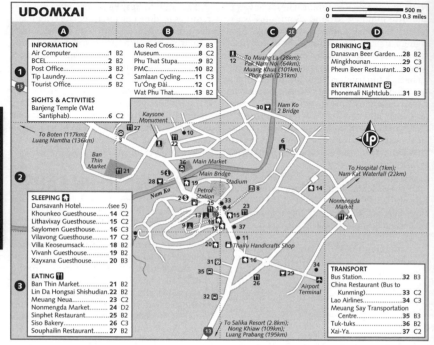

UDOMXAI

INFORMATION		Lao Red Cross............7 B3		DRINKING	
Air Computer..................1 B2		Museum..................8 C2		Danasvan Beer Garden....28 B2	
BCEL..........................2 B2		Phu That Stupa.............9 B2		Mingkhounan...............29 C3	
Post Office...................3 B2		PMC.......................10 B2		Pheun Beer Restaurant....30 C1	
Tip Laundry..................4 C2		Samlaan Cycling.............11 C3			
Tourist Office................5 B2		Tu'Óng Đài.................12 C1		ENTERTAINMENT	
		Wat Phu That..............13 B2		Phonemali Nightclub........31 B3	
SIGHTS & ACTIVITIES					
Banjeng Temple (Wat					
Santiphab).................6 C2					

SLEEPING	
Dansavanh Hotel.............(see 5)	
Khounkeo Guesthouse........14 C2	
Lithavixay Guesthouse........15 C2	
Saylomen Guesthouse........16 C3	
Vilavong Guesthouse.........17 C2	
Villa Keoseumsack...........18 B2	
Vivanh Guesthouse...........19 B2	
Xayxana Guesthouse.........20 B3	

EATING	
Ban Thin Market..............21 B2	
Lin Da Hongsai Shishudian....22 B2	
Meuang Neua................23 C2	
Nonmengda Market..........24 D2	
Sinphet Restaurant............25 B2	
Siso Bakery..................26 C3	
Souphailin Restaurant........27 B2	

TRANSPORT	
Bus Station..................32 B3	
China Restaurant (Bus to	
Kunming)..................33 C2	
Lao Airlines.................34 C3	
Meuang Say Transportation	
Centre....................35 B2	
Tuk-tuks....................36 B2	
Xai-Ya.....................37 C3	

To Muang La (28km);
Pak Nam Noi (64km);
Muang Khua (101km);
Phongsali (231km)

To Boten (117km);
Luang Namtha (136km)

Kaysone Monument

Ban Thin Market

Main Market

Main Bridge

Nam Ko

Petrol Station

Nam Ko 2 Bridge

To Hospital (1km);
Nam Kat Waterfall (22km)

Nonmengda Market

Stadium

Thailu Handicrafts Shop

Airport Terminal

To Salika Resort (2.8km);
Nong Khiaw (109km);
Luang Prabang (195km)

---

excellent free town maps can also be found in many guesthouses and on the bus station noticeboard. The office organises a selection of treks and tours and sells the GT-Rider *Laos* maps (65,000K).The office sometimes opens on weekends, but the hours are irregular.

Air Computer (☎ 312 479; per min 200K; ☯ 7am-10pm) is an internet cafe with great connection speeds. Lithavixay Guesthouse offers free wi-fi to guests. **BCEL** (☎ 211 260; Rte 13) has an ATM, changes US dollars, pounds sterling, euros, Australian dollars, Canadian dollars, Thai baht and Chinese yuan (RMB) and accepts some travellers cheques (2% commission).

To the right of the archaic **post office** (☯ 8am-4pm Mon-Fri, 8am-noon Sat) is a small kiosk-shop offering a single pay-to-use **telephone** (international calls 2500K per min; ☯ 7am-9pm). **Tip Laundry** (same-day/next-day per kg 25,000/20,000K; ☯ 8am-10pm) is handily central.

Sights

Stairways lead up from the main road to two facing hills each offering excellent views. One is topped by the pretty little **Phu That Stupa**, an historic structure that was totally rebuilt after

wartime destruction. Full-moon days see religious ceremonies here; there's cute little **Wat Phu That**, and a brand new standing Buddha. The other hill hosts a disappointing **museum** (admission free; ☯ 8-11am & 2-4pm) in a grand, new two-storey mansion featuring colonial style shutters and oriental gables. Along with unlabelled artefacts and poorly explained photos are odd, unexplained exhibits including two gigantic model bamboo shoots, several cases of sports trophies and a few old typewriters.

Udomxai's foremost monastery is **Banjeng Temple** (Wat Santiphab; ☯ dawn-dusk), which is modest but very attractively set on a riverside knoll. The most notable feature here is an imaginative concrete **'tree of life'**. Tinkling in the breeze, its metal leaves hide a menagerie of naively crafted animal and bird statues that illustrate a local Buddha myth.

On a hillock overlooking a beautiful riverbend, the **Lao Red Cross** (☎ 312 391; steam bath 10,000K; massage per 1/2hr 15,000K; ☯ 2-8pm) offers Lao Swedish–style massage and herbal steam baths in a modest bamboo-matted structure.

Along the Phongsali road several government offices occupy late-colonial era buildings, and near the edge of town is the **Tu'Óng Đài**, a Lao–Vietnamese solidarity monument where a white stupa is fronted by two endearingly cherubic gilded soldier-statues.

PMC (Productivity & Marketing Center of Oudomxay; www.pmc.odx.com; ☎ 020-330 9456; ☑ 8am-noon & 2-5pm) is a small exhibition room and shop introducing local fibres and selling handmade paper products, bags and local essences. If you're wondering why it's part-funded by the UN Office on Drugs and Crime, that's because these crafts are an attempt to find non-narcotic-based commerce for former poppy-growing communities. Hence its ironic nickname, the 'opium shop'.

Activities

The tourist office organises an interesting series of **papermaking workshops** (70,000-190,000K depending on group size) that include gathering the raw materials. Their **cooking courses** (total cost for one/two/three participants 195,000/240,000/285,000K) include shopping for ingredients, but the teacher speaks French better than English. They also offer one-day tours around Udomxai, a city walk, two- and three-day visits to the Chom Ong Caves (p213), plus two possible trekking routes staying at Khamu village homestays. To find potential fellow trekkers arrive at 4pm for a 'rendezvous meeting' the day before your proposed departure.

Samlaan Cycling (☎ 020-5560 9790; www.samlaancycling.com; ☑ irregular) organises excellent one-day cycling tours and multiday combination cycling/trekking adventures. Call ahead as their 'office', opposite the Thailu Handicrafts shop, frequently stays shut when staff are busy.

Sleeping

Udomxai has an abundance of accommodation, including several brand new, fair value if soulless Chinese hotels in the 100,000K range. Unappetising crash pads within the bus station yard charge from 25,000K if you don't mind sharing one squat toilet between a dozen flimsy guest-rooms. For an interesting rural alternative, you might also consider staying 28km north in pretty Muang La (p214), which hosts the region's most exclusive boutique resort as well as two simple guesthouses.

Khounkeo Guesthouse (☎ 312 483; r 40,000-70,000K; ☒) The cheapest rooms in this quiet, family-style guesthouse have hard mattresses and mild damp patches in bathrooms. However, from 60,000K, rooms are new, fresh and great value.

Saylomen Guesthouse (☎ 211 377; r with fan/air-con 50,000/100,000K; ☒) Simple, fair-sized fan rooms with hot water, top sheet and multicoloured coat stands are better value than most of Udomxai's 50,000K options.

Vilavong Guesthouse (☎ 212 503; r without/with TV 50,000/60,000K) A pleasantly inviting foyer leads through to decidedly ordinary rooms with hot shower, but the owners are helpful and prices are fair for such a central location.

Vivanh Guesthouse (☎ 212 219; r 60,000K) Right beside the main bridge, this compact guesthouse offers a handful of tiled, spacious rooms with comfortable double beds, fans and private bathrooms.

Xayxana Guesthouse (☎ 020-5578 0429; r with fan/air-con 60,000/80,000K, tr 120,000K; ☒) This quiet new place is remarkably professional for the price, has communal sitting areas and good hot showers. Wonky curtain rails and the odd mosquito are minor niggles.

Lithavixay Guesthouse (☎ 212 175; r 60,000-150,000K; ☒ ▣ ☎) The rooms are dated and bigger ones seem overpriced, but some English is spoken and the free wi-fi is a key attraction for some guests.

our pick **Villa Keoseumsack** (☎ 312 170; r 100,000K; ☒) This new, aristocratic-looking mansion features tasteful touches of grained woodwork and local fabrics. Generous-sized rooms have super-comfy beds, powerful air-con, fridges, desks and hot showers. The current bargain price may increase once construction of its bigger rear section is complete and the planned wi-fi is installed.

Dansavanh Hotel (☎ 212 698; r 220,000-400,000K; ☒) Supposedly Udomxai's top hotel, the facade has buckets of neocolonial grandeur but the large lobby space is used as an upmarket furniture gallery and the rooms, while large and properly equipped, lack pizazz. Many are oddly aligned, so that windows look onto corridors or are absent altogether. Ask for serious discounts.

Eating

Several snack stalls set up shop opposite Xai-Ya early in the evening. There's a Chinese supermarket opposite BCEL bank. The **Ban Thin** and **Nonmengda markets** peddle vegetables, fruit and meat including some live and dead exotica (particularly at weekends).

Sinphet Restaurant (mains 10,000-20,000K; ☺ 7.30am-10pm) Udomxai's old-time back-packer restaurant is decorated with dusty posters and a decorative hornet's nest. It's fine for Western breakfasts but MSG finds its way into many 'Lao' dishes, the 'cheese sandwich' (5000K) is a French-bread roll with separate triangle of processed cheese, and banana pancakes (10,000K) are simply pancakes with a sliced banana.

Siso Bakery (☎ 020-5546 3973; sandwiches 10,000-20,000K; filter coffee 10,000K; ☺ 7am-9pm) This tiny two-tabled place is widely reputed for making Udomxai's best bread and cakes. Udomkai (omelette burgers, 15,000K) are popular vegetarian options. Some items require advance notice – two hours for pizza, a day for croissants and foccacias.

Souphailin Restaurant (☎ 211 147; mains 15,000-30,000K; ☺ 7am-10pm) Souphailin creates culinary magic with authentic, northern Lao food like *mok phaa* (a banana-leaf fish dish) plus imaginative creations of her own. Her small, backstreet restaurant is a traditional bamboo-weave house whose decor is just the pots hung on the wall. It's unbeatable if you're patient but if other guests are ahead of you, you might wait an hour to be served.

Lin Da Hongsai Shishudian (☎ 020-5598 6168; mains 20,000-40,000K) Better than several lacklustre Chinese restaurants on the main drag, this family place is haphazardly decorated with lurid posters of mismatched foodstuffs. Ordering is an adventure – walk through to the kitchen, point at a selection of ingredients and hope they come out as you like them. Prices are fair for such hefty portions.

Meuang Neua (☎ 020-5567 3783; meals 20,000-50,000K, wine/cocktails 17,000/25,000K; ☺ 7am-11pm) This is the nearest Udomxai gets to a stylish Western restaurant, yet prices are little more than the competition once you note that most quoted menu prices include rice and drinking water. Soft Latin music serenades the cosy two-tiered interior and there's a three-table fairy-lit garden. Multifaceted menu choices include unusually convincing vegetable tempura, so-so pastas and mild, subtle yellow curry.

Drinking & Entertainment

Reasonably priced beer (but little else) is available at the **Danasvan Beer Garden** (☺ 6-11pm) beside the main bridge. **Pheun Beer Restaurant** (☺ 2-10pm) overlooks riverside vegetable gardens through bamboo fronds beside the Nam Ko 2 bridge. Several lively beer pavilions including **Mingkhounan** (☎ 020-5400 5010; ☺ 11am-11pm) line the airport road. Meuang Neua restaurant has a tiny two-seat cocktail bar.

Phonemali Nightclub (☎ 020-5568 0761; admission free; ☺ 8-11.30pm) is an amusingly unsophisticated youth venue where a typical evening's floor fillers start with Lao line dancing and progress through Thai disco to a few English-language pop tracks.

Getting There & Away

AIR

Lao Airlines (☎ 312 146, 312 047; ☺ 8am-5pm Mon-Sat) flies to/from Vientiane (895,000K) every

---

BUSES FROM UDOMXAI

Destination	Cost (kip)	Departs	Duration (hours)
Boten	28,000	8am	3*
Luang Prabang	50,000	9am, noon, 3pm	6
Luang Namtha	35,000	8.30am, 11.30am, 3.30pm	4*
Muang Houn	25,000	noon, 2pm, 4pm	2½
Muang Khua	30,000	8.30am, 11.30am, 3pm	3
Nong Khiaw	40,000	9am	4
Pak Beng	35,000	8.30am, 10am	4
Pak Mong	25,000	2pm, 4pm	3
Phongsali	65,000	8.30am & around 2am	9 to 15
Vientiane	110,000	11am	16 to 19
Vientiane (VIP)	155,000	4pm, 6pm	15 to 17

* = time should reduce once major roadworks are complete

Tuesday, Thursday and Saturday. Tickets are also available from Lithavixay Guesthouse.

BUS & SĂWNGTHĂEW
Long Distance
The **bus station** (☎ 212 218) is southwest of the centre. See the boxed text for destinations and departure times.

Regional
Săwngthăew to Muang La depart when full at around 8.30am and 11.30am from the **Meuang Say Transportation Centre**.

To China
An 8am minibus to Mengla leaves from the bus station. The Kunming-bound bed-bus from Luang Prabang bypasses the bus station but makes a short snack-break at the **China Restaurant** around 11.30am. Booking isn't possible but they'll take extra passengers if space allows – generally one of the less-comfy rear berths.

Getting Around
Xai-Ya (☎ 212 753; ⏰ 9am-10pm) bills itself as an internet service and sells mobile phone SIM cards, but most usefully it rents 100cc motorbikes (old/new 50,000/100,000K per day if returned by 5pm, 80,000/150,000K per 24 hours). New ones are well worth the extra kip. Lithavixay Guesthouse rents decent bicycles (per half-/full-day 20,000/40,000K) and Samlaan Cycling rents high-quality mountain bikes (per day US$10). Xai-Ya, Lithavixay and the tourist office can all help arrange chauffeured minivans from US$100 per day.

Tuk-tuks cost 5000K per person per hop within city limits.

AROUND UDOMXAI
Hop on a decent motorbike and head out in any direction and you'll quickly find attractive scenery and plenty of rural interest. A pleasant target to head for is **Nam Kat Waterfall**, a picnic site around 23km from the centre of town. Turn right in Ban Fan, continue to the parking area then walk the last half hour or so through protected forests. The access road is currently being improved and it's likely that an entry fee will be introduced.

Chom Ong Caves
Potentially the province's top tourist attraction, this extensive **cave system** burrows over

15km beneath a forested karst ridge near **Ban Chom Ong**, 48km from Udomxai. Often as high as 40m within, it's a veritable cathedral of a place whose first 450m have been lit with solar-powered lamps. Over millions of years the time-worn stalactites have been coated with curious crusts of minerals and sometimes studded with gravel from later wash-throughs. To gain access you'll need to borrow the gate-key and engage a guide (40,000K) in Ban Chom Ong, a large Khamu village from which the cave entrance is an hour's walk. The village commands a wide, attractive valley. Tall sentinel trees add character to the surrounding expanse of rice terraces backed by patches of mature woodland and bamboo-covered hills. It's a great place to observe weaving, spinning, milling, girls fetching water in hollow bamboos and red-toothed old ladies chewing betel. The village's simple, unmarked **'guesthouse'** (per person 15,000K) is a purpose-built local-style longhouse with roll-out bedding and the relative luxury of a tap and porcelain squat in the outside shared toilets. Note that the village has no electricity and that very little English is spoken (as yet). As there are no restaurants or shops, organising food as well as the guide and key will require some spoken Lao, Khamu or plenty of gesticulation. A bigger problem is that the uncomfortable access 'roads' are almost entirely unpaved, impassably muddy after rain and improbably steep and rutted in places.

GETTING THERE & AWAY
Two- and three-day tours, including meals, English-speaking guide and ample time to observe typical village scenes can be organised through the Udomxai tourist office but transport is by excruciatingly uncomfortable jeep-*săwngthăew*. Samlaan Cycling (p211) runs inclusive three-day guided loop-trips by mountain bike (per person US$65/155 in groups of seven/three, or US$195 for one person only).

In totally dry conditions when river fords are low it's possible, if challenging, to arrive by motorcycle. Turn west off Rte 13 just beyond Salika Resort (2.8km south of Udomxai bus station) on a road signed 'Homyen Restaurant'. After 1.4km turn right past fish ponds, left 600m later, fork right after Donnanoy Restaurant, then keep straight through Nam Lae village. Approaching the Ang Nam Hin reservoir around 3km beyond, keep left at the first turn, then right 1.2km later (over a concreted ford). Continue along the main track for 21km, passing through a series of villages (mostly Khamu, one Hmong) and a 2km stretch of steep, attractive forest. About 1km after Ban Mokkha village, take the obvious right-hand turn. Then, after 11.5km (having crossed extensive Nam Pla village part way), turn left and descend across a slippery ford. The last 4.5km are the toughest involving some seriously steep muddy slopes.

Muang La

Scenic **Muang La**, just 28km from Udomxai towards Phongsali, offers a charming rural alternative to the 'big city'. This Tai Lü village sits at the confluence of the Nam La and Nam Phak rivers, attractively awash with palm trees. Its central feature is a classically styled temple that hosts one of northern Laos's most revered Buddha statues, the Pra Singkham Buddha.

Dr Houmpheng Guesthouse (☎ 020-5428 0029; r without/with bathroom 50,000/60,000K) is Muang La's most conspicuous accommodation, a new orange-and-turquoise house with a small shared terrace amid palms. There's no hot water and the toilets are bucket-flush squats. Mind your head on low beams and doorways.

Just beyond is the **Nang Bei Chit Restaurant** (☎ 020-5533 2712; r without/with bathroom 30,000/ 50,000K), which has a separate selection of guest rooms one block behind, down by the river. Some rooms are very basic; the newest ones are still under construction.

Two minutes' walk south along a riverside footpath (via a road bridge across a side stream) brings you to Muang La's modest **hot spring** that bubbles into the river when water levels are high. Some of its waters are piped into the very discreet **Muang La Resort** (☎ 020-284 1264; www.muangla.com) directly behind. The resort hides an elegant rustic refinement behind tall, whitewashed walls. It accepts neither walk-in guests nor visitors, so you'll need to prebook a pricey package to enjoy the stylishly appointed *colombage* guestrooms, sauna, and curiously raised open-air hot tub, all set between palms and manicured lawns.

When river levels are low, a flimsy bamboo suspension bridge allows access from the hot springs to an area where **salt** is produced by a mud-leeching process.

Buses to Phongsali and Muang Khua pass through Muang La around an hour after departing Udomxai. The last bus returning to Udomxai usually rolls through around 5pm. There's no bus station, just wave the bus down. Additional *săwngthăew* to Udomxai

---

THE PRA SINGKHAM BUDDHA

You've got exams to pass? Want to get rich? Afraid you might be infertile? Don't worry. Whatever your concern, just ask the Pra Singkham Buddha and your wish will be granted…providing of course that you are pure of heart. And that when it all pans out, you pop back and leave the gift you promised him. It's a story common to a great many temples, but **Muang La**'s Pra Singkham Buddha is considered to be especially potent.

Inlayed with precious stones, the 200kg gold-and-bronze statue has an interesting history. Legend claims it was cast in Sri Lanka just a few generations after the historical Buddha's death, and reached Laos in AD 868 via Ayodhya in India. In 1355 it was reputedly one of five great Buddhist masterpieces sent out by Lan Xang founder Fa Ngum to inspire the faithful at the far reaches of his new kingdom. However the boat carrying the statue was sunk in a battle. Later found by a fisherman, Pra Singkham was dragged out of the water amid considerable tribulations and thereupon became the subject of a contest between residents of Muang La and Muang Khua regions. The sneaky folks from Muang Khua, downriver, suggested that the Buddha choose for himself and set the statue on a raft to 'decide'. However, the seemingly hopeless contest went Muang La's way when the raft magically floated upstream against the current, 'proving' it belonged in La. Kept initially in the **Singkham Cave**, by 1457 it had found a home in a specially built temple around which today's town of Muang La is now ranged. Like almost everything else in rural Laos, the temple was bombed flat during the 20th-century Indochina wars. However, the statue had been rehidden in the Singkham Cave. By the time a new temple was consecrated in 1987, the Buddha had turned a black-green colour 'with sadness at the destruction'. But today he's once again a gleaming gold.

depart at around 7am and 11am if there's sufficient custom.

Buddha Cave

The **Singkham Buddha Cave** (Tham Padjao Singkham), where the famous Buddha statue once rested, is 3.7km west of **Ban Samakisai** (Km15, Rte 2E), around halfway between Udomxai and Muang La. In Samakisai ask 'Khor kajeh tham noy' (may I have the cave key please) at the second hut south of the bridge. Then cross the bridge and take the second rough track west – that's just about passable by tuk-tuk. This terminates at a collection of huts from which it's just three minutes' walk to the cave, climbing a shallow staircase at the end. The cave isn't huge and obviously the statue inside is a modern replica but the setting is attractive – a woodland thicket opening into a fan of steep dry-rice valley slopes.

Udomxai to Pak Beng

Smoothly asphalted Rte 2W is very attractive for the first 40km or so from Udomxai passing through pretty Khamu villages and even crossing through a section of not-yet-burnt forest. After Muang Beng, and especially beyond bigger, unappealing Muang Houn, the undulating slopes and steeper backdrop ridges have almost all been pitilessly clear-cut for plantations of rubber and teak or for corn cultivation. There are guesthouses in both Muang Beng (one) and Muang Houn (five, the best at the southern city limits) but little reason to stop. Between Oudom and Pak Beng the ground becomes rocky, making the ongoing forest-burning seem particularly gratuitous, but a few steeper valley-sides retain a generous covering of older trees. At least for now.

BOTEN

ບໍເຕນ

If you want a taste of raw, commercial China without actually going there, take a brief excursion to the curious border settlement of **Boten**. It's the only Laos–China border open to foreigners and makes an easy short excursion while en route from Udomxai to Luang Namtha (it's more awkward in reverse). A decade ago Boten was a typically sleepy hamlet of thatched Lao cottages. Today there's a big casino-resort and a huge, ugly market complex where signage, telephone numbers and even the currency used are all Chinese.

At the top (north) end of the market on the main street the **Lao Development Bank** (8.30am-3.30pm Mon-Fri) changes major currencies, but for effortless yuan–kip exchange at fair rates use the supermarket diagonally across the road. Beside that is the high-tech internet cafe, **Season 3** (per hr RMB3.5-5; 24hrs).

Liveried bell-boys ferry guests about in electric golf cart–style buggies between the multiple buildings of the vast **Lao Royal Hotel** (China 1596-154 888; r US$30-1000). The cheapest of their 1000-plus rooms are in barrack-like apartment blocks near the big, greening **open-air swimming pool** (admission RMB15). More ornate blocks include an eccentric attempt at Napoleon III neoclassicism adorned with caryatids. The turreted main reception building is set behind a little fountain garden on the far west of the market. That building is almost entirely taken up with a seemingly endless **casino** but the games played are likely to be unfamiliar to most Western gamblers.

Boten's two cheaper hotels are near the petrol station but neither seem to accept falang guests so if you want budget accommodation

---

CROSSING THE CHINESE BORDER AT MOHAN & BOTEN

The **Lao immigration post** (7.30am-4.30pm Laos time, 8.30am-5.30pm China time) is seven minutes' walk north of Boten market. Tuk-tuks shuttle across no-man's land to the Chinese immigration post in Mohan (Bohan) or it's an easy ten-minute walk. Northbound you'd be firmly advised to have a Chinese visa in advance, though a few travellers claim to have bought 14-day entry passes on the spot here. From the Chinese immigration post it's around a 15-minute walk up Mohan's main street to the stand where little buses depart for Mengla (RMB15, 80 minutes) every 20 minutes or so till mid-afternoon. These arrive at Mengla's bus station No 2. You'll need to nip across that city to the northern bus station for Jinghong (RMB40, 2½ hours, frequent till 6pm) or Kunming (mornings only).

A much easier solution than all of the above is to take one of the growing number of handy Laos–China through-bus connections such as Udomxai–Mengla, Luang Namtha–Jinghong and Luang Prabang–Kunming.

you'd be better off sleeping 20km south at the junction hamlet of **Ban Na Theuy**. Marginally the best of three options there (all west of the bridge towards Luang Namtha) is the **Duang Chandy Guesthouse** (☎ 020-299 4085; r 50,000K), set in a garden behind the tiny market.

Getting There & Away

Although Boten taxi drivers try to persuade travellers otherwise, there are six daily *săwngthăew* to/from Luang Namtha (20,000K, two hours) plus assorted China–Laos through-buses. Chartered taxi-vans charge 120,000K to Luang Namtha and around 50,000K to Ban Na Theuy.

LUANG NAMTHA (NAMTHA)

ຫລວງນໍ້າທາ

☎ 086 / pop 18,000

Orderly, if dull, Namtha's grid-pattern centre offers all the facilities you need to head straight off into the wide surrounding rice-bowl valley, where mountain ridges form layered silhouettes in the golden glow of sunset. Nowhere in Laos offers a better range of outdoor activities or organised 'ecotreks' to get you into the region's forests and ethnically diverse villages.

Orientation

Virtually flat, Namtha is in fact a 10km-long collection of villages coalescing in an administrative hub at the northern end. Built since 1976, the administrative hub is a well-spaced grid within which there's a two-block traveller enclave dotted with guesthouses, internet cafes and tour agencies. A smaller, prettier second centre is 7km further south near the airport. This used to be Namtha's commercial heart before it was bombed to bits in the Second Indochina War. Today it's a mostly residential area called Meuang Luang Namtha or simply Ban Luang. The new long-distance bus station is 3km further south on the Rte 3 bypass, an improbable 10km out of the main centre.

Beware that locally distributed tourist maps are schematic and not at all to scale. Much better maps are available online at http://hobomaps.com/luangnamthamain.htm

Information

The **Provincial Tourism Office** (☎ 211 534; www.lu ang-namtha.org; ☉ 8am-noon & 1.30-8pm) doubles as Nam Ha Ecoguide Service. Several Internet cafes on the main strip charge 200K per minute

but two blocks further north **NIT Internet** (per min 100K; ☉ 8am-9pm) is equally fast for half the price. **BCEL** (☉ 8.30am-3.30pm Mon-Fri) changes major currencies (commission-free), travellers cheques (2% commission, minimum US$3) and has a 24 hour ATM. The **Manychan Guesthouse & Restaurant** (☎ 312 209; ☉ 6.30am-10.30pm) sells the GT-Rider *Laos* map (65,000K), the most accurate map of Laos currently available.

Sights

Renting a bicycle or motorbike saves a lot of sweat even within the main area and without wheels, getting much further will be a major pain. Tuk-tuks can be few and far between, and virtually disappear after dark.

WATS & STUPAS

By far Namtha's most striking landmark is a large **Golden Stupa** built in 2009, sitting on a steep ridge directly northwest of town. It gleams majestically when viewed from afar. Up close, the effect is a little tackier but the views over town are impressive. Smaller and much more historic is **That Phum Phuk** (admission 5000K), though the red-gold stupa you see when first approaching is a 2003 replica. Right beside it lies the brick and stucco rubble of an earlier version, blown over by the force of a US bombing raid during the Second Indochina War. Judging from the ferro-concrete protrusions, that wasn't the 1628 original either. The site is a hillock 3km northwest of the oddly isolated Phouvan Guesthouse, on a stony laterite road that initially parallels the airfield. An obvious set of *naga* stairs lead up to the stupa from a road junction in front – turning right here leads back an alternative way to the main market and Royal Hotel.

Visiting two 20th-century monasteries, **Wat Ban Vieng Tai** and **Wat Ban Luang Khon**, presents an excuse to wander into less-visited village-style parts of town.

MUSEUM

The odd, barn-like **Luang Namtha Museum** (admission 10,000K; ☉ 8.30-11.30am & 1.30-3.30pm Mon-Thu, 8.30-11.30am Fri) is just about worth a ten-minute flit. A few haphazardly labelled anthropological treasures include stone steles and three Khamu bronze drums. Dusty cases show off regional costumes and beyond the selection of craft implements and 20th-century ammunition lies an unexplained pile of old video recorders and film projectors.

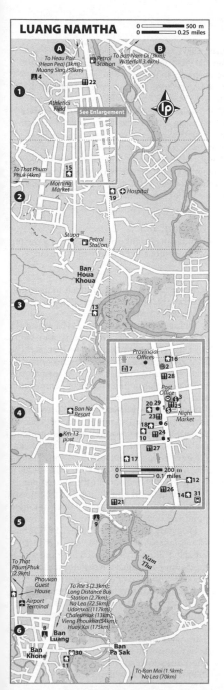

LUANG NAMTHA

BAN NAM DI (NAM DY)

Although barely 3km out of Luang Namtha, this hamlet is populated by Lao Huay (Lenten) people whose womenfolk still wear traditional indigo tunics with purple sash-belts and silver-hoop necklaces. They specialise in turning bamboo pulp into rustic paper, using cotton screens that you'll spot along the scenic riverbanks. At the eastern edge of the village, a three-minute stroll leads from a small **carpark** (parking fee bicycle/motorcycle/car 1000/2000/3000K) to a 6m-high **waterfall** (admission 2000K). You'll find it's more of a picnic site than a scenic wonder but your visit helps put a little money into village coffers. Unless the water level is really high there's no need to struggle up and over the hillside steps so ignore that sign and walk along the pretty streamside.

NORTHERN LAOS

NAM HA NPA

Within easy reach of Luang Namtha (p216), Muang Sing (p223), Vieng Phukha (p222) and even Muang Long (p226), the 2224-sq-km Nam Ha National Protected Area (NPA) is one of Laos's most accessible natural preserves. That accessibility is a blessing and a curse. Both around and within the mountainous park, woodlands have to compete with pressure from villages of various ethnicities including Lao Huay, Akha and Khamu. But the inhabitants of these villages are also learning the economic benefits of ecotourism. Since 1999, the prize-winning **Nam Ha Ecotourism Project** (www.unescobkk.org/culture/our-projects/sustainable-cultural-tourism-and-ecotourism/namha-ecotourism-project) has tried to ensure that tour operators and villagers work together to provide a genuine experience for trekkers while ensuring minimum impact to local communities and the environment. Tours are limited to small groups, each agent has its own routes and, in principle, each village receives visitors no more than twice a week. Authorities don't dictate what villagers can and can't do, but by providing information on sustainable forestry and fishing practices it's hoped that forest protection will become a self-chosen priority for the communities.

Activities

Luang Namtha is a major starting point for trekking, rafting, mountain biking and kayaking trips in the Nam Ha NPA. Many of the tours stop for at least a night in a minority village. Most photogenic for their costumes are those of the Lao Huay and Akha peoples but all are fascinating for genuine glimpses of village life.

Treks all follow carefully considered sustainability guidelines but they vary in duration and difficulty. In the wet season, leeches are a minor nuisance.

Namtha agents display boards listing their tour options and how many punters have signed up already, very helpful if you're trying to join a group to make things cheaper (maximum eight people). If you don't want others to join you, some agents will accept a 'private surcharge' of around US$50.

Around a dozen agencies operate, each with its own specialities, so don't limit yourself to the following options:

Nam Ha Ecoguide Service (☎ 211 534; ☉ 8am-noon & 1.30-8pm) A wing of the Provincial Tourism Office. Retains the rights to some of the best trekking routes.

Green Discovery (☎ 211 484; www.greendiscovery laos.com; ☉ 8am-9pm) Well regarded private outfit.

Jungle Eco Guide Service (☎ 212 025, 020-5578 6964; jungletours@gmail.com; www.thejungle-ecotour. com) Humorous, well informed and with very capable guides. Its jungle camp trip gets good reports and can be combined with kayaking options.

Namtha River Experience (☎ 212 047, 020-299 0344; www.namtha-river-experience-laos.com; Minority Restaurant) One of several kayaking outfits, but also specialises in guided motorbike tours into ethnic villages.

Sleeping

Popular places fill up fast, especially during the November to February high season.

CENTRAL

Most lodging in Luang Namtha is in the architecturally bland northern part of town around the traveller restaurants.

Soulivong Guesthouse (☎ 312 256; r without/with bathroom 30,000/40,000K) If price is your only concern you might be able to stomach the Soulivong's miserable shared bathrooms, thin mattresses and thinner walls. At least there's hot water, plus fading posters of Lenin, Stalin and friends to welcome you in.

Darasavath Bungalows (☎ 020-5560 7308; r 30,000-60,000K) Set behind an under-used backpacker restaurant, these wooden bungalows have matting walls and mosquito nets. The cheapest have squat toilets and cold showers but the rooms are a decent size. For 40,000K you get hot water and a little shared porch. Pay 60,000K and you'll find Rajasthani wall hangings and a rear balcony overlooking a pond.

Phengtavy Guesthouse (☎ 020-5555 7768; r without/with bathroom 40,000/60,000K) In a distinctive, vaguely Viking-style wooden building set behind a four-table garden restaurant, the large 60,000K rooms come with hot water and a sitting area featuring bamboo settees. Cheaper rooms are significantly more basic but do have attractive embroidered bedspreads.

Adounsiri Guesthouse (☎ 020-5544 5532; r 50,000K) This new place has a row of compact ground-floor rooms with a few local decor touches and good hot showers. It's central and quiet but the world looks in when you open your door.

Vieng Kham 2 (☎ 020-292 9234; pheng_vt@yahoo.com; fan/air-con r 60,000/80,000K; ❷) Handy for the district bus station, this ochre-coloured mansion provides sparkling clean rooms that are large if characterless.

ourpick Thoulasith Guesthouse (☎ 212 166; thoulasithguesthouse@gmail.com; r small/large 60,000/100,000K; ❞) This brand-new yet timeless hotel gives midrange quality at budget prices. Tucked in a garden just off the main strip, the long upper balcony is set off with two-colour woodwork and filigree edging. The rooms aren't enormous but the beds are stylish, even in the standard rooms that also squeeze in a desk and TV. Bigger rooms have a curious Aztec-style window through to a bathroom with tub. Free wi-fi is available.

Thavyxai Guesthouse (☎ 030-511 0292; r 60,000K) With its tall whitewashed pillar-facade this concrete villa would look right at home in an upmarket American suburb. Good-sized rooms without particular style have gleaming tiled floors and showers that run very hot – eventually. The location is quiet yet central and the rear, upper-floor balcony would make a pleasant reading spot.

Zuela Guesthouse (☎ 312 183; r standard/large 70,000/120,000K; ❷ ❞) Zuela consists of two sturdy timber-framed houses set just back from the main traveller strip in a calm, garden area. Cheaper fan rooms have exposed brick walls, high ceilings and decent clean bathrooms with hot water. Brighter, pricier ones have air-con and wood-panelled walls. All share plentiful sitting areas and terraces and the convivial restaurant spills out into the garden. Wi-fi is free, laundry costs 10,000K per kg and the family owners are delightfully obliging.

Royal Hotel (Huang-Ching Tajodian; ☎ 212 151; d/ste from RMB120/200) The brand new, six-storey Royal is Namtha's biggest, glitziest hotel. Standard rooms have excellent beds, walk-in showers and elements of modernistic style. The suites come with carpeting and luxurious bathrobes. Staff speak Chinese but not English and need calculators to work out room rates in Kip (from 150,000K).

FURTHER AFIELD

Chaleunsuk Homestays (☎ 020-5555 7768; 500m past Km 45, Rte 3; per person 50,000K) Beside the main Rte 3 highway, around 20km from central Luang Namtha, four rustic homes in Chaleunsuk village offer a real Khamu homestay experi-ence without the need to trek. At least one home even has a sit-down toilet, albeit in an outhouse. The fee should include breakfast, dinner and a contribution to the village development fund with a guided forest walk added for 15,000K more. It all sounds great in principle but as very little English is spoken, coming alone without language skills can feel awkward. Ask at the Luang Namtha tourist office for more information.

Namtha Riverside Guesthouse (☎ 212 025; www.thejungle-ecotour.com/web_jungle/guest/our_gest.htm; r first/subsequent nights US$25/20) Very much imitating the better-known Boat Landing Guesthouse, this four-bungalow place also offers a tranquil Nam Tha setting and copycat menu at the restaurant. Rooms are newer and similar in approach, albeit with slightly less aplomb. Pétanque is available and there are lounger-cushions on the balconies. It's 2km south of the centre.

Boat Landing Guesthouse (☎ 312 398; www.theboatlanding.laopdr.com; tw/d/ste/q incl breakfast US$40/45/55/55) Perched above the river, 7km south of the new town, this quiet lodge is a peaceful garden getaway comprising 11 wood-and-bamboo bungalows whose finest features are the river-facing porches. Curiously, the cheapest rooms have the best views of all. Each ecofriendly bungalow has a private bathroom with solar-heated shower. Local fabrics add colour to interiors that are tasteful but not overly luxurious. Although removed from most tourist facilities, the complex has bicycle rental (20,000K per day), organises kayaking and treks and has a truly excellent restaurant on the premises.

Eating & Drinking

The lively **night market** (☼ 7-10pm) is a good place for snack grazing.

Noodle Shops (noodle soup 8000K; ☼ 7am-2pm) Two basic, central eateries side-by-side on the main street serve excellent *fŏe*, *khào pìak sèn* and *khào sáwy*. Find more noodle stands in the morning market.

Cake Bread Store (snacks 2000-5000K; ☼ 7am-10pm) A grocery shop with a small selection of bread and pastries, including fluffily light banana muffins.

Panda Restaurant (☎ 020-5560 6549; mains 8000-15,000K; fruit shakes 5000K; ☼ 7am-11.30pm) This friendly, open-sided restaurant is decorated with birds nests and buffalo horns and built on a slope overlooking a fish pond, vegetable gardens and karaoke beer-garden. The menu offers very inexpensive, if slightly small, portions of Lao and Chinese classics along with pancakes and Western breakfasts.

Heuan Lao (☎ 211 111; mains 10,000-50,000K; ☯ 8am-10pm) This attractive upstairs corner-restaurant has a timber and bamboo-panelled interior and a shady wraparound terrace. The menu of Thai and Lao dishes is only partly translated into English.

Papaya Restaurant (mains 13,000-30,000K; ☯ 6.30am-10.30pm) Small, side-street eatery whose English language menu includes Akha and Tai Dam dishes and curious breakfast items like ginger scrambled eggs.

Minority Restaurant (☎ 212 047; mains 13,000-35,000K; ☯ 7am-10.30pm) Set behind the main strip in a high-ceilinged timber building with bamboo-blind sides, the menu offers original twists on local tribal recipes along with Lao, Chinese and Western options. The Tai Dam and Khamu soups are especially good.

Yamuna Restaurant (☎ 020-5557 1579; mains 14,000-26,000K; ☯ 7am-10.30pm) Moreish curries, including numerous vegetarian options, are made as spicy as you wish in this unassuming Indian restaurant. The richly delicious paneer butter masala substitutes tofu for Indian cheese. Dosai and western breakfasts are also available.

Heau Pair/Hean Pea (Km 3, Rte 17; mains 15,000-35,000K; ☯ 8.30am-11.30pm) If you've been biking towards Muang Sing, this pair of floating barge-pavilions make a peaceful place to break for an afternoon beer (10,000K) or wine cooler (12,000K). Well, at least until the karaoke sets in. The exotic food menu tempts with dishes such as grasshopper, baked frog and fried lungs.

Manychan Guesthouse & Restaurant (☎ 312 209; mains 15,000-40,000K; ☯ 6.30am-10.30pm; ☜) An inviting all-wood interior spilling out onto a fairy-lit street terrace keeps this place among the most popular *falang* venues in town. Wi-fi is free and the menu covers the gamut of possibilities. Beers arrive in cooler jackets with the restaurant's logo, and the coffee is Namtha's best.

Boat Landing Restaurant (☎ 312 398; Boat Landing Guesthouse; meals 17,000-65,000K; ☯ 7am-8.30pm) The relaxing riverside setting complements some of the best and most authentic northern Lao cuisine you'll find anywhere. From five-dish menus for two/three people (130,000/150,000K) to one-plate meals

(17,000K) the flavour combinations are divine. The menu explains each unfamiliar dish in detail but if you're still stuck for a choice try snacking on a selection of *jǎew* (from 8000K per fist-size mini bowl) used as dipping sauces for balls of sticky rice. Each bowl bursts with intense flavours, some sweet, some tangy, some fruity. You can choose how hot you want them so don't be put off by the translation 'chilli paste'. Wash it down with a superbly refreshing lemon mint shake. The restaurant is 7km south of the centre. Tuk-tuks charge around 70,000K return including waiting time.

Getting There & Away

AIR
Lao Airlines (☎ 212 072) flies to Vientiane (895,000K) on Tuesday, Thursday and Sunday.

BOAT
An inspiring alternative way to reach Huay Xai is on a two-day longboat odyssey down the Nam Tha, sleeping en route at a roadless village. But hurry – this option might be lost forever if a proposed dam project near Ban Phaeng were to be approved. For the ride, Luang Namtha agencies charge around US$200 per open longboat (very negotiable, maximum six people) to which you'll add 50,000K per person for accommodation paid directly to whichever family hosts you (the boatman will arrange one). You might get a slightly better deal from the **boat station** (☎ 312 014) right beside the Boat Landing Guesthouse. When river levels are low (typically January to June), the boat station closes and departures start from Na Lae, with agencies providing tuk-tuk transfers and prearranging a boat. If you just turn up in Na Lae and can handle negotiating in Lao, longboat prices are around 1,300,000K to Huay Xai but you might have to wait a while. You'll still need an overnight stop en route. If you have no deadlines, see p222 for a possible cheaper solution that avoids chartering.

BUS & SĂWNGTHĂEW
There are two bus stations. The **district bus station** is walking distance from the traveller strip – turn east where the sign says Two Sister Restaurant. The main **long distance bus station** is 10km south of town. In either case, prebooking a ticket doesn't guarantee a seat – you just have to arrive early and claim one in person, especially important for Muang

BUSES FROM LUANG NAMTHA

Destination	Cost ('000 kip)	Duration (hours)	Station	Departures
Boten	20	2	D	six daily 8am-3.30pm
Huay Xai ('Borkeo')	55	4	M	9am, 1.30pm bus
	75	4	M	8.30am minibus
Jinghong (China)	95	6	M	8.30am
Luang Prabang	80	9	M	9am bus
	100	8.5	M	8am minibus
Mengla (China)	50	3.5	M	8am
Muang Long	40	4	D	8.30am
Muang Sing	20	2	D	six daily 8am-3.30pm
Na Lae	35	3	D	9.30am, noon
Udomxai	35	4	M	8.30am, noon, 2.30pm
Vieng Phukha	20	1.5	D	9.30am, noon
Vientiane	150-160	21-24	L	8.30am, 2.30pm

M = Main long-distance bus station; D = District bus station
For Nong Khiaw take a Vientiane or Luang Prabang bus and change at Pak Mong (60,000K).

Long. For bus destinations, times and prices, see the boxed text.

Getting Around
Chartered tuk-tuks charge 10,000K per person (minimum 30,000K) between the bus station or airport and the town centre. Most agencies and guesthouses sell ticket packages for long-distance buses that include a transfer from your guesthouse and cost around 20,000K over the usual fare. If you're staying centrally it's a little cheaper to find fellow travellers and share a tuk-tuk of your own – try asking around at the Manychan Restaurant. Renting a bicycle (per day 6000-12,000K) or motorcycle (per day 30,000 to 50,000K) makes exploring far easier and there's plenty of choice from two **bicycle shops** (🕓 9am-6.30pm) in front of the Zuela Guesthouse.

AROUND LUANG NAMTHA
Luang Namtha to Vieng Phukha
Well-paved, scenic Rte 3 to Vieng Phukha (Km 87) makes for a pleasant day-trip by motorcycle from Luang Namtha. You'll cut through part of the Nam Ha NPA where, despite considerable felling for plantations and fields, there are still some stands of old-growth roadside forest. The most notable of these lie between Km 47 and Km 51 (albeit marred by brutal road cuttings) and along a steep karst ridge that parallels the road to the south between Km 69 and Km 76. Ban Prang at Km 63 sports a big shaggy banyan tree.

KAO RAO CAVES
Well signed beside Rte 3, 1.5km east of Nam Eng village, is this extensive, accessible **cave system** (Tham Nam Eng; 400m past Km 74; admission 10,000K) of which a 700m section is open to visitors. Hopefully on your arrival the guide/guardian will scurry out to meet you. He can't speak English but should guide you to the cave mouth (a five minute stroll between overgrown banana plants and buttressed old trees), open the cave gate and trot you past the main limestone formations including old stalactites encrusted with crystal deposits. Curious corrugations in the floor that now look like great old tree roots once formed the lips of carbonate pools like those at Turkey's Pamukkale. For now you'd be wise to bring a powerful torch (flashlight), though a feeble one is available on site. Extensive lighting, already wired up, should soon change the experience once Vieng Phukha gets connected to the power grid. Allow around 45 minutes for the visit.

VIENG PHUKHA (VIENG PHOUKHA)

Sleepy **Vieng Phukha** (Km 87, Rte 3) is an alternative trekking base for visiting the western limits of the Nam Ha NPA, notably on three day Akha Trail hikes. Such trails see fewer visitors than many from Luang Namtha and the partly forested landscapes can be magnificent, though many hills in Vieng Phukha's direct vicinity have been completely deforested. The tiny town centre consists of just three parallel streets. Within 500m you'll find a memorial plinth where Kaysone's bust is AWOL, seven guesthouses and three eco-tourism outfits: **Nam Ha Ecoguide Service Vieng Phoukha** (☎ 212 392, 020-5598 5289; ⊙ 8am-noon & 1.30-5pm) Has the least sexy looking office but Mr Vongsay is obliging and knowledgeable.

Vieng Phoukha Hilltrip (☎ 212 410; ⊙ 8am-6pm)
Akha Authentic Eco-guide Trekking Service (☎ 020-5570 8138; ⊙ 8am-noon & 1-8pm) Browse the interesting pamphlets on tribal histories.

Sights

Just 15 minutes' stroll south of Rte 3 near Km 85 but utterly hidden in thick secondary woodlands is the almost invisible site of the 1530 temple **Wat Mahapot**. What little had survived the centuries was mostly pillaged for building materials around 1977 when all the residents moved back after the war, so now all you'll see is the odd scattering of bricks poking out from a tree-choked muddy rise. Getting there involves walking along a steep V-shaped gulley that once protected the **Khúu Wíeng** ('ramparts') of a short-lived 16th-century 'city'. Again there's nothing but muddy banks to see but a good guide (essential) can fill in sketchy historical details and explain the medicinal uses of plants you encounter on a 40-minute walking tour. Such tours cost 25,000K per person (50,000K minimum) excluding transport for the 2km ride up Rte 3.

Sleeping & Eating

Virtually all Vieng Phukha accommodation is in simple thatched bungalows with cold showers. Twenty-four-hour power supply will soon be connected but for now electricity only operates from 6.30pm to 9.30pm.

Cryptically signed 'Restaurant Guesthouse', **Sainamchuk Guesthouse** (☎ 212 403; r 40,000K) has clean concrete rooms but those directly across the river at **Phuet Mung Khun Guesthouse** (☎ 020-5588 6089; r 30,000K) are slightly better value and the owner there speaks rudimentary English.

On the hilltop directly behind, up a steep 300m access lane, **Samlonchai** (☎ 020-5588 6089; r/bungalow 40,000/50,000K) has bungalows with comfy beds and balconies. There are sweeps of view from the garden area that features a rusty bulldozer as an incongruous 'sculpture'.

At the southern edge of town, **Mein Restaurant** (☎ 020-5408 0110; Rte 3; mains 10,000-30,000K; ⊙ 7am-9pm) has an English menu though precious little on it is actually available.

Getting There & Away

Săwngthăew for Luang Namtha (20,000K, 1½ hours) depart at around 9am and 1pm from beside the LN Restaurant on the main street. Or wave down a Huay Xai–Namtha through service (three daily).

Down the Nam Tha

For some 35km south of Luang Namtha, the pea-green Nam Tha flows across a series of pretty rapids tumbling between high-sided banks that are attractively shaggy with bamboo-choked forests. Luang Namtha tour agencies can organise one-day supported **kayaking** trips here (140,000/280,000K per person in a group of eight/two, or 600,000 for one person only), possibly combined with Nam Ha jungle treks. By bicycle or motorbike, the passably well-graded dirt road that runs along the river's eastern bank offers a quiet if potentially dusty way to enjoy some pretty views and see some interesting minority villages without the need for hiking.

NA LAE TO PAK THA

If you're trying to take a boat to Huay Xai or Pak Tha in the dry season, you'll need to start from Na Lae, a fair-sized market village with many newer concrete buildings. Of Na Lae's two guesthouses, **Vangmesay Guesthouse** (☎ 020-5540 7982; r 40,000-60,000K) is marginally the better one, with a family feel, an unfurnished upper-balcony terrace and clean, bright rooms with western toilet and cold shower. Upstairs rooms are smaller but have better mattresses. It's opposite the market where two daily *săwngthăew* arrive from Namtha. Longboats to various roadless riverside villages depart from beneath the conspicuous new bridge just two minutes' walk away. There are no set departure times. Unless you've prearranged things via a Luang Namtha agent, the best approach is generally to start by finding a ride to Ban Khon Kham (per person/

boat 50,000/300,000K, around 90 minutes). Climbing steeply up the riverbank, **Ban Khon Kham** is a traditional yet wealthy village of weavers and fishermen. There's a dinky little wat and tiny house-shop but the only electricity comes from solar panels. There's no formal accommodation but boatmen are accustomed to occasional visitors and informal homestays charge a standard 50,000K including breakfast and dinner. Don't forget a phrasebook.

From Ban Khon Kham there's a fair chance of finding a ride to Huay Xai (per person/boat 150,000/1,000,000K, about 10 hours) within a few days. If you leave much after 9am be aware that you probably won't reach Huay Xai that day because boats can't travel in the dark.

The river trip's scenic highlight is around **Ban Phaeng**, where a range of triangular karst peaks soar above the village and where some small stands of old-growth forest remain on the steepest slopes. Almost everywhere else, slash and burn has reduced the foliage to a bamboo fuzz but the riverine scenes are still mesmerising with roadless villages slipping by every ten to twenty minutes. In the dry season the calm, glistening waters are regularly punctuated by shallow rapids, which adds a slight frisson to the journey, and you'll need two skilled boatmen with punts and paddles to guide you through. From March the trip might prove outright impossible due to low water levels.

LUANG NAMTHA TO MUANG SING

This 58km route of bouncy asphalt cuts through the Nam Ha NPA. For the first 25km you might be thinking that Rubber Tree NPA would be a better name, such is the extent of the clear-felling of the steep slopes for plantations. However, between Km 30 and Km 49 you'll find a beautiful stretch of largely untouched old-growth forest covering steeply layered valley sides in all directions. A pleasant way to experience these woodlands without doing a major hike is to take a 15-minute streamside stroll to the 6m-high **Phagneung Phoukulom Waterfall** (admission 5000K). The well-signed trail starts at Km 40.8.

MUANG SING

ເມືອງສິງ

☎ 081 / pop 8000

Lying in the broad river valley of the Nam La, Muang Sing is a flat, dusty grid of mostly unpaved streets with a modest sprinkling of historic buildings. The town is a traditional

Tai Lú' and Tai Neua cultural nexus, plus a trade centre for Tai Dam, Akha, Hmong, Mien, Lolo and Yunnanese peoples, all of whom have villages within easy biking distance. Some older village women still wear elements of their traditional costumes, making for colourful people-watching, though don't forget to ask permission should you want to get trigger-happy with a camera.

History

In the late 18th century, a dowager of the Chiang Khaen principality founded the square, grid-plan citadel of Wiang Fa Ya (today's Muang Sing) along with the That Xieng Tung stupa (p224). In 1803 this area became vassal to Nan (now in Thailand) and was largely abandoned following the deportations of 1805 and 1813. But the Chiang Khaen princes returned, moving their capital here in 1884 from Xiang Khaeng on the Mekong. This kicked off a 20-year tug of war between France, Britain and Siam, causing the principality to be split in two, with the western sector including Muang Sing being absorbed into French Indochina. Muang Sing rapidly became the biggest opium market in the Golden Triangle, a function officially sanctioned by the French. In 1946, parts of town were devastated by Kuomintang troops who continued to operate here well into the 1950s after losing the Chinese civil war. In 1958 the famous American 'jungle doctor' Tom Dooley (see the boxed text, p226) set up his hospital in Muang Sing, which became the setting for a series of international intrigues.

Information

Note that old telephone numbers starting with 212 have been replaced. Local landlines now start with 400.

Lao Development Bank (☯ 8am-3.30pm Mon-Fri) Exchanges US dollars, euros, Thai baht and Chinese yuan (RMB) but at less than favourable rates.

Post Office (☯ 8am-4pm Mon-Fri) As tiny as the *petang* rectangle next to it.

Tourist Office (☯ 8am-4pm Mon-Fri) Displays of fact-scrolls are useful but the staff we met ranged from apathetic to aggressive and they seemed to find playing cards more fun that helping visitors. Some of the information they provided proved down-right misleading.

Sights

Sprinkled along the town's main street are a few classic Lao-French hybrid mansion-houses. These mostly 1920s structures have

NORTHERN LAOS

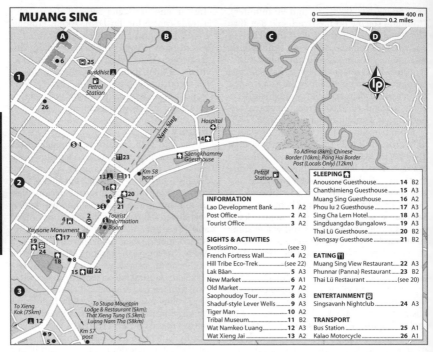

MUANG SING

0 — 400 m
0 — 0.2 miles

INFORMATION	
Lao Development Bank	1 A2
Post Office	2 A2
Tourist Office	3 A2

SIGHTS & ACTIVITIES	
Exotissimo	(see 3)
French Fortress Wall	4 A2
Hill Tribe Eco-Trek	(see 22)
Lak Bâan	5 A3
New Market	6 A1
Old Market	7 A2
Saophoudoy Tour	8 A3
Shaduf-style Lever Wells	9 A3
Tiger Man	10 A2
Tribal Museum	11 B2
Wat Namkeo Luang	12 A3
Wat Xieng Jai	13 A2

SLEEPING	
Anousone Guesthouse	14 B2
Chanthimieng Guesthouse	15 A3
Muang Sing Guesthouse	16 A2
Phou Iu 2 Guesthouse	17 A3
Sing Cha Lern Hotel	18 A3
Singduangdao Bungalows	19 A3
Thai Lü Guesthouse	20 B2
Viengsay Guesthouse	21 B2

EATING	
Muang Sing View Restaurant	22 A2
Phunnar (Panna) Restaurant	23 B2
Thai Lü Restaurant	(see 20)

ENTERTAINMENT	
Singsavanh Nightclub	24 A3

TRANSPORT	
Bus Station	25 A1
Kalao Motorcycle	26 A1

Buddhist
Petrol Station
Nam Sing
Hospital
Saengkhammy Guesthouse
Km 58 post
Petrol Station
To Adima (8km); Chinese Border (10km); Pang Hai Border Post (Locals Only) (12km)
Tourist Information Board
Kaysone Monument
To Xieng Kok (75km)
To Stupa Mountain Lodge & Restaurant (5km); That Xieng Tung (5.5km); Luang Nam Tha (58km)
Km 57 post

ground-floor walls of brick and stucco topped with a wooden upper storey featuring a wraparound roofed verandah. Classic examples house the tourist office and the Tai Lü Guesthouse. The most distinctive of these buildings is now home to the two-room **Tribal Museum** (admission 5000K; ⏱ 8.30am-4pm Mon-Fri), which boasts costume displays downstairs and six cases of cultural artefacts upstairs. Watching a 40-minute video on the Akha people costs 5000K extra.

In local wats, look for typical Tai Lü details such as silver-stencilled patterning on red pillars and ceilings, and the use of long vertical prayer flags. The most visually striking monastic buildings are at **Wat Xieng Jai** and **Wat Namkeo Luang**. The latter features an entry porch agog with red-tongued golden *naga* and an unusually tall and ornate gilded stupa. Some villagers still draw water from **shaduf-style lever wells** in the slowly gentrifying *bâan* opposite. Nearby you can also find a modest **Lak Bâan** spirit-totem, but touching it would cause serious offence.

The army barracks retains a pitiful, crumbling fragment of the former 19th-century **French fortress wall**. Were it not illegal to photograph the scene no one would think of doing so.

The **old market**, built in 1954, features a desultory handful of embroiderers selling so-so fabrics and a few half-hearted food sellers. The bustling **new market** is near the bus station.

Around 6km southeast of Muang Sing, **That Xieng Tung** is the famous stupa built by Muang Sing's founder dowager-queen in 1792. Shorter and less embellished than that at Wat Namkeo Luang, the octagonal layout is reminiscent of similar structures in Xishuangbanna, across the Chinese border. It's on a grassy plateau dotted with 'sacred trees', 1km up a very rough access track that branches south off the Luang Namtha road 200m after Km 52. This place really comes alive at festival time, ie full moon of the 12th lunar month, between late-October and mid-November, when hordes of merit-makers offer candles, flowers and incense around the base of the stupa, monks from around the province gather to collect alms and traditional dance performances add to a general carnival atmosphere that spills over into town.

Activities

The main reason visitors come to Muang Sing is to venture into the minority villages that dot the valley of rice paddies and sugar cane fields surrounding town. To do it yourself by bicycle or motorbike, start by purchasing Wolfgang Kom's helpful *Muang Sing Valley Map* (3000K) from the tourist office or Phou Iu 2 Guesthouse. The map shows major roads and labels the ethnicities of the valley's villages. To make the village-visiting experience somewhat less voyeuristic you can engage a guide for as little as 100,000K from one of Muang Sing's six ecotour agencies, which also offer a gamut of longer treks and homestay experiences. We found **Saophoudoy Tour** (☎ 400 012; www.muang-sing.com; ☑ 7.30am-6.30pm) to be relatively helpful and well organised. Other possibilities include **Tiger Man** (☎ 020-5546 7833), **Exotissimo** (☎ 030-511 0404; www.exotissimo.com) and **Hill Tribe Eco-Trek** (☎ 030-511 0578; somphonemx@ hotmail.com), a small outfit specialising in the more remote Xieng Khaeng district towards Burma. As always it's worth comparing several agents.

If you're staying at Adima, roughly 8km from Muang Sing, you'll find a series of very interesting villages within easy walking distance – the popular yet still authentic Akha village of **Nam Dath** is only 700m up the trail.

Some short-duration tours continue to **Pang Hai**, a locals-only China–Laos border crossing 12km east of Muang Sing. Middle-distance mountain views are certainly pleasant from the Mountain Overlook Guesthouse near here but the hilly scenery is largely one of newly planted rubber trees.

Sleeping

CENTRAL MUANG SING

Muang Sing Guesthouse (r 30,000K) Rooms are small, cell-like affairs but have mosquito nets and solar-heated showers. If the water's not warm head up to the roof and clean the solar panels…then linger for the views.

Thai Lü Guesthouse (s/d/tr 30,000/40,000/40,000K) This classic, if hardly plush 1920s building has a variety of ageing but well-kept budget rooms. The larger ones, accessed from the archaic looking upper balcony, have bamboo-matted walls and double-plus-single beds.

Viengsay Guesthouse (☎ 020-239 3398; r 40,000K) Three guest rooms in a newer block tacked behind a traditional-style wooden building have partly stained walls but sparkling clean

floors, good new mattresses and windows looking back towards the rice fields.

Sing Cha Lern Hotel (☎ 400 020; d/tw 50,000/70,000K) This ochre two-storey building offers 22 clean and neat, if characterless, rooms with hot water and fans. A breezy communal area has two lounge chairs, plus ageing mock-leather sofas where guests with nothing better to do can watch the single TV.

Chanthimieng Guesthouse (☎ 030-511 0834; r 60,000K) New rooms have decent bathrooms, water heaters and Western toilets, but the greatest attraction is the view across oceanic rice paddies from both upper rear guest rooms and from the appealing upstairs sitting area.

Anousone Guesthouse (☎ 030-511 0866; r 60,000K) This grand-looking mansion-guesthouse has well-equipped rooms in a proud, modern house fronted with pillars and gilded capitals, though on our last visit the whole place was deserted, Marie Celeste–style.

Singduangdao Bungalows (☎ 020-200 4565; r 60,000-70,000K) Three types of decently appointed bungalows are well spaced in a pleasant area behind the truck weighbridge. All have hot showers. The smaller bungalows come with bamboo walls and board floors, or brick walls with tiled concrete bases. The larger ones are on stilts. Bo speaks decent English.

Phou Iu 2 Guesthouse (☎ 020-5586 6909; phouiu@ yahoo.com; bungalow small/medium/large 80,000/ 200,000/400,000K) Set around a pleasant garden of lawn, young trees and banana fronds, the biggest bungalows have fun outdoor rock-clad shower spaces but furnishings are sparse and floorboards are rough. The small twin bungalows are better value. All have comfortable beds, fans and small verandahs, there's an on-site herbal sauna (10,000K) and massage (per hr 50,000K). The reception doubles as a handicraft shop and sells decent town maps.

OUTSIDE MUANG SING

Stupa Mountain Lodge & Restaurant (r 50,000K) Once-refined wooden bungalows with sweeping views now feel seriously neglected and the restaurant seems entirely dormant. It's 5km towards Namtha, handy for That Xieng Tung but not for anything much else.

our pick **Adima** (☎ 020-239 3398; r with thin/thick mattresses 50,000/60,000K) The huge selling point of Adima is that you're on the edge of exactly the kind of classic Akha village that most people come to the region to see. Many other minority villages are within easy walking distance. Adima's sturdy brick and thatch bungalows aren't especially stylish but do have hot showers and bucket-flush toilets. Their appealing rustic restaurant overlooks fishponds. From Muang Sing take the Pang Hai road to the far edge of Ban Udomsin (500m after Km 7), turn right and Adima is 600m south. A tuk-tuk from town costs 10,000K per person.

Eating

A variety of guesthouse-eateries along the main street tend to suffer a barrage of annoying sales-folk trying to peddle souvenirs and low-grade 'ethnic' tat.

Phunnar (Panna) Restaurant (☎ 400 004; mains 8000-15,000K; � 7.30am-8pm) Airy if unsophisticated place for inexpensive fried rice, noodles, *làap* and soups.

Thai Lü Restaurant (mains 10,000-20,000K; � 7.30am-8pm) Along with a typical selection of backpacker standbys, it serves a range of authentic local and northern Lao fare, well explained in the menu.

Muang Sing View Restaurant (mains 10,000-25,000K, rice 5000K; � 8am-7pm) This simple bamboo-floored stilt pavilion overlooks a seemingly endless sea of rice paddies, making it very much the most attractive place in town to eat. The menu is wide ranging but what's actually available is hit and miss.

Entertainment

Singsavanh Nightclub (� 7pm-11.30pm) Most of Muang Sing is dead asleep by 9pm except at the Singsavanh where the locals get down to live Lao and Chinese pop.

Getting There & Away

From the **bus station** in the northwest corner of town, *sǎwngthǎew* depart for Muang Long (25,000K, 1½ hours) at 8am, 11am and 1.30pm. To Luang Namtha (20,000K, two hours, 58km)

minibuses leave at 8am, 9.30am, 11.30am, 1pm, 2pm and 3pm. An extra 5pm service might be added if enough customers show up on the last *sǎwngthǎew* from Muang Long.

Getting Around

Despite the tourist office's denials, renting motorbikes is indeed possible through **Kalao Motorcycle** (per day 80,000K; � 8am-5pm) but bring a good phrasebook as nobody here speaks English. Bicycle rental (per day 30,000K) is available from several main-street agencies and guesthouses.

WEST OF MUANG SING

Dusty and unpaved but reasonably smooth and fast, the Xieng Kok road leads through a predominantly Akha district where an unusually large proportion of women wear distinctive silver 'coin' head-dresses and billowing indigo blouses. At **Ban Tao Home**, a traditional Akha swing is briefly visible from the main road (north side) on a rise at the village's western end.

Muang Long

Lacklustre in itself, **Muang Long** is the capital of this interesting district and its **tourist office** (☎ 020-5519 5561; � 8-11.30am & 1.30-4pm Mon-Fri) is the one place you're likely to find English-speaking tourist information. Keen Mr Tui can organise a variety of **treks** for next-day departure. There are seven guesthouses within two blocks of Muang Long's market/bus stand. Set back from the main road in a modest garden with sitting areas, some rooms at **Thatsany** (☎ 020-5534 8337; r 40,000-50,000K) are very large and all come with squat toilet and cold shower. Near the bus stand, the functional **Siseng Guesthouse** (☎ 020-5556 0225; r 50,000K) is new, very clean and has water heaters in the attached bathrooms (squat toilet).

Xieng Kok
ຊຽງກົກ

On market days (the 14th or 28th of any month) Xieng Kok attracts hill-tribe folks and traders from surrounding countries. Otherwise, despite its reputation as a smuggling route, it's a sleepy, attractive little place surveying a deep slice of Mekong Valley and the Burmese banks behind. In autumn, when river levels are high, Chinese barges call in at the river port and Xieng Kok attracts a trickle of travellers who come to find a boat along one of Laos's more attractive stretches of the Mekong. The area between here and Muang Mom (p178) is roadless and a speedboat should cost around 900/3500B per person/boat. Consider paying 1200/4500B and continuing to Tonpheung (p178), from which onward *sǎwngthǎew* to Huay Xai are easier to find. Although a daily 9am speedboat departure is touted by the Muang Long tourist office, if there are no fellow passengers you'll have to charter a boat. From late January to June the water levels are usually too low to make the river trip at all. If you manage to organise a ride on a cargo boat, be sure that it will be able to let you off in Laos – some dock only in Thai ports further south and that could leave you with serious immigration worries.

Arriving in Xieng Kok by boat you climb the steep riverbank to a loop of asphalt road that fronts the immigration booth. Veer left for the **Xieng Kok Resort** (☎ 030-511 0696; r 50,000K), a line of 11 simple timber bungalows overlooking the Mekong, each with balcony, private squat toilet, cold shower and grubby bathroom walls. Veer right instead for the marginally inferior **Wang Jiang Lou Guesthouse** (r without/with bathroom 30,000/50,000K) offering basic bamboo-walled rooms in a stilt building with disconcerting holes between the ageing floorboards. A second, newer building is under construction.

The two roads converge again within 300m where the minibus to Muang Long (20,000K, 35 minutes) leaves at 6am, 8am and 2pm from outside the town's little pharmacy. Finding any other vehicle can be hard here, even if you're prepared to charter.

PHONGSALI PROVINCE

No longer Laos, not yet China, Phongsali is a visual feast and home to some of the nation's most traditional hill tribes. Trekkers might feel that they've walked onto the pages of *National Geographic*. For travellers, the province's most visited settlement is Muang Khua, a useful transit point linked by river to Nong Khiaw and by rough road to Dien Bien Phu in Vietnam. Further north the province is kept well off the standard tourist trail by arduous journeys on seriously rough and/or muddy roads – the only asphalt links Muang Khua to Udomxai and Phongsali to Mengla (China). Annoyingly foreigners can't cross the Chinese border there nor anywhere else in the province (yet). The terrible Dien Bien Phu road is being totally rebuilt.

Plans to make Boun Neua the new provincial capital have yet to be realised though it's already home to misnamed 'Phongsali' Airport.

PAK NAM NOI
ປາກນ້ຳນ້ອຍ

Rte 2E from Udomxai via Muang La (p214) is newly paved and attractive, although most of the forest has long-since been burnt and replaced with bamboo fuzz. At Km 64, Pak Nam Noi (marked Sin Xai on some maps) is the junction at which rough Rte 1B to Phongsali strikes north. It's little more than a bus stand plus a few shop-stalls, some selling hard-to-identify creatures apparently intended for human consumption. Colourfully dressed Akha women are often in evidence here and many more appear every tenth day for the big *thalat nat* (special morning market). To watch their dawn arrival consider staying at the bus station's unmarked four-room **Guesthouse** (☎ 020-5440 1326; without/with bathroom 30,000/40,000K) where rooms have decent new mattresses. Two have ensuite squat toilets, the others no bathrooms whatsoever so you must pay to use the bus station's loo!

En route to Muang Khua, 800m after Km 75, **Monsavan** (literally 'paradise') is an appropriately named village famous for its *làoláo* production, whose various stages can be perused without charge if you're able to stop here for five minutes.

MUANG KHUA
ເມືອງຂວາ
☎ 088 / pop 3500

Pretty little Muang Khua is an inevitable stop if you're transiting between Laos and Dien Bien Phu in Vietnam or taking the Nam Ou river route between Hat Sa (Phongsali) and

Nong Khiaw. While not as spectacular as the latter, Muang Khua has oodles of small-town charm set amid starburst palms where the Nam Ou and Nam Phak rivers meet. If you're arriving from Dien Bien Phu, please relax. This is Laos, and unlike in neighbouring Vietnam, hard bargaining is neither required nor appropriate.

Information

There is no internet cafe and no ATM (nor in Phongsali, the nearest is in Udomxai) but you can change US dollars (clean new notes only), euros, Vietnamese dong and Thai baht at the **Lao Development Bank** (☒ 8.30am-3pm Mon-Fri). If you're heading downriver, remember to change enough for your stays in Muang Ngoi Neua and Nong Khiaw, where there are no banks at all. When the bank is closed, an un-signed **pots and pans shop** (☒ 7am-6pm) beside the Agricultural Promotion Bank can exchange dong for kip and vice versa. Some other shops sometimes exchange Thai baht.

The helpful **tourist office** (☎ 020-284 8020; ☒ 8.30-11.30am & 1.30-4.30pm Mon-Fri) opposite the Sernalli Hotel can answer questions and ar-range treks. If you want to book a trek out of office hours, call **Keo** (☎ 020-284 8020) to arrange a meeting.

Muang Khua was officially connected to the power grid in March 2010, but when we visited there were still days when the mains electricity didn't come on at all.

Sights & Activities

A pleasant short walk takes you to the rustic Khamu quarter across a high, creaky **suspen-sion bridge** (bike/pedestrian only) over the Nam Phak river. An even easier stroll passes the colourful little **wat** and heads into an-other palm dappled village area where the road turns muddy. The **Ethnic Handicrafts Shop** at Chaleunsuk Guesthouse sells a small but appealing range of local crafts. Photo-explanation boards explain their production and introduce the villages that your purchases support.

The tourist office organises several trekking options, including a very pleasant one-day trek to Ban Bakha, an Akha Pala village high on the heavily deforested ridges above Pak Nam Noi. The population only moved here 18

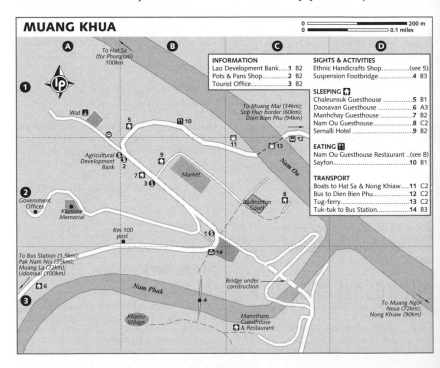

MUANG KHUA

0   200 m
0   0.1 miles

INFORMATION
Lao Development Bank.....**1** B2
Pots & Pans Shop..........**2** B2
Tourist Office................**3** B2

SIGHTS & ACTIVITIES
Ethnic Handicrafts Shop...............(see 5)
Suspension Footbridge................**4** B3

SLEEPING 🏠
Chaleunsuk Guesthouse **5** B1
Daosavan Guesthouse **6** A3
Manhchay Guesthouse **7** B2
Nam Ou Guesthouse...................**8** B2
Sernalli Hotel **9** B2

EATING 🍴
Nam Ou Guesthouse Restaurant ..(see 8)
Sayfon...................................**10** B1

TRANSPORT
Boats to Hat Sa & Nong Khiaw.....**11** C2
Bus to Dien Bien Phu...................**12** C2
Tug-ferry................................**13** C2
Tuk-tuk to Bus Station.................**14** B3

To Hat Sa
(for Phongsali)
100km

Wat

Agricultural
Development
Bank

Government
Offices

Kaysone
Memorial

Km 100
post

To Bus Station (1.5km);
Pak Nam Noi (35km);
Muang La (72km);
Udomxai (100km)

Nam Phak

Khamu
Village

Market

Badminton
Court

To Muang Mai (34km);
Sop Hun border (60km);
Dien Bien Phu (94km)

Nam Ou

Bridge under
construction

Manotham
Guesthouse
& Restaurant

To Muang Ngoi
Neua (72km);
Nong Khiaw (90km)

NORTHERN LAOS

years ago and many of the women still wear the traditional gaudy-coloured Pala aprons and metal-beaded top-knots.

Luang Prabang–based Tiger Trail (p159) is pioneering 'voluntourism' experiences for longer,, experience-based stays in such villages.

Sleeping & Eating

There are nearly a dozen options.

Manhchay Guesthouse (☎ 210 841; r 30,000K) Above a family shop beside the tourist office, the very simple box rooms come with shared squat toilets and cold shower. It's no worse than you'd expect for this price.

Nam Ou Guesthouse (☎ 210 844; s/tw without bathroom 25,000/40,000K, r 50,000K) This rambling guesthouse overlooking the Nam Ou tug-ferry has a hodgepodge of rooms. The best have a hot shower and shared terrace but the cheaper ones are very basic bamboo boxes.

Chaleunsuk Guesthouse (☎ 210 847; d/tw 50,000/60,000K, tw with separate bathroom 50,000K) Clean, generously sized rooms have large comfy beds and hot showers. Most also come with a desk and a ceiling patterned with stars and plastic planets. Free tea is available in the ample communal sitting terrace. Altogether it's the best deal in town, except when the mains power's off – it doesn't have a generator.

Daosavan Guesthouse (☎ 210 820; Rte 2; r 50,000K) On stilts above the Nam Phak riverbank, rooms here have more taste than most competitors but showers are cold and it's 1km from the boat landing on the main road to the bus station.

Sernalli Hotel (☎ 212 445; r 150,000K) Muang Khua's only 'hotel', the Sernalli's facade suggests a certain neo-colonial elegance and the small lobby is full of carved hard-wood furniture. The rooms are clean and perfectly adequate, with soft-wood fittings and Western bathrooms, but they're cramped and lacking any real verve.

Eating

Nam Ou Guesthouse Restaurant (☎ 210 844; mains 10,000-25,000K) Perched on stilts overlooking a range of lively riverside scenes, the Nam Ou cooks good, if wafer-thin, 'steak' and chips (25,000K) and a range of western breakfast options plus a selection of stirfries and Thai-Lao dishes.

Sayfon (☎ 210 843; mains 12,000-30,000K) Set high above the river with views through the palm trees, the Sayfon has a wide English-language menu, of which about half is actually available. The mushrooms in ginger are particularly good.

Getting There & Away

The bus to Dien Bien Phu in Vietnam (50,000K) departs from a point just across the Nam Ou from town; it costs 2000K by tug-ferry or motorised canoe to cross. Bus departures are currently around 5am in both directions taking more than ten gruelling hours. This should drop to five hours once road construction is complete, when departure times will doubtless become more sociable.

Muang Khua's inconvenient **bus station** (900m past Km 97, Rte 2E) is nearly 3km west of the river towards Udomxai. Very rare tuk-tuks (per person 5000K) head out there once full from near the Lao Development Bank. Buses to Udomxai (30,000K, three hours) depart at 8.30am, noon and 3pm. For Phongsali take the 8am *săwngthăew* to Pak Nam Noi (11,000K, one hour) and await the Udomxai–Phongsali bus there. It usually arrives around 10am.

Boat travel on the Nam Ou is a very attractive alternative, as long as you're not in a hurry. Upriver to Hat Sa, boats sometimes arrive too late to connect with the last bus to Phongsali. Downriver boats to Muang Ngoi Neua can prove easier to find than to Nong

---

CROSSING THE VIETNAMESE BORDER AT TAY TRANG & SOP HUN

Daily buses between Muang Khua and Dien Bien Phu cross the Laos–Vietnam border 26km east of Muang Mai. With a road that's rough but currently being entirely rebuilt, it's a picturesque route but making the trip in hops isn't recommended: you'll end up paying far more than the bus fare and risk getting stranded part way. There are no facilities or waiting vehicles at either border posts, which are separated by at least 3km of no-man's-land. The 31km road from Tay Trang to Dien Bien Phu is paved.

Heading for Laos this way it's essential to bring ample convertible currency (eg US$ cash) as the nearest ATM is in Udomxai. While not terribly far from Muang Khua, that's an annoying detour if you'd really prefer to jump on a riverboat towards chill-out Nong Khiaw or trek-worthy Phongsali.

Khiaw. Either way, be aware that the trip might therefore take a day (or more) longer than anticipated.

PAK NAM NOI TO PHONGSALI

The route north is an uncomfortably rough roller-coaster as far as Ban Yo. The scenery is attractive but the majority of villages are set well away from the road, especially south of Boun Tai where those on two wheels might welcome an overnight break.

Boun Tai
ບຸນໃຕ້
☎ 088 / pop 3500

Phongsali buses generally stop for ten minutes at **Boun Tai**, 79km north of Pak Nam Noi. That's long enough to nip across the road from the bus station and peruse the root-strangled brick ruins of a former French fortress (certainly not worth a special trip). Starting from Boun Tai, the fascinating three-day **Nam Lan Trek** passes through Yang, Laobit, Akha Djepia and Akha Nuqui villages and emerges on the last day at Ban Pakha in time for the onward bus to Boun Neua and Phongsali. However, with over 30 stream and river crossings, it should only be attempted later in the dry season. To organise guides, phone well ahead to Phongsali's tourist office. Your backpack can be sent on ahead to be picked up in Phongsali.

Unlovely but survivable, **Khem Nam Lan Guesthouse** (☎ 020-5509 5806; r 30,000K) is the unmarked peach-coloured house just across the river bridge as you arrive in town from the south. Prices are the same whether you take the small concrete box-rooms, bigger versions with new mattresses and en-suite toilet or the upstairs rooms with wooden walls and thin, aged beds. The ragged beer-house next door has river views and serves basic food if you're lucky.

Phonsevanh Guesthouse (☎ 020-5588 7118; tvp. info@gmail.com; bungalow 40,000K) has simple but pleasant bamboo-walled bungalows set around a lawn but despite a predominantly rural setting, there's a noisy warehouse plot directly behind and your fellow guests are likely to be Chinese log-truck drivers, possibly with paid companions. The location is some 3km out of central Boun Tai, 400m beyond the sawmill on a road that forms a T-junction with the Phongsali main road opposite Boun Tai fort. This road continues eventually to

Luang Namtha but crosses half a dozen fords en route so should only be attempted by trails bike, truck or sturdy 4WD.

Boun Tai to Boun Neua

Near Km 81, just 2.5km beyond Boun Tai, there's a pretty little village with the new **Tai Lü stupa** across a suspension footbridge. A kilometre beyond notice the **tobacco tower** and archaic **brick-making works**. Located 500m beyond Km 89, **Ban Singsai** has an attractive Tai Lü temple to the left of the road. Rubber plantations hog the hills to the left but some surviving stands of shaggy jungle remain to the right in the next valley. **Ban Yo** (Km 109 of Rte 1B, Km 62 of the Mengla–Phongsali road) is the northern end of painful Rte 1B. Turning left leads 19km to **Ban Pakha**, a locals-only border crossing to China). Turning right, smooth asphalt leads all the way to Phongsali, passing through **Phaphounkao** (Km 49), an Akha Phixo village where womenfolk wear distinctive raised, flat-topped cowls draped with silver baubles.

Boun Neua
ບຸນເໜືອ
☎ 088 / pop 2500

A local transport hub 41km west of Phongsali, Boun Neua is a diffuse scattering of mostly newer concrete houses that has been tentatively proposed as the unlikely new provincial capital. Staying here might prove handy if connecting to Ou Tai (p235) or for those doing the Phongsali 'Jungle Trek'. For information or 'call-n-trek' bookings contact **Mr Khampheng** (☎ 020-5578 7399) who operates a small tourist office beside the bus station.

The bus station, plus a few shops and basic eateries, lies around the main junction where Rte 1A to Ou Tai turns north off the Phongsali road. Facing the junction, the handy three-storey **Sivienkham Guesthouse** (☎ 210 784; r 50,000K) has well-kept new rooms with comfy beds, hot showers and sit-down toilets. Around 300m north, **Inthaseng Guesthouse** (☎ 030-510 0648; d/tr 50,000/60,000K) has a more rustic setting overlooking a fishpond but rooms are mustier and slightly worn. Around 600m further north is the relatively grand new **Houtsayalath** (Haoxayalath; ☎ 210 780; r 50,000K). At the crossroads beyond, the asphalted lane to the left leads 1km west to the misnamed 'Phongsali Airport'. **Lao Capricorn** (☎ 088-210 111; http://laocapricornair.net) flies to Vientiane (1,011,000K, 1½ hours) Wednesday and Saturday, though cancellations are all too common.

For Phongsali (20,000K, 1½ hours) use the through buses from Mengla, Boun Tai, Udomxai or Vientiane, typically departing around 1pm and between 4pm and 6pm. The rickety bus from Boun Neua to Ou Tai (at least 4½ hours) departs around 9.30am once the early bus from Phongsali arrives. If you're arriving from Vientiane you'll probably miss it.

Boun Neua to Phongsali

After Boun Neua (Km 41) the road to Phongsali climbs onto a ridgetop road surveying swaths of protected mountain forests. There's a signed viewpoint at 500m past Km 31 with ridgetop panoramas continuing for the next 15km. **Baka Luang** (200m beyond Km 17) is the first noticeably Phu Noi village en route where old women still wear distinctive Phu Noi leggings.

PHONGSALI

ຜົງສາລີ

☎ 088 / pop 6000 / elevation 1400m

Quite unlike any other Lao provincial capital, Phongsali sits high on a small ridgetop plateau above which the peak of Phu Fa ('Sky Mountain', 1625m) rises steeply. The location gives the town panoramic views and a refreshing climate that can swing from pleasantly warm to downright cold in a matter of hours. Bring a jacket and waterproofs in case, even in March. The town's population is a mix of Phu Noi and Haw/Yunnanese, both long-term residents and more recent immigrants.

History

According to tradition the Phu Noi were originally a warlike tribe who had migrated from Burma to Luang Prabang. Seeing danger and opportunity in equal measure, the Lan Xang king granted them land in the far north of his domains, today's Phongsali, where they maintained the borderlands against incursions from the Tai Lü kingdom of Sipsong Panna.

Information

BCEL New bank under construction that will soon have Phongsali's first ATM.

Lao Development Bank (� 8.30am-3.30pm Mon-Fri) Can change nine currencies to Kip and cashes US$ travellers cheques without commission. Western Union transfers possible but no ATM, no cash advance.

Lao Telecom International calls possible.

Tourist Office (☎ 210 098; www.phongsaly.net; ☼ 8am-11.30am & 1.30-4pm Mon-Fri) Helpful maps and brochures are also available online and free from most guesthouses. If you need emergency help or want to book a tour out of hours, call ☎ 020-5568 8396 or the mobile phone number of duty staff posted on the front door.

Wang Electronics Shop (per hr 15,000K; ☼ 7am-10pm) One computer with the internet, plus independent electricity to run it.

Sights

The town's modest but distinctive **old town** area includes a three-block grid of rough, stone-flagged alleys and a winding street mostly lined with traditional **Yunnanese style shop-houses** whose wooden frontages recall the architecture of old Kunming. Tiny, new and functional, the **Chinese Temple** overlooks a pond, behind which **Wat Keo** is more memorable for its *petang*-playing monks than its architecture.

For great views across town climb to the stupa-topped peak of **Phu Fa**, a punishing, tree-shaded climb up over 400 stone steps or a very bumpy, steep road that's just passable by motorbike in first gear. A 4000K toll is payable on the last section of the ascent from a picnic area. A new alternative descent returns to the Hat Sa road near a tea factory 2km east of town, 500m short of Jaidee, a bamboo-walled eatery where you might get a *tôm pąa* (fondue-style fish soup) lunch. Ten minutes is ample to see the **Museum of Tribes** (admission 5000K; ☼ 8am-11.30am & 1.30-4.30pm Mon-Fri) displaying local costumes of the province's diverse cultures. If the door is locked, ask for the key from the post office across the road.

Activities

Hill-tribe treks in Phongsali province are among the most rewarding in all of Laos. Tours have a heavy emphasis on ecological and cultural sensitivity, with a sizeable chunk of your fee going into development funds in the villages where you stay. Carefully thought-out treks are offered through the well-organised tourist office. Most treks can be organised for next-day departure, especially if you phone ahead. A popular option is the **Jungle Trek** (two short days starting from Boun Neua), visiting an Akha Phixo village as well as crossing a rare surviving stand of primary forest. Various multi-day start and finish treks include boat rides up the Nam Ou from Hat Sa and visiting

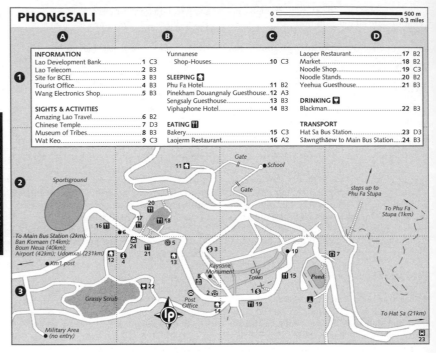

PHONGSALI

unforgettable Akha Nuqui villages linked by high ridgetop paths. One-way treks like the three-day Nam Lan Trek to Boun Tai (see p230) can be organised to include delivery of your backpack to the destination so that you don't have to backtrack.

Fixed prices per person per day are currently 200,000/150,000K in a pair/larger group, or 300,000K going it alone. This includes the guide's fee, food and ultra-basic homestays in real village homes. But you must add transport costs, which are very variable according to whether you'll use public transport or charter vehicles. Projected 'experience tours' allow you to spend more time with village folk including, perhaps, guided foraging trips to collect the ingredients for the local family dinner.

Amazing Lao Travel (Northern Travelling Center; ☎ 210 594; www.amazinglaos.com; ☺ 8am-5pm, often later) has its own selection of treks and may soon offer exciting river expeditions on the upper Nam Ou through the NPA.

Sleeping

All of the following have water heaters and the Phou Fa even has air-con and room-heaters.

However, such facilities require electricity, which is often limited to a few hours a day.

Sengsaly Guesthouse (☎ 210 165; r 40,000-60,000K) The best of three cheaper options on the main drag, the Sengsaly's 40,000K rooms have ageing bedding but even these have basic private bathrooms. Better rooms are newly built and comfy if overly colourful and come with hot showers.

Pinekham Douangnaly Guesthouse (☎ 020-239 5005; r 60,000-80,000K) Phongsali's newest guesthouse is compact but very clean, has warm duvets and small private bathrooms, albeit sometimes with plumbing problems.

Viphaphone Hotel (☎ 210 111; r 60,000-80,000K) A handily central three-storey hotel whose rooms are decent and include desks, wardrobes and TV. View rooms cost a little more but most such 'views' are now obscured by building works.

Phou Fa Hotel (☎ 210 031; tw/d 90,000/120,000; ☒) Western toilets, room heaters and golden bedcovers give the Phou Fa a marginal edge as Phongsali's top choice, though the concrete floors let the image down a little. It's a series of 26 one-storey courtyard rooms in what was a Chinese consulate until 1975. Three staff members speak English but finding them can be a challenge. There's no reception per se – look in the small room on the left beyond the groups-only restaurant building.

Eating

A basic, unmarked **noodle shop** (fõe 8000K; ✆ 6-11am) near the bank does the best noodle soup in town though there's also decent *khào sáwy* available from **noodle stands** (khào sáwy 5000K; ✆ 6.30am-5pm) hidden away in the northwest corner of the **market**, which is at its most interesting at dawn. None of the town's eateries make any attempt at decoration and restaurant food is predominantly Chinese. *Tôm pạa* (fondue-style fish soup) is a local speciality, notably served at simple places along the Hat Sa road (Km 2 and Km 4). In an archetypal Old Town shop-house, the tiny **'bakery'** produces bread some mornings but often stocks only doughnuts stuffed with coconut or bean paste.

Yeehua Guesthouse (☎ 210 186; mains 10,000-30,000K; 🖳) Beneath Phongsali's cheapest (but not recommended) guesthouse, the Yeehua's functional restaurant serves inexpensive traveller fare, French wines, Chinese beer (7000K) and thick Lao Coffee (3000K). The menu is in English.

Laojerm Restaurant (☎ 030-588 7448; mains 20,000-35,000K; ✆ 11am-10.30pm) Service ranges from lacklustre to odd but reliably good food comes in decent-sized portions and the menu's approximate English includes inscrutable offerings such as 'High-handed Pig's liver' and 'Palace Protects the Meat Cubelets'.

Laoper Restaurant (☎ 030-578 8283; mains 15,000-20,000K; ✆ 5-10pm) Locally considered to cook the best food in town, there's no menu, just a display box of the possible ingredients. Point to a selection and see what turns up. It's good for groups sharing a mixture of dishes but not ideal for single diners. *Tôm pạa* is available.

Drinking

Phongsali region, especially Ban Komaen is famous for Chinese-style green tea. The tourist office sells samples along with excellent local *lào-láo* (per half-litre 14,000K). The pale green tint comes from having been passed over raspberry leaves after fermentation. To sip a beer in a central yet semi-rural setting, try **Blackman** (beer 10,000K; ✆ 3-10pm).

Getting There & Away

Phongsali's airport is actually at Boun Neua (p230) but air tickets to Vientiane (1,011,000K) are also sold at the Viphaphone Hotel. Boats to/from Muang Khua depart/arrive at Hat Sa, to which buses (10,000K) leave daily at 8am and 1.30pm from the **Hat Sa bus station**, 10 minutes' walk east of town.

Phongsali's **main bus station** is at Km 3, west of town. A *sǎwngthǎew* shuttle runs there from the market area (5000K) at 6.30am but only very infrequently after that, so leave plenty of time. The daily bus to Vientiane (at least 25 hours) leaves at 7.30am and the bus to Udomxai (65,000K, nine to 15 hours) at 8am. As foreigners can't cross the Chinese border at Ban Pakha, the buses to Mengla (7am and 1.30pm) and the weekly Luang Namtha service (via Mengla) are only useful for reaching Boun Neua.

Amazing Lao Travel rents so-so motorbikes from 100,000K per day.

AROUND PHONGSALI

For Boun Neua see p230.

Ban Komaen

ບ້ານກຳແມນ

☎ 088 / pop 400

Phongsali's famous tea village is a very attractive place commanding stupendous valley views. These sweep nearly 360 degrees when you stand on the promontory behind the school, where a new ecolodge is planned eventually. A fair percentage of authentic Phu Noi homes are set on stone-pile platforms. Arriving from Phongsali (15km), you'll drive past plenty of tea bushes, but those beside the main road through the village centre are reputedly over 400 years old and are said to be the world's oldest. That doesn't mean they're huge – after all, the leaf pickers still need to clamber through the branches.

Ban Komaen makes a very pleasant part-day motorbike excursion. Take the Boun Neua road, turn left directly opposite the inspirationally named Km4 Nightclub (not the asphalt road just before) then curve steadily around on the main unpaved road, keeping left at most junctions but avoiding any turn that descends into the valley.

Hat Sa

ຫາດຊາ

☎ 088 / pop 500

Hat Sa is a tiny river 'port' village climbing the steep wooded bank of the Nam Ou. It's

SENSITIVE TREKKING

When visiting tribal villages you'll need to learn slightly different etiquette according to each local culture. The following notes focus particularly on the Akha, as Akha women's coin-encrusted indigo costumes make their villages popular trekking targets while their animist beliefs are also some of the most unexpected.

Shoes & Feet – Entering an ethnic Lao home it would be rude not to remove your shoes, but in mud-floored dwellings of Hmong, Akha and some other tribal peoples, leave them on. Of course you should still refrain from pointing your feet at anyone.

Toilets – If there's a village toilet, use it. When in the forest be sure to dump away from watercourses. But in remote villages with no toilets at all, check with your guide as to the local custom: although trekking etiquette usually dictates burying faeces, in some villages your solid deposits will be gobbled up greedily by the local pigs so shouldn't be wasted! Nonetheless, please do carry out your used toilet paper, tampons etc, however unpleasant that might seem.

Photos – While many hill-tribe boys are delighted to be photographed, most village women run squealing from a camera. Asking permission to snap a passing stranger often results in straight refusal, which should be respected. However, a great advantage of staying in a village homestay is that you become 'friends' with a family. Try snapping digital photos of babies and men, show those casually to your host ladies and eventually it's quite likely that they will want to see themselves on camera. Never force the issue, however, as a few really might believe the crusty old superstition that photographers are soul-stealers.

Gifts – If you want to give gifts, consider fruit and vegetable seeds or saplings that continue to give after you've left. Always ask your guide first if it's appropriate to give anything and if so, only give directly to friends or to the village chief. Giving gifts to children can encourage begging, which undermines societies that have always been self-sufficient.

Beds – In trekking villages you'll probably sleep in the house of the village chief. In traditional Akha homes all the men-folk sleep on one raised, curtained platform, most of the women on another (which it is absolutely taboo to visit) and the daughter-in-law gets a curtained box-space poignantly befitting her almost slave-like status. To make space for visitors, most men-folk move out for the night to sleep in other houses, leaving the guide, trekkers and maybe a village elder or two to snuggle up in a line in the male section. Bringing a sleeping bag gives a greater semblance of privacy. Note that female trekkers count as 'honorary men'.

Spirits – The spirit world is every bit as lively in hill-tribe cultures as it is in other Lao cultures and it would be exceedingly bad form for a visitor to touch a village totem (Tai Lü villages), a spirit gate (Akha) or any other taboo item. Ask your guide to explain and don't even think of dangling yourself on an Akha swing (hacheu).

Breasts & Babies – Akha women who display their bare breasts are neither being careless nor offering a sexual come-on, they're simply following a belief that young mothers who cover both breasts will attract harm to their newborn offspring. Eating stones while pregnant is an odder custom, while the brutal Akha attitude to twins is quite unpalatable.

21km east of Phongsali by unsealed road. There's a handful of noodle stalls and a market on the 15th and 30th of each month, which is liveliest from dawn and mainly sells Chinese goods to hill-tribe folk. That's directly above the river landing from where boats leave to Muang Khua (100,000K) and Watai (25,000K), around 30 minutes after the arrival of the first bus from Phongsali – assuming sufficient clientele and decent water levels. Finding the right boat is easy enough and an official tots up passenger numbers to calculate whether you'll need to pay a supplement. When water levels are low departures can drop to a couple a week and prices will be higher.

There's no guesthouse but if you're stuck in Hat Sa (quite possible for a night if you arrive late by boat from Muang Khua), you can sleep in one of three unfurnished bamboo-walled crash-pad rooms above **Wanna Ngyai Shop** (per person 20,000K), the first two-storey shack to the right as you climb from the boat landing. Mosquito nets and thin floor mats are available but it's preferable to bring your own sleeping bag. Wash in the river.

Buses to Phongsali (10,000K) depart at around 9am and 2pm from the market, taking up to 1½ hours westbound due to the steep climb. An additional *săwngthăew* will generally depart to Phongsali after the boat arrives from Muang Khua, charging 20,000K per person assuming the driver can make 100,000K minimum.

Phu Den Din NPA

This vast area of partly unexplored, relatively pristine forest is layered across inaccessible mountains that climax at almost 2000m near the Vietnamese border. At present the only legal way to get a glimpse of its grandeur is on irregular boating or kayaking trips down the Nam Ou river between Ban Tha and Hat Sa, for which you'll need to do a lot of organisation. You'll also need to carry your own camping necessities, as there's a lengthy section without any habitation whatever. Some tourists have made ill-considered attempts to drive into the park from Hat Sa. While there is a French-built suspension bridge and rough unpaved road leading there, it passes through rather monotonous slash-and-burn landscapes. Then, after slogging for 70km, you reach an army checkpoint that prevents any access to the NPA anyway. Sneaking past that is very unwise as you risk being shot as a suspected poacher.

NORTH OF BOUN NEUA

Despite some memorable scenery and many inspiring yet accessible roadside villages, virtually no tourists venture up the dusty but quite passable road north of Boun Neua. This is unlikely to change rapidly even if the Laos-China border at Nan Tuey finally opens to foreigners. Communication can be challenging, with Chinese spoken more widely than Lao in some places.

If you can find one, renting a van for a day trip from Boun Neua would be an ideal way to visit. By motorbike, come prepared for serious mud or dust according to the season.

Boun Neua to Ou Tai

This fascinating route passes briefly through very attractive forested slopes around Km 21 then reaches the Akha village of **Huoi Jing** at Km 24, where a buffalo-horn totem marks the entrance to town and there's a classic Akha swing at the top. Thereafter the road forms a spectacular skyline drive for several

kilometres. The large village of **Ngay Ngeu** (Ngay Neua; Km 34) is marred at first glance by its modern school complex. However, the main town, across the river by flimsy footbridges, is an elegant tight-packed mix of traditional shaggy-thatch and corrugated roof Tai Lü houses with a quaint little temple tucked away at the back. The main road curls around and above, then heads into another patch of older-growth forest that's only been partially burnt. At Km 63, a bridge across the Nam Ou leads into **Ban Tha** (confusingly marked as 'Yofam' on some maps), where the regular market is particularly busy on the 15th of each month. Phongsali Tourist Office has mooted three-day boating or kayaking trips to descend the wild Nam Ou rapids from here to Hat Sa. These have yet to start officially but would involve at least one night camping, another in a homestay.

At Km 65 the road climbs through **Ban Pankhai**, a tiny settlement of Akha Phixo people where the women wear archetypal head-dresses with rectangular indigo protrusions draped in strings of beads and silver coins. The climb continues with great views at Km 71 to Km 72 and again at around Km 77 where the road crosses a pass with classic 'sea of clouds' views at sunrise. Then there's a steady descent into the rice-bowl valley of **Ou Tai** (Km 93).

Ou Tai (Muang Nyot Ou)

ຂູໄຕ້ (ເມື່ອງຢອດຂູ)

☎ 088 / pop 2500

The main town of the Nyot Ou (Gnot Ou) district, Ou Tai features a rather brash, functional main street but its lower town has a good scattering of thatch- and tile-roofed wooden homes. The town's best-known attraction is the open-sided temple **Wat Luang,** originating from 1445 and long considered one of the finest temples of its style. Sadly a 2009 reconstruction has seriously compromised its appeal. The weather-beaten old terracotta roof tiles and ceiling timbers of the original structure remain in maudlin stacks around the rebuilt building, but fortunately the unusual four-way colonnaded approaches remain original. The central Buddha figure sits in an ornately gilded box-throne in the middle.

Tam Fan Binguan (☎ 0879-687 4969; r 50,000K) is the best guesthouse in town with slight elements of style to the new beds, though rooms are a little dusty and the curtains starting to sag. Private bathrooms are slightly musty and have squat toilets but solar-heated showers. It's opposite the motorbike showroom, just at the point where the spur road to the wat diverges from the main street. The sign is only in Chinese and staff speak minimal Lao, let alone English.

Manyvong Guesthouse (☎ 088-210 889; tw/d/ tr 45,000/50,000/50,000K) is rather grubby with stark unshaded light bulbs, cold showers and squat toilets but it's the one place where staff can manage a word or two of English. It's on the main street at the top of the rise where the main road swings around in front of the Bureau des Travaux. There's a simple but pricey restaurant, but for much cheaper meals visit one of the **noodle shacks** (noodle soup from 3000K) 600m beyond near the bus stand.

The 9am bus to Boun Neua (25,000K) should take 4½ hours but we've seen it take double that. By van, three hours is ample without stops. If there's sufficient custom, a *săwngthăew* might run from Ou Tai to Ou Neua once the bus has arrived from Boun Neua.

North of Ou Tai

Following the valley of the Nam Ou, the main road is comparatively fast, if less scenic and appallingly dusty. However, **Ou Neua** (Km 116) is a large, attractive Tai Lü village whose eastern flank is perched above a lake. The 90-year-old **Wat Pa** is a wonderfully authentic Tai Lü forest temple retaining all the old tiled roofing. Inside there's little to see and the open sides are wrapped in chicken wire, but the setting is a spiritually rewarding woodland glade at the southwestern edge of the settlement.

From all the cobwebs and missing curtain rails, Ou Neua's 14-room **Munkham Hotel** (☎ 020-301 2222; r 40,000K) looks abandoned but in fact it does accept guests. Upstairs rooms with timber walls seem slightly fresher than the concrete ones downstairs. Although it's Ou Neua's largest building, the hotel is oddly easy to miss, perched above the lakeside and accessed by a rough unmarked track from the middle of the village.

As you approach the border with China contours become milder and the landscape more deforested, largely replaced by sugar cane. Rumours suggest that in 2012 the Chinese border post might open to foreigners at **Nan Tuey**, where a decaying former casino was reportedly forced to close down once the power supply was cut from the Chinese side.

Central Laos

The area at the waist of the country has traditionally been skipped over by most travellers. But improved roads and several sustainable tourism initiatives, which give you a full-flavoured taste of the 'real Laos', mean central Laos is more open to exploration than ever.

You might not be the first person to trek into the medieval limestone karsts of the Phu Hin Bun National Protected Area (NPA), but it will probably feel like you are and there won't be a banana pancake or happy shake for miles.

Instead, you'll find a diverse mix of ecology, environment and ethnicity that is very different to the north – and as much tough and memorable travel as you like. The Mekong River towns of Tha Khaek and Savannakhet, with their Lowland Lao communities, slowly crumbling French histories and lethargic lifestyles, will be your bases. This part of the country claims the most forest cover and the highest concentrations of wildlife, including some species that have disappeared elsewhere in Southeast Asia.

To find them, you could do 'The Loop' through Khammuan and Bolikhamsai Provinces by motorbike, detouring via the incredible 7km-long cave Tham Kong Lo in the process. Or trek into far-off Dong Phu Vieng NPA in Savannakhet Province to sleep with the spirits in a Katang village. Branches of the Ho Chi Minh Trail await the most intrepid, or just go forth and create your own trail…

CENTRAL LAOS

HIGHLIGHTS

- Trek amid the gothic limestone karsts, subterranean caves and meandering rivers of the **Phu Hin Bun NPA** (p242)

- Do **The Loop** (boxed text, p252) and experience upcountry Laos; good roads, bad roads, stunning scenery, a big dam and unexpected challenges

- Soak up the colonial atmosphere of the historical districts of **Tha Khaek** (p244) and **Savannakhet** (p254)

- Stay in the remote villages of **Dong Phu Vieng NPA** (p262) and experience life in the spirit forests

- Go off the beaten track to **Tham Kong Lo** (p242) for a boat trip through this astonishing 7km-long limestone cave

Phu Hin Bun NPA ★   Tham Kong Lo ★

Tha Khaek ★

Savannakhet ★   Dong Phu Vieng NPA ★

Climate

The Mekong River valley is always pretty warm and from March to May Savannakhet is positively steaming. It gets cooler as you head east towards the Annamite Chain and Lak Sao, and the villages along Rte 8B can be close to freezing during winter nights. The southwestern monsoon brings bucket-loads of rain from June to October. Far-eastern areas around the Nakai-Nam Theun National Biodiversity Conservation Area (NBCA) also receive rain from the South China Sea that lasts longer, thus supplying enough water to maintain the thicker vegetation.

National Protected Areas

Central Laos is the most protected part of the country with eight National Protected Areas (NPAs) accounting for vast swathes of the region. Access to Nakai-Nam Theun NBCA, and Hin Namno and Se Ban Nuan NPAs, is limited to those with decent Lao language skills and plenty of time and money, but others are easy to get to.

In Khammuan the labyrinth of limestone karsts, caves and rivers in Phu Hin Bun NPA

(p242) is accessible either on your own or on a community-based or commercial trek. Similar treks lead to the sacred forests and animist villages of Dong Phu Vieng (p262) in Savannakhet Province.

Treks into the Nam Kading NPA in Bolikhamsai Province can be arranged at the Nam Kading Research and Training Centre (see p240).

Getting There & Around

Gone are the days when travelling anywhere south of Vientiane involved inordinately large amounts of time and incredible fortitude. These days Rte 13 is sealed and, somewhat surprisingly after nearly two decades, still pretty smooth; congratulations to the road maintenance teams. Other roads have graduated from 'bone-jarring nightmare' status to 'smooth as silk', including Rte 9 from Savannakhet to the Vietnamese border at Lao Bao, Rte 8 between Rte 13 and the Vietnamese border at Nam Phao, Rte 12 between Tha Khaek and the Vietnamese border, and most recently, the road to Tham Kong Lo.

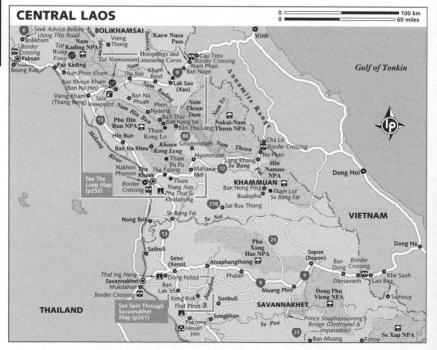

TREKKING IN CENTRAL LAOS

Underrated central Laos is a great place to combine a cultural and environmental experience. Most treks in central Laos are run by either the state-run Eco-Guide Units in Tha Khaek and Savannakhet or the private company Green Discovery, and range in cost from approximately US$40 to US$500 per person (prices drop significantly the greater the number of people in the group). Following are some particularly recommended trekking destinations in the region:

Phu Hin Bun NPA (p242) From Tha Khaek. For beauty, it's hard to beat these trekking and boating trips through the monolithic limestone karsts. Two- and three-day options are available at Tha Khaek's Tourism Information Centre (p246), or four days with Green Discovery (p246).

Tham Lot Se Bang Fai/Hin Namno NPA (p251) From Tha Khaek. Although trekking here is still in its infancy and mostly revolves around the eponymous Nam Lot cave, it is also possible to combine a homestay with walks in the spectacular Hin Namno NPA. Enquire at Tha Khaek's Tourism Information Centre or with Green Discovery.

Dong Natad Provincial Protected Area (PPA) (p261) From Savannakhet. One- and two-day trips to the provincial protected area near Savannakhet are cheap and popular for their homestays and explanations of how villagers use the sacred forest. Contact Savannakhet's Eco-Guide Unit (p254) for details.

Dong Phu Vieng NPA (p262) From Savannakhet. This three-day trek (with a fair bit of road time at either end) takes you to two Katang villages where animist beliefs come with a host of taboos. It's a real head-bending cultural experience, but the transport makes prices a bit steep. Organised by Savannakhet's Eco-Guide Unit (p254).

Apart from on the Nam Kading and Nam Hin Bun rivers, arranging boat transport is more difficult and you'll need a fat wad of persuasion if you want a boatman to take you more than an hour or two in any direction.

BOLIKHAMSAI & KHAMMUAN PROVINCES

Bolikhamsai and Khammuan straddle the narrow, central 'waist' of the country. Physically the land climbs steadily from the Mekong River valley towards the north and east, eventually reaching the Annamite Chain bordering Vietnam, via an area of moderately high but often spectacular mountains. Laid-back and well-connected Tha Khaek (p244) is the logical base.

Lowland Lao, who speak a dialect peculiar to these two provinces, dominate the population and, with smaller groups of tribal Thais, are the people you'll mostly meet. In remoter areas the Mon-Khmer-speaking Makong people (commonly known as Bru) make up more than 10% of the population of Khammuan, while you might see Hmong, Kri, Katang, Maling, Atel, Phuan and Themarou in the markets and villages of the mountainous east.

Much of the region is relatively sparsely populated and five large tracts of forest have been declared National Protected Areas (p238). These areas have become a major battleground between those wishing to exploit Laos's largely untapped hydroelectricity capacity and those wishing to preserve some of the most pristine wilderness areas in Asia. For now, the developers are winning.

PAKSAN
ປາກຊັນ
☎ 054 / pop 43,700

Located at the confluence of the Nam San (San River) and the Mekong River, Paksan (Pakxan or Pakxanh) is the capital of Bolikhamsai Province. Its position on Rte 13 between Vientiane and the nearest border with Vietnam makes it an increasingly busy highway town, and the traffic is expected to increase in the next five years when Rte 10 linking Phonsavan and Paksan is finally paved. But as it stands now there's really not a whole lot to do or see in Paksan. It's possible to cross into Thailand, though hardly anyone ever does.

There's a Lao Development Bank just east of the market, which is also where buses stop. It's a short walk from here east to the bridge over the Nam San and the hotels listed here. There's also a BCEL ATM about 200m east of the Paksan Hotel.

Sleeping & Eating
BK Guesthouse (☎ 212 638, 020-5561 2348; r 50,000-80,000K; ✵) This is Paksan's best budget choice.

CENTRAL LAOS

CROSSING THE THAI BORDER AT BEUNG KAN & PAKSAN

Few travellers use this Mekong crossing between Paksan and Beung Kan. Still, if you turn up at the Lao **immigration office** (☺ 8am-noon & 1.30-4.30pm) they should process the paperwork without too much fuss, though they do not issue visas on arrival. The boat (60B, 20 minutes) leaves when eight people show up or you charter it (480B).

In Thailand buses leave Beung Kan for Udon Thani and Bangkok (infrequently).

Rooms are poky, but they're spotless and the atmosphere is welcoming. Mr Koth is a good guy and speaks some English and French. Take the first right (south) east of the bridge and it's a few hundred metres along on the right.

Paksan Hotel (☎ 791 333; fax 791 222; Rte 13; r 50,000-180,000K; ❄) This new Vietnamese-run hotel just east of the bridge is probably the closest you'll come to luxury, with the 32 rooms all kitted out the same but varying in price depending on size.

You won't have any trouble finding noodle and *fŏe* (rice noodles soup) options around Talat Sao (Morning Market) and there are a couple of Lao restaurants near the junction of the Mekong and the Nam San that are great at sunset.

Viengxum Restaurant (mains 8000-30,000K) About 50m along the street from the BK Guesthouse, this restaurant is known up and down Rte 13 for its top-notch Lao, Vietnamese and Thai food.

Saynamsan Restaurant (☎ 212 068; mains 20,000-35,000K; ☺ 7am-9.30pm) In town, the family-run Saynamsan, at the northwest end of the bridge crossing the Nam San, serves decent fish dishes.

Getting There & Away

For buses from Vientiane, see p114. From Paksan, buses leave from Rte 13 outside the Talat Sao for Vientiane (25,000K, three to four hours, 143km) between 6.05am and 4.30pm, with most in the morning. *Săwngthăew* (passenger trucks) also leave frequently from the market, or you could just hail anything going west.

If you're heading to Vietnam, *săwngthăew* depart for Lak Sao (50,000K, five to six hours,

189km) at 5am, 5.30am and 6.30am, or when they fill. After this take a *săwngthăew* to Vieng Kham, usually known as Thang Beng (20,000K, 1½ to two hours), where Rte 13 joins Rte 8, then change for other transport along Rte 8 to Lak Sao (30,000K, 1½ to 2½ hours, 100km). For Pak Kading, take anything going south.

All buses heading south from Vientiane pass through Paksan about two hours after they leave the capital – wait outside the Talat Sao.

PAKSAN TO LAK SAO

If the hellish 24-hour bus journey between Vientiane and Hanoi doesn't appeal, take local transport instead and stop to enjoy some of central Laos along the way.

Nam Kading NPA
ປ່າສະຫງວນແຫ່ງຊາດນ້ຳກະດິງ

Heading east along Rte 13 you'll come to the sleepy yet picturesque village of **Pak Kading**, 187km from Vientiane. Pak Kading sits just upstream from the junction of the Mekong River and the **Nam Kading**, one of the most pristine rivers in Laos – for now (see boxed text, p81). Flowing through a forested valley surrounded by high hills and menacing-looking limestone formations, this broad, turquoise-tinted river winds its way into the **Nam Kading NPA**. The river is undoubtedly the best way into this wilderness, where confirmed animal rarities include the elephant, giant muntjac, pygmy slow loris, François' langur, Douc langur, gibbon, dhole, Asiatic black bear, tiger and many bird species. As usual in Laos, you'll count yourself very lucky to catch anything more than a glimpse of any of these.

There's basic accommodation and food available at the **Nam Kading Research and Training Centre** (NKRTC; ☎ 020-5571 9522; www.namkading.org; r 80,000K, meals 20,000-35,000K), located on the banks of the Nam Kading about 30 minutes upstream from Ban Phon Kham. A stay is best combined with a trip to **Tat Wang Fong**, a small waterfall in a wonderfully picturesque setting about 30 minutes upstream from the centre. Alternatively, the officials here can also arrange various treks into the Nam Kading NPA ranging from one to three days, and from US$30 to US$90, depending on how many nights and how many people are involved.

To get there, it's possible to charter a boat during the wet season from the Pak Kading side of the Nam Kading, underneath the bridge (250,000K per boat, 8am to 4pm Tuesday and Friday). However, it's simpler to continue east about 15km to the village of **Ban Phon Kham**; follow a blue sign along a laterite road until you reach the river and ask for a boat to Tat Wang Fong. Boats to the research centre cost 100,000/150,000K one-way/return. If you simply want to visit Tat Wang Fong, it costs 150,000K return, including waiting time while you swim and picnic at the falls – bring food and water as the falls are mercifully free of salespeople.

Falls or no falls, Pak Kading is a good place to stop for a meal at the **Bounxou Restaurant** (☎ 055-320 046; Rte 13; mains 10,000-25,000K; ☽ 8am-9pm), where the fish dishes are famous. If you have to stay there is one simple guesthouse directly across from the restaurant.

Ban Khoun Kham (Ban Na Hin)

Located at the edge of mountainous jungle, and with a village centre comprised primarily of hastily erected guesthouses and karaoke bars, Ban Khoun Kham (also known as Ban Na Hin) is the archetypal boomtown. All the fuss is due to the town's status as a base for the Nam Theun–Hin Bun Dam, essentially a 13km-long tunnel being bored directly through a nearby mountain. Despite this, the village only recently received electricity and still suffers from regular power outages.

Ban Khoun Kham's main role is as a base from which to visit the extraordinary **Tham Kong Lo** (p242). The other main attraction is the impressive twin-cataract of **Tat Namsanam**, 3km north of town. The falls are in a striking location surrounded by karst and the upper tier is quite high. Unfortunately, the path and signs leading to the falls aren't entirely clear, and more than one foreign visitor has become lost here. Proceed with caution, or better yet, hire a guide through the **Tourist Information Centre** (Rte 8), just south of the Tat Namsanam entrance. This centre, built by the Khammuan tourism office, wasn't staffed when we passed, but plans to run community-based treks from here into the Phu Hin Bun NPA.

As you approach Ban Khoun Kham from Rte 13, there is a **sala (open-sided shelter) viewpoint** near Km 36. Do not, whatever you do, miss the spectacularly dramatic scenery here.

SLEEPING & EATING

Ban Khoun Kham's main strip, which runs parallel to Rte 13, is home to several nearly identical guesthouses, all offering new but tiny and characterless air-con rooms with cable TV and hot water for 60,000K to 80,000K. Long-standing options include the tight rooms at **Sisouphanh Guest House** (☎ 020-285 5865; r 60,000K; ☒), about 300m north of the market, and the three simple but tidy fan rooms at **Seng Chen Guesthouse** (☎ 051-214 399; s/d 40,000/60,000K), opposite the market. You won't need the help of a guidebook to find the more recent options.

Xok Xai (☎ 051-233 629; Rte 8; r 50,000-100,000K; ☒) On Rte 8 this is about 300m north of the market. In addition to its 20 slightly aged rooms, it should have finished construction on eight new rooms in a Lao-style building by the time you read this.

Mi Thuna Restaurant & Guesthouse (☎ 020-224 0182; Rte 8; r 70,000-100,000K; ☒ ▯) About 800m south of the market on Rte 8, past the petrol station, Mi Thuna offers standard air-con rooms, as well as a restaurant (mains 25,000K to 40,000K) and motorcycle hire (per day 100,000K).

Sainamhai Resort (☎ 020-233 1683; www.sainamhairesort.com; fan/air-con 100,000/130,000K; ☒) The resort is outside of town, and comprises 12 semidetached bungalows at the edge of the Nam Hai (Hai River). There's an attached restaurant (mains 15,000K to 30,000K), and motorcycles (per day 80,000K) and bicycles (per day 30,000) are available for hire. It's really the only place in town with any character. The resort is 3km east of Rte 8; follow the sign near the junction of Rte 8 and the road that borders the Theun Hin Bun dam housing compound at the east end of town, or via a turn-off a few kilometres down the road that leads to Tham Kong Lo. They'll pick you up for free at the *săwngthăew* station if you call ahead.

For food, **Dokkhoun Restaurant** (☎ 020-246 9811; mains 8000-35,000K; ☽ 7am-10pm), opposite Sisouphanh Guest House, serves decent Lao food.

GETTING THERE & AWAY

If you're in Tha Khaek there's a single daily 7.30am departure for Ban Khoun Kham (50,000K, three to four hours). Alternatively, if you're starting your journey in Tha Khaek or Vientiane, another option is to simply hop on any north or southbound bus and get off at Vieng Kham (also known as Thang Beng), at the junction of Rtes 13 and 8, and continue by *săwngthǎew* (20,000K, 7am to 5pm, one hour) to Ban Khoun Kham.

All transport along Rte 8 stops in Ban Khoun Kham, including buses for Vientiane (40,000K) and Tha Khaek (40,000K, three hours, 143km), both of which you're more likely to catch in the morning. Later in the day you'll need to take any of the semiregular *săwngthǎew* to Vieng Kham (Thang Beng; 20,000K, 7am to 5pm) or if you're bound for the Vietnam border, Lak Sao (20,000K, 7am to 5pm) – both about one hour from Ban Khoun Kham – and change. To Tham Kong Lo, *săwngthǎew* leave at 10am, 1pm and 3.30pm (50,000K), taking about one hour. For *săwngthǎew* from Tham Kong Lo, see p243.

Phu Hin Bun NPA
ປ່າສະຫງວນແຫ່ງຊາດພູຫິນບູນ

The Phu Hin Bun NPA is a huge (1580 sq km) wilderness area of turquoise streams, monsoon forests and striking karst topography across central Khammuan. It was made a protected area in 1993 and it's no overstatement to say this is some of the most breathtaking country in the region. Passing through on foot or by boat it's hard not to feel awestruck by the very scale of the limestone cliffs that rise almost vertically for hundreds of metres into the sky. Flora clings to the cracks in the cliff face, at once wonderfully isolated and desperately exposed.

Although much of the NPA is inaccessible by road, local people have reduced the numbers of key forest-dependent species through hunting and logging. Despite this, the area remains home to the endangered Douc langur, François' langur and several other primate species, as well as elephants, tigers and a variety of rare species of deer.

A trip out to **Tham Kong Lo** (see p246) will give you a taste of what the NPA has to offer. But there are two better ways to really get into this area of almost mythical gothic peaks and snaking streams.

Khammuan Province runs five different community-based treks (see the boxed text, p239) of varying lengths into the NPA. From Tha Khaek, the popular two-day trip (1,200,000K for one person, 600,000K each for two, 550,000K for three to five) into the Phu Hin Bun is especially good. The route includes plenty of karst scenery, a walk through Tham Pa Chan, accommodation in a village and four different swimming locations, including

the stunning **Khoun Kong Leng** (aka the Blue Lagoon; see p250).

Although the prices aren't cheap (a result of the centre now being self-sufficient after several years of NGO subsidies) these treks were designed to bring tourist dollars into some of the poorest parts of Laos and they do; we highly recommend them. Bookings can be made through the **Tourist Information Centre** (☎ 030-530 0503; Th Vientiane; ⏰ 8am-5pm) in Tha Khaek (p246).

With a little more time and money **Green Discovery** (p246) offers similar treks plus one very tempting four-day kayaking trip between spectacularly sheer cliffs, as the Nam Hin Bun follows a large anticlockwise arc towards the Mekong (US$453 per person).

Tham Kong Lo
ຖ້ຳລອດກອງລໍ

Imagine a river disappearing at the edge of a monolithic limestone mountain and running 7km through a pitch-black, winding cave and you'll start to get an idea of **Tham Kong Lo**, truly one of the natural wonders of Laos. Pronounced *thàm kɑwng láw*, the cave-cum-tunnel is quite awesome – up to 100m wide in some places and almost as high. It takes a motorised canoe nearly an hour to pass through.

Boat pilots hired for the journey can lead visitors to natural *thâat* (stupas) that are actually groups of glittering stalagmites in a dry cavern branching off the main tunnel. Be sure to bring a torch (flashlight) and wear rubber sandals; the gravel in the riverbed is sharp and it's usually necessary to disembark and wade at several shallow points.

Besides snaking through the tunnel, the Nam Hin Bun meanders through some spectacular scenery – gothic mountains and cliffs of jagged black karst. Amazingly, a fair number of hardy trees have managed to take root on the cliffs. Keep an eye out for sago palms that have attained rare heights of more than 2m; in more accessible places these slow-growing trees have been dug up and sold to landscape gardeners in Thailand.

It costs 100,000K per boat for the return trip (about 2½ hours, maximum four people) through the cave, including a short stop on the far side. Cave entrance costs 5000K and there's a 5000K parking fee.

Since the sealing of the road to Tham Kong Lo, Khammuan Province has put together a day trip (700,000/750,000/800,000/1,400,000K per person in a group of four/three/two/alone) to the cave. Bookings can be made through the **Tourist Information Centre** (☎ 030-530 0503; Th Vientiane; ✆ 8am-5pm) in Tha Khaek (p246).

SLEEPING & EATING

Auberges Sala Hinboun (☎ 020-7775 5220; www.salalao .com; r incl breakfast 240,000-300,000K) At the edge of Phon Nyaeng on the banks of the Nam Hin Bun just past Km 9, Auberges Sala Hinboun has 12 comfortable but slightly overpriced Lao-style rooms with hot-water bathrooms and balconies; those with river views are the biggest and most expensive. Lao and Western dishes are available for about 15,000K to 40,000K, although you need to order in advance. If you can afford it, this is the best place to stay in the area.

Sala Kong Lor (☎ 020-7776 1846; www.salalao.com; r 50,000-250,000K) In Ban Tiou, about 3km closer to Ban Kong Lo, the same outfit runs Sala Kong Lor, where in addition to the somewhat aged original rooms, an additional six riverside bungalows were being built during our visit.

At the outskirts of Ban Kong Lo, the first place you'll come to is **Saylomyen Guest House** (☎ 020-7775 5216; r 40,000-80,000K), a handful of basic but tidy fan-cooled rooms and a basic restaurant looked after by a friendly local family. Across the way, **Chantha Guest House** (☎ 020-210 0002; r 80,000K) features 16 more modern rooms in a two-storey Swiss-lodgelike structure.

In the mazelike village of Ban Kong Lo, wonderfully named **Enjoy Boy Guesthouse** (☎ 020-7776 4896; r 80,000K) consists of two fan-cooled rooms near the Nam Hin Bun. Alternatively, say the word **'homestay'** (50,000K per person, incl dinner & breakfast) and you'll be hooked up with a family somewhere in the village. Homestay accommodation is also available on the opposite side of the cave, in Ban Na Tan and the prettier Ban Phon Kham, and costs 50,000K per person, including meals. Both villages are within walking distance of the drink stalls where the boats terminate; Ban Na Tan is a 2km walk along the left fork, and Ban Phon Kham is the second village you'll come to after about 1km along the right fork. The drink vendors are more than happy to point you in the right direction. For more on homestays, see the boxed text, p45.

Located just outside the entrance to the cave and run by the same people as the identically named guesthouse in Ban Khoun Kham, **Mithuna Restaurant** (mains 25,000-40,000K;

✆ 7am-8pm) serves a short menu of Lao and Western-style dishes.

GETTING THERE & AWAY

The 50km road from Ban Khoun Kham to Ban Kong Lo has been finished, making the former boat trip obsolete, and now getting to Kong Lo is an easy one-hour motorbike ride or *săwngthăew*. For departure times from Ban Khoun Kham, see p241. From Ban Kong Lo *săwngthăew* to Ban Khoun Kham (50,000K) depart at 6.30am, 7.30am and 3pm. Between 8am and 11am there are infrequent departures when there are enough people.

Tha Bak
ບ້ານທ່າບັກ

About 18km east of Ban Khoun Kham, Tha Bak sits near the confluence of the Nam Kading and Nam Theun rivers. The town itself is pretty, and pretty quiet; the real reason to stop is to take photos of the river or get out on the incredible **bomb boats**. The name is slightly misleading, as the boats are made out of huge missile-shaped drop tanks that carried fuel for jets operating overhead during the 1960s and '70s. Empty tanks were sometimes dropped and those that weren't damaged when they hit the deck have been turned into boats.

If you fancy a spin in a bomb boat just head down to the riverbank at the east end of the bridge and negotiate a price.

LAK SAO
ຫລັກຊາວ

☎ 054 / pop 31,400

While the forest, mountain and karst scenery along the upper stretches of Rte 8 on the way to Lak Sao (Lak Xao; literally, Kilometre 20) is strikingly beautiful, the town itself is a disappointment. In the eastern reaches of Bolikhamsai Province near the Vietnam border, Lak Sao is a frontier boomtown that has grown rapidly as the headquarters for logging operations that continue to decimate surrounding forests. And while it's the nearest real town to the border, that border is still 32km away – raising some good questions about why it's called 'Kilometre 20'.

Information

Lao Development Bank (Rte 8B) Located near the market, this bank changes Thai baht, US dollars, UK pounds and Vietnamese dong.

Post office (cnr Rte 8 & Rte 8B)

CENTRAL LAOS

CROSSING THE VIETNAMESE BORDER AT CAU TREO & NAM PHAO

The **Nam Phao (Laos)/Cau Treo (Vietnam) border** (🕐 7am-4.30pm) is at the Kaew Neua Pass, 36km from Lak Sao. *Săwngthăew* (20,000K, 45 minutes) leave every hour or so from Lak Sao market and drop passengers at the typically relaxed Lao border post. There is an exchange booth on the Lao side, though the rates aren't generous. You'll need to have your Vietnamese visa arranged in advance. Laos issues 30-day visas at the border; for details on Lao visas, see p328.

Inconveniently, the Vietnam border post is another 1km up the road, and once you pass this you'll be welcomed by an assortment of piranhas masquerading as transport to Vinh. Contrary to their claims, a minibus to Vinh doesn't cost US$30 per person – about US$5 for a seat is more reasonable, though you'll do very well to get that price. A metered taxi costs US$35 to US$40 while a motorbike fare is about 200,000d. Hook up with as many other people as possible to improve your bargaining position.

You can hopefully avoid these guys by taking a bus direct from Lak Sao to Vinh (120,000K, five hours); there are usually four buses leaving between about noon and 2pm. Once in Vinh you can take a bus or a sleeper on the **Reunification Express** (www.vr.com.vn) straight to Hanoi.

Coming from Vinh, buses to Tay Song (formerly Trung Tam) leave regularly throughout the day (70,000d, three hours, 70km). From Tay Son, it's another 25km through some richly forested country to the border. It should cost about 50,000d by motorbike or taxi, but drivers will demand several times that. Expect to be ripped off on this route (see the boxed text, p337).

Sleeping & Eating

You don't need 20/20 vision to see where this town made its money and it's nowhere more obvious than in the sleeping and eating establishments. There's enough high-quality timber in these places to keep a carpenter busy for several lifetimes. All the establishments are a short walk to both the market and bus station.

Phouthavong Hotel (☎ 341 074; Rte 8B; r 30,000-100,000K; 🖳) The ever-expanding Phouthavong, located a short walk from the intersection of Rte 8 and Rte 8B, now has 49 clean, spacious rooms with cable TV to complement the timber. Very good value.

Souriya Hotel (☎ 341 111; Rte 8B; r 50,000-80,000K; 🖳) Opposite the Phouthavong, this three-storey place has 50 clean twin and double rooms with cable TV.

Vongsouda Guest House (☎ 020-210 2020; r 60,000K; 🖳) About 300m north of Rte 8 along a dirt road, this family-run place has decent, relatively large rooms and a cosy communal area with a fireplace, though you'll be lucky if anyone else is around.

OnlyOne Restaurant (☎ 341 034; Rte 8B; mains 20,000-40,000K; 🕐 7am-10pm) Located near the Souriya Hotel, this long-standing restaurant has expanded, and the pretty good Lao dishes can be enjoyed in a large dining room that has live music in the evenings.

Several **small restaurants** (🕐 6am-8pm) and *fŏe* stalls serve Lao and Vietnamese dishes around the market.

Getting There & Away

Buses leave from east of the market for Vientiane (65,000K, six to eight hours, 334km) daily at 5am, 6am, 8am and 5.30pm. For services from Vientiane, see p114. These buses stop at Vieng Kham (Thang Beng; 30,000K, 1½ to 2½ hours, 100km), where you can change for regular buses heading south or get off at Paksan (50,000K, five to six hours, 189km). Other buses and *săwngthăew* head along Rte 8 to Vieng Kham/Thang Beng (between 8.30am and 5pm) and one bus goes to Tha Khaek (50,000K, five to six hours, 202km) at 7.30am.

THA KHAEK

ທ່າແຂກ

☎ 051 / pop 78,400

Who'd have thought it? In a couple of years Tha Khaek, the archetypal somnolent Lao riverside town, has gone from being a charming but relatively boring place to the base for an ever-growing range of adventure travel in central Laos. Idling attractively on the east bank of the Mekong River 332km south of Vientiane, Tha Khaek means 'guest landing', believed to be a reference to its earlier role as a boat landing for foreign traders. Appropriately,

DOG TRUCKS

If you spend enough time on Rte 8 you're likely to encounter eastbound lorries carrying cages filled with hundreds of dogs. And no, these dogs aren't bound for the local humane society, but rather are destined for dinner plates in Vietnam.

The dog trade actually begins in northeastern Thailand, where stray dogs are caught on a daily basis by what locals and journalists consider a local mafia. The vast majority of Thais actually eschew the idea of eating dog meat, but contribute to the trade nonetheless, alerting dog catchers of stray dogs in exchange for cash or plastic buckets. The trade is technically illegal, but local police choose to look the other way, claiming that enforcing the drug trade or illegal immigration is a better use of their resources.

The caught dogs are eventually brought to Tha Rae in Nakhon Phanom, the Thai province that borders the Mekong River opposite Tha Khaek, where they are temporarily held in pens, graded by quality, before being packed into wire cages and loaded onto a truck. A typical truck can hold as many as 1000 dogs, with five or more dogs crammed into each cage. The trucks then cross the Mekong on a barge, beginning a journey to Vietnam via Rte 8 that can take up to two or three days. The dogs aren't fed or given water during the trip, and many die along the way. We encountered one of these trucks during our research and the sight of dead dogs and the smell of dog fur and excrement coupled with the constant sound of howling and fighting was disturbing. A man we spoke to near the border with Vietnam claimed that the trucks pass every single day. 'Some days I see four trucks,' he added.

Arriving in Vietnam, the dogs can be worth as much as 10 times the price for which they were obtained in Thailand, making the trade highly lucrative. It's estimated that this particular cross-border trade in dog meat is worth US$3.6 million a year.

A four-part investigative report and video on the dog trade in Thailand by journalists Patrick Winn and Pailin Wedel can be seen at www.globalpost.com/dispatch/thailand/091123/eating-dogs-dog-meat-mafia-capture.

the capital of Khammuan Province is a place where you can soon feel comfortable.

Particularly around the old town near the riverfront, the surviving Franco-Chinese architecture, mixed with newer structures, is similar to that found in Savannakhet, with tall trees shading quiet streets and no one seeming in any particular hurry. The epicentre (if you can call it that) of the old town is the modest fountain square at the western end of Th Kuvoravong near the river. Riverside beer shops near here are a good place for sundowners.

It's busier around the markets, and traffic between Vietnam and Thailand is increasing. The population is mostly Lowland Lao, Thai and Vietnamese.

History

Once an outpost of the Mon-Khmer Funan and Chenla empires, when it was known as Sri Gotapura (Sikhottabong in Lao) and was ruled by King Suryavarman (r AD 578–614), Tha Khaek traces its present-day roots to French colonial construction in 1911–12. Evidence of this period can be found in the slowly decaying buildings around Fountain Sq, few of which have so far been restored. The town served as a port, border post and administrative centre during the French period, when a large number of Vietnamese were brought in to serve as administrators. More arrived during the 1950s and '60s, fleeing the Viet Minh movement in North Vietnam, and by the late 1960s Vietnamese made up about 85% of Tha Khaek's population. Their numbers dropped drastically in the late 1970s as many fled another Communist regime.

In the 1960s and early '70s the city also drew a large number of Thais, though these were mostly visiting on decadent day trips to gamble. The fun stopped when the North Vietnamese Army and Pathet Lao cut the road to Vientiane.

Information
EMERGENCY
Police (cnr Th Kuvoravong & Th Unkham)

Tha Khaek Hospital (cnr Th Chao Anou & Th Champasak) Fine for minor ailments or commonly seen problems such as malaria or dengue. For anything more serious, head to Thailand.

THA KHAEK

INFORMATION		SIGHTS & ACTIVITIES			Thakhek Mai	19	B2
BCEL	1 C1	Bounthong Petang Field	9	B3	Thakhek Travel Lodge	20	D2
BCEL ATM	(see 8)	Nang Linly	(see 9)		Thipphachanh Guesthouse	21	D2
BCEL ATM	2 B2	Phetmany	10	D2			
Green Discovery	(see 12)				EATING		
Immigration	(see 30)	SLEEPING			Duc Restaurant	22	A2
Lao Development Bank	3 D1	Hotel Riviera	11	A2	Grilled Meat Restaurants	23	A3
Lao Development Bank		Inthira Hotel	12	B2	Inthira Restaurant	(see 12)	
Exchange Service	(see 30)	Khamuane Inter Guest House	13	B2	Kesone Restaurant	24	B2
Main Post Office	4 C2	Mekong Hotel	14	A2	Local Food Place	25	A2
Police	5 B2	Phonepadidh Guesthouse	15	B2	Night Market	26	A2
Tha Khaek Hospital	6 B3	Phoukhanna Guesthouse	16	B1	Sabaidee Thakhaek	27	A2
Tourism Information Centre	7 B1	Sooksomboon Hotel	17	A2	Smile Barge Restaurant	28	A3
Wangwang	8 A2	Southida Guest House	18	A2			
					ENTERTAINMENT		
					Phudoi Disco	29	D1
					TRANSPORT		
					Mr Ku's Motorbike Rental	(see 20)	
					Passenger Ferry	30	A2
					Phavilai Restaurant	31	A2
					Talat Lak Săam (Sook Som Boon		
					Bus Terminal)	32	D2
					Vehicle Ferry	33	A2
					Wangwang	(see 8)	

INTERNET

There are a couple of places on Th Chao Anou, north of Fountain Sq, offering decent internet connection. Both are open approximately 10am to 10pm and charge 6000K per hour.

Wangwang (☎ 020-569 8535; Fountain Sq; per hr 6000K; ☉ 8am-9pm) Offers internet on a few laptops as well as motorcycle rental (see p249).

MONEY

BCEL (☎ 212 686; Th Vientiane) Has an ATM and exchange booth and can provide cash advances on Visa and MasterCard. There are also BCEL ATMs further east along Th Vientiane and at Fountain Sq.

Lao Development Bank (☎ 212 089; Th Kuvoravong) Changes cash and offers cash advances on Visa and

MasterCard. Another branch changes cash at the port immigration post.

POST & TELEPHONE

Main post office (Th Kuvoravong) Also offers international phone calls.

TOURIST INFORMATION

The excellent **Tourism Information Centre** (☎ 030-530 0503; Th Vientiane; ☉ 8am-5pm) is the place to get all the latest info on the various community-based trekking options, book yourself on a trip and meet your English-speaking guide. The centre has plenty of informative pamphlets and sells maps of the town and province, and can also provide information on everything from where to get online in Tha

Khaek to the town's best massage options. As trek prices vary depending on group size, it's worth calling **Mr Somkiad** (☎ 020-5575 1797) to coordinate with other travellers.

Green Discovery (☎ 251 237; www.greendiscovery.com; Inthira Hotel, Th Chao Anou; ☺ 8am-9pm) has a desk in the lobby of the Inthira Hotel and can arrange day trips to Tham Kong Lo (p242) or multiday treks in three of Khammuan's NPAs.

Sights & Activities

Other than wandering the streets and soaking up the atmosphere, there's not a lot to keep you occupied in Tha Khaek, but if you're looking for something (slightly) more active, the town has an abundance of organised *petang* (Lao pétanque; see the boxed text, p48) grounds. **Bounthong Petang Field** (☎ 020-5561 9331; ☺ 4-10.30pm) and **Nang Linly** (☎ 020-5522 2021; ☺ 4-10.30pm), next door to each other two blocks south of Fountain Sq, let you use their pitches and boules in exchange for the purchase of Beerlao or other drinks. If you're staying at the popular Thakhek Travel Lodge (p247), a more convenient option is the nearby **Phetmany** (☎ 020-9988 9789; ☺ 4-10pm).

Sleeping

Perhaps surprisingly, given it is the nearest big town to the vast Nam Theun 2 dam site, Tha Khaek has a pretty small range of rooms.

Thakhek Travel Lodge (☎ 030-530 0145; travell@ laotel.com; dm 25,000K; r 50,000-110,000K; ☒ ⬜) It's nearly 3km away from Tha Khaek's atmospheric old town, but the Travel Lodge is the clear favourite with travellers for its easy atmosphere, decent food, 17 clean rooms and welcoming staff. The internet, camp-style fire, decent food and coffee are other draws, topped off by the travellers' book, which has the latest feedback on The Loop (see the boxed text, p252). Motorcycle hire is also available via the adjacent Mr Ku's Motorbike Rental (p249).

Phoukhanna Guesthouse (☎ 212 092; Th Vientiane; r 35,000-80,000K; ☒) The English-speaking woman manager gives this place an easygoing atmosphere. Simple rooms without bathrooms are 35,000K, but the pick are those in the newer building at the back, which are bigger, quieter and generally better. The restaurant (open 7.30am to 11pm, mains 15,000K to 30,000K) serves a mix of Western and Asian food and gets good reviews.

Southida Guest House (☎ 212 568; Th Chao Anou; r 80,000-130,000K; ☒) Not far from the riverfront and Fountain Sq, the Southida has clean rooms with cable TV in a modern two-storey building. Most rooms have at least one balcony, but size can vary considerably, so ask to see several.

Phonepadidh Guesthouse (☎ 020-5672 6111; Th Setthathirat; r 80,000-100,000K; ☒) This two-storey complex, in a quiet courtyard just off Th Vientiane, offers featureless but new and clean rooms with air-conditioning and hot-water showers.

Mekong Hotel (☎ 250 777; Th Setthathirat; r 550-1200B; ☒ ☎) The bright blue exterior of this Vietnamese-run, four-storey hotel on the riverfront is impossible to miss. Rooms are well-equipped if a bit dim. Fair value.

our pick Inthira Hotel (☎ 251 237; www.inthirahotel. com; Th Chao Anou; r incl breakfast US$20-28; ☒ ⬜ ☎) This refurbished colonial-era shophouse is easily Tha Khaek's most stylish place to stay. The high-ceilinged loftlike rooms offer attractive touches such as exposed brick, teak furnishings and rain showerheads. The best rooms face the street and have balconies, while the cheaper rooms can be a bit dark. There's free wi-fi for those who need to be online, and the attached restaurant is one of the more consistent in town.

Hotel Riveria (☎ 250 000; www.hotelriveriathakhek .com; Th Setthathirat; r US$40-55, ste US$75-95; ☒ ⬜ ☎) Tha Khaek's largest and poshest hotel offers all the mod cons you'd expect in a hotel of this price range, except perhaps a pool. The river-view balconies in virtually every room are perhaps an attempt to make up for this.

Other hotels include the following:

Khammuane Inter Guest House (☎ 212 171; Th Kuvoravong; r 50,000-70,000K; ☒) Rooms here are some of the cheapest in town, which makes up for the lack of any atmosphere and the dubious plumbing.

Sooksomboon Hotel (☎ 212 225; Th Setthathirat; r 80,000-120,000K; ☒) In a colonial-era police station right on the Mekong, the exterior promises more than the surreal faux–art deco interior delivers.

Thakhek Mai (☎ 212 551; Th Vientiane; r 100,000-120,000K; ☒) Privatisation of public assets in Laos has opened this former government guesthouse to everyone.

Thipphachanh Guesthouse (☎ 212 762; r 50,000-100,000K; ☒) Motel-style place with clean rooms and TV.

Eating & Drinking

Several guesthouses and hotels also have restaurants, with kitchens in the Mekong Hotel,

Thakhek Travel Lodge and Thakhek Mai. A miniscule night market unfolds at Fountain Sq every evening, and the adjacent waterfront strip directly south of the night market features several outdoor **grilled meat restaurants** (mains 10,000-20,000K; ☺ 11am-11pm) specialising in duck (Ms Noy, Ms Kay and Ms Mo) and goat (Khem Kong).

Local food place (Th Chao Anou; mains 5000-10,000K; ☺ 7am-7pm) Head to the busy local food place, alongside the river, if you fancy tasty Lao favourites such as *pîng kai* (grilled chicken) and sticky rice for next to no money.

Duc Restaurant (mains 15,000K; ☺ 6am-10pm) On the riverfront, this place does a delicious *fŏe hàeng* (dry rice noodles served in a bowl with various herbs and seasonings but no broth). There's no English-language sign here, so look for the blue ETL sign.

Kesone Restaurant (☎ 212 563; mains 15,000-35,000K; ☺ 9.30am-11.30pm) With dining in the garden or indoors, this is a popular place serving a mix of Thai, Thai-Chinese and Lao dishes; the ice cream is also pretty good.

Smile Barge Restaurant (☎ 212 150; meals 15,000-40,000K; ☺ noon-1am) One of several floating restaurants set up along the Mekong, the Smile Barge has been so successful it now has a landlubbers' venue as well. It's hard to know whether the tasty food or the karaoke is more popular.

Sabaidee Thakhaek (mains 15,000-45,000K; ☺ 7am-10pm) The classic travellers' cafe, this place has a short menu of decent Western and local dishes, a TV tuned to the BBC, a book exchange and DVDs for sale.

Inthira Restaurant (☎ 251 237; Th Chao Anou; mains 15,000-130,000K; ☺ 7am-10pm; ☺) In addition to being the town's only design-conscious place to eat, the chefs in the kitchen of this hotel puts out some of the town's most consistently solid food. The menu, with its origins in Vientiane's Khop Chai Deu (p107), features everything from reasonably authentic Lao dishes to slightly less authentic pizzas. There's also a fully stocked bar.

Entertainment

Phudoi Disco (☺ 8pm-midnight) Behind the Phudoi Guest House, this place can be a fun Lao night out if you have plenty of energy and fancy getting down to lots of Thai pop, a bit of Lao pop and some cheesy Western classics with the local youth.

Getting There & Away
BUS

Tha Khaek's **bus station** (Rte 13) is about 3.5km from the centre of town and has a sizeable market and basic guesthouses to complement the regular services going north and south. For Vientiane (50,000K, six hours, 332km), buses originate in Tha Khaek at 4am, 5.30am, 7am, 8.30am and 9am, as well as a VIP departure at 9.15am (70,000K). From 9am to midnight buses stop en route from Pakse and Savannakhet every hour or so. Any bus going north stops at Vieng Kham (Thang Beng; 25,000K, 90 minutes, 102km), Pak Kading (30,000K, three hours, 149km) or Paksan (40,000K, three to four hours, 193km). For buses from Vientiane, see p114.

Heading south, buses for Savannakhet (25,000K, two to three hours, 125km) depart at 10.30am, 11am, 11.30am and noon, and there's an air-con departure for Pakse (60,000K, six to seven hours, 368km) at 8.30am. Otherwise, southbound buses are reasonably frequent between noon and midnight. There are two daily departures to Attapeu (75,000K, about 10 hours) at 3.30pm and 11pm. Buses originating in Vientiane leave at around 5pm for Don Khong (75,000K, about 15 hours, 452km) and around 5.30pm for Nong Khiang (75,000K, about 16 hours, 482km), on the Cambodian border. They stop at Tha Khaek between 5pm and 6pm, but you'd need to be in a hurry.

If you're heading to Vietnam, a bus for Hué (85,000K) leaves every Monday, Tuesday, Wednesday, Saturday and Sunday at 8pm. There are also departures for Danang (110,000K) every Monday and Friday at 8pm, to Dong Hoi (130,000K, 10 to 14 hours) at 7pm on Monday, Wednesday, Friday and Sunday, and for Hanoi (160,000K) at 8pm on Tuesday and Saturday.

SĂWNGTHĂEW

Săwngthăew depart when full from the Talat Lak Săam (Sook Som Boon Bus Terminal) into the Khammuan Province interior. Along Rte 12, *săwngthăew* leave every hour or so between 7am and 3pm for Mahaxai Mai (15,000K, one hour, 50km), Gnommalath (30,000K, 1½ to two hours, 63km) and Nakai (35,000K, two hours, 80km). There are daily departures at 8.15am and noon for Lang Khang, 18km short of the Vietnam border at Na Phao (35,000K, 3½ hours, 142km). There

---

CROSSING THE THAI BORDER AT NAKHON PHANOM & THA KHAEK

Crossing the Mekong from Tha Khaek to Nakhon Phanom in Thailand is simple. On the Lao side, the boat landing and **immigration office** (☉ 8am-6pm) are about 400m north of Fountain Sq and boats travel in both directions roughly every half-hour from 8am to noon and 1pm to 6pm. From Laos, the ferry costs 15,000K, while from Nakhon Phanom it's 60B. On weekends boats might be less frequent and you'll be asked for an extra 10,000K on the Lao side, and an extra 10B in Thailand.

In Tha Khaek, Lao immigration issues 30-day tourist visas on arrival and there's a **money exchange service** (☉ 8.30am-3pm Mon-Fri) at the immigration office. In Thailand, it's a 30B share tuk-tuk ride to the bus station, from where buses leave Nakhon Phanom for Udon Thani (regular) and Bangkok (at 7.30am and from 7pm to 8pm).

---

are departures at 8am and noon for Bualapha (40,000K, five to six hours) and there's also a single daily 7.30am departure for Ban Khoun Kham (Ban Na Hin; 50,000K, three to four hours), which should arrive in time for the 10am *săwngthăew* to Tham Kong Lo.

Getting Around

It should cost about 15,000K to hire a jumbo (motorised three-wheeled taxi) to the bus terminal, though you'll need to negotiate. From the bus terminal, jumbos don't budge unless they're full or you're willing to fork over 50,000K to charter the entire vehicle. Rides around town can cost from 5000K to 10,000K per person.

There are now a handful of places around town offering motorbike hire; the Tourism Information Centre (p246) carries a comprehensive list.

Mr Ku's Motorbike Rental (☎ 020-220 5070; per day 100,000K; ☉ 7am-7pm), located at Thakhek Travel Lodge (p247) gets good reviews for both service and the quality of the 110cc Korean bikes. Mr Ku has also put together a relatively accurate map of The Loop (see the boxed text, p252).

Phavilai Restaurant (Fountain Sq; per day 100,000K; ☉ 6am-9pm) has a few motorcycles for hire, and **Wangwang** (☎ 020-5697 8535; Fountain Sq; per day 70,000-110,000K; ☉ 8am-9pm) internet shop also hires motorcycles.

AROUND THA KHAEK
Pha That Sikhottabong

About 6km south of town is the much venerated **Pha That Sikhottabong** stupa which stands in the grounds of a 19th-century monastery of the same name. According to local lore the stupa was erected on the site of a 6th- to 10th-century *thâat* built by King Nanthasen during a time when Tha Khaek was part of a principality called Si Khotabun. Considered one of the most important *thâat* in Laos, Sikhottabong was first renovated by King Setthathirat in the 16th century, when it assumed its current general form. It was again restored in the 1950s and later augmented in the 1970s. It's the site of a major festival each February.

A *wihǎan* (temple hall) on the temple grounds contains a large seated Buddha, constructed by the order of King Anouvong (Chao Anou).

Adjacent to the temple is an interesting open-air museum consisting of nine wooden houses showing the various traditional architectural styles of Khammuan Province.

Tham Pa Fa (Buddha Cave)

When Mr Bun Nong used a vine to scramble 15m up a sheer 200m-high cliff in April 2004, he was hoping to make a dinner of the bats he'd seen flying out of the rock face. Instead he discovered a narrow cave mouth and, stepping into the cavern beyond, was greeted by 229 bronze Buddha images. The Buddhas, ranging from 15cm to about 1m tall, were sitting as they had been for centuries facing the entrance of a cave of impressive limestone formations. It took him a week but Mr Bun Nong eventually told friends in the nearby village of Ban Na Kan Sarng and the cave was named **Tham Pa Fa** (Buddha Cave; admission 2000K; ☉ 8am-noon & 1-5pm).

It's hard to say exactly how long the Buddha images have been there, but experts think they are more than 600 years old. Whatever their age, the cave has become a pilgrimage site for Buddhists from around Laos and Thailand.

Mr Bun Nong, now deceased, became a hero in Ban Na Kan Sarng because the village is now living fat off the fruits of his discovery. Electricity has arrived and a market selling food, drinks and forest products to visitors is bringing much-needed income. And perhaps best of all the new laterite road linking the cave site to Rte 12 has made going anywhere that much easier for the locals. Tourism, it would seem, is a force for good in the case of Ban Na Kan Sarng… mostly. The concrete staircase leading to the cave is undoubtedly practical, but it's hideous too.

Tham Pa Fa is about 18km from Tha Khaek. After crossing Rte 13, continue about 4km and look for a large green sign on the left-hand side. Hand-painted signs lead to the cave along what remains of a **railway line**, a French scheme aimed at connecting Thailand and Vietnam that was eventually abandoned when money ran out in the early 1920s. On the Vietnamese side the line runs right to the border, but here only a couple of concrete bridges remain.

If you don't have your own transport, tuk-tuks will do the return trip for about US$20 depending on your bargaining skills. Tha Khaek's Tourism Information Centre (p246) runs a one-day Buddha Cave trek (250,000/300,000/370,000K per person in a group of three to five/two/alone) and Green Discovery (p247) runs a Discover Buddha Cave day tour (US$30/38/54/102 per person in a group of four or more/three/two/alone plus group surcharge of US$34). Both stop at a beautiful swimming cave, reached via a wet, swampy walk.

Khoun Kong Leng
ຂຸມກອງແລງ

Nestled amid the limestone karsts of the southern reaches of the Phu Hin Bun NPA is the stunningly beautiful 'Evening Gong Lake'. The luminescent green waters spring from a subterranean river that filters through the limestone, making the water crystal clear. The lake is reputed to be 70m deep.

Khoun Kong Leng is named after a legend that describes a gong sounding on the full moon each month. Villagers from nearby Ban Na Kheu believe the lake is sacred and ask visitors to follow a few rules. First, you must ask at the village before swimming in the lake. Once you get approval, only swim in the stream that flows from the lake, near the wooden footbridge, and not in the lake itself. Fishing is banned.

Khoun Kong Leng is only about 30km northeast of Tha Khaek as the crow flies, but given you're not a crow and the road is terrible, it's going to be quite a trip. Head north along Rte 13 and turn right (east) at Km 29

onto a dirt road. After 2km, turn right (south) again, and bump up over hills and through villages for 16km until you reach Ban Na Kheu. It's another 1km to the lake.

Khoun Kong Leng can be visited as a one-day trip, or is one of the stops on the two-day trek into the Phu Hin Bun NPA run by both Tha Khaek's Tourism Information Centre (p246) and Green Discovery (p247).

East on Rte 12

Whether as a day trip or as part of The Loop (see the boxed text, p252), the first 22km of Rte 12 east of Tha Khaek is an area with several caves, an abandoned railway line and a couple of swimming spots that are worth a look. This is part of the vast Khammuan Limestone area, which stretches roughly between Rtes 12 and 8 and east towards Rte 8B. There are thousands of caves, sheer cliffs and jagged karst peaks.

All these places can be reached by tuk-tuk, bicycle or hired motorcycle. Alternatively, the sights can be visited on the day trip (250,000/300,000/370,000K per person in a group of three to five/two/alone) that's run by Tha Khaek's Tourism Information Centre (p246).

THAM XANG (THAM PHA BAN THAM)
ຖ້ຳຊ້າງ (ຖ້ຳຜະ ບ້ານຖ້ຳ)

The first cave is **Tham Xang** (Elephant Cave), also known as Tham Pha Ban Tham after the nearby village of Ban Tham. It's famous for its stalagmite 'elephant head', which is along a small passage behind the large golden Buddha; take a torch (flashlight). This cave has an unusually lively recent history. Before 1956 it was home to a limestone formation believed to resemble an evil monster's head. Various taboos were observed to avoid upsetting the monster's spirit, but when a wave of sickness hit the village in 1956 the locals decided the evil head had to go and promptly blew it to smithereens with dynamite. Soon after this the elephant's head miraculously appeared and village health improved. It's been revered ever since.

To find Tham Xang, take the right fork about 2.5km east of the Rte 13 junction. You'll see the large cave mouth in the distance – just keep following the road. In the wet season you might need to cross a river by foot, or it might be too flooded to cross at all. In this case, try continuing along Rte 12 and turn right (south) onto a dirt road shortly after a bridge.

Back on Rte 12 you can continue east or turn north to the **old railway** and **Tham Pa Fa** (p249).

THA FALANG
ທ່າຝລັ່ງ

At Km 11 (about 9km from Rte 13) a rough trail leads 2km north to the water-sculpted rocks at **Tha Falang** (French Landing) on the scenic Nam Don (Don River). Tha Falang features a wooded area on a stream where colonials used to picnic and, during the wet season, is a nice enough place for a swim. Tha Falang is much more easily accessed than Khoun Kong Leng (see p250) but is not nearly as attractive, especially in the dry season. In the wet season you'll probably need to hire a small boat from near the Xieng Liap bridge to get there.

THAM XIENG LIAP
ຖ້ຳຊຽງລຽບ

Follow the clear sign indicating the track heading south for about 400m, near the bridge over the Huay Xieng Liap and the village of Ban Songkhone (about 10.5km from Rte 13), to the stunning limestone cave **Tham Xieng Liap**, the entrance of which is at the base of a dramatic 300m-high cliff. It's named for a legendary former novice monk *(xieng)* who was sneaking around *(liap)* in the cave looking for the beautiful daughter of a local hermit; he eventually tracked her down at Tham Nang Aen. The cave is about 200m long and, in the dry season, you can walk/wade through and swim in the picturesque valley on the far side. *Paa faa* (soft-shelled turtles) live in the cave, while the cliffs outside are said to be home to the recently discovered *khan you* (Laotian rock rat).

THAM SA PHA IN (THAM PHANYA INH)
ຖ້ຳສະພາອິນ (ຖ້ຳພະຍາອິນ)

With high cliffs either side, Rte 12 continues through a narrow pass (about 11.5km from Rte 13) and immediately beyond a track leads north to **Tham Sa Pha In** (Tham Phanya Inh). This rarely visited Buddhist holy cave is said to have magical healing powers; swimming is not allowed. There's no sign here; look for the faded brick gateway.

THAM NANG AEN
ຖ້ຳນາງແອນ

The last cave along this stretch of Rte 12 is the touristy **Tham Nang Aen** (admission 10,000K; ⏰ 8am-

5pm), about 18km from Tha Khaek. Much concrete has been added to the limestone here though thankfully the large wooden *sala* (hall) that obstructed views of the front of the cave has recently been torn down. You certainly won't feel like you're the first person here, but at least you'll be able to see inside as it's pretty well lit.

The cave's name is also related to the legend of the sneaky novice monk of Tham Xieng Liap. He is believed to have tracked down his beautiful girl at the entrance to this cave before sitting *(nang)* with her and flirting *(aen kan)* – thus it's the Cave of Sitting and Flirting.

The turn-off to the cave is indicated by a clear sign just past a left-hand bend 16km from the junction with Rte 13. The 700m-long track should be passable at all but the wettest times, when you'll need to park and wade across the stream. The pitiful 'zoo' near the entrance will appeal to people who don't like animals.

THAM PHA CHAN & THE NAM DON RESURGENCE
ຖ້ຳຜະຈັນ/ຊນນນດໍ່ໂດນ

Further afield is **Tham Pha Chan**, with an entrance 60m high and about 100m wide. A stream runs about 600m through a limestone karst and in the dry season it's possible to walk to the far side. At its western end there is a sandalwood Buddha image in a crevice about 15m above the ground, hence the cave's name, meaning Sandalwood Buddha Cave.

Not far from Tham Pha Chan is the **Nam Don Resurgence**, a cave where the Nam Don emerges from the ground. It's quite a physical marvel to see the water coming up and out from the cave, and the lagoon that sits at the bottom of the tall limestone karst is a beautiful swimming spot.

Unfortunately, getting to these sights isn't easy. They are accessed via a rough road that runs 9km north from about 10km east of the junction with Rte 13. Go by motorbike, tuk-tuk or arrange an English-speaking guide through Tha Khaek's Tourist Information Centre (p246). In the wet season this road deteriorates quite badly.

Tham Lot Se Bang Fai
ຖ້ຳລອດເຊບັ້ງໄຟ

Almost certainly the most impressive, and yet least-visited cave in Khammuan is the

THE LOOP

The Loop is an off-the-beaten-track circuit through some of the more remote parts of Khammuan and Bolikhamsai Provinces. The trip is possible by bicycle, but is best done on a motorbike. Fuel is available in most villages along the way. Give yourself at least three days, though four is better if you want to see Tham Kong Lo and have time to find yourself after being lost.

In addition to providing transportation, Mr Ku (p249) has put together a reasonably accurate map of The Loop. Tha Khaek's Tourism Information Centre (p246) can also provide advice on the circuit. It's also probably a good idea to sit down with a cold Beerlao and the ever-expanding travellers' book at Thakhek Travel Lodge (p247) before you head off.

Once you've got your wheels, spend day one heading **east on Rte 12** (p250) from Tha Khaek, visiting the caves and swimming spots on the way. The 20km stretch north of **Mahaxai Mai**, about 40km from Tha Khaek, is where you'll find accommodation options for this leg of the loop. Just north of Mahaxai Mai there are two basic guesthouses, **Maniphone** (☎ 020-215 8699; fan/air-con 50,000/80,000K; ⊠) and **Mahaxai Mai** (☎ 020-216 4453; r 50,000K). The cement bungalows and restaurant at **Linxomphou Resort-Night Club** (☎ 020-5458 4453; fan/air-con 50,000/80,000K; ⊠), about 15km north of Mahaxai Mai offers another option. Just north of Km 55 is the Rte 12 turn-off to Vietnam and the expansive **Nam Theun 2 Main Camp**, across from which **Phothavong Guest House** (☎ 020-5663 5555; fan/air-con 40,000/90,000K; ⊠) is probably one of the better places to stay along this stretch of The Loop.

Continuing past **Gnommalath**, an additional 5km north of the Rte 12 intersection, where there's petrol and basic food, you'll reach **Nam Theun 2 Power Station** and virtually the last bit of paved road you'll have the pleasure of riding on until Lak Sao. At the top of the hill the road splits at a busy village called Ban Oudomsouk; keep straight for 3km to **Nakai,** where you can refuel your body at **Houaphou Restaurant** (☎ 051-620 111; mains 18,000-70,000K; ⊠ 7am-10pm) and refuel your bike at the petrol station.

The next 23km is a disturbing corridor of pristine jungle on your left and the environmental disaster zone created by the recent flooding of the Nam Theun 2 dam on your right. You'll also start to see successive *bâan jat sàn*, tidy villages created for those displaced by the flooding. Just before the road crosses the Nam Theun (Theun River) via a new bridge, you'll arrive in tiny **Ban Tha Lang**, where a shockingly basic **guesthouse** (r 60,000K), across from the signed Saynamtom Restaurant, is your last chance for accommodation before the very rough stretch to Lak Sao. From Mahaxai Mai to Ban Tha Lang took us about two hours.

After crossing the bridge at Ban Tha Long it's about 60km to Lak Sao along a road that's pretty rocky in places. This stretch is stunning as you drive through the corridor between the Nakai-Nam Theun NBCA and Phu Hin Bun NPA. After 17km keep straight at the junction (the left fork will take you to the Nam Theun 2 dam site). In the dry season this stretch took us about two hours.

When you finally hit the tarmac at **Lak Sao** (p243) you (and your butt) will offer up thanks to whichever god you're into. Accommodation and food are available here, and it's also a good place if you need bike repairs. Riding the 56km of smooth Rte 8 between Lak Sao and Ban Khoun Kham (Ban Na Hin) is like stepping into a video game – the road runs between walls of impregnable karst on one side, into winding hills of deep forest, and crosses the wide Nam Theun at **Tha Bak** (p243) where it's worth stopping for a look at the bomb boats.

Ban Khoun Kham (p241) has a petrol station and heaps of accommodation and is the base for trips into **Tham Kong Lo** – see p242 for details. From Ban Khoun Kham it's about 145km back to Tha Khaek. Good luck!

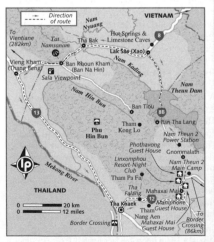

CROSSING THE VIETNAMESE BORDER AT CHA LO & NA PHAO

Despite the fact that Rte 12 is now fully paved, for *falang* (Westerners) the **Cha Lo/Na Phao crossing** (7am-4pm) remains one of the least-used and most inconvenient of all Laos's borders. This is partly because transport on both sides is slow and infrequent, though there are two daily *săwngthăew* from Tha Khaek (45,000K, 3½ to four hours, 142km) at 8.15am and noon bound for Lang Khang, 18km short of the border. If you're determined to cross here, take the early departure as there's no accommodation in the area and you'll almost certainly have to wait a while for transport all the way to the border.

On the Vietnam side the nearest sizeable city is Dong Hoi. A bus does run directly between Tha Khaek and Dong Hoi (130,000K, 10 to 14 hours), leaving Tha Khaek at 7pm on Monday, Wednesday, Friday and Sunday, making this the most logical way to cross this border.

amazing **Tham Lot Se Bang Fai**. Located at the edge of Hin Namno NPA, the cave is the result of Se Bang Fai river plunging 6.5km through a limestone mountain, leaving an underground trail of immense caverns, impressive rock formations, rapids and waterfalls that have been seen by only a handful of foreign visitors.

The earliest record of Tham Lot Se Bang Fai goes back to 1905 with details about a French explorer who traversed the length of the cave on a bamboo raft, allegedly taking 21 hours. During the Second Indochina War, the surrounding area was a conduit of the Ho Chi Minh Trail and locals left their homes and lived in the cave to escape American bombing. The cave wasn't professionally mapped until 2006, and the Canadian/American that led the expedition concluded that Tham Lot Se Bang Fai is among the largest river caves in the world.

Traversing the entire cave involves eight portages and is only possible during the dry season, from January to March. Local wooden canoes can only go as far as the first portage, about 1km into the cave, making inflatable rafts or kayaks the only practical option for traversing the entire length of the cave.

A branch of the Tham Lot Se Bang Fai, known locally as **Tham Pha Reusi**, is dry year-round and is accessible via an alternative entrance, a 1km walk uphill from the entrance of Tham Lot Se Bang Fai. The cave is home to some stunning porcelainlike formations, but until a designated walkway is created, they stand a huge risk of being permanently destroyed by tourists. If you do visit Tham Pha Reusi, be sure not to walk on or touch these formations.

The base for visiting the cave is Ban Nong Ping, a mixed Lao Loum/Salang village about 2km downstream from the cave entrance. Villagers here can provide homestay accommodation, but electricity isn't expected to reach the village until 2012.

Getting to Tham Lot is no easy task, and involves taking one of two daily (at 8am and noon) *săwngthăew* to Bualapha (40,000K, four to five hours) before chartering a *dok dok* (mini tractor) the remaining 14km to Ban Nong Ping (600,000K round trip), 1½ hours). Although visiting the cave independently could ostensibly be included as a (rather time-consuming) extension of The Loop (see the boxed text), the logistics are quite substantial, and at the very least you'd need to speak fairly fluent Lao. It's also worth mentioning that the lack of any tourism infrastructure and the dangerous nature of the cave make exploring it an expeditionlike endeavour that requires both experienced guides and proper equipment. For now, we recommend booking an organised tour through Tha Khaek's Tourism Information Centre (p246), which is in the initial stages of establishing a four-day, three-night trip to the cave (US$145/185/300 per person in a group of six to eight/three to five/two). In addition to exploring the cave in wooden canoes, this includes activities ranging from exploring Tham Pha Reusi and trekking in Hin Namno NPA to fishing with locals. Phetmexay, a guide known by his nickname Ey, is familiar with the area and comes recommended. Green Discovery (p247), in theory at least, also offers a three-day trek (US$135/169/237/441 per person in a group of four or more/three/two/alone, plus a group surcharge of US$147) that involves homestay, camping, exploring Hin Namno NPA and traversing the cave in inflatable kayaks.

CENTRAL LAOS

SAVANNAKHET PROVINCE

Savannakhet is the country's most populous province and is home to about 15% of all Lao citizens. Stretching between the Mekong and Thailand in the west and the Annamite mountains and Vietnam in the east, it has in recent years become an increasingly important trade corridor between these two bigger neighbours. With the luxuriously smooth tarmac of Rte 9 now complemented by yet another Thai-Lao Friendship Bridge, opened in December 2006, the province is witnessing even more traffic.

The population of approximately 926,000 includes Lowland Lao, Thai Dam, several small Mon-Khmer groups (Chali, Bru, Kaleung, Katang, Lave, Mangkong, Pako and Suay), and long-established and growing communities of Vietnamese and Chinese. Particularly in the lowland farming lands east of the Mekong, the villages of Savannakhet are among the most typically Lao in the country.

There are three NPAs wholly or partly in the province: Dong Phu Vieng (p262) to the south of Rte 9, Phu Xang Hae (p262) to the north and Se Ban Nuan straddling the border with Salavan Province. Eastern Savannakhet is a good place to see remnants of the Ho Chi Minh Trail (p263), the primary supply route to South Vietnam for the North Vietnamese Army during the Second Indochina War. It is also a major gateway for visitors arriving from Vietnam via Lao Bao.

SAVANNAKHET

ສະຫວັນນະເຂດ

☎ 041 / pop 139,000

The slowly crumbling colonial-era buildings of Savannakhet serve as reminders of the importance the French attached to what was their largest trading and administrative centre south of Vientiane. These days the city's riverside centre retains a languid ambience, with tall trees shading French-era buildings that are unfailingly appealing despite their evermore forlorn appearance. Unfortunately, many of these buildings will be lost in the coming years; the government is unsentimental about such colonial reminders and is unlikely to start spending money on their upkeep.

While central Savannakhet can seem like the land that time forgot, change has come since Laos's second bridge across the Mekong was opened in late 2006. The city's traditional role as a hub of trade between Vietnam and Thailand has grown, while the busy riverfront has become much slower. Which is a pity, because the trucks, customs office, overloaded merchants, labourers playing *petang* between jobs, food and drink stalls and general hubbub of the border was one of the most attractive aspects of the city. That's progress.

Outside the centre, Savannakhet (officially known as Muang Khanthabuli but more commonly known simply as Savan) is growing fast. The large and lively **Talat Savan Xai** (Th Sisavangvong; ◷ 7am-5pm), north of the centre near the bus terminal, is the centre of much of the city's commerce.

Savannakhet is on a simple north–south grid and although large, is pretty easy to navigate on foot.

Information

EMERGENCY

Police (☎ 212 069; Th Makhaveha)
Provincial Hospital (☎ 212 717; Th Khanthabuli)

INTERNET ACCESS

There are several internet cafes along the west side of Th Ratsavongseuk between Th Sutthanu and Th Chao Kim; most are open from about 8am to 10pm and charge 4000K per hour.

MONEY

BCEL Bank (☎ 212 722; Th Ratsavongseuk) Has an ATM and exchange booth, and can provide cash advances on Visa or MasterCard.
Lao Development Bank (☎ 212 226; Th Udomsin) Exchanges cash and can provide cash advances on Visa or MasterCard.
Phongsavanh Bank (☎ 300 888; Th Ratsavongseuk; ◷ 8.30am-4pm Mon-Fri, 8.30-11.30am Sat) Limited to cash exchange.

POST & TELEPHONE

Post office (☎ 214 817; Th Khanthabuli) For calls, use an internet cafe instead.

TOURIST INFORMATION

Tourist information in Savannakhet is plentiful and professional, and is provided in two locations. The **Tourist Information Centre** (☎ 212 755; Th Si Muang; ◷ 8am-noon & 1-4pm Mon-Fri) has English-speaking staff who can provide advice as well as a variety of informative pamphlets on everything from local food to self-guided day trips in the area. Nearby, the **Eco-Guide Unit** (☎ 214

SAVANNAKHET

CENTRAL LAOS

INFORMATION
BCEL Bank	1 C2
Eco-Guide Unit	2 B4
Exchange Office	(see 42)
Internet Cafes	3 C3
Lao Development Bank	4 C2
Phongsavanh Bank	5 C2
Police	6 B4
Post Office	7 B4
Provincial Hospital	8 B5
Savanbanhao Tourism Co	(see 30)
SK Travel & Tour	9 B2
Thai Consulate	10 B2
Tourist Information Centre	11 B4
Vietnamese consulate	12 D3

SIGHTS & ACTIVITIES
Herbal Sauna	13 C3
Musee des Dinosaures	14 B2
Red Cross	15 B3
Savannakhet Provincial Museum	16 B4
Wat Rattanalangsi	17 C3
Wat Sainyaphum	18 B3

SLEEPING
Boualuang Hotel	19 C5
Daosavanh Resort & Spa Hotel	20 B5
Hoongtip Hotel	21 B2
Leena Guesthouse	22 C3
Lelavade Guest House	23 D2
Nanhai Hotel	24 C2
Nongsoda Guest House	25 B2
Phonepaseud Hotel	26 D2
Phonevilay Hotel	27 C5
Saisouk Guesthouse	28 C4
Salasavan Guest House	29 B4
Savanbanhao Hotel	30 C3
Sayamungkhun Guest House	31 C4
Souannavong Guesthouse	32 C3

EATING
Baguette Vendors	33 C3
Cafe Anakot	(see 13)
Café Chez Boune	34 C2
Dao Savanh	35 B4
Khao Piak Nang Noy	(see 1)
Lao Derm Savan	36 B3
Local Breakfast Corner	37 C3
Riverside Snack and Drink Vendors	38 B3
Savan Restaurant	39 C5

DRINKING
Khanhom Khao	40 C4

TRANSPORT
Lao Airlines	41 D4
Pier for Passenger Ferry to Mukdahan	42 B4

CROSSING THE THAI BORDER AT MUKDAHAN & SAVANNAKHET

Since the construction of the Second Thai-Lao Friendship Bridge in 2006, non-Thai and non-Lao citizens are no longer allowed to cross between Mukdahan and Savannakhet by boat.

The Thai-Lao International Bus from Mukdahan's bus station (50B, 45 minutes) departs roughly every hour from 7.30am to 7pm, stopping at the **Thai border post** (☎ Thailand 0 4267 4274; ☺ 6am-10pm) and the **Lao border post** (☺ 6am-10pm), where a 30-day visa on arrival is available for US$20 to US$42, depending on your nationality (for more details on Lao visas, see p328). If you don't have a photo you'll be charged the equivalent of US$2, and an additional US$1 'overtime fee' is charged from 6am to 8am and 6pm to 10pm on weekdays, as well as on weekends and holidays. The last obstacle is a US$1/40B 'Entry Fee', and then the Thai-Lao International Bus will take you all the way to Savannakhet's bus station.

From Savannakhet, the Thai-Lao International Bus (13,000K to 14,000K, 45 minutes) departs approximately every 45 minutes from 8.15am to 7pm. Onward from Mukdahan, there are five daily buses bound for Bangkok between 5.30pm and 8.15pm.

203; www.savannakhet-trekking.com; Th Ratsaphanith; ☺ 8-11.30am & 1.30-5pm Mon-Fri, 8-11.30am & 2-5pm Sat & Sun) provides information ranging from bookings for treks to Dong Natad (p261) and Dong Phu Vieng (p262) NPAs, to bus times and where to hire a motorbike.

TRAVEL AGENCIES

Savanbanhao Tourism Co (☎ /fax 212 944; Th Saenna) In the Savanbanhao Hotel, these guys can arrange tours to Sepon and the Ho Chi Minh Trail and Heuan Hin, and sell bus tickets to Vietnam.

SK Travel & Tour (☎ 300 176/7; Th Chaimeuang; ☺ 8am-4pm) Can arrange air tickets.

Sights & Activities

Much of the charm of Savannakhet is in just wandering through the quiet streets in the centre of town, between the new and old buildings, the laughing children and, along Th Phetsalat near Wat Sainyamungkhun, among the slow-moving, *petang*-playing old men. If you require a bit more guidance, the Tourist Information Centre (p255) has put together a brochure called 'Savannakhet Downtown', which features a self-guided tour of the city's most interesting buildings. The centre also offers guided tours of the historic downtown district.

MUSEE DES DINOSAURES
ຫໍພິພິຖະພັນໄດໂນເສົ່າ

It might come as some surprise to learn Savannakhet Province is an exciting place for palaeontologists. In a colonial-era building, this small but well-presented **museum** (☎ 212 597; Th Khanthabuli; admission 5000K; ☺ 8am-noon & 1-4pm) displays some of the finds from the five sites where dinosaur bones or footprints have

been found. The curators' unfailing enthusiasm is infectious and they're willing to use their limited English or French on you. It's good Lao-style fun.

WAT SAINYAPHUM
ວັດໄຊຍະພູມ

The oldest and largest monastery in Savan, with more than 100 novices and monks in residence, **Wat Sainyaphum** (Th Tha He) is thought to have first been built in 1542, though most of what you see today dates from the 20th century. It's a pleasant place to wander, and the monks may be willing to show you around and practise their English in the process. Look for the workshop near the river entrance – it's a veritable golden-Buddha production line.

WAT RATTANALANGSI
ວັດລັຖຖະນະລັງສີ

Nearly as large as Wat Sainyaphum, **Wat Rattanalangsi** (Th Phagnapui) was built in 1951 and houses a monks' primary school. The *săm* (ordination hall) is unique in that it has glass windows (most windows in Lao temples are unglazed). Other structures include a rather gaudy Brahma shrine, a modern *săaláa lóng thám* (sermon hall) and a shelter containing a 15m reclining Buddha backed by Jataka (stories of the Buddha's past lives) paintings.

SAVANNAKHET PROVINCIAL MUSEUM
ພິພິຖະພັນແຂວງສະຫວັນນະເຂຖ

Despite having moved house to a beautifully refurbished French-era administrative building (the former site was being turned into a hotel at the time of research), this **museum** (Th Khanthabuli; admission 5000K; ☺ 8am-noon & 1.30-4pm

Mon-Fri) offers little of interest for those who can't read Lao. The bulk of the exhibition takes the form of hundreds of photos from various periods of Laos's modern history, none with English captions. In the front yard are a few rusting artillery pieces and the barely recognisable remains of an American-built T-28, the main combat aircraft of the Royal Lao Army.

HERBAL SAUNA

As if it wasn't already hot and humid enough in Savannakhet, there are a couple of places to take part in a Lao-style herbal sauna. The **Red Cross** (☎ 212 826; Th Kuvoravong; sauna 10,000K; ☯ 10am-8pm) offers Lao-style massage (per hour 30,000K) in addition to sauna. The offerings at the sporadically open no-name **herbal sauna** (Th Ratsavongseuk; sauna 10,000K; ☯ 1-8pm) are more straightforward.

Sleeping

Savannakhet has a reasonable range of budget options but little to excite if you're looking for luxury. Most guesthouses are located within walking distance of the attractive old town.

BUDGET

Saisouk Guesthouse (☎ 212 207; Th Phetsalat; r 30,000-70,000K; ☒) Just south of the centre of town, the atmosphere in this airy wooden house is almost invariably warm and welcoming. Rooms come in several shapes and sizes but are clean and some are quite big; ask to see a few. The husband-and-wife owners speak English. Recommended.

Leena Guesthouse (☎ 212 404, 020-5564 0697; Th Chao Kim; r 40,000-90,000K; ☒) While it's a little further from the river, the 40 smallish rooms here are clean and good value. All have attached bathroom, with hot water in the more expensive rooms.

Sayamungkhun Guest House (☎ 212 426; 84 Th Ratsavongseuk; r 50,000-70,000K; ☒) The superfriendly Sayamungkhun has spacious, spotlessly clean rooms (some with a fridge) and an inviting atmosphere in an appealing colonial-era building on the main road, which means front rooms are a bit noisy.

Souannavong Guesthouse (☎ 212 600; Th Saenna; fan/air-con 50,000/70,000K) In a rambling house, the six rooms here are simple but clean, and feature cable TV. Service is cheery and the owner hires out motorbikes for 70,000K per day.

Nongsoda Guest House (☎ 212 522; Th Tha He; r 400-600B; ☒) About 200m north of Wat Sainyaphum, this modernish house on the river's edge has great views from the elevated bar but not the rooms, which are comfortable if a bit dark. The owner hires out motorbikes for 360B per day.

Boualuang Hotel (☎ 300 106; Th Ratsavongseuk; s/d 600/800B; ☒) This tidy, bright blue complex, a few blocks from Savannakhet's old town, offers large rooms with TV, air-con and huge bathrooms.

Other budget places include the following:

Lelavade Guest House (☎ 212 732; Th Chaimeuang; r 400B; ☒) It's a fair hike to Savannakhet's historical district, but the rooms at this bright green compound are tidy and new. The attached restaurant comes recommended.

Phonevilay Hotel (☎ 212 284; 172/173 Th Phetsalat; r 25,000-70,000K; ☒) Phonevilay's air-con rooms with TV and fridge are decent enough, but the dingy fan rooms with cold water are not.

Savanbanhao Hotel (☎ 212 202; sbtou@laotel.com; Th Saenna; r 55,000-95,000K; ☒) In four buildings set around a soulless concrete courtyard, rooms here aren't bad but there's not much on the atmosphere front. All rooms have hot water, air-con and English-language TV.

MIDRANGE & TOP END

There aren't a lot of midrange options in Savannakhet, and only a couple of places worthy of being called 'top end'.

Hoongtip Hotel (☎ 212 262; cnr Th Phetsalat & Th Udomsin; r incl breakfast US$18-25; ☒ ☎) Rooms in the Hoongtip's two buildings have TV (English channels in the best rooms) and minibar but aren't as good as they could be. Those in the old building (US$18) are overpriced; and while those in the new building (US$25) are better, several have no window.

Salasavan Guest House (☎ 212 371; fax 212 380; 129 Th Kuvoravong; s/d US$20/25; ☒ ☎) Located in the former Thai consulate, a well-preserved colonial-era building dating back to 1926, the five rooms here are large and appear comfortable, but don't quite live up to the price tag or the potential this place has as a true boutique hotel. Nonetheless, if you want to stay in an old building in the heart of the historical district, this is virtually your only choice.

Nanhai Hotel (☎ 212 371; fax 212 380; Th Santisouk; r/ste incl breakfast US$25/45; ☒) The ugly, six-storey Nanhai has semiluxurious rooms with decent views, but has all the character of a Chinese business hotel – not much. Sadly, the pool remains (years on) closed.

Phonepaseud Hotel (☎ 212 158; fax 212 916; Th Santisouk; r US$25, ste US$35-100; ☒ ☎) The

Phonepaseud is a bit far from the Mekong, but is easily the best hotel in town for rooms and service. Rooms are spotlessly clean and have English TV, minibar and (in some) bathtubs, while the 'S.VIP' room (US$100) is a huge, wood-panelled affair with a flat-screen TV the size of a small cinema screen. Discounts might be possible in low season.

Daosavanh Resort & Spa Hotel (☎ 212 188; www.daosavanhhtl.com; Th Tha He; r incl breakfast US$66-97, ste incl breakfast US$163-174; ❉ 🖳 ⓢ ⓦ) This new venture, popular with Thai tour groups, is the flashest place to stay in Savannakhet, although don't come expecting a great deal of atmosphere. The riverside location and pool are pluses, but the rooms aren't particularly great value.

Savan Vegas (☎ 252 200-4; www.savanvegas.com; r incl breakfast 2000B, ste incl breakfast 5000-50,000B; ❉ 🖳 ⓢ ⓦ) This elephant-themed monstrosity, 8km from Savannakhet near the Friendship Bridge, is one of four casinos in Laos, and is virtually the sole reason that Thais now constitute the majority of tourists to Savannakhet. The rooms are nice enough, if a bit bland, and as if you needed a reminder that you're staying at a casino, the junior suite windows look directly over the gaming floor.

Eating & Drinking

Compared to most provincial capitals in Laos, Savannakhet has a decent food scene. Local specialities you're likely to encounter include *siin sawăn* (a slightly sweet, dried, roasted beef) and *nâm phák nòrk* (a refreshing drink made from Asiatic pennywort, a green herb).

For breakfast, several **baguette vendors** (cnr Th Ratsavongseuk & Th Phagnapui) along this strip sell *khào jìi sai khai* (baguettes filled with scrambled eggs). There's also a good **local breakfast corner** (cnr Th Phagnapui & Th Saenna) where you can get *khào pìak* (rice soup) and *bạn kụan* (Lao for *bánh cuôn*; a freshly steamed rice noodle filled with minced pork, mushrooms and carrots); look for the sign that says 'B. Lattanalangsy Tai'.

Khao Piak Nang Noy (☎ 020-7774 4248; Th Ratsavongseuk; mains 7000K; ❉ 7am-10pm) Nang Noy sells what is probably the most popular, and almost certainly the richest, *khào pìak sèn* (thick noodles served in a slightly viscous broth with crispy deep-fried pork belly or chicken), in Savannakhet. There's no English-language sign, so look for the busy stall under the purple Tigo sign.

Lao Derm Savan (☎ 020-5554 0348; Th Tha He; mains 10,000-70,000K; ❉ 11am-11pm) The former vehicle ferry is now a floating restaurant serving a solid selection of authentic Lao dishes. If you're dining with friends try *pạa phán míang*, a whole grilled fish served with various side dishes; likewise, try *jẹw* (spicy dipping sauces, here referred to as 'seasonal spicy sauce') and *kôy* (a spicy salad of fish) won't disappoint.

Cafe Anakot (☎ 020-7774 8154; Th Ratsavongseuk; mains 20,000-40,000K; ❉ 9.30am-9pm Tue-Sun) This Japanese-run place has a menu that's eerily similar to, but not quite as well executed as, Vientiane's YuLaLa Cafe (p106). Nonetheless, it's one of the better places to go for non-Lao food, and the Japanese-ish set meals, desserts, drinks and vegetarian options are bound to appeal to just about everybody.

Savan Restaurant (☎ 214 488; Th Khangluang; mains 20,000-50,000K; ❉ 6-11pm) In an oddly romantic outdoor setting with private compartments, this place is all about *sìin dàat* (Korean-style barbecue). There's no English menu but it's easy enough to just point and shoot.

Dao Savanh (☎ 260 888; Th Si Muang; mains 30,000-145,000K; ❉ 7am-10pm; ❉) Housed in a beautiful French-era building, this is probably Savannakhet's most upscale restaurant. The menu emphasises classic French dishes such as *bœuf bourguignon* and *poulet basquaise*, although the execution isn't always up to par. Several set meals and vegie options are also available.

Café Chez Boune (☎ 215 190; Th Chaimeuang; mains 30,000-150,000K; ❉ 7am-10pm) The owner of this attractive restaurant lived several years in Paris, a fact not entirely manifest in the rather uninspiring pizza/pasta/steak menu. Nonetheless, it's probably the best place in Savannakhet for casual Western-style food, and one of the only places serving Western-style coffee.

Opposite the Wat Sainyaphum the **riverside snack and drink vendors** (❉ 5-10pm) are great for sundowners and, as evening approaches, *sìin dàat* is also available.

Khanhom Khao (☎ 020-5552 2649; Th Ratsavongseuk; mains 10,000-25,000K; ❉ 6-10pm) Mostly a garden-style drinking place, fuelled by Beerlao and Thai rock, but there's also a comically mistranslated menu of drinking snacks ('fried habitually drunk big', anyone?).

Lao Lao Der (☎ 212 270; mains 28,000-120,000K; ❉ 10am-11pm) This riverside restaurant, 2km north of the old stadium, is one of the only

CENTRAL LAOS

places in town to offer great Mekong views. The hefty menu spans Lao, Thai and Chinese dishes, but Lao Lao Der functions equally well as a bar.

Getting There & Away
AIR
Savannakhet's **airport** (☎ 212 140; Th Kaysone Phomvihane) is served solely by Lao Airlines, with domestic connections to Vientiane (895,000K, 55 minutes) at 1.25pm on Wednesday, Friday and Sunday, and Luang Prabang (1,045,000K, 90 minutes) at 4.40pm on Monday, Thursday and Saturday. International flights connect Savannakhet to Siem Reap (US$150, 70 minutes) daily at 8.30am, and Bangkok (US$120, 80 minutes) on Wednesday, Friday and Sunday at 9.05am. Tickets can be purchased at the **Lao Airlines office** (☎ 212 140; Savannakhet Airport; ☼ 6.30am-4.30pm) or travel agents in town such as SK Travel & Tour (p256).

The airport is at the southeast edge of town and jumbos make the trip downtown for 50,000K.

BUS
Savannakhet's **bus terminal** (☎ 213 920; Th Sisavangvong), usually called the *khíw lot*, is near the Talat Savan Xai at the northern edge of town. Buses leave here for Vientiane (65,000K, eight to 11 hours, 457km) roughly every half-hour from 6.45am to 11.30am. From 1.30pm to 10pm you'll have to hop on a bus passing through from Pakse. They stop at Tha Khaek (25,000K, 2½ to four hours, 125km). There are also hourly *săwngthăew* and minivan departures (25,000K) to Tha Khaek from 8am to 4pm. A VIP bus (95,000K, six to eight hours) to Vientiane leaves at 9.30pm, or you could try to pick up a seat on one of the VIP buses coming through from Pakse. For buses from Vientiane, see p114.

Nine buses to Pakse (35,000K, five to six hours, 230km) originate here, the first at 7am and the last one at 10pm. Otherwise jump on one of the regular buses passing through from Vientiane. There's also a daily bus to Don Khong (70,000K, six to eight hours, 367km) at 7pm, and two daily buses to Attapeu (70,000K, eight to 10 hours, 410km) at 9am and 7pm.

Buses leave for the Laos–Vietnam border at Dansavanh (35,000K, four to six hours, 236km) at 7am, 9am and noon, stopping at Sepon (30,000K, four to five hours).

To Vietnam, there's a bus to Dong Ha (US$12, about seven hours, 350km), departing at 8am on even-numbered dates. For Hué, there's a local bus (90,000K, about 13 hours, 409km) daily at 10pm and a VIP bus (110,000K, about eight hours) at 10am from Monday to Friday. There's also a bus to Danang (170,000K, about 10 hours, 508km) on Saturday and Tuesday at 6pm; the same bus continues to Hanoi (200,000K, about 24 hours, 650km), but we reckon you'd have to be a masochist to consider this journey.

Getting Around
Savannakhet is just big enough that you might occasionally need a jumbo – or the Savannakhet equivalent, a *sakai-làep* ('Skylab'). Apparently someone thought a jumbo looked like the famed space station that fell to earth, though we suspect that whoever drew such a conclusion was probably on drugs at the time. *Sakai-làep* tend to loiter outside the passenger ferry pier. Trips cost from 5000K for shorter trips to 10,000K to the bus station, for the whole vehicle.

Motorcycles can be hired at Souannavong Guesthouse (p257) and Nongsoda Guest House (p257) for 70,000K to 100,000K per day. The Eco-Guide Unit (p254) provides a comprehensive list of places that hire out motorbikes. There are also a few places to rent bicycles, most along Th Ratsavongseuk, charging about 10,000K per day.

AROUND SAVANNAKHET
That Ing Hang
ຫາດອີງຮັງ
Thought to have been built in the mid-16th century, this well-proportioned, 9m-high *thâat* is the second holiest religious edifice in southern Laos after Wat Phu Champasak. Built on or near the spot where Chao Fa Ngum's forces were based during the takeover of Muang Sawa in the mid-14th century, **That Ing Hang** (admission 5000K; ☼ 7am-6pm) may occupy an earlier site sacred to the Si Khotabun kingdom. The Buddha is believed to have stopped here when he was sick during his wanderings back in ancient times. He rested by leaning *(ing)* on a hang tree (thus Ing Hang). A relic of the Buddha's spine is reputed to be kept inside the *thâat*.

Not including the Mon-inspired cubical base, That Ing Hang was substantially rebuilt during the reign of King Setthathirat

SPIN THROUGH SAVANNAKHET

Muang Champhone (Champhone District) southeast of Savannakhet city is home to several sites that might not be fascinating individually, but together make a fun motorcycle day trip through this archetypal Lao Loum area of scattered villages and rice paddies. Because it involves a river crossing, completing the trip as a loop is only possible during the dry season, between approximately November and May. Before you set out, read the boxed text, p342.

Savannakhet's tourism board has made doing the trip a bit easier by providing clear signs with distances along most of the route. They've also put together a brochure available at Savannakhet's Tourist Information Centre (p254) called 'Champhone', which features a map and brief background information on the stops.

After checking your odometer, head south from Savannakhet to Ban Lak 35, where you turn left (east) on the decent sealed road towards Keng Kok. After 11km turn left (north) onto a laterite road at Ban Khoum; look for the brown sign saying 'Monkey Forest' (similar signs will guide you the rest of the way). About 4km along turn right (east) at Ban Don Dok Mai; the turn is signposted. The first 'sight' is the **Sui Reservoir**, which you'll skirt for 3km until you'll come to an irrigation levee.

Beyond the levee (dry season only) follow the road a few kilometres and turn left (north), following the sign, at the T-junction in Ban Sakhon Neua, then immediately right (east). Soon you'll be in Ban Dong Mouang (Ban Tha Thouang) where you turn left (north). About 400m along here you'll come to the **Monkey Forest**, in a shaded area opposite a bunch of small white *thâat* (stupas). If you've picked up some bananas along the way, get them out and start feeding.

After monkeying around, follow the trail winding into the beautiful sacred forest. Before long you'll be at the Se Champhone for the most challenging part of this ride. After walking across the river to check its depth (or following the tyre trails to see where the locals go), put the bike in first and hit the gas. If you stall, you'll have to get off and push. Alternatively, you could wait for the occasional *dok dok* (mini tractor) that crosses here.

Once across, follow the road about 2km to Ban Nonglamchanh where you take the left fork to **Wat Nonglamchanh** (the sign says 'Hotai Pidok'). The wat is famous for its elevated wooden manuscript library (*hǎw tại* in Lao), which is said to be more than 200 years old. There's also an attractive wooden prayer hall that appears to date from the same period.

From Ban Nonglamchanh continue east about 1km and turn right (south). Follow this good laterite road about 17km to Ban Taleo Mai. Just before you approach the village, turn right at the sign that says 'Taleow Old Temple'. A short path will lead you to **Wat Kao Ban Taleo**, a temple originally built in 1918 and subsequently destroyed by American bombing in 1969.

Returning to the main road, turn right and continue to the four-way junction, proceeding straight and continuing 5km further to Ban Don Daeng. In the centre of the village is **Nong Luang** (Turtle Lake; admission 2000K), where dozens of soft-shelled turtles have been living as long as anyone can remember.

To get back to Savannakhet, ride back to the four-way junction and turn left (west). This road leads about 11km before terminating at a T-intersection. Turn left at the intersection and then right at the roundabout in Keng Kok; from there it's 19km of sealed road back to Ban Lak 35, and on to Savannakhet.

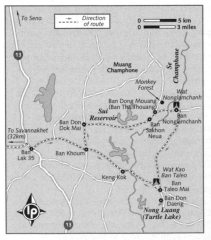

CROSSING THE VIETNAMESE BORDER AT LAO BAO & DANSAVANH

Crossing the **Dansavanh (Laos)/Lao Bao (Vietnam) border** (☉ 7am-7.30pm) is a relative pleasure. From Savannakhet, buses (35,000K, five to seven hours) leave at 7am, 9am and noon for the border. Alternatively, if you're passing this way it's worth breaking the journey for a night in Sepon as a base for seeing the Ho Chi Minh Trail.

The bus station in Dansavanh is about 1km short of the border; Vietnamese teenagers on motorbikes are more than happy to take you the rest of the way for about 5000K. The Lao border offers 30-day tourist visas on arrival and has an exchange booth. Vietnam visas must be arranged in advance, which can be done at the Vietnam consulate in Savannakhet (p319).

Once through, take a motorbike (10,000d) 2km to the Lao Bao bus terminal and transport to Dong Ha (50,000d, two hours, 80km) on Vietnam's main north–south highway and railway. Entering Laos, there are buses to Savannakhet (35,000K, four to five hours) at 7.30am, 9.30am, 10am and noon, as well as regular *sǎwngthǎew* to Sepon (20,000K, one hour) from 7am to 5pm. Simple accommodation is available on both sides of the border.

If you're in a hurry, an alternative is to take one of the various buses from Savannakhet bound for the Vietnamese cities of Dong Ha, Hué and Danang; see p259 for departure details.

(1548–71) and now features three terraced bases topped by a traditional Lao stupa and a gold umbrella weighing 40 *baht* (450g). A hollow chamber in the lower section contains a fairly undistinguished collection of Buddha images; by religious custom, women are not permitted to enter the chamber. The French restored That Ing Hang in 1930.

The That Ing Hang Festival is held on the full moon of the first lunar month.

That Ing Hang is about 11.5km northeast of Savannakhet via Rte 9, then 3km east; the turn-off is clearly signed. Any northbound bus can stop here, or you could haggle with a *sakai-làep* driver and will do well to knock him down below 100,000K return. Going by hired bicycle or motorbike makes more sense.

Dong Natad
ດົງນາທາດ

Dong Natad is a sacred, semievergreen forest within a provincial protected area 15km from Savannakhet. It's home to two villages that have been coexisting with the forest for about 400 years, with villagers gathering forest products such as mushrooms (in the rainy season), fruit, oils, honey (from March to May), resins and insects. If you visit, there's a good chance you'll encounter villagers collecting red ants, cicadas or some other critter, depending on the season; all are important parts of their diet and economy.

It's possible to visit Dong Natad on your own, by bicycle, motorbike or in a tuk-tuk from Savannakhet. However, it will be something of a 'forest-lite' experience. It's better to

engage one of Savannakhet's English-speaking guides through the Eco-Guide Unit (p254). The unit offers six different programs, ranging from multi-day homestays to one day cycling trips, and ranging in price from US$42 to US$189 for one person (prices drop substantially the more people there are). These community-based treks (see the boxed text, p79) have had plenty of positive feedback and the combination of English-speaking guide and village guide proves a great source of information about how the local people live. However, prices are relatively high compared with trekking elsewhere in Laos. Arrange trips at least a day ahead.

Heuan Hin
ເຮືອນຫີນ

On the Mekong River south of Savannakhet is this set of Cham or Khmer ruins (the name means Stone House), built between AD 553 and 700. Apart from a few walls, most of the stones of this pre-Angkorian site now lie in piles of laterite rubble. No carvings remain, the only known lintel having been carted off to Paris.

It's a long haul by public transport and you'd need to be a truly dedicated temple enthusiast to make the trip. *Sǎwngthǎew* (20,000K, two to three hours, 78km) leave Talat Savan Xai when full, usually in the mid-morning. With your own transport, head south along Rte 13 and turn west at Ban Nong Nokhian, near Km 490, from where it's a dusty 17km to the site. Guided tours are also available from Savannakhet.

CENTRAL LAOS

SLEEPING WITH SPIRITS

The Katang villagers of Dong Phu Vieng NPA live in a starkly different world to the Lao Loum of the Mekong River valley. They are not Buddhist, but instead believe strongly in the myriad spirits that surround them in the forest. One of the most important is the house spirit, one of which is believed to live in the home of every village family. Over the centuries a series of taboos have been developed in an effort to avoid disturbing this spirit and as a visitor it is vitally important you don't break the taboos. If the house spirit is seriously disturbed the village is obliged to call a meeting to work out how the spirit can be mollified. Usually a sacrifice must be made – ranging from a chicken all the way to a buffalo for the most serious indiscretions. As the villagers have little money, the unnecessary loss of a pig or buffalo can have a dire impact both socially and economically.

So, when you're in a Katang house:

■ never enter the owner's bedroom or touch the spirit place

■ do not sleep beside a person of the opposite sex, even if that person is your spouse: if you really can't be separated tell the Eco-Guide Unit and they can bring a tent for you

■ sleep with your head pointed towards the nearest outside wall; never point your feet at the outside wall or, spirits forbid, another person's head

■ do not bang on the walls of the house.

While clapping without first checking with the house spirit is also a no-no, the villagers decided this was no fun so they now clear it with the spirit as a matter of course before any trekking group arrives. It goes without saying that these villages are extremely sensitive to outside influence, which is why you can only visit them as part of the organised trek through the Eco-Guide Unit in Savannakhet. Guides have been trained, and the trek was established after extensive consultation with the villagers themselves.

DONG PHU VIENG NPA
ປ່າສະຫງວນແຫ່ງຊາດດົງພູວຽງ

One of the most fascinating treks in Laos is to Dong Phu Vieng NPA, which offers a rare chance to step into a rapidly disappearing world. The park, south of Muang Phin in the centre of Savannakhet Province, is home to a number of Katang villages, where you can stay if you behave yourself (see the boxed text, p262).

The trek involves a fair bit of walking through a mix of forests ranging from dense woodlands to bamboo forests and rocky areas with little cover, or paths only accessible during the dry season (November to May). There's a boat trip on the third day. All food is included and eating local forest specialities is a highlight. A village guide leads trekkers through a sacred forest where you'll see *lak la'puep* – clan posts placed in the jungle by village families. Animals regularly seen include the rare silver Langur leaf monkey and hornbill.

The three-day trek uses local transport for the 180km to and from the NPA, and it's the long trip that goes some way towards explaining the high prices (US$90/116/157/280

per person in a group of eight to 10/four to seven/two to three/alone). Clearly getting a bigger group together makes sense, and if you're interested it pays to go straight to the Eco-Guide Unit (p254) and put your name on a list as soon as you arrive in Savannakhet. Better still, call ahead to see when a trip is departing.

PHU XANG HAE NPA
Named after Wild Elephant Mountain, Phu Xang Hae NPA is a long expanse of forest stretching east–west across the remote north of Savannakhet Province, and its hills are the source of several smaller rivers. The Phu Thai people who live here, like the Katang of Dong Phu Vieng NPA, observe a series of taboos (see the boxed text, p262).

Unfortunately, the diabolical state of the roads means getting into Phu Xang Hae is very difficult. In theory the Eco-Guide Unit (p254) in Savannakhet runs a five-day community-based trek staying in villages and in the jungle. However, in 2009 a grand total of three groups did the trek, most likely due to the high cost (US$250 per person, two person minimum).

SEPON (XEPON) & THE HO CHI MINH TRAIL

ເຊໂປນ/ເສັ້ນທາງໂຮຈີມິນ

☎ 041 / pop 40,000

Like so many other towns that needed to be rebuilt following the Second Indochina War, Sepon (often spelt 'Xepon') today is fairly unremarkable. The main reason for coming here is to see parts of the Ho Chi Minh Trail and what's left of the old district capital, Sepon Kao, 6km to the east.

A trip to **Sepon Kao** (Old Sepon) is a sobering experience. On the banks of the Se Pon, Sepon Kao was bombed almost into the Stone Age during the war. Although a handful of villagers have since moved back, they live among reminders of the war, including the bomb-scarred facade of the wat and a pile of bricks surrounding a safe, which was once the town's bank. If you're on foot or bike, head east from Sepon and turn right just after Km 199; the sign says 'Ban Seponkao'.

HO CHI MINH TRAIL

The infamous Ho Chi Minh Trail is actually a complex network of dirt paths and gravel roads running parallel to the Laos-Vietnam border from Khammuan Province in the north to Cambodia in the south.

Although mostly associated with the 1963–74 Second Indochina War, the road network was originally used by the Viet Minh against the French in the 1950s as an infiltration route to the south. The trail's heaviest use occurred between 1966 and 1971 when more than 600,000 North Vietnamese Army (NVA) troops – along with masses of provisions and 500,000 tonnes of trucks, tanks, weapons and ordnance – passed along the route in direct violation of the 1962 Geneva Accords (see p35). At any one time around 30,000 NVA troops guarded the trail, which was honey-combed with underground barracks, fuel and vehicle repair depots, hospitals and rest camps as well as ever more sophisticated anti-aircraft emplacements.

The North Vietnamese denied the existence of the trail throughout most of the war. The USA denied bombing it. In spite of 1.1 million tonnes of saturation bombing (begun in 1965 and reaching up to 900 sorties per day by 1969, including outings by B-52 behemoths), traffic along the route was never interrupted for more than a few days. Like a column of ants parted with a stick, the Vietnamese soldiers and supplies poured southward with only an estimated 15% to 20% of the cargo affected by the bombardment. One estimate says 300 bombs were dropped for every NVA casualty. The Yanks even tried bombing the trail with canned Budweiser beer (incapacitation through intoxication!), Calgonite dishwasher detergent (to make the trail too slippery for travel), and massive quantities of defoliants and herbicides.

Contrary to popular understanding, the trail was neither a single route nor a tiny footpath. Several NVA engineering battalions worked on building roads, bridges and defence installations, and methods to hide the trails from the air were simple but ingenious. Bridges were built just below the water level and branches were tied together to hide what had become wide roads. As the war continued, the various trails stretched deeper into Laos, and virtually all roads running north–south in the southeast of Laos were once part of the trail.

Today the most accessible points are at Ban Dong (p264), east of Sepon, and the village of Pa-am (p310) in Attapeu Province, which sits almost right on the main thoroughfare. South of here the trail enters Cambodia, where (until March 1970 when a coup toppled Prince Sihanouk in Phnom Penh) it met up with the Sihanouk Trail, another Communist supply route running up from the Gulf of Thailand.

Seeing evidence of the trail, however, isn't easy. Except in the most remote and inaccessible areas, scrap-metal hunters have removed almost all of what was once a huge amount of war scrap. In Ban Dong and Pa-am, a couple of tanks and a surface-to-air missile remain, protected by government order. Elsewhere you'll need to get way out into the sticks and get locals to guide you.

In eastern Savannakhet, Salavan, Sekong and Attapeu Provinces, joint Lao-American teams are still searching for the remains of American soldiers missing in action. Eighty per cent of American servicemen still missing in Laos are thought to have gone down somewhere along the Ho Chi Minh Trail.

CENTRAL LAOS

Ban Dong, 20km east of Sepon, was on one of the major thoroughfares of the Ho Chi Minh Trail and is the easiest place to see what little materiel is left from the war. Most of what was previously scattered around the area has been gathered into the gated front lawn of the yet-to-open **War Museum**. These include two American-built tanks used during Operation Lam Son 719 – a disastrous ARVN (Army of the Republic of Vietnam) assault on the Ho Chi Minh Trail in February 1971. Despite support from US combat aircraft, the ARVN troops retreated across the border at Lao Bao after being routed by seasoned North Vietnamese Army (NVA) troops at Ban Dong. To see the tanks, part of a plane, guns and other scrap, the museum is at the east edge of Ban Dong and is bordered by a baby blue and pink fence. There's nobody looking after the area as far as we could tell, but the gate near the shops is left unlocked and locals assured us it was OK to go inside and have a look.

The dirt road that borders the museum was in fact one of the main branches of the **Ho Chi Minh Trail**. It is still used, and if you head another couple of kilometres south you'll come to a swing bridge built by the Vietnamese after the war ended.

In **Muang Phin**, 155km east of Savannakhet and 34km west of Sepon, stands an imposing Vietnamese-built monument to Lao-Vietnamese cooperation during the Indochina wars. Done in the stark 'Heroes of Socialism' style, the monument depicts NVA and PL soldiers waving an AK-47 and Lao flag aloft.

Savannakhet's Tourist Information Centre (p254) publishes a map-based guide of the area called 'Ho Chi Minh Trail'.

Sleeping & Eating

Ki Houng Heuang (Rte 9; fan/air-con 50,000/70,000K; 🕃) In the centre of Sepon, just past the market on the south side of Rte 9, this hotel offers a handful of comfortable, but forgettable rooms.

Vieng Xay Guesthouse (☎ 214 895; Rte 9; s/d 70,000/80,000K; 🕃) Next door to Ki Houng Heuang, the slightly nicer Vieng Xay has mostly large rooms with TV, air-con and hot water. A stairway bordered by bomb casings leads to more rooms out the back.

There are a few places to eat in Sepon, none of which is remarkable, and all of which can be identified by their yellow Beerlao signs. A small night market unfolds every evening at about 5pm near the market/bus stop.

Getting There & Away

Săwngthăew and the occasional bus leave from outside the market at Sepon for Savannakhet (35,000K, four to six hours, 196km) between about 8am and 3pm, or you can flag down any bus heading west for the same price. There are also relatively frequent *săwngthăew* to Ban Dong (10,000K) and the border at Dansavanh (20,000K, one hour) during the same times, or you could hop on any bus going in that direction – your best bet is in the afternoon.

Southern Laos

An enticing blend of archetypal Mekong River life, ancient Khmer temples, the cooler climes of the Bolaven Plateau and three remote and little-visited eastern provinces make southern Laos a region of stark contrasts for the adventurous traveller. The whole area remains refreshingly raw, but as with other parts of Laos a series of community-based tourism projects have made it possible to experience an authentic Laos far from the beaten track.

The obvious, almost unavoidable staging point is Pakse, the Mekong riverside capital of Champasak Province with a relaxed ambience for a 'city'. From here the Mekong flows south past the ancient Khmer religious complex at Wat Phu Champasak and Don Daeng, before expanding its girth at Si Phan Don, the 'four thousand islands' that straddle the Cambodian border. Among this stunningly beautiful maze of waterways are the palm-lined Don Khong, Don Det and Don Khon, where you can soak up the million-dollar sunsets from your hammock.

Heading east from Pakse you climb to the cooler climes of the Bolaven Plateau, with its picturesque waterfalls and high-grade coffee. Keep going and you start getting well off the beaten track and into the little visited provinces of Salavan, Sekong and Attapeu where minority ethnic groups are still surprised to see *falang* visitors. The adventurous at heart can tackle the southern swing motorbike loop. So whether you're seeking an offbeat experience or are happy just lazing in a riverside hammock, prepare to stay longer in southern Laos than planned.

SOUTHERN LAOS

HIGHLIGHTS

- Soak up the rural lifestyle from the horizontal perspective of your hammock on the laidback Mekong islands of **Si Phan Don** (p285)
- Wake up early for a dramatic sunrise at the ancient Khmer temple complex at **Wat Phu Champasak** (p278)
- Walk and wade your way into the jungles and stay in a remote Lavae village in the **Se Pian NPA** (p285)
- Gaze in awe at 100m-high waterfalls and sip fair-trade coffee on the cool **Bolaven Plateau** (p298)
- Ride out to the wild east of **Attapeu** (p308) and back via **Nam Tok Katamtok** (p307) on **the Southern Swing** (p297)

National Protected Areas

Southern Laos has six National Protected Areas (NPAs), covering habitats as diverse as the riverine forest along the Mekong River in Phu Xieng Thong NPA to the remote mountains of Se Xap NPA. For now Phu Xieng Thong (p275) and Se Pian NPA (p285) are the easiest to get in to, with village-based treks the best way to do it. Dong Hua Sao NPA, at the edge of the Bolaven Plateau, and the wilderness of Dong Amphan NPA can also be accessed with more time, money and organisation.

Climate

The Mekong Valley is hot most of the year but becomes hellishly so between March and May. Some relief comes from relatively soothing river breezes, but not much. The Bolaven Plateau, on the other hand, is relatively cool all year, and from November to February it's downright cold after dark. The plateau also has its own mini weather system, which brings rain right into December.

Getting There & Around

There are three border crossings into southern Laos – one each from Thailand, Cambodia and Vietnam. Once you're in the region, the main roads are smooth and well serviced by buses and *săwngthăew* (passenger trucks). The exceptions are Rte 18 between Attapeu and Thang Beng in Champasak Province, and all the roads running north

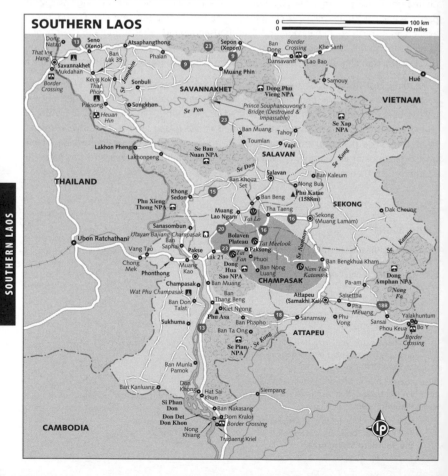

TREKKING IN SOUTHERN LAOS

Opportunities for trekking in southern Laos have really taken off in recent years, but despite the range of hikes available, it remains a raw experience compared with the more developed parts of northern Laos or neighbouring Thailand. Most of the hikes in southern Laos feature homestays with Lao families, a great way to immerse yourself in the Lao way of life. It is possible to organise some of these treks directly with local communities where there is an information centre, but you may struggle without an English-speaking guide to help set things up. The tourism office in Pakse is a useful starting point for the most popular treks in Champasak Province, or there are a couple of reputable tour operators (p268) in Pakse that can organise these treks with experienced guides to help interpret along the way. Costs average about US$20 to US$50 per day depending on numbers, plus transport to access the trek.

See the boxed text, p234, for trekkers' cultural tips, and visit the excellent website www.ecotourismlaos.com for plenty of helpful information. Some of the more popular trekking areas are:

Phu Xieng Thong NPA (p275) Starting from Pakse, take a three-day trek and river trip along the Mekong. The village homestay is much like others in southern Laos, but the hermit nuns maintaining a vow of silence for world peace are a famous fixture.

Se Pian NPA (p285) Striking out from Pakse, half-day elephant treks and nature walks around Kiet Ngong (p283) offer stunning views of the 700-hectare Kiet Ngong wetlands. Longer two- and three-day treks into Xe Pian's forest reach remote Ta Ong villages via dugout canoe. Kingfisher Lodge has knowledgeable English-speaking guides. Also accessible from remote Attapeu is a waterfall trek with a homestay in Ban Mai.

Tat Lo (p301) This picturesque series of waterfalls is an affordable base for some straightforward day-hikes to pretty villages. Costs are very reasonable, at 45,000K per person, and experienced English-speaking guides are available on the spot.

---

and east of Salavan. Cargo boats no longer operate on the Mekong.

CHAMPASAK PROVINCE

Headline attractions include Wat Phu Champasak, the Mekong River islands of Si Phan Don and the Bolaven Plateau, adding up to make Champasak one of the most popular provinces in Laos. Champasak has a long history that began during the Funan and Chenla empires between the 1st and 9th centuries AD. Between the 10th and 13th centuries it was part of the Cambodian Angkor empire. Following the decline of Angkor between the 15th and late 17th centuries, this region was absorbed into the nascent Lan Xang kingdom, but broke away to become an independent Lao kingdom at the beginning of the 18th century. The short-lived Champasak kingdom had only three monarchs: Soi Sisamut (r 1713–37), who was the nephew of the long-reigning Lao king Suriya Vongsa, Sainyakuman (r 1737–91), and Fai Na (r 1791–1811).

Today Champasak Province has a population of more than 500,000, including lowland Lao (many of them Phu Thai), Khmers and a host of small Mon-Khmer groups, most of whom inhabit the Bolaven Plateau region.

PAKSE

ປາກເຊ

☎ 031 / pop 75,000

Gateway to the south, Pakse sits at the confluence of the Mekong River and the Se Don (Don River) and is the capital of Champasak Province. It was founded by the French in 1905 as an administrative outpost and has grown rapidly since the Lao–Japanese Bridge across the Mekong opened in 2002. Trade with Thailand and Vietnam may be changing the face of the town, but tourism has also taken off in recent years as southern Laos emerges as an essential stop on the overland trail through the Mekong region. It's all about location, with Wat Phu, Si Phan Don and Cambodia to the south, the Bolaven Plateau and remote provinces to the east, and Thailand to the west. If you are travelling in the south, it is likely all roads will lead to Pakse at some time during your trip.

The centre of Pakse retains the sort of Mekong River lethargy found in towns like

---

CRUISING THE MEKONG IN SOUTHERN LAOS

For those who like life on the water, there are now two cruise ships plying the waters between Pakse and Si Phan Don. Both are very comfortable, but you're tied to the itinerary once you book. With smart accommodation now available in Champasak, Don Khong and Don Khone, you may prefer to plot your own course.

The luxurious **Vat Phou** (www.asian-oasis.com) was the pioneer, operating a 34m steel-hulled barge-cum-hotel. It offers 12 wooden staterooms with single berths and western bathrooms. A three-day, two-night trip between Pakse and Don Khong takes in Wat Phu Champasak, Uo Moung and Khon Phapheng falls. Fares vary, but start at €403 per person from May to October (when there is only one trip per week), and €528 at other times (three per week).

Newcomer **Mekong Islands Tours** (www.cruisemekong.com) offers a similar set-up aboard a converted wooden cargo boat. However, their cruises are slightly longer, lasting five days and include more time to explore Si Phan Don and surrounding villages. These trips start from €620 in the 'green season' (corresponding to May to October) or from €760 in the high season.

Savannakhet and Tha Khaek further north. Fewer colonial-era buildings remain, but do look for the grandiose, Franco-Chinese style **Chinese Society building** on Th 10 in the centre of town.

The vast Talat Dao Heung (New Market) near the Lao–Japanese Bridge is one of the biggest in the country, famous for its selection of fresh produce and coffee from the fertile Bolaven Plateau. Short day trips from Pakse can be made to Ban Saphai and Don Kho (p275), weaving centres, 15km north of town.

Information

EMERGENCY
Hospital (☎ 212 018; cnr Th 10 & Th 46)
Police (☎ 212 145; Th 10)

INTERNET ACCESS & TELEPHONE
There are several places to get a fast online fix, all charging around 100K per minute or 6000K per hour, including the following:
Skynet (Rte 13; ☸ 8am-10pm)
Next Step Internet (Th 24; ☸ 8am-10pm)
SD Internet (Rte 13; ☸ 7am-8pm)

MONEY
BCEL (☎ 212 770; Th 11; ☸ 8.30am-3.30pm Mon-Fri, 8.30-10am Sat) South of Wat Luang, BCEL has the best rates for cash and travellers cheques and makes cash advances on Visa and MasterCard. Also has ATMs around the city, including one opposite the Sang Aroun Hotel.
Lao Development Bank (☎ 212 168; Rte 13; ☸ 8am-4pm Mon-Fri, 8am-3pm Sat & Sun) Changes cash and travellers cheques in the smaller exchange office; cash advances (Monday to Friday only) in the main building.

ANZ Vientiane Commercial Bank (☎ 254 371; Rte 13; ☸ 8.30am-3.30pm Mon-Fri) ATM dispensing up to 2,000,000K in one hit, but with a US$5 charge.

POST
Main post office (cnr Th 8 & Th 1) South of the town centre.

TOURIST INFORMATION
Provincial Tourism Office (☎ 212 021; Th 11; ☸ 8am-noon & 1.30-4pm Mon-Fri) On the Se Don (Don River) near the Lao Airlines office, the well-organised English-speaking staff here can book you onto community-based treks in Se Pian NPA and Phu Xieng Thong NPA, and into homestays on Don Kho and Don Daeng. There's no charge for this service. They are also armed with all the latest schedules for buses heading anywhere from Pakse.

TOUR OPERATORS
Most hotels can arrange day trips to the Bolaven Plateau, Wat Phu Champasak and Si Phan Don. For longer and more adventurous trips, try the following reputable companies:
Green Discovery (☎ 252 908; www.greendiscovery laos.com; Rte 13) Operates rafting, kayaking, mountain biking and trekking trips. Development plans include a new jungle zip-line and ecoresort in the Paksong area.
Xplore-Asia (☎ 221 893; www.xplore-laos.com; Rte 13) Mountain biking, trekking and kayaking trips around the south, including the Bolaven Plateau, Si Phan Don and protected areas. During high season, day trips run to Wat Phu (190,000K) and the Bolaven Plateau (150,000K), including entry fees and guide.

Sights & Activities
Much more about being than seeing, Pakse's 'sights' are limited.

CHAMPASAK HISTORICAL HERITAGE MUSEUM

ພິພິດທະພັນມໍລະດົກທາງປະຫວັດສາດຈຳປາສັກ

Government-run museums in Laos do not necessarily make for compulsive viewing, and the **Champasak Historical Heritage Museum** (Rte 13; admission 10,000K; ⏱ 8.30-11.30am & 1.30-4pm) upholds this grand tradition. It has a few artefacts and

a lot of dull documents chronicling the history of the province. Once you get past the Lao and Communist hammer- and-sickle flags at the entrance you're in the best part of the museum – three very old Dong Son bronze drums and striking 7th-century sandstone lintels found at Uo Moung (Tomo Temple). The simple textile and jewellery collection

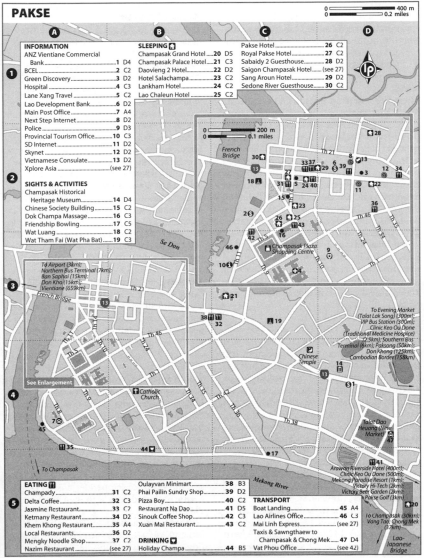

PAKSE

Se Don

To Airport (3km); Northern Bus Terminal (7km); Ban Saphai (15km); Don Kho (15km); Vientiane (659km)

French Bridge

See Enlargement

Catholic Church

To Champasak

French Bridge

French Bridge

Champasak Plaza Shopping Centre

Chinese Temple

To Evening Market (Talat Lak Song) (300m); VIP Bus Station (300m); Clinic Keo Ou Done (Traditional Medicine Hospice) (2.5km); Southern Bus Terminal (6km); Paksong (50km); Don Khong (125km); Cambodian Border (158km)

Talat Dao Heuang (New Market)

Mekong River

Arawan Riverside Hotel (400m); Clinic Keo Ou Done (500m); Mekong Paradise Resort (1km); Victory Hi-Tech (2km); Victory Beer Garden (2km); Pakse Golf (3km)

To Champasak (30km); Vang Tao; Chong Mek (37km)

Lao-Japanese Bridge

SOUTHERN LAOS

from the Nyaheun, Suay and Laven groups is also interesting for its large iron ankle bracelets and ivory ear-plugs, as these are rarely seen nowadays.

Also on the ground floor are musical instruments, stelae in the Tham script dating from the 15th to 18th centuries, a water jar from the 11th or 12th century, a small lingam (Shiva phallus), plus a scale model of Wat Phu Champasak.

Once you head upstairs you'll be experiencing your last five minutes in the museum. Apart from a small collection of Buddha images and forlorn-looking American weaponry, it's all headshots of Party members. Yawn.

WATS

There are about 20 wats in Pakse, among which Wat Luang and Wat Tham Fai, both founded in 1935, are the largest. A monastic school at **Wat Luang** (Th 11) features ornate concrete pillars, carved wooden doors and murals; the artist's whimsy departs from canonical art without losing the traditional effect. Behind the *sĭm* is a monks' school in an original wooden building. A *thâat* on the grounds contains the ashes of Khamtay Loun Sasothith, a former prime minister in the Royal Lao Government.

Wat Tham Fai (Rte 13) near the Champasak Palace Hotel, is undistinguished except for its spacious grounds, making it a prime site for temple festivals. It's also known as Wat Pha Bat because there is a small Buddha footprint shrine.

GOLF

Golf may seem an unlikely pursuit in southern Laos, but swingers can practice their putting at **Pakse Golf** (☎ 030-534 8280; www.paksegolf.com; Ban Phatana; ☯ 6am-6pm). The 18-hole golf course is a bargain by international standards, costing just 1150B per round, including green fees, clubs, caddy and a cart. Quite a technical course, it is located near the Mekong River, about 3km southeast of town. Head east from the Champasak Grand Hotel and follow signs to the right after about 500m.

BOWLING

Friendship Bowling (☎ 020-7786 8886; Th 11; ☯ 9am-11pm) is a bargain for those looking for some pin action. It is 7000K before midday, including shoes, and 12,000K thereafter. There wasn't that much friendship the evening we

bowled, as it was basically empty. Snooker is just 3000K.

GYM

The **Champasak Palace Hotel** (☎ 212 777; www.champasak-palace-hotel.com; Rte 13; ☯ 2-10pm) gym is free for guests and a cheap 7000K per day for visitors to use the weight room. There's also massage, sauna and jacuzzi.

MASSAGE & SAUNA

There are several good massage centres in Pakse if you need to rest those weary muscles after exploring the south.

Clinic Keo Ou Done (Traditional Medicine Hospice; ☎ 251 895, 020-5543 1115; ☯ 9am-9pm, sauna 3-9pm) This professional and popular massage centre has an air-con massage room and herbal sauna segregated by gender. A massage, usually with medicated balms, costs from 30,000K (body or foot) to 70,000K (aromatherapy) per hour. Unlimited use of the herbal sauna costs 10,000K. To get here, take a jumbo east of the Lao–Japanese Bridge. Turn right at the signpost after about 500m and the clinic is just a short distance away on the right-hand side.

Dok Champa Massage (☎ 020-7743 9278; Th 5; ☯ 9am-10pm, sauna 3-9pm) Conveniently located opposite the Pakse Hotel, this is the longest-running massage emporium in the centre of town. Prices are very reasonable for the stylish set-up: body massages start at just 35,000K or 70,000K with oils. Throw caution to the wind and have a body scrub journey for just 200,000K.

Sleeping

There has been a bit of a building boom in Pakse and there is now a cluster of higher-end hotels on the Mekong riverfront. This is good news for visitors, as it means plenty of downward pressure on room rates.

BUDGET

Sabaidy 2 Guesthouse (☎ /fax 212 992; www.sabaidy2tour.com; Th 24; dm 25,000K, r 40,000-87,000K; ☒ ▢) A long-running budget favourite, the friendly Sabaidy offers good travel information in homely surrounds. It can be very busy, so it is wise to book ahead. Four-bed dorms are a cheap-as-chips option, or secure some privacy in a room with shared facilities for just 40,000K. Motorbikes are available for rent, and the guesthouse operates a daily boat to Champasak and runs a tour of the Bolaven Plateau.

Sedone River Guesthouse (☎ 212 158; Th 11; s/d from 50,000/60,000K; ☒) When it comes to location, this place is certainly hard to beat, with a riverside setting on the Se Don. However, it's a tad lethargic and ageing compared with the Sabaidy. Air-con rooms start from 60,000K for a single and include hot water.

Lankham Hotel (☎ 213 314; lankhamhotel@yahoo. com; Rte 13; r 60,000-120,000K; ✖) Another popular spot for backpackers, the centrally located Lankham doubles as a motorbike rental business and noodle shop. Rooms come in size small or smaller: fan rooms are a cheap option, but have windows facing the corridor. Try and bag a larger air-con room at the front.

Lao Chaleun Hotel (☎ 251 333; Th 10; r 70,000-130,000K; ✖) A friendly spot just off the main drag, this can make for that extra hour of sleep on a busy morning. Singles are a little cell-like, but the larger doubles with air-con, satellite TV and hot water are worth considering. This is also a reliable place to rent transport.

Royal Pakse Hotel (☎ 410 192; Rte 13; r US$10; ✖) Located above Nazim Restaurant, this hotel has been recently refurbished, so the rooms are pretty good value given the shininess of the fixtures and fittings.

Daovieng Hotel 2 (☎ 214 331; Rte 13; r 85,000-150,000K; ✖ ⌨ 🛜) Before you ask where Daovieng 1 is (we did), it is out of town on Rte 13. So forget about that one and make for this new place with smart rooms, shiny tiles and free wi-fi.

Saigon Champasak Hotel (☎ 254 181; Rte 13; r 100,000-120,000K; ✖) Vietnamese-run, as the name suggests, this is a convenient base for anyone taking the Mai Lanh bus to Vietnam, as it departs from here daily. Don't be put off by the old building – the rooms are smart and sparkling clean.

MIDRANGE & TOP END

our pick **Hotel Salachampa** (☎ 212 273; salachampa@ yahoo.com; Th 14; r US$14-30; ✖) Set in an attractive French villa, the rooms in the original building are full of charm and character with high ceilings, wooden floors and heavy furnishings. Room 3 has views of the garden and room 4 is an immense suite with space to hold a conference. With a little more TLC, this would be the best boutique hotel in town. Cheaper garden rooms are rather bland by comparison.

Pakse Hotel (☎ 212 131; www.paksehotel.com; Th 5; r incl breakfast US$20-96; ✖ ⌨ 🛜) A reliable French-run hotel in the heart of Pakse, the cheaper rooms are not such a good deal as they have no window. Invest in a deluxe for Mekong River views. All rooms have air-con

and hot water, plus some decorative flourish in the shape of Lao textiles and tribal arts. Wi-fi is free in public areas, but charged at 300k per minute in rooms. Breakfast is included in the lobby restaurant, but by night it is well worth venturing up to Le Panorama on the rooftop, which offers one of the best hotel menus in town.

Sang Aroun Hotel (☎ 252 111; sangarounhotel@hot mail.com; Rte 13; r 135,000-240,000K; ✖ ⌨ 🛜) What it lacks in character, it more than makes up for in amenities and facilities. Rooms are smart, modern and include a fast wi-fi connection. Breakfast is included in some room rates, not with others.

Champasak Palace Hotel (☎ 212 777; www.cham pasak-palace-hotel.com; Rte 13; r incl breakfast US$23-200; ✖ ⌨) No one can miss the vast, wedding-cake style Champasak Palace, on Rte 13 about 1km east of the town centre. It was originally built as a palace for Chao Boun Oum na Champasak, the last prince of Champasak and the prime minister of the Kingdom of Laos between 1960 and 1962. Boun Oum started building the palace in 1969, fled to Paris in 1974 and died soon after. The 115 rooms are good value after extensive renovations in 2004, but it is worth investing in one of the VIP suites (US$60), which have parquet floors, ample space and panoramic views. Rooms in the Sedone building are less inspiring.

Mekong Paradise Resort (☎ 254 120; mekongpara dise@yahoo.com; r incl breakfast US$25-40; ✖) Under the same ownership as the Hotel Residence du Champa, this new riverside resort is a pretty escape from downtown Pakse. Set amid verdant gardens, most rooms have Mekong views. The newest rooms were still being finished during our visit and include breezy balconies and flat-screen TVs.

Arawan Riverside Hotel (☎ 260 345; www.arawan hotelpakse.com; r incl breakfast 1500-6000B; ✖ ⌨ 🛜 🍴) The five-star claim in their brochure is a tad ambitious, but it is one of the smarter establishments in southern Laos. Rooms are spacious and elegantly decorated, including the signature elephant on everything from drawer handles to towels. Facilities include an inviting pool by the Mekong River. Specials at 1000B are available during the low season.

Champasak Grand Hotel (☎ 255 111; www. champasakgrand.com; r incl breakfast 570,000-1,750,000K; ✖ ⌨ 🛜 🍴) Visible from all over town, this 12 storey giant is a smart new addition to the

Pakse hotel scene, despite the somewhat in-yer-face exterior. All rooms include Mekong views and an attractive wooden trim. Free internet is included, plus there is a kidney-shaped pool and fitness centre, available to nonguests at 54,000K per day.

Eating

Chowing down with the locals, especially at breakfast and lunch, is an immersive Lao experience. The restaurant under the **Lankham Hotel** and, just across the road, the **Mengky Noodle Shop** (Rte 13) are safe and popular places for noodles and soup. Mengky is justly famous for its duck *fŏe* breakfasts. Service at the Lankham can be indifferent to the point of being rude, but the soups are worth the struggle. Even better is the spread of **local restaurants** on Th 46, each one serving something slightly different; just wander along and take your pick. The restaurants are open all day.

Just west of the traffic lights, **Phay Pailin Sundry Shop** (Rte 13) sells decent *khào jì* in the morning and afternoon. Self-caterers should head to the market or try **Oulayvan Minimart** (Rte 13; ☼ 7am-10pm), Pakse's answer to 7-Eleven.

LAO, THAI AND VIETNAMESE

Xuan Mai Restaurant (☎ 213 245; Th 4; mains 13,000-30,000K; ☼ 6am-midnight) Popular Xuan Mai serves top-drawer *fŏe* (15,000K; the chicken is best), *khào pún* (white flour noodles with sweet-spicy sauce), fruit shakes and even garlic bread. The owners speak a bit of French and that may explain the 'gleam cheese' on the menu. It's one of the only places for a late feed.

Ketmany Restaurant (☎ 212 615; Rte 13; mains 15,000-40,000K; ☼ 6.30am-9.30pm) A good spot for authentic Lao and Vietnamese food, the Ketmany has an air-con interior which provides refuge on a hot day. The menu includes Western dishes and fry-up breakfasts.

Champady (☎ 030-534 8999; mains 15,000-40,000K; ☼ 7am-9pm) Popular with locals and visitors alike, the Champady has an extensive menu of Thai and Laotian dishes. Set in a French-era building, it's also a friendly spot to sip on some Dao Coffee from the Bolaven Plateau.

Khem Khong Restaurant (☎ 213 240; Th 11; mains 15,000-60,000K; ☼ 11am-10pm) Located just south of town on the Mekong, this is one of several floating restaurants and has a deserved reputation for excellent seafood. Go in a group so you can share several dishes, especially the *pîng pqa* (grilled fish). It also serves Beerlao

in 3L towers, but beware the gentle rocking of the restaurant on a windy night, as you'll feel like a drunken sailor.

WESTERN, INDIAN AND MORE

Delta Coffee (☎ 030-534 5895; Rte 13; mains 20,000-50,000K; ☼ 7am-10pm) Delta does a lot more than 'Coffee' suggests, including a hearty selection of Italian and Thai dishes. The lasagne, pasta and pizzas are strongly recommended, particularly if you've been on a steady diet of sticky rice in the boonies. Owners Alan and Siriporn serve some of the best coffee in town from their plantation near Paksong and raise money to build schools for the children of plantation workers.

Pizza Boy (☎ 212 982; Rte 13; mains 20,000-54,000K; ☼ 7am-10pm) Formerly Van Pisa, this little traveller cafe offers good-value pizzas, some tasty pastas and a smattering of Lao and Thai fare.

Sinouk Coffee Shop (☎ 212 552; cnr Th 9 & Th 11; ☼ 7am-7pm) In a renovated French shophouse this cafe is best-known for its coffee, sold both in the cup and by the bag. The menu includes designer coffees like mocha banana liquor or ice latte peppermint. Snacks include moist croissants and *pain au chocolat* daily, plus less-exciting hot dogs and fries.

Restaurant Na Dao (☎ 255 558; Th 38, opposite Talat Dao Heuang; mains 30,000-180,000K; ☼ 11am-11pm) Fine French dining has arrived in Pakse. Exiled from Vientiane, the family has migrated south to bring their cultured cuisine to southern Laos. Moreish moments include a salmon and sea bass carpaccio, Paksong goose with olives and a five-course menu degustation for 185,000K.

If it's the taste of India you crave, then you're in luck, as downtown Pakse boasts two restaurants almost opposite each other. **Jasmine Restaurant** (☎ 251 002; Rte 13; mains 15,000-50,000K; ☼ 7am-10pm) is the original and serves a good selection from the subcontinent, including tikka dishes and extensive vegetarian offerings. **Nazim Restaurant** (☎ 410 192; Rte 13; mains 15,000-50,000K; ☼ 7am-10pm) recently relocated across the road, easing the tensions between former partners, and has a similar menu of northern Indian cuisine.

Drinking

The rooftop bar at the **Pakse Hotel** is a nice stop for a sunset Beerlao or two. For more of a local touch, check out the riverside bars along the Mekong, to the north of the Khem

Khong Restaurant. Plastic chairs, fairy lights and oodles of cold Beerlao make for a Lao night out.

The popular grungy haunt of Lotty recently reopened as **Holiday Champa** (Th 11; � 7am-11pm), with a beer garden out front, but it remains to be seen if it will recapture its old form.

As the night unfolds, most locals head to **Victory Hi Tech**, a small nightclub on the new ring road. It is loud and dark and not exactly Vientiane, but it does stay open until, wait for it, 11.30pm. The nearby **Victory Beer Garden** is a more relaxed open-air place showing regular football (soccer to our American friends).

Getting There & Away
AIR
Pakse Airport has several domestic flight connections, including daily services to Vientiane (US$118) and several flights per week to Luang Prabang (US$155). There are also international flights to Siem Reap (US$119) and Bangkok (US$132), with several services per week. Be sure to check at the **Lao Airlines office** (☎ 212 252; www.laos-airlines.com; Th 11; � 8-11.30am & 1.30-4.30pm Mon-Fri) a day or two before.

The airport is 3km northwest of town and has a BCEL exchange office. A jumbo to the airport should cost about 20,000K.

BOAT
Like so many others, the public boat from Pakse to Champasak and Don Khong has stopped operating, unable to compete with soaring fuel prices and *săwngthăew* that do the trip in half the time for less money. Any chance of a recovery has evaporated with the new road to Champasak, running along the west bank of the Mekong.

Sabaidy 2 Guesthouse (p270) operates a daily boat to Champasak for those that like life on the water. It costs 65,000K per person and leaves at 8am. It is slightly slower (and a bit more expensive) than taking the new road, but infinitely more relaxing.

BUS & SĂWNGTHĂEW
Pakse has several bus and *săwngthăew* terminals. Most guesthouses and hotels offer tickets to the islands of Si Phan Don, including the boat transfer. Prices are usually around 50,000K to Don Khong and 60,000/70,000K to Don Det/Don Khon. This is a convenient, if slightly more expensive option than the local bus, as you get picked up in the centre

of town. When buying bus tickets at any of Pakse's bus stations, ensure you buy the ticket from the ticket counter or the bus driver and not from any intermediaries out to make some quick kip.

Mai Linh Express (☎ 254 149, 0592-211 211 in Vietnam) operates a daily minibus connecting Pakse with Kontum (118,000K) in Vietnam's Central Highlands. It travels via Paksong (15,000K), Sekong (34,000K), Attapeu (57,000K) and Ngoc Hoi (108,000K) on the Ho Chi Minh Highway. It departs at 7am from the Saigon Champasak Hotel (p271) in Pakse and arrives in Kontum around 3.30pm. For more information on crossing into Vietnam this way see p310.

VIP Bus Station
The **VIP Bus Station** (☎ 212 228; off Rte 13), also known as the Evening Market Bus Station or Km 2 Bus Station, is where most VIP buses to Vientiane (150,000-190,000K, eight to 10 hours, 677km) originate, though they also usually stop in town, around the Lankham Hotel and at the bus offices next to the Se Don. It's possible to take these buses to Seno (for Savannakhet) and Tha Khaek, but the arrival times are pretty unfriendly and you have to pay the full fare. Tickets for the various VIP buses are available in guesthouses, hotels and restaurants all over town; just ask where you need to be when the bus is leaving. This bus station includes the inviting KVT Coffee with air-conditioning and internet access for 8000K per hour.

The other service departing from here is the handy Thai–Lao International Bus; see p274 for details.

Dao Heung Market (Morning Market)
Buses and *săwngthăew* leave the *săwngthăew* farm at the edge of the Dao Heung Market for Champasak (20,000K, one to two hours, if you have to wait for a ferry) and for Ban Saphai (8000K, 40 minutes) regularly between about 6.30am and 3pm.

Northern Bus Terminal
At the **northern terminal** (☎ 251 508), usually called *khíw lot lák jét* (Km 7 bus terminal), 7km north of town on Rte 13, you'll find a steady procession of agonisingly slow normal buses (without air-con) heading north. Every 50 minutes or so between 6.30am and 4.30pm a slow bus starts the long haul to Savannakhet

---

CROSSING THE THAI BORDER AT CHONG MEK & VANG TAO

The **Vang Tao (Laos)/Chong Mek (Thailand) crossing** (⌚ 5am-6pm) is the busiest in southern Laos. From Pakse, *săwngthăew* (10,000K, 75 minutes, 44km) – and some of the most battered taxis (20,000K per person or 120,000K for a charter, 45 minutes) you're ever likely to see – run between Talat Dao Heuang (New Market) and Vang Tao. When your transport stops, walk about 300m up to the green-roofed building, where you'll be stamped out. Immigration is also here, plus an exchange office offering criminally low rates.

Walk through the throngs of traders and small-time smugglers loitering around the border, then another 100m or so to Thai immigration, located in a startling building that looks vaguely like a plate full of purple nachos minus the guacamole. They'll process your entry in short order. Taxi drivers usually wait outside immigration and want about B900 to B1200 for a whole air-con van to Ubon Ratchatani (one hour, 82km). The cheaper option is to walk to the end of the stall-lined street and find a *săwngthăew* (40B, one hour) to Phibun Mangsahan. It will drop you at a point where another *săwngthăew* will soon pick you up for the trip to Ubon (40B, one hour, 40km).

Much less stressful is the Thai–Lao International Bus (55,000K, 2½ to three hours, 126km) direct between Pakse and Ubon. Buses leave Pakse at 8.30am and 3.30pm, and run from Ubon's main bus station at 7.30am and 3.30pm. It is also possible to buy through tickets from Pakse to Bangkok (200,000K, 14 hours), departing at 3.30pm daily or a combination bus/sleeper train ticket to the Thai capital (280,000K), also departing at 3.30pm.

(35,000K, four to five hours, 277km), Tha Khaek (50,000K, eight to nine hours), and, for those of you with plenty of time, no money and a major masochistic streak, Vientiane (100,000K, 16 to 18 hours). The durations of these journeys are very flexible and depend on how long the bus stops in Savannakhet.

There are also a few international bus services from here, although journey times are interminably long. Daily services leave for Lao Bao (6am, 100,000K), Hue (6.30am, 150,000K) and Danang (7am, 180,000K). These 'direct' services usually involve one or two changes along the way, so it makes much more sense to break the journey if you have the time.

For details about buses to Pakse from Vientiane, see p114.

Southern Bus Terminal

For transport anywhere south or east, head to the **southern terminal** (*khíw lot lák pǎet* or 'Km 8 bus terminal'), south of town on Rte 13. The transport might be a bus, but it could just as easily be a *săwngthăew*. For Si Phan Don, there are regular departures for Muang Khong (35,000K including ferry, three hours, 120km) between 7am and 3pm and Ban Nakasang (30,000K, three to four hours) for Don Det and Don Khon. More comfortable are the Cambodian bus companies running international services to Phnom Penh that can drop travellers at Don Khong or Don Det/

Don Khon. Tickets cost 55,000K including the boat transfer. These buses also offer tickets to Stung Treng (120,000K, five hours), 60km south of the border in Cambodia. One *săwngthăew* runs to Kiet Ngong and Ban Phapho (25,000K, two hours or so), leaving around 12 noon.

Regular transport to the Bolaven Plateau leaves for Paksong (15,000K, 90 minutes), stopping at Tat Fan if you ask. Transport to Salavan (25,000K, three to four hours, 115km) leaves regularly until around 2pm and can drop you at Tat Lo. Buses to Sekong (30,000K, four hours, 135km) leave hourly between 7am and 11am and continue to Attapeu (40,000K, five to six hours, 212km).

Getting Around

Using any of Pakse's local transport on a shared basis costs between 3000K and 8000K, but as a foreigner you will need to bargain a bit to avoid being overcharged. A ride to either bus terminal costs about 5000K. For charter, the standard fares to the bus stations are 20,000K (*săam-lâaw*) or 30,000K (jumbo or tuk-tuk).

Several shops and guesthouses rent bicycles, usually for around 10,000K per day. Motorbikes are also readily available through popular budget guesthouses, including Sabaidy 2 Guesthouse, Lankham Hotel and Lao Chaleun Hotel. Prices start at about 60,000K for smaller bikes, rising to

80,000K for more powerful 120cc bikes. The Lankham Hotel has 250cc dirt bikes available for 210,000K per day if you rent for a week, perfect for tackling some of the trails on the Bolaven Plateau or remote roads beyond Attapeu, Sekong or Salavan.

AROUND PAKSE
Don Kho & Ban Saphai
ດອນໂຄ/ບ້ານສະພາຍ

The Mekong island of Don Kho and the nearby village of Ban Saphai, about 15km north of Pakse, are famous for their silk weaving. Women can be seen working on large looms underneath their homes producing distinctive silk and cotton *phàa salóng*, long sarongs for men, and are happy to let you watch.

Like Don Daeng further south, there are no cars on Don Kho and despite the advent of electricity it's easy to feel like you're stepping back to a more simple time. The 300 or so residents live in villages at either side of the 800m-wide island and farm rice in the centre. Believe it or not, Don Kho was briefly the capital of southern Laos following the French arrival in the 1890s, and it later served as a mooring point for boats steaming between Don Det and Savannakhet. These days, however, the only real sight is **Wat Don Kho**, which has some French-era buildings and an impressive drum tower. In the southeast corner of the grounds is a soaring tree that locals say is 500 years old, though 200 seems more realistic. These trees periodically have fires burned inside the trunks to extract a resin used to seal local boats.

The villages of Don Kho are some of the best places to experience a homestay (see the boxed text, p45) in southern Laos. Just turn up on the island and say 'homestay' and the villagers will sort you out. A homestay costs 30,000K per bed, with a maximum two people per house. Meals are taken with the host family and cost 20,000K. In our experience, the food is delicious.

If a homestay doesn't sound like your thing there's a **community guesthouse** at the edge of the **sacred forest** on the far side of the island. Bed and meal rates are the same as a homestay, and villagers will help you make a small offering to the forest spirit to smooth your stay. Just say 'guesthouse' when you turn up and someone will lead you there (it's about a 700m walk). Alternatively, the guys in the

small **Tourist Information Centre** near the boat pier in Ban Saphai speak some English and can phone ahead to arrange a bed. This is part of the Ban Saphai Handicraft Centre, where there are a couple of stalls selling local weaving.

A couple of villagers speak enough English to arrange the homestays, guided tours of the island (50,000K per day, one to four people), Lao-style fishing trips (25,000K for a half day) and even lessons in silk weaving (50,000K per day, plus thread). We have heard of one woman who spent four days 'homestaying' and learning to weave.

GETTING THERE & AWAY
Săwngthăew to Ban Saphai (8000K, 45 minutes) leave fairly regularly from Pakse's Dao Heung Market (Morning Market; p273), or hire a tuk-tuk or *săam-lâaw* for about 60,000K one way. From Ban Saphai to Don Kho boats cost 20,000K for one to five people. A boat tour around Don Kho costs 70,000K.

Phu Xieng Thong NPA
ປ່າສະຫງວນແຫ່ງຊາດພູຊຽງທອງ

Although the majority of the 1200-sq-km **Phu Xieng Thong NPA** (www.ecotourismlaos.com) lies in Salavan Province, its most accessible areas are about 50km upriver from Pakse. The area features scrub, mixed monsoon deciduous forest and exposed sandstone ridges and cave-like outcroppings, some of which contain prehistoric paintings. On the Thai side of the Mekong is Pha Taem National Park.

The Phu Xieng Thong NPA is home to a range of wildlife, including important concentrations of banteng, green peafowl and clouded leopard. Elephant, Douc langur, gibbon, Asiatic black bear and tiger might also pass through, but it is unlikely that visitors will see any of these. If the season is right you're much more likely to see some striking wild orchids.

The best way into Phu Xieng Thong NPA is on a two- or three-day community-based trek beginning in the Mekong village of **Ban Singsamphan**. The trip involves river transport, a homestay in Ban Singsamphan and a trek over historically important **Phu Khong** (Khong Mountain). It's best to start the four to five-hour trek early, as it can get pretty warm. Parts of the trek cross exposed rock outcroppings that allegedly resemble a turtle and a fish basket and provide a backdrop to mysterious archaeological ruins and amazing views. More enjoyable is the two-hour walk through beautiful forest, with the possibility of a lunch stop with some hermit nuns. The nuns lives in a cave underneath the dramatic Pa Peung (Bee Cliff) and have forsaken speaking and many foods for several years, all in the name of world peace. Bizarre, yes, but their dedication is quite inspirational if not yet successful on the international stage. The two-day trip finishes after the trek but we recommend the three-day version, which heads downriver to Don Kho for a homestay there.

Limited transport means it is possible but difficult to reach Ban Singsamphan independently – if you're interested, get the lowdown from the Provincial Tourism Office in Pakse (p268). A boat from Ban Saphai to Ban Singsamphan costs 350,000K. A slightly cheaper route involves road transport to Ban Buang Kha and a boat from there to Ban Singsamphan (200,000K).

CHAMPASAK
ຈຳປາສັກ
☎ 031

It's hard to imagine Champasak as a seat of royalty, but until only 30 years ago it was just that. These days the town is a somnolent place, the fountain circle in the middle of the main street alluding to a grandeur long since departed with the former royal family. The remaining French colonial-era buildings, including one that once belonged to Chao Boun Oum na Champasak and another to his father Chao Ratsadanai, share space with traditional Lao wooden houses. The few vehicles that venture down the narrow main street share it with buffaloes and cows who seem relaxed even by Lao standards. It's easy to spend a couple of days here.

The Angkor-period ruins of Wat Phu Champasak (p278) lie 8km southwest of town and are the main attraction, as Champasak has the only accommodation in the immediate vicinity of Wat Phu. The town also acts as a jumping-off point for Don Daeng (p281).

Just about everything in Champasak is spread along the one riverside street, either side of the fountain circle.

Information
The **Lao Development Bank** (8.30am-3.30pm Mon-Fri) changes cash and travellers cheques.

It is US$2 per cheque if you want dollars, no charge for kip.

The **Champasak District Visitor Information Centre** (☎ 020-220 6215; 8am-4.30pm Mon-Fri) should be your first point of call in Champasak. It has well-presented displays with information about the town, Wat Phu, Um Tomo and Don Daeng, and can arrange boats to Don Daeng and a bed in the guesthouse there. Local guides, some of whom speak English, lead day walks around Wat Phu and the ancient city, and to Um Tomo. Guides charge 40,000/80,000K for a half/full day, irrespective of numbers.

Internet Nam Oly (per hr 12,000K; 7am-6pm), about 150m south of the Inthira Hotel, has public internet access.

Sights & Activities
Champasak has a couple of mildly interesting temples. On a dirt road parallel to the main north–south street is the late 19th-century **Wat Nyutthitham**, more commonly known as Wat Thong. An old *sim* features an arched and colonnaded verandah, and has a washed pastel stucco relief on the front. This was the wat

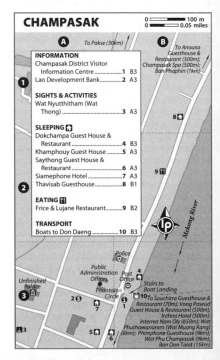

CHAMPASAK

INFORMATION
Champasak District Visitor
  Information Centre 1 B3
Lao Development Bank.............2 A3

SIGHTS & ACTIVITIES
Wat Nyutthitham (Wat
  Thong) 3 A3

SLEEPING
Dokchampa Guest House &
  Restaurant 4 B3
Khamphouy Guest House 5 A3
Saythong Guest House &
  Restaurant 6 A3
Siamephone Hotel 7 A3
Thavisab Guesthouse................8 B1

EATING
Frice & Lujane Restaurant.........9 B2

TRANSPORT
Boats to Don Daeng 10 B3

used by Champasak's royal family, and the *thâat kádụuk* here contain the ashes of King Nyutthitham (died 1885), Chao Ratsadanai (died 1946) and Chao Boun Oum (died 1975), among other royalty.

About 8km south of town on the Mekong stands the oldest active temple in Champasak, **Wat Phuthawanaram**, more popularly known as Wat Muang Kang. Like the *sĭm* at Wat Thong, the intriguing *hǎw tại* (Tripitaka library) at Wat Muang Kang combines elements of French-colonial and Lao Buddhist architecture. The three-tiered roofs of the *sĭm* and *hǎw tại* have coloured mosaics at the corners, and a small box with coloured crystal windows at the centre of the top roof ridge, reminiscent of Burmese architecture.

Ostensibly these crystal-sided boxes hold Buddha images, but local legend ascribes a more magical purpose to the one atop the *hǎw tại*. Supposedly at a certain moment in the annual lunar calendar (most say it's during the Wat Phu Festival), in the middle of the night, a mystic light beam comes from across the river, bounces through the *kâew* (crystal) and alights atop Sri Lingaparvata, the holy mountain above Wat Phu Champasak.

You can reach Wat Muang Kang by boat from Champasak, or come by bike on the narrow dirt road along the riverbank. You could combine a boat trip to Wat Muang Kang with a visit to Uo Moung (p282).

After exploring the region, treat yourself to a round of pampering at the **Champasak Spa** (☎ 020-5649 9739; www.champasak-spa.com; ☯ 10am-midday & 1-7pm). Set in a traditional wooden house on the riverbank, treatments include a foot massage (45,000K), body massage (45,000K), oil massage (80,000K) and a herbal massage with a hot compress (70,000K). Service is superb and the atmosphere very calming, very much the international spa experience at local prices. Relax in a riverside *sala* after the massage with some herbal tea and fruit. It's almost as essential as a visit to Wat Phu and is also a good cause as it creates local jobs to allow women to stay in Champasak rather than migrate to the city.

Sleeping & Eating

Finding a room in Champasak is straightforward enough except during the Wat Phu Champasak Festival (Magha Puja; usually in February, see p281), when you can sleep on the grounds of Wat Phu Champasak. If you do this, ask at one of the food tents for a safe spot and take particular care of your valuables. Accommodation, ranging from the basic (homestay) to the luxurious is available all year-round on nearby Don Daeng.

The restaurants in the following guesthouses are open for breakfast, lunch and dinner.

Vong Paseud Guest House (☎ 920 038; r US$2-15; ☒) Long a popular choice with backpackers thanks to the English- and French-speaking owners, attractively located riverside restaurant and free lift from the ferry. The original rooms are bare bones with just a fan, bathroom and paper-thin walls, but the newer air-con rooms are more substantial. The restaurant comes with river breezes and serves better-than-average travellers' fare. Motorbikes and bicycles are available for rent. It is located near the Inthira Hotel, about 600m south of the fountain circle.

Saythong Guest House & Restaurant (☎ 030-534 6603; r 30,000K) One of the first guesthouses in town, Mr Sing's place remains resolutely basic while all those around it upgrade. The Saythong is cheap, but a little musty. The restaurant (mains 15,000k to 30,000k) has one of the best locations in town.

Phimphone Guesthouse (☎ 020-227 4218; r 30,000K) This offers the closest beds to Wat Phu – it's just a few hundred metres from the entrance booth. The rooms are pretty basic but include an attached bathroom, and the family are friendly.

Khamphouy Guest House (☎ 252 700; r 30,000-40,000K) Just south of the circle, the simple rooms with hot-water bathrooms and overhead fans are a good choice. New beds are under construction during our visit, so expect a decent night's sleep.

Dokchampa Guest House and Restaurant (☎ 020-5535 0910; r 40,000-150,000K; ☒). The Dokchampa has undergone a serious facelift in recent years and the rooms are now some of the smartest at this price range. Try to bag room 6 for river views. Air-conditioned bungalows start from 100,000K and include spiffy bathrooms and satellite TV.

Souchitra Guesthouse (☎ 920 059; r 50,000-150,000K; ☒) These clean and comfortable rooms are a good deal if you opt for a fan, but not quite such a steal if you turn on the air-con. The spacious common verandah, riverside hammocks and restaurant are all good places to chill out.

Anouxa Guesthouse (☎ 213 272; r 100,000-150,000K; 🔀) Arguably the pick of the guesthouses, the friendly Anouxa offers some of the most appealing bungalows in Champasak. The air-conditioned bungalows that face the river are well-worth the money at 120,000K as they are spacious and smart. It's a bit of a hike from the middle of the action, but come on, there isn't that much action in Champasak, so who's complaining? The attached riverside restaurant (mains 15,000K to 30,000K) serves a tasty *mok pa* (fish curry in banana leaf).

our pick **Inthira Hotel** (☎ 214 059; www.inthirahotel. com; r US$60; 🔀 🖥 🛜) The classy Inthira brings a whole new experience to the Champasak accommodation scene. Set in a converted old shophouse, the rooms are tasteful in the extreme. Choose from split-level duplex suites with terrazzo bathtubs, flat-screen TVs and a double balcony or Lao-style garden houses with plenty of space and a Balinese-style alfresco rain shower. Mmmm, very nice indeed. The restaurant is one of the best in town, borrowing liberally from the menu of the Kop Chai Deu Restaurant in Vientiane, as it is also part of the Green Discovery family. Prices are reasonable from 15,000K to 45,000K or just wade into the Lao Discovery Menu at 69,000K, including a shot of *lào-láo* (rice whisky).

Frice & Lujane Restaurant (☎ 920 096; mains 40,000-60,000K) An unlikely find in Champasak, this Italian trattoria has a small menu of authentic dishes based on 19th-century family recipes. Try gnocchi, pasta or lasagne washed down with a glass of vino.

Other sleeping options:

Siamephone Hotel (☎ 920 128; r 150,000K; 🔀) Probably the biggest hotel in town, with smart, clean rooms, but not a lot in the atmosphere department.

Thavisab Guesthouse (☎ 920 081; r 50,000-150,000K; 🔀) Long-running guesthouse with large rooms including TV and hot water.

Getting There & Away

The big news is that Champasak is now connected to Pakse by a new road running along the west bank of the Mekong. It was still under construction at the time of writing, so some vehicles use it and others don't, but eventually it will cut the distance to 28km and the journey time to less than one hour. Buses and *săwngthăew* from Pakse leave throughout the day until about 3pm; see p273.

Ferries (2000K per person, 7000K for motorbikes) from Ban Muang on the eastern side of the Mekong to Ban Phaphin (1.8km north of Champasak) on the western side run regularly during daylight hours, and 24 hours a day during the Wat Phu Champasak Festival. Travel from Ban Phaphin to Champasak by any vehicle is about 2000K per person, more like 15,000K to charter.

Leaving Champasak, *săwngthăew and* buses depart for Pakse (20,000K) until about 3.30pm, with early morning the busiest. Going south, get to Ban Lak 30 on Rte 13 and hail anything going past.

Getting Around

Bicycles (10,000K per day) and motorbikes (50,000/80,000K per half/full day) can be rented at most guesthouses.

WAT PHU CHAMPASAK
ວັດພູຈຳປາສັກ

The ancient Khmer religious complex of **Wat Phu** (admission 30,000K, children 12 & under free; ⏰ 8am-4.30pm) is one of the highlights of any trip to Laos. Stretching 1400m up to the slopes of the Phu Pasak range (also known more colloquially as Phu Khuai or Mt Penis), Wat Phu is small compared with the monumental Angkor-era sites near Siem Reap in Cambodia. However, you know the old adage about location, location, location and the tumbledown pavilions, ornate Shiva-lingam sanctuary, enigmatic crocodile stone and tall trees that shroud much of the site in soothing shade add up to give Wat Phu an almost mystical atmosphere. These, and a layout that is unique in Khmer architecture, led to Unesco declaring the Wat Phu complex a World Heritage Site in 2001.

Sanskrit inscriptions and Chinese sources confirm the site has been a place of worship since the mid 5th century. The temple complex was designed as a worldly imitation of heaven and fitted into a larger plan that evolved to include a network of roads, cities, settlement and other temples. What you see today is the product of centuries of building, rebuilding, alteration and addition, with the most recent structures dating from the late-Angkorian period.

At its height, the temple and nearby city formed the most important economic and political centre in the region. But despite its historic importance, the 84-hectare site

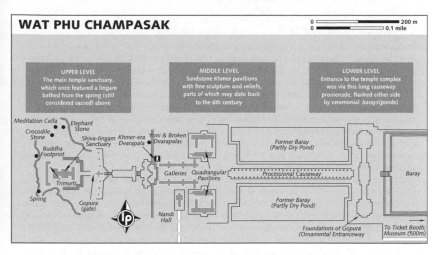

WAT PHU CHAMPASAK

0 _____ 200 m
0 _____ 0.1 mile

UPPER LEVEL
The main temple sanctuary, which once featured a lingam bathed from the spring (still considered sacred) above

MIDDLE LEVEL
Sandstone Khmer pavilions with fine sculpture and reliefs, parts of which may date back to the 6th century

LOWER LEVEL
Entrance to the temple complex was via this long causeway promenade, flanked either side by ceremonial *barays*(ponds)

Meditation Cella
Crocodile Stone
Elephant Stone
Buddha Footprint
Shiva-lingam Sanctuary
Khmer-era Dvarapala
Yoni & Broken Dvarapalas
Trimurti
Spring
Gopura (gate)
Galleries
Quadrangular Pavilions
Nandi Hall
Processional Causeway
Former Baray (Partly Dry Pond)
Former Baray (Partly Dry Pond)
Baray
Foundations of Gopura (Ornamental Entranceway)
To Ticket Booth; Museum (500m)

remains in considerable danger from the elements. Detailed studies reveal that water erosion is pressuring the site and without a systematic water-management plan the buildings will eventually collapse. Italian- and Japanese-funded projects have helped stabilise the southern of two ancient canals built to channel water away from the central structures. However, the equally important northern canal has collapsed completely, resulting in a slow but steady destruction of the northern side of the site. To see it, compare the relatively intact terraced steps and pavilions on the south of the site with those on the north.

Years of work by the Italian Archaeological Mission and the inimitable Dr Patrizia Zolese, the leading expert on Wat Phu who has been working at the site since 1990, have resulted in the first detailed map of the site and surrounding 400 sq km, revealing much about the way the ancients lived. During the last few years, archaeologists have restored the ceremonial causeway, replacing slabs and re-erecting stone lotus buds that had been scattered across the site. Restoration of the Nandi Hall has recently been completed.

Don't miss the **museum** (admission with Wat Phu ticket; ⏰ 8am-4.30pm) beside the ticket office. Extensive cataloguing work has recently been completed on the dozens of lintels, *naga* (mythical water serpents), Buddhas and other stone work from Wat Phu and its associated sites. Descriptions are in English, plus the building includes clean bathrooms.

The Archaeological Site

Wat Phu is situated at the junction of the Mekong plain and Phu Phasak, a mountain that was sacred to local peoples centuries before the construction of any of the ruins now visible. The original Austro-Asiatic tribes living in this area undoubtedly paid respect to animist spirits associated with the mountain and its rock shelter spring.

The archaeological site itself is divided into six terraces on three main levels joined by a long, stepped promenade flanked by statues of lions and *naga*.

LOWER LEVEL

A modern sala built by Chao Boun Oum in the 1960s stood at the western side of the great *baray* (ceremonial pond; *năwng sá* in Lao) until it was recently dismantled, revealing the sandstone base of the ancient main entrance. From here begins a causeway-style ceremonial promenade, flanked by two *baray*. Parts of both the northern and southern *baray* still fill with water, lotus flowers and the odd buffalo during the wet season and the site is in better shape since the stone lotus buds lining the promenade have been re-erected.

MIDDLE LEVEL

The middle section features two exquisitely carved **quadrangular pavilions** built of sandstone and laterite. Believed to date from the mid 10th or early 11th century, the style resembles Koh Ker in Cambodia. Some people (but not the Unesco experts) suggest these pavilions

CHAMPASAK IN ANTIQUITY

Under the palm trees and rice paddies 4km south of Champasak town is the remains of a city that was, about 1500 years ago, the capital of the Mon-Khmer Chenla kingdom. The site is known today as Muang Kao (Old City), but scholars believe it was called Shrestapura.

Aerial photographs show the remains of a rectangular city measuring 2.3km by 1.8km, surrounded by double earthen walls on three sides and protected on the east by the Mekong River. Other traces of the old city include small *baray* (a Khmer word meaning 'pond', usually used for ritual purposes), the foundations for circular brick monuments, evidence of an advanced system of irrigation, various Hindu statuary and stone carvings (including a lintel in the style of 7th-century Sambor Prei Kuk), stone implements and ceramics. The sum of all this is an extremely rare example of an ancient urban settlement in Southeast Asia, one whose design reveals how important religious belief was in the workings of everyday life.

The origin of the city remained a mystery until Southeast Asia's oldest Sanskrit inscription was discovered here. The 5th-century stele stated the city was founded by King Devanika and was called Kuruksetra and also mentions the auspicious Sri Lingaparvata nearby, a clear reference to the mountain near Wat Phu Champasak. 'Honoured since antiquity', the mountain was believed to be the residence or the manifestation of the Hindu god Shiva, and even today local people honour the mountain as the place of Phi Intha (the soul or protecting spirit of the mountain).

By the end of the 5th century the city was thriving. It continued as a major regional centre until at least the 7th century, as showed by two Nandi pedestal (Shiva's bull mount) sculptures discovered in 1994-95 bearing inscriptions by King Citrasena-Mahendravarman, the 'conqueror' who later shifted the kingdom's capital to Sambor Prei Kuk in northeast Cambodia. Archaeological material suggests the city was inhabited until the 16th century.

Ongoing research by Dr Patrizia Zolese and her team has revealed that a second city was built near Wat Phu after the 9th century. She believes the Ho Nang Sida (see p281) was at the centre of this city, which was probably Lingapura, a place mentioned in many ancient inscriptions but which has not been categorically identified by modern scholars.

---

were used for gender-segregated worship and they are sometimes called 'lady pavilion' and 'man pavilion'.

Wat Phu was converted into a Buddhist site in later centuries but much of the original Hindu sculpture remains in the lintels, which feature various forms of Vishnu and Shiva. Over the western pediment of the north pavilion is a relief of Shiva and Parvati sitting on Nandi, Shiva's bull mount. The building consists of four galleries and a central open courtyard, although entry is forbidden for safety reasons.

Just behind the southern pavilion stands a smaller building known as the **Nandi Hall** (dedicated to Shiva's mount) and two collapsed galleries flanking a set of laterite steps leading to the next level. From the Nandi Hall an ancient royal road once led south for about 1.3km to Ho Nang Sida (p281), and eventually to Angkor Wat in Cambodia. Six ruined brick shrines – only their bases remain – separate the lower two levels from the final and holiest level. Roots and mosses hold the bricks together in some places, and drive them apart in others.

An impressive **dvarapala** (sentinel figure) stands ramrod straight with sword held at the ready near what was once a *gopura* (ornate entranceway). If you step down off the walkway and onto the grassy area just north of here you'll come to the remains of a **yoni pedestal**, the cosmic vagina-womb symbol associated with Shaivism. Very near the yoni lie two unusually large, headless and armless **dvarapala statues** half-buried in the grass. These are the largest dvarapala found anywhere in the former Angkorian kingdom.

A steep *naga* stairway leads onwards to the sanctuary and probably dates from the 11th century. It is lined with *dàwk jąmpąa* (plumeria or frangipani), the Lao national tree.

UPPER LEVEL

On the uppermost level is the sanctuary itself, which once enclosed a Shiva lingam that was bathed – via a system of sandstone pipes – with waters from the sacred spring above and behind the complex. A lintel inside the southern entrance depicts the story of Krishnavatara in which Krishna kills his uncle

Kamsa. The sanctuary now contains a set of unsophisticated-looking Buddha images on an altar. The brick rear section, which might have been built in the 9th century, is a *cella* (cell), where the holy linga was kept.

Sculpted into a large boulder behind the main sanctuary is a Khmer-style **Trimurti**, the Hindu holy trinity of Shiva, Vishnu and Brahma. Further back, beyond some terracing, is the cave from which the holy spring flowed into the sanctuary.

East of the sanctuary and a newer wat building, a winding path leads north to the so-called **crocodile stone**, a boulder with a deep, highly stylised impression of a croc believed to date from the Angkor period. Crocodiles were semidivine figures in Khmer culture, but despite much speculation that the sculpture was used for human sacrifices its function, if there was one, remains unknown. Further along the same path is the **elephant stone**, a huge boulder bearing the likeness of an elephant thought to date from the 16th century. Nearby you can see remains of a stone **meditation cella**.

When you've seen everything here, just sitting and soaking up the wide-angle view of the *baray,* the plains and the Mekong is fantastic, especially in the morning before the crowds arrive.

Other Sites Associated with Wat Phu

South of Wat Phu are three smaller Angkor-era sites in very poor condition that will mainly interest die-hard fans of Khmer architecture. Each of the three stands beside the ancient road to Angkor Wat in Cambodia.

An easy 1.3km walk to the south of Wat Phu – stick to the trail heading south from the terraced promenade because there may be some UXO (unexploded ordnance) in the area – stands **Ho Nang Sida**. Its exact function is uncertain, though it probably dates from the early 10th century and might have been the central shrine for a second ancient city.

A further kilometre south stands another rubble pile, **Hong Tha Tao** (Lord Turtle Room). This structure, or what's left of it, resembles hospitals built during the reign of Khmer King Jayavarman VII in the early 13th century, so it might have been there to serve as a hospital for ill pilgrims.

Another few kilometres on, close to the village of Ban That, stand three Khmer *prasat* (square-based brick stupas) reminiscent of similar tripartite monuments in Thailand's

Lopburi. No doubt symbolic of the Hindu Trimurti of Shiva, Brahma and Vishnu, the towers are believed to date from the 11th century and were likely never completed; they are in poor condition. A large, dried-up *baray* can be seen nearby. Ban That can be reached by jumbo from Champasak or Ban Thong Khop.

Festivals

The highlight of the year in Champasak is the three-day Bun Wat Phu Champasak (Wat Phu Champasak Festival), held as part of Magha Puja (Makha Busa) during the full moon of the third lunar month, usually in February. The central ceremonies performed are Buddhist, culminating on the full-moon day with an early-morning parade of monks receiving alms from the faithful, followed that evening by a candlelit *wíen thíen* (circumambulation) of the lower shrines.

Throughout the three days of the festival Lao visitors climb around the hillside, stopping to pray and leave offerings of flowers and incense. The festival is more commercial than it once was, and for much of the time has an atmosphere somewhere between a kids carnival and music festival. Events include Thai boxing matches, cockfights, comedy shows and plenty of music and dancing. Food is available from vendors who set up along the road from Ban Thong Khop, and after dark several areas are cordoned off for open-air nightclubs featuring bands from as far away as Vientiane. After dark the beer and *lào-láo* flow freely and the atmosphere gets pretty rowdy.

Getting There & Away

Wat Phu Champasak is 46km from Pakse, 12km from Ban Phaphin and 10km from Champasak. A shared jumbo from Champasak to Ban Thong Khop, the village opposite Wat Phu, should cost about 6000K per person. More likely you'll have to haggle with a *sǎam-lâaw* or tuk-tuk driver who will do the return trip for about 60,000K to 80,000K. Cycling is also popular, but there's not much shade so it pays to start early.

DON DAENG

ດອນແດງ

Stretched out like an old croc sunning itself in the middle of the Mekong, Don Daeng is a little like an island that time forgot. It's classic middle Mekong, with eight villages scattered around its edge and rice fields in the middle.

The small and mostly shaded track that runs around the edge of the 8km-long island is mercifully free of cars – bicycles, slow-moving motorbikes and the odd *dok dok* (mini tractor) are all the transport that's required.

The remains of a square-based brick **prasat** in the centre of the island and another, hiding under the *sĭm* at **Wat Ban Boung Kham**, suggest the island has been inhabited since Khmer times, at least. But the attraction of Don Daeng is more about just soaking up village life. Walking or cycling around you'll find people refreshingly welcoming.

While life on Don Daeng is much as it has been for decades, the introduction of tourism will put some pressures on this timeless existence. The village elders told us specifically that they don't want Don Daeng to go the way of Don Det (p289). That means they don't want *falang* openly smoking spliffs or getting overly amorous in public, and women are asked to wear sarongs when they bathe, not bikinis; ditto for sunbathing. As you are a guest in their village, please respect these requests.

The village of **Hua Don Daeng**, at the northern tip of the island, is where the accommodation has been built. The simple **community guesthouse** (dm 30,000K), with two rooms and mattresses on the floor, makes a good base from which to visit Wat Phu Champasak and Uo Moung. There is a bathroom with bucket shower, but we recommend bathing local-style in the Mekong. Delicious meals (20,000K per meal) are prepared by the villagers, who also rent out bikes. Village homestays are possible and cost the same price as the guesthouse (30,000K per bed, 20,000K per meal).

In a rather different class is **La Folie Lodge** (☎ 030-534 7603; r incl breakfast US$95/140 low/high season; ✗ ▢ ☐), set on the riverbank facing Wat Phu. Rooms are housed in elegant wooden bungalows with lots of attention to detail, including Lao textiles, colonial motifs and polished wood floors. The resort includes an inviting pool with views across to Phu Pasak. The poolside restaurant is very atmospheric by night and includes a wide selection of Lao and international dishes. Rates include a boat transfer from Ban Muang to the lodge. La Folie is supporting several community projects on Don Daeng, including renovation of the Ban Bang Sai School.

To get to Don Daeng take a small boat from Ban Muang or Champasak for about 50,000K with a certain amount of negotia-

tion. Champasak guesthouses can assist but will likely charge 60,000K to 70,000K. The **Champasak District Visitor Information Centre** (p276) in Champasak can arrange boats and will let the villagers know you're coming, as will the **Provincial Tourism Office** in Pakse (p268).

UO MOUNG (TOMO TEMPLE)
ອຸໂມງ (ວັດໂຕະໂມະ)

The Khmer temple ruin of **Uo Moung** (Tomo Temple; admission 10,000K; ✹ 7.30am-4.30pm) is believed to have been built late in the 9th century during the reign of the Khmer King Yasovarman I. It's about 45km south of Pakse off Rte 13, in a wonderfully shaded forest beside a small tributary of the Mekong. The exact function of the temple is unknown, though its orientation towards the holy mountain Phu Pasak suggests its location was somehow related to Wat Phu.

The ruins include an entranceway bordered by distance markers (often mistaken for lingas) and two crumbling *gopura* (ornate entranceways). The more intact of the *gopura* contains an unusual lingam-style stone post on which two faces have been carved. It's unusual because *mukhalinga* usually have four *mukha* (faces), while most ordinary linga have no face at all. Several sandstone lintels are displayed on rocks beneath towering dipterocarp trees, but the best examples of lintels from this site are in the Champasak Historical Heritage Museum in Pakse (p269). The white building at the heart of the site houses a bronze Sukhothai-style Buddha.

Getting There & Away
The easiest way to get to Uo Muong is by boat from Don Daeng, Ban Muang (the village on the far side of the Mekong from Champasak) or Champasak. You can charter a boat to Ban Tomo (the riverbank village about 400m south of the ruins) for about 200,000K return, including waiting time of an hour or so while you locate and tour the ruins. Prices fall as the boat distance gets shorter, so riding a bicycle to Ban Sisouk at the south end of Don Daeng and taking a boat from there is cheapest (60,000K or so return).

From Ban Tomo, climb the riverbank and walk north through the village, following the road right, then left. The temple is in a forest. If in doubt, ask the kids along the way. The ruins can also be reached by vehicle from Pakse by turning west just before Km 42.

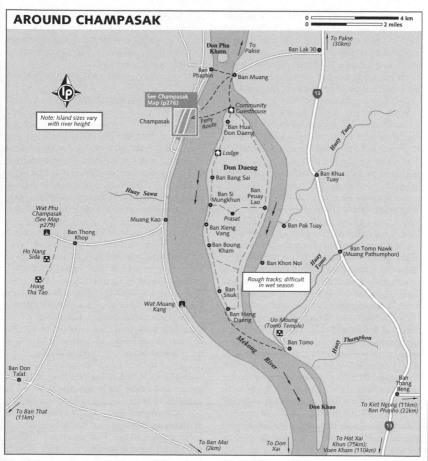

AROUND CHAMPASAK

By boat, you could combine a trip to Uo Muong with a stop at Wat Muang Kang on the west bank of the Mekong. Another option is to rent a bike on Don Daeng, take it by boat first to Uo Muong, then Wat Muang Kang, and ride the riverside path back to Champasak.

KIET NGONG & BAN PHAPHO
ບ້ານຜາໂພ/ກງດຍ່ງ

Perched on the edge of Se Pian NPA, the Lao Loum villagers of Kiet Ngong have had a centuries-long relationship with elephants. The elephants have traditionally worked moving logs or doing heavy work in the rice fields. Typically each elephant has a different owner and in many cases the relationship between owner and pachyderm has existed

for the majority of both lives. But as elephants are expensive to keep and machines now do much of their traditional work, the village has turned to tourism to help pay their way.

Kiet Ngong is at the edge of a wetland 11km from Rte 13 and is also home to Kingfisher Eco-Lodge, one of Laos's first real ecolodges. The wetland is used by an unusually large herd of buffalo and more than 90 species of bird have been sighted.

Almost everyone who comes to Kiet Ngong takes the elephant ride to the summit of a hill called **Phu Asa**, named for a group of 19th-century nationalists who fought against the Siamese. The flat-topped hill is topped by an expansive archaeological site. Unmortared slate brick columns, topped by larger slabs, stand about 2m high and enclose a rectangular space about 180m long and 50m wide. At the centre of the site is a crumbling and overgrown temple. At its far end a trail leads down to a Buddha footprint. The site has a Stonehenge feel to it but, contrary to what the locals will tell you, the columns are probably not 1000 years old.

From the top you can see across the wetlands and vast swaths of forest, though the 90-minute elephant trek (120,000K per elephant) follows a steep laterite road rather than a forest path. It is also possible to hire a guide and walk up and back through the forest (60,000K per four people or less).

Guides can be found at the new **Visitor Information Centre** (☎ 030-534 6547) at the entrance to the village, built as part of the Asian Development Bank's pro-poor tourism initiative, designed to bring tourist dollars to some of the poorest communities in the country. The centre arranges elephant rides and local accommodation, and has information about the local area and Se Pian NPA. If telephoning for information ask a Lao speaker to translate.

About 15km east of Kiet Ngong is the Suay village of **Ban Phapho** (22km east of Rte 13), a traditional breeding centre for working elephants. However, elephant breeding appears to be a dying art because the mahouts of Kiet Ngong and Ban Phapho won't let their female elephants mate for fear they will wind up with broken hips (not uncommon, apparently). The owners just can't risk the loss of income. Clearly this isn't a sustainable policy, but no one seemed to have any alternative plan when we asked.

Ban Phapho itself is old and quite attractive. Mr Bounhome, who runs the only guesthouse, arranges elephant rides (120,000K) or can take you to watch the elephants working (80,000K, in season). At either village it's worth arriving early or calling ahead as it takes a couple of hours to fetch and prepare the elephants.

Visitors heading to Kiet Ngong or Ban Phapho must pay a 10,000K entry fee for Se Pian NPA.

Sleeping & Eating

Kiet Ngong might seem an unlikely place for one of Laos's first real eco-lodges, but that is exactly what opened here in 2006. Run by a Lao-Italian family, **Kingfisher Eco-Lodge** (☎ 030-534 5016; www.kingfisherecolodge.com; r 180,000-765,000K) is set on 7ha at the edge of a wetland, about

700m east of Kiet Ngong. It's a beautiful spot and sitting on the balcony at dawn, watching a herd of buffalo splash their way across the wetland while mahouts ride their elephants towards work is memorable.

There are four classy bungalows (585,000/765,000K low/high season), which include balconies with large rattan hammocks, his and hers sinks and ethnic motifs. There are also four ecorooms (that's 'eco' for economy; 180,000/270,000K low/high season), which are nice enough with spotless shared bathrooms, but have thin walls. Lights and hot water are solar powered. The highlight is the restaurant and bar, which could easily be in an East African safari lodge. There is also free internet available for guests but no wi-fi.

Activities include elephant rides, birdwatching (November to January is best), mountain biking, trekking by foot and even a day-long course to learn how to become a mahout (600,000K). It's also the best place to arrange the Ta Ong trek into Se Pian NPA because they have the most-knowledgeable English-speaking guides. Kingfisher is extremely transparent about where the benefits of these activities go, including information on village income and lodge profits.

On the far side of the village, a 15-minute walk through rice fields, are five basic and ageing **community-run bungalows** (30,000K). The location is fantastic, but the bungalows are not. Instead, get the villagers to set up your mattress and mosquito net on the *sala* overlooking the wetland. Homestays for 30,000K per person are also possible. Arrange either of them at the Visitor Information Centre: for bungalows say '*heuan phak*', for homestays say 'homestay'.

In Ban Phapho, the **Boun Home Guest House** (☎ 030-534 6293; per bed 30,000K) has small, ultrasimple rooms in an authentic wooden house. The bathroom is shared and there's no hot water, but Mr Bounhome and his family are welcoming and speak some English and French. Order meals of *làap* (20,000K) and *khào nĭaw* in advance.

Getting There & Away

Kiet Ngong and Ban Phapho are off the sometimes diabolical Rte 18A that runs east from Ban Thang Beng, 48km south of Pakse on Rte 13, to Attapeu. The turn-off for Kiet Ngong is about 8.5km east of Rte 13 and the village is 1.8km further south. For Ban Phapho, continue along Rte 18 and soon after the Kiet Ngong turn-off take the right fork; it's about 15km along this road. These roads are easily travelled on small motorbikes and should be passable, if sometimes slippery, most of the year.

Săwngthăew (25,000K, 1½ to 2½ hours) leave Kiet Ngong at about 8am. From Ban Phapho *săwngthăew* leave at 8am or 9am (sometimes only one service runs). If you miss the 8am from Kiet Ngong, you should be able to jump on one of these when they pass on Rte 18. These same *săwngthăew* return from Pakse's southern bus terminal between about noon or so; Kiet Ngong is often misunderstood so ask instead for 'Phu Asa'.

Alternatively, board anything going south on Rte 13, get off at Ban Thang Beng and wait for transport bumping its way east.

SE PIAN NPA
ປ່າສະຫງວນແຫ່ງຊາດເຊປຽນ

Se Pian NPA (www.xepian.org) is one of the most important protected areas in Laos. Stretching between Rte 18 in the north, Rte 13 to the west and the Cambodian border in the south, the 2400 sq km is fed by three major rivers, the Se Pian, Se Khampho and Se Kong. It boasts globally significant populations of banteng, Asiatic black bear, yellow-cheeked crested gibbon and gaur, among others. There may also be a few tigers. It's also home to many birds, including the rare sarus crane, vultures and hornbills.

The reason Se Pian's wildlife population is so significant (unlike most other NPAs) is that barely anyone lives here, so the wildlife hasn't been hunted to the verge of extinction. The most southern permanent settlement is the ethnic Lavae (commonly known as Brou) village of **Ta Ong**, and it's in this extremely poor village that you'll stay if you do the two-day Ta Ong trek. This is the hardest of the treks we've done in Laos, but it's the only way to get into this way-off-the-beaten-track part of Se Pian. Much of the five-hour first day involves barely visible trails and wading through streams.

The villagers' belief system is a mix of animism and Buddhism and, if our experience is anything to go by, they know how to have fun – especially the guy playing the *kaen,* a bamboo instrument that looks like a long pan-flute but sounds more like an accordion. Brou bagpipes is how one of our party summed it up.

The second day starts with a fantastic dawn walk through the forest. If you're lucky you might hear the haunting call of rare yellow-cheeked crested gibbons. After breakfast you can choose an easy one-hour walk and boat trip, or a steamy three-hour bush bash via a spectacular natural viewpoint.

You can book the trek (dry season only) through either the Provincial Tourism Office in Pakse (p268) or Kingfisher Eco-Lodge in Kiet Ngong (p284). The latter trek is more expensive but includes an excellent English-speaking guide. There's no electricity in Ta Ong so bring a torch (flashlight).

SI PHAN DON (FOUR THOUSAND ISLANDS)
ສີພັນດອນ

Si Phan Don is where Laos becomes the land of the lotus eaters, an archipelago of islands where the pendulum of time swings more slowly and life is more laid-back, a world somewhat disconnected from the mainland beyond. Many a traveller has washed ashore here, succumbed to its charms and stayed longer than expected. The name literally means 'Four Thousand Islands', and the few you are likely to visit on this scenic 50km-long stretch of the Mekong are so tranquil that it's easy to understand the allure.

During the rainy season this section of the Mekong fills out to a breadth of 14km, the river's widest reach along its 4350km journey from the Tibetan Plateau to the South China Sea. During the dry months between monsoons the river recedes and leaves behind hundreds (or thousands if you count every sand bar) of islands and islets. The largest of the permanent islands are inhabited year-round and offer fascinating glimpses of traditional river-oriented village life – 'more detached from time than from the riverbank' as one source described it. Communities tend to be self-sufficient, growing most of their own rice, sugar cane, coconut and vegetables, catching fish and weaving textiles as needed. Women wash their clothes in the Mekong as long-tail boats weave around the bathing buffalo.

Island life is changing, however, and electricity and tourism are the big drivers. Don Khong attracts travellers looking for better lodgings while Don Det has become one of Southeast Asia's backpacker magnets, with all the good and bad that entails. Don Khon falls somewhere in between.

The villages of Si Phan Don are often named for their position at the upriver or downriver ends of their respective islands. The upriver end is called *hŭa* (head), the downriver end is called *hăang* (tail). Hence Ban Hua Khong is at the northern end of Don Khong, while Ban Hang Khong is at the southern end.

The French left behind a defunct short railway (the only railway ever actually completed in Laos), a couple of river piers, and a few colonial buildings. Other attractions include some impressive rapids and the Khon Phapheng (p295) waterfall, where the Mekong suddenly drops in elevation at the Cambodian border. The increasingly rare Irrawaddy dolphin (p292) also likes to hang out in the Mekong south of the falls.

Don Khong (Khong Island)
ດອນໂຂງ
☎ 031 / pop 13,000

Even in Laos, where 'sleepy' seems an almost universal adjective to describe provincial towns, Muang Khong, Don Khong's epicentre, is the epitome of the sleepy district capital. Life moves slowly here, like a boat being paddled against the flow on the Mekong, and you'll seldom be disturbed by a vehicle. It's no party town – keep going south for that – but the torpid pace of life here and the sights around the island make it an attractive place to pass a day or two, pedalling about on a bicycle or just chilling by the river. In some ways it is more relaxing that its sister islands, perhaps because of fewer foreigners and wider skies.

Named for the surrounding river (using the Thai pronunciation *khŏng* rather than the Lao *khǎwng*), this large island measures 18km long by 8km at its widest point. Most of the islanders live in and around two villages, Muang Khong on the eastern shore and Muang Saen on the west; an 8km road links the two.

As his surname suggests, the postman who went on to become president of Laos, Khamtay Siphandone, was born in Si Phan Don in 1924, in Ban Hua Khong at the north end of Don Khong. His family are quite influential here, although rumours that he is seeing out his retirement on the island are apparently untrue, as locals say he is living it up in the cool climes of Paksong.

INFORMATION
The police are a block back from the river in Muang Khong. If you have any minor ailments, Dr Soubane speaks English and French and is based at the hospital, midway between Muang Khong and Ban Huay. If it is something more serious, head for Pakse or Thailand.

Agricultural Promotion Bank (☯ 9.30am-4pm Mon-Fri) South of town, this bank offers poor rates for US dollars and Thai baht cash, and travellers cheques (8000K charge per cheque).

Khong Tourism Office (☎ 020-257 0373) Set in a dilapidated colonial villa dating from 1937, the period furnishings don't look to have changed in the days since the French departed. Mr Phan sits upstairs and speaks some English, but it's probably of more interest for the architecture than information.

Lao Telecom On the road to Muang Saen.

Phoukhong Guesthouse (☎ 213 673; per hr 30,000K; ☯ 7am-9pm) Has several computers, but the connection is not superfast.

Post Office Just south of the bridge.

SIGHTS & ACTIVITIES
Don Khong is a pretty island with rice fields and low hills in the centre and vegetable gardens around the perimeter, punctuated by small villages, most of which have their own wats. Bicycle (ecofriendly) or motorbike (ecolazy) is the best way to explore it.

Muang Khong is dominated by **Wat Phuang Kaew** and its towering modern '*naga* protected' Buddha image facing east. The locals believe the abbot used supernatural powers gained in meditation to defeat government efforts to oust him after the Revolution. Elsewhere in Muang Khong, the **market** is fascinating between 4.30am and 6.30am, when people come from throughout the islands to buy and sell. Many come by boat and getting yourself down to the **small beach** at dawn to watch the boats unload their fish, fowl and other fare is a fantastic way to start the day.

At Ban Xieng Wang, a neighbourhood at the northern end of Muang Khong, is **Wat Jom Thong**, the oldest temple on the island. Dating from the Chao Anou period (1805–28), the main *sim* features a unique cruciform floor plan in crumbling brick and stucco with a tile roof. Carved wooden window shutters are a highlight, and an old wooden standing Buddha in one-handed *abhaya mudra* (offering protection) is notable. The sandy temple grounds are shaded by coconut and betel palms and mango trees.

A kilometre or so north of Muang Khong, in some hills more or less behind the mayor's

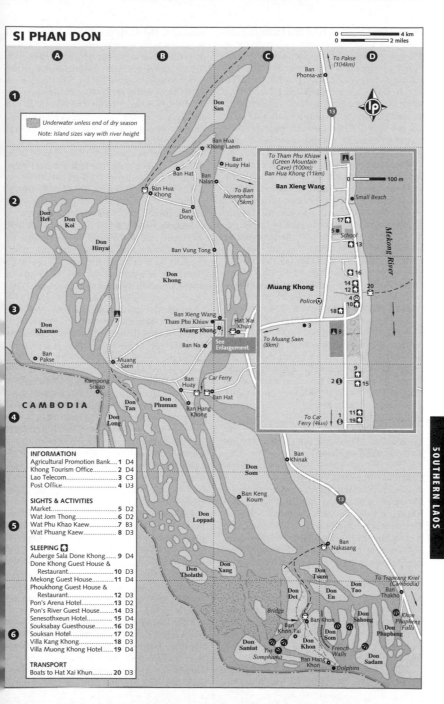

SI PHAN DON

0 ———— 4 km
0 ———— 2 miles

Underwater unless end of dry season
Note: Island sizes vary with river height

Don San
Ban Hua Khong Laem
Ban Hat
Ban Nalan
Ban Huay Hai
Ban Hua Khong
Ban Dong
To Ban Nasenphan (5km)
Don Het
Don Koi
Don Hinyai
Ban Vung Tong
Don Khong
Ban Xieng Wang
Tham Phu Khiaw
Muang Khong
Hat Xai Khun
Don Khamao
Ban Pakse
Muang Saen
Ban Na
See Enlargement
Kampong Sralao
Don Tan
Don Phuman
Ban Huay
Car Ferry
Ban Hat
CAMBODIA
Don Long
Ban Hang Khong

Ban Khinak
Ban Phonsa-at
To Pakse (104km)

Don Som
Ban Keng Koum
Don Loppadi
Ban Nakasang
Don Tholathi
Don Xang
Don Toum
Don Tao
To Trapeang Kriel (Cambodia)
Ban Thakho
Don Det
Don En
Bridge
Ban Khon
Ban Khon Tai
Don Som
Don Khon
Don Sahong
Don Phapheng
Khon Phapheng Falls
Don Saniat
Tat Somphamit
French Walls
Ban Hang Khon
Dolphins
Don Sadam

Enlargement (Muang Khong):

To Tham Phu Khiaw (Green Mountain Cave) (100m); Ban Hua Khong (11km)

Ban Xieng Wang

0 ———— 100 m

Small Beach

School
Mekong River

Muang Khong

Police
To Muang Saen (8km)

To Car Ferry (4km)

INFORMATION
Agricultural Promotion Bank....	1	D4
Khong Tourism Office............	2	D4
Lao Telecom.......................	3	C3
Post Office.........................	4	D3

SIGHTS & ACTIVITIES
Market..............................	5	D2
Wat Jom Thong....................	6	D2
Wat Phu Khao Kaew..............	7	B3
Wat Phuang Kaew.................	8	D3

SLEEPING
Auberge Sala Done Khong......	9	D4
Done Khong Guest House & Restaurant........................	10	D3
Mekong Guest House............	11	D4
Phoukhong Guest House & Restaurant........................	12	D3
Pon's Arena Hotel.................	13	D2
Pon's River Guest House........	14	D3
Senesothxeun Hotel..............	15	D4
Souksabay Guesthouse..........	16	D3
Souksan Hotel.....................	17	D2
Villa Kang Khong.................	18	D3
Villa Muong Khong Hotel......	19	D4

TRANSPORT
Boats to Hat Xai Khun...........	20	D3

SOUTHERN LAOS

office, a trail leads to **Tham Phu Khiaw** (Green Mountain Cave). The cave – actually more of an overhanging ledge – contains some old Buddha images and is the object of local pilgrimages during Lao New Year in April. To find it, head north from Muang Khong for 1.5km and take a track to the left, through a banana plantation. It's only a 15-minute walk (mostly uphill) to the cave entrance, marked by two tree trunks, but the track isn't always obvious so it's best to find a local to guide you.

Muang Saen, on the opposite side of the island from Muang Khong, is a bustling little town with boats servicing the islands to the west of Don Khong that have no road access whatsoever. If your trip doesn't include Cambodia, it is possible to take a boat across to the Cambodian village of **Kompong Sralao** on the west bank of the Mekong. There's nothing to see, but you can say that you've been to a part of Cambodia few others have visited and sample an Angkor Beer. There were no immigration facilities at the time of research. **Wat Phu Khao Kaew**, on a low hill north of Muang Saen (about 5km from the junction of the north–south and east–west roads), was built on the site of some Khmer ruins. It is believed to be home to a *naga*, though the entrance to its lair is covered. Look for a stand of frangipani trees on the eastern side of the hill to locate the path to the temple, or hire a motorcycle taxi in Muang Saen for around 30,000K return.

Two smaller villages at the southern tip of the island worth visiting for old wats are **Ban Huay** and **Ban Hang Khong**.

FESTIVALS & EVENTS

A boat-racing festival (Bun Suang Heua, also referred to as Bun Nam) is held on Don Khong in early December around National Day, usually the first or second weekend of the month. Four or five days of carnival-like activity culminate in races opposite Muang Khong, much closer to the shore than in larger towns.

SLEEPING

Muang Khong has the best range of accommodation anywhere in the islands and standards are generally higher than those on Don Det or Don Khon. They are all on, or just back from, the riverbank along a 700m-stretch. Most have attached restaurants.

ourpick Phoukhong Guesthouse & Restaurant (☎ 213 673; r 40,000-100,000K; ⚹ 🖵) This place has

gone up in the world thanks to an elegant new structure with four bedrooms, all boasting panoramic views to the Mekong. However, the windows are full frontal, so it may be better to take rooms 201 or 202 upstairs to avoid the public glare. The bathrooms are sparkling new and the air-con adds a chilled atmosphere to the place. The old rooms are disappointingly barren by comparison, but are very cheap.

Souksabay Guesthouse (☎ 214 122; r 50,000-80,000K; ⚹) A friendly guesthouse near the riverfront, the rooms are set around a leafy garden which gives the place a relaxing vibe. The 11 rooms include TV and hot water shower. Out front is a minimart with a basic menu of Lao dishes.

Souksan Hotel (☎ 212 071; r 60,000-100,000K; ⚹) Once one of the more pricey options in Muang Khong, rates are now very reasonable, possibly as it is the last place on the strip, about 250m north of the bridge. Souksan offers spacious rooms with hot water, the cheaper options with fan only. There is also an attached restaurant perched over the river.

Pon's River Guest House (☎ 214 037; r US$6-15; ⚹) A reliable spot thanks to English-speaking Mr Pon, the rooms are good value, as he has reduced the prices since opening his swish new Arena Hotel. Air-con rooms are spacious with smart bedding and a satellite TV. Pon's offers transport all over the southern Laos region.

Auberge Sala Done Khong (☎ 212 077; www.salalao. com; s/d incl breakfast US$20/25, ste from US$26/33; ⚹) One of the first auberges to welcome guests on Don Khong, this remains an atmospheric if somewhat time-warped place. Part of the Sala Lao group, one of the original French-era teak mansions is under renovation and this may lead to a hike in rates. Prices drop by 20% or more from May through September.

Pon's Arena Hotel (☎ 253 065; www.ponhotel.com; r US$40-50; ⚹ 🖵) Clearly the locals have been spurred on by the arrival of the Senesothxeun Hotel. Mr Pon has borrowed heavily from their blueprint to invest in this stylish villa with 21 rooms, including seven with a Mekong view. Furnishings are tasteful throughout, including the contemporary bathrooms, and rooms include a terrace or balcony.

Villa Muong Khong Hotel (☎ 213 051; www. khongislandtravel.com; r incl breakfast US$40/45; ⚹ 🖵) Another long-running place popular with tour groups, the Villa Muong Khong has somehow managed to squeeze 52 rooms into one riverfront site. Standards can differ much more significantly than the prices suggest, so it pays to look at a few. The big rooms are slightly spartan, but staff say an upgrade is in the pipeline. French and English are spoken.

Senesothxeun Hotel (☎ 030-526 0577; www.ssx hotel.com; r incl breakfast US$45-80; ✗ ▢ ☞) Let's agree to forgive the unpronounceable name (or the awful abbreviation), for this is the smartest hotel on Don Khong. Rooms offer tasteful linens, Lao silks and fine wood finishing, plus satellite TV and minibar. The bathrooms include a rain shower. River views start at US$50.

Other options are:

Done Khong Guest House & Restaurant (☎ 214 010; r 50,000-120,000K; ✗) In a prime position near the bridge, the upstairs fan-rooms open onto a balcony and are good value at 50,000K.

Mekong Guest House (☎ 213 668; r 50,000-120,000K; ✗) Sprawling over a family compound, the air-con rooms here are in pretty good shape for the kip.

Villa Kang Khong (☎ 213 539; r 60,000-100,000K; ✗) Set back from the river, this old-time favourite is set in a spacious teak house, but rooms are a little threadbare.

EATING

Apart from the odd place selling *fŏe* and Lao snacks, all the eating options are restaurants attached to the aforementioned accommodation. Most places serve Don Khong's famous *lào-láo*, which is often cited as the smoothest in the country.

Done Khong Guest House & Restaurant (mains 15,000-50,000K; ☘ 6.30am-10pm) In an appealing position by the river, this place serves tasty Lao dishes such as *làap*, the mysterious 'soup with chicken gallingly root' (we thought it was galangal on tasting), and plenty of rice dishes.

Pon's (mains 15,000-50,000K; ☘ 6.30am-10pm) Pon's fresh river fish are worth a shot; the *mok pa* (steamed fish in banana leaf) is particularly good. An extensive menu that includes Lao, Thai and traveller fare and an attractive riverfront terrace make this a travellers' favourite.

Auberge Sala Don Khong (mains 20,000-60,000K; ☘ 7am-10pm) The Lao and European fare here is enjoyable and the setting romantic by Don Khong standards. Dishes includes Laotian greatest hits, plus a smattering of French-accented creations. Nonguests should give the kitchen some notice.

Senesothxeun Hotel (mains 20,000-50,000K; ☘ 6.30am-10pm) The restaurant here is not as expensive as the room tariffs would suggest. It is also one of the only air-conditioned dining rooms in the Si Phan Don area. Fresh fish specialities are on the menu, plus comfort food like pasta and salads.

GETTING THERE & AWAY

Boat

The slow boat to Pakse is extinct, so plan on arriving by a combination of boat and road.

There are regular boats between Hat Xai Khun and Don Khong; it's 20,000K per boat for one person, or 10,000K per person for two or more. Bargaining is futile. The boatman will take you as near as possible to your guesthouse of choice. The vehicle ferry between Ban Hat and Ban Na charges 2000K per pedestrian and 7000K per motorcycle (including passengers).

Mr Pon operates boats for Don Det and Don Khon (40,000K per person one way, 60,000K return, 1½ hours) at 8.30am. Getting to Don Khon in the dry season will require a smaller boat. Chartering a private boat for this run will cost about 200,000K.

Bus, Săwngthăew & Minibus

Săwngthăew and buses head to Pakse (50,000K, 2½ to 3½ hours, 128km) until about 10am. After that, head over to Rte 13 and wait for anything heading north.

For the Cambodian border, there is usually a 9am connection that costs US$8 to Stung Treng, US$12 to Kratie, US$15 to Ban Lung and US$18 to Phnom Penh.

Finally, Pon's River Guest House has aircon minibuses that run at 11.30am daily to Pakse for 60,000K.

GETTING AROUND

Bicycles (8000K to 10,000K per day) and motorbikes (from 60,000K per day) can be hired from guesthouses and elsewhere along the main street. Alternatively, haggle with a jumbo driver.

Don Det & Don Khon
ດອນເດດ/ດອນຄອນ

Welcome to the travellers' mecca that is Don Det and Don Khon. Life on these twin islands feels so laid back that you can imagine them just drifting downriver into Cambodia with barely anyone blinking an eyelid. The land of the lotus eaters is writ true on Don Det, as many a traveller has found themselves in a hammock-bound slumber, unable to drag themselves away from the island's charms.

SOUTHERN LAOS

Vang Vieng, the town most often compared with these two islands, feels like Woodstock by comparison.

Don Det has developed dramatically in the past decade and is the more rock'n'roll of the two. Ban Hua Det, at the north end of the island has emerged as a sort of backpacker tractor beam. This market is serviced by music and TV, pool tables and restaurant-bars where travellers, for an extra 10,000K or so, can choose *anything* 'happy' – 'happy' mashed potatoes, 'happy' Lao coffee. Change may be on the way, however, as former president Khamtay Siphandon is concerned about the impact stoned foreigners are having on local life, not to mention his reputation thanks to the shared name.

The islanders are benefitting from the income tourism brings, but many are aware enough of the potential changes to cite Vang Vieng as an example of what they *don't* want to become. Having a spliff is part of backpacker experience and the locals we spoke with seemed to have accepted the arrival of marijuana in Ban Hua Det, but they'd prefer it was an incidental part of a visit rather than the sole reason for coming. They are not, however, that pleased about the arrival of harder drugs, worrying about the influence on their kids. Wherever you are it's polite to ask before you light up.

If this isn't your scene don't scratch the islands off your itinerary yet. Respite is only a short walk away and it's on Don Khon, or at the guesthouses along the southern bank of Don Det, where things are much more serene. This is more what the islands were like when people were first drawn to them, with a sort of timeless beauty best appreciated by riding a bicycle around the few sights, swinging in a hammock, reading a book and chatting with locals and travellers alike.

The islands were an important link for supply lines between Saigon and Laos during the French colonial era. In order to bypass the rapids and waterfalls in the Mekong River, the French built a narrow-gauge railway across the two islands, linked by an attractive arched bridge and terminating in concrete piers at either end. Small engines pulled cargo across the islands but the French dream of making the Mekong a highway to China never really materialised. The bridge and piers remain but no engine has run since WWII, and most of the track has long since been carted off.

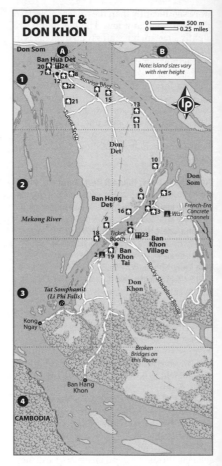

Don Khon, the larger of the two islands, is famous throughout Laos for the cultivation of coconut, bamboo and kapok. In the main village, **Ban Khon**, there are several crumbling French buildings that are about 100 years old. **Wat Khon Tai**, in Ban Khon Tai, towards the southwestern end of Ban Khon, is a Lao temple built on the former site of an ancient Khmer temple, the laterite remains of which are scattered around the site.

INFORMATION
There are plenty of internet cafes clustered along the main drag in Ban Hua Det, all charging a uniform 400K per minute. There are also a handful of places on Don Khon to the east of the bridge. There is no bank, no medical serv-

ices and not even a post office. Some guesthouses and restaurants will change money at poor rates: Mr Mo Guesthouse was offering the most generous rate during our visit.

Xplore-Asia (www.xplore-asia.com) has an office-cum-bar-cum-cafe in Ban Hua Det. It offers various boating options, including kayaking, rafting and sunset pleasure cruises, and can arrange all manner of transport, including connections to Cambodia. Most other guesthouses can also hook you up with onward transport north to Pakse and south to Cambodia. Shop around for the best price.

SIGHTS & ACTIVITIES
There are a few things to see while you're relaxing on the islands, all of which are best accessed on a bicycle hired for about 10,000K per day. Mr Mo Guesthouse has the best bikes available, including Trek, Giant and Merida mountain bikes, for 20,000K per day.

Floating around in inner tubes is a pretty popular way to pass the time. It costs 5000K per day but don't float too far downriver or you'll hit the fast currents that feed into the falls.

Don Khon has an official entrance charge to visit the island, which is set at 20,000K per day and is collected at a booth just below the bridge to Don Det. This charge includes a toll to cross the bridge, a visit to Tat Somphamit and a fee for the community fund to ensure tourist dollars trickle down to help provide village services.

Tat Somphamit (Li Phi Falls)
ຕາດສົມພາມິດ
About 1.5km downriver from Ban Khon is a raging set of rapids called Tat Somphamit but referred to by just about everyone as Li Phi Falls. Li Phi means 'trap spirit' and locals believe the falls act as just that – a trap for bad spirits (of deceased people and animals) as they wash down the river. You'll never see locals swimming here – mixing with the dead is clearly tempting fate a little too much – and it's both culturally insensitive and dangerous to do so. Water churns through the falls at a frenetic pace, especially during the wet season, and we are aware of two travellers who have drowned here in recent years.

Much less risky but thoroughly captivating is watching local fishermen edging out to clear the enormous bamboo traps. During the early rains, a well-positioned trap can catch half a tonne of fish a day. Some traps here and elsewhere in the area have an intake almost 10m long, funnelling fish into a huge basket at the end.

The falls can be reached via the main path heading southwest out of Ban Khon, or on a smaller, shaded and more attractive path that passes through the wat and avoids the trucks full of Thai tourists and their billowing dust. There are plenty of small eat-drink shops at the falls.

Railway Hike
On Don Khon you can make an interesting 5km trek across the island by following the old rail bed. Rusting locomotives sit near either end of the line, including one located about 75m from the south end of the bridge in an area that once doubled as the rail service yard. Heading south, the trail passes stretches of primary forest, rice fields, small villages and singing birds, eventually emerging at the French loading pier, which resembles the skeleton of an unfinished hotel from afar. Across the river to the right is Cambodia. The rail bed is quite a rocky road and tough on a bike. An alternative path runs nearer the island's

SOUTHERN LAOS

DOLPHINS ENDANGERED

The Irrawaddy dolphin (*Orcaella brevirostris*, called *pqa khaa* in Laos) is one of the Mekong River's most fascinating creatures, and one of its most endangered. From the thousands that populated the Mekong and its tributaries in Cambodia and southern Laos as recently as the 1970s, it's now estimated there are fewer than 100 remaining. The surviving few live primarily along a 190km stretch of the Mekong between the Lao border and the Cambodian town of Kratie.

The dark blue to grey cetaceans grow to 2.75m long and are recognisable by their bulging foreheads and small dorsal fins. They are unusually adaptable and can live in fresh or salt water, though they are seldom seen in the sea. The only other known populations in Myanmar and Bangladesh are thought to be equally, if not more at risk of extinction.

Among the Lao and Khmer, Irrawaddy dolphins are traditionally considered reincarnated humans and there are many stories of dolphins having saved the lives of fishermen or villagers who have fallen into the river or been attacked by crocodiles. These cultural beliefs mean neither the Lao nor the Khmer intentionally capture dolphins for food or sport.

In an attempt to crush these beliefs and to extract oil for their war machinery, the Khmer Rouge reportedly killed thousands of the dolphins in the Tonlé Sap, a large lake in Cambodia, during their 1970s reign of terror. Since then fishermen haven't actively targeted Irrawaddy dolphins, but general gill netting, and grenade and dynamite fishing in Cambodia has inevitably taken its toll on the dolphins. Education has reduced the amount of explosive fishing, but unintentional gill netting remains a constant threat – dolphins need to surface and breathe every two to three minutes, and will usually drown before fishermen even know they are in the nets. As if that wasn't bad enough, many juvenile calves have died mysteriously in recent years, suggesting water pollution is also taking its toll.

In Laos, dolphins have been seen as far north as Sekong in recent years, but you're most likely to see them in the conservation zones between 10m and 60m deep that have been established near the border, south of Don Khon. These areas are vital to the dolphins because they act as a refuge during the dry season, when river levels drop dangerously low.

Education and conservation programs to save the dolphins continue, particularly in Cambodia, but their survival is far from guaranteed.

western edge. The return trip, with breaks, should take about three hours on foot.

Eastern Loop Hike

A less onerous walk or cycle takes you to the waterways at the eastern edge of Don Khon where the French built a series of concrete channels used to direct logs. The logs, usually from forests in Sainyabuli Province west of Vientiane, were usually lashed together into rafts of logs. To prevent them going off-course, a Lao 'pilot' would board the raft and steer it through the maze of islands. When they reached the critical area at the north end of Don Khon, the pilots were required to guide the raft onto a reinforced concrete wedge, thus splitting the binds and sending the logs into the channels beyond. The poor 'pilot' would jump for his life moments before impact.

You can still see the walls if you go to the shaded village at the east end of Don Khon. To get here, head northeast from the bridge and turn south about 1km along, passing through a wat and following the path through rice fields to the riverbank. As you continue south you'll see the walls opposite a small village. The path continues along the river and becomes more of a road, eventually petering out at a stream near the southern end of the island. Nearby is the island of **Don Pak Soi**, which has been earmarked for tourism development, although when we visited it didn't have much to offer beyond some mighty big fish traps.

Dolphins

Rare Irrawaddy dolphins (see the boxed text) can sometimes be seen off the southern tip of Don Khon, mainly from December until May. Boats chartered (60,000K per boat, maximum three people) from the old French pier at the south end of Don Khon run out to a small island that looks over a deep-water conservation zone near Cambodian waters. Viewing dolphins is best in the early morning or late afternoon.

SOUTHERN LAOS

Don't expect Flipper-style antics from these dolphins. If they are there at all you'll see a brief flash as they surface to breathe, then they're gone.

SLEEPING

Almost every farmer and his cow on Don Det has jumped aboard the bungalow bandwagon and there are now dozens of guesthouses lining the edge of the island. The greatest concentration is in Ban Hua Det at the northern tip of Don Det, which has become the place to be if you want to live la vida loca into the night. From here a footpath known as Sunset Strip leads along the northwestern edge of the island to places that are relatively quiet and, not surprisingly, have good sunset views. The rest of the accommodation is spread along the pleasant eastern shore, known as Sunrise Boulevard. If you'd prefer to be further from the crowds, head for the quieter places on the southern shore of the island.

Note that things continue to change pretty fast on Don Det, so if the place you're looking at isn't listed here, that doesn't necessarily mean it's not up to scratch: it might be newer and smarter.

Don Khon is home to some more upmarket places, pleasant eateries on the water and a less youthful atmosphere than Don Det. Staying on Don Khon offers a more 'Lao' experience.

Pretty much all the guesthouses here also serve food and drinks all day.

Coming from Ban Nakasang (see p295), boatmen will usually drop you at your guesthouse of choice if you ask, although this may have an impact on price depending on the location.

Don Det

Sunset View (☎ 020-367 6803; Sunset Strip; r 20,000-60,000K) The creaking bamboo lean-tos are old-skool Don Det and start at a budget-friendly 20,000K. Across the path in a new home are some very smart (for Don Det) double rooms with shiny new bathrooms.

Mr Tho's Guesthouse (☎ 020-5656 7502; Sunrise Blvd; r 30,000-60,000K) Confusingly there are two Mr Tho's on Don Det, but this is the sturdier, more central option. Rooms are named after local products like 'Bamboo' and 'Sticky Rice' and the bigger ones include a bathroom and fan.

Mr B's Sunset View (☎ 030-534 5109; Sunset Strip; bungalows 30,000-60,000K) English-speaking Mr B

has some solid bungalows set amid extensive gardens, but Sunset View is popular more for the warm atmosphere and delicious food in the cafe (mains 15,000K to 35,000K). The pumpkin burger is the stuff of legend.

King Kong Resort (Southern Shore; bungalows 35,000-50,000K) Probably the most memorable name among the Don Det offerings, this Brit-run 'resort' has a couple of ensuite bungalows, two more with shared facilities and some rooms in an old house. The restaurant is a cut above the competition with Italian food, pub grub and Sunday roasts. Gay-friendly.

River Garden (☎ 020-7770 1860; Southern Shore; bungalows 40,000-80,000K) A small, friendly guesthouse with house-proud rooms featuring hanging silks and local handicrafts. The pavilion restaurant has a tranquil setting on the riverbank.

Dalom Guesthouse (Sunrise Blvd; r 40,000-80.000K) Set in a big building for this part of the village, the upstairs rooms are spacious, clean and include rare touches like towel and toilet paper. The nice garden includes some cheaper bungalows.

Souksan Hotel (☎ 030-534 5154; Ban Hua Det; r 40,000-100,000K) Hanging onto the northern tip of Don Det, the Souksan's solid rooms remain some of the better options on the island. Spacious doubles start from 60,000K, including bathroom, and staff speak reasonable English. The restaurant (mains 15,000 to 40,000K) has fine sunset views but it does get hot.

Mr Mo Guesthouse (☎ 020-5575 9252; Sunrise Blvd; r 60,000-80,000K) Another substantial cement building offering slightly smarter than average rooms with a fully equipped bathroom. The riverside restaurant is a good place for travel information.

ourpick Little Eden (☎ 020-7773 9045; www.littleedenguesthouse-dondet.com; Sunset Strip; r 150,000-200,000K; ❄) Probably the smartest rooms on Don Det are to be found here, located on the northern tip of the islands next to the Souksan. The bathrooms are bigger than some bungalows elsewhere and the air-con will ensure you're one of the cooler cats in town. The menu here is among the best on the island, with plenty of Western dishes and banana flambé.

Don Det Bungalows (☎ 020-7772 1572; lovely_laos@yahoo.com; Sunrise Blvd; r 150,000-250,000K; ❄) A new bungalow resort with twee little wooden bungalows with elaborate temple-style roofs. Nice touches include impressive bathrooms and some decorative touches rarely seen elsewhere

---

NOT AS SAME, SAME AS THEY LOOK

Standards might be rising, but for now there are still plenty of bungalows on Don Khon and particularly Don Det that look basically the same and cost around 25,000K a night. There are, however, a few things worth considering when making your choice, such as the following:

- **Bathroom** As competition intensifies many guesthouses are adding basic bathrooms to their bungalows. These can vary in standard, so take a look. Ditto for places with share bathrooms. If you don't want to squat, look for one with a throne.
- **Hammock(s)** Most bungalows have balconies with hammocks, but anyone travelling as a pair should check to see if there is room to string up two hammocks, and if there is a second one available.
- **Location** If it's the hot season and you plan on sleeping in, avoid Sunrise Blvd or anywhere facing east, where the morning sun makes your bungalow pretty toasty by 8am. By the same token, places on Sunset Strip can be oven-like in the afternoons.
- **Neighbours** Bamboo walls are paper thin. If you need privacy look for a detached bungalow.
- **Roof** Tin roofs are hotter than traditional palm-frond thatch roofs.
- **Window(s)** With the advent of electricity, all rooms have fans these days, but having two windows in the bungalow/room means that air circulation (and the night's sleep) is vastly improved.

---

on Don Det. Prices range widely between high and low season.

Be afraid, be very afraid, there are dozens more options:

Mekong Dream (Southern Shore; r 40,000-60,000K) New place boasting a hammock lounge, with 14 rattan hammocks in which to kick back. The four rooms include fan and bathroom.

Mr Bounehome's Bungalows (South Sunrise Blvd; bungalows 20,000-40,000K) True, the bungalows are among the most basic on the island, but it's a pretty setting with wide views and spacious grounds.

Mr Phao's Sunrise Bungalows (Sunrise Blvd; bungalows 20,000-40,000K) South of the pier, Mr Phao's has a warm, family feel and bungalows set in a pretty riverside garden.

Mr Tho's Bungalows (☎ 030-534 5865; Sunrise Blvd; bungalows 30,000-50,000K) Just south of the pier, the 'other' Mr Tho's has long been popular for the relaxed atmosphere and library/book exchange.

Paradise Bungalows (Sunrise Blvd; bungalows from 20,000K) As basic as it gets, with shared bathrooms. The book exchange helps fund a local school.

Santiphab Guesthouse (☎ 030-534 6233; bungalows 30,000-60,000K) Near the bridge, Santiphab was one of the first guesthouses on Don Det and is still a good option. The stilted restaurant has panoramic views.

Sidae's Bungalows (Sunrise Blvd; bungalows 30,000K) Nothing to write home about, but it is the only place promoting free *petanque* (boules) on the island.

Mama Tanon Bungalows (☎ 020-5546 5262; Sunrise Blvd; r 30,000-50,000K) Once known as the Rasta Cafe,

the spirit of Marley lives on thanks to the big communal balcony with superb views.

Tawan Daeng (☎ 020-5615 2173; Southern Shore; bungalows 50,000-60,000K) Friendly spot run by Mrs Daeng, rooms include a bathroom and the restaurant has bridge views.

Tena Bungalows (☎ 020-272 2730; Sunset Strip; bungalows 20,000-40,000K) Relaxed restaurant and chill-out area with bungalows dotted about the riverside garden. Just watch out for the resident buffalo.

Don Khon

All of Don Khon's sleeping and eating options are spread along the river either side of the bridge.

Guesthouse Souksanh (r from 30,000K; 💻) Still the cheapest place on the Don Khon strip, rooms are set in a bungalow block with a shared riverview terrace. The internet centre across the road is the cheapest on the island at 15,000K per hour.

Pan's Guesthouse & Restaurant (☎ 020-5534 6939; pkounnavong@yahoo.co.uk; bungalows 70,000-130,000K; 🍴 💻) These are pretty solid bungalows compared with those on Don Det. The air-con rooms include hot water, and some have a riverside setting. The small restaurant is set in a colonial shophouse across the track; internet is available.

Seng Ahloune Guesthouse & Restaurant (☎ 030-534 5807; r US$11-30; 🍴) Long a popular restaurant with visiting tour groups, the family are now providing quality accommodation as well. The fan rooms are a little pricey, but the aircon options are some of the smartest on Don Khon, including a two-star hotel trim. Book a bungalow with a riverside balcony. The restaurant, open from 7am to 10pm, has a huge riverside terrace and does bubbling hotpots for 70,000K.

Auberge Sala Don Khone (☎ 030-525 6390; www.salalao.com; r incl breakfast US$30-50) Formerly a small French-era hospital, the Auberge Sala Don Khone offers the most romantic location on the island. It is worth paying extra for rooms in the original building, as the bungalows aren't any more impressive than cheaper offerings elsewhere. It's a high price to pay for atmosphere, but a newer 'heritage' wing is under construction, which should raise standards.

Sala Phae (☎ 030-525 6390; www.salalao.com; r incl breakfast US$45) Under the same ownership as the Auberge, this is a floating hotel with bungalows set on bamboo rafts (*phae* means raft) in the Mekong. The smart rooms include wooden floors, a small safe, bio-safe toilet and hot water, plus a small balcony with unblemished river views. Nice, but pricey compared with upriver Don Khong.

EATING & DRINKING

When it comes to eating, with the exception of guesthouses noted above for their food, most places serve cold Beerlao and a range of Lao and Western favourites at prices ranging from 15,000K to about 40,000K.

Don Det

Lamphoune's Restaurant Bakery (Sunrise Blvd; cakes 10,000K, mains 15,000-35,000k) A real treat, particularly for those with a bout of the munchies, this bakery whips up delicious brownies, carrot cake and other comforting treats. The small Western menu includes dishes that don't turn up elsewhere, making it a top spot.

Khamphong Restaurant (Ban Hua Det; mains 15,000-40,000K) Occupying a strategic location above the 'beach' and boat landing, this relaxed restaurant offers a good selection of Lao food. Floor seating makes it a relaxed place to linger for a beer.

Jasmine Restaurant (☎ 020-5563 3572; Ban Hua Det; mains 15,000-50,000K) This is the Don Det branch of the Pakse institution serving up a selection of Indian favourites.

Pool Bar (Ban Hua Det) A popular drinking-hole with a busy pool table, this is one of the longer-running bars in town, also turning out pizzas and doubling as the Xplore-Asia office.

Other bars come in and out of fashion depending on whether or not a *falang* is steering the ship. Plenty of travellers are so taken with life on Don Det that they stick around for a while to help a local family with their restaurant-bar. Ban Hua Det is a good place to crawl. There seems to be a semi-official curfew of 11.30pm when the bars wind down and the action moves to the 'beach'. Beach bonfires and midnight dips are not unheard of, but proceed with caution if you have been drinking or smoking heavily.

Don Khon

Chanthounma's Restaurant (mains 15,000-35,000K; ☯ 7am-10pm) Chanthounma's 'good food to suit your mood' lives up to the advertising, delivering tasty and affordable Lao and Western dishes. Hopefully you'll be in a good mood by the time you finish here.

Fleur du Mekong (☎ 020-5676 3141; mains 20,000-50,000K; ☯ 7am-10pm) Run by a friendly French-speaking tour guide, this is the closest restaurant to the bridge. Lao dishes include a delicious duck curry and a fusion baked fish in banana leaf or *papillote*.

GETTING THERE & AWAY

Boat prices to the islands are fixed by a local boat association (that's according to budding communists, more like mafia to you and me). Ban Nakasang to Don Det costs 15,000K per person or 30,000K alone, or to Don Khon costs 25,000K per person or 50,000K alone. Boats can be hired to go anywhere in the islands for about 100,000K per hour.

For Pakse (30,000K, 2½ to 3½ hours, 148km), buses or *săwngthăew* leave Ban Nakasang regularly from 6am to 10am. Most travellers book through tickets on the island, including the local boat and a minibus transfer. There are usually a couple of services a day to Pakse (50,000K, 8am & 1.30pm), plus connections to Stung Treng (US$8) and Phnom Penh (US$11) in Cambodia.

See p274 for buses from Pakse.

Khon Phapheng Falls

ບ້ານຕົກຕາດຄອນພະເຟັງ

South of Don Khon the Mekong River features a 13km stretch of powerful rapids with several sets of cascades. The largest, and by

CROSSING THE CAMBODIAN BORDER AT TRAPAENG KRIEL & NONG KHIANG

Open since 2001, this remote **border** (7am-5pm) is a popular crossing point on the Indochina overland circuit. For many years, there was much confusion associated with crossing here due to not one but two immigration posts, one on the river and one on the road. Things have finally settled down, hence the new names, and a glitzy border gate is under construction as we go to press. Both Lao and Cambodian visas are available on arrival, although minor overcharging is common both sides of the border. In Laos, it's 'overtime', as every day seems to be a public holiday. In Cambodia, it's called 'tea money', as the poor border guards have been stationed at such a remote crossing. Negotiation is possible.

The route south goes to Stung Treng in northeast Cambodia. From the islands most travellers are taking a backpacker bus (minibus) to Stung Treng (US$8, three hours, including formalities), Kratie (US$12, five hours), Ban Lung in Ratanakiri (US$11, six hours) or Phnom Penh (US$18, 11 hours). From Pakse, it costs 120,000K to Stung Treng or 230,000K to Phnom Penh. It's cheaper to take the bus to Stung Treng and then board a Cambodian bus from there. Services to Siem Reap are also advertised, but we don't really recommend these, as they involve an overnight in Kompong Cham, a change of bus and occasional overcharging. Take your time and soak up the atmosphere in the laid-back riverside town of Kratie. Getting to Stung Treng by local transport is just about possible, but you will need lots of time and it will end up costing you more money, as you will need to charter transport to and from the remote border.

It is no longer possible to cross the border via the river and few boats operate the stretch to Stung Treng with the advent of the upgraded road. Xplore-Asia (see p268) may be able to help arrange something via their office in Stung Treng, but it will cost quite a bit more than the bus. They run a raft from Don Det to the border (US$20) between July and November, connecting with the minivan running through to Stung Treng. They also offer combination kayak trips from Si Phan Don to Stung Treng, taking in the flooded forest on the Cambodian side.

Heading north, tourist minibuses dominate the trade from Stung Treng to Don Det and Don Khon (US$9), Don Khong (US$11) or Pakse (US$13). There are also direct buses from Phnom Penh to Pakse, but it's a long haul and better broken up into bite-sized chunks.

far the most awesome anywhere along the Mekong, is **Khon Phapheng** (admission 20,000K), near the eastern shore of the Mekong not far from Ban Thakho. Khon Phapheng isn't as beautiful as the towering waterfalls of the Bolaven Plateau or the fairytale pools of Tat Kuang Si near Luang Prabang, but it is pure, unrestrained aggression as millions of litres of water crash over the rocks and into Cambodia every second. This is a spectacular sight, particularly when the Mekong is at full flood, and is one of the most-visited sites in Laos for Thai tourists, who arrive by the busload. Part of the attraction is the spiritual significance they hold for both Lao and Thais, who believe Khon Phapheng acts as a spirit trap in the same way as Tat Somphamit near Don Khon.

A pavilion on the Mekong shore affords a good view of the falls. A shaky network of bamboo scaffolds on the rocks next to the falls is used by daring fishermen who are said to have an alliance with the spirits of the cascades.

SLEEPING & EATING

Khonephapheng Resort & Golf Club (☎ 030-516 0777; www.khonphaphengresort.com; r incl breakfast US$25-70; ❄ 🖳 🏊) Few people tend to stay near the falls, preferring to bed down on nearby islands. However, this resort is pretty good value compared with the higher end options on Don Khon. Rooms include rain showers, satellite TV and air-con, luxuries on the islands, plus riverview balconies. There's a swimming pool with views to the river and a six-hole golf course. It is meant to be a nine-hole eventually, but things are upside down for the moment. It is about 3km north of Khon Phapheng.

There are lots of local stalls and restaurants beside the falls. **Khamphao Restaurant** (☎ 020-240 7704; mains 20,000-40,000K) served a fine feast on our visit and comes highly recommended.

GETTING THERE & AWAY
Most people book their trip through a guesthouse to go to see the waterfalls, often taking in both the falls and dolphins. If you're making the journey independently, it's best to get to Ban Nakasang and take a *săwngthăew* from there. From Ban Nakasang to Khon Phapheng Falls you can hire a motorcycle taxi for about 40,000K or a jumbo for 100,000K (this is a return fare for the whole jumbo and should

---

THE SOUTHERN SWING

The southern swing is a motorbike or bicycle trip starting in Pakse and taking in the Bolaven Plateau and other southern provinces, see Map p266. By motorbike it can take anywhere from three days to as long as you like, depending on how fast you go and how often you stop. The route we've laid out here takes five days but this is only a guide – everything about it is as flexible as you like. On a bicycle, doing it in reverse is a good idea. Distances are fairly accurate, if not exact (we didn't trust our bike's odometer). Most roads are sealed, and those that are not are in relatively good condition, meaning 110cc bikes are fine. Read the boxed text on p342 before you go.

Day 1 – Pakse to Tat Lo
Head south out of Pakse and up toward the plateau, keeping straight on at the bus station. After about 20km turn left (north) at the junction (labelled Lak 21) of routes 16 and 20, and go another 17km or so to **Utayan Bajiang Champasak** (Phasoume Resort, p301 which is good for lunch. Continue on Rte 20 towards **Tat Lo** (p301) and look for the **Katu village** with its textile market.

Day 2 – Tat Lo to Attapeu
It's easy to spend two nights in Tat Lo, but if not then head about 28km up the road for a look around **Salavan** (p303). If that doesn't appeal, go just 4km to Ban Beng and turn right on the road to Tha Taeng. This 30km-road climbs up onto the **Bolaven Plateau** through **Katu and Alak villages**. Look carefully and you'll see coffins stacked beneath buildings, and perhaps traditional graves in small clearings in the forest. The dead are always buried in the forest, and usually with a significant possession; in one case we saw a child's bicycle atop a grave, in another a farmer's hoe. Continue south on the 46km sealed road to **Sekong** (p306), which can be a useful lunch stop. The smooth 77km road from Sekong to **Attapeu** (p308) goes past a couple of smaller waterfalls, though there are plenty of those later on.

Day 3 – Around Attapeu
You could spend a few days exploring this province; check out the options on p310.

Day 4 – Attapeu to Paksong
We absolutely loved this ride, but would have loved it even more if we'd left Attapeu earlier. Do that (before 10am), and head 47km north on Rte 16 to Ban Bengkhua Kham. Top up your tank and check your odometer here before heading up the beautiful, shaded road through pristine jungle. You won't see many people, but the few Laven we saw included cheroot-sucking women in *sîn* (sarongs), and a couple of guys with unfeasibly long rifles slung over their shoulders with dead birds hanging from the end. After about 16km look for a waterfall in the distance to the north, and at 18km for the awesome but unsigned **Nam Tok Katamtok** (p307). Continue uphill and at about 27km you're on the **Bolaven Plateau**. Several villages dot this road towards Paksong, the last 15km of which is partly sealed but badly potholed. There is affordable accommodation in Paksong (p299) or smarter lodgings at Tat Fan (p298). The distance between Ban Bengkhua Kham and Paksong is 71km. Or you can push on to Pakse if time is tight.

Day 5 – Paksong & around
Check out some of the **waterfalls** (p300), take a trek from **Tat Fan** and drink some decent **coffee** (p299). And that's it – you're pretty much back in Pakse.

include at least two hours for taking in the atmosphere at the falls).

BOLAVEN PLATEAU

ພູພຽງບໍລະເວນ

Spreading across the northeast of Champasak Province into Salavan and Sekong, the fertile Bolaven Plateau (sometimes spelt Bolovens, known in Lao as Phu Phieng Bolaven) is famous for its cool climate, dramatic waterfalls, fertile soil and high-grade coffee plantations. It's also known for being one of the most heavily bombed theatres of the Second Indochina War.

The area wasn't farmed intensively until the French started planting coffee, rubber trees and bananas in the early 20th century. Many of the French planters left following independence in the 1950s and the rest followed as US bombardment became unbearable in the late '60s. Controlling the Bolaven Plateau was considered strategically vital to both the Americans and North Vietnamese, as evidenced by the staggering amount of UXO (unexploded ordnance) still lying around.

The slow process of clearing UXO continues, but in areas where it has been cleared, both local farmers and larger organisations are busy cultivating coffee (see the boxed text, p300). Other local products include fruit, cardamom and rattan.

The largest ethnic group on the plateau is the Laven (Bolaven means 'home of the Laven'). Several other Mon-Khmer ethnic groups, including the Alak, Katu, Ta-oy (Tahoy) and Suay, also live on the plateau. Katu and Alak villages are distinctive because they arrange their palm-and-thatch houses in a circle. One unique Katu custom is the carving of wooden caskets for each member of the household well in advance of an expected death. The coffins are stored beneath homes or rice sheds until needed.

Among other tribes, the best elephant handlers are said to be the animistic-shamanistic Suay (who call themselves Kui). Elephants were used extensively for clearing land and moving timber, although working elephants are a rare sight these days.

The Alak, Katu and Laven are distinctive for the face tattoos of their women, a custom slowly dying out as Lao influence in the area increases.

Several **Katu** and **Alak villages** can be visited along the road between Pakse and Paksong

---

THE KATU & ALAK BUFFALO SACRIFICE

The Katu and Alak are well known in Laos for an annual water buffalo sacrifice (usually performed on a full moon in March) in homage to the village spirit. The number of buffaloes sacrificed – typically from one to four animals – depends on their availability and the bounty of the previous year's agricultural harvest. During the ceremony, the men of the village don wooden masks, hoist spears and wooden shields, then dance around the buffaloes in the centre of the circle formed by their houses. After a prescribed period of dancing the men converge on the buffaloes and spear them to death. The meat is divided among the villagers and each household places a piece in a basket on a pole in front of their house as a spirit offering.

---

at the western edge of the plateau, and along the laterite road that descends steadily from Muang Tha Taeng (That Heng) on the plateau to Beng, in Salavan Province. There are also a few within walking distance of Tat Lo (p301), and on Rte 20. In **Lao Ngam** (not to be confused with Muang Lao Ngam on the road to Salavan), around 40km east of Pakse, is a large day market frequented by many tribal groups.

The plateau has several spectacular waterfalls, including **Tat Fan**, a few kilometres west of Paksong, and **Tat Lo** on Rte 20 to Salavan. Check out www.bolaven.com for some photos of the various waterfalls around the plateau.

Tat Fan & Dong Hua Sao NPA

ຕາດຟານ/ປ່າສະຫງວນແຫ່ງຊາດດົງຫົວຊາວ

Tat Fan is one of the most spectacular waterfalls in Laos. The twin streams of the Huay Bang Lieng plunge out of dense forest and tumble down more than 120m. Tat Fan (pronounced tàat fáan) is at the edge of the 1100-sq-km Dong Hua Sao NPA and the walking trails around here provide a good way to get a taste of the park. Dong Hua Sao is reputedly home to a small population of tigers who are said to munch through the occasional hunter, although the chances of actually seeing one are pretty much zero. You're more likely to see monkeys, large butterflies and, in the wet season, rare hornbills.

Tat Fan is 800m south of Rte 23 – look for the signs at Km 38. A path leads down to the top of the falls and affords fine views, though this is perilously slippery in the wet season and is often impassable. An easier viewing point is Tad Fane Resort (p299), a jungle lodge that looks down onto the falls from the top of a cliff opposite. The resort has a couple of professional English-speaking guides who can arrange fairly easy half- and full-day treks around the edge of the NPA. These might take in Laven and Katu villages, coffee plantations, and almost always at least one other waterfall.

A half-day trek costs US$3.50 to US$5.50, depending on numbers, and a full-day is US$10 including lunch. When possible, the morning trek leaves at 8.30am and takes the steep descent to the top of Tat Fan, returning about 12.30pm. The 1pm trek is usually more of a stroll and swim, walking through coffee plantations to 17m-high Tat Cham Pi (which means Small Banana Waterfall, although no one could tell us why). The large pool below is perfect for swimming, and private enough that women can usually get down to their swimwear without offending the locals. Adventure sandals are appropriate in the dry season but boots are better in the wet to deter leeches. As one guide told us, 'the flip-flop is not possible'.

Rafting and kayaking trips are possible on Huay Bang Lieng during the wet season from July to November. For details speak to Green Discovery or Xplore-Asia in Pakse (both p268).

Transport between Pakse and Paksong or beyond stops 800m north of Tat Fan (see p300 for details). When you arrive there's a small fee (5000K) for entrance and parking if you're not staying or eating at the resort. The popularity of Tat Fan with day-tripping Thai tourists has also prompted local residents to establish a small market in the car park. Some of the goods on sale are innocent enough, such as coffee and green tea grown locally. However, please don't buy the orchids, which come straight from Dong Hua Sao. Local guides report that orchids are now only marginally easier to spot than tigers in the area around Tat Fan.

SLEEPING & EATING

Tad Fane Resort (☎ 020-5553 1400; www.tadfane.com; s/d/fam incl breakfast US$30/32/40) These attractive wooden bungalows sit atop a cliff overlooking the falls, although only the two larger family rooms actually have a clear view of Tat Fan. All have a verandah and attached bathroom, but there is no fan or air-con due to cool nights. Ageing a little, they are still very atmospheric. The restaurant (mains 20,000 to 50,000K) has great views and serves sandwiches and tasty Lao and Thai food. In the high season (November to February) it pays to book ahead, and to pack something warm from Pakse.

E-TU Resort (☎ 020-276 9769; www.waterfallet upaksong.com; r incl breakfast US$45) Alright, so it's not strictly Tat Fan, but it's just a few kilometres down the road near Tat Etu and is signposted around the Km 35 mark. Set in the heart of a coffee and tea plantation, the bungalows are the smartest accommodation in the Bolaven area with polished wooden floors and striking Lao textiles. The nearby waterfall is easier to access than Tat Fan and swimming is possible.

Paksong & Around

Paksong, Laos's coffee capital, may not be much to look at, most of it having been obliterated in a storm of bombs during the Second Indochina War, but it boasts a temperate climate thanks to its altitude of 1300m. It is an affordable Bolaven base from which to explore the plateau, has a mildly interesting market and is refreshingly cool.

INFORMATION

The best place to seek out information on Paksong and its surrounding coffee plantations and waterfalls is **Ban Won** (Rte 16; 🛜), also known as Koffie's Coffee. There's currently no sign but look out for the free wi-fi sign…yes, this is the only place in Paksong with internet. Run by a Dutch coffee aficionado, who is appropriately nicknamed Koffie, and his Laven wife, this is the place to sample fresh coffee and green tea (5000K a cuppa) fresh from the plateau. Coffee workshops and plantation tours are available and start from 50,000K per person. For more on Paksong, visit the useful website www.paksong.info.

COFFEE

Coffee trees of varying sizes blanket the Bolaven Plateau and you can walk through them on the easy afternoon treks from Tat Fan. Those wanting to get closer to the action can head to **Phuoi** (Phuouy), which has become the unofficial headquarters for Jhai Coffee Farmers Co-op (see the boxed text, p300).

SOUTHERN LAOS

KĄA-FÉH LÁO (LAO COFFEE)

The high, flat ground of the Bolaven Plateau is ideal for growing coffee and the region produces some of the best and most expensive beans on earth. Arabica, Arabica Typica and Robusta are grown, much of it around the 'coffee town' of Paksong.

The French introduced coffee to the Bolaven Plateau in the early 1900s and the Arabica Typica shipped home became known as the 'champagne of coffee'. Plans to make the plateau a major coffee-growing centre died with the carpet bombing of the '60s and '70s.

Business began to pick up in the 1990s and was dominated by a few plantations and companies, the largest being Pakse-based Dao Heung. For the farmers, however, earning less than US$0.50 per kg wasn't really improving their living standards. These businesses still dominate today but a fair-trade project aimed at empowering small-scale farmers is gathering steam. The **Jhai Coffee Farmer Cooperative** (www.jhaicoffee.com) is a 500-member group formed in 2004 with help from the California-based Jhai Foundation and Thanksgiving Coffee in the US. Members come from 12 villages and several ethnic groups living mainly along the rough road running south from Rte 23 to Ban Nong Luang. Machinery has been bought, and cooperative farmers have been trained in modern cultivation methods to maximise the quality of the beans. And with Fairtrade certification the farmers are guaranteed US$1.36 per kg, more than three times what they made selling to larger wholesalers. However, when coffee prices climb above the fair trade price, such as to US$1.70 in 2007, farmers can choose to sell to other buyers if they want to guarantee the best price.

Lao Mountain Coffee (www.laomountain.com), a Vientiane-based roasting company, purchases from the Jhai Cooperative and their beans are available in Pakse, Vientiane and Luang Prabang.

To get to Phuoi head east on Rte 23 for about 1.5km and look for the big sign pointing right (south) down a dirt road to Ban Nong Luang. This spine-jarring road runs to the southern edge of the plateau and is home to the 12 mainly Laven villages that make up the Jhai Coffee Farmers Co-op. Phuoi is 4km along, but more adventurous souls with a few spare hours might want to continue another 7km to **Ban Nong Luang**. From this village it's possible to take a local guide and walk to two fairly impressive waterfalls, the seven-tiered **Tat Tha Jet** and **Tat Kameud**. The return trip takes a while so start early. If you get stuck, homestays in Ban Nong Luang are possible. Note that no one in the village speaks English, but they should understand 'homestay' if you want the experience.

WATERFALLS

As well as Tat Fan, numerous breathtaking other cascades drop off the Bolaven Plateau within striking distance of Paksong. Most are marked by a blue sign with a painted representation of the cataract in question. **Tat Yuang** (admission 5000K) is among the most impressive, with its twin torrents falling about 40m and flowing into lush jungle. Tat Yuang is hugely popular with day-trippers from Pakse and Thailand who like to picnic at the top, so getting here early is a good idea. It's OK to

swim at the bottom, but women should wear a sarong.

To get there, follow the signs right (south) off Rte 23 at Km 40 and go a further 2km. A scenic way to Tat Fan from here is the 45-minute walk along a beautiful forest trail that starts beside the bathrooms at Tat Yuang.

SLEEPING & EATING

Savanna Guesthouse (☎ 020-5579 0613; r 70,000-100,000K) A friendly spot near a pretty pond, the owner speaks some English. Rooms are modern and smart, including spiffy bathrooms and satellite TV. It is tucked away behind the market.

Paksong Phuthavada Hotel (☎ 030-534 8081; r from 600B; 🞫) Visible from all over town, this hotel sits atop a hillside overlooking Paksong. Sweep up the grand driveway and into a 600B room, which will be spacious and sparkling clean.

Borlaven Restaurant (☎ 020-5583 6326; mains 15,000-40,000K) Set in a thatched house with pretty flowers, this local restaurant has a small menu of Laotian food. Approaching town from the north, this is the first place in town, located on the left-hand side.

GETTING THERE & AWAY

Buses and *săwngthăew* between Paksong and Pakse's southern (Km 8) bus terminal leave frequently between about 8am and 4pm (15,000K, 90 minutes). For Tat Fan, get off at Km 38 and follow the signs to the falls and resort.

Utayan Bajiang Champasak (Phasoume Resort)

A Thai-owned 'ecoresort', **Utayan Bajiang Champasak** (☎ 031-251 294; off Rte 20; entry 5000k per person) 38km northwest of Pakse is scattered through a stretch of thick jungle either side of the small but beautiful Phasoume Waterfall. It's possible to stay here in one of the 14 Swiss Family Robinson–style tree houses (250,000K), but they're not great value compared with Tat Lo. More sensible is to drop by the restaurant (mains 20,000 to 40,000K) for a tasty Thai lunch, most likely accompanied by busloads of Thai tourists.

The resort itself might seem to be more a homage to big dead trees than to live trees – they're sliced and diced into chairs, tables, beams, posts, floor timbers, stepping stones and just about any other use you can imagine. However, we're assured that the tonnes of timber used to build this place were taken from trees rejected by local logging operations.

An appealing elevated jungle walk leads to a 'museum village' where families of Katu, Nge and Laven attempt to entertain visitors. The families seem happy enough, and you can even stay with them for 70,000K per person, but for us the whole experience is way too contrived – the museum lifestyle just feels surreal.

GETTING THERE & AWAY

There is no direct public transport to Phasoume. Take any transport heading up Rte 20 towards Salavan and get off at a turn-off 400m after the Houy Cham Pa bridge, about 36km from Pakse. Follow signs for Phasoume Falls and it is a 1.5km walk.

SALAVAN PROVINCE

Like Sekong and Attapeu Provinces to the south, Salavan is notable as much for its remoteness as any traditional tourism draws. Salavan (also spelt Saravan and Saravane) is not on the way to anywhere and upcountry roads remain some of the worst in Laos, but it is these very qualities and the lure of tough travel that have begun to attract a few hardy

visitors looking to get well-and-truly off the beaten track.

There are a handful of attractions. The province straddles the northern edge of the Bolaven Plateau and Tat Lo, just 30km from Salavan town, is an attractive village near some waterfalls and the best place to base yourself. Beyond waterfalls, however, the ethnic diversity of the region is the main lure. While more than half of the population of Salavan is ethnically Lao (Loum and Soung), none are native to this area. The remainder of the 350,000 inhabitants belong to relatively obscure Mon-Khmer groups, including the Ta-oy (Tahoy), Lavai, Katang, Alak, Laven, Ngai, Tong, Pako, Kanay, Katu and Kado.

Almost half the province is covered by natural forest but getting into the three protected areas is really tough. **Phu Xieng Thong NPA** is accessible from Pakse (see p275), but for now the **Se Ban Nuan NPA** near to Rte 13 and particularly the **Se Xap NPA** in the far east have no tourist infrastructure whatsoever – in fact, infrastructure of any kind is extremely limited.

Just about every major branch of the Ho Chi Minh Trail cut through Salavan at some point and UXO remains a serious problem. While Salavan town no longer has piles of rusting war detritus waiting for scrap merchants, plenty of towns to the north and east do. Clearance teams head out almost every day to continue the painstaking task of finding and neutralising these weapons of war, and expect to be busy for years to come. Despite plenty of interest from travellers keen to walk part of the trail, so far no such operation exists.

TAT LO

ຕາດເລາະ

☎ 034

Tat Lo (pronounced *tàat láw*) has the atmosphere of a backpacker retreat with cheap accommodation, an attractive setting and plenty of diversions, but very few backpackers. And herein lies its charm. Waterfalls are the town's *raison d'être* and they give it a serenity that sees many visitors stay longer than they planned. If you're wanting to explore deeper into the province, Tat Lo is the ideal base.

The town is a one-street affair, with most accommodation just east of the bridge. A **community guides office** here has information on nine different treks to surrounding sights and nearby Ngai villages (starting at 45,000K per person for a four-hour trip) and is where you get hooked up with a guide. It's run by Soulideth of Tim Guesthouse, who speaks great English and is a mine of information on nearby attractions. He also offers **internet access** (per min 500K) and can arrange motorbike hire (80,000K per day).

Sights & Activities
WATERFALLS
There are actually three waterfalls on this stretch of river. The nearest to town is **Tat Hang**, which can be seen from the bridge and some guesthouses. It's possible to swim here; just go where the local kids go. Note that during the dry season, dam authorities upstream release water in the evening, more than doubling the waterfall volume. Check out what time the release occurs so you're not standing at the top of the waterfall then, a potentially fatal error.

Tat Lo, about 700m upriver, is a little bigger but probably won't knock your socks off. To get there, cross the bridge and walk up through Saise Guest House, keeping to the path by the river. The spectacular third cascade is **Tat Suong**. It's about 10km out and accessible by motorbike or bicycle. Head uphill past the turn-off to Tadlo Lodge, turn right at the power station and left where the road ends. Look (hard) for the sign pointing left to Ban Sanummay and follow it to a parking area. It's not far from here to the stunning and precipitous top of the falls…don't get too close.

ELEPHANT RIDES
Tadlo Lodge offers rides on its two female elephants (85,000K per elephant, 90 minutes). The typical ride plods through forest, villages and streams full of slippery rocks you wouldn't dream of crossing on foot. Each elephant can carry two people and they depart from just outside the guides' office at 8am, 10am, 1pm and 3pm. You can book at the guides' office or Tad Lo Resort itself.

Sleeping & Eating
Palamei Guesthouse (☎ 020-333 9365; r 25,000-50,000K) This place may not be on the river, but it makes up for it with friendly service and a relaxed vibe. There are two large bungalows at the back of the compound with ricefield views and there is even a little lean-to kitchen if you fancy trying your hand at Lao cooking. Plus free transfers to the main road.

Tim Guesthouse & Restaurant (☎ 211 885; soulidet@gmail.com; r 40,000-60,000K; 💻) The simple rooms here all have shared bathroom and no views, but what they lack in luxuries is offset by atmosphere. English- and French-speaking Soulideth is a mine of local information and the restaurant (mains 6000k to 35,000K), serves the usual range of travellers' favourites plus seasonal specialities. There is a book exchange, and opposite the guesthouse is a classroom (built by Soulideth) where local kids learn computer skills.

Siphaseth Guest House & Restaurant (☎ 211 890; r 40,000-70,000K) In a great location by the bridge, the bungalows have a good garden location and include bathrooms. Solid rooms in the newer concrete building come with hot water and river views. The restaurant (mains 5000 to 25,000K) is the ideal place to have a sundowner Beerlao.

ourpick Saise Guest House (☎ 211 886; r US$8-35; 🐾) In lush gardens on the west bank of the river, this place sprawls from Tat Hang to Tat Lo. Rooms range from cheap 'tribe bungalows' for US$8 to sophisticated air-conditioned bungalows further upstream. The US$20 bungalows with air-con, hot water and views of the falls are a good deal. Check whether or not breakfast is included. The restaurant has been refurbished here and is beautifully set amid forest with views to Tat Hang. At night a spotlight picks out the falls making for a most romantic setting. Good Lao and Thai food, plus some spirits and mixers if you are feeling the urge.

Tadlo Lodge (☎ 211 889; www.tadlolodge.com; bungalows s/d incl breakfast US$39/44) This long-running lodge has a prime position straddling the river, overlooking the lower waterfall. The attractive bungalows have balconies and clean hot-water bathrooms, but are a touch overpriced when compared with the Saise. The pavilion-style restaurant (mains 25,000 to 100,000K) offers the best selection of European food in Tat Lo, but it was a case of 'sorry, no cooking' during our visit.

Other options include the following:

Mama Pap Guesthouse (r 25,000K) Set amid the village like a homestay, these basic bungalows are tended by friendly Mama Pap who promises 'big eat, small kips' at her roadside restaurant.

Sailomyen Guest House (r from 25,000K) Next door to Siphaseth, this place has simple fan-conditioned huts with balcony in a pretty riverside location. The restaurant has cheap meals with nothing costing more than 15,000K.

SOUTHERN LAOS

Getting There & Away

Just say 'Tat Lo' at Pakse's southern bus station and you'll be pointed in the right direction. It costs 25,000K and there are usually five or more buses a day. Tat Lo is 86km northeast of Pakse off the road to Salavan; you'll be dropped at Ban Khoua Set. There might be a motorbike or tuk-tuk (10,000K) to shuttle you the last 1.8km. Otherwise, it's an uphill walk.

If you're heading to Paksong, get to Ban Beng, and catch a bus coming from Salavan. It might go all the way to Paksong or change buses at Tha Taeng; either way, allow a few hours.

SALAVAN

ສາລະວັນ

☎ 034 / pop 25,000

Once a Champasak kingdom outpost known as Muang Mam and inhabited mostly by Mon-Khmer minorities, it was renamed Salavan (Sarawan in Thai) by the Siamese in 1828. The provincial capital of Salavan was all but destroyed in the Indochina War, when it bounced back and forth between Royal Lao Army and Pathet Lao occupation. The rebuilt town is a collection of brick and wood buildings, though if you look carefully you'll find more old buildings around than you might expect and it's not entirely without charm.

The town sits within a bend of the Se Don, which eventually meets the Mekong at Pakse. Functionally, Salavan serves mainly as a supply centre for farmers in surrounding districts. For most travellers, the backwater atmosphere isn't enough of a draw and instead they sensibly opt to stay at nearby Tat Lo.

Information

Lao Development Bank (8.30am-4.30pm Mon-Fri), a little west of the market, will change US dollars or Thai baht. The **post office** (8am-4.30pm) is around the corner from the market and next door is a **telecom office** (8am-5pm Mon-Fri).

The **Provincial Tourism Office** (☎ 211 528; Ground fl; 8am-noon & 1-4pm Mon-Fri), signposted on the main drag through town, is where the French- and English-speaking Mr Bounthone Sinachak resides and is worth a visit if you plan on heading further into the province.

Sleeping & Eating

Thipphaphone Guesthouse (☎ 211 063; r 40,000-70,000K;), Located near the market, this friendly guesthouse is set in an old wooden family house and the rooms are fine, if uninspiring. The wonderfully welcoming manager doesn't speak any English.

Phoufa Hotel (☎ 030-537 0799; r 50,000-140,000K;) This could be the main attraction of a visit to Salavan. Located on the road from Tat Lo, this pretty garden compound is home to the best digs in town. The 31 rooms include attractive bungalows with air-con and satellite TV. Take a cheaper room and you'll have to forsake such luxuries. The grounds include a chilling mound of war remnants and UXO from around the province.

Follow a short dirt road at the south end of town to discover a fish restaurant, the **Hong Lek**

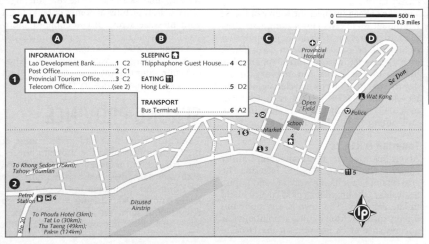

SOUTHERN LAOS

(mains 15,000–35,000K; 🕑 dinner), on the banks of the Se Don. It serves superb barbecued fish, fresh vegetables and icy Beerlao. Bring mosquito repellent and a Lao phrasebook.

Getting There & Away
BUS & SĂWNGTHĂEW
For buses from Pakse see p273. Salavan's bus terminal is 2km west of the town centre, where Rte 20 meets Rte 15. Buses for Pakse (25,000K, three hours, 124km) are scheduled to leave at 7.30am and 10am. Buses or *săwngthăew* leave for Sekong (20,000K, two to three hours, 93km) at 7.45am and 1.30pm. These go through Tha Taeng (10,000K, one to 1½ hours, 49km).

Lot dai săn, trucks with wooden cabins built on the back and seats sans legroom crammed inside, are the only beasts capable of tackling the roads north, east and directly west of Salavan. They run along rough Rte 15 to Khong Sedon (25,000K, three hours, 75km), on Rte 13, where you can pick up other transport to Savannakhet.

In the dry season they also take on the potholed stretches of earth that masquerade as roads running to Tahoy and Toumlan.

AROUND SALAVAN
Approach upcountry Salavan Province in the spirit of adventure, in part because getting to most destinations will be an adventure in itself.

Nong Bua
ໜອງບົວ
The lake of **Nong Bua**, near the source of the Se Don about 15km east of town along a seasonal road, is famous for its dwindling population of Siamese crocodiles (*khàe* in Lao). There aren't many left (two or three, apparently), but the tourism office can help organise a day trip to Nong Bua by bicycle. A guide and bicycle cost 40,000K per day each. Chances of actually seeing the crocs are slim. Instead, look out for 1588m-high Phu Katae nearby.

Toumlan & Rte 23
About 50km north of Salavan along bumpy Rte 23 is the Katang village of **Toumlan**. The area is famous for its silk weavings and Lapup festival (see the boxed text, p298) usually held in late February. The town is very poor but interesting both from a cultural point of view and because of its position on the Ho Chi Minh Trail. UXO continues to pose a threat here while also providing income from the sale of scrap.

North of Toumlan, Rte 23 heads towards Rte 9 and Muang Phin, via the site of **Prince Souvanaphong's Bridge**, named because it was built by the 'Red Prince' Souphanouvong (who was a trained engineer) in 1942. Unfortunately the bridge was blown up in 1968 and has never been rebuilt. In the dry season it should be possible to cross here with a small motorbike and continue on to Muang Phin on Rte 9, the journey between Salavan and Muang Phin taking about eight hours, sometimes much longer.

Tahoy & the Ho Chi Minh Trail
ເສັ້ນທາງໂຮຈີມິນ
Northeast along Rte 15, which can be impassable for days during the wet season, is **Tahoy** (Ta-oy), a centre for the Ta-oy ethnic group, who number around 30,000 spread across the eastern areas of Salavan and Sekong Provinces. The Ta-oy live in forested mountain valleys at altitudes between 300m and 1000m, often in areas shared with Katu and other Mon-Khmer groups. Like many Mon-Khmer groups in southern Laos, they practise a combination of animism and shamanism; during village ceremonies, the Ta-oy put up diamond-patterned bamboo totems to warn outsiders not to enter.

Tahoy town was an important marker on the Ho Chi Minh Trail and two major branches lead off Rte 15 nearby. If you want to see war junk ask a local to take you; you might need to draw pictures of bombs or tanks to get your message across. If you come to Tahoy you'll likely have to stay. The government lets out **rooms** (30,000K) in a simple building.

A *săwngthăew* leaves Salavan for Tahoy (30,000K, four to eight hours, 84km) at 11am every second day in the dry season.

SEKONG PROVINCE
Stretching from near the eastern edge of the Bolaven Plateau to the Vietnam border, this rugged and remote province is dotted with waterfalls, dissected by the impressive Se Kong and dominated in the east by the lesser-known Dak Cheung Plateau, which rises 1500m above sea level. With the massive cliff walls of the southern Se Xap NPA

(some are said to be more than 1000m high) and several sizable mountains in the province, Sekong has the potential to become an outdoor adventurers' paradise.

Alas, not yet. The province is among the poorest in Laos and a combination of terrible road infrastructure, virtually no facilities for tourism and a landscape that remains unsafe due to UXO dropped on the Ho Chi Minh Trail decades ago, mean much of it is off-limits to all but the most intrepid.

That's not to say there's no reason to come. There are waterfalls on the Se Nam Noy (Nam Noy River) and the breathtaking Nam Tok Katamtok waterfall (p307), which plunges more than 100m. The other reason to come is the

people. By population Sekong is the smallest of Laos's provinces, but among its 90,000 inhabitants are people from 14 different tribal groups, making it the most ethnically diverse province in the country. The vast majority are from Mon-Khmer tribes, with the Alak, Katu, Taliang, Yae and Nge the largest groups. These total more than 75% of the population. Other groups include the Pacoh, Chatong, Suay (Souei), Katang and Ta-oy. These diverse groups are not Buddhists, so you won't see many wats. Rather, their belief systems mix animism and ancestor worship. The Katu and Taliang tend towards monogamy but, unusually in a part of the world so traditionally male dominated, tolerate polyandry (two or more husbands).

WE'RE ON A ROAD TO NOWHERE   Nick Ray

It was August 2008 and the rains were already falling hard in Laos. I had been recruited by the BBC as the line producer for the popular *Top Gear* show, in readiness for the program's Vietnam special. Vietnam special? Quite what was I doing in Laos, you might ask? Well, the original brief was not motorbikes, but old cars (American, French, Russian), and the provisional route included both Cambodia and Laos. So I found myself in Laos trying to buy some old bangers and plot a challenging route for Clarkson and co.

Hooking up with fellow Lonely Planet author Andrew Burke, we decided to head south on our 250cc dirt bikes from Muang Phin to Salavan on abandoned Rte 23 (note the use of the word abandoned). It started so well. The beautiful route skirted Dong Phu Vieng NPA, and we made it to the Se Pon in no time at all. With Prince Souvanaphong's Bridge duly photographed, we crossed the river in rickety canoes and continued on our way. Then it all started to go wrong.

The trails kept dead-ending in ricefields and we couldn't find any locals to lead the way. Eventually we found the route, but time was ticking and it was a tough jungle ride. Four river crossings later, my battery was flooded and my bike had given up. We tried push starts, but in the end we had to abandon it in the forest for a later rescue. We continued on one bike until around 8pm, when we encountered a freshly fallen tree blocking the trail. It was too dark to find a workaround, so despondently we had to turn back. We ended up sleeping with a Lao family who we woke up around 10pm. They kindly plied us with sticky rice and *lào-láo* (rice whisky).

The next morning was a mission to recover the second bike. Towing motorbikes is a delicate art, particularly when the 'road' in question is a rocky, muddy jungle path. The person being towed can't blink. They simply have to follow the lead bike. If the lead rider hits a big rock, then bad luck, so does the rider being towed. Any deviation from the course and both riders will end up on the floor. We made it back to the river in one piece, despite a rather dramatic accident near the Se Pon. I ducked to avoid a branch at the last minute. My bike went right, Andrew's bike went left and he flew off the embankment like Superman. Luckily the bike didn't follow, and he managed to miss the rocks. We survived a wobbly crossing back over the Se Pon and eventually made it to Savannakhet later that night.

Incidentally, the *Top Gear* shoot eventually took place in October in Vietnam only and we made a madcap dash from Saigon to Hanoi in 10 days: Jeremy Clarkson on a Vespa, Richard Hammond on a Minsk and James May on a Honda Cub. Eventually arriving in Halong Bay, they converted the bikes to amphibious vehicles and became the first tourists to explore the bay by motorbike. I drove the whole length of the country on a customised Ural bike with a raised camera seat on the back to give the shooters maximum safety and comfort. I was right next to Clarkson when he came off his Vespa and can dispel all rumours at long last – it was a genuine accident and not staged. I mean, come on, tiny Vespas just aren't designed to be ridden by someone who's 6 ft 7 in.

Note that in the wet season travelling anywhere beyond Rte 16 can be difficult.

SEKONG (MUANG LAMAM)

ເຊກອງ(ເມືອງລະມາ)

☎ 038 / pop 15,000

Most visitors pass through Sekong, as the choice of accommodation is limited and the nearby attractions can usually be incorporated into a journey south to Attapeu. Carved out of the wilderness in the mid-1980s, the unnecessarily sprawling town is set on a basic grid with government buildings in the centre surrounded by areas of concrete, wooden and wood-and-thatch stilt homes. There are no street names.

The Se Kong wraps around the town on the southern and eastern sides, while the Bolaven Plateau rises precipitously to the west. At the **town market**, tribes from outlying areas trade cloth for Vietnamese goods while others sell an ever-dwindling number of birds, lizards and small mammals hunted in nearby forests.

Drop by **UXO Lao** (🕒 8am-5pm), opposite the Ministry of Finance office just west of the market. These guys have been clearing UXO for years and have a mildly interesting display of rusting munitions and weaponry in their yard. Visitors are welcome.

Information & Orientation

Sekong sits on a grid between Rte 16 in the north and the Se Kong to the south. Almost everything you need is in the streets just east of the market. The only real information offered here is in the Pha Thib Restaurant menu, which has stacks of information on local ethnic groups, villages and handicrafts, most of it prepared by a UN Development Programme (UNDP) caseworker.

The **Lao Development Bank** (🕒 9.30am-4pm Mon-Fri) is not far from the market and can change Thai baht and US dollars cash for kip only. The **post office** (🕒 8am-noon & 1-5pm Mon-Fri) is at the other end of this road.

Sleeping & Eating

Woman Fever Kosmet Centre Guesthouse (☎ 020-5415 1610; r 30,000K) Opposite the Pha Thib Restaurant, the simple rooms with share bathrooms here are very basic, but also very affordable. We haven't heard of any guests catching woman fever; proceeds actually go to a malaria education group.

Thida Hotel (☎ 020-233 7801; riverside; r 100,000K; ✵) Located on the banks of the Se Kong, this smart new hotel has little luxuries like satellite TV, a fridge and slick bathrooms. The riverside restaurant is arguably the most salubrious dining venue in town.

Hong Kham Hotel (☎ 211 777; Rte 16; r 125,000K; ✵) A big hotel on the main road, the Hong Kham is quite new, so consequently rooms are smart, clean and include satellite TV and bathrooms with hot water. The downstairs restaurant stays open later than most stalls around town and has a mix of Lao, Chinese and Vietnamese dishes.

Pha Thib Restaurant (mains 15,000-35,000K; 🕒 7am-8pm) Little more than a wooden shack, the friendly Viet owner cooks up tasty, fresh dishes, including Lao and Vietnamese favourites. Try the deep-fried fish with vegetables or sour fish soup. The bathrooms are somewhat less memorable than the food.

Getting There & Away

Sekong's dusty/muddy bus station is about 2km northwest of town off Rte 16; a jumbo there costs about 5000K. Few buses actually originate in Sekong; instead they stop here between Pakse and Attapeu. Schedules are flexible. For Pakse (30,000K, around four hours, 135km) there is at least one bus (usually 6am) then occasional buses/săwngthăew coming through from Attapeu until about 1pm. For Attapeu (25,000K, two hours, 76km) there is one dedicated departure at 8am, then every two hours or so until about 4pm. Transport to Salavan (25,000K, three hours, 93km) leaves intermittently from 6am 'til noon.

For transport from Pakse see p273.

Getting Around

Sekong has a few jumbos, look for them at the market. Pha Thib Restaurant can rent out motorbikes for 80,000K per day.

AROUND SEKONG

Off Rte 16 south of Sekong there are several villages and waterfalls that could be visited as part of a day trip; you'd have to hire a bicycle or motorbike in Sekong, or charter a tuk-tuk or jumbo (about 80,000K). About 3.5km south of town, turn right along a rough dirt road immediately after a school. Follow the dirt road about 2.5km to the relatively ordinary **Tat Hia** waterfall. A little further along Rte 16, another path heads southeast for about 3km toward the Se Kong and two Alak villages. The first is known for its fine *sín* (traditional sarongs). Similar villages can be found at the end of dirt roads leading east 12km and 14km from Sekong.

The road at Km 14 also leads to **Tat Faek**. On the Se Nam Noi not far upriver of the Se Kong, Tat Faek is about 5m high and there are two pools in which you can swim. Swimmers should use the one above the falls, as a diabolical-sounding puffer fish known as the *pa pao* is believed to lurk in the pool below. Locals report with a sort of gleeful dread how the evil *pa pao* can home in on and sink its razor-sharp teeth into the human penis with uncanny precision. Admittedly, the women are more gleeful about this than the men. Tat Faek is about 1.5km off the road; take the right fork after about 500m, then turn left another 800m beyond.

At Km 16 a long bridge crosses the Se Nam Noi and you enter Attapeu Province. Just south of the bridge a track leads east to **Tat Se Noi**, known locally as 'waterfall of the heads' (Tat Hua Khon), owing to a WWII episode in which Japanese soldiers decapitated a number of Lao soldiers and tossed their heads into the falls. The falls are about 100m wide and 7m deep.

Nam Tok Katamtok
ນ້ຳຕົກກະຕຳຕົກ

All of the above falls are small fry compared with the mighty Nam Tok Katamtok. Running off the Bolaven Plateau, the Huay Katam drops more than 100m out of thick forest at what some describe as Laos's highest waterfall. And while they may or may not be bigger than Tat Fan, these falls are easily as impressive because you need to be something of an explorer to find them.

When you're 31km south of Sekong, turn west along the laterite road that eventually leads to Paksong, 71km away. There are actually two falls to be seen from this road. The first is after 16km, where if you look off to the north you'll see a large cascade in the distance. Nam Tok Katamtok is about 2km further on. You'll know you're getting near when you cross three bridges and climb a hill, where a 25m-long trail leads back off to the left and out of the jungle appears this spectacular drop. There is no sign and both are easy to miss, so check your odometer and slow down when approaching.

ATTAPEU PROVINCE

Attapeu is the wild east of Laos. It's frontier territory in every sense, with the rugged and densely forested regions bordering Cambodia and Vietnam as well-endowed with wildlife as anywhere in the country. Tigers are still present in the province, and species as rare as the clouded leopard roam the more remote areas. However, this also makes it a rough and ready province to explore, with little in the way of information or infrastructure.

In reality, Attapeu is best experienced as part of a motorbike trip around the southern highlands. Coming here by public bus is not ideal, as it is difficult to arrange local transport and guides for further exploration. Anyone who wants an experienced guide may need to book a tour through travel companies based in Pakse (p268). It also offers a road less travelled for border enthusiasts, as the remote Phou Keua-Bo Y crossing links Attapeu with Kontum or Quy Nhon in Vietnam.

The province has hosted an important trading route since the Chenla period and Khmer-style brick *prasat* have been found in the jungles near the Vietnam border. During the Lan Xang period the area was known for being rich in gold and forest products. In the 16th century, it saw the demise of King Setthathirat. Historians believe the Lan Xang regent upset the locals and members of his court in Vientiane when, on an expedition to the area, he kidnapped a local woman and hauled her off to Vientiane. After getting her pregnant he returned to Attapeu to settle things down but wound up dead instead. The town of Saisettha is named after him and he is believed to be buried under a nearby stupa.

More recent history is just as violent. Every branch of the Ho Chi Minh Trail ran through Attapeu and the province was heavily bombed during the Second Indochina War. Rare pieces of ordnance are still visible, though most has been carted off for scrap – the missile launcher at Pa-am (p310) being the notable exception.

Sealed Rte 18B to the Vietnam border has brought the Vietnamese back in numbers. In several new guesthouses and restaurants in the provincial capital, a Vietnamese phrasebook will be more useful than a Lao dictionary.

Of the 11 ethnic groups found in Attapeu, Lavae, Nge and Talieng predominate, with Lao Loum, Chinese and a fast-growing number of Vietnamese concentrated in the capital. There are fewer than 20 Buddhist temples in the entire province.

ATTAPEU (SAMAKHI XAI)
ອັດຕະປື
☎ 036 / pop 19,200

It's officially known as Muang Samakhi Xai but even locals seem to find this a mouthful. The capital of Attapeu Province is set in a large valley and flanked by the mountains of the nearby Bolaven Plateau, 1000m above, and two rivers that meet nearby, the mighty Se Kong and the smaller Se Kaman. Attapeu is famed in southern Laos as the 'garden village' for its shady lanes and lush flora. While thoroughly deserved, this reputation is all the more remarkable given that Attapeu actually means 'buffalo shit' in Mon-Khmer dialects. Legend has it that when early Lao Loum people arrived they asked the locals what was the name of their town. In response, the villagers apparently pointed at a nearby pile of buffalo manure, known locally as *itkapu (ait krapeau* in contemporary Khmer*)*. Perhaps there was some misunderstanding. Maybe the Lao Loum didn't like the place or possibly the villagers were having a laugh. Either way, with some subsequent adjustment in pronunciation, the town is known as Attapeu.

While Attapeu has little in the way of 'sights' it's not a shitty town as such. Engaging locals and affordable accommodation make this a sensible base for exploring the wild east, a job made simpler by the completion of a bridge across the Se Kong and Rte 18B (the only street in town that actually has a name) to Vietnam.

Information

Attapeu Office of Tourism (☎ 211 056) Recently relocated to a smart new chalet 200m east of the water tower, English-speaking Mr Si Thanon Sai (☎ 020-244 0871) is the man in the know. Guides and transport (motorbike or 4WD) may be available with some notice, but don't expect to just rock up.

Internet (Attapeu Palace Hotel; 10,000K per hr; ☼ 7am-10pm) This hotel has one terminal in reception, plus a wi-fi connection for guests staying near enough to the lobby.

BCEL (Rte 18A; ☼ 8.30am-3.30pm Mon-Fri) Changes US dollars, euros or Thai baht for kip, plus it has Attapeu's first ATM, dispensing a miserly 700,000K at a time.

Lao Telecom (☼ 7am-5pm Mon-Fri)

Post office (☼ 8am-noon & 1-4pm Mon-Fri)

Sights & Activities

Despite being a largely Lao Loum place, Attapeu town is not renowned for its Buddhist temples. The most interesting is **Wat Luang Muang Mai**, usually known as Wat Luang, which was built in 1939 and features some older monastic buildings with original *naga* bargeboards. And that's about it. The real sights and activities lie beyond the town.

Sleeping

Souksomphone Guesthouse (☎ 211 046; r 40,000-65,000K; ✹) The place with the mother-of-all hardwood staircases protruding from the front. The cheaper rooms are cramped to the point of cells, but the air-con twins are pretty good value. The manager speaks some English and can arrange motorbike hire (80,000K).

Phoutthavong Guesthouse (☎ 020-9981 8440; r 60,000-70,000K; ✹) Forget the Lao name, this place is now Vietnamese-run like many businesses around town. Rooms are clean and spacious and come with satellite TV, fan or air-con, and hot water. A second building was nearing completion during our visit which may have a slightly smarter trim.

Dokchampa Hotel (☎ 211 061; Rte 18A; r 100,000-150,000K; ✹ ▢) A little out of town, the Dokchampa is a welcoming place to stay. Rooms are comfortable enough, if a slightly on the pricey side for what you get. There's a small restaurant out front that does reliable noodle soups.

Attapeu Palace Hotel (☎ 211 204; atp_palace@yahoo.com; r 100,000-310,000K; ✹ ▢ ☎) Before you get too excited, there is nothing very palatial about this place. However, the 44-room monolith has the best rooms in Attapeu, even if several of them are starting to show their age. Rooms are very spacious and fairly clean, and anything above 150,000K includes breakfast. VIP rooms (260,000K and up) have a bathtub and are big enough to play football in. The hotel has a (rare) computer terminal with an internet connection (10,000K per hour) but choose a room near the lobby if you want to take advantage of free wi-fi. The restaurant (mains 20,000 to 50,000K), however, isn't a highlight. If you want more than eggs for breakfast, venture elsewhere.

OUR PICK Saise Guesthouse (☎ 020-5659 8368; r 120,000-150,000K; ✹) Looking more like a modern mansion than a hotel, the Saise is the only

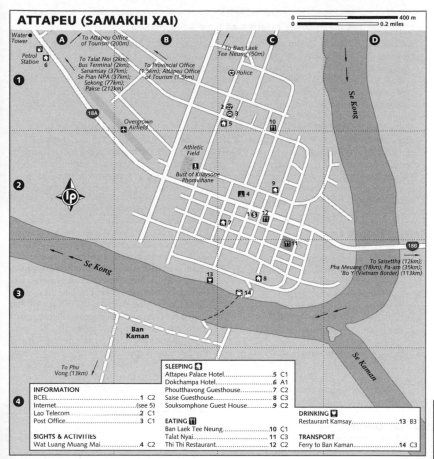

ATTAPEU (SAMAKHI XAI)

INFORMATION
BCEL...1 C2
Internet...(see 5)
Lao Telecom....................................2 C1
Post Office......................................3 C1

SIGHTS & ACTIVITIES
Wat Luang Muang Mai.......................4 C2

SLEEPING
Attapeu Palace Hotel.........................5 C1
Dokchampa Hotel.............................6 A1
Phoutthavong Guesthouse...................7 C2
Saise Guesthouse..............................8 C3
Souksomphone Guest House................9 C2

EATING
Ban Laek Tee Neung.........................10 C1
Talat Nyai......................................11 C3
Thi Thi Restaurant...........................12 C2

DRINKING
Restaurant Kamsay...........................13 B3

TRANSPORT
Ferry to Ban Kaman.........................14 C3

accommodation to take advantage of river views. The well-equipped rooms include polished wooden floors, air-con, satellite TV and hot showers. Clean and well-run, it's the best all-rounder in town.

Eating & Drinking

Attapeu is not a culinary destination by any means. Noodle dishes and *fŏe* are available during the morning at **Talat Nyai** (main market), near the bridge, and other snacks can be had at any time.

Thi Thi Restaurant (☎ 211303; Rte 18A; mains 10,000-40,000K; ⏰ 7am-9pm) This Vietnamese-run place has, unsurprisingly, decent Vietnamese food, including imported seafood from the Quy Nhon coast. However, the service is pretty

surly and we were ushered out after barely finishing our meal. Attapeu closes early.

Restaurant Kamsay (⏰ 11am-9pm) One of several mainly bamboo places overlooking the Se Kong, Kamsay is mainly about sunset Beerlaos but is also popular for its barbecued goat (25,000K per plate). If you buy the whole beast – they're usually tied up out the front praying for a busload of vegetarians – you get to drink the blood for free.

Ban Laek Tee Neung (☎ 020-5591 3580; mains 30,000-60,000K; ⏰ 11am-10pm) This restaurant is uniformly considered the best dining in town. The Korean barbecues are popular, the sukiyaki pretty good and the various *làap* are mouth-watering. It had just relocated to a new venue during our visit.

SOUTHERN LAOS

CROSSING THE VIETNAMESE BORDER AT BO Y & PHOU KEUA

Rte 18B is a dramatic mountain road that runs 113km to the **Bo Y (Vietnam)/Phou Keua (Laos) crossing**. The second half is all uphill and landslides are common during the wet season. Lao visas are now available on arrival at this border, but Vietnamese visas are definitely not, so arrange the paperwork in Pakse (US$40, available same day), Vientiane or Phnom Penh. The Vietnamese side of the border is an elaborate affair, with a massive duty free complex. Laos, by comparison, is a motley collection of wood cabins. It speaks volumes about the relative stages of development of the two countries.

Mai Linh Express (☎ 030-539 0216 in Attapeu, 0592-211 211 in Vietnam) operates a daily minibus connecting Kontum with Pakse (118,000K) via Attapeu (80,000K). It departs at 7am from both Pakse and Kontum, reaching Attapeu around 11.30am in either direction. It takes about four hours to Kontum. From Kontum it is possible to travel south to Pleiku or Quy Nhon and northeast to Hoi An and Danang. Tickets are sold at the Thi Thi Restaurant (p309) in Attapeu. It is also possible to charter a vehicle to the border and then arrange a transfer from Bo Y deeper into Vietnam, but this will cost an arm and a leg compared to the bus.

Getting There & Away

The Attapeu bus terminal is next to Talat Noi at Km 3 northwest of town. Rte 18A that runs south of the Bolaven Plateau remains impassable to most traffic, so all transport to or from Pakse goes via Sekong and Paksong. There are usually five or more buses to Pakse (40,000 to 60,000K, five to six hours, 212km) between 6am and midday. You can get off any of these buses at Sekong (25,000k, two hours, 77km) or Paksong (35,000k, four hours, 162km). For Tat Lo or Salavan you'll need to head off early, get a bus heading to Paksong, and change at Tha Taeng. Most buses servicing Attapeu are older, naturally cooled affairs.

Getting Around

A jumbo trip around town should cost about 4000K per person. To/from the bus terminal costs about 6000K, but you'll likely be charged US$1 or 10,000K. Bicycles (20,000K per day) and motorbikes (80,000K) can be rented at the Attapeu Palace Hotel.

AROUND ATTAPEU

Heading east on Rte 18B brings you to **Saisettha**, a sizable village 12km from Attapeu on the north bank of the Se Kaman. There is an attractive wat in use here and the whole town has a good vibe. Continue about 3km further east, across the Se Kaman (Kaman River) and take a sharp right just beyond Ban Hat Xai Khao. **Pha Meuang**, another 3km along a dirt road, is the main attraction because the Lan Xang king Setthathirat is buried here in Wat Pha Saysettha. The stupa in which he is interred is thought to have been built by his son around 1577. Just wandering around the village and wat is an experience.

The area southeast of Attapeu was an integral part of the Ho Chi Minh Trail (see the boxed text, p264) and as such was heavily bombed during the war. The bombers were particularly interested in the village of **Phu Vong**, 13km southeast of the capital, where two main branches of the trail split – the Sihanouk Trail continuing south into Cambodia and the Ho Chi Minh Trail veering east towards Vietnam. The village is a pleasant diversion for an hour or two, though you won't see much war junk. To get there, cross the Se Kong (3000K with motorbike) to Ban Kaman and ride the 13km to Phu Vong.

Pa-am

ພະອໍ

A day-trip to Saisettha could happily be combined with a visit to the modest, tree-shaded village of **Pa-am**. About 35km east of Attapeu, Pa-am straddles both the small Nam Pa (Pa River) and a road that was formerly a branch of the Ho Chi Minh Trail. The main attraction is a Russian **surface-to-air missile** (SAM), complete with Russian and Vietnamese stencilling, which was set up by the North Vietnamese to defend against aerial attack. It has survived the scrap hunters by government order and, apart from a few cluster bomb casings-cum-planter boxes, there's not much else to see – it's the trip that's most fun. Alak villagers sell textiles and basic meals are available.

When coming from Attapeu you need to cross the Nam Pa to reach the missile launcher. In the dry season you can walk, at other times there is an improvised passenger and motorbike ferry. Pa-am is easily reachable by motorbike; take Rte 18B 10km towards Vietnam and keep straight on the laterite road when the sealed road bends to the right. Otherwise *săwngthăew* run from Attapeu (15,000K, one hour, 35km) every morning.

Se Pian NPA
ປ່າສະຫງວນແຫ່ງຊາດເຊປ່ຽນ

While **Se Pian NPA** (www.xepian.org; admission 10,000K) is most accessible from Pakse (p285), it's also possible to get into the park from Attapeu. Community-based tourism projects have been established and involve village homestays and treks into the eastern reaches of the area. There are one-, two- and three-day treks concentrating on **Tat Saepha**, **Tat Samongphak** and **Tat Saeponglai**, three impressive waterfalls along branches of the Se Pian. In the rainy season some sections of the treks involve a boat ride. Talk to the Tourism Office about finding a guide, as having someone to translate for you makes the trip, and the mandatory homestay in the pretty village of **Ban Mai**, much richer.

Another way into this part of the Se Pian NPA is by taking a boat down the Se Kong towards the Cambodian border. If you fancy the road (or river) less travelled, then this might be for you. To do it, take a *săwngthăew* from the bus terminal in Attapeu to Sanamsay (15,000K, 75 minutes, 35km) along Rte 18A; *săwngthăew* leave Attapeu at 9am, noon, 2pm and 4pm, and the last one returns at 3pm. In Sanamsay, find a boatman to take you further downriver.

This trip is more about the travel than the destination, so don't expect a pot of gold at the end (or much in the way of services, either; BYO food, water and sun protection). The journey is, however, quite a trip, as the river is abutted by deep forest for much of the way.

To get back to Sanamsay on the same day start early (hiring a jumbo or motorbike from Attapeu might be best). There's no guesthouse in Sanamsay but if you are stuck, someone will find you a bed.

DONG AMPHAN NPA
ປ່າສະຫງວນແຫ່ງຊາດດົງອຳພານ

Dong Amphan NPA is a 1975-sq-km protected area wedged between the Se Kaman to the north and west, the Vietnamese border in the east and Rte 18B to the south. Timber and wildlife poaching threaten the pristine environment, but until recently it remained one of the most intact ecosystems in the country. However, hydroelectric projects on the Se Kaman and Se Su are changing this for the worse.

The main attraction in the protected area is fabled **Nong Fa**. This beautiful volcanic lake, similar to but larger than Yeak Lom in Cambodia's Ratanakiri Province, was used by the North Vietnamese as an R'n'R for soldiers hurt on the Ho Chi Minh Trail. It is now accessible by road from Attapeu, but it's a long ride involving 100km of surfaced road on Rte 18B and 76km on poor dirt roads. The journey takes about five hours, so it's not really possible as a day trip. If you're planning to visit Ratanakiri in Cambodia, you may want to save your volcanic crater experience for Yeak Lom, just 10 minutes from Ban Lung.

DIRECTORY

Directory

CONTENTS

ACCOMMODATION

The range and quality of accommodation in Laos is rapidly improving. That said, once you get off the beaten track (Vientiane, Luang Prabang, Pakse and Vang Vieng) the options are more modest, typically restricted to budget-priced guesthouses and hotels and the occasional midrange offering.

Paying in the requested currency is usually cheaper than letting the hotel or guesthouse convert the price into another currency using their unfavourable (to you, at least) exchange rates. If the price is quoted in kip, you'll do best to pay in kip; if priced in dollars, pay in dollars.

Accommodation prices listed in this book are high-season prices for rooms with attached bathroom, unless stated otherwise. An icon is included to indicate if air-con is available; otherwise, assume that a fan will be provided.

Homestays

Staying in a village home is becoming increasingly popular. Homestays are invariably in rural areas, cheap at about US$5 for your bed, dinner and breakfast, and provide a chance for travellers to experience life, Lao style. For an idea of what to expect, and what not to expect, see the boxed text, Feeling the 'Real Laos', p45.

PRACTICALITIES

■ The *Vientiane Times* (www.vientiane times.org.la), published Monday to Saturday, the country's only English-language newspaper, cleaves to the party line.

■ Francophones can read *Le Rénovateur* (www.lerenovateur.org.la), a government mouthpiece similar to the *Vientiane Times*.

■ The LPDR's single radio station, Lao National Radio (LNR; www.lnr.org.la), broadcasts sanitised English-language news twice daily.

■ Short-wave radios can pick up BBC, VOA, Radio Australia and Radio France International. A good frequency for BBC in the morning is 15360.

■ Lao National TV has two TV channels. Programming in Lao is limited so most people watch Thai TV and/or karaoke videos.

■ The LPDR uses 220V AC circuitry; power outlets usually feature two-prong round or flat sockets.

■ The metric system is used for measurements. Gold and silver are sometimes weighed in *bàat* (15g).

Guesthouses

The distinction between 'guesthouse', 'hotel' and 'resort' often exists in name only, but legally speaking a guesthouse in Laos has fewer than 16 rooms. They typically occupy large, two-storey homes of recent vintage, but occasionally you'll find them in more historic and charismatic wooden homes. In places such as Don Det (p289) in southern Laos or Muang Ngoi Neua (p207) in northern Laos you'll come across guesthouses consisting of simple bamboo-thatch huts with shared facilities, going for as little as US$3 a night.

Facilities are improving across the country, but the most inexpensive places might still have cold-water showers or simple Lao-style bathing, where you wash yourself using a plastic bowl to scoop cold water from large jars, tanks or even 44-gallon drums. Hot water is hardly a necessity in lowland Laos, but is very welcome in the mountains.

The price of simple rooms in most towns averages between US$5 and US$8 a night with shared bathroom. For an attached bathroom and hot shower expect to pay about US$9 to US$14; anything above this will usually also have air-conditioning and a TV, with cable TV in English if you're lucky. Some guesthouses have stepped up the style and offer upscale rooms for between about US$15 and US$30.

Hotels

Hotel rooms in Vientiane, Luang Prabang, Vang Vieng, Savannakhet and Pakse offer private bathrooms and fans as standard features for between about US$10 and US$20 per night. There is then a vast range of rooms with air-con, hot water and TV costing between about US$15 and US$70, differentiated by their location, the city and the levels of style and service.

Small and medium-size hotels oriented towards Asian business and leisure travellers and tour groups exist in the larger cities. In Vientiane, Luang Prabang and Pakse these may be housed in charming old French colonial mansions. Whether modern or historic, tariffs at hotels such as these run from about US$40 to US$100 for rooms with air-con, hot water, TV and refrigerator.

Then there are the few top-end hotels with better decor, more facilities and personalised service, often occupying more carefully-restored colonial villas or modern, purpose-built buildings. These typically cost between US$80 and US$200, occasionally even higher.

What is common among all hotels in Laos is that the rooms are great value compared with what you'd pay at home. Solid midrange places, that would cost US$80 or more at home, can be had for US$20 or US$40. And at the top-end boutique luxury, that would cost

---

ROOM RATES

In this guide all accommodation is listed by price order, starting at the cheapest, *not* in order of preference. We have divided accommodation by the price of a double room thus:

Budget	less than US$20
Midrange	US$20-80
Top end	more than US$80.

The overall quality of rooms in Laos has improved substantially in recent years but prices remain remarkably reasonable. By Western standards, they're a bargain. It's worth remembering this if you're trying to bargain the price down, particularly at the budget end where competition is fierce and margins are small.

For example, the farmers flogging bamboo bungalows on Don Det aren't making any money on their US$2 rooms, they're just hoping you'll buy some food and beer. Taking this into consideration, as well as the fact that international economic imperatives like inflation and the price of oil affect Laos as much as they do prices in your own country, it's important to understand that room rates may go up during the life of this book. When that happens, please don't just assume you're being ripped off.

By all means try to get the best rate you can; that's part of travelling. But be aware of the cultural context. Generally speaking, the Lao avoid conflict as much as they possibly can and while they are happy to bargain a little, they don't usually buy into protracted negotiations or arguments over price. If the rate seems unfair to you (as opposed to being beyond your budget) by all means make a counter offer. This will usually be accepted, or not, straight away.

two or three times as much in Europe, North America or Australia, can be had for US$80.

The trade-off, however, is in the service. Few hotels in Laos have managed to hone their service to Western standards, and English literacy is often frustratingly poor, even in the more expensive hotels. So prepare for lower standards of service than you're used to and you'll be more likely to have a good time.

Resorts

The term 'resort' in the Lao context may be used for any accommodation situated outside towns or cities. It does not imply, as it usually does in many other countries, the availability of sports activities, spa and so on.

Lao resorts typically cost about the same as a midrange hotel, ie from about US$15 to US$70 a night. A few, such as those outside Luang Prabang, come closer to the international idea of a resort, with prices to match.

ACTIVITIES
Boating

With only a handful of public riverboat routes still running (p142), do-it-yourself boating is increasingly the way to see the more remote corners of Laos. Rafting, canoeing and kayaking trips are all available, with varying degrees of comfort and cost. Operators in Luang Namtha, Luang Prabang, Vang Vieng, Tha Khaek, Pakse and Don Det offer guided rafting and kayaking trips, complete with the necessary equipment, along waterways in those areas.

As with bicycles, you shouldn't have any special customs difficulties bringing your own small boat to Laos. Because of the difficulties of overland transport, however, the smaller and lighter your craft is, the better.

For trained paddlers almost any of the major waterways draining from the western slopes of the Annamite Mountains towards the Mekong valley can be interesting. In the north, the Nam Ou, Nam Tha, Nam Khan and of course the Mekong River are navigable year-round. In central and southern Laos the Nam Kading, Nam Hin Bun and Se Kong as well as the Mekong are safe bets. The upstream areas of all these rivers can be accessed by road, so drop-offs and pick-ups are limited only by the availability of transport.

Several tributaries that feed into the Mekong between Vientiane and Tha Khaek are particularly recommended because they see so little boat traffic and run through spectacularly rugged limestone country. In particular the Nam Kading and Nam Hin Bun are wide and relatively clean rivers, though a proposed dam on the Nam Kading might change things there. Upstream put-in spots are limited but possible. If you'd prefer someone else looks after the logistics, **Green Discovery** (www.greendiscoverylaos.com) offers rafting and kayaking trips in this area.

Cycling

The overall lack of vehicular traffic makes cycling an attractive proposition in Laos, although this is somewhat offset by the general absence of roads in the first place. Bikes can be hired in the larger towns but they're generally cheap Chinese affairs unsuited to much more than pedalling around town. For any serious out-of-town cycling you're better off bringing your own bike, one that's geared to rough road conditions.

In terms of road gradient and availability of food and accommodation, the easiest long-distance ride is along Rte 13, which extends the entire north–south length of the country from Boten on the Chinese–Lao border to Nong Khiang on the Cambodian border. In the dry season this road may become very dusty on paved sections, and trucks can be a nuisance – though they're nowhere near as overwhelming as in Vietnam or Thailand.

For a list of outfits that offer guided cycling and mountain bike tours, go to p338.

Alternatively, for self-guided touring, any of the various loops described in this book are (usually) just as good on a bicycle as they are on a motorbike, just slower. There's the ride over the Bolaven Plateau and beyond (see the boxed text, p297); the shorter Savannakhet route (see the boxed text, p261); the West Vang Vieng loop (see the boxed text, p134); and of course the original loop (see the boxed text, p252) out of Tha Khaek. In northern Laos, heading east along Rte 7 towards the Plain of Jars is a good trip.

Hiking & Trekking

Trekking through the mountains and forests of Laos has become so popular it's almost a mandatory part of any visit to the country. And thanks to several projects aimed at getting money into poor communities, there are now more than 10 areas you can choose from; for a general rundown, see the boxed text, p79. Each organised trek is different, but most involve walking through a mix of forest and agricultural land and staying in homes or community guesthouses in remote villages. Prices, including all food, guides, transport, accommodation and park fees, start at about US$20 a day. In most cases you can trek with as few as two people, with per person costs falling the larger the group.

While the cultural side of a trip is limited without some language skills, trekking alone is possible in most of the country. Walking off the track in most of eastern Laos can be dangerous given the amount of unexploded ordnance (UXO; p318) still lying around.

If you do go it alone and have some language skills or a phrasebook it's often possible to spend the night in a remote village, though do offer to pay for your food and bed.

Finally, you can set off on a day hike from just about any town or village in Laos. Take a hat, sunscreen and plenty of water.

Rock Climbing

The limestone karsts of Laos are perfect for rock climbing, and routes have been established at two main sites: near Vang Vieng (p133) and Nong Khiaw (p205). Vang Vieng has the most established scene, with dozens of climbs ranging from beginner to very tough indeed. Climbers have compared the routes and guides here favourably with the high-profile climbing at Krabi, in Thailand.

Adam's Rock Climbing School (www.laos-climbing .com) Based out of Vang Vieng, Adam has heaps of experience climbing the area, his guides get good reports and equipment rental is also available.

Green Discovery (www.greendiscoverylaos.com) is a large operator and has a good reputation; its website has more detail on equipment, prices and routes.

BUSINESS HOURS

Government offices are typically open from 8am to 11.30am or noon and from 1pm to 5pm Monday to Friday. Some offices may open for a half day on Saturday, but this custom was generally abandoned in 1998 when the official two-hour lunch break introduced by the French was reduced to one hour. Does this mean you can expect to find Lao officials back in their offices promptly at 1pm? Probably not.

Shops and private businesses open and close a bit later and usually stay open during lunch.

> ### RESTAURANT HOURS
>
> Business hours for restaurants vary according to their clientele and the food they serve.
>
> ■ Shops selling noodles and/or rice soup are typically open from 7am to 1pm.
>
> ■ Lao restaurants with a larger menu of dishes served with rice are often open from 10am to 10pm.
>
> ■ Tourist restaurants offering both Lao and *falang* (Western) food, and open for breakfast, lunch and dinner, usually open their doors around 7.30am and serve till 10pm.
>
> ■ Tourist restaurants that don't open for breakfast generally serve from 11am to 11pm.

On Saturday some businesses are open all day, others only half a day. Most businesses, except restaurants, are closed on Sunday.

For a list of standard business hours see the inside front cover. If hours vary from these, they are stated in individual reviews.

CHILDREN

Like many places in Southeast Asia, travelling with children in Laos can be a lot of fun as long as you come prepared with the right attitudes, physical requirements and the usual parental patience. Lonely Planet's *Travel with Children* contains useful advice on how to cope with kids on the road and what to bring along to make things go more smoothly.

Practicalities

Amenities geared towards children – such as high chairs in restaurants, child-safety seats for vehicles, or nappy-changing facilities in public restrooms – are virtually unknown in Laos. Thus parents will have to be extra resourceful in seeking out substitutes or follow the example of Lao families (which means holding smaller children on their laps much of the time).

Outside of Vientiane, day-care centres are likewise unknown, though this is rarely a problem. The Lao adore children and in many instances will shower attention on your off-spring, who will readily find playmates among their Lao peers and a temporary nanny service at practically every stop.

DIRECTORY

Baby formula and nappies (diapers) are available at minimarkets in the larger towns and cities, but for rural areas you'll need to bring along a sufficient supply.

For the most part parents needn't worry too much about health concerns, though it pays to lay down a few ground rules – such as regular hand-washing – to head off potential medical problems. All the usual health precautions apply; see the Health chapter for details. Children should especially be warned not to play with animals encountered along the way as rabies is disturbingly common in Laos.

Sights & Activities

Younger children usually don't find the historic temples and French colonial architecture of Luang Prabang and Vientiane as inspiring as their parents do, but travelling with children does tend to give you a different perspective to what you might be used to. The chicken's-eye view of a three-year-old, for example, means they tend to notice all sorts of things at ground level their parents often miss. As long as they don't try to put any of them in their mouths, this is usually no problem.

If boredom does set in, the best cure in Laos is always the outdoors. In Luang Prabang the waterfalls at Tat Sae (p170) and Tat Kuang Si (p170) can amuse most kids for days. Boat trips (p142) are usually well-received too.

Most children also take to the unique Hindu-Buddhist sculpture garden of Xieng Khuan (p96) outside Vientiane. The capital also has a few more mainstream activities, such as swimming pools and ten-pin bowling alleys (p97).

Elsewhere, the Plain of Jars (p193) invites the kind of fantasy exploration most kids are prone to.

CLIMATE CHARTS

The annual monsoon cycles that affect all of mainland Southeast Asia produce a 'dry and wet monsoon climate' with three basic seasons for most of Laos. The southwest monsoon arrives in Laos between May and July and lasts into November.

The monsoon is followed by a dry period (from November to May), beginning with lower relative temperatures and cool breezes created by Asia's northeast monsoon (which bypasses most of Laos), lasting until mid-February. Exceptions to this general pattern include Xieng Khuang, Hua Phan and

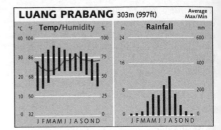

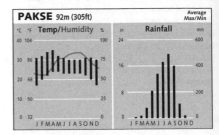

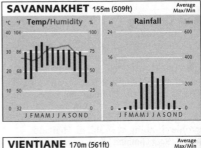

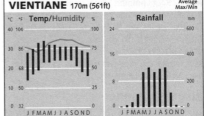

Phongsali Provinces, which may receive rainfall coming from Vietnam and China during the months of April and May.

Rainfall varies substantially according to latitude and altitude, with the highlands of Vientiane, Bolikhamsai, Khammuan and eastern Champasak Provinces receiving the most.

Temperatures also vary according to altitude. In the humid, low-lying Mekong River valley, temperatures range from 15°C to 38°C, while in the mountains of Xieng Khuang it can drop to 0°C at night. See p13 for comment on the best times to travel in Laos.

COURSES
Cooking
Lao cooking courses are available to tourists in Luang Prabang (p157), Udomxai (p211) and Vientiane (p99).

Language
At the time of research, regular courses in spoken and written Lao were only available at one institute.

Centre Culturel et de Coopération Linguistique (Map p90; ☎ 021-215 764; www.ambafrance-laos.org; Th Lan Xang, Vientiane)
Summer Study Abroad in Laos (SAIL; www.laostudies. org/sail) An intensive eight-week language study program at a variety of levels hosted by the Lao-American College in Vientiane.

Meditation
If you can speak Lao or Thai, or can arrange an interpreter, you may be able to study *vipassana* (insight meditation) at Wat Sok Pa Luang (p97) in Vientiane.

CUSTOMS
Customs inspections at ports of entry are lax as long as you're not bringing in more than a moderate amount of luggage. You're not supposed to enter the country with more than 500 cigarettes or 1L of distilled spirits. All the usual prohibitions on drugs, weapons and pornography apply, otherwise you can bring in practically anything you want, including unlimited sums of Lao and foreign currency.

DANGERS & ANNOYANCES
Over the last 15 years or so Laos has earned a reputation among visitors as a remarkably safe place to travel, with little crime reported and few of the scams so often found in more touristed places such as Vietnam, Cambodia and Thailand. And while the vast majority of Laotians remain honest and welcoming, things aren't quite as idyllic as they once were. The main change has been in the rise of petty crime, such as theft and low-level scams, which are more annoying than actually dangerous.

That's not to say Laos is danger free. However, most dangers are easy enough to avoid.

Queues
The Lao follow the usual Southeast Asian method of queuing for services, which is to say they don't form a line at all but simply push en masse towards the point of distribution, whether at ticket counters, post-office windows or bus doors. It won't help to get angry and shout 'I was here first!' since first-come, first-served simply isn't the way things are done here. Rather it's 'first-seen, first-served'. Learn to play the game the Lao way, by pushing your money, passport, letters or whatever to the front of the crowd as best you can. Eventually you'll get through.

Road Travel
Better roads, better vehicles and fewer insurgents mean road travel in Laos is quite safe, if not always comfortable. It's not yet possible to totally rule out the threat from armed bandits or insurgents, though it is miniscule. And while the scarcity of traffic in Laos means there are far, far fewer accidents than the daily horror on Vietnam's roads, accidents are still the major risk to travellers.

ARMED ATTACK
With the Hmong insurgency virtually finished, travel along Rtes 7 and 13, particularly in the vicinity of Phu Khoun and Kasi, is as safe as it has been for decades. There have been no reported attacks on traffic since 2004. If you're still nervous – and it's true that two Swiss cyclists were murdered during an ambush on Rte 13 in 2003 – ask around in Vientiane or Luang Prabang to make sure the situation remains secure before travelling along Rte 7 to Phonsavan or Rte 13 between Vang Vieng and Luang Prabang.

ACCIDENTS
After speedboats, and assuming you'll not be walking through any minefields, the law of averages suggests travelling by road is probably the most dangerous activity in Laos. Having said that, there are relatively few reports of bus crashes and the like, and the lack of traffic and quality of roads makes collisions less likely too.

When riding in buses, you may be able to cut your risk of serious injuries if you choose an aisle seat towards the middle of the bus; these are generally more comfortable too. If you can't get an aisle seat, the right side is usually safer as it cuts down the risks in the event

DIRECTORY

your conveyance is side-swiped by oncoming traffic. It's worth carrying on your person the number of your embassy in Vientiane and the number of **Aek Udon Hospital** (☎ 0066 4234 2555) in Udon Thani, Thailand, to call for help if necessary.

MOTORBIKES
As motorbikes become increasingly popular among travellers, so the number of accidents is rising. Even more likely is the chance of earning yourself a Lao version of the 'Thai tattoo' – that scar on the inner right calf caused by a run-in with a hot exhaust pipe. For tips on motorbiking, see p342.

Speedboats
The speedboats that career along the Mekong in northern Laos are as dangerous as they are fast. We recommend that you avoid all speedboat travel unless absolutely necessary.

Theft
While Lao are generally trustworthy people and theft is much less common than elsewhere in Southeast Asia, it has risen in recent years. Most of the reports we've heard involve opportunistic acts that, if you are aware of them, are fairly easily avoided.

Money or goods going missing from hotel rooms is becoming more common, so don't leave cash or other tempting items (such as women's cosmetics) out on show. If you ride a crowded bus, watch your luggage and don't keep money in your trouser pockets. If you ride a bicycle or motorcycle in Vientiane, don't place anything of value in the basket – thieving duos on motorbikes have been known to ride by and snatch bags from baskets. Also in Vientiane, we've had several reports of (usually) women having daypacks stolen after they've changed money near the BCEL bank on the riverfront. Be especially careful around here.

Other reports involve theft on buses between Vientiane and Luang Prabang, and on the slow boat between Huay Xai and Luang Prabang. Simple locks on your bags are usually enough to discourage the light-fingered.

UXO
Large areas of eastern Laos are contaminated by unexploded ordnance (UXO) left behind by nearly 100 years of warfare (see the boxed text, p199). According to surveys by the Lao National UXO Programme (UXO Lao) and other nongovernment UXO clearance organisations, the provinces of Salavan, Savannakhet and Xieng Khuang fall into a category of most severely affected provinces, followed by Champasak, Hua Phan, Khammuan, Luang Prabang, Attapeu and Sekong.

Statistically speaking, the UXO risk for the average foreign visitor is low, but travellers should exercise caution when considering off-road wilderness travel in the aforementioned provinces. Put simply, if you walk where other people have walked you should be OK. Never touch an object that may be UXO, no matter how old and defunct it may appear.

EMBASSIES & CONSULATES
Of the 75 or so nations that have diplomatic relations with Laos, around 25 maintain embassies and consulates in Vientiane. Many of the remainder, for example Canada and the UK, are served by their embassies in Bangkok, Hanoi or Beijing.

Opening hours for the embassies of neighbouring countries with valid border crossings are given here. Be sure to bring a photo when applying for a visa to any Southeast Asian country.

Australia (Map p86; ☎ 021-353 800; fax 012-353 801; www.laos.embassy.gov.au; Km 4, Th Tha Deua, Ban Wat Nak, Vientiane) Also looks after nationals of the UK, Canada and New Zealand.

Cambodia (Map p86; ☎ 021-314 952; fax 314 951; Km 3, Th Tha Deua, Ban That Khao, Vientiane; ☑ 7.30-11am & 2-5pm Mon-Fri) Tourist visas issued the same day for US$20.

China (Map p86; ☎ 021-315 105; fax 012-315 104; Th Wat Nak Nyai, Ban Wat Nak, Vientiane; ☑ 9-11.30am Mon-Fri) Issues visas in four working days.

France (Map p90; ☎ 021-215 258, 021-215 259; www.ambafrance-laos.org; Th Setthathirath, Ban Si Saket, Vientiane)

Germany (Map p86; ☎ 021-212 111, 021-212 110; Th Sok Pa Luang, Vientiane)

GOVERNMENT TRAVEL WARNINGS

Most governments have travel advisory services detailing potential pitfalls and areas to avoid, including:

Australia (www.smartraveller.gov.au)
Canada (www.voyage.gc.ca)
New Zealand (www.safetravel.govt.nz)
UK (www.fco.gov.uk)
US (www.travel.state.gov)

Myanmar (Burma; Map p86; ☎ 021-314 910; Th Sok Pa Luang, Vientiane; ☉ 8.30am-noon & 1-4.30pm Mon-Fri) Issues tourist visas in four days for US$20.

Thailand Embassy (Map p86; ☎ 021-214 581; www.thaiembassy.org/vientiane; Th Kaysone Phomvihane, Vientiane; ☉ 8.30am-noon & 1-3pm Mon-Fri); Consulate in Vientiane (Map p86; ☎ 021-214 581; 15 Th Bourichane, Vientiane; ☉ 8.30am-noon & 1-3pm) Come here for visa renewals, extensions etc; Consulate in Savannakhet (Map p255; ☎ 041-212 373; cnr Th Tha He & Th Chaimeuang, Savannakhet; ☉ drop-off 9-11am & collection 2-4.30pm Mon-Fri) Tourist and non-immigrant visas (1000B) issued the same day.

USA (Map p90; ☎ 021-267 000; fax 021-267 190; http://laos.usembassy.gov; Th Bartholomie, Vientiane; ☉ 8-11am Monday & Friday, 1-4pm Mon-Fri)

Vietnam Embassy (Map p86; ☎ 021-413 400; Th That Luang, Vientiane; ☉ 8-11.30am & 1.30-4.30pm Mon-Fri) Issues tourist visas in two working days for US$50, or in three days for US$45; Consulate in Luang Prabang (Map p146; ☎ 071-254 748; ☉ 7.30-11.30am & 1.30-4pm Mon-Fri) Issues tourist visas within a few minutes for US$60 or for US$45 if you wait three days; Consulate in Pakse (Map p269; ☎ 031-214 199; www.vietnamconsulate-pakse.org; Th 21; ☉ 7.30-11.30am & 2-4.30pm Mon-Fri) This consulate issues same-day visas for US$40; Consulate in Savannakhet (Map p255; ☎ 041-212 418; Th Sisavangvong, Savannakhet; ☉ 7.30-11am & 1.30-4.30pm Mon-Fri) A one-month tourist visa costs US$50 and a three-month visa US$60.

FESTIVALS & EVENTS

Festivals in Laos are mostly linked to agricultural seasons or Buddhist holidays. The word for festival in Lao is *bun* (or *boun*). Most festival dates change according to the lunar calendar, though even these are not set in stone and some festivals are celebrated at different times depending on where you are. All of this makes advance planning difficult. The website of the **Lao National Tourism Administration** (www.tourismlaos.org) has more details and lists the current year's dates for the larger celebrations.

JANUARY
International New Year (1-3 January) Public holiday.
Bun Khun Khao (mid-January) The annual harvest festival sees villagers perform ceremonies offering thanks to the land spirits for allowing their crops to flourish.

FEBRUARY
Makha Busa (Magha Puja or Bun Khao Chi, Full Moon) This commemorates a speech given by the Buddha to 1250 enlightened monks who came to hear him without prior summons. Chanting and offerings mark the festival, culminating in candlelit circumambulation of wats throughout the country. Celebrations in Vientiane and at Wat Phu (p278) are most fervent.

Vietnamese Tet & Chinese New Year (Tut Jiin) Celebrated in Vientiane, Pakse and Savannakhet with parties, fireworks and visits to Vietnamese and Chinese temples. Chinese- and Vietnamese-run businesses usually close for three days.

MARCH
Bun Pha Wet This is a temple-centred festival in which the *Jataka* (birth tale) of Prince Vessantara, the Buddha's penultimate life, is recited. This is also a favoured time (second to Khao Phansa) for Lao males to be ordained into the monkhood. Bun Pha Wet is celebrated on different days in different villages so relatives and friends from different villages can invite one another to their respective celebrations.

APRIL
Bun Pi Mai (Lao New Year, 14-16 April) Lao new year is the most important holiday of the year. Houses are cleaned, people put on new clothes and Buddha images are washed with lustral water. In wats, you'll see fruit and flower offerings at altars or votive mounds of sand or stone in the courtyards. Later, people douse one another and sometimes random tourists with water, which is an appropriate activity as April is usually the hottest month of the year. This festival is particularly picturesque in Luang Prabang (see the boxed text, p154), where it includes elephant processions and lots of traditional costuming. The 14th, 15th and 16th of April are public holidays and the vast majority of shops and restaurants are closed.

MAY
Visakha Busa (Visakha Puja, Full Moon) This falls on the 15th day of the sixth lunar month, which is considered the day of the Buddha's birth, enlightenment and *parinibbana* (passing away). Activities are centred on the wat, with much chanting, sermonising and, at night, beautiful candlelit processions.

Bun Bang Fai (Rocket Festival) This is a pre-Buddhist rain ceremony now celebrated alongside Visakha Busa in Laos and northeastern Thailand. It can be one of the wildest festivals in the whole country, with music, dance and folk theatre (especially the irreverent *măw lám* performances), processions and general merrymaking, all culminating in the firing of bamboo rockets into the sky. The firing of the rockets is supposed to prompt the heavens to initiate the rainy season and bring much-needed water to the rice fields. Dates vary from village to village.

JULY
Bun Khao Phansa (Khao Watsa, Full Moon) This is the beginning of the traditional three-month 'rains retreat',

during which Buddhist monks are expected to station themselves in a single monastery. At other times of year they are allowed to travel from wat to wat or simply to wander the countryside, but during the rainy season they forego the wandering so as not to damage fields of rice or other crops. This is also the traditional time of year for men to enter the monkhood temporarily, hence many ordinations take place.

AUGUST/SEPTEMBER

Haw Khao Padap Din (Full Moon) This sombre festival sees the living pay respect to the dead. Many cremations take place – bones being exhumed for the purpose – and gifts are presented to the Buddhist order (Sangha) so monks will chant on behalf of the deceased.

OCTOBER/NOVEMBER

Bun Awk Phansa (Ok Watsa, Full Moon) At the end of the three-month rains retreat, monks can leave the monasteries to travel and are presented with robes, alms bowls and other requisites of the renunciate life. The eve of Awk Phansa is celebrated with parties and, near any river, with the release of small banana-leaf boats carrying candles and incense in a ceremony called Van Loi Heua Fai, similar to Loy Krathong in Thailand.

Bun Nam (*Bun suang héua;* Boat Racing Festival) In many river towns, including Vientiane and Luang Prabang, boat races are held the day after Awk Phansa. In smaller towns the races are often postponed until National Day (2 December) so residents aren't saddled with two costly festivals in two months.

NOVEMBER

Bun Pha That Luang (That Luang Festival, Full Moon) Centred around Pha That Luang in Vientiane, this increasingly commercial celebration lasts a week and includes fireworks, music and drinking across the capital. There is also a procession between Pha That Luang and Wat Si Muang. Early on the first morning hundreds of monks receive alms and floral offerings. The festival ends with a fantastic candlelit procession circling That Luang.

DECEMBER

Lao National Day (2 December) This public holiday celebrates the 1975 victory over the monarchy with parades, speeches etc. Lao national and Communist hammer-and-sickle flags are flown all over the country. Celebration is mandatory, hence many poorer communities postpone some of the traditional Awk Phansa activities until National Day, saving themselves considerable expense (much to the detriment of Awk Phansa).

Luang Prabang Film Festival (early December; www.lpfilmfest.org) sees eight days of free screenings at several venues around town. The focus is on the blossoming work of Southeast Asian production houses and all films have English subtitles.

FOOD

Virtually all restaurants in Laos are inexpensive by international standards, hence we haven't divided them into budget, midrange and top-end categories.

See the Food & Drink chapter, p61, for thorough descriptions of the cuisine and the kinds of restaurants in Laos.

GAY & LESBIAN TRAVELLERS

For the most part Lao culture is very tolerant of homosexuality, although lesbianism is often either denied completely ('Lao women don't do that, why would they?' men have been heard to say) or misunderstood. The gay and lesbian scene is not nearly as prominent as in neighbouring Thailand. Strictly speaking, homosexuality is illegal, though we haven't heard of police busting anyone in recent years. In any case, public displays of affection – whether heterosexual or homosexual – are frowned upon.

HOLIDAYS
Public Holidays

Schools and government offices are closed on these official holidays, and the organs of state move pretty slowly, if at all, during the festivals mentioned on p319.

International New Year (1 January)
Army Day (20 January)
International Women's Day (8 March) For women only.
Lao New Year (14-16 April)
International Labour Day (1 May)
International Children's Day (1 June)
Lao National Day (2 December)

INSURANCE

As always, a good travel-insurance policy is a wise idea. Laos is generally considered a high-risk area, and with medical services so limited it's vital to have a policy that covers being evacuated (Medivaced), by air if necessary, to a hospital in Thailand. Read the small print in any policy to see if hazardous activities are covered; rock climbing, rafting and motorcycling often are not.

If you undergo medical treatment in Laos or Thailand, be sure to collect all receipts and copies of the medical report, in English if possible, for your insurance company.

See p345 for recommendations on health insurance, and p343 for vehicle insurance.

INTERNET ACCESS

The days in which most Lao people thought the internet was some sort of newfangled fishing device are fast disappearing. Internet cafes are popping up fast, and you can get online in most, but not all, provincial capitals. Generally speaking, if tourists go there in numbers, someone will have established a connection.

In places where there's plenty of competition – such as Vientiane and Luang Prabang – rates are usually very low, about 5000K or 6000K an hour. In towns where there are only one or two places offering such services, or where they need to call long-distance to reach the server, rates will be higher: between US$3 and US$6 an hour. Broadband is spreading across the country and speeds are usually pretty fast; though in the sticks they can be excruciatingly slow.

Computers in most internet cafes have instant-messaging software such as Yahoo! and MSN Messenger loaded and increasingly Skype, though you might need to search around for a headset.

If you're travelling with a laptop, internet cafes usually allow you to plug into their bandwidth for the same cost as using a fixed computer. Many hotels, restaurants and cafes in Vientiane, Luang Prabang and Vang Vieng have wi-fi, often for free.

LEGAL MATTERS

Revolutionary Laos established its first national legal code in 1988, followed by a constitution two years later – the reverse order of how it's usually done. Although on paper certain rights are guaranteed, the reality is that you can be fined, detained or deported for any reason at any time, as has been demonstrated repeatedly in cases involving everything from a foreigner marrying a Lao national without government permission, to running a business that competes too efficiently with someone who has high government connections.

Your only consolation is that it's usually much worse for locals, and Lao officials generally don't come after foreigners for petty, concocted offences. In most cases you must truly have committed a crime to find yourself in trouble with the law. However, as documented by Amnesty International (and corroborated by local expats), you could easily find yourself railroaded through the system without any legal representation.

If you stay away from anything you know to be illegal, you should be fine. If not, things might get messy – and expensive. Drug possession (see p131) and using prostitutes are the most common crimes for which travellers are caught, often with the dealer or consort being the one to inform the authorities (and later take a cut of any 'action' you might be forced to cough up).

If you are detained, ask to call your embassy or consulate in Laos, if there is one. A meeting or phone call between Lao officers and someone from your embassy/consulate can result in quicker adjudication and release, though unless you are genuinely innocent (as opposed to having been set up) the diplomats can do little and will probably advise you to just cough up the cash.

Police sometimes hint at bribes for traffic violations and other petty offences. In such cases the police typically offer a choice along the lines of 'Would you like to come down to the station to pay your fine, or would you like to take care of it here and now?' Presented with such a choice, it's up to you whether to expedite matters by paying a bribe, or fight corruption in Laos by doing things by the book.

The legal age for voting and driving in Laos is 18.

Sexual Relationships

Sexual relationships between foreigners and Lao citizens who are not married are illegal. Permission for marriage or engagement to a Lao citizen must be submitted in a formal application to Lao authorities. Penalties for failing to register a relationship range from US$500 to US$5000, and possibly imprisonment or deportation. Catching men in the act, or just witnessing them leaving a bar with a working girl, is a favourite excuse of the authorities for deporting *falang* they don't like.

Otherwise, the age of consent for sexual relations in Laos is 15. Travellers should note that they can be prosecuted under the law of their home country regarding age of consent, even when abroad.

MAPS

Good maps of Laos are difficult to find. The best all-purpose country map that's generally available is GT-Rider.com's *Laos*, a sturdy laminated affair with a scale of 1:1,650,000. It's available at bookshops in Thailand and at many guesthouses in Laos, as well as online at www.gt-rider.com. At the time of research the latest edition was published in 2009. The Reise Know-How (www.reise-know-how.com) map also gets very good reports, though it's almost impossible to find outside Germany.

Chiang Mai–based Hobo Maps (www.hobomaps.com) has produced a series of good maps of Vientiane, Luang Prabang and Vang Vieng. These are available in book shops and some hotels in the relevant destinations. The Lao National Tourism Administration (LNTA) has also produced a few city maps in recent years, available at their Tourist Visitor Centre (p89).

MONEY

The official national currency in Laos is the Lao kip (K). Although only kip is legally negotiable in everyday transactions, in reality three currencies are used for commerce: kip, Thai baht (B) and US dollars (US$); see the boxed text.

The Lao kip is not convertible to any currency outside of the Lao PDR. Because of this, the only reliable sources of foreign exchange information are those inside the country.

See p13 for an idea of the costs involved in travelling in Laos.

ATMs

In stark contrast to the previous edition of this guide, ATMs are now found in much of Laos, and in cities like Vientiane and Luang Prabang, are relatively ubiquitous. But before you get overexcited, ATMs dispense a maximum of 700,000K to 2 million K (about US$83 to US$240) per transaction, depending on the bank, not to mention a variable withdrawal fee (ANZ ATMs, for example, charge 40,000K, about US$5, per transaction). If, like most of us, you also have to pay extortionate charges to your home bank on each overseas withdrawal, that doesn't work out so well. So taking your plastic into the bank itself might still work out cheaper; see p323.

Banking

Foreign residents of Laos can open US dollar, baht or kip accounts at several banks in Vientiane, including branches of at least four Thai banks. Unfortunately, if you already have an account at a Thailand-based branch of a Thai bank, you won't be permitted to withdraw any money in Laos; you must open a new account. Alternatively, expatriates living in Vientiane use Thai banks across the river in Nong Khai because interest rates are higher and more banking services are available.

Black Market

There is no real black market in Laos, and unless there's an economic crash that's unlikely to change. Unlicensed moneychangers can be found in larger towns, and sometimes offer marginally better rates, but it's hardly worth seeking them out unless you're changing enough cash to fill a wheelbarrow (admittedly, that's not as hard as it sounds in Laos).

Cash

Laos relies heavily on the Thai baht and the US dollar for the domestic cash economy. An estimated one-third of all cash circulating in Vientiane, in fact, bears the portrait of the Thai king, while another third celebrates US presidents.

MONEY MATTERS

Although kip is the official currency of the Lao PDR, and despite the government's recent push to encourage the Lao people to use their own currency, the Lao continue to do commerce in a mixture of kip, Thai baht (B) and US dollars (US$). Kip is usually preferred for small purchases (eg snacks and meals), while slightly more expensive goods and services (eg hotel rooms, long-distance boat hire) may be quoted in kip, baht or dollars. Anything costing the equivalent of US$100 or more is likely to be quoted in US dollars. In this book, we're listing prices in the currency quoted to us on the ground. Although this may seem inconsistent, and at times confusing, this is the way it's done in Laos and the sooner you get used to thinking comparatively in kip, dollars or baht, the easier your travels will be.

A quick kip tip: the word kip is pronounced less like the first syllable of the word kippers, and more like the nonsense word *geep*.

However, the vast majority of transactions will be carried out in kip, so it's always worth having a wad in your pocket. Notes come in denominations of 500, 1000, 2000, 5000, 10,000, 20,000 and 50,000 kip. Small vendors, especially in rural areas, will struggle to change the 20,000K and 50,000K notes. Also, both of these larger notes are red, so watch you don't go handing out 50,000K notes thinking they're 20,000K.

For larger transactions the dollar and the baht are favoured. They also make carrying money less of a hassle; five 1000B notes – about US$150 worth – are quite a bit easier to carry than 129 10,000K notes. If you plan on making frequent transactions of over US$20, you can save luggage space by carrying most of your cash in baht and/or dollars, along with smaller amounts of kip.

Once you leave Laos no one – except perhaps other travellers on their way into Laos – will want your kip, so spend it before you go.

Credit Cards

A growing number of hotels, upmarket restaurants and gift shops in Vientiane and Luang Prabang accept Visa and MasterCard, and to a much lesser extent Amex and JCB. Outside of these two towns, credit cards are virtually useless.

Banque pour le Commerce Extérieur Lao (BCEL; *thanáakháan kŏan khâa taang páthêht láo* in Lao) branches in Vientiane, Luang Prabang, Vang Vieng, Tha Khaek, Savannakhet and Pakse offer cash advances/withdrawals on MasterCard and Visa credit/debit cards for a 3% transaction fee. Other banks may have slightly different charges, so if you're in Vientiane (where there are options) it might be worth shopping around; the various commissions/transaction fees are listed on p88.

Exchanging Money

After years of volatility the kip has in recent times remained fairly stable at about 10,000 to the US dollar. Don't, however, count on this remaining the same.

Exchange rates are usually virtually the same whether you're changing at a bank or a moneychanger. Both are also likely to offer a marginally better rate for larger bills (US$50 and US$100) than smaller bills (US$20 and less). Banks also tend to offer better rates for travellers cheques, though the whole process

of exchange is much more protracted. in Vientiane and Luang Prabang can gener change UK pounds, euros, Canadian, US anu Australian dollars, Thai baht and Japanese yen. Elsewhere most provincial banks change only US dollars or baht, though you might get lucky.

Licensed moneychangers maintain booths around Vientiane (including at Talat Sao) and at some border crossings. Their rates are similar to the banks and they stay open longer.

Therefore, organising your stash of cash before you leave a big town is highly recommended. If you plan on carrying US dollars or baht, stock up before you arrive in Laos. If you want to buy these currencies in Laos head to a market in a larger town or city, ask around for a money changer and don't expect great rates.

Exchange rates at country banks tend to be slightly lower than what you'd get in Vientiane, despite the fact that the national bank mandates a single daily rate for all government banks. For the latest rates from BCEL, check www.bcellaos.com. For a list of exchange rates as we went to press see the inside front cover.

Tipping

Tipping is not customary in Laos except in upmarket restaurants, where 10% of the bill is appreciated – but only if a service charge hasn't already been added.

Travellers Cheques

Travellers cheques can be cashed at most banks in Laos, but normally only in exchange for kip. Cheques in US dollars are the most readily acceptable, and in fact outside Vientiane they might be the only cheques accepted. It can sometimes be difficult to change travellers cheques because the bank won't have enough kip, especially in more remote provinces, so check that the bank can cover your cheques before you sign. Very few merchants accept travellers cheques.

PHOTOGRAPHY & VIDEO

Laos is a fantastic destination for photography and if you take the following into account there is no reason why you won't come away with some great shots – without upsetting anyone.

Digital photography has reached Laos and, particularly in popular tourist centres such as

...rabang, Vang Vieng and ...nge of batteries, memory ...limited range of cameras

...afes have card readers and can write photos to either CD or DVD for about US$1 or US$2.

Photographing People

In rural areas people are often not used to having their photos taken, so smile and ask permission before snapping away. In tribal areas *always* ask permission before photographing people or religious totems; photography of people is taboo among several tribes. Breaking such taboos might not seem like a big deal to you, but it is to your subject. See Sensitive Trekking (p234) for details.

Use discretion when photographing villagers anywhere in the country, and think before you shoot.

Restrictions

Lao officials are sensitive about photography of airports and military installations; when in doubt, refrain, and if you get stopped be as apologetic and dumb-tourist as you can be.

Technical Tips

As in other tropical countries, the best times of day for photography are early to mid-morning and late afternoon. A polarising filter is helpful for cutting glare and improving contrast, especially when photographing temple ruins or shooting over water.

Moisture is the biggest threat to your gear so during the rainy season (from June to October) pack some silica gel with your camera to prevent mould growing inside the lenses. Also always carry a plastic bag, at least, to keep your gear dry when the heavens open.

The wet season isn't all bad. The skies are clearer and the greens of the forest are much brighter, compared with the hot season (March to May) when you'll often find a layer of dust or smoke damping down the colours and adding glare to the skies.

Outside major cities and towns electricity is not always available. This is a problem if you need to recharge batteries, so be sure to pack enough and keep them charged. Standard camera batteries are readily available in big towns but you'll be lucky to find them out in the sticks, so carry all you'll need.

Lonely Planet's *Travel Photography* contains tips on how to get the most out of your camera.

Tours

A handful of outfits now offer photography-based tours of Laos.

Foto Fugitive (http://tours.fotofugitive.com) Seasonal photo tours of Laos led by experienced humanitarian photographers.

Grasshopper Tours (www.grasshopperadventures.com) This bicycle touring outfit also offers elephant-centric photo tours of Laos.

Rustic Pathways (www.rusticpathways.com) Teen-oriented photography tours of Laos.

Video

Blank videotapes in popular formats, including DV, are readily available for sale in Vientiane and Luang Prabang, and to a lesser extent in Savannakhet, Pakse and a few other provincial capitals.

POST

Sending post from Laos is not all that expensive and is fairly reliable, but people still tend to wait until they get to Thailand to send parcels. If you're heading to Cambodia, you're better off posting your parcels from Laos.

When posting any package you must leave it open for inspection by a postal officer. Incoming parcels might also need to be opened for inspection; there may be a small charge for this mandatory 'service'.

Waiting for mail to arrive, however, is not as certain, especially for packages. The main post office (p89) in Vientiane has a poste restante service. To send something here address it:

    Person's Name
    Poste Restante
    Vientiane
    Lao PDR

Note that there is no home mail-delivery service in Laos; you need to rent a post-office box. Throughout the country you can recognise post offices by the colour scheme: mustard yellow with white trim. See inside front cover for opening hours.

SHOPPING

Shopping in Laos is improving fast. The growth in tourist numbers has been matched, if not exceeded, by the number of stores flogging fabrics, handicrafts and regional favourites from Vietnam and Thailand. Vientiane and Luang Prabang are the main shopping centres and in these cities it's easiest to compare quality and price. It is, however, always nice to buy direct from the producer, and in many villages that's possible.

There is a *total* ban on the export of antiques and Buddha images from Laos, though the enforcement of this ban is slack.

Bargaining

Bargaining is a tradition introduced by early Arab and Indian traders, however, in most places in Laos it's not nearly as aggressive as in other parts of Southeast Asia. Good bargaining, which takes practice, is one way to cut costs. Most things bought in a market should be bargained for and it can't hurt to try in a shop, though increasingly prices are fixed.

In general the Lao are gentle and very scrupulous in their bargaining practices. A fair price is usually arrived at quickly with little attempt to gouge the buyer (tour operators may be an exception to this rule). The amount they come down is usually less than what you see in neighbouring countries. Laos definitely has a 'two-tier pricing system' when it comes to quoting prices to foreigners, but it's nowhere near as evident as in Vietnam.

For tips on bargaining in Laos, see below.

Antiques

Vientiane and Luang Prabang each have a sprinkling of antique shops. Anything that looks old could be up for sale in these shops, including Asian pottery (especially porcelain from the Ming dynasty of China), old jewel-

lery, clothes, carved wood, musical instruments, coins and bronze statuettes. Because of the government's lax enforcement of the ban on the export of antiques, due to an overall lack of funds and personnel, you might be tempted to buy these objects. However, bear in mind not only that it is illegal to take them out of the country but that if you do so you will be robbing the country of its precious and limited heritage. For more on the fight against antiquity theft in Southeast Asia, see www.heritagewatchinternational.org.

Carvings

The Lao produce well-crafted carvings in wood, bone and stone. Subjects include anything from Hindu or Buddhist mythology to themes from everyday life. Authentic opium pipes can be found, especially in the north, and sometimes have intricately carved bone or bamboo shafts, along with engraved ceramic bowls. The selection, though, gets smaller every year.

To shop for carvings, look in antique or handicraft stores. Don't buy anything made from ivory; quite apart from the elephant slaughter caused by the ivory trade, many countries will confiscate any ivory items found in your luggage.

Fabric (Textiles)

Textiles are among the most beautiful, most recognisable and easiest items to buy while you're in Laos. Together with a hanger that was once part of a loom, these can look great on a wall at home and, unlike many handicrafts that are ubiquitous throughout Indochina, these are unmistakably Lao.

BARGAINING 101

Many of your purchases in Laos will involve an ancient skill that has long been abandoned in the West: bargaining. Contrary to what you may have seen on Bangkok's Th Khao San, bargaining (in Lao, *tor lákhá*) is not a terse exchange of numbers and animosity. Rather, bargaining Lao style is a generally friendly transaction where two people try to agree on a price that is fair to both of them.

The first rule to bargaining is to have a general idea of the price. Ask around at a few vendors to get a rough notion. When you're ready to buy, it's generally a good strategy to start at 50% of the asking price and work up from there. If you're buying several of an item, you have much more leverage to request and receive a lower price. If the seller immediately agrees to your first price you're probably paying too much, but it's bad form to bargain further at this point. In general, keeping a friendly, flexible demeanour throughout the transaction will almost always work in your favour. And remember, only begin bargaining if you're really planning on buying the item. Most importantly, there's simply no point in getting angry or upset over a few thousand kip. The locals, who inevitably have less money than you, never do this.

DIRECTORY

Silk and cotton fabrics are woven in many different styles according to the geographic provenance and ethnicity of the weavers. Although Lao textiles do have similarities with other Southeast Asian textiles, Lao weaving techniques are unique in both loom design and weaving styles, generating fabrics that are very recognisably Lao.

Generally speaking, the fabrics of the north feature a mix of solid colours with complex geometric patterns – stripes, diamonds, zigzags, animal and plant shapes – usually in the form of a *phàa nung* or *sin* (a women's wraparound skirt). Sometimes gold or silver thread is woven in along the borders. Another form the cloth takes is the *phàa bîang,* a narrow Lao–Thai shawl that men and women wear singly or in pairs over the shoulders during weddings and festivals.

The southern weaving styles are often marked by the *mat-mii* technique, which involves 'tie-dyeing' the threads before weaving. The result is a soft, spotted pattern similar to Indonesian *ikat. Mat-mii* cloth can be used for different types of clothing or wall-hangings. Among Lao Thoeng and Mon-Khmer communities in the southern provinces there is a *mat-mii* weaving tradition that features pictographic storylines, sometimes with a few Khmer words, numerals or other nonrepresentational symbols woven into the pattern. In Sekong and Attapeu Provinces some fabrics mix beadwork with weaving and embroidery.

Among the Hmong and Mien tribes, square pieces of cloth are embroidered and quilted to produce strikingly colourful fabrics in apparently abstract patterns that contain ritual meanings. In Hmong these are called *pandau* (flower cloth). Some larger quilts feature scenes that represent village life, including both animal and human figures.

Many tribes among the Lao Soung and Lao Thoeng groups produce woven shoulder bags in the Austro-Thai and Tibetan-Burmese traditions, like those seen all across the mountains of South Asia and Southeast Asia. In Laos, these are called *nyaam*. Among the most popular *nyaam* nowadays are those made with older pieces of fabric from 'antique' *phàa nung* or from pieces of hill-tribe clothing. Vientiane's Talat Sao (Morning Market; p113) is one of the best places to shop for this kind of accessory.

The best place to buy fabric is in the weaving villages themselves, where you can watch how it's made and get 'wholesale' prices.

Failing this, you can find a decent selection and reasonable prices at open markets in provincial towns, including Vientiane's Talat Sao. Tailor shops and handicraft stores generally charge more and quality is variable. In Vientiane and Luang Prabang several stores are dedicated to high-quality textiles, with high prices to match.

Jewellery
Gold and silver jewellery are good buys in Laos, although you must search hard for well-made pieces. Some of the best silverwork is done by the hill tribes. Gems are also sometimes available, but you can get better prices in Thailand.

SOLO TRAVELLERS
Travelling alone in Laos is very common among both men and women. Lone women should exercise the usual caution when in remote areas or out late at night (see p330).

TELEPHONE
Laos has come a long way in a short time on the telephone front. While most Lao people are still not connected, the introduction of mobile phones and, in recent years, WIN phones (fixed satellite phones without a landline) has allowed some truly remote villages to get connected without the need for expensive landlines.

You can make international calls from Lao Telecom offices in most provincial capitals, or if there is no Lao Telecom office, from the post office, which is usually nearby. Operators cannot place collect calls or reverse phone charges. You must pay for the call in kip when it is completed. A faded list of rates is usually stuck on a wall near the phone. Where a separate phone office exists, hours typically run from 7.30am to 9.30pm or from 8am to 10pm.

International calls are also charged on a per-minute basis, with a minimum charge of three minutes. Calls to most countries cost about 2000K to 4000K per minute. Nowadays it's almost always cheaper to use an internet cafe (most provide international call services), if there is one.

Mobile Phone
Laos has bought into mobile telephony big time. Lao Telecom and several private companies offer mobile phone services on the GSM and 3G systems. Competition is fierce and you can buy a local SIM card for as little

as 10,000K from almost anywhere. Calls are cheap and recharge cards are widely available for between 15,000K and 60,000K each.

Network coverage varies depending on the company and the region. In our experience, Lao Telecom and Enterprise of Telecommunications Lao (ETL) – another government-affiliated company – have the widest coverage. These are more expensive than Tango Lao and M-Phone, but Tango's coverage is limited to larger cities and towns.

In some areas (such as Si Phan Don where M-Phone reigns supreme), one company is so dominant that it can be hard to find recharge cards for other companies. So if you really need to make that call, buy ahead.

In 2010, many mobile numbers in Laos gained an extra digit. See the boxed text, p17, for more information.

Phone Codes

Until a few years ago most cities in Laos could only be reached through a Vientiane operator. These days you can direct-dial to and from most of the country.

The country code for calling Laos is ☎ 856. For long-distance calls within the country, dial ☎ 0 first, then the area code and number. For international calls dial ☎ 00 first, then the country code, area code and number.

All mobile phones have a ☎ 020 code at the beginning of the number. Similar to this are WIN phones, which begin with ☎ 030. See the inside front cover and under individual towns and villages for area codes inside Laos.

Phonecards

In theory, Tholakham Lao (Lao Telecom), a private company, issues telephone cards *(bát thóhlasáp)* to be used in special card phone booths. In reality, they don't. These phones have been superseded by mobile phones and no one uses them anymore.

TIME

Laos is seven hours ahead of GMT/UTC. Thus, noon in Vientiane is 10pm the previous day in San Francisco, 1am in New York, 5am in London, 1pm in Perth and 3pm in Sydney. There is no daylight saving (summer) time.

TOILETS

While Western-style 'thrones' are now found in most midrange and top-end accommoda-

tion, if you're a budget traveller expect the rather-less-royal 'squat toilet' to be the norm. Whether you consider squat toilets an inconvenience, anatomically healthy or part of 'the real Laos', there's really no cause for alarm – they're not that bad.

Instead of trying to approximate a chair or stool like a modern sit-down toilet, a traditional Asian toilet sits more or less flush with the surface of the floor, with two footpads on either side of the porcelain abyss. Next to the typical squat toilet is a bucket or cement reservoir from which water is scooped using a plastic bowl. Firstly, toilet-goers use the scoop and water to clean their nether regions while still squatting over the toilet. Secondly, a couple of extra scoops are poured into the toilet basin to flush the waste away. The more rustic toilets in rural areas may simply consist of a few planks over a hole in the ground.

Even in places where sit-down toilets are installed, the plumbing may not be designed to take toilet paper. In such cases there will usually be a rubbish bin for the used toilet paper.

Public toilets are uncommon outside hotel lobbies and airports. While you are on the road between towns and villages it's perfectly acceptable to go behind a tree or use the roadside.

TOURIST INFORMATION

For years a visit to the Lao National Tourism Administration (LNTA) was little more than a waste of time, with a brochure or two to prove you wasted it. But things have changed. It's still not like map-crazy neighbours such as Thailand, but the LNTA now has offices in Vientiane and Luang Prabang that are well worth visiting, plus three very good websites that offer valuable pre-departure information:

Central Laos Trekking (www.trekkingcentrallaos.com)
Lao Ecotourism (www.ecotourismlaos.com)
Lao National Tourism Administration (www. tourismlaos.org)

Many offices are well-stocked with brochures, maps (usually), have easily understood displays of their provincial attractions and English-speaking staff to answer your questions. Fanstastic! Offices in Tha Khaek, Savannakhet, Pakse, Luang Namtha, Sainyabuli, Phongsali and Sam Neua are all pretty good, with staff trained to promote treks and other activities in their provinces and able to hand out brochures and first-hand knowledge about them. They should also be able to help with local transport options and bookings.

However, change hasn't reached everywhere. All provincial capitals have an LNTA office but English is often rudimentary and the lack of information can be profound; in some cases visiting such an office might even be more hindrance than help. If you find the local LNTA officials to be unhelpful, you can usually get up-to-date information from a busy guesthouse (if there is one).

TRAVELLERS WITH DISABILITIES

With its lack of paved roads or footpaths (sidewalks) – even when present the latter are often uneven – Laos presents many physical obstacles for people with mobility impairments. Rarely do public buildings feature ramps or other access points for wheelchairs, nor do most hotels make efforts to provide access for the physically disabled, the few exceptions being in the top end. Hence you're pretty much left to your own resources. Public transport is particularly crowded and difficult, even for the fully ambulatory.

For wheelchair users, any trip to Laos will require a good deal of advance planning. Fortunately a growing network of information sources can put you in touch with those who may have wheeled through Laos before. International organisations with information on travel for the mobility-impaired:

Access-Able Travel Source (www.access-able.com)
Accessible Journeys (www.disabilitytravel.com)
Mobility International USA (www.miusa.org)
Society for the Accessible Travel & Hospitality (www.sath.org)

VISAS

Getting into Laos is easier than ever and travellers from many countries can get 30-day tourist visas at nearly all border points (see the boxed text).

Tourist Visa on Arrival

The Lao government issues 30-day tourist visas on arrival at nearly all of its official international border crossings and at the international airports at Vientiane, Luang Prabang, Pakse and most recently, Savannakhet.

The whole process is dead easy. You need between US$20 and US$42 cash or the equivalent in Thai baht (travellers cheques and other currencies, including Lao kip, are not accepted); one passport-size photo of yourself; and the name of a hotel you will be staying at (pick any one from this guidebook). If you don't have a photo you'll have to pay an additional fee of about US$2, and if you're arriving on a weekend or holiday, or outside of office hours, you'll have to pay an 'overtime fee' of US$1. In theory you also need the name of a contact in Laos but it's OK to leave that section blank. For airport arrivals you're also supposed to possess a valid return air ticket, but we've never heard of anyone who's actually been asked to show it.

The visa fee varies depending on what passport you're carrying, with Canadians having to fork out the most (US$42), and most others between US$30 and US$35. If possible, set aside US$ for the fee, otherwise you'll likely be stuck with a flat rate of 1,500B (US$46) – no amount of arguing about the correct exchange rate will change this. Moneychangers at these places are unlikely to be able to give you dollars in exchange for Thai baht or any other currency, so be sure to bring enough. We've seen several travellers get stuck in airport limbo because they arrived without cash to pay for their visas. In such cases the immigration officers may allow you to go into town and try to get dollars from another source. They will, however, keep your passport at the airport in the meantime.

The 30-day tourist visa is extendable an additional 90 days at a cost of US$2 per day, although this can only be done in Vientiane and Luang Prabang. Depending on where you are, it's probably cheaper to leave the country and apply for a new tourist visa on arrival if you need to extend your stay in Laos for more than 30 days.

Tourist Visa

If you don't want, or aren't eligible for a visa on arrival, Lao embassies and consulates abroad offer 30-day tourist visas. The process involves roughly the same cost and documentation as described above and generally takes three working days. In Bangkok you can get your visa on the same day for an additional 200B express fee.

Nonimmigrant & Business Visas

A person who has a short-term professional or volunteer assignment in Laos is generally issued a nonimmigrant visa good for 30 days and extendable up to one year. As with the visitor visa, the application fee is around US$35.

Journalists can apply for the journalist visa, which has the same restrictions and validity as

---

VISA ON ARRIVAL – PORTS OF ENTRY

At the time of writing, these were the ports of entry where tourist visas were available on arrival (visas are also available on arrival at the international airports at Vientiane, Luang Prabang, Pakse and Savannakhet). See p334 for a full list of border posts.

Cambodia
- Trapaeng Kriel/Nong Khiang (p296)

China
- Mohan/Boten (p215)

Thailand
- Chiang Khong/Huay Xai (Hoksay; p172)
- Huay Kon/Muang Ngeun (p185)
- Tha Li/Kaen Thao (p172)
- Nong Khai/Vientiane (p117)
- Nakhon Phanom/Tha Khaek (p249)
- Mukdahan/Savannakhet (p256)
- Chong Mek/Vang Tao (p274)

Vietnam
- Tay Trang/Sop Hun (p229)
- Na Meo/Nam Soi (p202)
- Nam Can/Nam Khan (p196)
- Cau Treo/Nam Phao (p244)
- Cha Lo/Na Phao (p253)
- Lao Bao/Dansavanh (p262)
- Bo Y/Phou Keua (p310)

---

the nonimmigrant and visit visas except that the applicant must also fill in a biographical form.

Business visas, good initially for 30 days, are relatively easy to obtain as long as you have a sponsoring agency in Laos. Many brokers in Vientiane (and a few in Thailand) can arrange such visas with one to two weeks notice. Like nonimmigrant visas, these can extended up to a year.

Visa Extensions

As long as your Lao visa has yet to expire, getting an extension is easy, but is only possible in Vientiane (p85) and Luang Prabang (p148). You'll need your passport and a photo and can expect to pay US$2 per day for the extra time you want (plus a US$3 processing fee). You can extend a tourist visa a maximum of two 30-day periods, although depending on

where you are, this is probably more expensive than simply exiting Laos and requesting a new tourist visa on arrival. The whole process can be completed in one hour.

Nonimmigrant visas, journalist visas and business visas have to be extended through the sponsoring person or organisation.

Overstaying Your Visa

Overstaying your visa is not seen as a major crime but it is expensive. You'll have to pay a fine of US$10 for each day you've overstayed at the immigration checkpoint when you leave. Simple as that.

VOLUNTEERING

Volunteers have been working in Laos for years, usually on one- or two-year contracts that include a minimal monthly allowance.

The volunteer is often placed with a government agency and attempts to 'build capacity'. These sort of jobs can lead to non-volunteer work within the non-government organisation (NGO) community.

The alternative approach to volunteering, where you actually pay to be placed in a 'volunteer' role for a few weeks or months, has yet to arrive in Laos in any great capacity. A couple of groups in Luang Prabang (see the boxed text, p161) need volunteers occasionally. The website **Stay Another Day** (www. stayanotherday.org) is a good resource for unpaid volunteer opportunities.

Check out these agencies for more information:

Australian Volunteers International (www.aust ralianvolunteers.com) Places qualified Australian residents on one- to two-year contracts.

Earthwatch (www.earthwatch.org) Places paying volunteers in short-term environmental projects around the globe.

Global Volunteers (www.globalvolunteers.org) Co-ordinates teams of volunteers on short-term humanitarian and economic development projects.

UN Volunteers (www.unv.org) Places volunteers with qualifications and experience in a range of fields.

Volunteer Service Abroad (www.vsa.org.nz) Organises professional contracts for New Zealanders.

Voluntary Service Overseas (VSO) UK (www.vso.org. uk); Canada (www.vsocanada.org); Netherlands (www.vso. nl) Places qualified and experienced volunteers for up to two years.

WOMEN TRAVELLERS

Laos is an easy country for women travellers, though you still need to be sensitive to a set of cultural mores that hasn't been watered down as much as in many parts of Thailand. Laos is very safe (see p317) and violence against women travellers is extremely rare. And while everyday incidents of sexual harassment are more common than they were a few years ago, they're still much less frequent than in virtually any other Asian country.

The relative lack of prostitution in Laos, as compared with Thailand, has benefits for women travellers. While a Thai woman who wants to preserve a 'proper' image often won't associate with foreign males for fear of being perceived as a prostitute, in Laos this is not the case. Hence a foreign woman seen drinking in a cafe or restaurant is not usually perceived as being 'loose' or available as she might be in Thailand. This in turn means that there

are generally fewer problems with uninvited male solicitations.

That, however, is not an absolute. Lao women rarely travel alone, so a foreign female without company might be judged by Lao – male and female – as being a bit strange. And while this is less prevalent in the larger towns and cities where society is generally more permissive, in rural areas Lao men might see a woman travelling alone as a woman who wants company. Generally, though, if your bus or *săwngthăew* has other women on board, you shouldn't have any problems.

The best way to avoid unwanted attention is to avoid overly revealing clothes. It's highly unusual for most women (even in more modern places like Vientiane and Vang Vieng where they're used to seeing tourists), to wear singlet tops or very short skirts or shorts. So when travellers do, people tend to stare. Being stared at isn't much fun for the traveller, but if you try putting yourself in their shoes it's easier to understand. Relatively speaking, if a woman walked down Oxford St in London or Broadway in New York wearing nothing but a bikini, people would look.

Lao people will almost never confront you about what you're wearing, but that doesn't mean they don't care. As one woman in Vang Vieng told us: 'I wouldn't say anything, but I'd prefer it if they put on a sarong when they get out of the river. It's not our way to dress like that [a bikini only] and it's embarrassing to see it.' It's good advice – if you're planning on bathing in a village or river, a sarong is essential.

Elsewhere, just keep your eyes open and dress in a way that's not too different from women around you. This doesn't mean you need to get wrapped up in a *sin,* but you'll notice that shirts with at least a tiny strip of sleeve are universally popular, as are shorts or skirts that come to somewhere near the knee. Show this small measure of respect for Lao culture, and it will be repaid in kind.

Traditionally women didn't sit on the roofs of riverboats, because this was believed to bring bad luck. These days most captains aren't so concerned, but if you are asked to get off the roof while men are not, this is why.

WORK

With a large number of aid organisations and a fast-growing international business community, especially in energy and mining, the number of jobs available to foreigners is increasing, but still relatively small. The greatest number of positions are in Vientiane.

Possibilities include teaching English privately or at one of the handful of language centres in Vientiane, work which pays about US$5 to US$10 an hour. Certificates or degrees in English teaching aren't absolutely necessary, but they do help.

If you have technical expertise or international volunteer experience, you might be able to find work with a UN-related program or an NGO providing foreign aid or technical assistance to Laos. These jobs are difficult to find; your best bet is to visit the Vientiane offices of each organisation and inquire about personnel needs and vacancies, then start seeking out potential employers socially and buying them lots of Beerlao. For a list of NGOs operating in Laos, see the excellent www.directoryof ngos.org.

Transport

CONTENTS

Getting around Laos can be pretty tough. Although a growing number of main roads are sealed, and there are more domestic flights than ever, domestic transport is still infrequent, unreliable and extremely time-consuming. Most of Laos's main highways are sealed, but the vast majority of roads are very rough, and traversed by infrequent and equally uncomfortable vehicles.

Many travellers are choosing to come and go via Laos's numerous land and river borders, something we've acknowledged in this book by giving detailed descriptions of all border crossings that were open to foreigners when we researched this edition. While there are many border options, flying into Laos is refreshing in that you don't need to shop around much – only a few airlines service Laos and prices don't vary much. Flights and tours can be booked online at www.lonelyplanet.com/travel_services.

GETTING THERE & AWAY

ENTERING LAOS

It's possible to enter Laos by land or air from Thailand, Cambodia, Vietnam or China. Land borders are often remote and the travelling can be tough either side, but the actual frontier crossing is usually pretty simple.

Passport

The only real prerequisite for entering Laos is a passport with six months' validity and a visa if you are crossing at one of the few borders where you can't get a visa on arrival, such as the Mekong River crossing between Beung Kan and Paksan.

AIR

Airports & Airlines

There are four international airports in Laos. **Wattay International Airport** (VTE; ☎ 021-512 165) in Vientiane; **Luang Prabang International Airport** (LPQ; ☎ 071-212 173); **Savannakhet International Airport** (ZVK; ☎ 041-212 140) and **Pakse International Airport** (PKZ; ☎ 031-251 921). The following operate international flights to/from Laos although Lao Airlines is the national carrier and monopolises the majority of flights in and out of the country:

Air Asia (airline code AK; Map p86; Wattay Airport International Terminal, Vientiane; ☎ 021-513 029; www.airasia.com; ⏰ 8am-5pm)

Bangkok Airways (airline code PG; Map p150; Th Sisavangvong, Luang Prabang; ☎ 071-253 334; www.bangkokair.com)

China Eastern Airlines (airline code MU; Map p86; Th Luang Prabang, Vientiane; ☎ 021-212 300; www.flychinaeastern.com; ⏰ 8.30-11.30am & 1.30-4.30pm Mon-Sat, 8.30-11.30am Sun)

Lao Airlines (airline code QV; Airport Map p86; Wattay Airport International Terminal, Vientiane; ☎ 021-512 028; Central Vientiane Map p90; Th Pangkam, Vientiane; ☎ 021-212 051; www.laoairlines.com; ⏰ 8am-midday & 1-4pm Mon-Sat, 8am-midday Sun)

Thai Airways International (airline code TG; Map p86; Th Luang Prabang, Vientiane; ☎ 021-222 527; www.thaiairways.com; ⏰ 8am-5pm Mon-Fri, 8am-midday Sat)

Vietnam Airlines (airline code VN; Map p90; 1st fl, Lao Plaza Hotel, Th Samsènethai, Vientiane; ☎ 021-217 562; www.vietnamairlines.com; ⏰ 8am-midday & 1.30-4.30pm Mon-Fri, 8am-midday Sat)

Tickets

Unless you're in a country bordering Laos, your first mission is to find a flight to Bangkok. Luckily there are plenty of flights to the Thai capital, but fares fluctuate sharply. Generally, you'll pay less but it will take longer if you fly to Bangkok with a stop on the way. For example, if you're flying from the UK you'll probably

---

THINGS CHANGE!

The information in this chapter is particularly vulnerable to change: prices for international travel are volatile, routes are introduced and cancelled, schedules change, special deals come and go, and rules and visa requirements are amended. You should check directly with your airline or a travel agent to make sure you understand how a fare (and ticket you may buy) works, and be aware of the security requirements for international travel.

The upshot of this is that you should get opinions, quotes and advice from as many airlines and travel agents as possible before you spend your hard-earned cash. Details given in this chapter should be regarded as pointers and are not a substitute for your own careful and up-to-date research.

---

get a better deal with airlines such as Gulf Air, Emirates, Singapore Airlines, Garuda or, for those on the breadline, Biman Bangladesh – all of which involve a stop in the airline's home city – than you would on a direct flight with British Airways or Thai International Airways (THAI). Once you're in Bangkok, there are trains, planes and buses heading to Laos.

Asia

Almost any travel agency in Asia can book you a flight to Laos. STA Travel is always a safe bet, and has branches in **Bangkok** (☎ 0 2236 0262; www.statravel.co.th), **Singapore** (☎ 6737 7188; www.statravel.com.sg) and **Japan** (☎ 03 5391 2922; www.statravel.co.jp) among others. In Hong Kong try **Concorde Travel** (☎ 2526 3391; www.concorde-travel.com).

The only flights directly into Laos come from the following five countries – all prices listed are for one-way flights.

CAMBODIA
Phnom Penh
Between Phnom Penh and Vientiane, Lao Airlines operates a daily code-share flight with Vietnam Airlines (US$165, 1½ hours). There's also talk of a Phnom Penh–Pakse flight operated by Lao Airlines, but details weren't available at the time of research.

Siem Reap
Lao Airlines flies between Siem Reap and Vientiane (US$165, 2½ hours) daily, stopping at Pakse (US$119, 50 minutes), between Siem Reap and Luang Prabang (US$180, 3½ hours) daily, also via Pakse (1,345,000K), and between Siem Reap and Savannakhet (US$150, 70 minutes).

CHINA
Kunming
Lao Airlines flies daily between Kunming and Vientiane (US$155, 2½ hours). China Eastern Airlines flies the same route for slightly more.

MALAYSIA
Kuala Lumpur
Air Asia conducts a daily flight between Kuala Lumpur and Vientiane (US$152, 2½ hours).

THAILAND
Bangkok
THAI has one flight daily between Bangkok and Vientiane (9200B, 70 minutes), while Lao Airlines has two flights daily in each direction (US$115), a thrice-weekly flight between Savannakhet and Bangkok (US$120, 80 minutes) and a flight between Pakse and Bangkok ($132).

Some people save money by flying from Bangkok to Udon Thani in Thailand and then carrying on by road to Nong Khai, over the Friendship Bridge to Vientiane (see the boxed text, p117). Udon Thani is 55km south of Nong Khai and Bangkok–Udon Thani tickets on Air Asia start at about 900B. Likewise, if you're bound for central Laos, **Nok Air** (www.nokair.com) flies to Nakhon Phanom, from where it's only a short Mekong River crossing to Tha Khaek.

Bangkok Airways and Lao Airlines fly twice daily between Bangkok and Luang Prabang (US$160, 1¾ hours).

Chiang Mai
Lao Airlines has five flights a week between Vientiane and Chiang Mai (US$155, 2½ hours), via Luang Prabang (695,000K, one hour).

VIETNAM
Hanoi
There are several daily flights between Vientiane and Hanoi (US$125, one hour) on Lao Airlines and for slightly more, Vietnam Airlines. Both airlines also fly between Hanoi and Luang Prabang (US$130, one hour).

Ho Chi Minh City

Vietnam Airlines flies daily from Ho Chi Minh City to Vientiane (US$190, three hours) via Phnom Penh. Lao Airlines may also start flying between Ho Chi Minh City and Pakse, although details weren't available at the time of research.

Australia

Qantas, THAI, British Airways and several other airlines fly to Bangkok from Sydney, Melbourne and Perth, with discount fares starting at about A$1200 return (once you've added in all the taxes). For online bookings also check www.travel.com.au.

Flight Centre (☎ 133 133; www.flightcentre.com.au)
STA Travel (☎ 134 782; www.statravel.com.au)

Canada

Fares from Canada are similar to those from the US. **Travel Cuts** (☎ 866-246 9762; www.travelcuts.com) is Canada's national student travel agency. Also try **Travelocity** (www.travelocity.ca).

Continental Europe

Europeans can pick up discounted seats from about €700. Middle Eastern airlines are usually cheapest. The following agents are worth a look:
Lastminute (www.lastminute.com) Click through to various national sites.
Nouvelles Frontières (☎ 0825-000 747; www.nouvelles-frontieres.fr)
STA Travel (☎ 01805-456 422; www.statravel.de)
Voyages Wasteels (www.wasteels.fr)

New Zealand

Both **Flight Centre** (☎ 0800-243 544; www.flightcentre.co.nz) and **STA Travel** (☎ 0800-474 400; www.statravel.co.nz) have branches throughout the country. Low season fares start at about NZ$1100.

The UK

It's not hard to find a bargain from London to Bangkok, with discount prices starting at about £400. OmanAir, Sri Lankan, Etihad Airways and Kuwait Airways are worth looking at.

Recommended agencies:
North-South Travel (☎ 01245-608 291; www.northsouthtravel.co.uk) Donates some profit to projects in the developing world.
STA Travel (☎ 0871-230 0040; www.statravel.co.uk)
Trailfinders (☎ 0845-058 5858; www.trailfinders.co.uk)
Travel Bag (☎ 0871-703 4698; www.travelbag.co.uk)

The USA

Fares from New York to Bangkok range widely, with the cheapest (via places like Moscow) starting at about US$1100 return in the low season. From Los Angeles it's cheaper, and more direct, with airlines like All Nippon Airways, Cathay Pacific Airways, China Airlines, Korean Airlines and EVA Airways. Nondiscounted fares are several hundred dollars more. The following are good for online comparisons and bookings:
Cheapflights.com (www.cheapflights.com)
Cheap Tickets (www.cheaptickets.com)
Expedia (www.expedia.com)
Orbitz (www.orbitz.com)
STA Travel (www.sta.com)
Travelocity (www.travelocity.com)

OVERLAND

Laos shares land and/or river borders with Thailand, Myanmar, Cambodia, China and

---

CLIMATE CHANGE & TRAVEL

Every form of transport that relies on carbon-based fuel generates CO_2, the main cause of human-induced climate change. Modern travel is dependent on aeroplanes and while they might use less fuel per kilometre per person than most cars, they travel much greater distances. It's not just CO_2 emissions from aircraft that are the problem. The altitude at which aircraft emit gases (including CO_2) and particles contributes significantly to their total climate change impact. The Intergovernmental Panel on Climate Change believes aviation is responsible for 4.9% of climate change – double the effect of its CO_2 emissions alone.

Lonely Planet regards travel as a global benefit. We encourage the use of more climate-friendly travel modes where possible and, together with other concerned partners across many industries, we support the carbon offset scheme run by ClimateCare. Websites such as climatecare.org use 'carbon calculators' that allow people to offset the greenhouse gases they are responsible for with contributions to portfolios of climate-friendly initiatives throughout the developing world. Lonely Planet offsets the carbon footprint of all staff and author travel.

Vietnam; see the colour map at the front of this book for their locations.

The following overviews discuss the various overland options that are feasible for foreigners (several border crossings being limited to local citizens) and are cross-referenced to more detailed descriptions of the journeys and frontier posts in the relevant chapters. Of course border-crossing details change regularly, so ask around and check the **Thorntree** (http://thorntree.lonelyplanet.com/) before setting off

It's possible to bring your own vehicle into Laos from Thailand, Vietnam and Cambodia with the right paperwork (see p341) and Lao customs don't object to visitors bringing bicycles into the country.

Cambodia

There are daily buses and minibuses connecting Pakse with Stung Treng (four hours), Kratie (six hours) and Phnom Penh (11 hours). These also call at Ban Naksang and Ban Hat Xai in both directions for travellers planning to relax in Si Phan Don. It's best to take one of these through-buses, as it's pretty tough to arrange transport yourself at the border, as there is nothing much available at the new crossing at Nong Khiang (Laos) and Trapaeng Kriel (Cambodia). See the boxed text, p296, for more information.

China

Handy through-buses link major towns in Yunnan to northern Laos. Luang Namtha–Jinghong (six hours), Udomxai–Mengla (five hours) and Kunming–Luang Prabang (around 24 hours on a Chinese sleeper bus). It's also perfectly feasible to make the journey in hops via Boten (see the boxed text, p215), the only China–Lao border crossing currently open to foreigners. From Mohan on the Chinese side it's around a two-hour minibus ride to Mengla, the nearest large town.

A proposal to open the Nan Tuey border to foreigners would massively increase traveller interest in currently obscure towns like Ou Tai (p235) and Ou Neua (p236) at the north of fascinating Phongsali province.

Myanmar

Locals cross into Myanmar at Muang Mom (p178) and Xieng Kok (p227) but foreigners, even with the visa and relevant travel permits, would have to arrange a guide to lead them to/from Tachilek. As that town is on the Thai

border opposite Mae Sai it simply isn't worth the trouble – simply hop through northern Thailand to/from Mae Sai and cross the border there. You'll still need awkward permits and a tour guide to go between Tachilek and Kengtung, from which the only permitted link to the rest of Myanmar is by air.

Thailand

There are eight crossings to Thailand open to foreigners. Some involve taking a boat across the Mekong, or crossing the river on one of the Friendship Bridges.

THAILAND TO VIENTIANE

Through-buses run regularly between Vientiane and the Thai towns of Khon Kaen (four hours), Nakhon Ratchasima (seven hours), Nong Khai (1½ hours) and Udon Thani (2½ hours) via the Friendship Bridge (see the boxed text, p117). There are also several daily trains (www.railway.co.th/english) from Bangkok to Nong Khai (about 12 hours), as well as four daily departures between Nong Khai and Vientiane's Dongphasy Station. For details on entering Laos via train, see p116. From Udon Thani there are budget flights to Bangkok and Phuket on Air Asia (www.airasia.com).

THAILAND TO NORTHERN LAOS

The majority of visitors are heading to or from Luang Prabang. There are three main options but no route allows you to make the trip in a single journey. The Chiang Rai–Huay Xai–Luang Prabang route is by far the most tourist-friendly and potentially the quickest route (around 24 hours using buses, two days by a more interesting bus-boat combination). And it's ideal if you want to stop en route for the Gibbon Experience, treks at Luang Namtha or to see Nong Khiaw and do the last section by Nam Ou riverboat.

Travel this way is via Chiang Khong (p172) where you'll need to use tuk-tuks and a cross-river ferry to reach Huay Xai (p172). If you depart from Chiang Rai on the first bus of the day you should reach Huay Xai in time for the slowboat ride to Luang Prabang arriving two evenings later. Or you could leave Chiang Rai as late as noon and still have time to comfortably reach the 5pm overnight bus (faster but not really recommended), arriving in Luang Prabang late next morning. Many travellers buy through-packages from Chiang Mai or

Chiang Rai agencies. While these save a little minor hassle, in our experience they are rarely good value. Some work out twice the price of doing things yourself and can also leave you waiting around at times because you are effectively required to stick with the group.

Two other possibilities are perfectly feasible but see almost no foreign tourists so you'll need to be comfortable with local languages or gesticulations. The Nan–Muang Ngeun–Luang Prabang route, which leaves Thailand at Huay Kon (see the boxed text, p185), is a little fiddly with only one connection a day on most sections and a possibility that you'll have to walk several kilometres from the border into Muang Ngeun (p182). If you start at 8am from Nan, in theory you should be able to reach Hongsa the same day and continue next day on a super-rough pick-up ride to Chomphet/Luang Prabang, though that doesn't always operate. An alternative from Muang Ngeun is to head up to desolate Pak Kaen, take the afternoon boat to Pak Beng then continue next morning down the river to Luang Prabang. Either way you're looking at two days and one night but should allow an extra day's leeway in case of eventualities.

The third possibility is Loei–Pak Lai, crossing near Kaen Thao (see the boxed text, p187), but until the Pak Lai–Sainyabuli road is rebuilt this is somewhat masochistic and you're likely to miss connections such that the trip will probably take two nights and three days.

THAILAND TO CENTRAL LAOS

Although relatively few tourists use them, the border crossings that straddle the Mekong between northeastern Thailand and central Laos are almost universally convenient and straightforward.

The river crossing between Nakhon Phanom and Tha Khaek (see the boxed text, p249) is a breeze and there are several daily buses between Bangkok and Nakhon Phanom (12 hours). This crossing is also a popular overland route to Vietnam, with buses linking Tha Khaek to Hue, Danang, Dong Hoi and Hanoi (for details see p248).

The bridge between Mukdahan and Savannakhet (see the boxed text, p256) is the southernmost Mekong River crossing open to non-Thai and non-Lao nationals. Several buses link Bangkok and Mukdahan (about 10 hours), and the Thai-Lao International Bus runs between the latter and Savannakhet's

bus station (45 minutes), making this an extremely convenient and hassle-free crossing. From Savannakhet, there are also regular but very time-consuming buses to Danang and points north in Vietnam (p259).

The exception to the traveller-friendly border crossings between Thailand and northern Laos is the river crossing between Beung Kan and Paksan (see boxed text, p240), where a dearth of regular transport on the Thai side and no available visas on arrival at the Lao side make this the most inconvenient method of crossing between Thailand and central Laos.

THAILAND TO SOUTHERN LAOS

International buses connect Pakse with Ubon Ratchathani (four hours including crossing) via the Vang Tao (Laos) and Chong Mek (Thailand) border twice daily, plus there is one through service a day to Bangkok. Combination bus and train tickets can also be purchased in Pakse or you can take the bus as far as Ubon and arrange a train ticket from there. It is also possible to do this by a combination of local transport, but by the time you've been overcharged on both sides you're not likely to save much money. Save the headaches instead and get the international bus. For more on this crossing, see the boxed text p274.

Vietnam

At the time of writing, foreigners could cross between Laos and Vietnam at seven different border posts. Laos issues 30-day tourist visas at all of these, but you'll need to get your Vietnamese visa in advance – now quickly and easily done in Luang Prabang, Vientiane, Savannakhet and Pakse (see p318). In every case we'd advise using a through bus rather than trying to make the trip in hops. Even then you can expect some haggling (see the the boxed text p337), but with border crossings in isolated territory, it's not always easy to arrange onward transport from border posts – at least for a decent price. Some of the Vietnamese towns near the borders have a reputation for deliberately making 'escape' difficult.

VIETNAM TO NORTHERN LAOS

Before you buy a ticket for the hellish 24-hour bus ride between Hanoi and Vientiane, consider breaking your journey up, passing through some of Laos's most remote and

VIETNAM BORDER WOES

If we had a Beerlao for every email we've received from travellers who've been scammed while crossing the border between Vietnam and Laos, we'd be able to have a very big party. There are several different scams you might encounter, and plenty of lies you'll be told that won't necessarily cost you money but will most certainly piss you off.

Among the most common is the '12-hour' bus between Vientiane and Hanoi, which is in fact a 20- to 24-hour trip including several hours spent waiting for the border to open. Once across the border (mainly at Nam Phao/Cau Treo but also Dansavanh/Lao Bao) another common scam involves the suddenly rising price. You'll know this one when your bus stops and demands an extra, say, US$20 each to continue. This one also applies to local transport from the border further into Vietnam, be it by motorbike, public bus, truck or – the worst – tourist-oriented minibuses.

The nastiest part about these scams is you can't do much to avoid them, no matter how many questions you ask or assurances you seek. The best thing to do is just go with the flow and hope your crossing is trouble free, as many are. If you do come across a problem, try to keep a smile on your face (yes, we know it's hard) and get the best result – usually paying a lower amount. As attractive as it might sound, venting your frustrations through your fists makes matters much worse.

Alternatively you could tell the scammers where to go and hope for the best. And as we discovered years ago (these scams have been running forever), sometimes it will pay off. For us, it happened on Rte 8 coming from Vinh to Cau Treo. Our minibus stopped halfway up the Annamite range and the driver demanded more money. We refused, got out and the driver left. No sooner had we asked ourselves 'What now?' than a truck loaded up with bags of cement lumbered over the hill and stopped. 'To the border?' I asked. 'Yes, yes, no problem,' came the smiling reply even after I'd shown him we only had 1300d between us. Sitting atop the truck as we wound our way slowly up through the cloud forests was fantastic and almost as good as the gesture itself, which had restored some of our faith in humanity. We had the last laugh as well, when we found our greedy driver at the border trying to rip off a Canadian couple. We enjoyed telling them: 'Don't, whatever you do, go with that guy.'

beautiful land crossings. An increasingly popular alternative is to start from north-western Vietnam then use the daily Dien Bien Phu–Muang Khua bus, crossing the border at Tay Trang (see the boxed text, p229), before arriving in fascinating Phongsali province. The bus is daily and although currently a painfully slow, bumpy route, road reconstruction should be finished within the life of this book. Reaching Luang Prabang from Dien Bien Phu would be possible in two days (one night in Muang Khua, buses with a change in Udomxai). But you'd be far wiser to allow at least three days (better one week) and take the Nam Ou riverboats – ideally planning stops in Muang Ngoi Neua as well as Nong Khiaw.

Other decent alternatives start from the Vietnamese towns of Thanh Hoa and Vinh. Thanh Hoa–Sam Neua buses (daily), which pass through the border at Nam Soi (see the boxed text, p202), take a beautiful route and are ideal for visiting the disturbing Vieng Xai caves. Indeed, the bus can drop you 1km outside Vieng Xai but that will be around 6.30pm, so getting Lao money probably won't be pos-

sible till the next morning – bring a few snacks to tide you over just in case. Having slept in Sam Neua you could get to Luang Prabang in one very long day but we'd recommend stopping in Vieng Thong and Nong Khiaw en route.

Buses on the Vinh–Phonsavan route, which pass the border at lonely Nam Can (see the boxed text, p196), allow you to visit the enigmatic Plain of Jars but don't run daily.

VIETNAM TO VIENTIANE & CENTRAL LAOS

Yes, there are direct buses from both Hanoi and Ho Chi Minh City to Vientiane (see the boxed text, p337), but do you really want to spend 24 hours (or 48 hours in the case of Ho Chi Minh City) or more on a bus? An alternative to this is to break up your trip in beautiful but seldom-visited central Laos.

If you're starting out in central Vietnam, you have a few different options. The border at Lao Bao (see the boxed text, p261), easily accessed from Dong Ha, is the largest and easiest of all crossings to/from Vietnam. Once in Laos, you can break up your journey with stays in Sepon, visiting what's left of the Ho Chi Minh Trail (p263), or in Savannakhet (p254). Moving north, there's a crossing at Cha Lo (see the boxed text, p253), but it's a quiet area, with few places to stay, and virtually the only traffic is the buses that run between Dong Hoi and Tha Khaek. The most popular crossing is at Cau Treo (see the boxed text, p244), which is easily accessed via Vinh, and which is also the route that the direct buses between Vientiane and Hanoi use. Punctuate your journey with a visit to the spectacular underground river at Tham Kong Lo (p242) or with a stay in Tha Khaek (p244).

VIETNAM TO SOUTHERN LAOS
There is a daily bus service (in both directions) between Pakse and Kontum, passing through both Sekong and Attapeu, as well as the Phou Keua (Laos) and Bo Y (Vietnam) border. The shuttle takes about eight to nine hours to complete the entire journey or about half that between Attapeu and Kontum. This crossing is in an extremely remote area of Laos, so coming under your own steam is difficult and expensive, involving a chartered vehicle. This border is one way to combine southern Laos and central Vietnam, as it is possible to make your way to Hoi An via Quy Nhon. For more on this crossing see the boxed text, p310.

GETTING AROUND

AIR
Airlines in Laos
Lao Airlines is the main airline in Laos, though smaller destinations are handled by Lao Air and Lao Capricorn. For domestic flights, Vientiane is the main hub. The Laos Airfares map (p339) gives you an idea of all Laos's scheduled air routes and prices, both domestic and international; for the latest fares check Lao Airlines' website (www.laoairlines.com).

Prices have been fairly steady in recent years and are reasonable value. Except at Lao Airlines' offices in Vientiane and Luang Prabang, where credit cards are accepted for both international and domestic tickets, you must pay cash in US dollars.

Domestic flights, especially to smaller airports like Boun Neua (Phongsali) or Nathong (Sam Neua), suffer fairly frequent cancellations due to fog and, in March, due to heavy smoke during the forest-burning season. Some such flights are only confirmed once the plane comes into view! During the holiday season it's best to book ahead as flights can fill fast. At other times, when flights are more likely to be cancelled, confirm the flight is still going a day or two before.

In its previous incarnation as Lao Aviation, Lao Airlines had a bad reputation and travellers still ask whether it's safe. The answer is 'pretty much'. Almost everything about the airline – the planes, maintenance and pilots – has improved and there haven't been any serious incidents for several years. French ATR-72 planes operate most international routes and many domestic flights, though some of the domestic flights use older and less-reliable Chinese or Russian planes.

BICYCLE
The stunning roads and light, relatively slow traffic in most towns and on most highways make Laos arguably the best country for cycling in Southeast Asia.

Hire
Simple single-speed bicycles can be hired in most places that see a decent number of tourists, usually costing about 10,000K per day.

These mostly Thai- or Chinese-made bikes come in varying degrees of usability, so be sure to inspect them thoroughly before hiring. Common problems include loose seats or handlebars and broken bells. Ask and you can usually get the seat adjusted to suit your height.

Purchase
You can buy a new bicycle for between US$70 and US$100. The Chinese bikes are sturdier, the Thai bikes more comfortable. Low-quality Chinese or Taiwanese mountain bikes cost more.

Tours
Several tour agencies and guesthouses offer mountain-biking tours, ranging in duration from a few hours to several weeks.

Green Discovery (www.greendiscoverylaos.com) Laos-based company offers a few cycling tours of the country.

Grasshopper Adventures (www.grasshopperadventures.com) Established bicycle touring outfit that offers a handful of Laos-based tours.

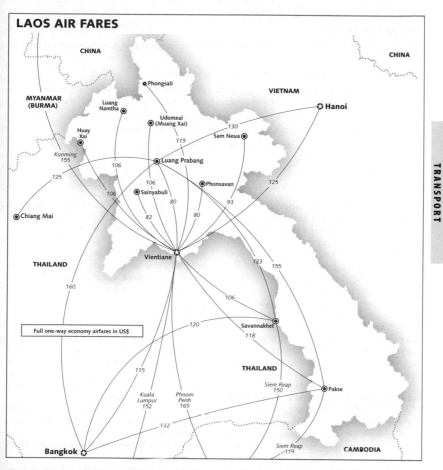

LAOS AIR FARES

Full one-way economy airfares in US$

CHINA

MYANMAR
(BURMA)

Phongsali

Luang
Namtha

Udomxai
(Muang Xai)

Huay
Xai

Kunming
155

Sam Neua

130

119

106

Luang Prabang

106

Sainyabuli

Phonsavan

125

125

Chiang Mai

106

80

93

82

80

Vientiane

123

155

THAILAND

160

106

Savannakhet

120

118

THAILAND

115

Kuala
Lumpur
152

Phnom
Penh
165

Siem Reap
150

Pakse

132

Siem Reap
119

Bangkok

CAMBODIA

VIETNAM

Hanoi

CHINA

Laosabaidee Travel (www.laosabaidee.com) Family-run outfit that specialises in bicycle tours of Laos.
North-by-Northeast Tours (www.north-by-northeast. com) Thailand-based company offering two cycling tours of Laos.
Spice Roads (www.spiceroads.com) Specialises in cycling tours.

BOAT

More than 4600km of navigable rivers are the highways and byways of traditional Laos, the main thoroughfares being the Mekong, Nam Ou, Nam Khan, Nam Tha, Nam Ngum and Se Kong. The Mekong is the longest and most important route and is, in theory if no longer in practice, navigable year-round between Luang Prabang in the north and

Savannakhet in the south (about 70% of its length in Laos). Smaller rivers accommodate a range of smaller boats, from dugout canoes to 'bomb boats' made from junk dropped from the skies during the Second Indochina War.

Sealed roads and buses, however, mean that the days of mass river transport are as good as finished. Every time a new road is opened more boatmen go out of business, unable to compete with the price and pace of those modern conveyors of the masses – buses and *sǎwngthǎew*. This aspect of progress means local people have access to faster and cheaper travel, and it's not our place to begrudge them that. However, from a travellers' point of view, the gradual death of river transport is a great shame. There were few things more romantic

---

KNOW YOUR BOAT

Following are some of the *héua* (boats) that you may encounter in your adventures along Laos's many waterways:

- *héua sáa* (double-deck boats) – big, old boats; almost extinct
- *héua duan* (express boat) – roofed cargo boats, common on the Huay Xai to Luang Prabang route; they're slow, but called 'express' because they're faster than double-deck boats
- *héua wái* (speedboat) – these resemble a surfboard with a car engine strapped to the back; very fast, exhilarating, deafeningly loud, uncomfortable and dangerous
- *héua hang nyáo* (longtail boat) – boats (usually roofed but not always) with engine gimbal-mounted on the stern; found all over Laos
- *héua phái* (rowboat) – essentially a pirogue; common in Si Phan Don.

---

than sitting on a slow boat, tacking from one riverside village to another as the boat worked its way along the river, picking up people, produce and animals on the way.

While there are barely any regular local boats on the Mekong anymore, there are still a few places left where you can do this, if you're prepared to get right off the beaten river and seek out the adventure…and you can be certain it will be a memorable trip, one way or another. So whether it's on a tourist boat from Huay Xai to Luang Prabang or on a local boat you've rustled up in some remote corner of the country, it's still worth doing at least one river excursion while in Laos.

River Ferries (Slow Boats) & River Taxis

The most popular river trip in Laos – the slow boat between Huay Xai and Luang Prabang – is still a daily event and relatively cheap at about US$24 per person for the two-day journey. From Huay Xai, boats are often packed, sometimes overloaded, while from Luang Prabang there should be plenty of room. It's also important to note that standards of luxury fall far short of the *Queen Mary*. Most river-boats were designed for cargo transport and facilities range from nonexistent to ultra-basic. Passengers sit, eat and sleep on the wooden decks. The toilet (if there is one) is an enclosed hole in the deck at the back of the boat.

For shorter river trips, such as Luang Prabang to the Pak Ou Caves, it's usually best to hire a river taxi. The *héua hang nyáo* (long-tail boats) are the most typical, though for a really short trip (eg crossing a river) a *héua phái* (rowboat) or one of the small improvised ferries can be hired. The *héua hang nyáo* are around US$10 an hour for a boat with an eight- to 10-person capacity.

Along the upper Mekong River between Huay Xai and Vientiane, Thai-built *héua wái* (speedboats) are common. They can cover a distance in six hours that might take a ferry two days or more. Charters cost at least US$30 per hour, but some ply regular routes so the cost can be shared among passengers. They are, however, dangerous.

Tours

With public boat routes becoming increasingly hard to find, tour companies are offering kayaking and rafting trips on some of the more scenic stretches of river. The best places to organise these are Luang Namtha, Luang Prabang, Nong Khiaw, Vang Vieng, Tha Khaek and Pakse.

For something a bit more luxurious, **Asian Oasis** (www.asian-oasis.com), **Luang Say** (www.luangsay.com), **Mekong Cruises** (www.mekong-cruises.com) and **Mekong River Cruises and Mekong Islands Tours** (www.cruisemekong.com) all offer multiday cruises along the Mekong on refurbished river barges.

BUS, SĂWNGTHĂEW & LOT DOI SAAN

Long-distance public transport in Laos is either by bus or *săwngthăew* (literally 'two rows'), which are converted pick-ups or trucks with benches down either side. Buses are more frequent and go further than ever before in Laos, and destinations that were all but inaccessible a few years ago now see regular services, though 'regular' in Laos can mean a few every day. Private operators have established services on some busier routes – particularly along Rte 13 and on international routes – offering faster and more-luxurious air-con buses. These buses are known as VIP buses and cost about 50% more than the normal bus price, but are only available on the most major of routes and you might find it's worth booking ahead. You'll usually have to go to the bus station to do this, though increasingly guesthouses can book tickets for a small fee. For an idea of prices, see the boxed text p114).

Săwngthăew usually service shorter routes within a given province. Most decent-sized villages have at least one *săwngthăew,* which will run to the provincial capital and back most days. Like local buses, they stop wherever you want but are generally slower given that the roads they ply are usually unpaved.

CAR & MOTORCYCLE

Driving in Laos is easier than you might think. Sure, the road infrastructure is pretty basic, but outside of the large centres there are so few vehicles that it's a doddle compared to Vietnam, China or Thailand.

Motorcyclists planning to ride through Laos should check out the wealth of information at **Golden Triangle Rider** (www.gt-rider.com). Doing some sort of motorbike loop is becoming increasingly popular among travellers. For some tips see the boxed text p342.

Bring Your Own Vehicle

Bringing a vehicle into Laos is easy enough if you have proof of ownership and a *carnet de passage.* You simply get the *carnet* stamped at any international border (p334) – there is no extra charge or permit required.

If you don't have a *carnet* – likely the case if you bought your vehicle in Thailand, which doesn't recognise the *carnet* system – you'll need an International Transport Permit, known in Thailand as the *lêm sĭi mûang* (purple book). This is available at **Nong Khai's**

Land Transport Office (☎ Thailand 0 4241 1591 ext 103; ⊗ 8.30am-4.30pm), or any other Land Transport Office in Thailand, for 55B. You'll need your vehicle's official registration book and tax receipts, your passport and an International Driving Permit or the newest version of the Thai driver's licence.

On the Lao side you'll need all the documents mentioned above and will also need to arrange Lao vehicle insurance (about 300B for a week).

Exiting into Thailand or Cambodia is fairly hassle free if your papers are in order. Vietnam is a different story. As friends of ours reported (read their account at www.landcruising.nl), some borders just don't have the necessary papers. They crossed at Na Meo but had to leave their vehicle at the border while they went 200km to Thanh Hoa to sort out the permit with the police, which took two days and copies of their *carnet,* licence, registration and insurance papers. Vietnam usually won't issue permits to right-hand drive vehicles.

If you're heading to China it's virtually impossible to drive a vehicle larger than a bicycle across the border.

Driving Licence

Officially at least, to drive in Laos you need a valid International Driving Permit, which you must get in your home country. If you're only renting motorbikes you'll never be asked for any sort of licence.

Fuel & Spare Parts

At the time of research fuel cost about US$1.12 a litre for petrol, slightly less for diesel. Fuel for motorcycles is available from drums or

---

ON THE BUSES

The buses of Laos probably won't be what you're used to, so what should you expect? For starters, it will almost certainly take longer than the advertised time. The ride itself depends on how lucky you are on a given day. It could be relatively smooth, moving at something approaching 60kph on an ageing but relatively modern bus, with two seats to yourself and no karaoke. Or it might not…

The bus itself might be a relic that's so bad it makes an otherwise flat road feel like a potholed monster. The music might be as loud as it is bad, and you might be sharing the bus with a menagerie of farmyard animals. One bus we took stopped for an hour outside of Savannakhet in order to stuff live goats into the luggage storage. Things break, too. Between Phonsavan and Sam Neua two of the day's buses had broken down the day we went by, luckily in the opposite direction.

Our advice is don't look at your watch too much and just soak it up. These sort of trips are actually more fun than they sound. They're inevitably social events and make much better stories than a few uneventful hours on a VIP bus where the only chicken to be seen has already been barbecued. And don't assume VIP buses won't break down either!

MOTORCYCLE DIARIES

There are few more liberating travel experiences than renting a motorbike and setting off; stopping where you want, when you want. The lack of traffic and stunningly beautiful roads make Laos about the best place in the region to do it. There are, however, a few things worth knowing before you hand over your passport as collateral on a rent bike.

- The bike – Price and availability mean that the vast majority of travellers rent Chinese 110cc bikes. No 110cc bike was designed to be used like a dirt bike, but Japanese bikes deal with it better and are worth the extra couple of dollars a day.

- The odometer – Given that many roads have no kilometre stones and turn-offs are often unmarked, it's worth getting a bike with a working odometer. That's easier said than done. The good news is that almost any bike shop can fix an odometer in about 10 minutes for about US$3 or US$4. Money well spent, we think, as long as you remember to note the distance when you start.

- The gear – Don't leave home without sunscreen, a hat, plastic raincoat or poncho, bandanna and sunglasses. Even the sealed roads in Laos get annoyingly dusty, so these last two are vital. At dusk your headlight will act as a magnet for all manner of suicidal bugs, but unfortunately their aim isn't so good and more often than not they end up smacking into your face. This soon gets tedious and you might find yourself doing a Corey Hart and wearing your sunglasses at night. Helmets are a good idea (ask for one if they don't offer), as is wearing pants and shoes, lest you wind up with the ubiquitous burnt leg.

- The problems – Unless you're very lucky, something will go wrong. Budget some time for it. However, short of a head-on with a *sǎwngthǎew* it shouldn't be the end of the world.

- The responsibility – In general, you can ride a motorbike in Laos without a licence, a helmet or any safety gear whatsoever, but for all this freedom you must take all the responsibility. If you have a crash there won't be an ambulance to pick you up, and even when you get to the hospital, facilities will be basic. Carrying a basic medical kit and phone numbers for hospitals in Thailand and your travel insurance provider is a good idea. The same goes for the bike. If it really dies you can't just call the company and get a replacement. Laos doesn't work like that, so you'll need to load it onto the next pick-up or *sǎwngthǎew* and take it somewhere they can fix it. Do not abandon it by the road, or you'll have to pay for another one.

Beerlao bottles in villages across the country, though prices are almost always higher than at service stations. Diesel is available in most towns. It's best to fuel up in bigger towns at big-brand service stations because the quality of fuel can be poor in remote areas. Villages with petrol seem to pop up every 30 to 50km on the remotest roads so it's advisable to fill a motorbike wherever you see petrol – often just a thatched shack with a hand pump on a metal drum or a few bottles on the side of the road.

Spare parts for four-wheeled vehicles are expensive and difficult to find, even in Vientiane.

Hire

Chinese- and Japanese-made 100 and 110cc step-through motorbikes can be hired for approximately 40,000K to 90,000K per day in most large centres and some smaller towns, although the state of the bikes can vary greatly. No licence is required. Try to get a Japanese bike if you're travelling any distance out of town. In Vientiane 250cc dirt bikes are available for about US$25 per day.

It's possible to hire a self-drive vehicle, but when you consider that a driver usually costs no more, takes responsibility for damage and knows where he's going, it seems pointless. Informal charters can be arranged almost anywhere, with small Japanese pick-ups costing between US$40 and US$100 per day, depending on where you're going; the rougher the road, the higher the price.

The following Vientiane-based companies have good reputations:

Europcar (Asia Vehicle Rental; Map p90; ☎/fax 021-223 867; www.avr.laopdr.com; 354-356 Th Samsenthai,

Vientiane) Undoubtedly the most reliable place to hire vehicles, with or without drivers. Offers 4WDs, vans, sedans. Recommended.

jules classic rental (Map p90; ☎ 020-7760 0813; www.bike-rental-laos.com; Th Setthathirath, Vientiane; per day US$25-50; ⏰ 7am-9pm). Jules specialises in larger dirt and road bikes, provides comprehensive insurance, trip consultation, one-way service and a full range of equipment and clothing.

LaoWheels (☎ 021-223 663, 020-5550 4604; laowheels @yahoo.co.uk) Christophe Kittirath speaks fluent French, ok English, knows the country inside out and is a good driver.

Elsewhere, larger hotels usually have a van for rent or can find one, or ask at the local tourism office.

Insurance

Car-hire companies will provide insurance, but be sure to check exactly what is covered. Note that most travel insurance policies don't cover use of motorcycles.

Road Conditions

While the overall condition of roads is poor, work over the last decade has made most of the main roads – originally laid out by the French as part of a network that covered Indochina – quite comfortable.

Elsewhere, unsurfaced roads are the rule. Laos has about 23,000km of classified roads and less than a quarter are sealed. Unsurfaced roads are particularly tricky in the wet season when many routes are impassable to all but 4WD vehicles and motorbikes, while in the dry the clouds of dust kicked up by passing traffic makes travel highly uncomfortable, especially in a *săwngthǎew* or by motorbike. Bring a facemask. Wet or dry, Laos is so mountainous that relatively short road trips can take forever; a typical 200km upcountry trip could take more than 10 hours.

Road Hazards

Try to avoid driving at dusk and after dark; cows, buffaloes, chickens and dogs, not to mention thousands of people, head for home on the unlit roads, turning them into a dangerous obstacle course. Unsigned roadwork, like a huge hole in the road, is also a challenge in fading light.

Road Rules

The single most important rule to driving in Laos is to expect the unexpected; Western-style 'tunnel vision driving' just doesn't work here. Driving is on the right side, but it's not unusual to see Lao drivers go the wrong way down the left lane before crossing over to the right – a potentially dangerous situation if you're not ready for it. At intersections it's normal to turn right without looking left, and while changing lanes people almost never look behind because the person behind is responsible for avoiding whatever happens in front of them.

Tours

A handful of companies offer motorcycle tours of Laos. Guided tours are all-inclusive, and in addition to accommodation, food and petrol, typically include rental of a 250cc dirt bike and protective gear.

Explore Indochina (www.exploreindochina.com) Guided tours of the Ho Chi Minh Trail on vintage Soviet motorcycles.

L.A.R.A (Laos Adventure Riders Association; www. ride-lara.com) Riders on this Laos-based company's tours are shadowed by a 4X4 truck with a spare motorcycle and parts.

Remote Asia (www.remoteasia.com/Motorbike.html) Self-guided motorcycle tours of Laos ranging in duration from four to 12 days are on offer here. Motorcycle and equipment rental are also available.

Siam Enduro (www.siamenduro.com) This Thailand-based outfit has brought together its two decades of experience in the region to put together a two-week tour of northern Laos.

HITCHING

Hitching is possible in Laos, if not common, though it's never entirely safe and not recommended for women as the act of standing beside a road and waving at cars might be misinterpreted. If you are hitching, cars with red-on-yellow (private vehicle) or blue-on-white (international organisations and embassies) number plates might be the best ones to target, though some aid agencies strictly forbid their drivers to give hitchers a lift. Long-distance cargo trucks are also a good bet.

LOCAL TRANSPORT

Although most town centres are small enough to walk around, even relatively small settlements often place their bus stations several kilometres out of town in what appears at times to be a blatant scam at providing business for tuk-tuk drivers.

TRANSPORT

Bus

Vientiane is the only city with a network of local buses (p116), though they're not much good to travellers.

Jumbo, Săam-lâaw, Sakai-làep, Tuk-tuk

The various three-wheeled taxis found in Vientiane and provincial capitals have different names depending on where you are. Larger ones are called *jąmbǫh* (jumbo) and can hold four to six passengers on two facing seats. In Vientiane they are sometimes called tuk-tuk as in Thailand (though traditionally in Laos this refers to a slightly larger vehicle than the jumbo), while in the south (eg Pakse and Savannakhet) they may be called *sakai-làep* (Skylab) because someone, probably on opium at the time, once thought they looked like the famous space station that crashed to earth. But wait, there's more…these three-wheeled conveyances are also labelled simply *thaek-sii* (taxi) or, usually for motorcycle sidecar-style vehicles, *săam-lâaw* (samlor or three-wheels). Whatever you call it people will usually know what you're after. The old-style bicycle *săam-lâaw* (pedicab), known as a *cyclo* elsewhere in Indochina, is an endangered species in Laos.

Taxi

Vientiane has a handful of car taxis that are used by foreign businesspeople and the occasional tourist, though in other cities a taxi of sorts can be arranged. They can be hired by the trip, by the hour or by the day. Typical all-day hire within a town or city costs between US$35 and US$45 depending on the vehicle and your negotiating powers.

TOURS

A growing number of tour operators run trips in Laos and it's cheaper to book directly with them rather than through a foreign-based agency. A common two-week tour might take in Vientiane, Luang Prabang, the Plain of Jars, Savannakhet and Champasak; the better operators can customise itineraries. More specialised tours are also becoming popular, with cycling (p338), boat tours (p340), motorcycling (p343) and even photographic tours (p324) all available.

The following are also worth investigating:

Carpe Diem Travel (www.carpe-diem-travel.com) Environmentally and socially responsible tours, focussing on pro-poor tourism and aiding communities through sponsorship projects.

Exotissimo (www.exotissimo.com) Large company with a mix of pure sightseeing and adventure tours.

Green Discovery (www.greendiscoverylaos.com) Biggest adventure tourism operator in Laos. Well-organised kayaking, trekking, cycling, rock climbing and rafting trips. Easy to book locally and fair value.

Inter-Lao Tourisme (www.interlao.com) Vientiane-based agency that subcontracts to several larger international tour operators.

Lao Youth Travel (www.laoyouthtravel.com) Multi-day tours between Vientiane, Vang Vieng and Luang Prabang, plus trips to minority villages further north.

Tiger Trail (www.tigertrail-laos.com) Established Luang Prabang-based company with big range of tours, including trekking, rafting and kayaking. No tigers, though.

Viengchampa (www.viengchampatour.com) Long-standing operator with a good reputation and variety of tours.

Xplore-Asia (www.xplore-asia.com) Popular with backpackers for their cheap adventure tours, especially from Pakse, Si Phan Don and Vang Vieng.

Health Dr Trish Batchelor

Health issues and the quality of medical facilities vary enormously depending on where and how you travel in Laos. Travellers tend to worry about contracting infectious diseases when in the tropics, but infections are a rare cause of serious illness or death in travellers. Pre-existing medical conditions such as heart disease and accidental injury (especially traffic accidents) account for most of the life-threatening problems. Becoming ill in some way, however, is relatively common. Fortunately, most common illnesses can either be prevented with common-sense behaviour or be treated easily with a well-stocked traveller's medical kit.

The following advice is a general guide only and does not replace the advice of a doctor trained in travel medicine.

BEFORE YOU GO

Pack medications in their original, clearly labelled, containers. A signed and dated letter from your physician describing your medical conditions and medications, including generic names, is also a good idea. If carrying syringes or needles, be sure to have a physician's letter documenting their medical necessity. If you have a heart condition bring a copy of your ECG taken just prior to travelling.

If you happen to take any regular medication, bring double your needs in case of loss or theft. In Laos it can be difficult to find some newer drugs, particularly the latest antidepressant drugs, blood pressure medications and contraceptive pills.

INSURANCE

Even if you are fit and healthy, don't travel without health insurance – accidents do happen. Declare any existing medical conditions you have – the insurance company *will* check if your problem is pre-existing and will not cover you if it is undeclared. You may require extra cover for adventure activities such as rock climbing. If your health insurance doesn't cover you for medical expenses abroad, consider getting extra insurance – check lonelyplanet.com for more information. If you're uninsured, emergency evacuation is expensive; bills of over US$100,000 are not uncommon.

Find out in advance if your insurance plan will make payments directly to providers or reimburse you later for overseas health expenditures. (In many countries doctors expect payment in cash.) Some policies offer lower and higher medical-expense options; the higher ones are chiefly for countries that have extremely high medical costs, such as the USA. You may prefer a policy that pays doctors or hospitals directly rather than you having to pay on the spot and claim later. If you have to claim later, keep all the documentation. Some policies ask you to call back (reverse charges) to a centre in your home country where an immediate assessment of your problem is made.

VACCINATIONS

The only vaccine required by international regulations is yellow fever. Proof of vaccination will only be required if you have visited a country in the yellow-fever zone within the six days prior to entering Southeast Asia. If you are travelling to Southeast Asia from Africa or South America you should check to see if you require proof of vaccination.

Specialised travel-medicine clinics are your best source of information; they stock all

HEALTH

RECOMMENDED VACCINATIONS

The World Health Organization (WHO) recommends the following vaccinations for travellers to Southeast Asia:

- Adult diphtheria and tetanus – Single booster recommended if you've had none in the previous 10 years. Side effects include a sore arm and fever.
- Hepatitis A – Provides almost 100% protection for up to a year; a booster after 12 months provides at least another 20 years' protection. Mild side effects such as headache and a sore arm occur for between 5% and 10% of people.
- Hepatitis B – Now considered routine for most travellers. Given as three shots over six months. A rapid schedule is also available, as is a combined vaccination with Hepatitis A. Side effects are mild and uncommon, usually a headache and sore arm. Lifetime protection occurs in 95% of people.
- Measles, mumps and rubella – Two doses of MMR required unless you have had the diseases. Occasionally a rash and flu-like illness can develop a week after receiving the vaccine. Many young adults require a booster.
- Polio – Since 2006, India, Indonesia, Nepal and Bangladesh are the only countries in Asia to have reported cases of polio. Only one booster is required as an adult for lifetime protection. Inactivated polio vaccine is safe during pregnancy.
- Typhoid – Recommended unless your trip is less than a week and only to developed cities. The vaccine offers around 70% protection, lasts for two to three years and comes as a single shot. Tablets are also available; however, the injection is usually recommended as it has fewer side effects. Sore arm and fever may occur.
- Varicella – If you haven't had chickenpox, discuss this vaccination with your doctor.

Long-term travellers

These vaccinations are recommended for people travelling for more than one month, or those at special risk:

- Japanese B Encephalitis – Three injections in all. Booster recommended after two years. A sore arm and headache are the most common side effects. Rarely, an allergic reaction comprising hives and swelling can occur up to 10 days after any of the three doses.
- Meningitis – Single injection. There are two types of vaccination: the quadrivalent vaccine gives two to three years protection; meningitis group C vaccine gives around 10 years protection. Recommended for long-term backpackers aged under 25.
- Rabies – Three injections in all. A booster after one year will provide 10 years protection. Side effects are rare – occasionally a headache and sore arm.
- Tuberculosis – Adult long-term travellers are usually recommended to have a TB skin test before and after travel, rather than vaccination. Only one vaccine is given in a lifetime.

available vaccines and will be able to give specific recommendations for you and your trip. The doctors will take into account factors such as past vaccination history, the length of your trip, activities you may be undertaking, and underlying medical conditions, such as pregnancy.

Most vaccines don't produce immunity until at least two weeks after they're given, so visit a doctor four to eight weeks before departure. Ask your doctor for an International Certificate of Vaccination (otherwise known as the yellow booklet), which will list all the vaccinations you've received. In the US, the yellow booklet is no longer issued, but it is highly unlikely the Lao authorities will ask for proof of vaccinations (unless you have recently been in a yellow-fever affected country). See Recommended Vaccinations for possible vaccinations.

INTERNET RESOURCES

There is a wealth of travel health advice on the internet. The **World Health Organization** (WHO; www.who.int/ith) publishes a superb book called

International Travel & Health, which is revised annually and is available online at no cost. Another website of general interest is **MD Travel Health** (www.mdtravelhealth.com), which provides complete travel health recommendations for every country and is updated daily. The **Centers for Disease Control and Prevention** (CDC; www.cdc.gov) website also has good general information.

FURTHER READING

Lonely Planet's *Healthy Travel – Asia & India* is a handy pocket-size book that is packed with useful information including pretrip planning, emergency first aid, immunisation and disease information and what to do if you get sick on the road. Other recommended references include *Traveller's Health* by Dr Richard Dawood and *Travelling Well* by Dr Deborah Mills – check out the website (www. travellingwell.com.au).

IN TRANSIT

DEEP VEIN THROMBOSIS (DVT)

Deep vein thrombosis (DVT) occurs when blood clots form in the legs during plane flights, chiefly because of prolonged immobility. The longer the flight, the greater the risk. Though most blood clots are reabsorbed uneventfully, some may break off and travel through the blood vessels to the lungs, where they may cause life-threatening complications.

The chief symptom of DVT is swelling or pain of the foot, ankle, or calf, usually on just one side. When a blood clot travels to the lungs, it may cause chest pain and difficulty in breathing. Travellers with any of these symptoms should immediately seek medical attention.

To prevent the development of DVT on long flights you should walk about the cabin, perform isometric compressions of the leg muscles (ie contract the leg muscles while sitting), drink plenty of fluids, and avoid alcohol and tobacco.

JET LAG & MOTION SICKNESS

Jet lag is common when crossing more than five time zones; it results in insomnia, fatigue, malaise or nausea. To avoid jet lag try drinking plenty of fluids (nonalcoholic) and eating light meals. Upon arrival, seek exposure to natural sunlight and readjust your schedule (for meals, sleep etc) as soon as possible.

HEALTH ADVISORIES

It's usually a good idea to consult your government's travel-health website before departure, if one is available:
Australia (www.smartraveller.gov.au/tips/ travelwell.html)
Canada (www.travelhealth.gc.ca)
New Zealand (www.safetravel.govt.nz)
UK (www.fco.gov.uk/en/travel-and-living-abroad/ staying-safe)
US (www.cdc.gov/travel)

The winding mountain roads in Laos can be beautiful, but they're also a problem if you suffer from motion sickness. The section of Rte 13 between Vang Vieng and Luang Prabang is particularly bad, and we heard from one guy who was ill for three days after making this trip. Antihistamines such as dimenhydrinate (Dramamine) and meclizine (Antivert, Bonine) are usually the first choice for treating motion sickness. Their main side effect is drowsiness. A herbal alternative is ginger, which works like a charm for some people.

IN LAOS

AVAILABILITY OF HEALTHCARE

Laos has no facilities for major medical emergencies. The state-run hospitals and clinics are among the worst in Southeast Asia in terms of the standards of hygiene, staff training, supplies and equipment, and the availability of medicines.

For minor to moderate conditions, including malaria, **Mahasot Hospital's International Clinic** (☎ 021-214 022) in Vientiane has a decent reputation. Some foreign embassies in Vientiane also maintain small but professional medical centres, including the **Australian Embassy Clinic** (☎ 021-353 840) and the **French Embassy Medical Center** (☎ 021-214 150).

For any serious conditions, you're better off going to Thailand. If a medical problem can wait until you're in Bangkok, then all the better, as there are excellent hospitals there.

For medical emergencies that can't be delayed before reaching Bangkok, you can call ambulances from nearby Nong Khai or Udon Thani in Thailand. **Nong Khai Wattana General Hospital** (☎ 0066 4246 5201; fax 0066 4246 5210) in Nong Khai is the closest. The better **Aek**

HEALTH

MEDICAL CHECKLIST

Recommended items for a personal medical kit:

- antifungal cream, eg Clotrimazole
- antibacterial cream, eg Muciprocin
- antibiotics for skin infections, eg Amoxicillin/Clavulanate or Cephalexin
- antibiotics for diarrhoea, eg Norfloxacin or Ciprofloxacin; Azithromycin for bacterial diarrhoea; and Tinidazole for giardiasis or amoebic dysentery
- antihistamines for allergies, eg Cetrizine for daytime and Promethazine for night
- anti-inflammatories, eg Ibuprofen
- antinausea medication, eg Prochlorperazine
- antiseptic for cuts and scrapes, eg Betadine
- antispasmodic for stomach cramps, eg Buscopan
- contraceptives
- decongestant for colds and flus, eg Pseudoephedrine
- DEET-based insect repellent
- diarrhoea 'stopper', eg Loperamide
- first-aid items such as scissors, plasters (Band Aids), bandages, gauze, thermometer (electronic, not mercury), sterile needles and syringes, and tweezers
- indigestion medication, eg Quick Eze or Mylanta
- iodine tablets (unless you are pregnant or have a thyroid problem) to purify water
- laxative, eg Coloxyl
- migraine medication (your personal brand), if a migraine sufferer
- oral-rehydration solution for diarrhoea, eg Gastrolyte
- paracetamol for pain
- permethrin (to impregnate clothing and mosquito nets) for repelling insects
- steroid cream for allergic/itchy rashes, eg 1% to 2% hydrocortisone
- sunscreen and hat
- throat lozenges
- thrush (vaginal yeast infection) treatment, eg Clotrimazole pessaries or Diflucan tablet
- urine alkalisation agent, eg Ural, if you're prone to urinary tract infections.

Udon Hospital (☎ 0066 4234 2555; www.aekudon.com) in Udon Thani is an hour further from the border by road. **Lao Westcoast Helicopter** (☎ 021-512 023; www.laowestcoast.com; Hangar 703, Wattay International Airport) will fly emergency patients to Udon Thani for about US$1500, subject to aircraft availability and government permission. From any of these hospitals, patients can be transferred to Bangkok if necessary.

Self-treatment may be appropriate if your problem is minor (eg traveller's diarrhoea), you are carrying the appropriate medication and you cannot attend a recommended clinic. If you think you may have a serious disease, especially malaria, do not waste time – travel to the nearest quality facility. It is always better to be assessed by a doctor than to rely on self-treatment.

Buying medication over the counter is not recommended, as fake medications and poorly stored or out-of-date drugs are common in Laos.

INFECTIOUS DISEASES
Dengue Fever
This mosquito-borne disease is becomingly increasingly problematic throughout Laos, especially in the cities. As there is no vaccine

it can only be prevented by avoiding mosquito bites. The mosquito that carries dengue bites day and night, so use insect avoidance measures at all times. Symptoms include high fever, severe headache and body ache (dengue was once known as 'breakbone fever'). Some people develop a rash and diarrhoea. There's no specific treatment, just rest and paracetamol – do not take aspirin as it increases the likelihood of haemorrhaging. See a doctor to be diagnosed and monitored.

Filariasis

This is a mosquito-borne disease that is very common in the local population, yet very rare in travellers. Mosquito-avoidance measures are the best way to prevent it.

Hepatitis A

A problem throughout the region, this food- and water-borne virus infects the liver, causing jaundice (yellow skin and eyes), nausea and lethargy. There is no specific treatment for hepatitis A, you just need to allow time for the liver to heal. All travellers to Southeast Asia should be vaccinated against hepatitis A.

Hepatitis B

The only sexually transmitted disease that can be prevented by vaccination, hepatitis B is spread by body fluids, including sexual contact. In some parts of Southeast Asia, up to 20% of the population are carriers of hepatitis B, and usually are unaware of this. The long-term consequences can include liver cancer and cirrhosis.

Hepatitis E

Hepatitis E is transmitted through contaminated food and water and has similar symptoms to hepatitis A, but is far less common. It is a severe problem in pregnant women and can result in the death of both mother and baby. There is currently no vaccine; prevention is by following safe eating and drinking guidelines.

HIV

According to Unaids and WHO, Laos remains a 'low HIV prevalence country'; Unaids reported a range of between 1000 and 1800 as of 2001. However, it's estimated that only about one fifth of all HIV cases in Laos are actually reported. Heterosexual sex is the main method of transmission in Laos.

The use of condoms greatly decreases but does not eliminate the risk of HIV infection. The Lao phrase for 'condom' is *thœng anáamái*. Condoms can be purchased at most *hâan khǎi yáa* (pharmacies), but it is worth bringing your own condoms from home.

Influenza

Present year-round in the tropics, influenza (flu) symptoms include high fever, muscle aches, runny nose, cough and sore throat. It can be very severe in people over the age of 65 or in those with underlying medical conditions such as heart disease or diabetes; vaccination is recommended for these individuals. There is no specific treatment, just rest and paracetamol.

Japanese B Encephalitis

While a rare disease in travellers, at least 50,000 locals are infected with Japanese B Encephalitis each year in Southeast Asia. This viral disease is transmitted by mosquitoes. Most cases occur in rural areas and vaccination is recommended for travellers spending more than one month outside of cities. There is no treatment, and a third of infected people will die while another third will suffer permanent brain damage.

Malaria

For such a serious and potentially deadly disease, there is an enormous amount of misinformation concerning malaria. You must get expert advice as to whether your trip actually puts you at risk. Many parts of Laos, particularly populated areas, have minimal to no risk of malaria, and the risk of side effects from the antimalaria medication may outweigh the risk of getting the disease. For some rural areas, however, the risk of contracting the disease far outweighs the risk of any tablet side effects. Remember that malaria can be fatal. Before you travel, seek medical advice on the right medication and dosage for you.

Malaria is caused by a parasite transmitted by the bite of an infected mosquito. The most important symptom of malaria is fever, but general symptoms such as headache, diarrhoea, cough or chills may also occur. Diagnosis can only be made by taking a blood sample.

Two strategies should be combined to prevent malaria – mosquito avoidance, and antimalarial medications. Most people who catch malaria are taking inadequate or no antimalarial medication.

Travellers are advised to prevent mosquito bites by taking these steps:

- Choose accommodation with screens and fans (if not air-conditioned).
- Impregnate clothing with Permethrin in high-risk areas.
- Sleep under a mosquito net impregnated with Permethrin.
- Spray your room with insect repellent before going out for your evening meal.
- Use a DEET-containing insect repellent on exposed skin. Wash this off at night, as long as you are sleeping under a mosquito net. Natural repellents such as citronella can be effective, but must be applied more frequently than products containing DEET.
- Use mosquito coils.
- Wear long sleeves and trousers in light colours.

MALARIA MEDICATION

There are a variety of medications available. The effectiveness of the Chloroquine and Paludrine combination is now limited in most of Southeast Asia. Common side effects include nausea (40% of people) and mouth ulcers. It is generally not recommended.

Lariam (Mefloquine) has received much bad press, some of it justified, some not. This weekly tablet suits many people. Serious side effects are rare but include depression, anxiety, psychosis and seizures. Anyone with a history of depression, anxiety, other psychological disorders or epilepsy should not take Lariam. It is considered safe in the second and third trimesters of pregnancy. It is around 90% effective in most parts of Southeast Asia, but there is significant resistance in parts of northern Thailand, Laos and Cambodia. Tablets must be taken for four weeks after leaving the risk area.

Doxycycline, taken as a daily tablet, is a broad-spectrum antibiotic that has the added benefit of helping to prevent a variety of tropical diseases, including leptospirosis, tick-borne disease, typhus and melioidosis. The potential side effects include photosensitivity (a tendency to sunburn), thrush in women, indigestion, heartburn, nausea and interference with the contraceptive pill. More serious side effects include ulceration of the oesophagus – you can help prevent this by taking your tablet with a meal and a large glass of water, and never lying down within half an hour of taking it. It must be taken for four weeks after leaving the risk area.

Malarone is a new drug combining Atovaquone and Proguanil. Side effects are uncommon and mild, most commonly nausea and headaches. It is the best tablet for scuba divers and for those on short trips to high-risk areas. It must be taken for one week after leaving the risk area.

Derivatives of Artesunate are not suitable as a preventive medication. They are useful treatments under medical supervision.

A final option is to take no preventive medication but to have a supply of emergency medication should you develop the symptoms of malaria. This is less than ideal, and you'll need to get to a good medical facility within 24 hours of developing a fever. If you choose this option the most effective and safest treatment is Malarone (four tablets once daily for three days). Other options include Mefloquine and Quinine but the side effects of these drugs at treatment doses make them less desirable. Fansidar is no longer recommended.

Measles

Measles remains a problem in some parts of Southeast Asia. This highly contagious bacterial infection is spread via coughing and sneezing. Most people born before 1966 are immune as they had the disease in childhood. Measles starts with a high fever and rash and can be complicated by pneumonia and brain disease. There is no specific treatment.

Melioidosis

This infection is contracted by skin contact with soil. It is rare in travellers. The symptoms are very similar to those experienced by tuberculosis sufferers. There is no vaccine but it can be treated with medication.

Opisthorchiasis (Liver Flukes)

These are tiny worms that are occasionally present in freshwater fish in Laos. The main risk comes from eating raw or undercooked fish. Travellers should in particular avoid eating uncooked pọa dàek (an unpasteurised fermented fish used as an accompaniment for many Lao foods) when travelling in rural Laos. The pọa dàek in Vientiane and Luang Prabang is said to be safe (or safer) simply because it is usually produced from noninfected fish, while the risk of infestation is greatest in the southern provinces.

A rarer way to contract liver flukes is by swimming in the Mekong River or its tributaries around Don Khong (Khong Island) in the far south of Laos.

At low levels, there are virtually no symptoms at all; at higher levels, an overall fatigue, a low-grade fever and swollen or tender liver (or general abdominal pain) are the usual symptoms, along with worms or worm eggs in the faeces. Opisthorchiasis is easily treated with medication. Untreated, patients may develop serious liver infections several years after contact.

Rabies

This uniformly fatal disease is spread by the bite or lick of an infected animal – most commonly a dog or monkey. You should seek medical advice immediately after any animal bite and commence post-exposure treatment. Having a pretravel vaccination means the postbite treatment is greatly simplified. If an animal bites you, gently wash the wound with soap and water, and apply iodine based antiseptic. If you are not vaccinated you will need to receive rabies immunoglobulin as soon as possible.

Schistosomiasis

Schistosomiasis (also called bilharzia) is a tiny parasite that enters your skin when swimming in contaminated water – travellers usually only get a light, symptomless infection. If you are concerned, you can be tested three months after exposure. On rare occasions, travellers may develop 'Katayama fever'. It can occur some weeks after exposure, as the parasite passes through the lungs and causes an allergic reaction – symptoms are coughing and fever. Schistosomiasis is easily treated with medications.

STDs

Sexually transmitted diseases most common in Laos include herpes, warts, syphilis, gonorrhoea and chlamydia. People carrying these diseases often have no signs of infection. Condoms will prevent gonorrhoea and chlamydia but not warts or herpes. If after a sexual encounter you develop any rash, lumps, discharge or pain when passing urine seek immediate medical attention. If you have been sexually active during your travels have an STD check on your return home.

Strongyloides

This parasite, also transmitted by skin contact with soil, rarely affects travellers. It is characterised by an unusual skin rash called larva currens – a linear rash on the trunk which comes and goes. Most people don't have other symptoms until their immune system becomes severely suppressed, when the parasite can cause an overwhelming infection. It can be treated with medication.

Tuberculosis

Tuberculosis (TB) is very rare in short-term travellers. Medical and aid workers, and long-term travellers who have significant contact with the local population should take precautions, however. Vaccination is usually only given to children under the age of five, but adults at risk are advised to get pre- and post-travel TB testing. The main symptoms are fever, cough, weight loss, night sweats and tiredness.

Typhoid

This serious bacterial infection is also spread via food and water. It gives a high, slowly progressive fever and headache, and may be accompanied by a dry cough and stomach pain. It is diagnosed by blood tests and treated with antibiotics. Vaccination is recommended for all travellers spending more than a week in Southeast Asia, or travelling outside of the major cities. Be aware that vaccination is not 100% effective so you must still be careful with what you eat and drink.

Typhus

Murine typhus is spread by the bite of a flea, whereas scrub typhus is spread via a mite. These diseases are rare in travellers. Symptoms include fever, muscle pains and a rash. You can avoid these diseases by following general insect-avoidance measures. Doxycycline will also prevent them.

TRAVELLER'S DIARRHOEA

Traveller's diarrhoea is by far the most common problem affecting travellers – between 30% and 50% of people will suffer from it within two weeks of starting their trip. In over 80% of cases, traveller's diarrhoea is caused by a bacteria (there are numerous potential culprits), and therefore responds promptly to treatment with antibiotics. Treatment with antibiotics will depend on your situation –

how sick you are, how quickly you need to get better, where you are etc.

Traveller's diarrhoea is defined as the passage of more than three watery bowel-actions within 24 hours, plus at least one other symptom such as fever, cramps, nausea, vomiting or feeling generally unwell.

Treatment consists of staying well hydrated. Rehydration solutions like Gastrolyte are the best for this. Antibiotics such as Norfloxacin, Ciprofloxacin or Azithromycin will kill the bacteria quickly.

Loperamide is just a 'stopper' and doesn't get to the cause of the problem. It can be helpful, for example if you have to go on a long bus ride. Don't take Loperamide if you have a fever, or blood in your stools. Seek medical attention quickly if you do not respond to an appropriate antibiotic.

Amoebic Dysentery

Amoebic dysentery is very rare in travellers but is often misdiagnosed by poor-quality labs in Southeast Asia. Symptoms are similar to bacterial diarrhoea, ie fever, bloody diarrhoea and generally feeling unwell. You should always seek reliable medical care if you have blood in your diarrhoea. Treatment involves two drugs; Tinidazole or Metronidazole to kill the parasite in your gut and then a second drug to kill the cysts. If left untreated complications such as liver or gut abscesses can occur.

Giardiasis

Giardia lamblia is a parasite that is relatively common in travellers. Symptoms include nausea, bloating, excess gas, fatigue and intermittent diarrhoea. 'Eggy' burps are often attributed solely to giardiasis, but work in Nepal has shown that they are not specific to this infection. The parasite will eventually go away if left untreated but this can take months. The treatment of choice is Tinidazole, with Metronidazole being a second-line option.

ENVIRONMENTAL HAZARDS
Food

Eating in restaurants is the biggest risk factor for contracting traveller's diarrhoea. Ways to avoid it include eating only freshly cooked food, and avoiding shellfish and food that has been sitting around in buffets. Peel all fruit, cook vegetables, and soak salads in iodine

---

DRINKING WATER

- Never drink tap water.
- Bottled water is generally safe – check the seal is intact at purchase.
- Avoid fresh juices – they may have been watered down.
- Boiling water is the most efficient method of purifying it.
- The best chemical purifier is iodine. It should not be used by pregnant women or those people who suffer with thyroid problems.
- Water filters should filter out viruses. Ensure your filter has a chemical barrier such as iodine and a small pore size, ie less than four microns.

---

water for at least 20 minutes. Eat in busy restaurants with a high turnover of customers.

Heat

Many parts of Southeast Asia are hot and humid throughout the year. For most people it takes at least two weeks to adapt to the climate. Swelling of the feet and ankles is common, as are muscle cramps caused by excessive sweating. Prevent these by avoiding dehydration and excessive activity in the heat. Take it easy when you first arrive. Don't eat salt tablets (they aggravate the gut) but do drink rehydration solution and eat salty food. Treat cramps by resting, rehydrating with double-strength rehydration solution and gently stretching.

Dehydration is the main contributor to heat exhaustion. Symptoms include feeling weak, headache, irritability, nausea or vomiting, sweaty skin, a fast, weak pulse and a normal or slightly elevated body temperature. Treatment involves getting out of the heat and/or sun, fanning the victim and applying cool wet cloths to the skin, laying the victim flat with their legs raised and rehydrating with water containing a quarter of a teaspoon of salt per litre. Recovery is usually rapid, though it is common to feel weak for some days afterwards.

Heatstroke is a serious medical emergency. Symptoms come on suddenly and include weakness, nausea, a hot dry body with a body temperature of over 41°C, dizziness,

HEALTH

confusion, loss of coordination, seizures and eventually collapse and loss of consciousness. Seek medical help and commence cooling by getting the person out of the heat, removing their clothes, fanning them and applying cool wet cloths or ice to their body, especially to the groin and armpits.

Prickly heat is a common skin rash in the tropics, caused by sweat being trapped under the skin. The result is an itchy rash of tiny lumps. Treat by moving out of the heat and into an air-conditioned area for a few hours and by having cool showers. Creams and ointments clog the skin so they should be avoided. Locally bought prickly heat powder can be helpful.

Tropical fatigue is common in long-term expats based in the tropics. It's rarely due to disease and is caused by the climate, inadequate mental rest, excessive alcohol intake and the demands of daily work in a different culture.

Insect Bites & Stings
Bedbugs don't carry disease but their bites are very itchy. They live in the cracks of furniture and walls and then migrate to the bed at night to feed on you. You can treat the itch with an antihistamine. Lice inhabit various parts of your body but most commonly your head and pubic area. Transmission is via close contact with an infected person, although body lice can come from contaminated bedclothes. They can be difficult to treat and you may need numerous applications of an anti-lice shampoo such as Permethrin, or in the case of body lice, with medicated creams or ointments. Pubic lice are usually contracted from sexual contact.

Ticks are contracted during walks in rural areas. They are commonly found behind the ears, on the belly and in armpits. If you have had a tick bite and experience symptoms such as a rash (at the site of the bite or elsewhere), fever or muscle aches you should see a doctor. Doxycycline prevents tick-borne diseases.

Leeches are found in humid forest areas. They do not transmit any disease but their bites are often intensely itchy for weeks afterwards and can easily become infected. Apply an iodine-based antiseptic to any leech bite to help prevent infection.

Bee and wasp stings mainly cause problems for people who are allergic to them. Anyone with a serious bee or wasp allergy should carry an injection of adrenaline (eg an Epipen) for emergency treatment. For others pain is the main problem – apply ice to the sting and take painkillers.

Parasites
Numerous parasites are common in local populations in Southeast Asia; however, most of these are rare in travellers. The two rules to follow if you wish to avoid parasitic infections are to wear shoes and to avoid eating raw food, especially fish, pork and vegetables. A number of parasites can be transmitted via the skin by walking barefoot including strongyloides, hookworm and cutaneous larva migrans.

Skin Problems
Fungal rashes are common in humid climates. There are two common fungal rashes that affect travellers. The first occurs in moist areas that get less air, such as the groin, armpits and between the toes. It starts as a red patch that slowly spreads and is usually itchy. Treatment involves keeping the skin dry, avoiding chafing and using an antifungal cream such as Clotrimazole or Lamisil. *Tinea versicolor* is also common – this fungus causes small, light-coloured patches, most commonly on the back, chest and shoulders. Consult a doctor for treatment.

Cuts and scratches become easily infected in humid climates. Take meticulous care of any cuts and scratches to prevent complications such as abscesses. Immediately wash all wounds in clean water and apply antiseptic. If you develop signs of infection (increasing pain and redness) see a doctor. Divers and surfers should be particularly careful with coral cuts as they become easily infected.

Snakes
Southeast Asia is home to many species of both poisonous and harmless snakes. Assume all snakes are poisonous and never try to catch one. Always wear boots and long pants if walking in an area that may have snakes. First-aid in the event of a snakebite involves pressure immobilisation via an elastic bandage firmly wrapped around the affected limb, starting at the bite site and working up towards the chest. The bandage should not be so tight that the circulation is cut off, and the fingers or toes should be kept free so the circulation can be checked. Immobilise the limb

HEALTH

with a splint and carry the victim to medical attention. Do not use tourniquets or try to suck the venom out. Antivenom is available for most species.

Sunburn

Even on a cloudy day, sunburn can occur rapidly. Always use a strong sunscreen (at least factor 30), making sure to reapply after a swim, and always wear a wide-brimmed hat and sunglasses outdoors. Avoid lying in the sun during the hottest part of the day (from 10am to 2pm). If you are sunburnt stay out of the sun until you have recovered, apply cool compresses and take painkillers for the discomfort. One percent hydrocortisone cream applied twice daily is also helpful.

WOMEN'S HEALTH

Pregnant women should receive specialised advice before travelling. The ideal time to travel is in the second trimester (between 16 and 28 weeks), when the risk of pregnancy-related problems are lowest and pregnant women generally feel at their best. During the first trimester there is a risk of miscarriage and in the third trimester complications such as premature labour and high blood pressure are possible. It's wise to travel with a companion. Always carry a list of quality medical facilities available at your destination and ensure you continue your standard antenatal care at these facilities. Avoid travel in rural areas with poor transportation and medical facilities. Most of all, ensure travel insurance covers all pregnancy-related possibilities, including premature labour.

Malaria is a high-risk disease during pregnancy. WHO recommends that pregnant women do *not* travel to areas with Chloroquine-resistant malaria. None of the more effective antimalarial drugs are completely safe in pregnancy.

Traveller's diarrhoea can quickly lead to dehydration and result in inadequate blood flow to the placenta. Many of the drugs used to treat various diarrhoea bugs are not recommended in pregnancy. Azithromycin is considered safe.

In the urban areas of Southeast Asia, supplies of sanitary products are readily available. Birth control options may be limited though so bring adequate supplies of your own form of contraception. Heat, humidity and antibiotics can all contribute to thrush. Treatment is with antifungal creams and pessaries such as Clotrimazole. A practical alternative is a single tablet of Fluconazole (Diflucan). Urinary tract infections can be precipitated by dehydration or long bus journeys without toilet stops; bring suitable antibiotics.

TRADITIONAL MEDICINE

Throughout Southeast Asia, traditional medical systems are widely practised. There is a big difference between these traditional healing systems and 'folk' medicine. Folk remedies should be avoided, as they often involve rather dubious procedures with potential complications. In comparison, traditional healing systems such as traditional Chinese medicine are well respected, and aspects of them are being increasingly utilised by Western medical practitioners.

All traditional Asian medical systems identify a vital life force, and see blockage or imbalance as causing disease. Techniques such as herbal medicines, massage, and acupuncture are utilised to bring this vital force back into balance, or to maintain balance. These therapies are best used for treating chronic disease such as chronic fatigue, arthritis, irritable bowel syndrome and some chronic skin conditions. Traditional medicines should be avoided for treating serious acute infections such as malaria.

Be aware that 'natural' doesn't always mean 'safe', and there can be drug interactions between herbal medicines and Western medicines. If you are utilising both systems ensure you inform both practitioners what the other has prescribed.

Language

CONTENTS

The official language of the LPDR is Lao as spoken and written in Vientiane. As an official language, it has successfully become the lingua franca between all Lao and non-Lao ethnic groups in Laos. Native Lao is spoken with differing tonal accents and with slightly differing vocabularies as you move from one part of the country to the next, especially in a north to south direction, but it is the Vientiane dialect that is most widely understood.

Modern Lao linguists recognise five basic dialects within the country: Vientiane Lao; northern Lao (spoken in Sainyabuli, Bokeo, Udomxai, Phongsali, Luang Namtha and Luang Prabang); northeastern Lao (Xieng Khuang and Hua Phan), central Lao (Khammuan and Bolikhamsai); and finally southern Lao (Champasak, Savannakhet, Salavan, Attapeu and Sekong). Each of these can be further divided into various subdialects; the differences between the Lao spoken in the neighbouring provinces of Xieng Khuang and Hua Phan, for example, are readily apparent to those who know the language well.

All dialects of Lao belong to the Thai half of the Thai-Kadai family of languages and are closely related to languages spoken in Thailand, northern Myanmar and pockets of China's Yunnan and Guangxi Provinces. Standard Lao is indeed close enough to standard Thai (as spoken in central Thailand) that for native speakers the two are mutually intelligible. In fact, virtually all of the speakers of Lao west of the Annamite Chain can easily understand spoken Thai.

Among educated Lao, written Thai is also easily understood, because many of the textbooks used at the college and university level in Laos are actually Thai texts.

Even more similar to Standard Lao are Thailand's northern and northeastern Thai dialects. There are actually more Lao speakers living in Thailand than in Laos, so if you're travelling to Laos after a spell in Thailand (especially the northeast), you should be able to put whatever you learned in Thailand to good use. It doesn't work as well in the opposite direction; native Thais can't always understand Lao, since they've had less exposure to it.

In the cities and towns of the Mekong River valley, French is intermittently understood. In spite of its colonial history, French remains the official second language of the government and many official documents are written in both Lao and French. Shop signs sometimes appear in French (alongside Lao, as mandated by law), though signs in English are becoming more common. As in Vietnam, the former colonial language is increasingly viewed as irrelevant in a region that has adopted English as the lingua franca of business and trade, and among young Lao students English is now much more popular than French. Lao over the age of 50 may understand a little English, but to a lesser extent than French.

Many Russian-trained Lao can also speak Russian, though the language has drastically fallen from favour.

It pays to learn as much Lao as possible during your stay in the country, since speaking and understanding the language not only enhances verbal communication

LANGUAGE

but garners a great deal of respect from the Lao people you come into contact with.

For a more in-depth guide to Lao than we have room for in this guide, get a copy of Lonely Planet's *Lao Phrasebook*. If you plan to travel extensively in any Lao Sung areas, Lonely Planet's *Hill Tribes Phrasebook* could also be useful.

SCRIPT

The Lao script today consists of 30 consonant symbols (formed from 20 basic sounds) and 28 symbols for vowels and vowel combinations (15 individual symbols used in varying combinations). Complementing the consonant and vowel symbols are four tone marks, only two of which are commonly used in creating the six different tones (in combination with all the other symbols). Written Lao proceeds from left to right, though vowel-signs may appear in a number of positions relative to consonants: before, after, above, below or 'around' (ie before, above *and* after).

TONES

Basically, Lao is a monosyllabic, tonal language, like the various dialects of Thai and Chinese. Borrowed words from Sanskrit, Pali, French and English often have two or more syllables, however. Many identical vowel-consonant combinations are differentiated by their tone only. The word *sao*, for example, can mean 'girl', 'morning', 'pillar' or 'twenty' depending on the tone. For people from nontonal language backgrounds, it can be very hard to learn at first but even when they 'know' the correct tone, their tendency to denote emotion, emphasis and questions through tone modulation often interferes with uttering the correct tone. So the first rule in learning and using the tone system is to avoid overlaying native intonation patterns onto the Lao language.

Vientiane Lao has six tones. Three of the tones are level (low, mid and high) while three follow pitch inclines (rising, high falling and low falling). All six variations in pitch are relative to the speaker's natural vocal range, so that one person's low tone is not necessarily the same pitch as another person's.

Low Tone

Produced at the relative bottom of your conversational tonal range – usually flat level, eg *dĭi* (good). Note, however, that not everyone pronounces it flat and level – some Vientiane natives add a slight rising tone to the end.

Mid Tone

Flat like the low tone, but spoken at the relative middle of your vocal range. No tone mark is used, eg *het* (do).

High Tone

Flat again, this time at the relative top of your vocal range, eg *héua* (boat).

Rising Tone

Begins a bit below the mid tone and rises to just at or above the high tone, eg *săam* (three).

High Falling Tone

Begins at or above the high tone and falls to the mid level, eg *sâo* (morning).

Low Falling Tone

Begins at about the mid level and falls to the level of the low tone, eg *khào* (rice).

On a visual curve the tones might look like this:

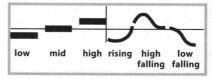

TRANSLITERATION

The rendering of Lao words in the Roman alphabet is a major problem, since many of the Lao sounds, especially certain vowels, do not occur in English. The problem is compounded by the fact that because of Laos's colonial history, transcribed words most commonly seen in Laos are based on the old colonial French system of transliteration, which bears little relation to the way an English speaker would intuitively write a Lao word.

There is no official method of transliterating the Lao language (the government is incredibly inconsistent in this respect, though they tend to follow the old French methods). This book uses a custom system of transliteration based on the Royal Thai General Transcription system, since Thai and Lao have very similar writing and sound systems. The only exceptions are where there may be confusion with terms that are already in common use.

The public and private sectors in Laos are gradually moving towards a more internationally recognisable system along the lines of Royal Thai General.

PRONUNCIATION

Vowels

Lao vowels can be written before, after, above and below consonants – in the following vowel chart we demonstrate this by using '×' to represent any consonant.

×ິ	**i**	as in 'it'
×ີ	**ii**	as in 'feet' or 'tea'
ໃ×, ໄ×	**ai**	as in 'aisle'
×າ	**aa**	long 'a' as in 'father'
×ະ	**a**	half as long as **aa**
ແ×	**ae**	as the 'a' in 'bad' or 'tab'
ເ× ະ, ເ ×ັ×	**e**	as in 'hen'
ເ×	**eh**	as the 'a' in 'hate'
ເ×ິ, ເ×ີ	**oe**	as the 'u' in 'fur'
×ຶ, ×ື	**eu**	as in French *deux*, or as the 'i' in 'sir'
×ຸ	**u**	as in 'flute'
×ູ	**uu**	as in 'food'
×າຍ	**aai**	as the 'a' in 'father' plus the 'i' in 'pipe'
ເ×ົາ	**ao**	as in 'now' or 'cow'
×ໍ	**aw**	as in 'jaw'
ໂ×ະ, ×ົ×	**o**	as in 'phone'
ໂ×	**oh**	as in 'toe'
ເ×ືອ	**eua**	combination of 'eu' and 'a'
×ຽ×, ເ×ັຍ	**ia**	as the 'i-a' sound in 'Ian'
×ວ×, ×ົວ	**ua**	as the 'u-a' sound in 'tour'
×ວຍ	**uay**	'u-ay-ee'
×ິວ, ×ີວ	**iu**	'i-oo' (as in 'yew')
×ຽວ	**iaw**	'ee-a-oo'
ແ×ວ	**aew**	as the'a' in 'bad' plus 'w'
ເ×ວ	**ehw**	as the 'a' in 'care' plus 'w'
ເ×ັວ	**ew**	same as 'ehw' above, but shorter (not as in 'yew')
ເ×ີຍ	**oei**	'oe-i'
×ອຍ	**awy**	as the 'oy' in 'boy'
ໂ×ຍ	**ohy**	'oh-i'

Consonants

An 'aspirated' consonant is produced with an audible puff of air. An 'unvoiced' or 'voiceless' consonant is produced with no vibration in the vocal chords.

ກ	**k**	as the 'k' in 'skin'; similar to the 'g' in 'good', but unaspirated and unvoiced
ຂ, ຄ	**kh**	as the 'k' in 'kite'
ງ	**ng**	as in 'sing'; used as an initial consonant in Lao
ຈ	**j**	similar to 'j' in 'join' or more closely, the second 't' in 'stature' or 'literature' (unaspirated and voiceless)
ສ, ຊ	**s**	as in 'soap'
ຍ	**ny**	similar to the 'ni' in 'onion'; used as an initial consonant in Lao
ດ	**d**	as in 'dodo'
ຕ	**t**	a hard 't', unaspirated and unvoiced – a bit like 'd'
ທ, ຖ	**th**	as in 'tip'
ນ, ໜ	**n**	as in 'nun'
ບ	**b**	as in 'boy'
ປ	**p**	a hard 'p' (unaspirated and unvoiced)
ພ, ຜ	**ph**	'p' as in 'put' (but never as in 'phone')
ຟ, ຝ	**f**	as in 'fan'
ມ, ໝ	**m**	as in 'man'
ຢ	**y**	as in 'yo-yo'
ລ, ຫລ	**l**	as in 'lick'
ວ, ຫວ	**w**	as in 'wing' (often transliterated as 'v')
ຮ, ຫ	**h**	as in 'home'

ACCOMMODATION

hotel	ໂຮງແຮມ	*hóhng háem*
guest house	ຫໍຮັບແຂກ	*hǎw hap kháek*

Excuse me, is there a hotel nearby?
ຂໍໂທດ ມີໂຮງແຮມຢູ່ໃກ້ນີ້ບໍ່
khǎw thǒht, mǐi hóhng háem yuu kâi nîi baw?

Do you have a room?
ມີຫ້ອງບໍ່
míi hàwng baw?

How many people?
จักคิน   *ják khón?*

one person
มิ่งคิน (คินๆจอ)   *neung khón (khón diaw)*

two persons
สองคิน   *săwng khón*

How much ...?   ... เท่าใด   *... thao dại?*
  per night   คิນละ   *khéun-la*
  per week   อาทິດละ   *qathit-la*

air-conditioning
แอເຢັນ   *qe yăn*

bathroom
ท้อງบ่ำ   *hàwng nâm*

blanket
ຜ້າห່ม   *phàa hom*

double room
ท້อງบอบຕຽງคู่   *hàwng náwn tĭang khuu*

fan
ພັດລົມ   *phat lóm*

hot water
บ่ำร้อบ   *nâm hâwn*

key
ກະแຈ   *kájqe*

sheet
ผ้าปูบ่อบบอบ   *phàa pụu bawn náwn*

single room
ท້อງบອບຕຽງจอ   *hàwng náwn tĭang diaw*

soap
ສະບູ   *sábuu*

toilet
ສ້ວມ   *sùam*

towel
ผ้าເຊັດໂຕ   *phàa set tŏh*

I/we will stay two nights.
ຊິພັກຢู่ສอງคิน   *si phak yuu săwng khéun*

Can I/we look at the room?
ຊຳເບิ່ງท້อງได้บ่   *khăw boeng hàwng dâi baw?*

Do you have other rooms?
ມີท้อງอิกบ่   *mĭi hàwng ĭik baw?*

cheaper   ถืກກວ່າ   *théuk-kwaa*
quieter   ມິດກວ່າ   *mit-kwaa*

CONVERSATION & ESSENTIALS

Greetings.
ສະບາຍดี   *sábqai-dĭi*

Goodbye. (general farewell)
ສະບາຍดี   *sábqai-dĭi*

Goodbye. (person leaving)
ลาກ່อบໄປກ່อบ   *láa kawn pại kawn*

Goodbye. (person staying)
ໂສກดี   *sŏhk dĭi*

See you later.
ພົບກັບໃໝ່   *phop kạn mai*

Thank you.
ຂອບใจ   *khàwp jại*

Thank you very much.
ຂອບใจຫລາຍๆ   *khàwp jại lăi lăi*

It's nothing/You're welcome.
ບ່ເປັນຫยัງ   *baw pẹn nyăng*

Excuse me.
ຂໍໂທດ   *khăw thôht*

How are you?
ສະບາຍดีบ่   *sábqai-dĭi baw?*

I'm fine.
ສະບາຍดี   *sábqai-dĭi*

And you?
ເຈົ້າເດ້   *jâo dêh?*

What's your name?
ເຈົ້າຊື່ຫยัง   *jâo seu nyăng?*

My name is ...
ຂ້อยຊື່ ...   *kháwy seu ...*

Glad to know you.
ดีใจທີ່ຮູ້ກັບເຈົ້າ   *dĭi-jại thii hùu káp jâo*

Where are you from?
ເຈົ້າມາແຕ່ໃສ   *jâo máa tae săi?*

I'm from ...
ຂ້อยມາແຕ່ ...   *kháwy máa tae ...*

DIRECTIONS

Where is the ...?   ... ຢູ່ໃສ   *... yùu săi?*

Which ...   ບ່อນນີ້ ...   *bawn nĭi ...*
is this?   ຫยัງ   *nyăng?*
  street   ຖນົນ   *thanŏn*
  city   ເມືອງ   *méuang*
  village   ຫມู่ບ້าน   *muu bâan*
  province   ແຂວງ   *khwăng*

Turn left/right.
ລ້ຽວຊ້າຍ/ຂວາ   *lĭaw sâai/khwăa*

How far?   ໄກເທ່าใด   *kại thao dại?*
straight ahead ໄປຊື່ๆ   *pại seu-seu*
near/not near ໃກ້/ບ່ໃກ້   *kâi/baw kâi*
far/not far   ໄກ/ບ່ໄກ   *kại/baw kại*
north   ທິດເໜືອ   *thit nĕua*

EMERGENCIES

Help!
ຊ່ວຍແດ່   *suay dae!*
Fire!
ໄຟໃໝ້   *fái mài!*
It's an emergency!
ສຸກເສີນ   *súk sŏen!*
Go away!
ໄປເດີ້   *pai dôe!*

Call a doctor!
ຊ່ວຍຕາມຫາໝໍ ໃຫ້ແດ່
suay tqam hǎa mǎw hài dae!
Call an ambulance!
ຊ່ວຍເອີ້ນລົດໂຮງໝໍ ໃຫ້ແດ່
suay ôen lot hóhng mǎw hài dae!
Call the police!
ຊ່ວຍເອີ້ນຕຳຫລວດແດ່
suay ôen tam-lùat dae!
Could you help me please?
ເຈົ້າຊ່ວຍຂ້ອຍໄດ້ບໍ່
jqo suay khàwy dqi baw?
I'm lost.
ຂ້ອຍຫລົງທາງ
khàwy lŏng tháang
Where are the toilets?
ຫ້ອງສ້ວມຢູ່ໃສ
hàwng sùam yuu sǎi?

south	ທິດໃຕ້	*thit tǎi*
east	ທິດຕາເວັນອອກ	*thit tqawén àwk*
west	ທິດຕາເວັນຕົກ	*thit tqawén tók*

EATING

Please bring (a) ... ຂໍ ... ແດ່   *khǎw ... dae*

bill	ແຊັກ	*saek*
bowl	ຖ້ວຍ	*thùay*
chopsticks	ໄມ້ທູ່	*mâi thuu*
fork	ສ້ອມ	*sâwm*
glass	ຈອກ	*jàwk*
knife	ມີດ	*mǐit*
menu	ລາຍການ	*lái-kqan*
	ອາຫານ	*qa-hǎan*
plate	ຈານ	*jqa*
spoon	ບ່ວງ	*buang*

Do you have ...?
ມີ ... ບໍ່   *mǐi ... baw*

I'd like to try that.
ຂ້ອຍຢາກລອງກິນເບິ່ງ *khàwy yàak láwng kin boeng*
I eat only vegetables.
ຂ້ອຍກິນແຕ່ຜັກ   *khàwy kin tae phák*
(I) don't like it hot and spicy.
ບໍ່ມັກເຜັດ   *baw mak phét*
(I) like it hot and spicy.
ມັກເຜັດ   *mak phét*

HEALTH

I'm not well.
ຂ້ອຍບໍ່ສະບາຍ   *khàwy baw sábqai*
I need a doctor.
ຂ້ອຍຕ້ອງການໝໍ   *khàwy tâwng-kqan mǎw*
I have a fever.
ເປັນໄຂ້   *pęn khài*
I have diarrhoea.
ລົງທ້ອງ   *lóng thâwng*
It hurts here.
ເຈັບຢູ່ນີ້   *jép yuu nǐi*

allergic	ແພ້	*phâe*
asthma	ໂລກຫືດ	*lôhk hèut*
malaria	ໄຂ້ປ່າ	*khài paa*
pregnant	ຖືພາມານ	*thěu pháa-máan*
	(ມີທ້ອງ)	*(mǐi thâwng)*
toothache	ເຈັບແຂ້ວ	*jép khàew*

LANGUAGE DIFFICULTIES

Can you speak English?
ເຈົ້າປາກພາສາອັງກິດໄດ້ບໍ່
jâo pàak pháasǎa qngkít dâi baw?
I can't speak Lao.
ຂ້ອຍປາກພາສາລາວບໍ່ໄດ້
khàwy páak pháasǎa láo baw dâi
Do you understand?
ເຈົ້າເຂົ້າໃຈບໍ່
jâo khào jqi baw?
I don't understand.
ບໍ່ເຂົ້າໃຈ
baw khào jqi
Please speak slowly.
ກະລຸນາເວົ້າຊ້າໆ
kálunáa wâo sâa-sâa
Please repeat.
ກະລຸນາເວົ້າໃໝ່ ເບິ່ງດູ
kálunáa wâo mai boeng dųu
What do you call this in Lao?
ອັນນີ້ພາສາລາວວ່າຍັງ
qn-nǐi pháasǎa láo waa nyǎng?

NUMBERS

0	ສູນ	sǔun
1	ນຶ່ງ	neung
2	ສອງ	ǎwng
3	ສາມ	sǎam
4	ສີ່	sii
5	ຫ້າ	hàa
6	ຫົກ	hók
7	ເຈັດ	jét
8	ແປດ	pàet
9	ເກົ້າ	kǎo
10	ສິບ	síp
11	ສິບເອັດ	síp-ét
12	ສິບສອງ	síp-sǎwng
20	ຊາວ	sáo
21	ຊາວເອັດ	sáo-ét
22	ຊາວສອງ	sáo-sǎwng
30	ສາມສິບ	sǎam-síp
40	ສີ່ສິບ	sii-síp
50	ຫ້າສິບ	hàa-síp
60	ຫົກສິບ	hók-síp
70	ເຈັດສິບ	jét-síp
80	ແປດສິບ	pàet-síp
90	ເກົ້າສິບ	kǎo-síp
100	ຮ້ອຍ	hâwy
200	ສອງຮ້ອຍ	sǎwng hâwy
1000	ພັນ	phán
10,000	ໝື່ນ(ສິບພັນ)	meun (síp-phán)
100,000	ແສນ(ຮ້ອຍພັນ)	sǎen (hâwy phán)
1,000,000	ລ້ານ	lâan

PLACES & LAND FEATURES

Buddhist temple	ວັດ	wat
cemetery	ປ່າຊ້າ	paa sâa
church	ສິມຄຣິດ	sǐm khlit
forest	ປ່າ	paa
jungle	ດົງ	dǒng
mountain	ພູເຂົາ	phúu khǎo
park/garden	ສວນ	sǔan
rice field (wet)	ນາ	náa
river	ແມ່ນ້ຳ	mae nâm
sea	ທະເລ	thaléh
stupa	ທາດ	thâat
swamp	ບຶງ	beung
trail/footpath	ທາງຫຼວ/	tháang thíaw/
	ທາງຍ່າງ	nyaang
waterfall	ນ້ຳຕົກຕາດ	nâm tók tàat

SHOPPING & SERVICES

bank	ທະນາຄານ	thanáakháan
barber shop	ຮ້ານຕັດຜົມ	hâan tát phǒm
bookshop	ຮ້ານຂາຍໜັງສື	hâan khǎai nǎng sěu
hospital	ໂຮງໝໍ	hóhng mǎw
museum	ພິພິທະພັນ	phiphithaphán
pharmacy	ຮ້ານຂາຍຢາ	hâan khǎai yǫa
post office	ໄປສະນີ	pǫi-sá-nii
	(ໂຮງສາຍ)	(hóhng sǎai)

I want to change ...	ຂ້ອຍຢາກປ່ຽນ ...	khàwy yàak pian ...
money	ເງິນ	ngóen
travellers cheques	ເຊັກເດີນທາງ	sek dôen tháang

I'm looking for ...
ຂ້ອຍຊອກຫາ ...   khàwy sàwk hǎa ...
How much (for) ...?
... ເທົ່າໃດ   ... thao dǫi?
Do you have something cheaper?
ມີຖືກກວ່ານີ້ບໍ່   mii thèuk-kwaa nǐi baw?
The price is very high.
ລາຄາແພງຫລາຍ   láakháa pháeng lǎai

TIME & DATES

today	ມື້ນີ້	mêu nîi
tonight	ຄືນນີ້	khéun nîi
this morning	ເຊົ້ານີ້	sáo nîi
this afternoon	ບ່າຍນີ້	baai nîi
all day long	ຕລອດມື້	talàwt mêu
now	ດຽວນີ້/ຕອນນີ້	diaw nîi/tqwn nîi
sometimes	ບາງເທື່ອ	bqang theua
yesterday	ມື້ວານນີ້	mêu wáan nîi
tomorrow	ມື້ອືນ	mêu eun

Monday	ວັນຈັນ	wán jqn
Tuesday	ວັນອັງຄານ	wán qngkháan
Wednesday	ວັນພຸດ	wán phut
Thursday	ວັນພະຫັດ	wán phahát
Friday	ວັນສຸກ	wán súk
Saturday	ວັນເສົ້າ	wán sǎo
Sunday	ວັນອາທິດ	wán qathit

January	ເດືອນມັງກອນ	dǫuan mángkqwn
February	ເດືອນກຸມພາ	dǫuan kqmpháa
March	ເດືອນມີນາ	dǫuan míináa
April	ເດືອນເມສາ	dǫuan méhsǎa
May	ເດືອນພຶດສະພາ	dǫuan pheutsápháa

June	ເດືອນມິຖຸນາ	dǫuan mithúnáa
July	ເດືອນກໍລະກົດ	dǫuan kǫwlakót
August	ເດືອນສິງຫາ	dǫuan sǐnghǎa
September	ເດືອນກັນຍາ	dǫuan kǫnyáa
October	ເດືອນຕຸລາ	dǫuan túláa
November	ເດືອນພະຈິກ	dǫuan phajík
December	ເດືອນທັນວາ	dǫuan thánwáa

TRANSPORT

aeroplane	ເຮືອບິນ	héua bǐn
bus	ລົດ	lot
boat	ເຮືອ	héua
minivan	ລົດຕູ້	lot tûu

What time will the ... leave?
... ຈະອອກຈັກໂມງ
... já àwk ják móhng?

What time (do we, does it, etc) arrive there?
ຈະໄປຮອດພຸ້ນຈັກໂມງ
já pai hâwt phûn ják móhng?

Where do we get on the boat?
ລົງເຮືອຢູ່ໃສ
lóng héua yuu sǎi?

I want to go to ...
ຂ້ອຍຢາກໄປ ...
khàwy yàak pai ...

I'd like a ticket.
ຂ້ອຍຢາກໄດ້ປີ້
khàwy yàak dâi pîi

How much to ...?
ໄປ ... ເທົ່າໃດ
pai ... thao dại?

How much per person?
ຄົນລະເທົ່າໃດ
khón-la thao dại?

May I sit here?
ນັ່ງບ່ອນນີ້ໄດ້ບໍ່
nang bawn nîi dâi baw?

Please tell me when we arrive in ...
ເວລາຮອດ ... ບອກຂ້ອຍແດ່
wéhláa hâwt ... bàwk khàwy dae

Stop here.
ຈອດຢູ່ນີ້
jàwt yuu nîi

I'd like to hire a ...
ຂ້ອຍຢາກເຊົ່າ ...   *khàwy yàak sao ...*

car	ລົດ(ໂອໂຕ)	lot (ŏh-tŏh)
bicycle	ລົດຖີບ	lot thìip
motorcycle	ລົດຈັກ	lot ják
taxi	ລົດແທກຊີ	lot thâek-síi
samlor (pedicab)	ສາມລໍ້	sǎam-lâw
săwngthăew (passenger truck)	ສອງແຖວ	sǎwngthǎew
tuk-tuk (jumbo)	ຕຸ໊ກ ຕຸ໊ກ	túk-túk

Also available from Lonely Planet:
Lao phrasebook and
Southeast Asia phrasebook

LANGUAGE

Glossary

For a list of Lao words for food and drink, see p67.

ąahaan – food
anatta – Buddhist concept of nonsubstantiality or non-essentiality of reality, ie no permanent 'soul'
anicca – Buddhist concept of impermanence, the transience of all things
Asean – Association of South East Asian Nations

bâan – the general Lao word for house or village; written Ban on maps
bąasǐi – sometimes spelt basi or *baci;* a ceremony in which the 32 *khwǎn* (guardian spirits) are symbolically bound to the participant for health and safety
baht – *(bàat)* Thai unit of currency, commonly negotiable in Laos; also a Lao unit of measure equal to 15g
BCEL – Banque pour le Commerce Extérieur Lao; in English, Lao Foreign Trade Bank
bja – beer; *bja sót* is draught beer
bun – pronounced *bųn,* often spelt boun; a festival; also spiritual 'merit' earned through good actions or religious practices

corvée – enforced, unpaid labour

Don – pronounced *dɔwn;* island
dukkha – Buddhist concept of suffering, unsatisfactoriness, disease

falang – from the Lao *falang-sèht* or 'French'; Western, a Westerner
fǒe – rice noodles, one of the most common dishes in Laos

hǎi – jar
hǎw tại – monastery building dedicated to the storage of the Tripitaka (Buddhist scriptures)
héua – boat
héua hang nyáo – longtail boat
héua phái – row boat
héua wái – speedboat
hùay – stream; written Huay on maps

Jataka – (Pali-Sanskrit) mythological stories of the Buddha's past lives; *sáa-dók* in Lao
jęhdii – a Buddhist stupa; also written Chedi
jịin hǎw – Lao name for the Muslim Yunnanese who live in northern Laos
jumbo – a motorised three-wheeled taxi, sometimes called tuk-tuk

kháen – a wind instrument devised of a double row of bamboo-like reeds fitted into a hardwood soundbox and made air-tight with beeswax
khào – rice
khào jịi – bread
khào nǐaw – sticky rice, the Lao staple food
khào-nǒm – pastry or sweet; sometimes shortened to *khanǒm*
khúu-bąa – Lao Buddhist monk
khwǎn – guardian spirits
kip – pronounced *kìip;* Lao unit of currency

làap – a spicy Lao-style salad of minced meat, poultry or fish
lák méuang – city pillar
lám wóng – 'circle dance', the traditional folk dance of Laos, as common at discos as at festivals
Lao Issara – Lao resistance movement against the French in the 1940s
lào-láo – distilled rice liquor
Lao Loum – 'Lowland Lao', ethnic groups belonging to the Lao–Thai Diaspora
Lao Soung – 'Highland Lao', hill tribes who make their residence at higher altitudes, for example, Hmong, Mien; also spelt Lao Sung
Lao Thoeng – 'Upland Lao', a loose affiliation of mostly Mon-Khmer peoples who live on midaltitude mountain slopes
lingam – a pillar or phallus symbolic of Shiva, common in Khmer-built temples
LNTA – Lao National Tourism Administration
LPDR – Lao People's Democratic Republic
LPRP – Lao People's Revolutionary Party

mae nâm – literally, water mother; river; usually shortened to *nâm* with river names, as in Nam Khong (Mekong River)
mǎw lám – Lao folk musical theatre tradition; roughly translates as 'master of verse'
meuang – pronounced *méuang;* district or town; in ancient times a city state; often written Muang on maps
múan – fun, which the Lao believe should be present in all activities
Muang – see *meuang*
muu bâan – village

náang sǐi – Buddhist nuns
naga – *nâa-kha* in Lao; mythical water serpent common to Lao and Thai legends and art

nâm – water; can also mean 'river', 'juice', 'sauce': anything of a watery nature

néhn – Buddhist novice monk; also referred to as *samanera*

NGO – nongovernmental organisation, typically involved in the foreign-aid industry

nibbana – 'cooling', the extinction of mental defilements; the ultimate goal of Theravada Buddhism

NPA – National Protected Area, a classification assigned to 20 wildlife areas throughout Laos

NVA – North Vietnamese Army

pąa – fish

pąa dàek – fermented fish sauce, a common accompaniment to Lao food

Pathet Lao – literally, Country of Laos; both a general term for the country and a common journalistic reference to the military arm of the early Patriotic Lao Front (a cover for the Lao People's Party); often abbreviated to PL

pha – holy image, usually referring to a Buddha; venerable

phàa – cloth

phàa bjang – shoulder sash worn by men

phàa nung – sarong, worn by almost all Lao women

phàa salòng – sarong, worn by Lao men

Pha Lak Pha Lam – the Lao version of the Indian epic, the Ramayana

phúu – hill or mountain; also spelt phu

săaláa lóng thám – a *sala* (hall) where monks and lay people listen to Buddhist teachings

săam-lâaw – a three-wheeled pedicab; also written *samlor*

sakai-làep – alternative name for *jumbo* in southern Laos due to the perceived resemblance to a space capsule (Skylab)

sala – pronounced *săa-láa;* an open-sided shelter; a hall

samana – pronounced *săamanáa;* 'seminar'; euphemism for labour and re-education camps established after the 1975 Revolution

samanera – Buddhist novice monk; also referred to as *néhn*

săwngthăew – literally, two-rows; a passenger truck; also written *songthaew*

se – also spelt *xe;* southern Laos term for river; hence Se Don means Don River, and Pakse means *pàak* (mouth) of the river

shophouse – two-storey building designed to have a shop on the ground floor and a residence above

sĭi – sacred; also spelt *si*

sĭm – ordination hall in a Lao Buddhist monastery; named after the *sima*, (pronounced *sĭimáa*) or sacred stone tablets, which mark off the grounds dedicated for this purpose

soi – lane

tàat – waterfall; also *nâm tók;* written Tat on maps

talàat – market; *talàat sâo* is the morning market; *talàat mèut* is the free, or 'black', market; written Talat on maps

thâat – Buddhist stupa or reliquary; written That on maps

thaek-sĭi – taxi

thanŏn – street/road; often spelt Thanon on maps; shortened to 'Th' as street is to 'St'

tuk-tuk – see *jumbo*

UXO – unexploded ordnance

Viet Minh – the Vietnamese forces who fought for Indochina's independence from the French

vipassana – insight meditation

wat – Lao Buddhist monastery

wihăan – (Pali-Sanskrit vihara) a temple hall

The Authors

AUSTIN BUSH   Coordinating Author, Vientiane & Around, Central Laos

After graduating from the University of Oregon, Austin Bush received a scholarship to study Thai at Chiang Mai University and has remained in Thailand ever since. Several years of working at a stable job were encouragement enough to make the questionable decision to pursue a career as a freelance photographer/writer. This choice has since taken him as far as northern Pakistan and as near as Bangkok's Or Tor Kor Market. Examples of his work can be seen at www.austinbushphotography.com.

MARK ELLIOTT   Northern Laos

Mark Elliott's career path has proved as crooked as any cross-Laos highway. A trained chemistry teacher, he spent three years entertaining bemused Japanese villagers, danced rain dances in Gambia and has crossed the world's deepest lake – in a truck. He has been visiting Laos since 1995 and previously covered the country for numerous travel publishers. He lives in Belgium with an understanding wife who found him at a Turkmenistan camel market. The camel would have been cheaper.

NICK RAY   Southern Laos

A Londoner of sorts, Nick comes from Watford, the sort of town that makes you want to travel. He first travelled to Laos in 1995, spending a few days on a cargo barge from Luang Prabang to Vientiane. Nick jumped at the chance to tackle southern Laos and spent time exploring the hinterland by motorbike. Nick lives in Phnom Penh with his wife Kulikar and his young children Julian and Belle. When not writing, he is often out exploring the remote parts of Indochina as a location scout and manager for the world of TV and film and has worked on productions such as the movies *Tomb Raider* and *Two Brothers*.

LONELY PLANET AUTHORS

Why is our travel information the best in the world? It's simple: our authors are passionate, dedicated travellers. They don't take freebies in exchange for positive coverage so you can be sure the advice you're given is impartial. They travel widely to all the popular spots, and off the beaten track. They don't research using just the internet or phone. They discover new places not included in any other guidebook. They personally visit thousands of hotels, restaurants, palaces, trails, galleries, temples and more. They speak with dozens of locals every day to make sure you get the kind of insider knowledge only a local could tell you. They take pride in getting all the details right, and in telling it how it is. Think you can do it? Find out how at **lonelyplanet.com**.

CONTRIBUTING AUTHORS

Martin Stuart-Fox wrote the History chapter. Martin is Professor Emeritus in the School of History, Philosophy, Religion and Classics at the University of Queensland, Australia. He first worked in Laos from 1963 to 1965 as a journalist, before covering the Vietnam War for two years. On his return to Australia, Martin joined the University of Queensland. He retired in 2005 after five years as Head of History. He has written dozens of articles and seven books on Laos, including *A History of Laos* (1997), *The Lao Kingdom of Lan Xang* (1998) and *Buddhist Kingdom, Marxist State* (2nd ed, 2002). His latest books are *Naga Cities of the Mekong* (2006), narrating the histories of Luang Prabang, Vientiane and Champasak, and *Festivals of Laos* (with Somsanouk Mixay).

Steven Schipani wrote the Ecotourism in Laos boxed text (p73). Steven was born in New York City and raised on the Atlantic coast of Long Island, New York. He first went to Asia as a United States Peace Corps volunteer, serving in Thailand from 1994 to 1996. He has worked as a professional guide, fisherman, Thai and Lao language interpreter, and has travelled extensively in Southeast Asia. Since 1999 Steven has been employed by Unesco, the Asian Development Bank, and a number of other international organisations advising on sustainable ecotourism development and heritage management in Laos. His interests include fishing, forest trekking, indigenous knowledge and Lao food. He has one son named Michael.

Dr Trish Batchelor wrote the Health chapter (p345). Trish is a general practitioner and travel medicine specialist who works at the CIWEC Clinic in Kathmandu, Nepal, as well as being a Medical Advisor to the Travel Doctor New Zealand clinics. Trish teaches travel medicine through the University of Otago, and is interested in underwater and high-altitude medicine, and in the impact of tourism on host countries. She has travelled extensively through Southeast and East Asia and particularly loves high-altitude trekking in the Himalayas.

Behind the Scenes

THIS BOOK

This 7th edition of Laos was researched and written by Austin Bush (coordinator), Nick Ray and Mark Elliott. Professor Martin Stuart-Fox wrote the History chapter, Dr Trish Batchelor wrote the Health chapter and Steven Schipani penned the Ecotourism in Laos boxed text in the Environment chapter. The previous edition was authored by Andrew Burke and Justine Vaisutis. This guidebook was commissioned in Lonely Planet's Melbourne office and produced by the following:

Commissioning Editors Shawn Low, Tashi Wheeler, Ilaria Walker

Coordinating Editors Jessica Crouch, Jocelyn Harewood

Coordinating Cartographer Csanad Csutoros

Coordinating Layout Designer Carol Jackson

Senior Editors Helen Christinis, Katie Lynch

Managing Editors Bruce Evans, Liz Heynes

Managing Cartographers David Connolly, Amanda Sierp, Herman So

Managing Layout Designer Celia Wood

Assisting Editors Justin Flynn, Anne Mulvaney

Cover Research Naomi Parker

Internal Image Research Aude Vauconsant

Language Content Laura Crawford

Thanks to Melanie Dankel, Ryan Evans, Errol Hunt, Corey Hutchison, Indra Kilfoyle, Lisa Knights, Averil Robertson

THANKS
AUSTIN BUSH

I can't thank former Laos author Andrew Burke enough, not only for recommending me for this gig, but also for being a patient teacher and a great example as a Lonely Planet writer.

I also owe many thanks to the kind, generous and helpful people on the ground in Laos and Thailand including Steven Schipani and Rik Ponne; Carl Middleton; The Man with the Van, Christophe Kittirath; Martin Stuart-Fox; Delphine and Tinay; Wat at Green Discovery; Somkiad at the Khammuan Eco-Guide Unit; David Phabmixay and the other kind folks involved with Nam Lik Eco-Village; and my Local Voices, Jonny Olsen, Sangthong Nieselt and yet again, David Phabmixay.

A handful of friends were brave enough to join me in Laos, namely Nick Grossman, Richard Hermes, Wes Hsu, Yaowalak Ittichai-Warakom, Andy Ricker and Patrick Winn.

At Lonely Planet, I'd like to thank my excellent co-authors, Nick '4am' Ray and Mark 'Mouth Harp'

THE LONELY PLANET STORY

Fresh from an epic journey across Europe, Asia and Australia in 1972, Tony and Maureen Wheeler sat at their kitchen table stapling together notes. The first Lonely Planet guidebook, *Across Asia on the Cheap*, was born.

Travellers snapped up the guides. Inspired by their success, the Wheelers began publishing books to Southeast Asia, India and beyond. Demand was prodigious, and the Wheelers expanded the business rapidly to keep up. Over the years, Lonely Planet extended its coverage to every country and into the virtual world via lonelyplanet.com and the Thorn Tree message board.

As Lonely Planet became a globally loved brand, Tony and Maureen received several offers for the company. But it wasn't until 2007 that they found a partner whom they trusted to remain true to the company's principles of travelling widely, treading lightly and giving sustainably. In October of that year, BBC Worldwide acquired a 75% share in the company, pledging to uphold Lonely Planet's commitment to independent travel, trustworthy advice and editorial independence.

Today, Lonely Planet has offices in Melbourne, London and Oakland, with over 500 staff members and 300 authors. Tony and Maureen are still actively involved with Lonely Planet. They're traveling more often than ever, and they're devoting their spare time to charitable projects. And the company is still driven by the philosophy of *Across Asia on the Cheap*: 'All you've got to do is decide to go and the hardest part is over. So go!'

Elliott; my Commissioning Editors, Tashi Wheeler, Shawn Low and Ilaria Walker; language guru Bruce Evans; and the dedicated cartographers, in particular David Connolly.

And last but not least, I must confess my particularly heartfelt gratitude to the talented brewers at Beerlao.

MARK ELLIOTT
As always, my work is dedicated to my beloved wife, Dani Systermans, and to my unbeatable parents. Their love is my freedom. Thank you to Dave Anderson; Roy and Rexley for the Judo send off; Tashi Wheeler for the opportunity; Andrew Burke, Paul Eshoo, Tara Gujadhur and Khoun Soutthivilay for getting me into gear and to Britt Bisk as an ever inspiring companion. Hats off to David Connolly and crew for getting the maps redrawn in double-quick time. A heartfelt *kipato* to Phonesai, Arnauld Paillusson and Nicolas Ledem in Akha-land; Stefan Auth in Phongsali; Julie Van den Bergh in Phonsavan; Wie (Fue Vue) and Frankie on the Phakeo trek; Rik Ponne; Steven Schipani; ever-smiling 'Mr New' Pa-nyu; Lola; Jo; Andy; Sean; Paul; Gabriel; Fuang for defeating the evil replicating fonts; Carine and Florian; Paul, Siegfried, Luisa, Filip et al in Udomxai; Monica in Hongsa; Ingrid, Gilles et al from Elefantasia; Ines and Saysamone 'The' Phengdouang in Sainyabuli; Geno Geng and the Pak Beng 'escapees'; Noël Rousset, my trusty shipmate down the Nam Tha; Mr Tui in Muang Long; Dtae in Vieng Thong; Boan Mee in Pak Tha; Sai in Muang Ngoi; Son Sim in Huay Xai; Keo in Muang Khua; Nathan Browne; Ian Skelton...and so many other kind, helpful folk who made the research such a very pleasurable experience.

NICK RAY
Firstly, a big thanks to the people of Laos, whose spirit and sense of humour make the country such a fascinating place to visit. Biggest thanks are reserved for my lovely wife Kulikar Sotho, as without her support and encouragement the adventures would not be possible. And to our young children Julian and Belle for enlivening our lives immeasurably and bringing a new perspective to travelling in Asia.

Thanks to fellow travellers and contacts in Laos who have helped shape my experience of this country. In particular, thanks to Alex Aziz of X-plore Asia, Inthy Deuansavan of Green Discovery, and long-time ecotourism consultants Steven Schipani and Paul Eschoo. There are many more good folk to thank, but whose names are too numerous to mention.

Thanks also to my co-authors Austin Bush and Mark Elliott. Authors are all too often islands, working in isolation, so it was great to pull off a meeting in Vientiane during the research.

Finally, thanks to the Lonely Planet team who have worked on this edition. The author may be the public face, but a huge amount of behind-the-scenes work went into making this a better book.

MARTIN STUART-FOX
Over the years, many Lao friends have provided me with invaluable information about Lao history, politics, society and culture. I have also learned much from the work of other scholars, for the serious study of any country is always a collaborative project. My friends and informants are far too numerous to be individually named, but I would like to mention the late Claude Vincent, Drs Mayoury and Pheuiphanh Ngaosrivathana, Khamsing Khammanivong, Dr Somphou Oudomvilay, Dr Grant Evans, Dr Michel Lorrillard, and my former student, Martin Rathie. My special thanks also to Somsanouk Mixay, former editor of the *Vientiane Times,* for his contribution as co-author on our book *Festivals of Laos.*

OUR READERS
Many thanks to the travellers who used the last edition and wrote to us with helpful hints, useful advice and interesting anecdotes:

A Bob Ackerman, Khun Aek, Mavis Airey, Johanna Akkerman, Mark Allen, Michel Alov, Steffen Ammundsen, Angela Anderson, Pete Appleyard, Sebastian Arabito, Helmut Arlt, Nikki Arthur, Kristin Ashley, Jules Atkins, **B** Rachel Bachmann, Reinier Bakels, Jessica Barbay, Christian Barbier, James Barbush, Shelley Barnes, James Barr, Tina Barrett, Hugh Barton, Elisabeth Baxter, Geoff Becque, Tim Beil, Emma Berry, Klaus Bettenhausen, Anjali Bhasin, Sandrine Bieckert, Amei Binns, Daniela Bischof Boesch, Rudi Blacker, Alex O Bleecker, Karin Blokziel, Michael Boddington, Thomas Bolton, Benjamin Boorstein, Ludovic Boulicaut, Somnuek Bounsa, Victor Bourdeau, Valerie Bourke, Anya Bramich, John Bramley, Charlotte Breinersdorf, Grainne Brick, Jade Brockley, Alex Brown, Lieve Bruggeman, Janet Brunckhorst, Joseph Brunning, Abram Buijs, John Bulcock, Susanne Bulten, Jakob Bumke, **C** Erika Cadeot, Gerlynn Cai, Christine Campens, Steve Canning, Sarah Cardenas, K Cherhabil, Joan Chihan, Roscoe Chubb, Olga Cirera Hontecillas, Tom Clark, Adam Clarke, Isabel Clough, Elizabeth Coatsworth, Richard Coe, Richard Cotton, Tom Cox, Krista Cramer, Krister Cromm, Matthew Crowther, Dugan Cummings, Agnies Cynkowska, **D** Kathrin Damm, Wim De Paepe, Cathrine Dean, Bill Delorme, Lindsay Diduck, Fredrik Divall, Sabine Dohmel, Eleanor Draughb, Yvonne Duijst, **E** Philipp Eichenberger, Albrecht Eisen, Or Eitan, Rachel Ellison, Dawn Eriksen, Peter Evans, Laura Ewles, **F** Therese Fällman, Harry Fenzl, Jill Filipovic, Alexander Findlay,

Jonny Finity, Fern Freeman, **G** Wendy Garrity, Lia Genovese, Philip Gibson, Susannah Gill, Noga Gissis, Graeme Goldsworthy, Charlie Gower-Smith, Tristan Graham, Abby Grayzel, Polly Griffith, Emily Grimes, Urs Grischott, Helmut Grossmann, Sylvain Guillemot, Marek Gutkowski, Jardena Guttmann, **H** Chris Hall, Dr Bashar Hamarneh, Mijnke Hamel, Joe Hammes, Miriam Hanley, Susan Hanley, Paul Hansen, Avital Harari, John Haren, Nienke Harmsen, Ian Harry, Simone Hauser, Kathryn Hayden, David Herel, Jose Hernandez, Will Hill, Simon Hill, Richard Hindle, Christopher Hoare, Rob Hodges, James Hodgson, Simone Hohoff, Julian Hopkins, Johnny Hopper, Mark Hughes, Esmaralda Huijbregts, Russell Huntington, **I** Kristine Isaacson, **J** Ariel Jacob, Richard James, Rich Jenkins, Will Jennings, Anna Jervaeus, Catherine Jewell, Zhang Jinpeng, Richard Joel, Adam Jones, Guido Jouret, **K** Sophie Kasriel, Kamel Kaverdi, Ingrid Kelly, Laura Kenny, Somsanith Keohoung, Philip Keulemans, Alomlack Khiosomphone, Pat Kiely, Kalle Kiisto, Darl Kleinbach, Mark Kobdish, Wolfgang Krueger, **L** Yvonne Lam, Silke Lassen, Michael Leboldus, Brenda Legget, John Leupold, Lewis Levine, Li Huey Tan, Michel Ligthart, Markus Lindner, Giorgia Liviero, Michael Loy, Mike Loy, Wayne Lynch, **M** Stephann Makri, Vongsamay Malibayphit, Samuel Malivoir, Linda Mannion, Dominique Martin, Sarah Mathers, Thomas A Mayes, Jim Mayhercy, Andrew McConville, Jane McCord, Michael McGowan, Larry McGrath, Caroline McKelvie, Tamar Meijers, Jeronimo Mejia, Ronald Meyerq, Elisabeth Mills, Ned Mitchell, Alex Montaigne, Kevin Mora, Tim Morison, James Mousley, Rayan Mroueh, D Muylaert, **N** Barbara Nardelli, Jonathan Nemani, Paul Newton, Jen Northey, David Nowlen, Hannele Nystrom, **O** Peter Ogier, Jonathan O'Keeffe, Siobhan O'Neill, Petra O'Neill, Mark O'Neill, Daniel Oredsson, Emil Orloff, Matthias Ott, Yai Outhai, Anna Oxenstrand, **P** Norman Paley, Romano Paparazzo, Tim Parkin, John Pavelka, Alice Pearson, Vicky Peeters, Ian Percy, Norman Peters, Parima Phetsiriseng, Phetmany Philasouk, Paul Phillips, Jenny Phonsouk, Eli Pik, Markus Planmo, Wolf Podlinski, Nathalie Pouliot, Julia Powell-Rogers, Chanel Pranic, Allen Prosser, **R** Pascal Raats, Francis Reardon, Rupert Reed, Frances Rein, Keith Resnick, Gerhard & Ruth Rieder, John Riley, Antonio Riquelme Lidon, Alexander Robb-Millar, Claire Roberts, Mike Robinson, Patrick Roman, Jolanda Romein, Derek Rosen, Sibylle Rotzler, Sarah Russwurm, Andy Ryder, **S** Joaquin Salas, Bernard Salez, Alison Salisbury, Radim Sarapatka, Martin Schatke, Jim Scheyvaerts, Mieneke Schiebaan, Dominik Schmid, Claudia Schmitt, Rainer Schulze, Steffen Schulze-Ketelhut, Samantha Schupack, Michael Schwartz, Ralph Schwer, Chip Scialfa, Lauren Scollick, Kim Serca, Bill Shaw, Liis Sibrits, Reesa Simmonds, Somchit Siri, Zofia Sitarz, Andrew Sloan, Melisa Smuts, Pablo Soledad, Tanya Spiteri, Ursula Stauffer, Bill Stephens, Sharon Stern, David Stern, Colin Steward, Greg Stitt, Anupma Sud, Stacey Sudlow, Helga Svendsen, Kathy Szybist, **T** Chris Taiaroa, Fleur Talbot, Ian Taylor, Gaz Teeven, Gerda Tettweiler, Caroline Theyse, Gordon Thompson, Lam Thuyni, Becky Tibbenham, Ep Tissing, Ariane Triebfürst, Kevin Triggle, Katharina Tt, Tu Kien Dang, April Turner, Jennifer Tutuska, Charles Tyler, **U** Caroline Ulmer, Wanlop Uthaivanichvatana, **V** Emmanuelle Valmy, Alexander van der Heiden, Wineke van der Linden, Derk van Kampen, Helena Van Niewenhuysen, Caris Vanghetti, Roy Verbrugge, Bart Verbruggen, Andrea Vercikova, Christian Vignali, Yvonne Vintiner, Jeroen Voogt, Marianne Vrouwenvelder, **W** Kelly Walsh, Jens Walter, Simon Ward, Sajith Weerasinghe, Willem Weiland, Peter Welton, Ellen West, Tony Wheeler, Roy Wijlens, Jo Williams, Konstantin Willmann, Danielle Wolbers, Alison Woolley, Sarah Wren, **Y** Adi Yehezkeli, Bill Young, **Z** Feng Zhu, May Zimmerli, Birgit Zuegg

ACKNOWLEDGMENTS
Many thanks to the following for the use of their content:

Globe on title page ©Mountain High Maps 1993 Digital Wisdom, Inc.

Index

GreenDex

MAP LEGEND

ROUTES

Primary	Mall/Steps
Secondary	Tunnel
Tertiary	Pedestrian Overpass
Lane	Walking Tour
Under Construction	Walking Trail
Unsealed Road	Walking Path
One-Way Street	Track

TRANSPORT

Ferry	Rail
Bus Route	Rail (Underground)

HYDROGRAPHY

River, Creek	Canal
Intermittent River	Water
Swamp	Lake (Dry)
Mangrove	Lake (Salt)
Reef	Mudflats

BOUNDARIES

International	Regional, Suburb
State, Provincial	Ancient Wall
Disputed	Cliff
Marine Park	

AREA FEATURES

Airport	Land
Area of Interest	Mall
Beach, Desert	Market
Building	Park
Campus	Reservation
Cemetery, Christian	Rocks
Cemetery, Other	Sports
Forest	Urban

POPULATION

◎ CAPITAL (NATIONAL)	◉ CAPITAL (STATE)
● Large City	● Medium City
● Small City	○ Town, Village

SYMBOLS

Sights/Activities
- Beach
- Buddhist
- Christian
- Monument
- Museum, Gallery
- Point of Interest
- Pool
- Ruin
- Taoist
- Zoo, Bird Sanctuary

Eating
- Eating

Drinking
- Drinking
- Café

Entertainment
- Entertainment

Shopping
- Shopping

Sleeping
- Sleeping
- Camping

Transport
- Airport, Airfield
- Border Crossing
- Bus Station
- Cycling, Bicycle Path
- General Transport
- Parking Area
- Petrol Station
- Taxi Rank

Information
- Bank, ATM
- Embassy/Consulate
- Hospital, Medical
- Information
- Internet Facilities
- Police Station
- Post Office, GPO
- Telephone
- Toilets

Geographic
- ▲ Mountain, Volcano
- National Park
-) (Pass, Canyon
- River Flow
- + Spot Height
- Waterfall

LONELY PLANET OFFICES

Australia (Head Office)
Locked Bag 1, Footscray, Victoria 3011
☎ 03 8379 8000, fax 03 8379 8111
talk2us@lonelyplanet.com.au

USA
150 Linden St, Oakland, CA 94607
☎ 510 250 6400, toll free 800 275 8555
fax 510 893 8572
info@lonelyplanet.com

UK
2nd fl, 186 City Rd,
London EC1V 2NT
☎ 020 7106 2100, fax 020 7106 2101
go@lonelyplanet.co.uk

Published by Lonely Planet Publications Pty Ltd
ABN 36 005 607 983

© Lonely Planet 2010

© photographers as indicated 2010

Cover photograph: Contemplative monk in sim window, Wat Xieng Thong, Luang Prabang, Laos, Bethune Carmichael/Lonely Planet Images. Many of the images in this guide are available for licensing from Lonely Planet Images: lonelyplanetimages.com.

Printed by Toppan Security Printing Pte. Ltd.
Printed in Singapore

MIX
Paper from responsible sources
FSC™ C021741
www.fsc.org